Approaches to Global Sustainability, Markets, and Governance

Series Editors

Approaches to Global Sustainability, Markets, and Governance takes a fresh and global approach to issues of corporate social responsibility, regulation, governance, and sustainability. It encompasses such issues as: environmental sustainability and managing the resources of the world; geopolitics and sustainability; global markets and their regulation; governance and the role of supranational bodies; sustainable production and resource acquisition; society and sustainability.

Although primarily a business and management series, it is interdisciplinary and includes contributions from the social sciences, technology, engineering, politics, philosophy, and other disciplines. It focuses on the issues at a meta-level, and investigates the ideas, organisation, and infrastructure required to address them.

The series is grounded in the belief that any global consideration of sustainability must include such issues as governance, regulation, geopolitics, the environment, and economic activity in combination to recognise the issues and develop solutions for the planet. At present such global meta-analysis is rare as current research assumes that the identification of local best practice will lead to solutions, and individual disciplines act in isolation rather than being combined to identify truly global issues and solutions.

Elena I. Lazareva · Anton D. Murzin ·
Baiba A. Rivza · Victoria N. Ostrovskaya
Editors

Innovative Trends in International Business and Sustainable Management

Springer

Editors
Elena I. Lazareva
Southern Federal University
Rostov-on-Don, Russia

Anton D. Murzin
Southern Federal University
Rostov-on-Don, Russia

Baiba A. Rivza
Latvian Academy of Sciences
Riga, Latvia

Victoria N. Ostrovskaya
Center of Marketing Initiatives LLC
Stavropol, Russia

ISSN 2520-8772 ISSN 2520-8780 (electronic)
Approaches to Global Sustainability, Markets, and Governance
ISBN 978-981-19-4007-1 ISBN 978-981-19-4005-7 (eBook)
https://doi.org/10.1007/978-981-19-4005-7

This Springer imprint is published by the registered company Springer Nature Singapore Pte Ltd.
The registered company address is: 152 Beach Road, #21-01/04 Gateway East, Singapore 189721, Singapore

Introduction—Sustainable Management of International Business: Conceptual Essence and Overview of Innovative Trends

Sustainable development is a new approach to the management of economic systems based on the principles of the social market economy. On the one hand, these principles include the classical principles of economic efficiency—market competition, mutually beneficial cooperation and integration, the international division of labor, productivity growth, economic growth based on innovative development, stimulation of employment, and improvement of living standards. On the other hand, these principles are supplemented by new principles of social efficiency—disclosing human potential and improving the quality of life—and environmental efficiency—decarbonization (combating climate change), circularity (reducing waste and increasing resource efficiency), etc.

The preconditions for the formation of the new approach described above have been growing since the end of the twentieth century; at the beginning of the twenty-first century, this approach started to receive an increasing practical application. The adoption of the Sustainable Development Goals (SDGs) by the global community has contributed to the widespread support and global dissemination of this approach to the management of economic systems. International business has launched a process of continuous adaptation to the global economic landscape, which changes as sustainability evolves. The basis of this adaptation is sustainable management, which is understood as a mechanism for managing international business on the principles of sustainable development in the unity of economic, social, and environmental efficiency.

At the current stage of evolution of the approach to the sustainable development of economic systems, associated with the active implementation of the SDGs in the "Decade of Action," four innovative trends in sustainable management of international business have emerged. The first trend is the popularization of corporate social responsibility and mass support of ESG principles by international businesses. This trend contributes to expanding the boundaries of corporate social responsibility assumed by international business.

A few decades ago, the boundaries of corporate social responsibility were narrow and included only responsibility to employees for safe and comfortable working conditions and responsibility to consumers for the quality and safety of products sold. Nowadays, these boundaries have expanded and now cover responsibility to employees in ensuring knowledge-intensive and highly productive employment, extended social guarantees, and gender and culture neutrality of corporate culture.

Moreover, corporate social responsibility now includes extended responsibility to consumers—for supporting local values, as well as the responsibility to the communities and territories of operation of international business—environmental protection, improvement of natural and climatic conditions, energy conservation, and the preservation of biodiversity and resource heritage for future generations. The entirety of corporate social responsibility is carried out based on sustainable management of international business through ESG investments.

The second trend is the modernization of the legal field and flexible government regulation of international business to stimulate its sustainable management. The laws of the countries around the world have become increasingly inclusive for international business under the influence of globalization and the development of international trade. For their part, government regulators impose ever-higher requirements and strengthen market incentives for sustainable international business management.

Integration processes in the business environment play an important role in this process. Collaboration between businesses and universities through technology parks and innovation networks strengthens scientific and technical support for sustainable management of international businesses and enhances their competitiveness in local markets. Supported by the government, business integration based on sectoral economic clusters promotes the coexistence of international businesses with local business structures.

In this case, the sustainability of international business management lies in the transition from displacement or absorption of local competitors to cooperation and "healthy competition" with them. Public–private partnerships and special (free) economic zones provide international businesses with access to improved infrastructure and public assets under the conditions of sustainability as a responsibility for the areas in which they do business.

The third trend is the increase in the social orientation of sustainable management of international business. Human resources play a crucial role in the competitiveness of international business, and sustainable human resource management (HRM) involves a mutually beneficial collaboration between employees and companies based on the principles of responsibility and long-term orientation. Training for international business is essential for its sustainable development.

The higher education systems of countries and integration unions of countries become more unified and adjusted to the current needs of international business. With the intensive development of high technology, much attention is paid to the training of digital personnel for international business and the improvement of management training aimed at developing sustainable management practices.

The fourth trend is the increased use of digital technologies in the practice of sustainable management of international business. The use of these technologies is specific to each sector of the economy; it requires special sustainable management practices for international business. For example, green innovations aimed at developing environmentally responsible production are most demanded and widespread in industry. Digitalization based on industrial robots allows for increasing the controllability of business processes, and artificial intelligence provides intelligent decision support to optimize production and distribution processes.

Sustainable management relies on organizational and digital marketing innovations in the service sector. Global e-commerce opens up opportunities for international businesses to explore new markets. In this case, sustainable management acquires an interpretation related to flexible adaptation to the changes in demand, reorientation to alternative markets when solvent demand decreases, and the maintenance of the break-even point of international business.

These trends are discussed in the available literature. Nevertheless, they are studied separately, which does not allow us to form a holistic view of sustainable management of international business at the current stage of development of economic systems. This book aims to solve this problem by providing systemic coverage and scientific rethinking of innovative trends in sustainable management of international business in the "Decade of Action." Five parts of the book detail the trends described.

Part One examines contemporary trends, challenges, and opportunities in international management and business. Part Two reveals the imperatives of smart and sustainable management in the digital environment. Part Three describes human capital as the main factor of the innovative economy and offers new managerial guidelines. Part Four presents sustainable development in close connection with innovation management. Part Five offers applied recommendations for the development of the blue economy and environmentally friendly management of sustainable development.

The novelty of this book lies in the comprehensive consideration of all innovative trends in sustainable management of international business in the "Decade of Action" based on the fundamental and methodological provisions of the systemic approach, which allows us to comprehensively study the emerging trends and offer scientific and practical recommendations for flexible and integrated sustainable management, considering these trends with the synergistic effect of the most comprehensive and large-scale support of the SDGs in the practice of international business.

The book is intended primarily for scholars whose research interests include sustainable development and international business. The book contains the results of a scientific review and critical analysis of innovative trends in sustainable management of international business, as well as the theoretical postulates of the systemic implementation of the SDGs in international business based on the mechanism of sustainable management.

The book can also be of interest to practitioners in the implementation and regulation of international business. In the book, practitioners will find a scientific review of the best practices of sustainable management of international business with broad coverage of international experience on the example of Russia, China, the BRICS countries as a whole, the OECD countries, and the Black Sea region and Eurasian countries, in particular the Republic of Tatarstan.

Numerous case studies and examples collected in the book will be useful for developing one's own applied sustainable management solutions for every international business structure. For state and supranational regulators, the book offers applied recommendations for developing the legal framework and improving state regulation of markets and international business, enabling the dissemination and enhancement of sustainable management practices.

Contents

Human Capital as the Main Factor of an Innovative Economy: New Managerial Guidelines

Contemporary Trends in International Management and Business: Challenges and Opportunities

The Sustainability Formula: A Human-Centred Strategy for Managing Economic Trends in the Context of ESG-Transformation

Elena I. Lazareva, Baiba A. Rivza, and Julia V. Gavrilova

Abstract The study identifies human-centred changes in the management strategy of multi-level economic trends under the influence of ESG-transformation. The objective of the article is to find ways of strategy for building human capital and minimizing HR risks installations in the management system of the specified economic trends. The research methodology provides for a consistent macro-meso-microanalysis of the impact of the changed conditions on the basic aspects of strategic management, starting from the macro level, with the definition of qualitative and quantitative parameters of likely HR benefits/risks related to implementing of human-oriented principles of sustainable management at all levels. The result of the study is a theoretical and methodological foundation and empirical verification of the strategy for increasing human capital in the sustainable management system. It has been justified that in the face of new global challenges, the systemic algorithm for the formation of this complex strategy should provide a complete, objective and internally consistent three-level expert-econometric analysis of human-oriented macro-, meso- and micro-economic strategies for managing economic trends. The requirements for strategic decision-making tools are formulated at the macro-, meso- and micro-level of the sustainable HR management system, as well as recommendations for economic actors on the use of expert-econometric tools for analyzing the reasons for slowing down the process of accumulation of human capital in the post-pandemic area, as well as for developing suitable public policy measures aimed at sustainable development of human capital are given.

Keywords Human capital · HR-risks · Strategic management · Economic trends of sustainable and innovative development · ESG transformation

JEL Classification J24 · C54 · J64

E. I. Lazareva (✉) · J. V. Gavrilova
Southern Federal University, Rostov-on-Don, Russia
e-mail: elazareva@sfedu.ru

B. A. Rivza
Latvian Academy of Sciences, Riga, Latvia
e-mail: baiba.rivza@llu.lv

E. I. Lazareva et al. (eds.), *Innovative Trends in International Business and Sustainable Management*, Approaches to Global Sustainability, Markets, and Governance,
https://doi.org/10.1007/978-981-19-4005-7_1

1 Introduction

The COVID-19 pandemic has become an unprecedented challenge for all planets, giving an important push for universal awareness of the important role of human and ESG factors in economic activity. Effective strategic management of human capital in the context of new global challenges is becoming a key condition for increasing the sustainability of socio-economic systems' innovative development. The study aims to find ways to install strategies for increasing human capital and minimizing HR risks in the management system of multi-level economic trends in the context of ESG transformation.

The difficulty in achieving this aim is due to three facts.

The first fact is the global spatio-temporal nature of the pandemic, which leads not only to a reduction in the number of jobs, a decrease in production but also is accompanied by negative social effects (the level of social segmentation of society increasing, income inequality, etc.). As a result, the process of human capital accumulation—the basic asset of innovation-oriented socio-economic development of countries and regions—is significantly slowed down/interrupted. In addition, there is a radical transformation of the labour market, and as a result, the demand for highly qualified personnel is significantly increasing (Fedorova et al., 2020; Jílková, 2021; Pritadrajati et al., 2021).

The second fact is that conservative directions are failing decisively and innovative technologies are replacing the traditional ones. The formation of a national strategic policy to support the development of human capital, innovation (especially in the sector of small enterprises and startups), research and development, should become a key priority in these conditions (Butowski, 2021; Lenihan et al., 2019; Michele & Dipboye, 2004).

The third fact is that the process of introducing ESG (Environmental, Social, Governance) principles into development strategies, which define the sustainability of the multi-level decision-making, is becoming very important for the world community (Clementino & Perkins, 2021; Cogan, 2006; EBA, 2021; Gassmann et al., 2021; Sciarelli et al., 2021). This thesis is supported by the following facts. The value of assets managed by organizations implementing the United Nations Responsible Investment Principles (UNPRI) amounted to USD 86 trillion in 2019; the global issue of green securities in 2020—more than 258 billion US dollars (Stern, 2020; United Nations, 2021).

The problem of ensuring the sustainability of economic trends based on ESG standards goes far beyond corporate policy, becoming a significant factor in national stability (Barnett & Salomon, 2002; Zhou et al., 2021). As a result, the number of ESG rating assessments of the development trajectories of corporations, regions and countries is growing, which make it possible to assess environmental and social risks, as well as the quality of management on a single scale, and make management decisions suitable to the current situation on this basis.

The increasing importance of ESG factors in the modern knowledge economy has served as a precondition for the gradual human-oriented transformation of the system of strategic regulation of multi-level socio-economic trends. According to the SD (Sustainable Development) of socio-economic systems concept, which is finding more and more supporters, the level of well-being achieved by one generation or another is consistently determined by the qualitative characteristics of the accumulated resource base, the most significant role in which is assigned to human capital (Ali et al., 2016; Buevich et al., 2020; Geissdoerfer et al., 2018; Laskowska & Danska-Borsiak, 2016; Lazareva et al., 2016).

The formation of an effective human-oriented strategy for managing economic trends of new global challenges must necessarily be systemic in the above-mentioned conditions. The novelty of the research consists in substantiating the algorithm of a three-level systematic expert-econometric analysis of human-oriented strategies for managing economic trends. The correlated levels of macro-, meso- and microeconomics are identified as the basic levels of strategies, which ensures completeness, objectivity and inter-level consistency of strategic measures in a complex management system of the human resource component of sustainable innovative economic trends.

The results of the study can serve as a basis for analyzing the reasons for slowing down the process of accumulation of human capital in the post-pandemic area, as well as for developing suitable public policy measures aimed at sustainable development of human capital.

2 Materials and Methods

The methodological basis of the author's approach was the innovation-cyclical and resource paradigm of economic development, according to which human capital in modern society has a rent-forming function and acts as a multi-parameter socio-resource component of the vector of sustainable innovative development of the economy (Lazareva et al., 2016) (Fig. 1).

Most of the theoretical approaches to identifying the systemic levels of sustainable economic development management are based on the assumption that to ensure the efficiency of its functioning, this system should have a multi-level character. The system-forming basis for the allocation of levels was the administrative division within Russia and interstate division when creating interstate and global levels of a sustainable management system for economic trends (Anopchenko et al., 2018).

In conditions of multi-level management of sustainable economic development, three levels of the system "macroeconomics–mesoeconomics–microeconomics" (MMM-systems) should be considered as the basic.

The human-oriented management strategy of the three-level MMM system is based on inter-related socio-ecological and economic strategies aimed at increasing human capital as a key resource factor of innovative and sustainable economic dynamics.

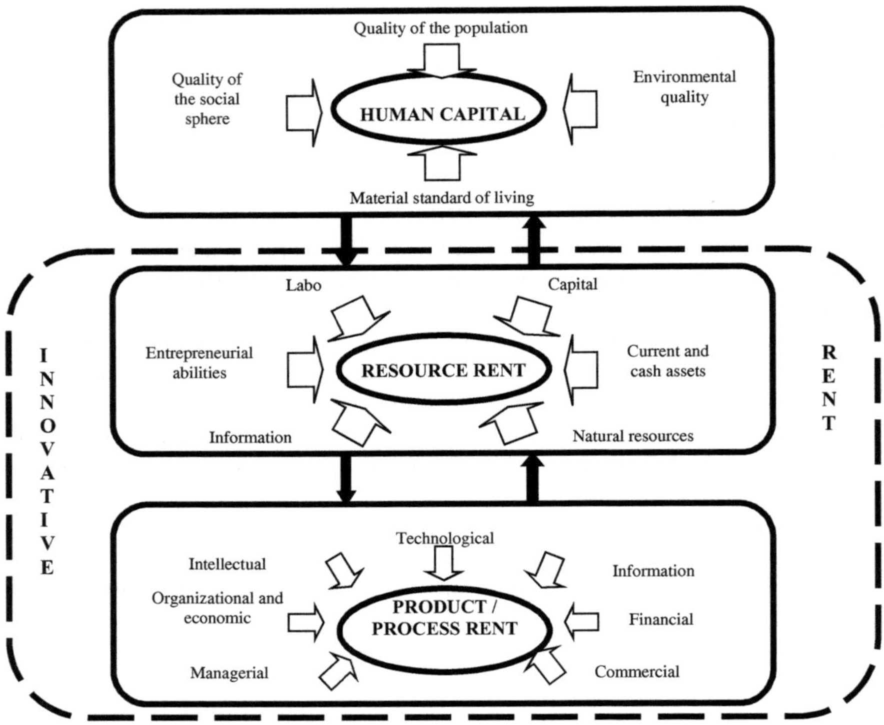

Fig. 1 Human capital as a rent-forming factor of the innovative process. *Source* Developed by the authors

At each level, the management system for sustainable development of the human potential of the economy consists of three standard modules: a comprehensive assessment of the potential and factors of an increase in human resources, a monitoring subsystem and a subsystem of managerial decisions (Anopchenko et al., 2018; Lazareva et al., 2016).

A comprehensive assessment of the potential consists in studying the properties of a specific human resource system in an economy of an innovative type, its material and non-material subsystems and the formed vectors of their multichannel impact on the formation of innovation-oriented economic development trends. The principles of a two-stage assessment of the potential of human capital as an integrated resource of an innovative economy are shown in Table 1.

Knowledge of the properties of the components of the human resource system, the characteristic of their influence on innovation-oriented economic processes serve as the foundation for the construction of the second module of the management structure—monitoring. At the same time, monitoring is understood as a subsystem of regular control of the parameters of human resources, as well as the forecast of their changes in space–time coordinates to ensure the adoption of innovation-oriented economic decisions.

Table 1 Principles of two-stage assessment of human capital potential as an integrated resource of innovative economy

Stage I. Human Resource Potential Assessment (HRP)				
The principle of "normative" identification of the level of sufficiency of HRP		The principle of comparative analysis of the mismatch between the actual and standard parameters of the HRP		Resource-targeting principle parameterization
Stage II. Assessment of the strategy for increasing the level of conversion of HRP into resources for innovative growth				
The principle of synchronization of the criteria of economic efficiency, social justice and environmental stability of strategies for the increment of HRP	Modified Hartwick-Solow principle	The principle of a full-fledged non-market assessment of the social and environmental components of the HRP	The principle of preserving the components of the HRP on a non-decreasing (constant) level	The principle of the socio-ecological and economic balance of strategies for increasing the HRP

Source Developed by the authors

Monitoring the state of the potential of human capital as an integrated resource for innovation-oriented economic development is based on the "resource-resultant" structuring of the PHR—its resource component reflects the impact on the innovative processes of certain human resources, and the resultant one reflects the effect of the use of these resources.

The final module of the sustainable management system is a subsystem of management decisions that are taken by the relevant controlling and managing state/administrative organizations to optimize the socio-economic situation in terms of increasing the innovation/economic effect of strategic actions. The whole complex of management decisions forms the main directions of socio-ecological and economic policy in the field of increasing human capital.

The development and substantiation of management strategies at the national and regional levels are implemented using expert and analytical tools that integrate synchronized calculation procedures for a comprehensive assessment of human resource potential by methods of system analysis and econometric assessment of the parametric characteristics of human-oriented strategies for managing economic trends (taking into account the potential innovation and economic effect of their implementation). The information base for calculations is the set of evolutionary and functionally related human resources of Russia, as well as some foreign countries (and their parametric characteristics).

The advantage of this tool is its holistic nature, which ensures mutual consistency of the instruments used in state strategic policy to stimulate economic trends. Indeed, both methods of system analysis, in particular, the Analytic Hierarchy method (Lazareva et al., 2016), and methods of econometrics (Li & Wang, 2018;

Pavlova et al., 2020; Shahjahan et al., 2016; Xu & Li, 2020) and simulation modelling (Anopchenko et al., 2018) are actively used in the modern human resource management system. However, these methods focus on separate, divorced from each other, aspects of the formation and implementation of human-oriented strategies of economic development. Understanding of the consistency and interdependence of management decisions aimed at minimizing HR risks is reflected in the need to integrate these tools into single decision support tools.

The development of a scenario model for the accumulation of human resource potential in order to ensure innovative economic growth (one of the modules of the tool) is implemented in the context of each of the parametric characteristics of the integral potential. Thus, the expert-analytical tool makes it possible to assess the factors of reducing the unemployment rate and to develop, on this basis, a strategy for increasing the level of employment of the population (Fig. 2). It also makes it possible to justify regionally differentiated strategies aimed at improving the quality of the population and the socio-ecological sphere, increasing the level of well-being.

The solution to the problem of minimizing HR risks at the micro-level is based mainly on the methodology of system analysis, which allows assessing complex structured factors and qualitative risk indicators. One of the most relevant methods of systemic risk assessment in the HR management structure is the Dematel multi-criteria analysis method, which has demonstrated effectiveness in identifying the

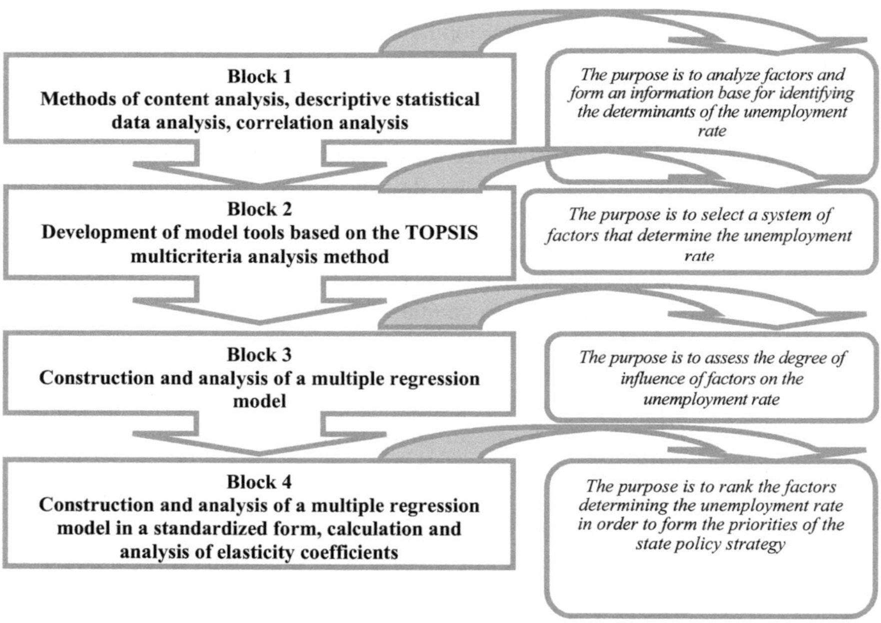

Fig. 2 An algorithm for developing an expert econometric model for identifying factors—determinants of the unemployment rate. *Source* Developed by the authors

causes-effects pattern in a complex HR risk management system, as well as ranking the HR risks of an organization (Lazareva et al., 2021).

3 Results

Using the author's tools, a comprehensive assessment of the current state of the potential of human resources in Russia in global coordinates were obtained, strategies for increasing the HRP in the context of ESG-transformation were substantiated and empirically verified, including managerial decisions on increasing the quality of accumulated potential in a four-component perspective (the level of well-being and the quality of the population, social, ecological subsystems).

A comprehensive assessment of strategies has shown that the most significant factors—resource sources for increasing the sustainability of post-pandemic economic trajectories—are a decrease in unemployment levels and social differentiation of society.

Consequently, priority strategies are to increase the level of employment of the population and a sustainable increase in the quality of the social infrastructure of innovatively targeted economic dynamics, characterized by positive network effects.

The results of expert econometric modelling of the unemployment rate showed that GNI per capita has the greatest impact on it, then, in order of decreasing influence, there are, respectively, the number of self-employed (% of total employment), the level of inflation in consumer prices, the number of tax revenues (% of GDP), the number of employers (% of total employment). These results were used as the basis for recommendations on the formation of a strategic policy aimed at the sustainable development of human capital.

When forming a policy, both federal-level actions, including those aimed at stabilizing the inflation rate, and regional-level actions, such as increasing the number of employers, are important.

The state policy strategies in the sphere of sustainable reduction of the level of social differentiation are ranked for each of the four types of Russian regions, differing in the degree of innovative activity of economic agents (Table 2).

Assessment of integrated HR risks in the organization management system (Kant Baltic Federal University) using the Dematel method made it possible to form a system of relationships between them in the coordinates "cause-effect" and to identify on this basis the priorities of the strategy for minimizing HR risks—overcoming "Failures" in strategic and motivational policies.

The transformation of the system of non-material motivation, as well as the stimulation of innovative activity based on an individual approach to the involvement of employees in the decision-making process, are becoming important priorities of the HR strategy.

Table 2 Ranking of strategies to reduce social differentiation

<table>
<tr><th rowspan="2">Type of region</th><th colspan="4">Rating</th></tr>
<tr><th>1</th><th>2</th><th>3</th><th>4</th></tr>
<tr><td>A</td><td>Development of social infrastructure</td><td rowspan="2">Increasing the level/conditions of employment</td><td>Small business development, liberty of entrepreneurship</td><td rowspan="2">Increasing access to science and technology, developing Information infrastructure</td></tr>
<tr><td>B</td><td rowspan="2">Small business development, liberty of entrepreneurship</td><td>Development of social infrastructure</td></tr>
<tr><td>C</td><td>Increasing access to science and technology, developing information infrastructure</td><td rowspan="2">Development of social infrastructure</td><td rowspan="2">Increasing the level/conditions of employment</td></tr>
<tr><td>D</td><td>Increasing access to science and technology, developing information infrastructure</td><td>Small business development, liberty of entrepreneurship</td></tr>
</table>

Source Developed by the authors

4 Conclusion

The novelty of the author's approach is defined by the methodological substantiation of the macro-meso-micro-level strategy of reproduction of the widely interpreted human resource potential of innovation-oriented dynamics, which allows to comprehensively take into account the effects of systemic regulation of economic trends in the process of making long-term decisions.

A systems approach to management means a mutually correlated three-level human-centred transformation of priorities and key channels for achieving them. The multistructural unity of tiered human resource systems initiates the implementation in order to develop the priority areas of ESG transformation of the strategy of the proposed tool.

The priority tasks of the strategic management of economic trends are the expansion of the list of regulated human resource subsystems (installation of both material and non-material components in the management system), material and non-material incentives for various forms of long-term employment, sustainable development based on the Hartwick-Solow methodological principle of social infrastructure in order to reduce the level of social differentiation in society, the implementation of investment policy that stimulates innovation activity and social responsibility of business.

The author's developments can be used by economic actors to analyze the reasons for the slowdown in the accumulation of human capital in the post-pandemic area and to form a strategy aimed at the sustainable reproduction of human resources.

References

Ali, M., Cantner, U., & Roy, I. (2016). Knowledge spillovers through FDI and trade: Moderating role of quality-adjusted human capital. *Journal of Evolutionary Economics, 26*(4), 323–351.

Anopchenko, T. Yu., Gorbaneva, O. I., Lazareva, E. I., Murzin, A. D., & Ougolnitsky, G. A. (2018). Systems methodology and model tools for territorial sustainable management. *Advances in Systems Science and Applications, 1*(4), 136–150.

Barnett, M., & Salomon, R. (2002). Beyond dichotomy: The curvilinear relationship between social responsibility and financial performance. *Strategic Management Journal, 27*(11), 1101–1122.

Buevich, A. P., Varvus, S. A., & Terskaya, G. A. (2020). Investments in human capital as a key factor of sustainable economic development. *Lecture Notes in Networks and Systems, 9*, 397–406.

Butowski, L. (2021). Sustainable tourism: A human-centered approach. *Sustainability, 2021*(13), 1835. https://doi.org/10.3390/su13041835.

Clementino, E., & Perkins, R. (2021). How do companies respond to Environmental, Social and Governance (ESG) ratings? Evidence from Italy. *Journal of Business Ethics, 171*, 379–397.

Cogan, D. G. (2006). *Corporate governance and climate change: Making the connexion*. Ceres. https://www.ceres.org. Accessed November 23, 2021.

EBA Report on Management and Supervision of ESG Risks for Credit Institutions and Investment Firms EBA/REP/2021/18. https://www.eba.europa.eu. Accessed November 20, 2021.

Fedorova, A., Dvorakova, Z., & Koropets, O. (2020). Transformation of labour relations in the context of global economic and social risks. *International Journal of Monetary Economics and Finance, 13*(3), 206–214.

Gassmann, P., Herman, C., & Kelly, C. (2021). *Are you ready for the ESG revolution? Societal need and business opportunity are coming together to transform the way companies craft strategy, drive performance, and report results*. Strategy+Business. PwC. https://www.pwc.com. Accessed November 23, 2021.

Geissdoerfer, M., Vladimirova, D., & Evans, S. (2018). Sustainable business model innovation: A review. *Journal of Cleaner Production, 198*, 401–416.

Jílková, P. (2021). Sustainable corporate strategy: The role of human capital in the time of COVID-19 crisis. *TEM Journal, 10*(2), 699–706.

Laskowska, I., & Danska-Borsiak, B. (2016). The importance of human capital for the economic development of EU regions. *Comparative Economic Research, 19*(5), 63–79.

Lazareva, E., Anopchenko, T., & Lozovitskaya, D. (2016). Identification of the city welfare economics strategic management innovative model in the global challenges conditions. In *SGEM 2016 Conference Proceedings* (pp. 3–10).

Lazareva, E. I., Gavrilova, J. V., & Murzin, A. D. (2021). Development of HR-management tools for an innovation-oriented organization using system analysis. In O. G. Shakirova, O. V. Bashkov, & A. A. Khusainov (Eds)., *Current problems and ways of industry development: Equipment and technologies* (Vol. 200, pp. 985–996). Lecture Notes in Networks and Systems. Springer.

Lenihan, H., McGuirk, H., & Murphy, K. R. (2019). Driving innovation: Public policy and human capital. *Research Policy, 48*(9), 103791.

Li, T., & Wang, Y. (2018). Growth channels of human capital: A Chinese panel data study. *China Economic Review, 51*, 309–322.

Michele, E. A. J., & Dipboye, R. L. (2004). Leveraging diversity to improve business performance. *Human Resource Management, Wiley, 43*(4), 409–424.

Pavlova, L. L., Kolesnik, E. A., & Filatova, E. L. (2020). Human capital valuation at the level of regional economic complexes. *Asia Life Sciences, 22*(2), 71–85.

Pritadrajati, D. S., Kusuma, A. C. M., & Saxena, S. C. (2021). Scarred for life: Lasting consequences of unemployment and informal self-employment: An empirical evidence from Indonesia. *Economic Analysis and Policy, 70*, 206–219.

Sciarelli, M., Cosimato, S., Landi, G., & Iandolo, F. (2021). Socially responsible investment strategies for the transition towards sustainable development: The importance of integrating and communicating ESG. *The TQM Journal, 33*(7), 39–56.

Shahjahan, A., Khandaker, J. A., & Md. Thuhid, N. (2016). An econometric analysis of human capital development and economic growth in Bangladesh. *Journal of Economics and Sustainable Development, 7*(17), 30–38.

Stern, H. J. (2020). *Better bonus plans for ESG*. Working Paper, SSRN. https://www.readcube.com. Accessed November 20, 2021.

United Nations, Inter-agency Task Force on Financing for Development, Financing for Sustainable Development Report 2021. (New York: United Nations, 2021). https://development.nance.un.org/fsdr2021. Accessed November 20, 2021.

Xu, Y., & Li, A. (2020). The relationship between innovative human capital and interprovincial economic growth based on panel data model and spatial econometrics. *Journal of Computational and Applied Mathematics, 365*, 112381.

Zhou, X., Caldecott, B., Harnett, E., & Schumacher, K. (2021). *The effect of firm-level ESG practices on macroeconomic performance*. Working Paper No. 20-03, University of Oxford. https://www.smithschool.ox.ac.uk. Accessed November 20, 2021.

Assessment of Country Political Risks as an International Business Management Tool

Tatiana E. Kochergina and Asia I. Ryaboshapka

Abstract *Purpose* The purpose of this article is to define methodological approaches to assessing country political risks as a tool for managing international business and substantiate the effectiveness of competitive analysis based on a point-rating assessment of the level of country risk. *Methodology* The authors, based on the global competitiveness index, taking into account the corrective influence of assessments of the country's international rating position, apply methods of competitive analysis and point-rating assessment of the country's political risks to determine specific, unique signs of this risk, which contributes to ensuring effective management of international business. *Results* It is determined that the country risk assessment can be based on the systematic application of a list of indices through which the country is described from the standpoint of real/potential risks in the political sphere. The proposal to use publicly available ratings data of international organizations or institutions engaged in research in the field of country risks as sources of information is substantiated. An algorithm for conducting a competitive analysis of countries based on selected criteria of country risks is presented. *Originality/value* The methodological approach to the assessment of country political risks proposed in the form of an algorithm can be considered as a theoretical and methodological tool for structural analysis of potential partners in the implementation of international business activities. In practical application, it makes it possible to assess the risks of specific forms of organization and areas of international business, as well as to assess the risks in the implementation of management functions in international business.

Keywords International business · Country risk · International rating · Competitiveness index · Competitive analysis

JEL Classification E01 · F23 · F42 · F68

T. E. Kochergina (✉) · A. I. Ryaboshapka
Rostov Branch of the Russian Customs Academy, Rostov-on-Don, Russia
e-mail: tpodgurskaya@mail.ru

E. I. Lazareva et al. (eds.), *Innovative Trends in International Business and Sustainable Management*, Approaches to Global Sustainability, Markets, and Governance,
https://doi.org/10.1007/978-981-19-4005-7_2

1 Introduction

Assessment of country risks in transactions related to international business is necessary to obtain the planned commercial results by all actors of an international transaction, for example, the state, the seller, the buyer in the implementation of foreign trade operations. Thus, the country risk assessment in customs risk management provides the state with the solution of a number of tasks related to the calculation of customs duties; filling of the revenue base of the state budget; suppression of smuggling; prohibition of the import of goods, which are harmful to society, consumers, the environment, etc. For the buyer, the knowledge of insurance risks allows him to insure himself in order to receive goods of a certain quantity and quality, in accordance with the contract price, to get the goods into ownership and pay for it. The seller, being familiar with the country risks of his foreign partner, receives the opportunity to correctly formulate the terms of the transaction and provide guarantees of their execution. Consequently, the planned commercial results will be obtained only in the absence of any risk situations, which indicates the theoretical and practical relevance of the study of the problem of methodological approaches to assessing country risks.

The problem of insurance risk assessment is comprehensively covered in the works on the assessment of investment and banking risks, due to the fact that they are largely influenced by political events and actions (Investing in Stocks Cousera, 2021; Demkin et al., 2016; Pereiro, 2002; WTO, 2021). Active actions to assess country risks are being taken by international organizations and analytical institutions. The results of this work are reflected in the relevant publications. Methodological approaches to assessing country risks based on BERI, Pricewaterhouse Coopers models, SWOT analysis, PEST analysis, country risk assessment by country index (CREAM), McKinsey global confidence index, etc. are recognized and practically significant (Country Risk Rating and - (CRM), 2021; Hermes, 2020; Index of Attractiveness of Offshore Placement, 2021; McKinsey Global Confidence Index, 2021; CREAM, 2021; Opacity Index (O-factor), 2021; Rating of the global competitiveness of the countries of the world, 2021). No less interesting and significant are the results of research concerning the country's international rating position, which presents data on the location of a particular country in accordance with the risk indicators selected for analysis and reflecting the national macroeconomic conditions of conducting international business (Comprehensive Risk Assessment and Business Risk Service (BRS), 2021; Kochergina, 2021; McKinsey Global Confidence Index, 2021; Reflection of Country Risk in Ratings, 2018).

The conceptualization of the proposed methodology is determined by the recognition of the priority of assessing political risks in international business, which is necessary in the conditions of dynamically developing geopolitical processes, increased competition and changes in the conjuncture of world markets in modern conditions. The working hypothesis is that on the basis of already applied methodological approaches, it is possible to concretize the methodology for assessing country political risks to ensure its greater adequacy, timeliness and instrumental orientation in the organization and conduct of international business.

The purpose of this work is to determine methodological approaches to the procedure of assessing country political risks as a tool for managing international business, taking into account the characteristics of country political risk, identifying indicators of country political risk based on international rating positions of countries and their comparative analysis using a point-rating assessment.

The realization of this goal necessitated the following tasks: to concretize country risks taking into account the changing global conditions of international business activity; to identify sources of quantitative indicators in order to form indicators of country political risks; to present a methodological approach to assessing country political risks based on competitive and comparative analysis conducted using risk indicators.

2 Methodology

The definition of country risk indicators is based on the identification of risk factors that include such areas as politics, economics, social relations, technology, culture and others. Therefore, the procedure for assessing country markets as an international business management tool included the identification and characterization of country risk factors that have developed in modern conditions, primarily under the influence of the COVID-19 pandemic.

In our opinion, today the political factor has the greatest influence on determining the macroeconomic conditions for doing international business. The macroeconomic environment that determines the results of individual international business operations develops under the influence of global social and political events, as well as the actions of states. Political risk is characterized as being unmanageable or hidden. The sources of risk are external factors. The specifics of the situation in a particular country do not allow us to predict the probability of its occurrence. There are three degrees of influence on the implementation of an international business project: weak, medium or strong.

Thus, according to the WTO, the spread of COVID-19 and the struggle for people's lives led to the use of unprecedented restrictive measures by countries, which together caused a reduction in international trade as the main direction of international business by 5.3% (Covid-19 and International Trade, 2020).

The main restrictive measures, according to the results of OECD studies, include economic and administrative measures. Among the economic restrictive measures, the following are highlighted: an increase in the prices of air cargo, for example, in the direction of China–North America by more than 60%; an increase in labor protection costs, etc. Administrative measures include such as cancellation of passenger flights; restriction of cargo transportation; changing port protocols and reducing cargo volumes by 10–20% compared to 2019; biosafety requirements and quarantine measures for food products; additional requirements for examination documentation, etc. (Covid-19 and International Trade, 2020).

The specificity of political risk lies in the fact that it occurs due to the instability of macroeconomic development under the influence of intended, adopted, implemented and/or unrealized political decisions and indirectly and/or partially manifested in the volumes and dynamics of GDP and GNP. It is known that countries with large fluctuations in GDP and GNP are perceived as countries with higher risk than countries with positive dynamics of these indicators.

The consequences of political decisions in the form of indices reflect the situation in a particular country in various ratings, such as the Corruption Perception Index (Transparency International Index—CIP); Sovereign Credit Rating; Index of Economic Freedom; Opacity Index (O-factor); Economic Vulnerability Index; Global Retail Development Index; E-Business Readiness Index; Ease of Doing Business Index; Global Competitiveness Index; Global Foreign Direct Investment Country Attractiveness Index; Ranking of countries in terms of per capita income; OECD methodology, etc.

Each of the designated ratings contains parameters characterizing the political situation in a particular country, which makes it possible to use them to assess the country's political risk for the implementation of an international business project. The need to adapt the indices of international ratings of countries to determine the level of country risks is due to the varying degree of influence of various factors on the execution of international contracts.

For example, the country rating index "Comprehensive Risk Assessment" (BRS-BERI) (Kochergina, 2021) includes an assessment of working conditions, political and currency risks that allow determining the rating positions of these countries. The sub-indices are calculated in three directions: the political risk index (PRI); the operational risk index (ORI) and the coefficient of money transfers and repatriation (Refactor), which are combined into an "Overall Score". The country risk assessment model "Country Index (CREAM)" (Comprehensive Risk Assessment and Business Risk Service (BRS), 2021) predicts violence and political risks, including: wars, terrorism, civil unrest and other non-business risks. This model presents four main risk categories:

1. War.
2. Terrorism.
3. Civil unrest.
4. Political risk (the risk of a significant change in foreign and/or domestic policy).

The consolidated assessment of the "O-factor" (The Opacity Index) for each country is based on data on opacity in five different areas that affect capital markets: corruption; the legal system; state macroeconomic and fiscal policies; accounting standards and practices (including corporate governance and information openness); regulatory regime (Opacity index (O-factor), 2021).

The purpose of the Country Risk Model (CRM) is to provide complete, internationally comparable and regularly updated country risk assessments for 100 highly indebted developing countries, as well as to obtain credit ratings of relative risks from a macroeconomic and financial point of view.

The risk assessment methodology (CRM) includes:

(1) identification of risk categories grouped into analytical categories of a political nature, economic policy, economic structure and liquidity factors;
(2) assessment of exposure to the risk associated with investing in certain types of financial instruments, i.e. certain investment risks. First of all, the assessment of this risk is related to the assessment of currency risk in relation to the US dollar, foreign currency loans to the state and loans to banks in foreign currency (Pereiro, 2002).

The Country Risk Rating (WMRC) (2021) includes two risk models: one evaluates the climate for foreign direct investment (FDI) for corporations; the other evaluates sovereign credit as a rating of international financial institutions. The country risk rating model evaluates the FDI climate based on six individual ratings in each country, including political, economic, legal, tax, operational and security.

The ratings of the International Country Risk Guide (ICRG) (2021) assess economic, political and financial risks and warn of serious changes. The rating includes 22 variables in three risk subcategories: political, financial and economic. A separate index is created for each subcategory.

Based on the selected indices for assessing country risks, a competitive analysis of countries is carried out in accordance with the goals and objectives of international business management.

The algorithm of the methodological approach of competitive analysis is presented in the following sequence of actions:

1. Definition of country risk criteria.
2. Identification of information sources based on country risk criteria.
3. Building a matrix of comparison of countries according to the selected criteria.
4. Determination of weights of criteria.
5. Collection of statistical data by countries according to the selected criteria.
6. Calculation of compliance indices according to the selected comparison criteria.
7. Conducting a comparative country analysis taking into account the weight of the criteria.
8. Conducting a comparative analysis of country indicators with assigned ranges of risk levels.

Thus, the algorithm of competitive analysis provides for research and analytical work, the result of which can be a system of quantitative and qualitative characteristics and indicators of political risks of a particular country.

3 Results

The use of rating systems to assess country political risks makes it possible to determine a country's rating position in accordance with publicly available, recognized, updated, mainly annually or several times a year indices in the global system. Thus, according to the global competitiveness index, countries are ranked by 333 indicators. These indicators reflect the state of the economy, the effectiveness of the government, the quality of the business environment, the condition of infrastructure, which provides an opportunity to obtain an overview of a particular country and macroeconomic conditions for international entrepreneurship (Rating of the Global Competitiveness, 2021).

As an example, data on the rating of the global competitiveness index for the EAEU countries were used, namely: Kazakhstan took 55th place in the ranking at the end of 2019 and improved its position by 4 points; Russia remained in 43rd place; Armenia improved its position by 1 point and took 69th place; Kyrgyzstan, taking 96th place, rose by 1 point (2021, p.14).

Table 1 shows data on the position of the EAEU countries in accordance with individual indicators of the Global Competitiveness Index 4.0. The country's place in the ranking of 141 countries is indicated in parentheses.

Table 1 Country indicators on the global competitiveness index of the EAEU countries, 2019

Indicator	Russia	Kazakhstan	Kyrgyzstan	Armenia
GDP per capita, US dollars	11,326.8	9237.0	1268.0	4149.3
Unemployment rate, %	4.7	4.9	7.2	17.7
Gini Index, 0–100	37.7	27.5	27.3	33.6
Corruption Level 0–100 (best)	28.0 (116)	31.0 (107)	29.0 (111)	35.0 (91)
The state ensuring the political stability 1–7 (best)	3.7 (88)	4.5 (46)	3.2 (111)	4.2 (58)
Transport infrastructure	(49)	(73)	(129)	(74)
Inflation, %	3.3 (3)	6.7 (119)	2.4 (1)	1.7 (1)
Trade openness	(116)	(79)	(109)	(84)
Prevalence of non-tariff barriers 1–7 (best)	4.1 (103)	4.5 (62)	4.1 (108)	4.4 (72)
Trade tariffs, 1–7 (best)	4.38 (57)	4.29 (54)	4.52 (60)	4.27 (55)
Complexity of tariffs 1–7 (best)	3.7 (109)	4.3 (104)	3.6 (111)	4.2 (105)
The effectiveness of the border crossing 1–5 (the best)	2.4 (99)	2.7 (64)	2.8 (56)	2.6 (81)
Financial system	(95)	(104)	(112)	(69)
Administrative requirements	(50)	(32)	(67)	(68)
Commercialization	(77)	(89)	(115)	(51)
Buyer Level 1–7 (best)	3.5 (80)	3.6 (68)	3.3 (91)	4.1 (33)

Source Compiled by the authors based on the source (2021, pp. 62–65, 314–317, pp. 330–333, pp. 482–485)

For the competitive analysis, individual indicators on the global competitiveness index of countries were selected as criteria in order to determine risk factors.

The factors of country risks of the business environment were:

1. Criterion 1—"The state ensuring political stability" (1–7 best);
2. Criterion 2—transport infrastructure according to the country's place in the ranking of 142 countries;
3. Criterion 3—prevalence of non-tariff barriers (1–7 best);
4. Criterion 4—trade tariffs (1–7 best);
5. Criterion 5—complexity of tariffs (1–7 best);
6. Criterion 6—efficiency of border crossing (1–7 best);
7. Criterion 7—the financial system according to the country's place in the ranking of 142 countries.

Next, a matrix of concrete and comparative analysis was formed, which is a template, i.e. a tool of competitive comparative analysis, the main criteria of which are the following: comparisons, weight of criteria, countries being compared, the index of compliance of the studied country with the comparison criteria (compliance index), the total indicator (Total). The weight of the criterion shows the significance of the criterion.

Usually, the weight of the criterion is assigned in the range from 1 to 10, but this is not very convenient, since the difference of one point is difficult to distinguish. Therefore, the Fibonacci series was applied as a sequence of numbers, where each subsequent one is the sum of the two previous numbers. Eight numbers were used to assess the significance of the criterion (weight): 1, 2, 3, 5, 8, 13, 21, 34.

The criteria with the indicated weight were presented in tabular form. To determine the compliance index, the parameters characterizing the selected criteria are assigned. Usually, the highest/lowest value is assigned an index of 10, and the remaining indexes are determined proportionally.

For example, for criterion 1, index 10 is assigned to the value of parameter 4.5 (the highest is for Kazakhstan). For Russia, the index indicator after calculating the score will be equal to 8.2. Similarly, calculations were carried out for criteria 3,4,5,6.

For criterion 2 (similarly for criterion 7), the calculation is performed as follows: first, we determine the weight of points for the 141st country, which will be equal to 0.07, and then we calculate the index for Russia, which will be equal to 6.4.

After making the necessary calculations, we obtain the compliance indices for the selected comparison criteria, which is reflected in Table 2.

Next, we conduct a comparative analysis taking into account the assigned weight of the criterion. Criterion 1 was assigned a weight of 34, criterion 2—13, criterion 3—34, criterion 4—21, criterion 5—21, criterion 6—13, criterion 7—21.

To calculate the Total, the weight of the criterion is multiplied by the index of compliance of the selected system, we do this with each criterion, and sum up the resulting products (formula 1).

$$\text{Total }(m) = \sum \text{Criterion weight} \times \text{Compliance Index }(n) \tag{1}$$

Table 2 Compliance indices according to the selected comparison criteria

N	Criterion	Russia		Kazakhstan		Kyrgyzstan		Armenia	
		Parameter value	Index	Parameter value	Index	Parameter value	Index	Parameter value	Index
1	The state ensuring policy stability 1–7 (best)	3.7	8.2	4.5	10	3.2	7.1	4.2	9.3
2	Transport infrastructure, ranked out of 141 countries	49	6.4	73	4.8	129	0.8	74	4.7
3	Prevalence of non-tariff barriers 1–7 (best)	4.1	9.1	4.5	10	4.1	9.1	4.4	9.8
4	Trade Rates 1–7 (best)	4.38	9.7	4.29	9.5	4.52	10	4.27	9.5
5	Complexity of tariffs 1–7 (best)	3.7	8.6	4.3	10	3.6	8.3	4.2	9.8
6	The effectiveness of the border crossing 1–5 (the best)	2.4	8.6	2.7	9.7	2.8	10	2.6	9.3
7	Financial system, ranked out of 141 countries	95	3.2	104	2.6	112	2.0	69	5.0

Source Developed by the authors

Ranges of country political risk levels can be assigned both by individual criteria (from 1 to 10) and by the total value (in our case, from 1 to 1570).

4 Conclusion

Thus, as a result of the study, it was revealed that the assessment of country political risks can be based on the identification of a list of indices through which the country is described from the standpoint of real/potential risks in the political sphere. Based on the characteristics of the indices of international ratings, the proposal to use publicly available ratings data from either international organizations or institutions engaged in research in the field of country risks as sources of information is substantiated. The presented algorithm for conducting a competitive analysis of countries based on selected criteria of country risks is aimed at increasing the reliability of the data used and reducing time spent in managing international business.

The proposed methodological approach to the assessment of country risks in the management of international business can be applied to the assessment of country risks not only on a geographical basis, but also to individual risk factors, commodity groups, logistics organization, choice of financial partners, ways to enter the foreign market, etc. In this case, the main tasks will be formulated as follows: to specify the object of risk, set parameters for risk indicators and identify reliable sources of information. Since the proposed algorithm involves generating a huge amount of information, it is advisable to use special technologies for storing and processing large amounts of data (Big Data).

As a result of this research, a methodological approach was formed in the form of an algorithm for assessing country political risks as a tool for managing international business.

References

Adjustments of multipliers for country risks. How can companies from different countries be compared? (2021). *Investing in stocks Cousera.* https://ru.coursera.org/lecture/investicii-akcii/vidieo-10-korriektsii-mul-tiplikatorov-na-stranovyie-riski-kak-sravnivat-MtsLp. Data accessed October 15, 2021.

Comprehensive Risk Assessment, Business Risk Service (BRS). *Business Environment Risk Intelligence.* http://www.beri.com/brs.asp. Data accessed October 28, 2021.

Country Risk Rating (WMRC). (2021). http://www.wmrc.com/wma_caf_sample.html. Data accessed October 22, 2021.

Covid-19 and international trade: issues and actions. (2020). http://media.rspp.ru/document/1/8/2/82dc16365b4fde7d1d3b0838a9ca9cae.pdf. Data accessed November 02, 2021.

Demkin, I. V., Vlasov, D. A., Gabrielov, A. O., Barkhatov, V. D., & Lukyanovich, N. V. (2016). Index approach to assessing country risks of real investments. *Risk Analysis Problems, 13,6*(13), 30–47.

EIU Country Risk Rating—(CRM). (2021). *Economist Intelligence.* http://country.eiu.com/AllCountries.aspx. Data accessed October 28, 2021.

Euler Hermes downgraded risk ratings for 18 countries and 126 sectors. (2020). Euler Hermes. https://www.eulerhermes.com/ru_RU/latest-news/euler_hermes_country_ratings_downgrade.html. Data accessed October 15, 2021.

Index of attractiveness of offshore placement. (2021). http://www.atkearney.com/main.taf. Data accessed October 28, 2021.

Kochergina, T. E. (2021). Country risks in foreign trade: Characteristics and methodological approaches for identifying them. *Innovative Economy: Prospects for Development and Improvement, 1*(51), 93–101. https://doi.org/10.47581/2021/FA-07/IE/51/01.014.

McKinsey Global Confidence Index. (2021). Mckinseyquarterly.com. http://www.mckinseyquarterly.com/. Data accessed October 28, 2021.

Model of assessment and assessment of country risks. Country Index (CREAM). (2021). http://www.exclusive-analysis.com. Data accessed October 30, 2021.

Opacity index (O-factor). http://www.kurtzmangroup.com/opacity.pdf. Data accessed October 15, 2021.

Pereiro, L. (2002). *Valuation of companies in emerging markets.* Wiley.

Rating of the global competitiveness of the countries of the world. (2021). Humanitarian Portal. https://gtmarket.ru/ratings/imd-world-competitiveness-ranking. Data accessed November 02, 2021.

Ratings of the International Country Risk Guide (ICRG). (2021). http://www.prsgroup.com/icrg/icrg.html. Data accessed October 22, 2021.

Reflection of country risk in ratings. (2018). *Commercial evaluation of investments.* https://bstudy.net/704238/ekonomika/otrazhenie_stranovogo_riska_reytingah. Data accessed October 15, 2021.

WTO: International trade is recovering faster than expected. (2021). United Nations. UN News. https://news.un.org/ru/story/2021/03/1400002. Data accessed October 28, 2021.

Trends of Inequality and Their Manifestation in China

Vyacheslav V. Volchik, Weichang Chen, Weili Zhao, and Yuchan Wang

Abstract With the gradual reduction of extreme poverty, the primary manifestation of inequality is the transition from extreme poverty to relative poverty; the standard of defining poverty changes from simple material consideration to the multidimensional evaluation of feasibility ability. The focus is no longer only on income inequality but on the analysis of the reasonable and unreasonable factors of income inequality from the dual perspectives of inequality of opportunity and inequality of effort. The way to alleviate inequality is to change uncontrollable external factors (e.g., the system and environment) and create equal opportunities. The proportion of wealth inequality in income inequality is on the rise, which is the primary manifestation of the widening gap between the rich and the poor, also deepening inequality to a certain extent. The change in inequality is inseparable from the role of the system. The system is not only the source of inequality but also the way to solve it.

Keywords Inequality · Extreme poverty · Relative poverty · Feasibility ability · Income inequality · Inequality of opportunity · Wealth inequality · System

JEL Classification R01 · F22 · F63

1 Introduction

As the world has continued to grow, the persistence of extreme poverty and the growing gap in the incomes and well-being between the world's poorest and richest people have become unconscionably high. Extreme inequality deprives the masses of

V. V. Volchik
Southern Federal University, Rostov-on-Don, Russia
e-mail: volchik@sfedu.ru; volchik@mail.ru

W. Chen (✉) · W. Zhao · Y. Wang
Henan University of Economics and Law, Zhengzhou, China

Y. Wang
e-mail: wych1221@163.com

E. I. Lazareva et al. (eds.), *Innovative Trends in International Business and Sustainable Management*, Approaches to Global Sustainability, Markets, and Governance,
https://doi.org/10.1007/978-981-19-4005-7_3

sharing the benefits of economic development, robbing the disadvantaged of voice; it also has a propensity to erode democracy. Growth is very important, and it is agreed that it is the right direction to strive to mitigate poverty and inequality. However, growth does not necessarily lead to the reduction of poverty. In fact, inequality has continued to grow, such as the segment of the population that is currently non-poor but faces a heightened risk of falling back into poverty. The analysis of equality of opportunity has contributed significantly to our understanding of the determinants of inequality of outcomes and has become an important part of the institution's analysis. To peer into the future, attention must turn to the drivers of poverty and inequality. The inequality of opportunities would replace the inequality of income.

Thus, we should care not only about reducing poverty but also about equality of opportunities. The relationship between poverty and inequality is important to study, but we also should try to understand the contemporary patterns and regularities, including income inequalities, inequalities of opportunity, and inequalities of wealth. We will analyze the new inequality trends to dissect the phenomenal increase in inequality that has occurred in recent times and better understand the relationship between inequality and development. The increased attention to the inequality of opportunity and other styles significantly contributed to the economy and policy.

2 Literature Review

Although the understanding of inequality is different, there is basically a consensus. In the initial stage of market economy development, poverty and backwardness are the main problems; with economic development, it is mainly manifested in the inequality of distribution, such as the gap between capital returns and labor returns. Simultaneously, income gaps continue to widen (Cai et al., 2020), and opportunity inequality is getting worse, mainly manifesting in the inequality of starting point and inequality of participation in the market (Gaosan, 2021).

In recent years, the focus of income distribution research at home and abroad has gradually shifted from income inequality to opportunity inequality. The factor affecting social stability is not income inequality but opportunity inequality. Income inequality comes not only from the efforts made by economic subjects but also from the key factors that economic subjects cannot self-regulate from birth (Guo, 2020). Opportunity equity is often more important than effort equity. Therefore, people begin to pay attention to opportunity inequality that people cannot control.

Roemer (1998) believes that the inequality caused by individual effort is the inequality of effort, which is the good one and can be accepted by people. However, the inequality caused by the different environments is the inequality of opportunities, which is the bad one. Thus, what the public is worried about and deeply resented is not only the imbalance of income distribution but the factors of unequal opportunities hidden behind income inequality, such as family background, social relations, age, gender, regional geographical location, etc. (Jiang & Liu, 2020a). The opportunity inequality brought by these factors is the fundamental factor affecting the economy.

With economic development, inequality is sharply increasing, making economic performance weaker (Jiang & Liu, 2020b); market reforms will increase social inequality. The role of institutional factors is more apparent (Kaushik & Stiglitz, 2016).

In the future, relative poverty, relative backwardness, and the relative gap will exist for a long time (Li et al., 2020). The institutional segmentation of the labor market makes migrant workers face the barrier of identity and rights that separate them from urban citizens and encounter unequal job opportunities, industry and occupational thresholds in the labor market (Li, 2020); institutional restrictions and structural restrictions make priority factors such as family background, household registration, and ownership, which have caused inequality in the employment (Li & Lv, 2019); intergenerational wealth inheritance based on the gap between the rich and the poor directly causes "unequal starting point." The structure of social inequality in China has begun to be transferred or inherited from generation to generation; a trend of class monopoly has been rising.

3 Results

According to the poverty reduction goal set in the United Nations post-2015 development agenda, it is necessary to eradicate extreme poverty among the world's population by 2030. China has completed its overall poverty alleviation in 2020, and extreme poverty has been eliminated historically. Affected by the pandemic, the number of people living in poverty worldwide has increased by about 120 million. Nowadays, about 600 million people are living in poverty worldwide. Extreme poverty is gradually decreasing. However, relative poverty will exist for a long time. The performance of inequality is changing. The evaluation criteria and the focus of attention show new trends. The study of these trends will help us better understand inequality and seek corresponding countermeasures according to different reasons.

3.1 The Criteria of Poverty Have Changed from Single to Multiple, and Relative Poverty Has Become the Focus

Sen (2009, 2020) proposes that poverty is not only a reduction in income but also a state in which capabilities are deprived. At least five aspects should be considered—individual heterogeneity, environmental diversity, differences in a social atmosphere, differences in interpersonal relationships, distribution within families, etc. Thus, the essence of poverty is "the lack of ability to meet some basic and necessary needs." The core of the problem points to functional activities and feasible ability, not limited to direct wealth, goods, or utility. In this process, goods and income are the means to achieve the goal, "we must focus on what kind of life we live." Meeting the minimum basic needs such as food and security is a key element of evaluating extreme poverty (Li & Peng, 2009). Whether the World Bank, the United Nations Development Programme, or China's poverty standard, they have always measured extreme poverty by average annual income or average daily income. This approach is simple, direct, and convenient for statistics. It is also the main consideration index for the reduction or even elimination of extreme poverty. However, simple material supply cannot form a stable state of getting rid of poverty and cannot reflect the complexity and multi-dimensional nature of poverty. Alleviation of material poverty alone cannot really touch the essence of poverty, and the ability to meet "basic needs" should be fully considered (Liu & He, 2020).

Relative poverty measures the income imbalance of different groups in a society, which is not only related to the wealth and income owned by different groups but is also closely related to the concept of social equity and personal self-identity. It means relative exclusion and deprivation. It is the relative difference and inequality of social members in the same economic environment in terms of resource access and public services, and it is a sense of social exclusion that is difficult to meet the needs of basic abilities such as education and health (Liu & He, 2020). Relative poverty is reflected in the relative poverty of economic material level and in health, rights, ability, etc. The degree of relative poverty will strengthen the awareness of social injustice and make it have a stronger sense of relative deprivation (Lu, 2017). As long as there is wealth and class, there is no absolute fairness and equality. Thus, relative poverty becomes the main obstacle to economic development and social progress.

Although extreme poverty has become history in China, relative poverty, such as urban–rural differences or regional differences, is more prominent. Poverty is mainly manifested in relative poverty, relative backwardness, and relative gap. China's poverty governance directions are the following:

1. In terms of setting the standards of poverty, we should go beyond the concept of absolute line and material poverty, conform to the connotation of relative poverty, comply with the overall requirements of the national poverty reduction strategy, and consider the practical ability of financial transfer payment;
2. The direction is from solving rural poverty to solving urban and rural poverty as a whole;
3. The focus is to narrow the income gap and the difference in public services and clarify the establishment and improvement of the social security system for low-income groups in a series of policies for economic and social development (Luo, 2018).

3.2 The Perspective of Considering Inequality Has Shifted from Income Inequality to Opportunity Inequality

Income is affected by an uncontrollable environment and by efforts related to individual decision-making and choice. Therefore, there are both reasonable and acceptable income gaps and unreasonable income gaps that cannot be recognized and even affect people's enthusiasm. Thus, income inequality consists of inequality of effort and inequality of opportunity. Opportunity inequality is the deep-seated reason for the unreasonable distribution results, and income inequality is only a result of economic development (Wu & Cao, 2018). People can often accept the income gap caused by the difference in effort but cannot tolerate the income inequality caused by other uncontrollable factors. The former can produce an incentive effect, which is conducive to the improvement of efficiency and economic development; the latter breaks the social environment of fairness and justice, which is easy to lead to the gap between the rich and the poor (Fig. 1).

In China, the degree of opportunity inequality is relatively serious. Currently, China is still in a transitional society and belongs to a developing country; a considerable number of markets are divided (regional or urban, and rural), and educational opportunities and employment opportunities are unequal (Yao & Wang, 2019).

We take the proportion of rural students in higher education as an example. In 1999, China's higher education began to carry out an enrollment expansion. Nowadays, the number of rural college students has accounted for more than 50%, and opportunities to receive higher education are improved as a whole. Nevertheless, they were mainly distributed in local colleges and higher vocational colleges with relatively weak education levels. In key universities, the proportion of rural students has been declining since 1990. The proportion has dropped from 30% to 40% in the 1980s to 15%–20% at present (Zhang, 2020a). On the one hand, the proportion of rural students entering high school has decreased. On the other hand, it is due to the regional differences in the proportion of enrollment in key universities. The unfair distribution of education indirectly leads to unequal opportunities, which is more serious with the solidification of the stratum and the increase in education investment.

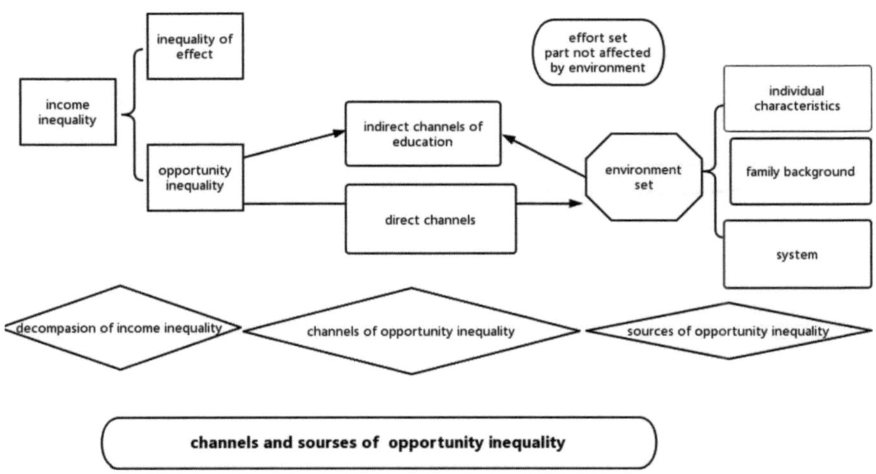

Fig. 1 Channels and sources of opportunity inequality. *Source* developed and compiled by the authors

3.3 *Wealth Inequality is on the Rise*

Property income is the economic embodiment of the rights enjoyed by individuals by virtue of property. Wealth inequality is closely related to income inequality. The inequality of wealth distribution will lead to income inequality, and the difference in property rights will amplify the difference in income opportunities (Zhang, 2020a). Moreover, because income is a flow, it can be investigated, counted, and adjusted relatively easily. However, wealth is a statistically difficult stock that is also difficult and slow to adjust. Therefore, once wealth inequality is formed, it is difficult to change. From Fig. 2, we can see that the more developed countries are, the more serious the phenomenon of wealth inequality is. Most of the wealth is concentrated in the hands of a few people: 1% of the top shared over 40% of the world's wealth (Suisse, 2021). According to the changing trend, the degree of inequality has strong stability.

The Gini coefficient is an indicator obtained by accounting for the total assets of families. The Gini coefficient of major countries in the world is basically above 0.6 and has been on the rise. COVID-19 has made this situation more serious. The impact of wealth on the gap between the rich and the poor is increasing, and the gap has a trend of continuous expansion.

Since 2006, the gap between the rich and the poor within cities and towns has widened in China. Due to the unfair capital stock, the wealth increment is unfair. For example, the rapid rise of real estate prices has led to the rapid appreciation of real estate. It becomes easier for capital to make money and more challenging for labor to make money. Changes in economic life often bring opportunities for the rich and losses to the poor. The top 1% of households occupy about one-third of the country's wealth, while the bottom 25% of households own only about 1%. The Gini coefficient of wealth raised from 0.45 in 1995 to 0.704 in 2020. Wealth increases

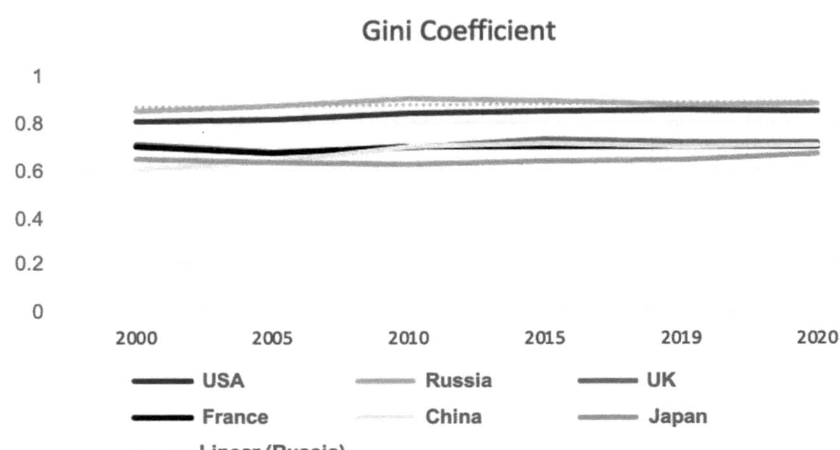

Fig. 2 Gini coefficient. *Source* compiled by the authors based on Suisse (2021)

the gap between the rich and the poor (Zhang, 2020b). If the inequality of wealth continues to increase, the downward trend of the income gap is likely to rebound.

Inequality is a dynamic change process, and different forms affect and interweave with each other. In the absence of equal opportunities, the people being at the bottom of the social distribution are likely to always be at the bottom of society. As a result, inequality will continue, and relative poverty will always exist. Opportunity inequality accounts for a relatively high proportion of income inequality. Each generation is an independent individual closely related to the previous generation. The income inequality of the previous generation will lead to unequal opportunities for the next generation. Combined with the unequal efforts, it leads to a new round of unequal results. With the continuous enhancement of inequality of results and the continuous weakening of equality of opportunity, the low level of equality of opportunity and the high level of wealth inequality may deteriorate further (Zhang, 2015).

4 Conclusion

The evaluation of feasible ability can find more serious problems of poverty. To solve poverty, we should consider the low income (opportunity) and the difficulty of transforming income into feasible ability, which requires establishing and improving the social security system.

The most important thing to reduce income inequality is to reduce the inequality of opportunities as much as possible and provide a starting point for equality. Simultaneously, it is also necessary to encourage individuals to achieve upward mobility in social strata to continuously improve the sense of acquisition and happiness and reduce the sense of relative deprivation (Zhang & Yang, 2019). Equality of opportunity can be realized only when individuals have the opportunity to put forward their own independent needs and put forward universal equality demands in labor and mutual relations.

We should pay attention to income inequality and take measures to curb wealth inequality.

The system is not only the root of inequality but also the main way to solve it. According to North's definition, a "system is a social game rule, or more formally, some human-made constraints that shape people's interactive relationship." Therefore, the most important thing to alleviate inequality is the regulatory role of the system. However, the behavior choice of both sides in the game to maximize their own interests can be changed by the formal rule of the system and inevitably affected by a series of informal constraints such as customs and traditions (Ping, 2021). To reduce poverty, inequality of opportunity and wealth, the establishment and adjustment of formal rules such as policies and systems are necessary and important. Simultaneously, the effects of a series of informal constraints such as customs and traditions must be used fully. This is not only the conclusion but also the topic of further research.

References

Cai, Y. Y., Guo, J. Q., & Fei, S. L. (2020). Trends and causes of income opportunity inequality in China: 1989–2015. *Zhejiang Social Sciences, 10*, 13–23.

Credit Suisse. (2021). *Global wealth report 2021*. Retrieved from https://www.credit-suisse.com/about-us/en/reports-research/global-wealth-report.html. Accessed June 21, 2021.

Gaosan. (2021, June 21). *Admission rate of Peking University and Tsinghua University in 2020*. Retrieved from http://www.gaosan.com/2021/6/21/gaokao/377728.html. Accessed June 21, 2021.

Guo, D. J. (2020). China's social mobility mechanism from the perspective of institutional change. *ZheJiang Social Sciences, 11*(09), 70–80.

Jiang, S. G., & Liu, M. Y. (2020a). From absolute poverty to relative poverty: Theoretical relationship, strategic transformation and policy focus. *Journal of South China Norm University (Soc Sci Ed)*, 18–29.

Jiang, S. G., & Liu, M. Y. (2020b). From absolute poverty to relative poverty: Theoretical relationship, strategic transformation and policy focus. *Social Sciences Digest, 12*.

Kaushik, B., & Stiglitz, J. E. (2016). Inequality and growth: Pattern and policy. In *Volume I: Concepts and Analysis*. Palgrave Macmillan.

Li, S., Terry, S., & Finn, T. (2020). Income inequality in China: Development, transformation and policy. *Journal of Beijing Technology and Business University (Social Sciences), 35*(4), 28.

Li, Y. (2020). Evolution trend, formation mechanism and reduction countermeasures of opportunity inequality in China's income distribution. *Development Research, 9*(7), 9–15.

Li, Y., & Lv, G. M. (2019). Research on the sources and channels of inequality of opportunity in China. *China Ind Econ, 9*, 60–78. https://doi.org/10.19581/j.cnki.ciejournal.2019.09.004.

Li, Z. W., & Peng, Z. F. (2009). An analysis of institutional factors affecting the income gap between urban and rural areas: An analysis framework based on the theory of opportunity inequality. *Special Zone Economy, 8*, 255–257.

Liu, C. K., & He, Y. M. (2020). Environment, effort and income inequality. *Research on Labor Economy, 8*(5), 70–92.

Lu, H. Y. (2017). Institutional defects and correction path of income distribution of Chinese residents. In *21st symposium on fiscal theory* (pp. 1–7). Retrieved from http://cpfd.cnki.com.cn/Article/CPFDTOTAL-CZXH201704001060.htm. Accessed June 21, 2021.

Luo, C. L. (2018). Polarization of residents' income distribution and property distribution in China. *Statistical Research, 11*.

Ping, Z. (2021). From absolute poverty to relative poverty: A study on the poverty of agricultural migrant population—A review based on domestic literature. *Journal of the Party School of CPC Ningbo, 239*(43), 120–128.

Roemer, J. (1998). *Equality of opportunity*. University of Chicago Press. Retrieved from https://www.researchgate.net/publication/37713578_Equality_of_Opportunity. Accessed June 21, 2021.

Wu, X. Z., & Cao, D. W. (2018). Analysis of "Unreasonable factors" of income distribution inequality in China. *Journal of Anhui Normal University, 5*.

Yao, S. J., & Wang, J. F. (2019). Economic development and anti-poverty road in the 70 years since the founding of New China. *Journal of Zhongnan University of Economics and Law, 237*(9), 4–15.

Zhang, N. (2020a). Objectivism, subjective utility, feasible capability: Amartya Sen's perspective on poverty alleviation. *Contemporary Economic Research, 5*, 58–65.

Zhang, Q. (2020b). On the long-term mechanism for alleviating relative poverty. *Journal of SJTU. Series: Philosophy and Social Science, 12*.

Zhang, Y. S. (2015). Thoughts on narrowing the gap between the rich and the poor under the new normal. *Journal of Qiqihar University. Series: Philosophy and Social Science, 8*, 60–63. https://doi.org/10.13971/j.cnki.cn23-1435/c.2015.08.018.

Zhang, Y. S., & Yang, C. H. (2019). The impact of social system on the intergenerational transmission of income inequality—A discussion based on cultural background. *Journal of Shanxi University, 7*.

Development of China's High-Tech Exports Under the Implementation of the Dual Circulation Strategy

Halina A. Shmarlouskaya, Natallia S. Shalupayeva, Ina V. Babyna, and Tatiana Yu. Sinyuk

Abstract The paper aims to reveal trends in the development of China's high-tech exports under the dual circulation strategy and identify the main problems and challenges for developing China's high-tech exports. The methodological basis of the research is presented by the foreign trade theories. During the research, the authors applied general scientific methods, systematic approach, and economic-statistical methods. Information basis is presented by the data of China's National Bureau of Statistics, World Bank, UNCTAD, and WIPO. China has become one of the world's centers for high-tech production. It plays a vital role in global high-tech value chains. Simultaneously, there are some considerable challenges for developing high-tech exports in China, including a low level of national value-added, domination of processing trade and foreign-invested enterprises. Nowadays, China's export-oriented development model based on the absorption of foreign technologies and foreign direct investment loses its effectiveness and does not result in sustainable economic growth. Thus, strengthening independent innovation and mastering smart technologies are the top priorities of China's industrial transformation. The paper reveals the trends in the development of China's high-tech products exports under the implementation of a dual circulation strategy. Moreover, it identifies the main problems and challenges for its development.

H. A. Shmarlouskaya (✉)
Belarus State Economic University, Minsk, Belarus
e-mail: galina.shmarlovskaya@gmail.com

N. S. Shalupayeva · I. V. Babyna
Francisk Skorina Gomel State University, Gomel, Belarus
e-mail: nshalupaeva@mail.ru

I. V. Babyna
e-mail: inna_babyna@tut.by

T. Yu. Sinyuk
Rostov State University of Economics, Rostov-on-Don, Russia
e-mail: t_sinyuk@mail.ru

E. I. Lazareva et al. (eds.), *Innovative Trends in International Business and Sustainable Management*, Approaches to Global Sustainability, Markets, and Governance,
https://doi.org/10.1007/978-981-19-4005-7_4

Keywords High-technology production · High-tech products exports · Innovation-driven economy · Dual circulation strategy · Foreign direct investment · China

JEL Classification F10 · F14 · L52 · O00 · O25 · O30

1 Introduction

For many years, China's export-oriented development model based on foreign direct investment (FDI) and exports of labor-intensive goods with low value-added has been effective. Nowadays, the economic growth mechanism, relying on cheap labor and foreign technologies, loses its effectiveness and cannot guarantee a sustainable long-term growth of the economy (Kostecka-Tomaszewska, 2018). To face new challenges, China is radically changing its economic and trade strategies. Faced with the COVID-19 pandemic that has revealed the extreme fragility of global market structures, Beijing decided to adopt an economic internalization plan, seeking to create measures to prioritize the domestic consumer market and strengthen its economy from the inside. In 2020, a new economic model was proposed—the "dual circulation strategy" (DCS). It tends to stimulate China's domestic demand ("internal circulation") and, at the same time, foreign investment and exports ("international circulation") (Zhang, 2020). Thus, the "dual circulation" strategy is a two-purpose development strategy that seeks to allow domestic and foreign markets to boost each other and make a shift toward an innovation-driven economy.

China is currently building a new pattern of integration into the world economic system and opening-up policy; its foreign trade is going through a critical period of rapid development and transformation. One of the most important issues of the development of China's foreign trade is the exports of high-technology products. In China, the exports of high-tech products present a large part of its total foreign trade. It has become an important engine to promote China's economic development. With the implementation of the concept of high-quality development and corresponding innovative and industrial policies, the high-tech industry in China has developed rapidly. However, recent changes in the global trade environment, promoting economic protectionism over a free market economy, have made the issue of exports development and economic diversification more urgent for China. The *COVID-19 pandemic* has additionally provoked global concerns on supply chain dependency, which will likely accelerate supply chain shifts out of China that can bring new difficulties to China's export of high-tech products. Additionally, the widening rift with the USA poses additional challenges for the development of China's exports. To achieve a more sustainable long-term economic growth and hedge against the impact of external shocks, China needs to diversify its exports markets, range of exported products, and trade methods that determine the significance and the relevance of the selected research topic.

The paper aims to reveal the trends in the development of China's high-tech products exports under the implementation of the DSC and identify the main problems and challenges for the development of China's high-tech exports.

2 Methodology

The methodological basis of the research is presented by the foreign trade theories. The authors applied general scientific methods, systematic approach, and economic-statistical methods. The information basis of the research was drawn from the scientific literature and data from China's National Bureau of Statistics, the World Bank, UNCTAD, and WIPO.

In recent years, some scholars have carried out research on China's innovative development and exports of its high-tech products. The major studies are summarized as follows.

Hu and Zheng analyzed the complex structure of export technology in the high-tech manufacturing industry in China and the USA. The authors built the PRODY and EXPY indexes to analyze the export technical characteristics and development trends of the high-tech industries in China and the USA (Hu & Zheng, 2019).

Zhang and Sun investigated the factors affecting the export of high-tech products in China under the trade war with the USA (Zhang & Sun, 2019).

Wang and Wang substantiated that the development of the high-tech industry played a leading role in guiding the transformation of China's economy from "investment-driven" to "technology-driven" (Wang & Wang, 2020).

Hammer and Yusuf described the paradox of China's economy as a high-tech but low productivity economy. In their research, the authors explained why China's rapid technological development did not provide a real total factor in productivity growth (Hammer & Yusuf, 2020).

Babenko et al. studied the current state of China's innovation development based on a comparative analysis of individual macroeconomic indicators characterizing the national innovation system between countries (Babenko et al., 2020).

Li investigated key factors of China's economic transition from factor-driven to innovation-driven development and gave policy recommendations for further innovation-driven development (Li, 2020).

Yang and Li analyzed the innovative development in China. Based on it, the system of indicators according to the "input–output" model in the field of innovation efficiency was formed and tested, which allowed the authors to divide the subsectors of advanced manufacturing into the groups according to the innovation efficiency growth rate (Yang & Li, 2021).

Wang et al. provided a theoretical basis to understand smart manufacturing and intelligent manufacturing (Wang et al., 2021).

Based on big data analysis and regression verification, Wang, Ziqi, and Wang analyzed the influence of industrial agglomeration on industrial export complexity (Wang et al., 2021).

3 Results

In recent years, China's exports of new and high-tech products have grown rapidly. Their proportion in the country's merchandise export has been continuously increasing. According to World Bank data, in 2019, China's exports of new and high-tech products reached $715.8 billion. As a result, *China is* leading the globe in this sector, ranking the first in the high-tech exports by countries in 2019, followed by Hong Kong with $322.0 billion of high-tech products exports, Germany with $208.7 billion, the USA with $156.1 billion, and South Korea with $153.6 billion of high-tech products exports.

Simultaneously, the amounts and dynamics of high-tech products exports do not fully show their role in China's foreign trade. If we regard the share of high-tech exports in the whole manufactured exports, in 2019, China was the eighth in the world with 30.8%, which is still higher than the world average at 21.1% (Fig. 1). For comparison, in 2001, the exports of the high-tech products equaled only 17.5% of total China's commodity exports.

According to the data of the China Statistical Yearbook (2020), the value of China's high-tech products exports continued to grow, from $218 billion in 2005 to more than $730 billion in 2019 (Table 1).

Despite high growth rates, the development of China's high-tech exports faces several challenges, among serious of which are the following ones, closely related to each other:

(1) Low level of national value-added in high-tech exports;
(2) High concentration of trade modes in high-tech products exports;
(3) High dependence on foreign-invested enterprises in high-tech exports development.

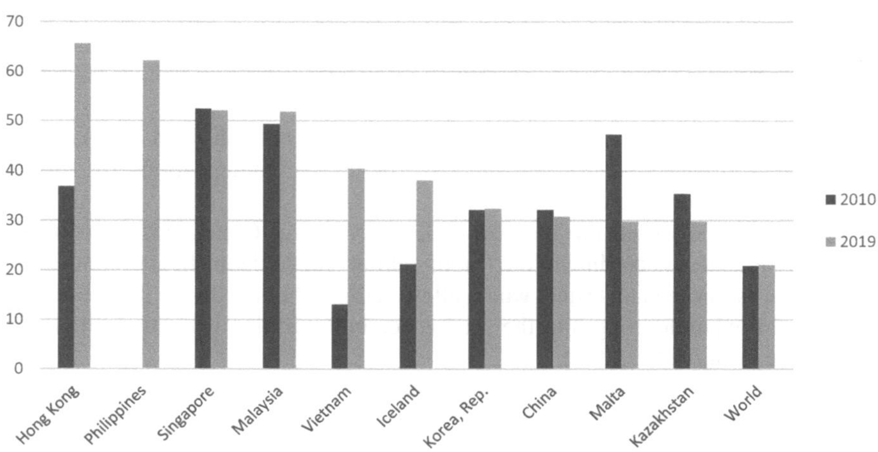

Fig. 1 Exports of high-tech products by country (% of manufactured exports). *Source* Compiled by the authors based on the data of World Bank (2021)

Table 1 China's imports and exports of new and high-tech products in 1995–2019

Item	1995	2000	2005	2010	2015	2018	2019
Value ($100 million)							
Total value of exports	1488	2492	7620	15,779	22,749	24,867	24,995
Manufactured goods	1273	2237	7129	14,962	21,710	23,517	23,655
New and high-tech products			2182	4924	6552	7468	7307
Balance of exports and imports							
Manufactured Goods	196	454	2007	5339	9620	9177	10,171
New and high-tech products			206	797	1072	752	929
Percentage (%)							
Total value of export = 100							
Manufactured goods	85.6	89.8	93.6	94.8	95.4	94.6	94.6
New and high-tech products			28.6	31.2	28.8	30.0	29.2

Source Compiled by the authors based on the data of China Statistical Yearbook (2020)

(1) *Low level of national value-added in high-tech exports.*

The trade data show that China is the largest exporter of high-tech products. However, some scientists (e.g., Yuqing Xing) substantiate that China's leadership in the world's high-tech exports "...is a myth created by outdated trade statistics, which are inconsistent with the trade based on global supply chains" (Xing, 2014). It is explained by the fact that assembled products made with imported components account for about 82% of China's exports of high-tech products. Nevertheless, trade statistics put the total values of these assembled products to China's exports, thus greatly overestimating its high-tech exports. Therefore, China, playing an important role in the high-tech global value chains, has a low level of national value-added in its high-tech exports.

(2) *High concentration of trade modes in high tech products exports.*

The processing trade, which is at the low end of the value chain, is the main trade mode of China's high-tech products exports. Although it shows a downward trend in recent years, processing trade still accounted for more than 60% in 2015. Total imports and exports of processing trade in China increased by about 250 times in 30 years, from the initial $1.67 billion in 1980 to $417.43 billion in 2010 (Xiong & Qureshi, 2013).

The foreign-led processing trade is a serious driving factor of China's economic growth. The merchandise structure of China's processing trade considerably upgraded from labor-intensive products to capital- and technology-intensive products (e.g., electronic products) (Xiong & Qureshi, 2013). Simultaneously, integration into the international division of labor by processing trade makes China's high-tech products exports seriously affected by economic fluctuations, including the impact of the 2008 economic crisis and the COVID-19 crisis. The reason is that China only controls the processing links, and the production, technology, and marketing channels are in the hands of foreign parties. Thus, the profit depends on cheap labor, not advanced technology (Wang et al., 2021), which negatively impacts independent innovation and accelerates industrial upgrading.

(3) *High dependence on foreign-invested enterprises in high-tech exports development.*

The foreign-owned enterprises play a significant role in China's foreign trade as a whole. For example, in 2019, the exports of foreign-owned enterprises equaled $966.0 billion, or 38.6% of the total exports in goods of China. In 2019, the imports of foreign-owned enterprises equaled $857.8 billion, or 41.3% of the total imports in goods of China. The same situation is observed in the area of high-tech exports, where most exported goods are produced by foreign-funded enterprises (Grimes & Sun, 2014). For example, in 2002, foreign-funded firms and enterprises with funds from Hong Kong, Macau, and Taiwan accounted for more than 55% of total China's high-tech products exports; in 2009, this number already equaled 68%. If we take 2016 as an example, almost 67% of high-tech exports were made by foreign-funded enterprises and enterprises with funds from Hong Kong, Macau, and Taiwan. It shows the high dependence of the development of China's high-tech exports on FDI. As Jieping Chen notes, the current science and technology policy "…focusing on indigenous innovation since 2006 does not significantly reduce the dominant role of foreign companies in Chinese economy…" (Chen, 2018).

Thus, FDI has a significant impact on China's exports of high-tech products. Nevertheless, it is necessary to note that, after the financial crisis, this impact has significantly decreased. One of the main reasons is that, after the financial crisis, the developed economies (the USA and the EU countries) began implementing the "reindustrialization" strategy to revitalize their manufacturing industries. Most of the high-tech products can no longer rely on the absorption and transformation of foreign technology to enhance their competitiveness. However, many high-tech products absorb more advanced foreign high-tech products. Thus, the impact of FDI on China's exports of high-tech products is still significant, but it is lower than that before the crisis.

Therefore, the dominant position of foreign companies in China's high-tech sector and the high level of its dependency on foreign technology make the development of independent innovation and mastering of smart technologies the top priorities in China's industrial transformation and development.

Nowadays, China makes efforts to push its economy toward a greater focus on indigenous innovation and deepen national technological and innovative potential. A new economic model being adopted by China—the "dual circulation strategy"—being an economic internalization plan, is a way to overcome new challenges, strengthen its economy from the inside, and make a shift toward an innovation-driven economy.

It should be noted that this process started in 2006 through the implementation of "Medium- and long-term program for science and technology development," "Made in China 2025," and "Thirteenth five-year science and technological innovation" and "Fourteenth five-year" plans. These programs and plans were reinforced by increasing amounts of research and development spending and acquisitions of foreign technology (Hammer & Yusuf, 2020).

The best illustration for this shift toward internal innovations is the global innovation index, indicating that China's innovation capacity has been steadily improving. China is moving up in cross-country rankings, from 29th in 2011 to 12th in 2021; it is the highest-ranking middle-income country and the third country in the region rank after the Republic of Korea and Singapore (WIPO, 2021). China is one of a few economies that has consistently demonstrated high innovation performance.

To identify the reasons for the success of the Chinese economy in the innovation area, we studied the main indicators of the innovative development of the national economy. These indicators can be divided into two groups: indicators describing the innovation spending and indicators describing the results of innovative activity. The indicators of the first group include the full-time equivalent of R&D personnel, expenditure on R&D, and the ratio of expenditure on R&D to GDP. The second group is presented by a number of patent applications.

According to Table 2, China's investment in R&D and the full-time equivalent of R&D personnel have risen rapidly in recent years. Thus, expenditures on R&D have increased by 55.6% over the last five years. China ranks second in the world by expenditure on R&D after the USA. In 2020, China's total expenditure on R&D amounted to 54% of the level of the USA and was 3.1 times higher than Japan's level. As follows from Table 2, China also creates conditions for increasing the number of researchers. Thus, China has built an extensive national innovation system to supply the innovation and technologies required for productivity growth. As a result, the number of patent applications raised 1.5 times for the last five years and amounted to 5.2 million pieces in 2020.

In China, the ratio of expenditure on R&D to GDP is still not so high. In 2020, China spent 2.4% of GDP on R&D, compared with 2.1% in 2016. In the countries that lead in innovative development, this indicator was much higher. For example, in 2018, this indicator equaled 2.8% in the USA, 4.9% in Israel, and 3.3% in Sweden.

The data on technology acquisition and technology transformation shows that the last three years have been characterized by high growth rates of expenditure for purchasing domestic technology in China (Table 2). It increased more than two times from 20,090 million yuan in 2017 to 45,670 million yuan in 2020. This fact indicates a high potential for creating domestic technologies in China.

On the contrary, the expenditure for the acquisition of foreign technology demonstrates the exhaustion of their potential, remaining almost unchanged in the last five years. The reasons for this trend are the loss of China's traditional competitive advantages for FDI (low cost of labor), reindustrialization policy of developed countries, the US–China trade war, the COVID-19 crises, and contraction of global value chains. Moreover, in 2019, the expenditure for the purchase of domestic technologies exceeded the expenditure for acquiring foreign technology in China. The same trend is typical for the expenditure for the assimilation of technology. Its amount decreased by 31.8% for the last five years (Table 2).

Table 2 Indicators on science and technology activities in China in 2016–2020

Indicator	2016	2017	2018	2019	2020	Growth rate, %
Full-time equivalent of R&D personnel, 10,000 people	387.8	403.4	438.1	480.1	523.5	135
Ratio of expenditure on R&D to GDP, %	2.1	2.12	2.14	2.24	2.4	114.3
Expenditure on R&D, 100 million yuan	15,676.7	17,606.1	19,677.9	22,143.6	24,393.1	155.6
Number of patent applications, piece	3,464,824	3,697,845	4,323,112	4,380,468	5,194,154	149.9
Expenditure for the acquisition of foreign technology, 100 million yuan	475.4	399.3	465.3	476.7	460	96.8
Expenditure for assimilation of technology, 100 million yuan	109.2	118.5	91	96.8	75.6	69.2
Expenditure for purchase of domestic technology, 100 million yuan	208	200.9	440.2	537.4	456.7	219.6

Source Compiled by the authors based on the data of China Statistical Yearbook (2020)

Such a reorientation from foreign technologies to domestic ones can serve as a basis for changing China's strategic development goals and ensure the transition from "Made in China" to "Created in China" (Wei et al., 2017). Simultaneously, while China's high R&D expenditures have resulted in technological advances in some areas (e.g., machine learning and 5G technology), it is not the case in other core technologies (e.g., semiconductors, integrated circuits, airplanes, etc.) (Hammer & Yusuf, 2020).

Thus, the implementation of the high-quality development concept and corresponding policies in China stimulated the rapid development of the high-tech industry in the country; its foreign trade in high-tech products has also shown a trend of rapid growth. In its turn, the continuous expansion of the FDI-led high-tech exports resulted in the gradual growth of high-tech industries in China, which significantly promoted the optimization and upgrading of China's economic structure. Thus, these two processes complement and support each other in creating an innovation-driven economy in China.

4 Conclusion

1. The analysis of China's high tech exports dynamics showed that China is the world leader in high-tech exports. With the implementation of the concept of high-quality development and corresponding innovative and industrial policies, the high-tech industry in China has developed rapidly; the foreign trade of high-tech products has also shown a trend of rapid growth. If we consider the share of high-technology exports in the whole manufactured exports, in 2019, China was only eighth in the world.
2. China has become one of the world's centers for high-tech production and plays an essential role in high-tech global value chains. Despite high growth rates, the development of China's high-tech exports faces several challenges, the most serious of which are the following ones: low level of the national value-added in high-tech exports; high concentration of trade modes of China's high-tech products exports; high dependence on foreign-invested enterprises in high-tech exports development. It should be noted that these problems are closely related to each other.
3. The problems and challenges for high-tech production and exports in China revealed in the research show that strengthening independent innovation and mastering smart technologies are the top priorities of China's industrial transformation and upgrading development. A new economic model adopted by China—the "dual circulation strategy"—being an economic internalization plan, is a way to overcome new challenges, strengthen its economy from the inside, and make a shift toward becoming a demand and innovation-driven economy.
4. In recent years, in China, the basic indicators on science and technology activities, such as R&D investments, the full-time equivalent of R&D personnel, the number of researchers, and the number of patent applications, have risen rapidly. During the last years, in China, the expenditure for the purchase of domestic technology has been characterized by high growth rates. This fact indicates a high potential for the creation of domestic technologies. On the contrary, the expenditures for the acquisition of foreign technology in China demonstrate the exhaustion of their potential, remaining virtually unchanged in the last five years. The same trend is typical for the expenditure for the assimilation of technology. Thus, we may say that China has built an extensive national innovation system to supply the innovation and technologies required for productivity growth. Such a reorientation from foreign technologies to domestic ones can serve as a basis for changing China's strategic development goals and ensure the transition from "Made in China" to "Created in China."

References

Babenko, V., Pravotorova, O., Yefremova, N., Popova, S., Kazanchuk, I., & Honcharenko, V. (2020). The innovation development in China in the context of globalization. *WSEAS Transactions on Business and Economics, 17*, 523–531. https://doi.org/10.37394/23207.2020.17.51.

Chen, J. (2018). *Innovation in China: The promise and the challenge in a transition economy.* (Dissertation of Doctor of Economics). Mannheim, Germany: University of Mannheim.

Grimes, S., & Sun, Y. (2014). Implications of China's on-going dependence on foreign technology. *Geoforum, 54*, 59–69. https://doi.org/10.1016/j.geoforum.2014.03.010.

Hammer, A. B., & Yusuf, S. (2020). *Is China in a high-tech, low-productivity trap?* Economic Working Paper Series (Working Paper 2020–07-B). U.S. International Trade Commission.

Hu, Y., & Zheng, X. (2019). Analysis of export technology complexity structure of high-tech manufacturing industry in China and the US. *Advances in Economics, Business and Management Research, 68*, 85–91. https://doi.org/10.2991/ssmi-18.2019.16.

Kostecka-Tomaszewska, L. (2018). Economic security of China: The implications of the belt and road initiative. *Optimum Economic Studies, 4*(94), 166–182. https://doi.org/10.15290/oes.2018.04.94.14.

Li, P. (2020). The outlook for China's innovation-driven development beyond COVID-19. *Cultures of Science, 3*(4), 232–244. https://doi.org/10.1177/2096608321995294.

National Bureau of Statistics of China. (2020–2021). *China statistical yearbook*, 2020, 2021. Beijing, China.

Wang, B., Tao, F., Fang, X., Liu, C., Liu, Y., & Freiheit, T. (2021). Smart manufacturing and intelligent manufacturing: A comparative review. *Engineering, 7*(6), 738–757. https://doi.org/10.1016/j.eng.2020.07.017.

Wang, J., Ziqi, Z., & Wang, H. (2021b). Research on influencing factors of export complexity of Chinese high-tech industry based on big data analysis. *E3S Web of Conferences, 235*. https://doi.org/10.1051/e3sconf/202123503013.

Wang, L. Y., & Wang, B. H. (2020). Spatial statistical analysis and comprehensive evaluation of high-tech industry development. *Open Journal of Statistics, 10*(3), 431–452. https://doi.org/10.4236/ojs.2020.103028.

Wei, S.-J., Xie, Z., & Zhang, X. (2017). From "made in China" to "innovated in China": Necessity, prospect, and challenges. *The Journal of Economic Perspectives, 31*(1), 49–70. Retrieved from http://www.jstor.org/stable/44133950. Accessed August 15, 2021.

World Bank Data. (n.d.). *High-technology exports (% of manufactured exports)*. Retrieved from https://databank.worldbank.org/reports.aspx?source=2&series=TX.VAL.TECH.MF.ZS&country=. Accessed August 15, 2021.

World Intellectual Property Organization (WIPO). (2021). *Global Innovation Index 2021: Tracking innovation through the COVID-19 crisis*. WIPO. Retrieved from https://www.wipo.int/edocs/pubdocs/en/wipo_pub_gii_2021.pdf. Accessed August 15, 2021.

Xing, Y. (2014). China's high-tech exports: The myth and reality. *Asian Economic Papers, 13*(1), 109–123. https://doi.org/10.1162/ASEP_a_00256.

Xiong, J., & Qureshi, S. (2013). The quality measurement of China high-technology exports. *Procedia Computer Science, 17*, 290–297. https://doi.org/10.1016/j.procs.2013.05.038.

Yang, S., & Li, L. (2021). A study on evaluation on innovation efficiency of advanced manufacturing in China. *E3S Web of Conferences, 235*. https://doi.org/10.1051/e3sconf/202123502074.

Zhang, J., & Sun, F. (2019). Research on the factors affecting the export of high-tech products in Jiangsu province under Sino-US trade war. *Advances in Economics, Business and Management Research, 68*, 468–475. https://doi.org/10.2991/ssmi-18.2019.78.

Zhang, Z. (2020, September 25). *What is China's dual circulation strategy and why should foreign investors take note*. Available via China Briefing. Retrieved from https://www.china-briefing.com/news/what-is-chinas-dual-circulation-strategy-and-why-should-foreign-investors-take-note/. Accessed August 15, 2021.

Development of the Russian Consumer Market in Conditions of Global Instability

Maxim V. Prokopenko, Natalia F. Cheremisova, and Anastasiya Yu. Chmyryova

Abstract The state of the world economy is characterized by growing crisis phenomena caused by the coronavirus epidemic and measures to combat it. One of the important features of the modern period is the high rates of global inflation and the logistics crisis. In Russia, the state of the consumer market is further influenced by the decline in real incomes of the population that has been going on for several years. The article examines the challenges faced by the consumer market at the present stage, analyzes its current situation and suggests ways out of the crisis.

Keywords International trade · Consumer market · Economic crisis

JEL Classification F14 · F41 · L81

1 Introduction

The current situation in the global economy is characterized by an increase in crisis phenomena caused by the consequences of the coronavirus pandemic. Global production and logistics chains have been disrupted. This, combined with high inflation rates, which is partly a consequence of measures to combat the effects of the pandemic, and partly the result of ill-considered energy policies in Western countries and China, has led to crisis phenomena in the consumer market. We believe that the Russian consumer market, being part of the global system, is subject to the same risks as the consumer markets of developed countries, and has every chance of encountering the same problems that are currently observed in the USA, the EU and China.

M. V. Prokopenko (✉)
South-Russian Institute of Management of the Russian Presidential Academy of National Economy and Public Administration, Rostov-on-Don, Russia
e-mail: prokopenko-mv@ranepa.ru

N. F. Cheremisova · A. Yu. Chmyryova
Rostov Institute of Entrepreneur Protection, Rostov-on-Don, Russia
e-mail: cheremisova81@list.ru

E. I. Lazareva et al. (eds.), *Innovative Trends in International Business and Sustainable Management*, Approaches to Global Sustainability, Markets, and Governance,
https://doi.org/10.1007/978-981-19-4005-7_5

The purpose of this article is to analyze the current situation in the consumer market of Russia and suggest ways to neutralize the negative manifestations of the crisis. This goal made it necessary to solve the following tasks:

- analysis of the situation in the global economy;
- study of macroeconomic indicators of the Russian economy at the present stage in the context of their impact on the level of consumer activity;
- consideration of the directions of development of the consumer market at the present stage.

2 Methodology

The study examines statistical materials characterizing the situation in the global economy, in the Russian economy, as well as in the consumer market of the Russian Federation. As a general method of research, a consistent consideration of the situation is used at levels, starting from the general situation in the world economy and ending with the market of an individual product. This approach makes it possible to identify factors influencing the consumer market and suggest ways to solve existing problems.

Statistical data and analytical materials of Gaidar Institute for Economic Policy and Russian Presidential Academy of National Economy and Public Administration under the President of the Russian Federation were used to substantiate the key provisions of the study. In addition, the publications devoted to the development of the Russian and world economy at the present stage were analyzed.

3 Results

All the processes taking place in the Russian consumer market, which is part of the global economic system, are conditioned to one degree or another by the general state of the world economy. At the same time, the situation in the global economy can be described as unstable. The scope of our work does not allow us to consider in detail all aspects of the problem, so we will limit ourselves to the main points that characterize the situation of developed economies and have a direct impact on the global consumer market.

The key factor determining the economic situation at the present stage is the high level of inflation. In October 2021, consumer inflation in the United States reached its highest level in 31 years, amounting to 6.2% in annual terms. In September, the inflation rate was 5.4%. The growth was provided by high prices for energy, housing, vehicles and food. Core inflation, excluding food and energy, was 4.6% (Inflation in U.S., 1990). In September, the annual inflation in the 27 EU countries was 3.6%, and in the eurozone countries—3.4%. At the same time, in Germany, the price growth was 4.1%, in France—2.7%, in Italy—2.9. The highest inflation rate was recorded in Estonia and Lithuania—6.4% (Inflation in the Eurozone, 2021). In China, the producer price inflation accelerated to the fastest pace in 26 years and amounted to 13.5% (China Factory Inflation, 2021). Consumer prices increased by 1.5% (Consumer Price Index (CPI) in China, 2021).

At the same time, the economy has faced a number of problems that negatively affect the overall level of economic development. High rates of inflation in the United States are largely due to rising energy prices. The increase in gasoline prices from November 2020 to November 2021 was 62% (from $2.11 to $3.42 per gallon) (Falling Back, 2021). In the UK and EU countries, there is a "gasoline crisis", expressed in a shortage of fuel and rising prices for it.

The port and container crises are a big problem for the global economy. The disruption of production and logistics chains, the introduction of coronavirus restrictions led to an acute shortage of sea containers (according to the portal "China MacroEconomy" in 2020, the shortage of containers was 70–72 million, but the entire industry of China, which produces 96% of sea containers in the world, produced only 2.6 million (South China Morning Post, 2021)) and their higher prices (the cost increased from 1200 to 10,000 dollars (Global Container Traffic Turns to Mush, 2021)). At the same time, the same coronavirus restrictions, as well as the consequences of management decisions of previous years aimed at warehouse optimization, personnel and railway infrastructure, led to overstocking of ports. The work of the ports was paralyzed, which, in turn, affected the supply of manufacturers with components, and the consumer market with goods. For example, in the United States, a number of the country's largest ports switched to round-the-clock operation only thanks to the personal intervention of President Biden, which underlines the importance of the situation (Rozhdestvenskaya Ya, 2021). The shortage of personnel was also a big problem for the United States. As of September 2021, 10.4 million jobs are vacant in the United States (SmartMoney, 2021). The shortage is caused by the coronavirus consequences, as well as significant payments to the population, which have reduced the motivation for more active job search among low-skilled personnel.

The Chinese economy has faced great difficulties. A huge number of enterprises are forced to stand idle due to lack of electricity. This is the result, on the one hand, of the strategic goal set earlier by the PRC authorities to abandon coal as part of the struggle to improve the environmental situation, on the other hand, of the peculiarities of state regulation of electricity prices, which led to the fact that with an increase in the cost per kWh of electricity, the official price remained the same. This has caused an acute shortage of supply from generating companies. At the same time, the government cannot sharply raise electricity tariffs, as this may negatively affect the overall economic performance and social stability. The problems of production in China, due to its place in the international division of labor, are having and will continue to have a dramatic effect on the economic situation of all countries of the world.

It is also advisable to consider the macroeconomic situation in the Russian Federation in 2021. The year began with hopes that the pandemic would soon pass and recovery growth would begin. However, the observed trends proved to be multidirectional. The key factor of the last two years—the spread of the coronavirus epidemic—has not slowed down, and hopes for the developed vaccines have turned out to be too optimistic. As a result, during the year the country experienced several waves of the disease, and the Government was forced twice, in May and November, to introduce a regime of non-working days, the purpose of which was to reduce rates of infection. This has had and continues to have an impact on production and consumption activities.

Another important factor was the recovery of global commodity markets, which led to increased demand for Russian exports. In the first half of the year, prices for metallurgy products showed a sharp increase. Steel fittings, iron ore and scrap have risen in price by more than 1.5 times, rolled steel—by more than 2 times compared to 2020 (Milkin et al., 2021). Brent Crude oil price increased from January to the end of October from 51.5 to 85.9 dollars per barrel, that is, more than 1.6 times. Gas prices on the European market have increased by 1.8 times. Mineral fertilizers have risen in price by 60–65% in ten months of 2021 (Pirogov, 2021). All this has affected the results of foreign trade. According to Rosstat, foreign trade turnover in January–August 2021 increased by 1.37 times, and exports—by 1.44 times (Socio-Economic Situation of Russia, 2021, p. 111). The trade surplus for 8 months of this year amounted to 106 billion dollars, which is 47.8 billion, or 82% higher than the same indicator last year. The current account surplus for nine months amounted to $82.2 billion (The Bank of Russia, 2021). The inflow of foreign exchange made it possible to reach the maximum level of gold and currency reserves – $623.2 billion (Key indicators, 2021). However, at the same time, in the first nine months of the year, capital exports amounted to $ 59 billion, which actually negates the positive results of commodity exports.

It should be noted that the increase in exports caused a rise in domestic prices. The reorientation of supply to foreign markets led to an increase in prices within the country and, as a result, an increase in the cost of domestic products. According to the Chairman of the Board of Directors of Osnova Group of Companies A. Ruchyev, the share of metal in the cost price of construction reaches about 10–12%, in the automotive industry, the share of metal in the cost price, according to D. Babansky, is 35–40%. The share of metals in the cost price of a freight car is 65–75% (Milkin et al., 2021). Similarly, it is possible to consider the influence of other commodity groups, in particular, energy commodities. This had a negative impact on economic activity within the country.

Inflation in 2021 shows high growth rates. In general, from the beginning of the year to November 8, the consumer price index was 106.62% (Rosstat, 2021). Annual inflation was 8.1% (Key indicators, 2021).

In our opinion, the U.S. dollar overvalued relative to the ruble also contributed to the development of inflation. It should be recalled that the sharp drop in oil prices on March 9, 2020 from $ 45.27 to $ 34.36 per barrel, that is, by 24.1%, led to the devaluation of the ruble by 8.8%, and at the height of the crisis, the exchange rate reached 80.88 rubles, that is, it fell by more than 20% compared to the pre-crisis level. However, the recovery of oil prices did not contribute to the recovery of the exchange rate. In November 2020, oil returned to the price of $ 46, and the ruble exchange rate remained at 76 rubles, that is, 15% cheaper than before the devaluation

(Dynamics of the official US dollar exchange rate, 2021). This can be explained by the deliberate actions of the Government and the Central Bank. In particular, the low level of key interest rate of 4.25%. Only an increase in the rate to 7.5% in November 2021 allowed to lower the dollar exchange rate to 70.7 rubles. At the same time, the price of oil was already $82.57 per barrel (Brent Oil Futures, 2021).

High inflation rates have a negative impact on the consumer market, reducing the incomes of the population. Although according to Rosstat data, real incomes of the population show significant growth. In the third quarter of 2021, real disposable incomes increased by 8.1%, and in nine months—by 4.15% compared to the same period last year (Socio-Economic Situation of Russia, 2021, p. 199). However, this growth was not a stable trend and was due to payments made by the state to families with children in August and to pensioners and law enforcement officers in September 2021. According to the Minister of Finance of the Russian Federation A. Siluanov, more than 500 billion rubles were allocated for these purposes (Kommersant, 2021). This has led to the fact that the share of social payments in the total income of the population has peaked in recent years and amounted to 23.1% in quarterly terms and 21.42% for 9 months of 2021. Table 1 contains data on the dynamics of income by type of sources.

As can be seen from the table data, the share of income from entrepreneurial activity is steadily decreasing. Since 2016, the decline has been 0.6% in total revenue, and the rate of decline is 9.3%. Given the improved quality of tax administration, it can be concluded that the role of entrepreneurship in the economy is declining. But the share of social payments increased by 2.6% in the total structure or by 13.8% compared to 2016, which indicates an increase in the dependence of the population on public assistance. These processes, in turn, have an impact on consumer expectations of the population and on consumer demand.

Lending provides some support to the consumer market. From January to October 2021, citizens of the Russian Federation took 15.8 million loans in cash, which exceeds by 36% the level of the same period last year (11.6 million loans). At the

Table 1 The structure of income of the population in 2016–2021

Year	Share in total income, %				
	Income from entrepreneurial activity	Compensation of employees	Social benefits	Income from property	Other income
2016	6.4	54.0	18.8	5.1	15.7
2017	6.3	55.1	19.3	4.6	14.7
2018	6.1	57.3	19.0	4.6	13.0
2019	5.9	57.6	18.9	5.1	12.5
2020	5.2	58.4	20.8	4.3	11.3
2021 (January–September)	5.8	60.4	21.4	3.76	8.61

Source Compiled by the authors on the basis of Rosstat (2021)

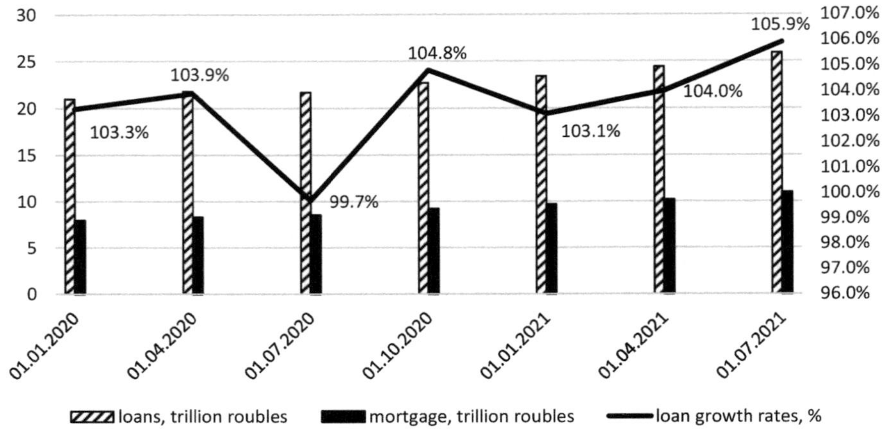

Fig. 1 Dynamics of lending in 2020–2021. *Source* Compiled by the authors based on Financial Assets and Liabilities (2021)

same time, only 14.5 million loans were taken for the whole year of 2020, and 15.3 million loans were taken for the whole year of 2019 (Izvestiya, 2021). The pace of lending was not affected even by the increase in the key rate. Given the low growth rates of the consumer market, it can be assumed that a significant part of the loans is used for debt restructuring.

Figure 1 shows the dynamics of lending for the period 2020–2021.

The increase in external and internal prices affects the various sectors of the Russian economy in different ways. A.S. Kaukin and E.M. Miller analyzed the dynamics of industrial production in the third quarter of 2021 (Kaukin & Miller, 2021). As can be seen from the research data, the mining industry, which is largely export-oriented, demonstrates steady economic growth. The manufacturing industry and the production of electricity, gas and water are in a situation of stagnation. Wholesale and retail trade, as well as paid services for the population show weak growth, which indicates the weakness of the domestic market. Anti-epidemic restrictions imposed in the country continue to have a negative impact on the service sector.

Thus, we can draw an interim conclusion that the global economic recovery has not had a significant positive impact on the domestic consumer market. The restoration phase affected, first of all, export-oriented industries. The trade surplus ensured a high level of capital outflow, which, combined with a low refinancing rate, did not allow the ruble exchange rate to strengthen. At the same time, the rise in prices for export goods affected the cost of domestic products, increasing inflationary pressure. The incomes of the population, despite the official growth achieved by lump-sum payment, continued to stagnate, as well as the credit burden on the population continued to grow.

It is worthwhile to analyze the consumer market. First of all, attention should be paid to the recovery of retail trade turnover that has begun. If in 2020 it decreased to

96.8% compared to the level of 2019, including 98.4% for food and 95.4% for non-food products, then in January–September 2021 the turnover amounted to 108.4% compared to the same period in 2020 (Socio-Economic Situation of Russia, 2021, p. 94).

The change in the structure of retail trade turnover in 2020 compared to the pre-pandemic years is demonstrated by the data in Table 2, which shows the dynamics of consumer spending in Russia by various groups of goods for 2016–2020.

As can be seen from the table data, the structure of retail trade turnover in 2020 differs from the structure of previous years. First of all, it is worth noting the increased share of food products. If it gradually decreased from year to year before that, it increased in 2020. Among food products, it is worth paying attention to the increase in the share of groats and macaroni. This can be explained both by the fact that citizens were stocking up on food at the beginning of the epidemic, and by the fact that they were saving on food due to a drop in their incomes.

Considering the turnover of non-food products, it should be noted that there was a decrease in sales of clothing and shoes and, conversely, an increase in sales of computers, phones and medicines. The growth in sales of mobile phones and computers can be explained by the growing demand in conditions of self-isolation and the transition to remote work, and medicines—by the need for people to be treated and to stock up.

A distinctive feature of the consumer market during the pandemic is the explosive growth of online sales. According to research conducted by the Association of E-Commerce Companies and Sberbank, the volume of online trade in 2020 increased by 58.5% compared to 2019 from 2032 billion rubles to 3221 billion rubles, while the volume of domestic trade showed an increase of 92.3%—from

Table 2 Commodity structure of retail goods turnover, %

Product name	Year				
	2016	2017	2018	2019	2020
Food products	48.6	48.4	47.7	47.9	49
Including					
Meat	3.6	3.4	3.3	3.3	3.3
Groats	0.6	0.6	0.6	0.6	0.7
Macaroni	0.5	0.5	0.5	0.5	0.6
Non-food products	51.4	51.6	52.3	52.1	51
Including					
Clothing	5.6	5.6	5.3	5.2	4.8
Shoes	2.1	2.3	2.3	2.2	2.0
Mobile phones	0.9	1.0	1.1	1.1	1.3
Computers	0.6	0.6	0.6	0.6	0.8
Medicines	–	3.4	3.5	3.7	4.0

Source Compiled by the authors based on Commodity structure of retail trade turnover (2021)

1446 billion rubles to 2781 billion rubles (Online Trading in Russia, 2020). In 2021, this growth continued. According to Rosstat, the volume of sales via the Internet in September 2021 increased by 1.4 times compared to September 2020. The share of online sales increased from 5.7% to 7.2%. At the same time, OZON, WILDBERRIES and Citylink stores became Internet leaders, accounting for 48% of the market. Clothing (15%), computers (6.8%), shoes (6.4%), household electrical goods (5%) predominate in the sales structure (Socio-Economic Situation of Russia, 2021, p. 99).

Another feature of the market is the active process of mergers and acquisitions, due to increased competition in the face of declining consumer demand. In May 2021, Magnit retail chain announced the acquisition of Dixy retail chain. 2612 outlets operated under Dixy brand and another 39 under Megamart brand. The total volume of the transaction is estimated at 82.4 billion rubles. A major player in the market of mergers and acquisitions was the Lenta retail chain, which in May 2021 acquired 161 supermarkets of Austrian chain Billa for 215 million euros. In June 75 stores of the Family chain were acquired. X5 Retail Group company continued the reduction of Karusel chain stores started at the end of 2019. According to the company's plans, Karusel hypermarkets will be closed or transformed into Perekrestok chain stores by the end of 2021.

Although the growth in real incomes of the population has been declared, an important trend is the development of the format of so-called hard discounters, that is, stores with prices 10–15% lower than in conventional supermarkets. An example of such networks are the networks Svetofor, Chizhik, Yes!, Myprice, FixPrice. A feature of discounters is the search for solutions to reduce costs, which, in particular, affects the product range, sales conditions, service, etc. However, consumers focused primarily on saving money prefer the opportunity to purchase goods cheaper, even in worse conditions compared to a conventional supermarket.

It should also be noted that one of the important features of the consumer market during the pandemic period is a return to the practice of state regulation of prices. On December 30, 2020, amendments to the Federal Law No. 381-FZ of December 28, 2009 "On the fundamentals of state regulation of trade in the Russian Federation" came into force, enshrining the right of the Government "to set maximum permissible retail prices for these types of goods for a period of no more than ninety calendar days" (Federal Law, 2021). In particular, agreements regulating wholesale and retail prices for sugar and sunflower oil were concluded. We consider this trend dangerous, since the intervention in market principles of pricing can contribute to the emergence of an imbalance of supply and demand and, as a result, the formation of a commodity deficit. In our opinion, the Government, instead of directive methods of influencing the final price of goods, should analyze the entire supply chain, find links where there is an excessive increase in costs, and work with them based on the particularities of each specific case.

It is worth paying attention to the solution of issues of the macroeconomic level. In particular, at the present stage, in our opinion, it can be recommended to abandon the purposeful underestimation of the ruble exchange rate and preferences to exporters. Export growth should be considered as a means of pumping up the economy with money, but in conditions of large-scale capital outflows, it only leads to an increase in domestic prices, a decrease in the profitability of domestic industry and a drop in real incomes of the population. At the same time, the development of exports contributes to a decrease in the volume of production of vital products on the domestic market.

As an example, we consider it important to analyze the situation on the potato market, considered in detail by Ternovsky and Shagaida (2021). During 2020, potatoes rose in price by 36% compared to the end of 2019. In October 2021, the annual price increase was 79.6%. In the same month, potatoes were sold 82.1% higher than the average price over the past five years. The reason for such a significant increase was not food inflation and not its exports, but an increase in domestic consumption (the population is switching to more affordable food products) against the background of a long-term decline in production. The population has been reducing potato production in private subsidiary farms for the past twenty years, farms produce potatoes in insufficient quantities and do not have the opportunity to sell them through retail chains, and large producers prefer export-oriented products—wheat and oilseeds. The profitability of potato production is lower than that of cereals, oilseeds and sugar beet. As a result, there was a shortage of potatoes on the market. It is impossible to solve the problem with imports due to global food inflation and an overvalued dollar. In this particular case, the solution can be found in subsidizing potato production. However, we believe that in general it would be appropriate to solve the problem through an appreciation of the ruble, which would reduce exports, relieve pressure on domestic prices and promote the expansion of domestic production by reducing cost inflation. A significant increase in imports would not have occurred due to high global inflation. In general, the situation would have a positive impact on the real incomes of the population, the level of consumption and the development of the consumer market.

4 Conclusion

The conducted research of the consumer market allows us to draw a number of conclusions:

- the situation in the world economy is in an unstable state, the development of crisis phenomena continues, which entails a number of negative consequences, including a decrease in production and an increase in inflation;
- the Russian economy has actually been divided into two segments: working for export and for the domestic market. The export sector is experiencing a period of significant growth, but this leads to a reduction in products on the domestic market and an increase in prices. Industries working for domestic consumption are experiencing a state of stagnation;
- the consumer market is beginning to recover compared to 2020, but its dynamics are negatively affected by high inflation, multidirectional vectors of changes in household incomes and a high level of debt;

- important trends in the consumer market are the rapid development of online commerce, the processes of mergers and acquisitions that strengthen its monopolization and the spread of the format of discounters that focus on demand from citizens with a reduced income level;
- the state practice of regulating food prices can be recognized as dangerous and threatening to cause shortages. The state needs to reconsider the policy of supporting producers, in particular, to abandon export incentives and undervaluation of the national currency, which will contribute to the growth of real incomes of the population and will support the production of products oriented to the domestic market.

References

Brent oil futures: quotes for past periods. Investing.com. https://ru.investing.com/commodities/brent-oil-historical-data. Data accessed November 10, 2021.

China Factory Inflation Surges to 26-year High CPI Picks Up. (2021). Bloomberg. https://www.bloomberg.com/news/articles/2021-11-10/china-factory-inflation-surges-to-26-year-high-cpi-picks-up. Data accessed November 11, 2021.

Commodity structure of retail trade turnover. Rosstat. https://rosstat.gov.ru/storage/mediabank/rozn_41.xls. Data accessed November 10, 2021.

Consumer Price Index (CPI) in China. *Investing.com—quotes and financial news*. https://ru.investing.com/economic-calendar/chinese-cpi-459. Data accessed November 6, 2021.

Dynamics of the official US dollar exchange rate. (2021). Bank of Russia. https://cbr.ru/currency_base/dynamics/?UniDbQuery.Posted=True&UniDbQuery.so=1&UniDbQuery.mode=1&UniDbQuery.date_req1=&UniDbQuery.date_req2=&UniDbQuery.VAL_NM_RQ=R01235&UniDbQuery.From=01.03.2020&UniDbQuery.To=12.11.2021. Data accessed November 10, 2021.

Estimate of key aggregates of the balance of payments of the Russian Federation in January–October 2021. The Bank of Russia. https://cbr.ru/statistics/macro_itm/svs/bop-eval/. Data accessed November 10, 2021.

Falling Back: Will Shorter Days Lead To Less Demand For Gas? (2021). Gas Prices. https://gasprices.aaa.com/falling-back-will-shorter-days-lead-to-less-demand-for-gas/. Data accessed November 10, 2021.

Federal Law No. 381-FZ of 28.12.2009 (as amended on 02.07.2021). *On the Fundamentals of State Regulation of Trade in the Russian Federation.* Legal reference system "ConsultantPlus". http://www.consultant.ru/document/cons_doc_LAW_95629. Data accessed November 9, 2021.

Financial assets and liabilities of the households sector by the type of financial instruments. Bank of Russia. https://cbr.ru/statistics/macro_itm/households/. Data accessed November 10, 2021.

Global container traffic turns to mush: shortages and higher prices are looming. (2021). Retail Detail. https://www.retaildetail.eu/en/news/general/global-container-traffic-turns-mush-shortages-and-higher-prices-are-looming. Data accessed November 09, 2021.

Inflation in the eurozone accelerated to 3.4% in September, to 3.6% in the EU. (2021). Finmarket: Rconomic news. http://www.finmarket.ru/news/5571755. Data accessed November 6, 2021.

Inflation in U.S. Builds With Biggest Gain in Prices Since 1990. (2021). Bloomberg. https://www.bloomberg.com/news/articles/2021-11-10/inflation-builds-with-biggest-gain-in-consumer-prices-since-1990?srnd=premium-europe&sref=fgHqaWRV. Data accessed November 11, 2021.

Kaukin, A. S., & Miller, E. M. (2021). Dynamics of industrial production in the III quarter of 2021. Monitoring of the economic situation in Russia. *Trends and Challenges of Socio-Economic*

Development 2021, 8(15). https://www.ranepa.ru/images/newMedia/about/1.pdf. Data accessed November 10, 2021.
Key indicators. The Bank of Russia. https://cbr.ru/key-indicators/. Data accessed November 9, 2021.
Milkin, V., Ilyushenko, V., & Patsaeva, K. (2021). How metal prices have spurred inflation. *Vedomosti*. https://www.vedomosti.ru/business/articles/2021/06/21/874859-inflyatsii-metall. Data accessed November 9, 2021.
Online Trading in Russia: Results of 2020. (2021). *Autonomous non-profit organization "Center for the Promotion of Entrepreneurship in the Novosibirsk region"*. https://mbnso.ru/company/analytics/internet-torgovlya-v-rossii-2020/. Data accessed November 10, 2021.
On the assessment of the consumer price index from November 2 to November 8, 2021. Rosstat. https://rosstat.gov.ru/storage/mediabank/201_10-11-2021.htm. Data accessed November 10, 2021.
Pirogov, S. (2021). *Phosagro, Mosaic and Akron are beneficiaries of the increase in fertilizer prices*. Investing.com. https://ru.investing.com/analysis/article-200285655. Data accessed November 10, 2021.
Putin signed decrees on the payment of 15,000 rubles to the military and security forces. (2021). Kommersant. https://www.kommersant.ru/doc/4966361. Data accessed November 10, 2021.
Rozhdestvenskaya Ya. (2021). *Ports and logistics companies in the United States are switching to round-the-clock work to cope with the flow of cargo*. Kommersant. https://www.kommersant.ru/doc/5030837. Data accessed November 8, 2021.
Russians ahead of schedule have set a record for the number of cash loans taken out in a year. (2021). Izvestiya. https://iz.ru/1248219/2021-11-11/rossiiane-dosrochno-ustanovili-rekord-po-chislu-vziatykh-za-god-kreditov-nalichnymi. Data accessed November 11, 2021.
Shipping containers becomes new buzz word as coronavirus leaves industry struggling to meet demand. (2021). South China Morning Post. https://www.scmp.com/economy/china-economy/article/3117257/shipping-containers-becomes-new-buzz-word-coronavirus-leaves?module=perpetual_scroll&pgtype=article&campaign=3117257. Data accessed November 10, 2021.
Socio-economic situation of Russia—2021. (2021). Rosstat. https://rosstat.gov.ru/storage/mediabank/osn-09-2021.pdf. Data accessed November 10, 2021.
Ternovsky, D. S., & Shagaida, N. I. (2021). The price of potatoes: growth factors and ways to reduce. Monitoring of the economic situation in Russia. *Trends and challenges of socio-economic development 2021, 8*(15). https://www.iep.ru/ru/doc/36816/tsena-na-kartofel-faktory-rosta-i-sposoby-snizheniya.pdf. Data accessed November 11, 2021.
The number of open vacancies in the US labor market decreased in September. (2021). SmartMoney. https://smartmoney.one/news/chislo-otkrytyh-vakansiy-na-rynke-truda-ssha-23/2178812. Data accessed November 12, 2021.
The volume and structure of monetary incomes of the Russian population by sources of income. Rosstat. https://rosstat.gov.ru/storage/mediabank/urov_13kv-nm(2).xls. Data accessed November 10, 2021.

A Mechanism for Overcoming the Negative Consequences of COVID Lockdowns in Russian Organizations

Gulnaz F. Galieva, Olga V. Shugaeva, Irina N. Shvetsova, Andrey V. Yakovlev, and Olga A. Olenina

Abstract The research is aimed at analyzing and systematizing the consequences for organizations from the COVID-19 pandemic and the introduction of restrictive lockdowns, as well as finding effective tools for levelling them in the conditions of Russian reality. It is determined that the COVID-19 pandemic and the measures taken by the state to combat it have become catalysts for structural changes in organizations of an organizational and economic, technological and socio-psychological nature. The positive effects and negative consequences of the pandemic and the restrictive lockdowns introduced were assessed using the method of interviewing representatives of Russian business structures. Among the negative consequences, a decrease in the organization's income, a decline in demand for products, a reduction in economic opportunities for most types of business, a lower efficiency of staff, organizational problems of switching to a remote work format are highlighted. The directions of overcoming the negative consequences of the pandemic for Russian organizations are determined, including the search for additional sources of income, optimization of internal processes, digital transformation. In order to neutralize objectively developing negative processes and potential socio-economic risks and their consequences, the author's mechanism of adaptation of the organization to new conditions is proposed.

G. F. Galieva (✉)
Financial Research Institute of the Ministry of Finance of the Russian Federation, Moscow, Russia
e-mail: economresearch@mail.ru; galievagf@mail.ru

Ufa State Petroleum Technological University, Ufa, Russia

O. V. Shugaeva
Southwest State University, Kursk, Russia

I. N. Shvetsova
Pitirim Sorokin Syktyvkar State University, Syktyvkar, Russia

A. V. Yakovlev
Voronezh State University of Forestry and Technologies Named after G.F. Morozov, Voronezh, Russia

O. A. Olenina
Russian University of Transport (MIIT), Moscow, Russia

E. I. Lazareva et al. (eds.), *Innovative Trends in International Business and Sustainable Management*, Approaches to Global Sustainability, Markets, and Governance,
https://doi.org/10.1007/978-981-19-4005-7_6

Keywords Enterprises · Pandemic · Lockdown · Structural changes · Digitalization · Personnel efficiency · Adaptation

JEL Classification D21 · D23 · F61

1 Introduction

The COVID-19 pandemic has become an extraordinary challenge for the entire world community and the economic systems of the countries of the world. The nature of the epidemiological impact, the rate of spread, the globality and the forms of the pandemic cannot be compared with any of the previous epidemics. Naturally, States do not and could not have experience in preventing it and levelling the consequences. Governments of many countries intuitively took sanitary measures, introduced lockdowns, suspending the activities of enterprises and self-isolation regimes for citizens. Such non-standard measures in March–April 2020 were perceived as urgent and necessary. However, their prolongation led to the closure of some sectors of the economy and the creation of prerequisites for the development of crisis phenomena in the economy (Karpunina et al., 2020, 2021). The so-called pandemic crisis, according to experts, differs significantly from the traditional cyclical crisis. Its key feature is a controlled decrease in activity due to government actions and an extremely uneven distribution of costs due to the complete shutdown of some industries, the transfer to a remote format of work in compliance with strict sanitary and epidemiological measures (Karpunina & Konishchev, 2021; Zimovets et al., 2020). In addition, its development is taking place against the background of global changes in the field of technology and the social environment, on the one hand, exacerbating the manifestations of crisis phenomena, and on the other hand, accelerating the process of transition to the digital economy (Steblyakova, 2021). Meanwhile, the measures taken by the State to combat the pandemic and protect the population have had a strong impact on enterprises, in many cases causing structural changes (Gukasyan et al., 2022). However, the nature and extent of the impact of the pandemic, as well as the benefits and possible damage to the organization, will depend on its adaptability, speed of response to changes in business conditions and competent behaviour of staff and administration.

2 Literature Review

At the beginning of the COVID-19 pandemic in April 2020, the drop was 6.6%, and later reached 9.9% (Analysis of Macroeconomic Trends, 2021). Production in specific industries decreased by 60–70%, which proves that enterprises are unprepared for critical external events (Ivankovich & Chuprina, 2021). Special attention of researchers is drawn to the processes of organizing the activities of enterprises during the pandemic. In particular, (Zimovets et al., 2020) note the relationship between the dynamics of the self-isolation index in the regions of Russia and the restrictive measures implemented by the state. The authors note that the pandemic has not had a negative impact on large businesses, and small businesses have become the most susceptible to the pandemic crisis. Karpunina et al. (2021) analyze the impact of the pandemic on the sectors of the Russian economy and identify the most affected sectors as a result of the pandemic. Ivankovich and Chuprina (2021) note that the main affected sectors of the Russian economy are those that produced their product at the beginning of the pandemic on a small scale. Enikolopov (2020) emphasizes that, in general, the Russian Federation has approached the pandemic crisis with quite favourable prerequisites. During this period, the country had a low level of public debt (less than 15% of GDP compared to the world average of 80%); a significant level of reserves; relatively low inflation; non-zero bank interest rates; an adequate package of business assistance is not related to economic components, but political actions. How are Russian organizations coping with the spreading crisis? Some of them are moving to implement market diversification strategies to achieve competitive advantages (Geroski & Gregg, 1997), others are trying to reduce costs (organizational costs, working hours and employment, staff development and training costs, research costs) (Gukasyan et al., 2022; Shama, 1993). Some simply did not survive a new economic and epidemiological collapse. But there are also those organizations that purposefully implement an adaptation strategy and are ready to adapt to new business conditions, no matter how tough and inconvenient they may be at the initial stage of implementation (development of new products and orientation to new market niches (Clifford, 1977); increased marketing expenses (Roberts, 2003).

3 Methodology

The purpose of the study is to conduct systematic analysis and systematization of the consequences for organizations from the COVID-19 pandemic and the introduction of restrictive measures, as well as to search for effective tools for levelling them in the conditions of Russian reality.

Research objectives: (1) to analyze the impact of the COVID-19 pandemic on the activities of organizations; (2) to systematize the positive and negative consequences of the pandemic and the imposed restrictive lockdowns; (3) to determine the directions of overcoming the negative consequences of the pandemic by Russian organizations.

Research methods: theoretical analysis, interview method, economic and statistical analysis, graphical method, comparative analysis, systematic approach.

4 Results

The effectiveness of organizations is determined by the factors of the external and internal environment. Both in the internal and external environment, risks arise that can not only destabilize the stable functioning of the organization but also cause changes and launch a new vector of its development. One of these environmental risks was the coronavirus pandemic that swept the world in 2020 (Steblyakova, 2021). The nature of the impact of the COVID-19 pandemic can be assessed as a global macroeconomic shock, unprecedented in scale and duration. It has epidemiological, economic, social and other consequences. Russia is in 5th place in the world in the incidence of coronavirus, following the USA, India, Brazil, United Kingdom (Coronavirus, 2021). The reasons for the high incidence of coronavirus in Russia are its large territory, high population density, expansion of domestic tourism programs that increase the mobility of the population, as well as the lack of readiness of hospitals and outpatient staff to provide the necessary assistance to those in need. The epidemiological consequences of a pandemic can cause a further increase in morbidity and mortality, they are aggravated by the redistribution or depletion of resources intended for general medical care, as well as limited access to it due to the inability to move by transport, fear and other factors (Kholikov, 2020). Pandemics, as a rule, either cause an acute, short-term financial shock or cause long-term damage to economic development. The COVID-19 pandemic is characterized by the second option, when measures to contain the spread of the disease (contact tracing, quarantine, isolation of the sick, etc.), as well as restrictive measures introduced for non-proliferation of COVID-19, which led many companies to both temporary shutdowns of production and complete closure, were prolonged in time. The greatest economic losses were caused by the forced restrictive measures imposed by most countries and the global recession that followed (Kashepov, 2021). In particular, there was a simultaneous decrease in aggregate demand (especially for certain groups of goods and services related to tourism, transport, hotel business, cafes and restaurants, cultural and sports events, etc.), and a decline in aggregate supply (due to a reduction in labour, disruption of supplies of material resources, etc.). The pandemic has affected economic sectors unevenly. On the one hand, the inevitable embedding of the COVID-2019 pandemic into the economic dynamics of organizations has reached the expected sharp acceleration, accompanied by a powerful spread of the impact of negative effects, causing a record decline in the pace of development for certain types of activities (HSE, 2020). The special nature of the recession triggers, coupled with the secondary destabilizing trends that have arisen (deformation of consumer behaviour due to a reduction in household budgets and strict social distancing measures that additionally block the business activity of certain industries), have caused significantly increased risks and led to a serious loss of business stability of some of them. On the other hand, during this period there was the growth of the IT industry, as well as the intensive development of the field of pharmacology, bioengineering, medical research, etc.

However, the growth of some industries did not compensate for the general decline in the economy. In 2020, Russia's GDP decreased by 2.7 compared to 2019 (RBC, 2021). The dynamics of GDP were influenced by a drop in final demand within the country and an increase in net exports of goods and services due to a sharp 12.1% drop in imports. Final consumption expenditures decreased by 4.9%, due to a drop in demand for services and non-food products (excluding cars). Household spending on final consumption fell by 7.3%. In Russia in 2020, the number of operating enterprises decreased by 300 thousand or 9.6% (net reduction, taking into account newly opened businesses), to 2.82 million units (Klerk, 2021a). In addition, overcoming the consequences of the pandemic also requires significant human resources and financial costs. These are investments in the construction of additional medical facilities for the treatment of infected people, the provision of medical equipment and consumables, additional costs for maintaining sanitary conditions in public institutions, the development of testing systems, the creation of new vaccines and vaccine prophylaxis.

A survey of experts from among representatives of Russian business structures conducted by the authors allowed us to highlight the consequences of the impact of the pandemic and lockdowns on organizations. Only 25% of respondents assessed the consequences of the pandemic as positive (Table 1).

Experts attributed the positive effects of the pandemic on the activities of organizations to the intensification of digitalization of business processes (29% of respondents noted), personnel optimization (24%), improvement of intra-organizational communications (22%), increased transparency of the activities of Russian organizations (14%), the emergence of new niches for doing business (11%). Note that the positive effects of the pandemic were noted mainly by representatives of the IT sector (35% of respondents). Meanwhile, in the pre-pandemic period, most organizations were focused on tactical solutions rather than strategic digital transformation. The transition to a remote format of work for an indefinite period pushed organizations to the so-called forced digitalization, which has become a kind of tool for adapting organizations to new conditions (Kulaga, 2021). The share of companies that use the Internet has increased by 2% since the beginning of February 2020, the share of organizations with mobile business applications has grown by 9%, and the share of companies with full-fledged websites and pages in social networks has raised by 19% and 12%, respectively, over the same period (Shpileva, 2021). During the pandemic, every fifth organization began to use Internet technologies to organize events and meetings online (NAFI, 2020). HR optimization and improvement of intra-organizational communications were also noted by experts as positive effects of restrictive lockdowns. Maintaining the financial viability of an organization during a pandemic is often associated with the dismissal of staff, maintaining the work of the most competent employees, as well as ensuring their probable conversion (Homks, 2020). The pandemic forced employers to "freeze" bonus payments on a legitimate basis, reduce staff costs, while there is no qualitative change in approaches to staff incentives (Ryabukhin, 2020). In addition, during the pandemic, organizations received a powerful incentive to eliminate bureaucratic units that perform only a supporting function.

Table 1 Ranking of positive consequences of the pandemic for Russian organizations

Parameter	Expert assessment 1	Expert assessment 2	Expert assessment 3	Expert assessment 4	Expert assessment 5	The sum of the estimates for each parameter	Weight	Rank
Activation of digitalization of business processes	0.31	0.25	0.27	0.28	0.33	1.44	0.288	1
Personnel optimization	0.24	0.24	0.14	0.25	0.31	1.18	0.236	2
Increasing the transparency of the activities of Russian organizations	0.1	0.17	0.18	0.2	0.06	0.71	0.142	4
Improving intra-organizational communications	0.19	0.23	0.26	0.2	0.24	1.12	0.224	3
The emergence of new niches for doing business	0.16	0.11	0.15	0.07	0.06	0.55	0.11	5
Total	1	1	1	1	1	5	1	-

Source Compiled by the authors based on their survey

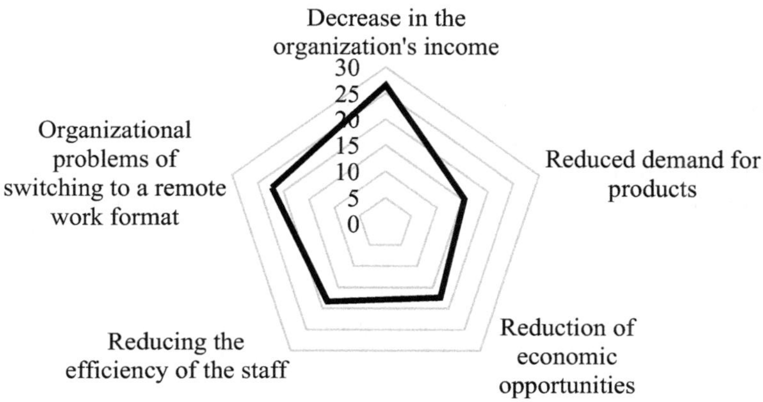

Fig. 1 Map of the negative impact of the pandemic and restrictive lockdowns on Russian organizations. *Source* Compiled by the authors based on their survey

We systematize the negative consequences of the pandemic and the restrictive knockdowns introduced using the method of interviewing experts from Russian organizations. Comparison of expert opinions through statistical analysis, the five most significant negative consequences of the pandemic for organizations were selected: reduction of the organization's income, decrease in demand for products, the decline in economic opportunities, lower staff efficiency, organizational problems of switching to a remote work format (Fig. 1).

The decrease in the organization's income as a result of the negative impact of the pandemic was noted by 26.6% of the surveyed experts. This fact is confirmed by the report of the audit company FinExpertiza, where it is noted that only in the spring of 2020, more than a third of Russian organizations were at a loss of 1.65 trillion rubles, and the rest earned 3.05 trillion rubles. As a result, the profit of Russian businesses amounted to 1.4 trillion rubles, which is 67% less than in the spring of 2019 (Sberbank, 2020). In addition, certain types of activities have suffered losses to a greater extent. For example, organizations in the field of tourism, catering, non-food products sector. According to Rosstat, in April 2020, the turnover of the non-food sector decreased by 36.7% compared to April 2019, which is more than 400 billion rubles. In May, the decline slowed to 19.2%.

According to the survey, 22.2% of organizations faced organizational problems of switching to a remote work format. The main reason for organizational problems is the forced nature of the transition to remote work (Izvestiya, 2020; Stakhiev, 2021). During the pandemic, there was a transformation of the team culture. In the conditions of geographically distributed work, methods of visual control over employees and traditional forms of organization management have become impossible (WCIOM, 2020). The IT/Telecom industries turned out to be the most resistant to the transition to a remote format of work (Rostelecom, 2020).

18.4% of the experts we interviewed indicated a decrease in the efficiency of the staff. It was revealed that the transfer of personnel to remote work in every fifth organization caused a decrease in the efficiency of employees (Klerk, 2021b). A decrease in economic opportunities as a result of the impact of the pandemic was noted by 17.4% of the experts surveyed, and a decrease in demand for products was observed in 15.4% of cases. The pandemic has become a catalyst for structural changes in organizations that have gradually "matured" and are now able to be implemented (Russian Council, 2020) (Table 2).

In order to offset the negative consequences of the pandemic, it is necessary to implement a mechanism for adapting the organization to new conditions, taking into account the identified structural changes (Fig. 2).

Organizations should direct their management efforts towards finding additional sources of income, implementing digital transformation, as well as optimizing internal processes. Firstly, the sources of additional income during the pandemic can be the funds released as a result of emergency cost optimization (for example, reducing marketing costs, employee salaries, minimizing rental payments, lowering production costs, spending on IT solutions and services, social packages for employees) (Sberbank, 2020). Secondly, organizations have redesigned their businesses to adapt to the new realities of knockdowns and self-isolation, and have started using different channels, including online stores, social media groups and marketplaces. Changing demand forces organizations to become more flexible and provides an opportunity to gain new strategic advantages (Barton et al., 2002). It is in conditions of crisis of the old foundations and uncertainty that the organization can find new opportunities and make a serious strategic breakthrough (Gukasyan et al., 2022). In this case, it is necessary to monitor changes in legislation that release hidden consumer demand, and implement an investment adaptation strategy based on the creation of a new product, thereby ensuring significant growth of the organization. Increasing the organizations' efficiency and reducing costs during the pandemic began to take the form of digitalization. The key areas of digital transformation of organizations are analysis of the effectiveness of activities as a whole and individual processes in the organization; effective tools for monitoring the work of employees; increasing the speed of decision-making and identifying new opportunities for monitoring their execution; effective technologies for tracking the work of teams. In addition to the obvious use of digital solutions in IT management, organizations intend to use digital technologies in the analysis of markets and consumers and logistics, that is, in those business processes that radically differ in tasks and mechanisms of influence on the competitiveness of the organization (Ranepa, 2020). Optimization of internal processes will be facilitated by the formation of a culture of constructive feedback in real-time; the use of system controls (for example, project management tools, regular management, task setting, planning, step-by-step acceptance of results); changing the methods of employee evaluation (in particular, emphasis should be placed on evaluating the individual contribution of an employee to achieving a common result); combining employees into teams and determining joint responsibility for the result; a clear definition of tasks delegated to the team; use of working day planning procedures; redistribution of roles and statuses of employees in terms of contribution to the result, completed tasks and assigned responsibilities; creation of employee motivation mechanisms. During the pandemic, one of the strongest

Table 2 Structural changes triggered in organizations as a result of pandemics and lockdowns

Prerequisites for the emergence of structural change	New requirements
Organizational and economic	
Transfer of employees to remote work	Changing approaches and principles of the organization of work in general, building a new model of interaction with employees, in remote mode. Improvement of the regulatory framework regulating labor relations with employees in a remote format
Reducing the efficiency of the organization's staff	Introduction of new metrics to track the effectiveness of work and business processes. The use of digital technologies to organize the work of teams. Elimination/reorganization of inefficient departments in the organization
High transaction costs	Digital transformation that reduces transaction costs
Idle office and production areas during lockdowns, high rent	Optimization of leased/own space
Narrowing the corridor of business opportunities	Search for new product niches and directions, implementation of a breakthrough strategy and launch of a new product
Technological	
Low level of digitalization of organizations, implementation of tactical solutions in the field of digital development	Activation of digitalization processes, implementation of strategic digital transformation in conditions of high socio-economic uncertainty
Low decision-making speed	Introduction of digital technologies that increase the speed of decision-making and provide new opportunities for monitoring their execution. Overall acceleration of business processes and communications
Lack of remote communication channels between employees	Establishing information flows in the organization. Maintaining an open dialogue between managers about the state of affairs in the organization
Socio-psychological	
High level of anxiety of the organization's employees due to the threat of dismissal	Transformation of internal processes and management culture, personnel optimization based on personnel cost management, labour productivity management and loyalty management
Non-compliance of digital competencies with the requirements of remote work	Improving the quality of professional training and retraining of employees, developing motivational mechanisms to ensure continuous training of personnel

(continued)

Table 2 (continued)

Prerequisites for the emergence of structural change	New requirements
Lack of a social package for employees	Ensuring the effective work of personnel in conditions of uncertainty requires the availability of tools for social support of personnel. This contributes to an increase in the level of trust and motivation of staff for self-development, mastering new competencies and ensuring their loyalty to the organization during a crisis

Source Compiled by the authors

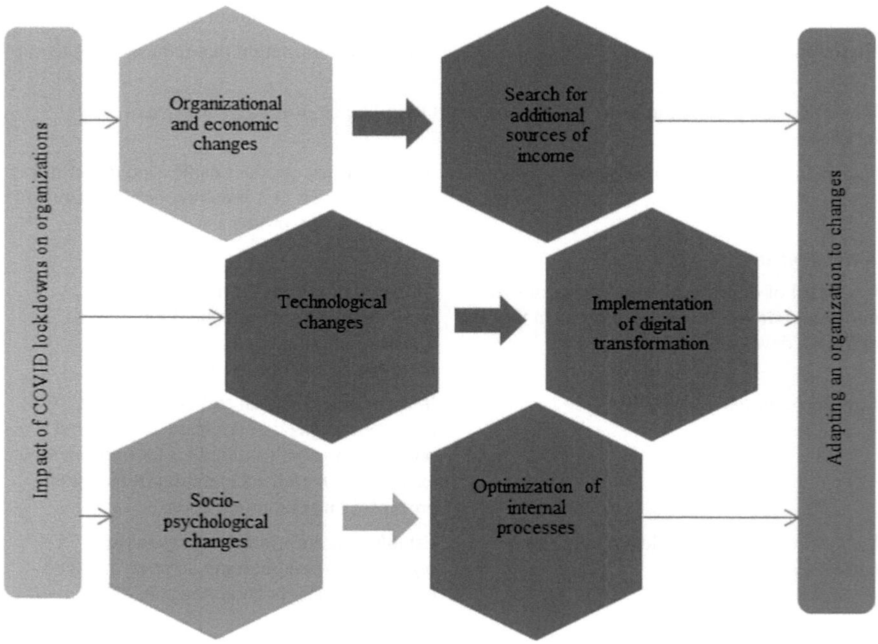

Fig. 2 The mechanism of overcoming the negative consequences of COVID lockdowns in Russian organizations. *Source* Compiled by the authors

motivators for employees is the ability to link personal contribution to work with the strategic goal and mission of the organization in real-time.

5 Conclusion

Firstly, the article systematizes the consequences for organizations from the COVID-19 pandemic and the introduction of restrictive measures. The survey conducted by the authors allowed us to establish the positive effects and negative consequences for Russian organizations from the impact of the pandemic and the restrictive lockdowns introduced. The negative consequences of the pandemic include a decrease in the organization's income, a decline in demand for products, a reduction in economic opportunities for most types of businesses, a lower efficiency of staff, organizational problems of switching to a remote work format. Secondly, the authors proved that the pandemic and COVID lockdowns contributed to the launch of structural changes in organizations. Thirdly, the authors have identified ways to overcome the negative consequences of the pandemic by Russian organizations. In particular, the article suggests the author's mechanism for adapting an organization to new conditions based on the implementation of three key areas: the search for additional sources of income, optimization of internal processes, digital transformation.

References

Barton, D., Newell, R., & Wilson, G. (2002). *Dangerous markets: Managing in financial crises*. Wiley.

Center for Macroeconomic Analysis and Short-Term Forecasting. (2021). *Analysis of macroeconomic trends*. http://www.forecast.ru/_ARCHIVE/Mon_MK/2021/macro21.pdf. Accessed January 02, 2022.

Clifford, D. (1977). Thriving in a recession. *Harvard Business Review, 55*(4), 57–65.

Coronavirus. (2021). *Coronavirus: Statistics*. https://yandex.ru/covid19/stat#statistics-table. Accessed January 02, 2022.

Enikolopov, R. (2020*). Crisis: Is the current one similar to the previous ones?* https://www.nes.ru/files/EVENTS/Economics%20and%20life/Enikolopov-Economic-Crises-PDF.pdf. Accessed January 02, 2022.

Geroski, P., & Gregg, P. (1997). *Coping with recession: UK company performance in adversity*. Cambridge University Press.

Gukasyan, Z., Tavbulatova, Z., Aksenova, Zh., Gasanova, N., & Karpunina, E. (2022). Strategies for adapting companies to the turbulence caused by the Covid-19 pandemic. In *Business 4.0 as a subject of the digital economy*. Springer.

Homks, R. (2020). *What personnel decisions need to be made in a pandemic*. https://hbr-russia.ru/biznes-i-obshchestvo/uroki-stoikosti-2020/832769. Accessed January 02, 2022.

HSE. (2020). Economic and social consequences of coronavirus in Russia and in the world. *Analytical Bulletin of the HS*. https://www.hse.ru/pubs/share/direct/435321841.pdf. Accessed January 02, 2022.

Ivankovich, D., & Chuprina, A. (2021). Industrial enterprises in a pandemic coronavirus infection. *Business Education in the Knowledge Economy, 1*, 35–38.

Izvestiya. (2020). *Negligent attitude: A third of Russians complain about the difficulties of working from home*. https://iz.ru/990930/ekaterina-iasakova-anna-ivushkina/khalatnoe-otnoshenie-tret-rossiianzhaluetsia-na-trudnosti-raboty-iz-doma. Accessed January 02, 2022.

Karpunina, E., Butova, L., Sobolevskaya, T., Badokina, E., & Pliusnina, O. (2021). The impact of the Covid-19 pandemic on the development of Russian national economy sectors: Analysis of dynamics and search for stabilization measures. In *Proceeding of the 37th IBIMA Conference* (pp. 1213–1226), 1–2 April 2021, Cordoba, Spain.

Karpunina, E., & Konishchev, E. (2021). Challenges for the economic security of Russia's regions during the pandemic. Izvestiya Yugo-Zapadnogo gosudarstvennogo universiteta. Economics series. Sociology. *Management, 11*(6), 105–121.

Karpunina, E., Zabelina, O., Galieva, G., Melyakova, E., & Melnikova, Y. (2020). Epidemic threats and their impact on the economic security of the state. In *Proceeding of the 35th IBIMA Conference* (pp. 7671–7682), 1–2 April 2020, Seville, Spain.

Kashepov, A. (2021). Factors and economic consequences of the coronavirus pandemic. *Bulletin of the Altai Academy of Economics and Law, 2*, 38–45.

Kholikov, I. (2020). The spread of epidemics, pandemics and mass diseases as a global challenge of modernity. *Paths to Peace and Security, 2*(59), 27–40.

Klerk. (2021a). In 2020, *2.4 times more businesses closed than opened*. https://www.klerk.ru/buh/news/509680/. Accessed January 02, 2022.

Klerk. (2021b). *Reduced labor efficiency and deterioration of financial results: Is the remote woman to blame?* https://www.klerk.ru/blogs/msfo/521804/. Accessed January 02, 2022.

Kulaga, A. (2021). The impact of the COVID-19 pandemic on the processes of digitalization of small business. *Business Strategies, Analysis, Forecast, Management, 9*(5), 1–4.

NAFI. (2020). *Otkritie Bank: The pandemic has not changed the index of digitalization of SME companies*. https://nafi.ru/analytics/bank-otkrytie-pandemiya-ne-izmenila-indeks-tsifrovizatsiikompaniy-msb/. Accessed January 02, 2022.

Ranepa. (2020). *The consequences of the pandemic for business*. https://cdto.ranepa.ru/digital_turn_research/3-1-strategii-preodoleniya-posledstvij-pandemii. Accessed January 02, 2022.

RBC. (2021). In 2020, *Russia's GDP decreased by 2.7%, follows from a new Rosstat estimate*. https://www.rbc.ru/economics/30/12/2021/61cd8bab9a79477466646954. Accessed January 02, 2022.

Roberts, K. (2003). What strategic investments should you make during a recession to gain competitive advantage in the recovery? *Strategy and Leadership, 31*(4), 31–39.

Rostelecom. (2020). *20% of Russian companies, managers on the "remote" burn out and quit*. https://rt-solar.ru/events/news/2044/. Accessed January 02, 2022.

Russian Council. (2020). *Inflection point: The world after the COVID-19 pandemic*. https://russiancouncil.ru/analytics-and-comments/columns/global-governance/tochka-infleksii-mir-posle-pandemii-covid-19/. Accessed January 02, 2022.

Ryabukhin, A. (2020). *The impact of the COVID-19 pandemic on personnel management practices in industrial companies*. https://elar.urfu.ru/bitstream/10995/99832/1/978-5-91256-519-9_2021_052.pdf. Accessed January 02, 2022.

Sberbank. (2020). *Went into negative territory: How much Russian business lost in the crisis*. https://www.sberbank.ru/ru/s_m_business/pro_business/poteri-rossijskogo-biznesa-ot-koronavirusa/. Accessed January 02, 2022.

Shama, A. (1993). Marketing strategies during recession: A comparison of small and large firms. *Journal of Small Business Management, 31*(3), 62–72.

Shpileva, A. (2021). Digitalization processes in small and medium-sized businesses in a pandemic. *Economics, Entrepreneurship and Law, 11*(2), 299–312.

Stakhiev, N. (2021). Organizational problems of the transition to teleworking in the context of the COVID-19 pandemic in Russia. *Telescope: Journal of Sociological and Marketing Research, 2*, 147–150.

Steblyakova, L. (2021). Features of the application of anti-crisis measures to overcome the consequences of the coronavirus pandemic in the context of the manifestation of the challenges of the information society. *Drucker's Bulletin, 4*, 28–38.

WCIOM. (2020). *Digital literacy and remote work in a pandemic*. https://wciom.ru/analytical-reviews/analiticheskiiobzor/czifrovaya-gramotnost-i-udalennaya-rabota-v-usloviyakh-pandemii. Accessed January 02, 2022.

Zimovets, A., Sorokina, Yu., & Khanina, A. (2020). Analysis of the impact of the COVID-19 pandemic on the development of enterprises in the Russian Federation. *Ekonomika, predprinimatelstvo i pravo, 10*(5), 1337–1350.

Digital Transformation of Business Through Diagnostics of Its Core Competencies

Ekaterina P. Garina, Alexander P. Garin, Irina P. Denisova, Irina N. Semykina, and Elena V. Romanovskaya

Abstract Continuous technological progress defines business transformation using digital technologies, which creates a clear link between the implementation of integrated digital processes and economic performance. The first step in digital transformation is deciding which new digital offerings and in which areas of economic activity they should be implemented. The issues of IT system architecture, the cost and scale of digital transformation, and the structure of the system platform are also important. The answers to the questions determine the choice of options based on the conditions of iteration and flexibility of production, identifying the emphases of the study. In the study, the introduction of integrated digital technologies is proposed to be based on the diagnosis of the core competencies of the business unit; it is proposed to build a digital information model in the form of a matrix, assessing promising areas of informatization, competencies in development, applicability/inapplicability of the model. It is proposed to focus on the implementation of integrated digital technologies in the context of their impact on the operating activities of a manufacturer of domestic mechanical engineering related to the production of a complex, high-tech product.

Keywords Digital transformation of the business model · Predictive analytics · Operational support · Monitoring of the effectiveness of digitalization · Training complexes · Data management

---

E. P. Garina (✉) · A. P. Garin · E. V. Romanovskaya
Minin Nizhny Novgorod State Pedagogical University, Nizhny Novgorod, Russia
e-mail: e.p.garina@mail.ru

A. P. Garin
e-mail: garinsasha@icloud.com

E. V. Romanovskaya
e-mail: alenarom@list.ru

I. P. Denisova
State University of Economics (RINH), Rostov-on-Don, Russia

I. N. Semykina
Rostov State Transport University, Rostov-on-Don, Russia

E. I. Lazareva et al. (eds.), *Innovative Trends in International Business and Sustainable Management*, Approaches to Global Sustainability, Markets, and Governance,
https://doi.org/10.1007/978-981-19-4005-7_7

JEL Classification D22 · L23 · O21

1 Introduction

Digital transformation of a business is a holistic continuous process involving automation, as well as other digital alternatives (digitization, use of payment systems, personalized data, resources of banking instruments, implementation of technologies in production) to manual operations and traditional business processes, aimed at a deep and fundamental change of processes, at business transformation. Changing processes, in turn, requires a complete assessment of the corporate culture, operations, technology, and value chain. Key technologies such as data analysis, systems and software engineering, cloud computing, big data, and IT security are driving digital transformation (Akberdina, 2019; Merzlov et al., 2020). Digital transformation can be represented in the form of cloud services, smart devices, the Internet of Things, or blockchain (Armashova-Telnik, 2020). An additional direction of company's development can be the development and maintenance of digital information models and data management processes.

The purpose of the study is to form an approach to digital business transformation; to assess the change in the manufacturer's operating activities caused by the introduction of integrated digital technologies.

The object of the research is an enterprise in the domestic engineering industry, which is a manufacturer of a complex, high-tech products.

2 Methodology

The directions of digital business transformation are proposed to be determined through diagnostics of the current state of the main competencies in the following areas: organizational structure, personnel management, IT systems, knowledge management, preparation and participation in tenders (bidding), R&D, design, production, interaction with customers and subcontractors considering the scope of potential changes. The study proposes to focus on the IT system in the context of the impact of its change on the manufacturer's operating activities by forming a competency matrix for digital transformation of production (Stromberg matrix).

3 Results

In the surveyed company, we study the IT system from the point of view of subparameters:

- Interactive knowledge base integrated with design software—the knowledge base is developed in accordance with best practices, however, in production departments, internal developments are stored on the server as separate files.
- The use of automated design tools—modern automation tools are used. At the same time, the use of modern design tools did not allow to abandon the use of paper assignments for related departments.
- Project management programs integrated with external contractors—project management programs are applied in accordance with best practices.
- Integrated financial accounting and control system—financial accounting and control programs are fully applied.

Diagnostics of the current state of the main competencies of the manufacturer made it possible to determine the following.

- the business unit has a sufficient level of competence development to work within the framework of the business model, which is being implemented: better than those of comparable companies in the industry in the Russian Federation, the main functions related to design are developed; business processes are maximally adapted to the requirements of the main customer; the main emphasis is on meeting deadlines and passing expertise in the development of project documentation; the Center of Competence for increasing production efficiency has been formed and is developing;
- for the digital transformation of the business model, it is additionally required: to strengthen the project component in the design and functional activities, to create conditions to stimulate the increase in employee productivity, to form a KPI system to measure the economic efficiency of each project;
- to increase the productivity of business processes and the development and implementation of measures to improve the efficiency of production activities, it is necessary: to develop quantitative (cost) indicators characterizing the economic efficiency (value) of each project and project portfolio; to allocate a group independent of the participants in the process to calculate and track these indicators; to use these indicators to prioritize projects, to build a portfolio of projects and to manage the portfolio, to enter all participants in the process into KPIs.

An additional direction of the company's development can be the development and maintenance of digital information models and data management processes.

The Stromberg matrix for digital transformation can be structured in two directions: to include elements of digital transformation—technological steps along the X-axis, activities—along the Y-axis.

Dwelling in more detail on technological steps, we define competencies that may be subject to digital transformation:

1. Predictive analytics, diagnostics, and monitoring of the state of technological equipment (Aspen mTell) (Gileva, 2019; Usmanov, 2019), incl. (1) development of technical specifications (TS), (2) support of the process of implementation of predictive analytics systems, (3) examination of executive documentation for

the systems being implemented, (4) construction of predictive models of technological equipment failure; (5) formation and provision of proposals for building an optimal algorithm for the interaction of production services of the Companies in the implementation of predictive analytics systems; (6) integration of predictive analytics systems with real-time databases (RTDB) of enterprises and/or information systems (IS) of Companies; (7) monitoring and recommendations to improve the efficiency of the use of predictive analytics systems;

2. Implementation of technological process optimization systems based on machine learning tools (Garina et al., 2020; Kupriyanova, 2019), incl. (1) development of technical specifications for the creation of systems based on machine learning; (2) creation and expert assessment of documentation regarding the creation and use of machine learning tools; (3) development of predictive models of technological and business processes based on machine learning; (4) development of advanced virtual analyzers («Virtual assistants») based on machine learning for use in technological processes; (5) development of optimization models of technological and business processes based on machine learning; (6) development of tools for assessing and using (stands) models based on machine learning; (7) advice on the use of machine learning tools in technological processes; (8) integration of machine learning-based tools into the process control system and IT systems; (9) evaluation of the results of the implementation of machine learning tools in production;
3. Monitoring the effectiveness of using the advanced process control system, support, accompaniment at the stages of implementation and operation (APC, RTO, GDOT) (Babkin & Pestova, 2019), including: (1) development of TS; (2) advice and support for the implementation of advanced process control systems; (3) examination of design and as-built documentation; (4) finalization of the basic designs of the advanced process control system in terms of the inclusion of APC + modules; (5) examination of reports on the effectiveness of the advanced process control system; (6) the introduction of information systems for monitoring the system of advanced control of technological processes; (7) addition of APC solutions with high-precision models; (8) audit of existing systems of advanced process control; (9) monitoring of advanced process control systems; (10) performance of a full range of works on the implementation of systems for improved control of technological processes; (11) implementation of systems of hierarchical management and optimization (RTO) (Antonov, 2019);
4. Maintenance of the implementation of computer training complexes (CTC) for the training of technological personnel, including: (1) development of technical specifications; (2) support for the implementation of CTC; (3) examination of documentation; (4) testing of rigorous models for compliance with the real technological process; (5) testing of means of pre-exercise training (testing knowledge of accident and emergency response plan); (6) full range of works on CTC implementation; (7) development of dynamic 3D models of the technological process for practicing field operations with reference to the process model (including in VR); (8) construction of rigorous models of complex technological objects; (9) integration of CTC and machine learning-based models;

5. Supporting the implementation of information systems for monitoring and managing the efficiency of production sites (dashboards) (Garin et al., 2020), Including: (1) development of technical specifications; (2) support and expertise of IS implementation processes; (3) development of formulas for calculating key performance indicators of those participating in the implemented IS; (4) evaluation of results and acceptance of works; (5) participation in the development of IS integration plans; (6) integrated development of monitoring systems;
6. Development and maintenance of digital information models and data management processes (Usmanov M.R.), including: (1) assessment of existing information systems and data arrays for completeness, reliability, applicability, sufficiency, etc.; (2) carrying out the whole range of works on the creation of CIM (creation, implementation, support, training, development, etc.); (3) carrying out work on the integration of CIM with existing information systems; (4) development of CIM modules to support new and existing business processes; (5) support for the formation of technical specifications, control and acceptance of work during design and construction using CIM (including design in 3D);
7. Support in the field of information technology in education, incl. provision of consulting services in the field of information technology in education in terms of writing technical specifications, evaluating selected solutions, and accepting results (taking into account related competencies).

Dwelling in more detail on the types of activities using the example of the business unit in question, we define the following. The effects of the proposed ideas for the implementation of information systems are calculated in relation to the physical indicators of production and, as a rule, physical effects are not translated into value ones. Prioritizing digital business transformation solutions across an entire portfolio of projects is challenging. The degree of elaboration of solutions provides an opportunity to clarify capital costs. Work on a number of projects showing low efficiency has been discontinued. There is no formalized and structured work to maximize the effectiveness of the solutions. Projects for technical support of production that have no formal effect are highlighted.

4 Conclusion

Pilot testing of digital business unit alternatives allowed to:

- Partially formalize the operating activities of the manufacturer: to divide the design work into «elementary» components with the subsequent detailing of the scope of work; to determine the standards of labor costs for the implementation of «elementary» components of the design, and, starting from the standards, to recalculate the amount of work per man-hours. The result was: a decrease in the contribution of the subjective component of planning and identification of points of inefficiency.

- Adjust the incentive system: to add commercial criteria (project budget/margin) to the KPI; analysis and extraction of lessons learned at the end of each project into practice.

The prolongation of the results was the need to develop «cross-cutting» quantitative indicators to assess the effectiveness of the process. The proposed quantitative indicators are different for different types of projects.

References

Akberdina, V. V. (2019). Digital transformation of the industrial complex of Russia. Collection of reports of the St. Petersburg International Economic 2394 Journal of Economics, Entrepreneurship and Law # 9'2020 (September) Congress (SPEC-2018) «Foresight «Russia»: New Industrial Society. The Future». – Saint Petersburg, pp. 11–24.

Antonov A. (2019). Improved management in the metallurgical and mining industry. Digital transformation: ideas, solutions, results. https://www.honeywellprocess.com/en-US/online_campaigns/EUCyberSecuritySummit/Documents/2019-presentation/APC-for-MMM.pdf. Data accessed: November 05, 2021.

Armashova-Telnik, G. S. (2020). On the issue of digital economy tools. *Vestnik VGUIT [Proceedings of VSUET]. 82*(2), 243–250 (in Russian). https://doi.org/10.20914/2310-1202-2020-2-243-250

Babkin, A. V., & Pestova, A. Yu. (2019). Algorithm for assessing the level of digitalization of an industrial enterprise. Digital transformation of the economy and industry: Collection of proceedings of a scientific and practical conference with foreign participation, June 20–22, edited by Doctor of Economics, prof. A.V. Babkina. – SPb.: POLYTECH-PRESS, pp. 683–680.

Garin, A. P., et al. (2020). Research of the tools of influence on the behavior of market subjects. *Lecture Notes in Networks and Systems, 91*, 156–162

Garina, E. P., Romanovskaya, E. V., Andryashina, N. S., Kuznetsov, V. P. & Shpilevskaya, E. V. (2020). Organizational and economic foundations of the management of the investment programs at the stage of their implementation. *Lecture Notes in Networks and Systems, 91*, 163–169.

Gileva, T. A. (2019). Enterprise digital maturity: Assessment and management methods. *Bulletin USPTU. Science, Education,* Economy. *Series Economy, 1*(27), 38–52.

Kupriyanova, M. V. (2019). Methodological approaches to assessing the level of digitalization of industrial production. Law, economics and management: Topical issues: Collection of materials of the All-Russian scientific and practical conference with international participation, pp. 28–34

Merzlov, I. YU., Shilova, E. V., Sannikova, E. A., & Sedinin, M. A. (2020). Comprehensive methodology for assessing the level of digitalization in the organizations. *Economics, Entrepreneurship and Law, 10*(9), 2379–2396.

Usmanov, M. R. (2019). Assessment of the potential of a system of continuous improvement as a condition for innovative technological development of systems «product-production». *Scientific Review: Theory and Practice, 9*(10(66)), 1496–1151

Assessment of Production Development During the Digitalization of Continuous Improvement Systems and Increasing Its Efficiency

Ekaterina P. Garina, Alexander P. Garin, Irina E. Gurr, Veranika N. Gasanova, and Natalia S. Andryashina

Abstract The article studies the result obtained—the development of business processes from the digitalization of two systems: the system of continuous improvement and the production efficiency improvement system. The assertion that the maximum long-term positive effect (profit) with the minimum cost of finance and time resources of the organization's employees is possible within the framework of digitalization of systems is confirmed by the example of a pilot project. The study shows that the use of modern information products by manufacturers can significantly increase labor productivity. At the same time, in the perspective of three to five years, the decisions do not show unequivocal effectiveness. OPENSPASE and Bottleneck analysis technologies act as digital tools for continuous improvement. The digitalization tools for increasing production efficiency are the control system of the ACS IORD, SAP, Primavera, and the information system for managing overhaul.

Keywords Digitalization of continuous improvement · Digitalization of increasing production efficiency · Development as a result

JEL Classification D22 · L23 · O21

E. P. Garina (✉) · A. P. Garin · N. S. Andryashina
Minin Nizhny Novgorod State Pedagogical University, Nizhny Novgorod, Russia
e-mail: e.p.garina@mail.ru

A. P. Garin
e-mail: garinsasha@icloud.com

N. S. Andryashina
e-mail: natali_andr@bk.ru

I. E. Gurr
Volga State University of Water Transport, Nizhniy Novgorod, Russia

V. N. Gasanova
Rostov State Transport University, Rostov-on-Don, Russia

E. I. Lazareva et al. (eds.), *Innovative Trends in International Business and Sustainable Management*, Approaches to Global Sustainability, Markets, and Governance,
https://doi.org/10.1007/978-981-19-4005-7_8

1 Introduction

The digitalization of systems of continuous improvement and increasing production efficiency presupposes changes in the basic structure of managing processes, people, technologies that are laid down in the design of a product. At the same time, the value design of the product focuses on the final solution, for example, on the constructed and commissioned facility, on the means and methods of working with it, as well as on the directions for further use of the facility when creating new business values. The main losses, in addition to the vagueness of the assessment of the need and criteria for digitalization, as well as the difficulties arising in the optimization of competing values, in this case are: the increased final cost of realization and ownership of the asset; the lack of complete, holistic understanding of all the nuances of the digitalization process, the limitations of the created technical complexes (Shipshova, 2017). Further, when the basic structures are changed, supplemented by the introduction of a value design system, it is possible to use almost the entire arsenal of lean manufacturing tools (systems of continuous improvement) (Kuznetsov et al., 2019). At the same time, the opposite statement is also equivalent: the introduction of these tools and methods of the lean manufacturing system inevitably leads to a change in the basic structures of the value design system.

Mastering the principles and techniques of lean production, continuous improvement of design, management, production processes lead to an increase in labor productivity and a decrease in the costs of the enterprise as a whole. The tools of continuous improvement in the areas of optimizing business processes (increasing productivity, reducing costs) can be the technology of organizing the workspace according to the open space system—OPENSPASE (Usmanov et al., 2019); the key performance indicators (KPIs), which allow tracking potential improvements at key points in the activities of performers; the technology for identifying system limitations—Bottleneck analysis (Usmanov, 2020).

Let us dwell on the first result in more detail. In connection with the continuous improvement of design and production activities, new systems and software for automating manual labor, optimizing workflow, increasing the speed of operations, aimed at minimizing one of the types of losses in accordance with TIM WOODS—Skills Unused—untapped human potential, are constantly appearing on the market. In this case, personnel management acts as a component of the system of continuous improvement at enterprises for the following reasons: insufficient productivity and qualifications; uneven load; inconsistency or duplication of personnel functionality during data exchange, etc. The tools for minimizing losses in this case can be (Shushkin et al., 2016): 5S, Heijunka (Heijunka), Hoshin Kanri policy (Hoshin Kanri), Continuous improvement (Kaizen), key indicators (KPI), Poka-Yoke, «poka-yoke» («error protection», «foolproof»); SMART goals; standardized work, Visual Factory (visualization). The examples of personnel management software are Primavera Oracle, TDMS, Business Studio, «KASKAD», etc.

As for the second result—reduction of producer costs in general, it is difficult to assess the direct economic effect obtained from the implementation of measures for the digitalization of economic activities, because, according to open sources, 99% of the created system can operate at maximum productivity, however, a failure of digitalization of a business process by at least 1% can completely «zero» expectations from its implementation (Poddubny, 2021). In addition, productivity gains by reducing losses over a three to five-year perspective do not show unequivocal effectiveness. There are a number of reasons for this. Measures to increase productivity require significant material (financial) resources during implementation, but the effect is large scale, widespread and long term. At the same time, solutions to reduce losses at the initial stage of deployment of the «Lean Six Sigma» methodology require a significant amount of time for employees to train, create and launch a business process (mechanism) for continuous improvement (Kaidzen). The economic effect of improvements at the initial stage is quite high, but it has a clearly pronounced negative correlation by time. Keeping the process of continuous improvement on a constant level also requires maintaining a permanent staff of specialists in the organization. More details about this are written in the lean manufacturing literature and all-Union State Standards (Garina et al., 2017, 2018, 2020; Management of Design Estimates. 2021).

2 Methodology

The study of open source data shows that the use of modern information products based on high-performance software by manufacturers can significantly increase labor productivity. At the same time, it should be noted that a certain time from the moment of making a decision on the implementation of these information systems in the current activities of the enterprise to the transition of the company's employees to work «according to the system» is required—as a rule, from 2 to 6 years. This is a significant period of time during which the external environment of the company, as well as the goals and objectives facing it, can radically change. Significant investments, training of employees of the enterprise in the use of new technologies in the main production activity are required additionally, this entails the diversion of a significant amount of resources, for example, the time of specialists. The transition to new information systems causes a performance failure at the beginning of implementation very often. Identifying and eliminating shortcomings in the work takes a lot of time, both for the employees of the organization and for the employees of the provider firms. In the case of implementation, one-time failures and shortcomings are realized at once in the entire value chain of the product. All shortcomings are eliminated over time, and the system begins to function with the desired consumer properties. System setup time is usually from 2 to 4 months.

The maximum long-term positive effect (profit) with the minimum cost of finance and time resources of the organization's employees within the framework of digitalization of systems of continuous improvement and increasing production efficiency is proposed to be determined by the formula (1):

$$\text{Development} = \frac{\text{Increase in productivity} + \text{Cost reduction}}{d\text{T (Time)}} \quad (1)$$

3 Results

The considered areas of improving business processes—digitalization of continuous improvement systems and increasing production efficiency, are inextricably linked and complement each other with a positive synergistic effect. For example: when implementing the 5S system in the work of designers, the time spent on finding the necessary documents, tools, materials is reduced, this, in turn, leads to an increase in productivity, because the net working time (hereinafter referred to as «NWT») increases during the working day. Productivity during the execution of work is increased due to the avoidance of paper-based information carriers and an increase in the speed of communication of employees during joint work with the introduction of an automatic control system (ACS «IORD») (Usmanov et al., 2019). On the other hand, the same system is a kind of Poka-Yoke («protection against errors»—a tool for eliminating losses), not allowing the operation (action) to be performed in any other way, except as implemented in the software (Babkin & Pestova, 2019). This leads to significant savings in the time spent by specialists to identify and eliminate defects.

The priority task of the organization's management is to determine the optimal combination of elements of the formula (1) when introducing new high-performance technologies in the design and implementation of tools for reducing losses. Skewing to either side can have negative consequences for the organization in the short term and especially in the long term. Consider an example of an information system developed for the purpose of project management during major overhauls, which allows tracking errors in the formation of orders, controlling the timing and volume of work performed. Tasks that the use of the information system solves: providing access to information on current work from a mobile device, as well as from a «field» workplace; electronic approval of the work performed, including with the possibility of rejecting previously confirmed work; operational control of the fact of work performed; the ability to distribute tasks between performers online; photographic recording of the work performed; consolidation of data in one system; automatic generation of reports on the work performed.

Information on the work of the upcoming overhaul, before the initial loading of data into the information system, passes through several main stages: formation of orders in SAP by the manufacturer; loading order information from SAP to Primavera; formation and approval of the calendar network schedule (CNS) in Primavera; Loading information on orders with due dates from Primavera to the information system. As a result, an overview card of the project, which contains information about the number of open and closed sub-operations, project participants, as well as accounting for the time spent on work, will open.

In order to quickly find the work needed by the performer or controller, the information system provides a panel with «saved requests»: *work for today*—tasks that are scheduled for the current day; *search by equipment* - grouping by type and marking of equipment; *all open orders* - all orders that have not yet been closed; *construction work*—all sub-operations related to equipment painting, finishing and earthworks; *electrical work*—a list of sub-operations that relate to electrical work; *in progress*—all tasks to which the contractor has assigned the status «in work»; *closed*—a list of sub-operations that were closed by the specialists of the R&D plant; *confirmed*—a list of all tasks that have been approved by the executor of this request; *rejected*—sub-operations that were rejected by the specialists of the R&D plant; *by different types of equipment*—a list of inquiries by type of equipment. Sub-operations in requests are grouped by equipment marking, which allows you to quickly find the task you are looking for in the list when you are on the site next to the equipment to which the work requiring confirmation belongs. That is, the «Time» element from Formula 1 shows the development.

To confirm the work performed by the contractor, the performer selects it in the list, and as a result, a task card opens. Then the contractor changes the status of the task, fills in the field «Actual volume», attaches photographic materials, if necessary, adds notes and clicks on the button «Apply»—the work is confirmed!

Based on the results of filling in the information system with data, the performers organized the possibility of providing daily reporting: online reporting and automated generation of a daily report in Power Point. It is also possible to automatically enter actual costs from the information system for installations into checklists, this predetermines the possibility of comparing and choosing the optimal option for reducing them. That is, the «Cost reduction» element from Formula 1 shows the development.

A modern way of digitalizing systems of continuous improvement and increasing production efficiency, including organizing and monitoring various types of activities in order to ensure the required quality of work and compliance with the prescribed requirements, allows an objective increase in labor productivity, equipment productivity. That is, the element «Performance» from Formula 1 shows the development.

4 Conclusion

The study examines an approach to assessing the development of an enterprise in the engineering industry based on the interdependence of performance indicators, cost price and time on the example of a separate pilot project to digitize systems of continuous improvement and production efficiency. The conclusions allow us to conclude that there is a direct correlation of indicators in the conditions of domestic production. The digitalization tools for continuous improvement are the technology of organizing the workspace according to the open space system—OPENSPASE, the technology for identifying system limitations—Bottleneck analysis. Minimization tools are—5S, Heijunka, Hoshin Kanri, Kaizen, Poka-Yoke, SMART, Visual Factory.

The digitalization tools for increasing production efficiency are the automatic control system (ACS «IORD»—a variant of document flow, electronic archiving), SAP, Primavera, the information system for project management during major repairs. Minimization tools are—Kaizen, Poka-Yoke.

References

Babkin, A. V., & Pestova, A. Yu. (2019). Algorithm for assessing the level of digitalization of an industrial enterprise. Digital transformation of the economy and industry: A collection of proceedings of a scientific and practical conference with foreign participation, June 20–22, Edited by Doctor of Economics, prof. A.V. Babkina. – SPb.: POLYTECH-PRESS, pp. 683–680.

Garina, E. P., Kuznetsov, V. P., Egorova, A. O., Romanovskaya, E. V., & Garin, A. P. (2017). Practice in the application of the production system tools at the enterprise during mastering of new products. *Contributions to Economics* № 9783319606958, pp. 105–112.

Garina, E. P., Kuznetsov, V. P., Romanovskaya, E. V., Andryashina, N. S., & Efremova, A. D. (2018). Research and generalization of design practice of industrial product development (by the example of domestic automotive industry). *Quality—Access to Success, 19*(S2), 135–140.

Garina, E. P., Romanovskaya, E. V., Andryashina, N. S., Kuznetsov, V. P., & Shpilevskaya, E. V. (2020). Organizational and economic foundations of the management of the investment programs at the stage of their implementation. *Lecture Notes in Networks and Systems, 91*, 163–169.

Kuznetsov, V., et al. (2019). Re-engineering the business process of sales in view of life cycle stage and the company organisational structure. *International Journal of Trade and Global Markets (IJTGM), 12*(3/4), 412–423.

Management of Design Estimates. (2021). Technical data management system. https://tdms.ru/solution/functional-solution/management-design-and-estimate-documentation.html. Data accessed: November 05, 2021.

Poddubny, A. (2021). Calculation of the economic effect of the implementation of the automation system. *Antegra Consulting*. https://antegra.ru/expert/raschet-ekonomicheskogo-effekta-ot-vnedreniya-sistemy-avtomatizatsii/. Data accessed: November 10, 2021.

Shipshova, O. A. (2017). An innovative component of the formation of competitive advantages in production systems in the context of change in technological structures: Monograph. In O. A. Shipshova and others (Eds.), Moscow, 142p.

Shushkin, M. A., Aleksandrovsky, S. V., & Fomenkov, D. A. (2016). Research of the practices of implementing the strategy for catching up innovative development by companies: Monograph. National Research University Higher School of Economics. Nizhny Novgorod, 187p.

Usmanov, M. R. (2020). Generalization of management practices of continuous improvement and increasing the efficiency of the formed corporate systems on the example of the production and design complex of the Russian Federation. *Leadership and Management, 7*(1), 33–48.

Usmanov, M. R., Odnolko, I. S., Gimaletdinov, R. R., & Firsov, A. V. (2019). Improving productivity and operational efficiency of production assets. Implementation of a system of continuous improvement in manufacturing enterprises and in research and development and design complexes (Vol. 2, 224p). Nizhny Novgorod: Quartz.

Pandenomic Transformation of the Modern World Economy and International Business

Elena V. Fomicheva, Alla V. Temirkanova, and Kseniya Y. Boeva

Abstract The purpose of the article is to analyze the changing conditions of the world economy and the transformation of the mechanism of international business during the COVID-19 pandemic, as well as the formation of a system of pandenomics and its impact on the directions and conditions of the development of the world community. The authors highlight the structural shifts of the modern world economy associated with the pandemic conditions, in which it has to operate. The main systemic changes include: pandenomic disruption of supply chains, changes in the structure of international trade and other forms of international economic relations, changes in the role and priority of the development of industries and the conversion of enterprises in accordance with the requirements of pandenomics, restructuring of the consumption system, transformation of the globalization process itself, its content and forms of manifestation. It is shown that the COVID-19 pandemic has changed most of the basic principles of the functioning of the world economy and international business, affected and transformed all aspects of life, in one way or another changed the activities of all actors of the world economy. The presented systematic view of the transformational processes that have occurred and are occurring in the modern practice of international business and the entire global economic system allows us to understand the new reality that is being formed under the influence of changes taking place in life in the conditions of pandenomics.

Keywords World economy · International business · COVID-19 pandemic · Transformation · Pandemonics

JEL Classification F02 · F20 · F50

E. V. Fomicheva (✉) · A. V. Temirkanova · K. Y. Boeva
Southern Federal University, Rostov-on-Don, Russia
e-mail: efomicheva@sfedu.ru

A. V. Temirkanova
e-mail: temirkanova@sfedu.ru

K. Y. Boeva
e-mail: kyboeva@sfedu.ru

E. I. Lazareva et al. (eds.), *Innovative Trends in International Business and Sustainable Management*, Approaches to Global Sustainability, Markets, and Governance,
https://doi.org/10.1007/978-981-19-4005-7_9

1 Introduction

The processes of consistent development, in one direction or another, progress or regression, occur in such a complex system as the world economy, always under the influence of a huge number of factors operating in various spheres of life. Transformational processes very often become an objective consequence of the crisis stages of the development of a respective system, including economic one.

The level of development of the modern world economy, both of the entire system as a whole and of its individual components, the multi-vector nature of its trends, the complexity of cause-and-effect relationships, the multisphere and multifactorial nature of the models being implemented, imply a complex hierarchy of relationships between its subjects, characterized by fierce competition, the search for strategic partners, joint cooperation, competition for spheres of influence and access to markets and factors of production, geopolitical cooperation and confrontation, etc. (Arkhipov & Fomicheva, 2020).

The COVID-19 pandemic has become the point of bifurcation in the development of the world economy, which radically, dramatically and inevitably, without time for preparation and adaptation, has changed most of the basic elements and principles of its functioning. It affected and transformed all aspects of life, as well as the activities of all actors of the world economy. A whole system of pandenomics has been formed, which has its own principles and specifics of functioning (Fomicheva, 2021).

According to the authors, the experience and lessons learned from the systemic crisis caused by COVID-19 can become an additional incentive for global cooperation in all areas of international business and the establishment of the system of international communications taking into account the new economic conditions and interaction.

2 Methodology

During the two years of the pandemic, a fairly large number of scientific papers have already appeared. They are devoted to the study of its impact on various aspects of society, including the economy. The authors emphasize the need to analyze the ongoing changes, increase the role of state management of the economy and support of the population in this period, assess the probabilistic transformations that are occurring and will occur for a long time, as well as the formation of new trends in the development of the world economy (Osipov et al., 2020). Views are expressed about the attempt of individual countries to use the pandemic conditions of the development of the world economy to strengthen global hegemony (Glazyev, 2020) and even subordinate to their interests using the achievements of the scientific and technological progress (Katasonov, 2020). The growing volume of publications on these issues characterized, almost chronologically, the increasing impact of the pandemic on the development and forms of international and domestic business and economic systems as a whole (Genkin & Frumkin, 2020).

At the same time, the growing interest in this issue and the need for its further study are determined by the ongoing pandemic and the ever deeper penetration of its consequences into the mechanism of functioning of the world economy and international business.

The object of this study is the world economic system as a complex mechanism of cause-effect and subject-functional relationships in a situation of objective necessity of rapid forced transformation, slowing down of economic activity and attempts to overcome both external destructions and breakdown of the usual system of established interactions.

The subject of the study is structural shifts in the system of the modern world economy and international business, taking place under the comprehensive, dominating impact of the pandemic on the entire world economy as a whole and actors of all levels of economic processes in particular.

In the process of researching the chosen topic, based on the principles of a systematic approach and general scientific methodology, methods of logical, statistical and comparative analysis, synthesis and selective scientific abstraction were applied.

The information and empirical base of the research is the data of statistical agencies, analytical reviews of international economic organizations, materials of periodicals, as well as the results of research by Russian and foreign economists.

3 Results

Considering the main directions of transformation of the modern world economy and international business, the following main manifestations of interaction of entities and structural mega-economic shifts of a pandenomic nature can be distinguished.

The pandenomic interruption of supply chains. The spread of the COVID-19 pandemic has led to the disruption of the largest supply chain networks in China, the United States and Europe. The industries that have faced a sharp break in production chains due to quarantine restrictions and changes in the structure of consumption and the priority of the development of industries can be attributed to the automotive industry, all types of passenger transportation and transport in general, retail, electronic industry, clothing production, etc. The consequence of this was a drop in industrial production, a decrease in the volume of export–import operations, in some cases there was a sharp decline in production, suspension and even shutdowns of production.

For example, Nissan, due to interruptions and suspension of the supply of components from China, faced an acute global shortage of parts and was forced to make a decision to stop the production of cars around the world. The production of Nissan cars uses a wide range of Chinese parts from brake discs to climate sensors. More than 800 types of components were purchased in the Chinese province of Hubei, which the government completely quarantined, ànd at the same time supplies were suspended for an indefinite period. In mid-February 2020, there was an acute shortage of components at the factories of Nissan, as well as a number of other major automakers. According to Nissan, since February 2020, assembly lines at enterprises in Japan, Malaysia, the USA, Mexico, the UK and Spain have been under different termination or suspension regimes.

Disruptions in the supply chains of electronic goods of Chinese origin caused delays in the delivery of computers and smartphones to the retail sector. Disruptions in supply chains in the electronics industry have a stronger impact on smartphones, headphones and computers, as retailers prefer not to make large stocks due to the constant updating of models and instability of demand, especially in conditions of a special pandenomic regime. According to a survey of a number of experts conducted by the Financial Times, some companies underestimate the consequences of these supply disruptions, which will affect foreign economic activity for a very long time. A common situation has become a warning to electronics manufacturers from the possibility of delaying the delivery of personal computers and components to a threefold increase in standard terms to several months. In such conditions, ensuring sufficient production capacity is very problematic. In business practice, fears of disruptions in the supply chain have taken a leading position in the list of risks associated with COVID-19. It is this risk that company managers consider the most dangerous for internal and corporate growth (The coronavirus effect on global economic sentiment, 2021).

According to a survey by the Institute for Supply Management (ISM), almost 75% of American companies are experiencing supply problems due to restrictive and protective measures introduced in connection with the pandemic, 16% of them lowered their revenue targets by an average of 5.6% in this regard. At the same time, the number of large businesses facing problems related to supply chains is 44%, medium and small businesses—32% (The impact of the COVID-19 pandemic on industry & the environment, 2020).

Changing the structure and dominant forms of international trade and other forms of international economic relations. There have been quite obvious changes affecting the volume, structure and conditions for the implementation of international trade in goods and services: a decrease in the absolute volume of trade in goods and services due to the coronavirus pandemic and related restrictions (2020: a reduction in trade in goods by 8%, trade in commercial services by 21%); a sharp reductions in all tourist flows and related services for movement, accommodation, escort, insurance and other related services and the production of goods (for example, in the second quarter of 2020, international travel expenses decreased by 81%, transport by 29%) (Overview of world trade statistics for, 2021, 2021); uneven impact on the development of trade in services (the sectors connected with physical labor and personal contact, such as construction, cultural and recreational services, etc.) sharply decreased, but financial services, online education and medicine, e-commerce, etc. continued to grow.; the growth of trade in goods of a pandenomic nature (the growth of trade in medical goods in 2020 was 16.3%, and in 2019, when the pandemic was just beginning, 4.7%), while the trade in personal protective equipment increased by 47.2% (Overview of world trade statistics for, 2021, 2021); the uneven impact of the pandemic on the economy of various regions of the world associated with varying degrees of involvement in the system of international division of labor, the harshness of limitations imposed, the speed and coverage of the spread of morbidity, etc. The new wave of the pandemic and the tightening of global financial conditions hinder the flow of capital to emerging markets and developing countries, which consequently negatively affects the international movement of capital. Against the background of pressure from external factors, the pandemic has led to large government borrowings to dramatically increase the funding for the healthcare system and provide socio-economic support to the population and companies, which affects the implementation of almost all forms of interaction with other states.

In its latest issue of the External Sector Report, the IMF notes that as a result of measures taken in the world in connection with the pandemic, the global current account balance—the sum of absolute deficits and surpluses among all countries—has increased, from 2.8% of global GDP in 2019 to 3.2% of GDP in 2020. This balance is expected to grow as the pandemic continues in most countries of the world (Kaufman & Lee, 2021).

The change of the role and priority of the development of industries and the conversion of enterprises in accordance with the requirements of pandenomics. The pandemic of a previously unknown virus and the severe economic crisis that followed it, coincidentally, were aggravated by the crisis phenomena in the oil market, which only increased the degree of their negative impact. Unlike the 2008 financial crisis, the coronavirus pandemic caused a supply-side shock, as production in a number of industries closed, as mentioned above. The list of areas that was most severely affected by the coronavirus and the quarantine imposed in most countries include: tourism, logistics, automotive manufacturing, air transportation and hospitality, international trade, catering, retail, real estate sales. The border closures caused to massive job losses in airlines and international transportation companies, which led to a negative multiplier effect in a large number of industries. The list of industries affected by COVID-19 included the entertainment industry: lockdown and widespread restrictions sharply destabilized the work of shopping malls and parks, the filmmaking was almost completely suspended, festivals and concerts were postponed indefinitely. The spheres of education, sports and culture were seriously affected. Due to quarantine measures, the number of unemployed is increasing around the world, and according to forecasts of the International Labor Organization, by the end of the epidemic, more than 300 million people will lose their jobs, and 1.6 billion may be left in a destitute condition (Abramov, 2021).

Among the industries affected by the COVID-19 crisis were exhibitions and exhibition activities, which are one of the channels for promoting goods and services, serve as a platform for concluding foreign trade contracts and investment cooperation. The potential damage (lost contract income), according to the World Association of the Exhibition Industry, is 134.2 billion euros (The impact of the COVID-19 pandemic on industry & the environment, 2020).

However, despite the severity of the economic situation in the world, a number of industries remain protected during the coronavirus epidemic, and some companies have even achieved record growth for themselves. First of all, biotech and pharmaceutical companies, companies providing online services, or companies that managed to adapt to work online in time, remain the winners. For example, against the background of a sharp jump in the popularity of streaming services, the shares of the online cinema Netflix surged by 3%, increasing the total capitalization to $ 187 billion, surpassing the cost of such a giant of the film industry as Disney. Since the coronavirus pandemic broke out, the use of Zoom, Team, Skype, etc. has increased tenfold all over the world.

According to the World Economic Forum (WEF), the growing demand for personal protective equipment and ICU ventilators has led to the production line conversion of a number of enterprises. For example, the American company General Motors (GM), specializing in the production of cars, has signed a contract with the US Department of Health and Human Services for the production of 30 thousand ICU ventilators, with volume of funding 489 million US dollars. By order of the UK government, Mercedes Formula One has developed and started production of an adapted device capable of providing continuous positive airway pressure (CPAP) and delivering oxygen to the lungs without invasive ventilators (The impact of the COVID-19 pandemic on industry & the environment, 2020).

According to the forecasts of the WEF, pandenomics will contribute to the wider introduction of robotics and artificial intelligence, which can reduce the participation of people in production and marketing processes, lower the risk of infection and dependence on human resources, provide a socially painless and rapid adaptation to a sharp reduction or increase in demand.

The change of the consumption system. According to the results of a fairly large-scale study (15 countries, 3000 consumers) conducted by Accenture, it can be said that the COVID-19 pandemic has changed consumer behavior and the structure of retail trade. The hierarchy of consumer preferences and the priority of consumer purchases has changed dramatically. Consumer spending has mostly shifted from services to consumer goods, mainly basic necessities and medical supplies, while the population's propensity to save has increased, motivated, on the one hand, by the situation of lockdown and global slowdown in economic activity and by a protective mechanism in conditions of total uncertainty in the development of the situation, on the other.

Respondents stated that they are currently buying more personal hygiene and cleaning products, as well as food, but at the same time they began to buy fewer clothes and shoes, beauty products, as well as consumer electronics. In addition, respondents note that they began to: spend more time taking care of themselves and their mental well-being—60%; play sports more actively at home—57%; pay serious attention to reducing food waste, and plan to do so in the future—64%; take their health and environmental consequences of shopping more seriously, make more purchases for health, and will continue to do so in the future—50%; be more rational in their purchasing behavior—45% (Accenture analysts have identified long-term changes in consumer behavior, 2020). The results of the study allow us to conclude that many consumer approaches and trends that have emerged in connection with the pandemic will continue in the future. In addition, we can even say that this tendency will remain for a long time.

Transformation of the globalization process itself, its content and forms of manifestation. The unpredictability of the directions of development of the world economy in the near future, the lack of clarity about the government's actions regarding trade, fiscal and monetary policy, sanctions and anti-sanctions confrontation, trade wars of powerful countries, political confrontation, and all this is complicated by the specifics of interaction in pandemic situations—these are the real risks and risky realities of the modern world economy. Globalization in the former, pre-crisis, version is no longer there and, most likely, will not be. The structural characteristics and principles of the new model of "globalization 2.0" are already emerging, and it should restore the desire for interaction and cooperation of the main actors of the world economy, which are under the strong pressure of the events of the current stage of its development.

According to the UN (Reports and Messages of UN Secretary-General Antonio Guterres, October 11, 16 and 24, 2021), the COVID-19 pandemic has sharply worsened the financial situation, pushing more than 120 million people into poverty, 160 million faced hunger, about 100 million children are experiencing difficulties with education; at the same time, more than 4 billion people do not have access to social support and the necessary level of medical care, their nominal and real income levels are falling sharply and there are no mechanisms to protect them (Messages from the Secretary-General, 2021).

On the one hand, the danger associated with the pandemic is an external challenge to all of humanity, which is not related to competition, access to resources, redistribution of spheres of influence or any other contradictions Therefore, it would seem that this challenge should have generated a sense of unity in the fight against its manifestations, should have contributed to the unification of efforts in this battle while reducing the confrontation between the countries. But at the same time, the economic side of the process of combating the pandemic by each individual entity of the world economy (the need to transform national economies, search and redistribution of resources, reduction of development potential, etc.) raises even more acute issues of competitiveness (at all levels, from nano- to mega-economy), as well as problems of economic and political sovereignty, economic and foreign economic security. Geopolitical problems have worsened in the international relations of the pandemic period, economic and political competition has become tougher, sanctions confrontation continues, etc.

4 Conclusion

Consequences of the Great Quarantine (in IMF terminology) will affect the main indicators of the development of the world economy for a long time, since COVID-19, which plunged the world economy into a state of "economic coma", had a great impact not only on demand, but also on the competitiveness of countries. A number of countries were able to successfully resist new challenges by applying a system of additional protectionist restrictions. But at the same time, it is important to understand that the events in the world economy system, as well as the actions of states and other entities, taking into account the achieved level of interdependence of its individual subsystems, are, in essence, the process of adaptation of the economic policy of most countries to the realities and contradictions of globalization, which, changing and transforming, will remain the defining trend in the development of the world economy. As a result, globalization is intensifying, which is being realized in increasing importance and specificity of regions and regional associations; the multipolar and multi-layered nature of the world economic system is being formed; issues of priority for the implementation and protection of national interests and economic and foreign economic security are becoming more important and relevant.

Of course, these are only some transformational manifestations in the system of the world economy associated with the COVID-19 pandemic, which is still ongoing and the consequences of which will be complex, often latent and multilevel. The main trends in the development of the world economy will manifest themselves differently in each individual country, being specified depending on: the duration and depth of the pandemic impact and the economic crisis caused by it; directions and personification of state assistance, its extent and forms; the existing level of economic development and technological structure; the readiness of the population for future changes and many other factors. But it is absolutely clear that neither the world economy itself, nor its actors in various forms of interaction, nor the nature and content of relations between them, nor globalization and protectionism as the key directions of its development, will no longer be able to exist in the former pre-crisis, pre-pandemic version. Further improvement of the efficiency of the economy and the well-being of the entire world community, which is ultimately the key goal of the global economy, is possible only with interaction and active constructive cooperation.

References

Abramov, D. (2021). Experts assessed the impact of coronavirus on the labor market in the world. RIA Novosti. https://ria.ru/20200429/1570746746.html. Data Accessed: October 27, 2021.

Accenture analysts have identified long-term changes in consumer behavior. (2020). Accentere. https://www.accenture.com/ru-ru/about/company/company-news-release-long-term-changes-consumer-behavior. Data Accessed: October 28, 2021.

Arkhipov, A. Yu., & Fomicheva, E. V. (2020). Human development and STR: The main directions of the economic breakthrough of Russia. In E. G. Popkova & M. L. Alpidovskaya (Eds.), *Human and technological progress towards the socio-economic paradigm of the future* (Part 1, pp. 129–142). Berlin, Boston: De Gryeter Oldenbourg. https://doi.org/10.1515/9783110636147-015. Data Accessed: October 27, 2021.

Fomicheva, E. V. (2021). New realities of the modern world economy: Pandenomics and protectionism 2.0. In *Proceedings of the VIII International Scientific and Practical Conference in Memory of A. Y. Arkhipov "Multipolar Globalization and Russia"*, pp. 309–312.

Genkin, A. S., & Frumkin, K. G. (2020). *Koronaeconomics. Chronicle of the economic consequences of the 2020 pandemic*. Publishing Solutions.

Glazyev, S. Yu. (2020). *The plague of the XXI century: How to avoid a catastrophe and overcome a crisis?* Book World.

Katasonov, V. Yu. (2020). *Postcapitalism. From liberal democracy to a digital concentration camp.* Book World.

Kaufman, M., & Lee, D. (2021). *How the pandemic increased the global current account balance.* IMF BLOG. https://www.imf.org/ru/News/Articles/2021/08/02/blog-how-the-pandemic-widened-global-current-account-balances. Data accessed: August 3, 2021.

Messages from the Secretary-General. (2021). The United Nations. Official website. https://www.un.org/sg/ru/content/sg/declarations-and-messages. Data accessed: October 9, 2021.

Osipov, Yu. M., Arkhipov, A. Y., & Zotova, E. S. (2020). *Crowned pandemic and the Enchanted World.* Monograph. Rostov-on-Don, Taganrog: Southern Federal University Press. http://ukros.ru/wp-content/uploads/2020/08/%D0%9A%D0%BE%D1%80%D0%BE%D0%BD%D0%BE%D0%B2%D0%B0%D0%BD%D0%BD%D0%B0%D1%8F-%D0%BF%D0%B0%D0%BD%D0%B4%D0%B5%D0%BC%D0%B8%D1%8F-%D0%BD%D0%BE%D0%B2.pdf. Data accessed: September 23, 2021.

Overview of world trade statistics for 2021. (2021). Roscongress. https://roscongress.org/materials/statisticheskiy-obzor-mirovoy-torgovli-za-2021-god/. Data accessed: September 23, 2021.

The coronavirus effect on global economic sentiment, December, 2021. Survey. (2021). McKinsy&Company. https://www.mckinsey.com/featured-insights/mckinsey-global-surveys. Data accessed: October 31, 2021.

The impact of the COVID-19 pandemic on industry and the environment. (2020). Accounts Chamber of the Russian Federation. https://ach.gov.ru/upload/pdf/Covid-19-prom.pdf. Data accessed: October 27, 2021.

Innovation and Development of Social Responsibility Models of Chinese Internet Companies Under COVID-19

Yang Yang

Abstract The COVID-19 outbreak has led to a stagnation of economic activity in many countries and a significant decline in trade and investment, causing a fatal impact on the global economy. However, many Chinese Internet companies have seized the opportunity of the digital transformation of the epidemic, taken the initiative to adapt to the new situation, changed the traditional social responsibility model, implemented digital intelligence to fulfil the social responsibility model, created flexible and diverse social responsibility platforms, provided safe and reliable online charity platforms, promoted scientific and technological innovation, used big data to develop epidemic screening applications, and artificial intelligence technology to help vaccine research and development to protect the people's basic needs. It is found that, unlike traditional corporate social responsibility, Internet enterprises change the form of traditional social responsibility and broaden the content of social responsibility, and the Internet corporate social responsibility model in the digital era has an innovative role in the development of corporate social responsibility.

Keywords COVID-19 · Epidemic · Internet companies · Corporate social responsibility · Innovation · Practice

JEL Classification R01 · F22 · F63

1 Introduction

Internet companies have penetrated all walks of life in various informational and digital forms and have subtly influenced people's lives. In the cyberspace platform created by Internet companies, Internet users are the most directly involved subjects. As of June 2020, the size of China's Internet users has reached 940 million, and the Internet penetration rate has reached 67%. On 22 January, 2020, the COVID-19

Y. Yang (✉)
Southern Federal University, Rostov-on-Don, Russia
e-mail: 393567991@qq.com

E. I. Lazareva et al. (eds.), *Innovative Trends in International Business and Sustainable Management*, Approaches to Global Sustainability, Markets, and Governance,
https://doi.org/10.1007/978-981-19-4005-7_10

epidemic outbreak occurred in Wuhan, Hubei Province, and at 10:00 a.m. on 23 January, Wuhan was declared "lockdown", and China launched full-scale prevention and control of the COVID-19 outbreak, timely contain the spread of the epidemic. For Internet companies, it is more important to take social responsibility, participate in the prevention and control of the epidemic, cooperate with the government, and implement the main responsibility for the prevention and control of the epidemic in the industry.

According to the latest data on the whole epidemic, it is difficult for the epidemic to end in a short period, and it is impossible to determine the exact time when the epidemic will end. Internet enterprises should fulfil their epidemic prevention responsibilities in the long term, optimize their products and services by using their professional advantages, such as developing epidemic screening applications, big data epidemic dynamic prediction, and applying artificial intelligence technology to vaccine research and development, to promote the transformation of the digital economy as soon as possible by effectively pulling social resources. This study enriches the connotation and mode of social responsibility of Internet enterprises, which is conducive to the unified development of Internet enterprises and society.

2 Materials and Methods

According to stakeholder theory and sustainable development theory, the stakeholders of an enterprise should include at least shareholders, creditors, employees, community and society, government, and the public (Shu, 2020). In addition, Internet enterprises and two special objects—Internet users and network environment. Internet corporate social responsibility should ensure the interests of all stakeholders.

The pyramid model of corporate social responsibility was proposed in 1983 by the American management scientist Archie B. Carroll. It is a theory widely accepted in academic and business circles. In Carroll's study, CSR is divided into four levels: economic responsibility, legal responsibility, ethical responsibility, and philanthropic responsibility (Luo et al., 2021).

In this paper, we selected the 2020–2021 social responsibility reports of representative Chinese Internet companies such as Alibaba, Tencent, and Jingdong. The study found that Internet companies have performed in epidemic prevention and control by (1) using technology to invent health codes to identify patients, using big data to distribute materials and provide charitable platforms; (2) using online platforms to sell products and change sales patterns, prohibiting monopolistic practices and eliminating counterfeiting; (3) ensuring the safety of the online environment; (4) caring for employees and protecting the interests of relevant stakeholders, and these actions advance Internet companies' social responsibility innovation development.

3 Results

3.1 *Financial Responsibility*

Large-scale information technology ensures the transportation of medical supplies and daily necessities and promotes economic recovery.

Internet companies use the "Internet+" model in the delivery of medical supplies and livelihood protection of the worried city and the basic life of residents (Zhao & Feng, 2021). Takeaway platform launched a "contactless delivery" service, Jingdong also used delivery robots, drones and other intelligent equipment, to maximize the possibility of human contact is reduced (Rao et al., 2020).

According to the report on the business income of 41 companies in Hubei in the first quarter of 2020 published by Hubei Province. The higher turnover growth is in medical enterprises and Internet enterprises. Based on the operating income report of small- and medium-sized listed companies in Hubei Provincial Bureau of Statistics, in the first quarter of 2020, among the 12 companies, only one medical company and one Internet company's operating income increased by 30–50%, and most companies continued to decline during the epidemic (Li, 2020).

3.2 *Innovation Responsibility*

Artificial intelligence set up online medical consultations to help vaccine research and development.

Internet companies promote AI algorithms and arithmetic power for the first time in large-scale application to the research and application of viral infectious diseases, in some directions such as viral gene sequencing, vaccine and drug development, protein screening and other medical devices, and drug development and research and development, greatly improving the efficiency of research and the speed of application placement, and the intelligent research of viral infectious diseases has taken shape. The professional medical consultation service of the Internet medical platform relieves the pressure of hospital outpatient clinics most efficiently and conveniently, reduces the risk of crowded cross-infection, and leaves precious medical resources and limited medical workers to the neediest diagnosed patients (Xu & Pei, 2020).

3.3 *Innovation Responsibility*

Online office learning can effectively avoid infection. iFLYTEK (Asia AI leader) has opened its "AI+ Office" platform to provide remote office services for enterprises and individuals to help prevent and control the epidemic (Ou, 2020). There are more than 10 million enterprises working online on Alibaba's DingTalk. Online education platforms such as "Job Help" and "Net Education" also provide live online courses to help teachers and students achieve online education and online learning (Tian, 2020). In addition, many provinces have also used smart government systems to improve the efficiency of online business and avoid offline contact. In Henan province, more than 95% of government services are available online, more than 50% of matters can be done without a single trip, and the number of registered users of the «Henan Affairs» APP has exceeded 8.5 million. The government encourages enterprises and individuals to apply online to avoid the spread of the COVID-19 epidemic and reduce cross-infection caused by the movement of people (Carnevale & Hatak, 2020).

3.4 Charity Responsibility

Corporate provides a reliable charity platform and ensures the fair use of donations.

Internet companies can rely on their own advantages to provide an honest and reliable charity platform. Through the fulfilment of charitable responsibilities, Internet enterprises can also get more support and build up a good corporate image. China Xiongnu Group developed a charitable donation management traceability platform, and on February 10, "Good Track" was officially launched (Su, 2016). Blockchain technology features to improve the transparency of donation information, management of social institutions donated materials, donation funds use, to provide the community with a full process of public traceability, feedback and supervision, and to promote the ability to see and believe the whole process of donation.

3.5 Environmental Responsibility

Protect the internal network environment and external ecological environment.

The environmental responsibility of Internet companies includes the responsibility for the internal network environment and the external ecological environment (Luo et al., 2021). Internet enterprises should strengthen industry self-discipline, safeguard network security sovereignty and national security, resist unethical internet practices, do not spread information such as obscene text, picture and video advertisements, do not provide false information, do not spread violent and obscene games, actively carry out network security days, remind the public to prevent telecommunication network fraud, and provide a safe and stable internal network environment (Mercedes, 2017). In addition, more and more Internet companies have begun to pay attention to the protection of the environment and help energy conservation and emission reduction, producing positive social effects (Li & Yan, 2016). We are familiar with Alibaba's "Ant Forest" public welfare project, the social impact of which should not be underestimated. As of August 2020, the Ant Forest online 500 million users accumulated 7.99 million tons of carbon emissions reduction, planting 132 million real trees on the earth, and some Internet companies with new technologies to upgrade the operation of equipment to actively help energy saving and emission reduction (Zhang, 2021).

4 Conclusion

This paper concludes that the social responsibility of Internet companies during the epidemic is changing and innovating in life and practice. To develop harmoniously with society and the environment, Internet companies must do three things. First, Internet companies identify sensitive information and judge social issues through data mining and semantic analysis and use big data and information technology, intelligent algorithms, and artificial intelligence to provide data support for corporate social responsibility strategies and help them participate in epidemic prevention and control. Secondly, Internet enterprises should classify information, turn high-quality information resources into economic benefits, and give full play to their own advantages in the process of fulfilling social responsibility to find business opportunities and develop them. Finally, Internet enterprises should establish a multi-dimensional social responsibility system and form a multi-dimensional value system of "economic value, social value, environmental value, and cultural value" to promote innovation and development of enterprises.

Acknowledgements First of all, I would like to thank my supervisor, Professor Lazareva Elena Iosifovna, for his help from the initial selection of the topic to the framework of the thesis, from the academic attitude to the research methodology, Professor Lazarava's academic rigour, his patience with students and his scientific spirit of excellence during the thesis supervision process, all of which I deeply admire.

Thanks to the teachers of the faculty of management, I have gained a comprehensive and systematic knowledge of management under the guidance of the experts and professors, and with their help, I have truly discovered my strengths and weaknesses in management knowledge and skills, which will have a great impact on my future career development.

References

Carnevale, J. B., & Hatak, I. (2020). Employee adjustment and well-being in the era of COVID-19: Implications for human resource management. *Journal of Business Research, 116*, 83–187.

Li, J. R. (2020). A study of new employment patterns in the context of the COVID-19. The "Shared Staff" model as an Example. *Industrial Economics Review, 06*, 27–31.

Li, Y., & Yan, X. (2016). The enlightenment of American computer enterprise environmental responsibility practice to my country. *A Modern Commerce, 01*, 107–108.

Luo, Z., Sheng, H., Li, X., Song, M., & Liu, Z. (2021). COVID-19 backdrop report on the business situation of enterprises in the context of the COVID-19 epidemic–a study mainly in Wuhan City, Hubei Province. *Research on the United Front, 02*, 176–183.

Mercedes, A. (2017). Corporate sustainability and institutional shareholders: The pressure of social responsible pension funds on environmental firm practices. *Business Strategy and the Environment, 28*(6), 1060–1071.

Ou, L. L. (2020). Study on the impact of COVID-19 on small and medium-sized enterprises in Hubei Province and countermeasures. *Journal of Hubei College of Economics (humanities and Social Sciences Edition), 10*, 255–263.

Rao, F., Tang, Q., Wang, H., & Ma, J. (2020). The impact of the COVID-19 epidemic on employment in Sichuan Province analysis and countermeasures. *Economic Research Reference, 12*, 56–59.

Shu, X. Z. (2020). Research on the current situation and countermeasures of social responsibility fulfillment of Internet enterprises. *Economist, 8*, 277–279.

Su, X. (2016). Corporate sustainability and institutional shareholders: The pressure of social responsible pension funds on environmental firm practices. *Business Management Consulting, 5*, 456–478.

Tian, Q. (2020). Research on coping strategies of small and medium-sized logistics enterprises under the background of epidemic situation. *Management and Technology of SME, 9*, 140–145.

Xu, W. L., & Pei, X. (2020). Research on the enhancement of corporate value by the performance of corporate social responsibility under the background of major epidemics. *Financial Management Research, 8*(3), 8–48.

Zhang, Z. (2021). Research on the legal regulation of environmental protection responsibility of e-commerce enterprises. *Management Trend, 8*(19), 135–138.

Zhao, W. Z., & Feng, J. (2021). Research on new employment patterns in the context of the COVID-19 epidemic. *Management Trend, 16*, 267–274.

The Ease of Doing Business and International Indices in the BRICS Countries: Evaluating Their Relationship

Nadezhda K. Savelyeva and Victoria A. Saidakova

Abstract *Purpose* The purpose of the research is to analyse favourable conditions for doing business amongst the BRICS countries and assess how international criteria influence the Ease of Doing Business IndexIndex. *Methodology* The main methods of the research are statistical ones: correlation analysis and regression analysis. The authors use comparative analysis, synthesis, and method of analysis of cause-and-effect relationships. *Findings* The authors analyse the countries of the international association BRICS. The results of the study show that the Ease of Doing Business Index has close ties with some international indices designed to determine the place of the state according to a certain criterion. However, the effective trait can form a statistically significant regression equation, but not with every factor. *Originality* The article shows that it is possible to compare various international ratings to identify the relationship and mutual influence within any interstate group.

Keywords Sustainable development · Doing business · COVID-2019 · Statistical analysis · Regression · Correlation

JEL Classification C10 · C22 · F02 · F20 · F53 · O11 · O19

1 Introduction

The new decade of the twenty-first century has faced a global challenge—the COVID-19 pandemic. The global economy must be flexible and able to adapt to changing reality.

An important sector for any economy is business, which must be able to adapt to the changing external environment and increase the business activity of the state. However, for many countries, positioning in international rankings is the main reference point in the national economic system.

N. K. Savelyeva (✉) · V. A. Saidakova
Vyatka State University, Kirov, Russia
e-mail: nk_savelyeva@vyatsu.ru

E. I. Lazareva et al. (eds.), *Innovative Trends in International Business and Sustainable Management*, Approaches to Global Sustainability, Markets, and Governance,
https://doi.org/10.1007/978-981-19-4005-7_11

Rating systems help conduct a comparative analysis by any criterion and identify competitive advantages in comparison with other member states of the international union (organization). The issue is relevant due to COVID-19 when the business sector has great losses.

Third International Municipal Forum of the BRICS countries (the members of this international group are leaders in terms of GDP, calculated at purchasing power parity) has shown that small and medium-sized businesses have significantly been affected during the pandemic. About 40% of enterprises cannot work longer.

The purpose of the study is to analyse favourable conditions for doing business amongst the BRICS member states and assess how other international criteria influence the Ease of Doing Business Index.

2 Methodology

Favourable conditions for doing business are reflected in the Doing Business rating, which was developed by the World Bank and is calculated annually. Currently, the number of objects of assessment is 190 economies of countries. The favourable conditions are established by monitoring modifications to the regulations governing the activities of small and medium-sized businesses.

The issue of the favourable conditions for doing business at the national level is important and scientists carry out various types of research, using economic and mathematical methods: (Alshubiri, 2021; Doing Business 2018; Dzhukha, 2017; Fabbris & Scioni, 2021; Hao et al., 2020; Inshakova et al., 2021; Ivashchenko & Orlova, 2017; Kozyr et al., 2018; Mezentceva & Mezentceva, 2017; Necadova, 2020; Nianko et al., 2021; Pirogova et al., 2021; Rajabova et al., 2021; Roszko-Wójtowicz & Grzelak, 2020; Savelyeva et al., 2019; Sozinova et al., 2017a, 2017b; Sozinova et al., 2021a, 2021b, 2021c; Swamy & Narayanamurthy, 2018; Volkodavova et al., 2017; Vorontsova & Palesheva, 2021; Zayats, 2020) etc.

In addition to the specified rating, the authors use other data necessary to assess the degree of influence on the ease of doing business:

- Index of Economic Freedom allows tracking progress in the field of economic freedom, opportunities to promote ideas. It is determined based on the regulatory framework, government restrictions, government regulation, market openness (Index of Economic Freedom, 2021);
- Global Innovation Index tracks global innovation trends and assesses the efficiency of the economy in terms of innovations, the ability to use them (Global Innovation Index, 2020);
- Global Competitiveness Index allows to assess the ability to ensure a high level of well-being of the population, stable rates of economic development (Global Competitiveness Report Special Edition, 2020);
- The Loan Receipt Index consists of two indicators: an index of the effectiveness of legal rights (an assessment of legislation on collateral and insolvency) and an

Table 1 Statistics for correlation and regression analyses in the BRICS countries

State	Ease of doing business index	The number of COVID-19 cases per 1 million people	Loan receipt index	Government's responsiveness to change	Index of economic freedom	Global innovation index	Global competitiveness index
	y	X_1	X_2	X_3	X_4	X_5	X_6
Brazil	59.1	36,249	50	29.2	53.7	31.94	60.93
India	71	7,429	60	55.9	56.5	35.59	61.36
China	77.9	62	80	49.8	59.5	53.28	73.3
Russian Federation	78.2	23,311	80	47.4	61	35.63	66.74
South Africa	67	17,746	60	33.2	58.8	32.67	62.44

Source Compiled by the authors

index of the depth of credit information (an assessment of the coverage, volume, and availability of credit information) (Doing Business, 2018, 2019, 2020).

As part of the study of the favourable conditions for doing business in the BRICS countries, the authors have compiled a table for further statistical analysis (Table 1).

3 Data Availability

Data on the results of the regression analysis of the Ease of Doing Business Index for the BRICS member states for 2020, which are described in the following section of the study, are available at Ease of Doing Business Index for the BRICS member states for (2020).

4 Results

At the beginning of the study, the authors have analysed the ratings of the BRICS member states according to DB data for 2018–2020 in order to assess the current situation as a whole in terms of the Ease of Doing Business Index (Fig. 1).

The diagram shows that the situation is developing in the best way in Russia since it has the best rating amongst the BRICS countries. It can be concluded that the level of business support is higher and has better conditions. In terms of progressive actions to improve an enabling environment, India is the best, moving up from 100 to 31 in the rankings. The situation in Brazil is less favourable.

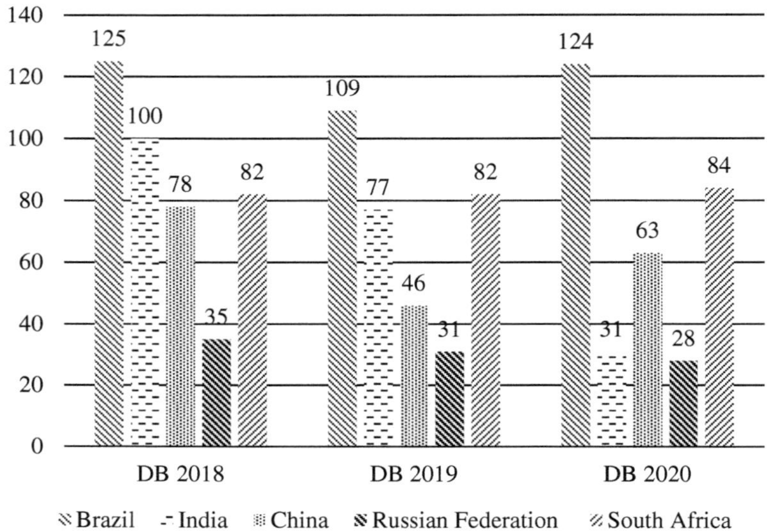

Fig. 1 Ease of doing business index in the BRICS countries for 2018–2020. *Source* Compiled by the authors

For the correlation analysis, the authors took 2020 as the base period, reflecting the impact of the COVID-19 pandemic. The results of the analysis based on the data in Table 1 are shown in Fig. 2.

Analysing the diagram, the closest relationship of the Ease of Doing Business Index can be seen with such indicators as the Loan Receipt Index, Index of Economic Freedom and Global Competitiveness Index. The least impact on the Ease of Doing Business Index in the BRICS countries is made by the Global innovation index and the number of cases of COVID-19 per 1 million people.

Variables with the greatest impact on the Ease of Doing Business Index were used for regression analysis—Loan Receipt Index, Index of Economic Freedom, Government's responsiveness to change, and Global Competitiveness Index (Table 2).

Let us consider the first relationship between the Ease of Doing Business Index and the Loan Receipt Index. This dependence is best described by a linear function of the form $y = a_2 + b_2{*}x_2$.

According to the results of regression statistics, multiple R is 0.9584, respectively, 95.84% change in the dependent factor is explained by the change in the independent variable. At the same time, the normalized R-square is at the level of 0.8914, which indicates the high accuracy of the approximation.

According to the results of the analysis of variance, the actual value of the Fisher criterion is 33.83. When referring to the F-distribution according to the significance level $\alpha = 0.05$, the correspondence of k_1 and k_2 to the values 1 and 3, respectively, the tabular value of F is 10.1. When comparing the two Fisher criteria, we can talk

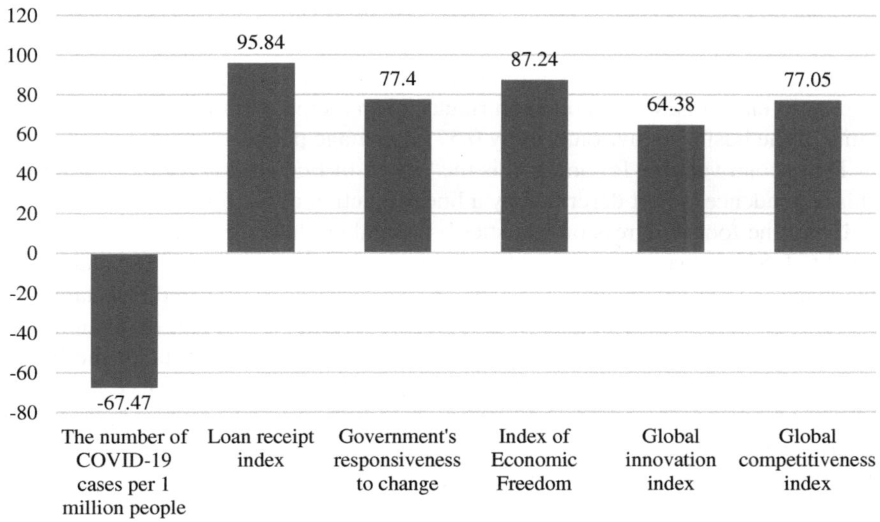

Fig. 2 Correlation analysis of the dependence of the ease of doing business index on factors. *Source* Compiled by the authors

Table 2 Regression statistics

Indicator	Loan receipt index	Index of economic freedom	Government's responsiveness to change	Global competitiveness index
Multiple *R*	0.958409	0.872432	0.773996	0.770534
R-square	0.918548	0.761137	0.599069	0.593722
Normalized *R*-square	0.891397	0.681516	0.465426	0.458296
Standard error	2.638515	4.518379	5.853871	5.892779
Observations	5	5	5	5

Source Compiled by the authors

about the recognition of the equation as statistically significant, since the actual value of the F-criterion is greater than the table.

The calculated coefficients of the regression equation allow us to obtain the following model: $y = 32.89167 + 0.571944{*}x_2$. The significance of the regression coefficient is determined by the value of the Student's t-test: for the coefficient $b_2 = 5.816$. At a significance level of 0.05 and degrees of freedom = 4, the tabular value of the t-test = 3.183. According to this criterion, the regression coefficients are recognized as statistically significant, due to the excess of the actual value of the t-criterion over the tabular one. The P-value indicates the likelihood that determines the significance of the regression coefficient. If the P-value is greater than 0.05, the coefficient can be considered zero, therefore, the independent variable has practically no effect on the dependent variable. In our case, we do not have such a picture, since the P-value is at the level of 0.01.

Thus, the conducted regression analysis shows that an increase in the level of lending to enterprises by 1 point contributes to an increase in the index of the well-being of the business environment by 0.57 percentage points.

The second variable for analysis is the "Index of Economic Freedom" criterion. This dependence is best described by a linear function of the form $y = a_4 + b_4{*}x_4$.

Using the tool "Regression statistics", the authors have determined multiple R, equal to 0.8724, respectively, 87.24% change in the effective factor is explained by the change in the independent variable. In this case, the normalized R-square is at the level of 0.7611, which indicates a sufficient accuracy of the approximation.

Analysing the results of the analysis of variance, the actual value of the Fisher criterion is 9.56. When referring to the F-distribution at the significance level $\alpha = 0.05$, the tabular value of F is 10.1. When comparing the actual and tabular Fisher criteria, we talk about the recognition of the regression equation which is considered statistically insignificant (10.1 > 9.56) and unreliable.

In the framework of subsequent regression analyses, the variables are Government's responsiveness to change (x_3) and the Global Competitiveness Index (x_6). A linear function best describes the dependence on the effective factor.

The value of the multiple R for the variable x_3 is 0.774. It indicates a change in the effective factor by 77.4% due to the modification of the selected variable. According to the results of regression statistics, the multiple R for the variable x_6 is 0.771, indicating that the 77.1% change in the effective indicator depends on the selected variable. However, R-squared is <0.6 based on the analysis for both variables, respectively, the model requires certain improvements and for the BRICS countries, this criterion is not essential.

Thus, the study shows that not all selected international criteria fully reflect the change in the Ease of Doing Business Index. Therefore, the issue of finding factors that have a significant impact and have statistical significance in the construction of equations will be reflected in further scientific research.

5 Conclusion

To overcome the consequences of the pandemic, the BRICS member states are adopting business support programs, which include soft loans, tax holidays, grants, etc.

At the same time, it is necessary to more actively develop tools for cross-border e-commerce between countries. There is also a need to establish links between postal operators of the BRICS countries to reduce the cost of delivering products to the final consumer.

Therefore, in order to increase the level of the Ease of Doing Business Index, it is necessary to intensify cooperation between entrepreneurs in the field of achieving sustainable development goals.

References

Alshubiri, F. (2021). Investment obstacles to sustainable development and competitiveness index. *Marketing Intelligence & Planning, 39*(2), 234–248. https://doi.org/10.1108/MIP-02-2019-0118

Cehlar, M., Culkova, K., Pavolova, H., & Khouri, S. (2019). Sustainability of business with earth sources in V4 countries. *E3S Web Conference, 105*, 04038. https://doi.org/10.1051/e3sconf/201910504038

Doing Business. (2018). https://www.doingbusiness.org/en/reports/global-reports/doing-business-2018. Accessed: November 15, 2021.

Doing Business. (2019). https://www.doingbusiness.org/en/reports/global-reports/doing-business-2019. Accessed: November 15, 2021.

Doing Business. (2020). https://www.doingbusiness.org/en/reports/global-reports/doing-business-2020 Accessed: November 15, 2021.

Dzhukha, V. M. (2017). Research and development intensity in business: Russia and EU. *European Research Studies Journal, XX*(1), 64–76. https://doi.org/10.35808/ersj/596

Ease of Doing Business Index for the BRICS member states for 2020. https://doi.org/10.6084/m9.figshare.17069888

Fabbris, L., & Scioni, M. (2021). Pooling Rankings to obtain a set of scores for a composite indicator of erasmus + mobility effects. *Social Indicators Research, 156*, 481–497. https://doi.org/10.1007/s11205-020-02513-6

Global Competitiveness Report Special Edition. (2020). How countries are performing on the road to recovery. https://www.weforum.org/reports/the-global-competitiveness-report-2020. Accessed: November 15, 2021.

Global Innovation Index. (2020). https://www.wipo.int/publications/ru/details.jsp?id=4514. Accessed: November 16, 2021.

Hao, L., Zobia, B., Qaiser, A., Ishtiaq, A., Nadeem, I., & Babar, A. (2020). Measuring low carbon energy, economic and environmental sustainability performance of BRICS. *The Singapore Economic Review*. https://doi.org/10.1142/S0217590820500617

Index of Economic Freedom. https://www.heritage.org/index/visualize. Accessed: November 16, 2021

Inshakova, A. O., Sozinova, A. A., & Litvinova, T. N. (2021). Corporate fight against the COVID-19 risks based on technologies of industry 4.0 as a new direction of social responsibility. *Risks, 9*(12), 212. https://doi.org/10.3390/risks9120212

Ivashchenko, A., & Orlova, N. (2017). Comparative analysis of some EU member states and EU associated countries to identify the phenomenon of business development in post-socialist countries. *Economic Annals-XXI, 163*(1–2(1)), 22–25. https://doi.org/10.21003/ea.V163-04

Kozyr, N. S., Petrovskaya, N. E., & Zazimko, V. L. (2018). Modern approaches assessing global competitiveness. *European Research Studies Journal, 21*(4), 1034–1041.

Mezentceva, O., & Mezentceva, A. (2017). Macroeconomic factors, entrepreneurial performance and economic growth in emerging markets. *World Review of Science, Technology and Sustainable Development, 13*(1), 74–92. https://doi.org/10.1504/WRSTSD.2017.083717

Necadova, M. (2020). Impact of aggregation methods on countries' ranking in composite index of national competitiveness. *Malaysian Journal of Economic Studies, 57*(1), 39–58. https://doi.org/10.22452/MJES.vol57no1.3

Nianko, V., Purtov, V., Yekimov, S., Lopatynskyi, Y., & Nemtsova, A. (2021). The problem of state support and increasing the investment attractiveness of agriculture. *IOP Conference Series: Earth Environmental Sciences, 839*. https://doi.org/10.1088/1755-1315/839/2/022007

Pirogova, O., Lysova, E., & Sozinova, A. (2021). Post-COVID 2019 sustainable economic development: A new cycle of digital development. *E3S Web of Conferences, 284*, 04017. https://doi.org/10.1051/e3sconf/202128404017

Rajabova, M. G., Makkaeva, R. S., & Mahluff, A. (2021). Strategic framework for sustainable enterprise development. In J. V. Ragulina, A. A. Khachaturyan, A. S. Abdulkadyrov, & Z. S. Babaeva (Eds.), *Sustainable development of modern digital economy. Research for development*. Cham: Springer. https://doi.org/10.1007/978-3-030-70194-9_4

Roszko-Wójtowicz, E., & Grzelak, M. M. (2020). Macroeconomic stability and the level of competitiveness in EU member states: A comparative dynamic approach. *Oeconomia Copernicana, 11*(4), 657–688. https://doi.org/10.24136/oc.2020.027

Savelyeva, N. K., Kuklin, A. V., Lapteva, I. P., & Malysheva, N. V. (2019). The investment attractiveness of a regional market of educational services as the basis of its global competitiveness in Industry 4.0. *On the Horizon, 27*(3–4), 239–244. https://doi.org/10.1108/OTH-07-2019-0042

Sozinova, A. A., Fokina, O. V., & Fufacheva, L .A. (2017a). Reorganization of entrepreneurial structures within global crisis management: Problems and perspectives. In E. Popkova (Ed.), *Overcoming uncertainty of institutional environment as a tool of global crisis management. Contributions to Economics*. Cham: Springer. https://doi.org/10.1007/978-3-319-60696-5_1

Sozinova, A. A., Fokina, O. V., & Shchinova, R. A. (2017b). Marketing tools for increasing company's reorganization effectiveness. In: Popkova, E. (Eds.), *Overcoming uncertainty of institutional environment as a tool of global crisis management. Contributions to economics*. Cham: Springer. https://doi.org/10.1007/978-3-319-60696-5_40

Sozinova, A., Savelyeva, N., & Alpidovskaya, M. (2021a). Post-COVID marketing 2019: Launching a new cycle of digital development. *Global Challenges of Digital Transformation of Markets*, 419–431.

Sozinova, A. A., Kosyakova, I. V., Kuznetsova, I. G., Stolyarov, N. O. (2021b). Corporate social responsibility in the context of the 2020 economic crisis and its contribution to sustainable development. In E. G. Popkova, B. S. Sergi (Eds.), *Modern global economic system: Evolutional development vesus revolutionary leap. ISC 2019. Lecture notes in networks and systems* (Vol. 198). Cham: Springer. https://doi.org/10.1007/978-3-030-69415-9_10

Sozinova, A. A., Sofiina, E. V., Safargaliyev, M. F. & Varlamov, A. V. (2021c). Pandemic as a new factor in sustainable economic development in 2020: Scientific analytics and management prospects. In E. G. Popkova, & B. S. Sergi (Eds.), *Modern global economic system: Evolutional development versus. Revolutionary leap. ISC 2019. Lecture notes in networks and systems* (Vol. 198). Cham: Springer. https://doi.org/10.1007/978-3-030-69415-9_86

Swamy, V., & Narayanamurthy, V. (2018). What drives the capital flows into BRICS economies? *World Economy, 41*, 519–549. https://doi.org/10.1111/twec.12606

Volkodavova, E. V., Zhabin, A. P., Yakovlev, G. I., & Evdokimov, A. N. (2017). Development of favorable conditions for the entrepreneurial activity in the Russian Federation. *International Journal of Applied Business and Economic Research, 15*, 139–156.

Vorontsova, N., & Palesheva, N. (2021). Analysis of the modern methodology of calculating consumer price index in the Russian federation and the perspectives of its digital economy's sustainable development. https://doi.org/10.1007/978-3-030-70194-9_34

Zayats, O. (2020). The EU global competitive force index. *Economic Annals-XXI, 183*(5–6), 17–25.

Features of the Formation and Development of Competitive Relations in the Conditions of Digitalization

Nataliya S. Nemykina

Abstract The processes of globalization and digitalization have penetrated into all spheres of society, including the economy. The development of competitive relations is a necessary component of the process of stimulating economic growth. Globalization and digitalization have made it possible to expand the composition of competitors and the geographical boundaries of markets in the framework of the Pull Economy. But, at the same time, they have created a platform to activate unfair competitors. This article reveals the features of the formation of competitive relations due to the widespread introduction of digitalization. The article also analyzes the opportunities for the development of competitive relations, the problems that arise when competitors carry out economic activities and also suggests measures to stimulate competition to ensure the economic growth of the national economy.

Keywords Digitalization · Globalization · Competition · Unfair competition · Competitive advantage

JEL Classification D21 · D22 · D43 · F62 · M31 · M38

1 Introduction

Competition is an indicator of the development of the economic system since it is thanks to competitive relations between economic entities that technological development takes place in the market and a variety of goods and services is created. Therefore, the development of competition is an important task facing the states.

The processes of globalization and digitalization contribute to accelerating the development of competitive relations and expanding the circle of people who can be called competitors. At the same time, this creates a problem in regulating competition, since economic entities often violate the principles of good faith in relation

N. S. Nemykina (✉)
Southern Federal University, Rostov-on-Don, Russia
e-mail: pechnikova@sfedu.ru

E. I. Lazareva et al. (eds.), *Innovative Trends in International Business and Sustainable Management*, Approaches to Global Sustainability, Markets, and Governance,
https://doi.org/10.1007/978-981-19-4005-7_12

to other participants in the commodity market, gaining competitive advantages and redistributing demand in their favor. The problem of stimulating the development of competition in conjunction with measures to control the fair conduct of market entities is currently an urgent problem for states.

Therefore, it is important to analyze the features of the formation and development of competition in the conditions of widespread digitalization and globalization of economic relations, to study the forms of competitive relations, as well as to identify signs of unfair competition. As a result of such a study, a set of measures for the development of competitive relations within the framework of the requirements of the current legislation is proposed.

Currently, the control over competitive relations in the Russian Federation is carried out by the Federal Antimonopoly Service and its territorial administrations. They are faced with the task of balancing the situation on the market in order to avoid the redistribution of demand in favor of one of the economic entities, including by conducting an unfair policy against competing companies.

2 Methodology

In carrying out the research, general scientific methods were used, including methods of analysis, synthesis, and forecasting, which made it possible to systematize and characterize the features of competition in the conditions of digitalization and globalization of economic relations. As a result of the application of the above methods, it was possible to retrospectively trace the evolution of competitive relations between economic entities and determine the vector of improving control while encouraging the development of competition as an indicator of the level of economic development.

3 Results

3.1 Features of the Formation and Development of Competition in the Conditions of Digitalization

If we take as a basis the legislative definition of the concept of "competition", it means the rivalry of economic entities, in which the independent actions of each of them exclude or limit the possibility of unilaterally influencing the general conditions of circulation of goods in the relevant market (Federal Law No. 135-FZ of July26, 2006, 2021). At the same time, the challenges of our time result in an expansion of the list of situations that can be called competition.

In the context of widespread globalization and digitalization, borders between states and, accordingly, between commodity markets lose the functions of barriers on the trajectories of commodity flows, and therefore competition now arises not only between economic entities operating within certain geographical boundaries but also between those located on different continents.

Digitalization and globalization have made it possible to simplify logistics processes, now a larger number of business entities can distribute products outside the region where goods are produced, which has become possible thanks to electronic commerce.

In addition, globalization and the development of international relations create megacorporations that have spread their influence throughout most of the planet. These companies have gone a long way to form their own brand and have established themselves in a certain commodity market, became extremely popular, and gained good reputation, giving them an advantage over other business entities in this market. On the one hand, this can lead to the formation of a monopoly, on the other, to unfair competition from other market participants. They often do not need to create a personal brand and marketing strategy, since unscrupulous competitors use such tools as product duplication and imitation of a well-known brand. These actions create unfair competition not only for the company, whose logos and stylistic solutions in the design of goods, and trademarks are copied in one form or another. An example is the situation when a company starts copying Adidas brand products on the sportswear market, in this case, the actions will be not only an act of unfair competition against the copyright holder and manufacturer of Adidas products, but also to other economic entities, the so-called "noname", since when choosing a product between an unknown and popular company, the buyer will prefer the latter, and therefore an unscrupulous competitor gets a competitive advantage.

There is also a problem associated with the fact that unscrupulous competitors by "parasitic" actions redistribute demand not only in the market of certain goods but also by misleading consumers of another adjacent commodity market. It should be noted here that such actions are possible only in adjacent commodity markets, when a consumer, without special knowledge, can confuse products and buy goods of one brand under the guise of another. An example is the situation when the manufacturer of the cosmetic product Aquasol, through the use of a similar stylistic design, color scheme, and phonetic similarity with the medical product Aqualor, created the impression that the hygiene product refers to medical products that have certain properties and guarantee a therapeutic effect, while hygiene products do not have a clear confirmation of such qualitative characteristics and, as a result, cannot guarantee the expected therapeutic effect (The database of decisions and legal acts of the FAS of Russia, 2021).

Along with the above-mentioned tool of unscrupulous competitors, there is also an official way to use a popular brand to promote your business. A franchise is a relatively new phenomenon for commercial activity, it provides an opportunity to use a trademark, business ideas, and management decisions of a well-known company, while the brand owner accompanies the franchisee's activities by transferring a brand book, decorating premises for the sale of goods and services, creating an advertising campaign, consulting and technical support when doing business. At the same time, the franchisee must make a lump-sum payment and constantly pay royalties to the brand owner.

Perhaps it is the obligation to constantly pay royalties to the franchisor that pushes competitors to illegally copy and imitate the style of a well-known brand.

Another tool for promoting products on the market and at the same time creating a competitive environment is the Internet. Currently, the Internet makes it possible to conduct a marketing campaign much more efficiently and provide more coverage to potential consumers, which has allowed many companies to gain worldwide fame. Business entities form a personal style that distinguishes them from other market participants, as a result of which there is a constant need to maintain interest in the brand. From that moment on, companies enter into an often aggressive competition for the attention of consumers through a marketing campaign. This is often not only direct brand advertising, but also the dissemination of negative information about a competitor.

In this case, the Internet is damaging to business, since previously negative information was distributed within certain geographical boundaries and did not receive so much publicity. In modern conditions, negative information can spread over a much larger territory and it is difficult to assess the reputational risks of an economic entity from these actions. At the same time, publications refuting false information do not always reach those who have previously received negative reviews, which does not allow restoring a damaged reputation and, as a result, returning lost profits.

Currently, many organizations create websites to promote and sell their own products. This leads to the problem of creating duplicate sites containing the same designation in the domain name as in the goodwill domain, also made using the same color scheme, graphic images, and stylistic solutions when designing a page for the sale of goods under the guise of original products of a well-known brand.

Another feature of the formation of competitive relations at the present time is that the sale of goods is increasingly carried out in trade network structures. Now the place of production of the goods does not matter, since the distribution of goods flows takes place on the Internet and organizations that may not even know about each other's existence can become competitors. T Also, the emergence of e-commerce platforms such as Amazon, Alibaba Group, eBay, and others contributes to this. In the Russian Federation, Ozon, Yandex Market, and SberMegaMarket marketplaces are also being created to develop e-commerce and maintain business. These platforms contribute to business development, as they provide an opportunity to sell products on a larger territory, which leads not only to a direct increase in profits but also promising opportunities for product promotion, bringing it to a new level of recognition among consumers.

3.2 *The Role of Public Policy in the Development of Competition*

An important factor in the development of competition is the state policy implemented through monitoring activities by the Federal Antimonopoly Service (hereinafter—the FAS of Russia).

Due to the fact that competition has a stimulating and innovative impact on the development of the economic system, the state must maintain the dynamics of these processes (Botkin et al., 2017).

The FAS of Russia carries out activities in several areas: monitoring and control of the competitive environment and regulatory and methodological advice.

Monitoring and control are implemented by monitoring the market situation and preventing unfair actions on the part of business entities. The FAS of Russia and its regional divisions issue warnings to violators, mandatory for the elimination of violations committed, as well as the imposition of penalties.

To modernize antimonopoly regulation, the FAS of Russia has developed a "fifth antimonopoly package" to ensure compliance with the realities of the digital economy. Digitalization carries not only opportunities for the development of competition, but also potential risks associated with the possibility of abuse by economic entities using the opportunities of globalization and digitalization. In this regard, there is a need to regulate and control the economic power of digital platforms (Federal Antimonopoly Service, 2021).

Another area of activity of the antimonopoly service is the granting of preferences to economic entities, including for the development of the social sphere. In addition, the FAS of Russia coordinates the purchase by economic entities of other economic entities in order to prevent organizations from gaining a dominant position and to ensure equal conditions for the implementation of production and economic activities. Over the past year, the FAS of Russia has approved the acquisition of Vostochny Bank by Sovcombank, as well as the sale of Reebok Authentic Brands Group. All these processes are accompanied by market analysis and assessment of potential impacts on market conditions to ensure the stable development of all economic entities.

At the same time, business entities began to abuse their rights by gaining access to confidential information about a competitor's commercial activities and applying to the FAS of Russia and its regional divisions in order to force a competitor out of the market.

4 Conclusion

The challenges of digitalization and globalization contribute to the development of competition and at the same time create new risks in the form of the appearance of unscrupulous competitors, as a result of which it is necessary to restructure the antimonopoly policy by both state authorities and economic entities.

In order to ensure the dynamic and stable development of competition and, accordingly, stimulate economic growth, the state should conduct regular monitoring and control activities, especially on the Internet, since it is this platform that has become the most frequent place for acts of unfair competition in the conditions of digitalization. Another direction of state policy should be clear regulation of activities in the field of procurement and bidding, since the transition of this area to digital platforms has led to the emergence of new types of acts of unfair competition, including fraud.

On the part of economic entities, first of all, it is necessary to refrain from conduct contrary to the law, as well as the ideas of decent, reasonable, and fair behavior that have developed in civil circulation (Resolution of the Plenum of the Supreme Court of the Russian Federation of 04 03 2021 No. 2, 2021, paragraph 30) when conducting economic activity. In addition, as a tool for protecting their own rights, business entities can register trademarks and service marks with the Federal Service for Intellectual Property.

Due to the overcoming of territorial and border barriers between commodity markets, competition in the conditions of digitalization is reaching a new level, which encourages economic entities to develop production, introduce innovations, reduce the cost of goods and services, accelerate logistics processes and "develop" new territories. Now competitors must step up their activities in order to be prominent among a large number of manufacturers of identical goods and services and maintain their positions in the market. To do this, it is necessary to form a brand and enter the global network, constantly conduct marketing campaigns to attract attention to their products.

Entry into the international market entails large organizational consequences for an economic entity. The international arena in the long term may allow it to become a megacorporation that occupies a dominant position in the market. At the same time, this goal encourages the company to develop technologies and introduce innovations, which has a positive impact on the market situation. Taking into account competitive relations, each of the economic entities strives to occupy a dominant position, and this is what allows for the dynamic development of the national economy.

The more companies work to attract potential consumers for subsequent profit, the more this results in an increase in the variety of products and services offered, which, in turn, leads to a gradually increasing problem of oversaturation of the market, while stimulating the creation of a better, unique product to surpass a competitor.

These processes cause constant rivalry between economic entities for potential consumers, which, in turn, leads to technological development and, accordingly, economic growth of the national economy. At the same time, the issue of combating acts of unfair competition remains relevant, due to the fact that digitalization provides an additional impetus and opportunities for the latter.

References

Botkin, O. I., Sutygin, A. I., & Sutygin, P. F. (2017). Competition as a basis for the strategy of sustainable development of market structures. *Problems of Regional Economy, 3–4*, 62–72. Lan: Electronic Library System. https://e.lanbook.com/journal/issue/302501. Data accessed: November 13, 2021.

Federal Antimonopoly Service. (2021). https://fas.gov.ru/news/31112. Data accessed: November 14, 2021.

Federal Law No. 135-FZ of July 26, 2006 (2021) "On protection of competition" (as amended in 2021). Federal Antimonopoly Service of the Russian Federation. https://en.fas.gov.ru/documents/documentdetails.html?id=15366. Data accessed: November 13, 2021.

Resolution of the Plenum of the Supreme Court of the Russian Federation of 04 03 2021 No. 2 (2021) On some issues arising in connection with the application of antimonopoly legislation by courts. https://www.vsrf.ru/documents/own/29742/. Data accessed: November 13, 2021.

The database of decisions and legal acts of the FAS of Russia. https://br.fas.gov.ru/cases/624adfb5-2c98-400a-b4a8-e5b17d8f1dd3/. Data accessed: November 13, 2021.

The Imperatives of Smart and Sustainable Management in the Digital Environment

Tax Incentives for Sustainable Development in the Context of Digitalization

Yuri A. Kolesnikov

Abstract The problems of the environment and society hindering further economic development were the reason for the creation of the concept of sustainable development (hereinafter referred to as SD or ESG) on the international agenda in the second half of the twentieth century. The Russian Federation, as a significant player on the international agenda, cannot remain aloof from the principles of sustainability, but it is still inferior to developed countries in terms of the level of implementation and operationalization of ESG transformation. In the modern world, an important component of economic growth is the development of ESG infrastructure, which in the future will be able to be independent of climatic conditions and contribute to a comfortable life for people. In developed countries, since the early 2000s, sustainability factors have been taken into account when deciding on the implementation of investment projects, and international organizations, in turn, are implementing their own corporate policy to assess the sustainability of their investments. Such projects contribute to the achievement of national and international development goals and strategies—the UN SDGs, the Paris Agreement, the QII principles, etc.

Keywords Tax incentives for low-carbon economy · ESG transformation · CBAM tax · Decarbonization of the economy · Sustainable development · Green finance

JEL Classification K34

1 Introduction

There is no doubt that the green transformation and the energy transition affect large-scale transformations at the global level—this is reflected in all spheres of society: from the everyday life of ordinary citizens to the reformatting of the world's political elites. In this case, we are more interested in how this will affect the transformation of

Y. A. Kolesnikov (✉)
Southern Federal University, Rostov-on-Don, Russia
e-mail: yakolesnikov@sfedu.ru

E. I. Lazareva et al. (eds.), *Innovative Trends in International Business and Sustainable Management*, Approaches to Global Sustainability, Markets, and Governance,
https://doi.org/10.1007/978-981-19-4005-7_13

legislation, namely tax law, normative legal acts regulating the financial and banking sector, etc. The essence and timing of amendments to this legislation directly affect the quality and duration of the transformation process, and its acceleration depends on the availability of funds.

2 Methodology

Due to the fact that the level of development of the Russian Federation in the field of localization and implementation of the sustainable development goals (SDGs), as well as carbon development is at a low level compared to European countries, we cannot neglect the necessary actions in this area. This means that SD is even more relevant for our country. We propose to use the content analysis method to solve these problems and as a subject to consider the main global proposals for the introduction of tax preferences or restrictions for the development and support of the green economy.

3 Results

Environmental, social, and corporate governance (ESG) is the concept of sustainable development, which is complex in its content and is based on a variety of factors and not only environmental ones. Social and economic factors are of no small importance, and they should be used to preserve nature, as well as the prosperity to the people of the world.

The ESG is a sustainable development triad, which includes three aspects: economy, society, and environment. The ecological aspect is responsible for the issues of the state of the environment, resource consumption, air pollution, water and energy use, etc. The social aspect solves issues related to the quality of life of people and their well-being, the economic aspect—the state of the economy, its capabilities and development.

The government, the financial sector, and business act as the driving force of the economy, which, in turn, depends entirely on the activities of society and the state of the environment, since the latter are responsible for the necessary resources for the production of goods, services, and the existence of private capital. If legal instruments are not provided for the proper regulation of natural resources, they will be negatively affected and depleted, threatening the economic development of countries in the near future.

Therefore, in order to achieve the goals of sustainable development and solve these tasks, it is necessary to involve all economic entities in this process. This is due to the fact that for balanced development, everyone must perform their specific functions, but with those features that are necessary as a part of fulfilling these goals. For example, the state through the use of incentive tools, economic entities through the introduction of "greener" technologies, etc., the population through rational consumption of goods and services.

One of such steps was the approval by the Government of the Russian Federation on 29.10.2021 of the "Strategy of socio-economic development of the Russian Federation with low greenhouse gas emissions until 2050" (Decree of the Government of the Russian Federation No. 3052-r, 2021). The content of this document is to establish measures aimed at reducing greenhouse gas emissions associated with human activity in various areas of the economy and using inefficient carbon-containing processes by transforming fiscal and budgetary policy. The strategy also includes other measures designed to transform the policy in the customs and budgetary spheres, taking into account the challenges of developing an economy with low levels of greenhouse gas (GHG) emissions. Moreover, in each region, the above measures may vary depending on the results of the establishment of special legal regimes. In turn, the state bodies that carry out financial regulation create priority areas and economic entities, based on this, solve the problems of sustainable development directly in economic activity. On this basis, we can get an effective result in several areas at once: in the environmental, social, and financial spheres (Bobylev & Solovyova, 2017).

It takes considerable time to achieve the SDGs. The first important step in this activity is to identify, analyze, and coordinate the capabilities of economic entities in accordance with the priorities that have been identified in the strategy. Digitalization is one of the tools in achieving these objectives, as it can help industrial enterprises increase their efficiency, including introducing more advanced control technologies and clearly see their potential based on the data obtained. Therefore, the use of digitalization is most often the next step for business entities actively implementing the SDGs. Further, in the process of achieving certain indicators, newer ways of using digital technologies will be applied, as well as the technologies themselves will be improved, which will further reduce the negative impact on nature and society (Dunaev & Nagornov, 2017).

The tax system is used by the state as one of the ways to influence and develop a market economy. Through the tax system, it is possible to both stimulate and restrict the implementation of entrepreneurial activity in the country. In this regard, the state simultaneously affects the social and environmental spheres.

It is worth noting that the tax system is based on the tax policy of the state, accordingly, any change in the vector in tax policy entails the necessary changes to the regulations of the tax system. This is evident in the example of many amendments to tax legislation, which are associated with adjustments to the goals and objectives of state policy in this area. National policy is rapidly being transformed under the influence of international requirements for the transition to a green economy, and this strengthens the role of tax policy as a tool to support and stimulate those economic entities that follow the new requirements.

It is necessary to consider the existing mechanisms of tax support from the state. The tax law doctrine distinguishes two groups among the instruments of tax incentives:

1. tax incentives;
2. tax preferences.

The first group is tax incentives, which are one of the important ways to encourage investment activity. By granting or eliminating certain tax benefits, the state has the opportunity to increase or, conversely, reduce investment activity. The paragraph 1 of Article 56 of the Tax Code of the Russian Federation (Federal Law No. 146, 1998) defines this concept: "benefits for taxes and levies are recognized as advantages provided to certain categories of taxpayers in comparison with other taxpayers, including the opportunity not to pay taxes or levies or to pay them in a smaller amount."

In addition, the definition of the concept of an investment tax credit is also legally fixed: "This is a change in the tax payment period in which an organization is given the opportunity to reduce its tax payments within a certain period and within certain limits, followed by a phased payment of the loan amount and accrued interest" (Article 66 of the Tax Code of the Russian Federation).

Investment tax credits (ITC), depending on the type of tax, can be granted for a period of 1–5 years, and in a particular case for residents of the development zone for up to 10 years. The disadvantages of this method of stimulation include: difficulty in obtaining, which is associated with a complex procedure of interaction between public authorities and business entities; a long list of necessary documents; the need to formalize a guarantee contract and its confirmation. Other similar requirements, combined with a relatively short period of provision, make the ITC less attractive to entrepreneurs.

Considering the experience of foreign countries in this matter, it is possible to identify approaches to granting tax holidays. This tool consists in the temporary abolition of mandatory fees and payments so that an economic entity can start its activities at the initial stage with less costs and difficulties, or vice versa, restore its financial situation while already in the process of operation.

As part of the tax incentive, it is worth mentioning depreciation deductions. The essence of state influence in this situation is accelerated depreciation of equipment for scientific and technical activities, which entails a reduction in income tax. Such steps by public authorities make it possible to indirectly subsidize the economy. As a result of these actions, the volume of investments received at the expense of funds that should have been paid as part of income tax when calculating depreciation of fixed assets (Lanshina et al., 2019).

For the Russian Federation, the most widely used instrument of investment benefits remains a reduced income and property taxation. State authorities in the regions, within their competence, have the right to reduce the rate of calculation of income tax to 13.5%. In some regions, the property tax rate may even be reduced by half. In this example, we see a simple, clear, and effective tool for increasing investment activity.

Thus, the above-mentioned measures of the state tax policy assist economic entities in improving or replacing the technologies they use. Moreover, thanks to such incentives, the necessary financial conditions are created for the transition to new "green" requirements for economic activity.

However, the EU countries have resorted to another way to encourage the transition to a green economy, namely by establishing or raising taxes for companies that emit industrial greenhouse gases above the established quota as a result of the extraction of natural resources or the production of their products.

The system of regulation of harmful emissions in the EU consists in the acquisition by economic entities of carbon credits that allow them to emit no more than a certain quota of greenhouse gases into the atmosphere when carrying out their activities. Such a system has been operating in the EU for more than 15 years and is called The European Union Emissions Trading System (EU ETS). The policy of European countries in this case is aimed at limiting harmful emissions with the help of a tax (CBAM) and the application of liability measures for violations, which have already been applied in many aspects of production.

The emissions trading system redistributes carbon rights between those who need them and those who do not fully realize their rights to harmful emissions. Moreover, the draft of the European Commission stipulates the obligation of each entity to submit a declaration with data on the indicators of harmful emissions produced during their activities.

It should be noted that in our country there are no legally established requirements regarding the volume of greenhouse gas emissions, but in the next few years, a new law (Decree of the President of the Russian Federation No. 666, 2020) on their limitation should come into force.

It is planned to create a competent authority that will carry out state regulation and accounting within the framework of the mechanism for carbon taxes with the issuance of appropriate certificates. It is designed to monitor payments for carbon dioxide emissions and prevent the situation of importing goods to European countries without these payments from other countries where they are not installed.

In accordance with the current climate legislation, CBAM will initially be applied to the import of goods with a high risk of CO_2 emissions (carbon leakage) into the atmosphere during the production of goods from the following groups: cement, ferrous metals and steel (including pipes and rails), fertilizers, and aluminum. At the same time, the European Commission published a proposal to expand the list of imported goods. But it should be noted that at the moment the list of goods does not include oil and its refined products, as well as hydrogen and ammonia, and there are disputes about whether it is worth including them in the named list in the future.

The formation of carbon market and the organization of carbon regulation are currently being discussed in the Russian Federation. One of these steps was the above-mentioned law "On limiting greenhouse gas emissions". Its goal is to reduce emissions of harmful greenhouse gases and create conditions for the sustainable development of the national economy. The legislator consolidated the creation of state greenhouse gas accounting and also, by analogy with European countries, provided for the creation of a carbon market, introduced indicators aimed at reducing the amount of harmful substances emitted, and other measures.

Another act in the field of management of harmful substances was the introduction of a bill "On conducting an experiment on special regulation of emissions and absorption of greenhouse gases in the Sakhalin region". It is aimed at the formation of carbon neutrality in the specified region in three years, and it is planned to begin its implementation from 2022.

Summarizing all the measures of the state policy of the Russian Federation on sustainable development, we can say that they are insufficient:

- first, there is no single developed system for the implementation of sustainable development goals;
- secondly, the sustainable development goals have not been transformed taking into account the specifics of our country.

The national "green" policy coincides with the international sustainable development goals only in certain directions, which may be a negative factor that increases the lag of the Russian Federation from European countries, since the world community adheres to the generally accepted vector of implementing the goals of the green economy (Sakharov & Kolmar, 2019).

4 Conclusion

Sustainable development is becoming a priority issue on the international strategic agenda, and its achievement depends on the joint efforts of macroeconomics participants—states, financial organizations, and business. Companies' investment policies increasingly take into account ESG factors when making decisions on financing new projects.

The construction of an appropriate sustainable infrastructure plays an important role in achieving the sustainable development goals, and its adaptability to the new norms is an integral factor in the stable functioning of society in the twenty-first century. To date, the sustainable market infrastructure is actively developing: Appropriate legislation is being adopted; special green finance instruments are being introduced, with their inherent features (green, social, sustainable, blue, and transition bonds); international grant projects are being developed to stimulate sustainable infrastructure and standards for assessing its quality, etc.

Russia, as a leading country in the global system, is obliged to take into account international trends in ESG transformation—abandoning traditional facilities in favor of sustainable ones that take into account new economic, social, and environmental instruments for the development of society.

Based on the results of the study, it is reasonable to assume that the Russian Federation will pursue the following tax policy in relation to ESG transformation and CBAM:

- tax incentives for economic entities at all levels;
- raising taxes on wealthy people;

- provision of tax holidays for companies extracting and exporting natural resources for the period of their modernization under new environmental standards;
- introduction of tax incentives on investment related to basic services: from clean energy in healthcare facilities to electrification of transport and modernization of networks.

References

Bobylev, S. N., & Solovyova, S. V. (2017). Sustainable development goals for the future of Russia. *Problems of Forecasting, 3*, 26–33.

Decree of the Government of the Russian Federation No. 3052-r of October 29, 2021. Strategy of socio-economic development of the Russian Federation with low greenhouse gas emissions until 2050. Official internet portal of legal information. http://publication.pravo.gov.ru/Document/View/0001202111010022. Data accessed January 12, 2022.

Decree of the President of the Russian Federation No. 666 of November 4, 2020. On reducing Greenhouse gas emissions. Official internet portal of legal information. URL: http://publication.pravo.gov.ru/Document/View/0001202011040008. Data accessed: January 12, 2022.

Dunaev, O. I., & Nagornov, V. A. (2017). Harmonization of corporate social responsibility practices to achieve sustainable development goals. *Public-Private Partnership, 2*(4), 93–102.

Federal Law No. 146 of 31.07.1998. Tax code of the Russian Federation. Collection of legislation of the Russian Federation of 1998, No. 31, Article 3824. URL: https://www.szrf.ru/szrf/oglavlenie.php?md=1&nb=100&year=1998. Data accessed: January 12, 2022.

Lanshina, T. A., Barinova, V. A., Loginova, A. D., Lavrovsky, E. P., & Monday, I. V. (2019). Experience of localization and implementation of the sustainable development goals in the leading countries in this field. *Bulletin of International Organizations, 1*(14), 207–224.

Sakharov, A. G., & Kolmar, O. I. (2019). Prospects for the implementation of the UN sustainable development goals in Russia. *Bulletin of International Organizations, 1*, 189–206.

ESG-Oriented Model for Assessing the Quality of Company Management in a Sustainable Economy

Elena I. Lazareva, Olga V. Karaycheva, and Ding Haoming

Abstract The subject of the research in this article is the current trends of sustainable economic development and their impact on the quality of company management. In particular, the authors emphasize the shift of priorities of economic strategies toward ESG guidelines. The analysis of one of the most popular tools in the current period for assessing the place of business companies in the economic space—ESG ratings—is carried out. The result of the study was the conclusion that, despite the progressiveness and relevance of this tool, the lack of a unified methodology for compiling ESG ratings requires the development of system tools that provide a complete, objective and internally consistent multi-criteria analysis of environmental, social and managerial factors. As such a tool, the authors proposed, substantiated and empirically verified a model of multi-criteria assessment of the quality of company management based on such a method as analytical hierarchy process. Criteria for ESG evaluation of alternatives have been developed. Recommendations on the use of model tools to develop directions for improving the quality of the management system in the context of ESG transformation of economic trends are formulated.

Keywords ESG-oriented model · ESG rating · Quality of company management · Economy of sustainable development · The method of analytic hierarchy process (AHP) · Business reputation

JEL Classification J24 · C54 · J64

E. I. Lazareva (✉) · O. V. Karaycheva · D. Haoming
Southern Federal University, Rostov-on-Don, Russia
e-mail: elazareva@sfedu.ru

O. V. Karaycheva
e-mail: okaraycheva@sfedu.ru

D. Haoming
e-mail: haomdin@sfedu.ru

E. I. Lazareva et al. (eds.), *Innovative Trends in International Business and Sustainable Management*, Approaches to Global Sustainability, Markets, and Governance,
https://doi.org/10.1007/978-981-19-4005-7_14

1 Introduction

ESG standards have recently become part of economic and social theory and practice. If not so long ago the main criteria for assessing the quality of company management were commercial success and the effectiveness of a business strategy, today it is impossible to imagine this strategy itself without the triad "Environmental, social and corporate governance" (Barnett & Salomon, 2002; Gassmann et al., 2021).

ESG is a set of company performance standards that are taken into account, in particular, when deciding whether to invest in a company. These parameters ensure the management of sustainable development. Today, ESG has become a kind of "business philosophy", according to which a company should be not only commercially successful, but also socially active, aimed not only at generating income, but also at meeting environmental, social and other needs of society (Clementino & Perkins, 2021; Cogan, 2006; European Banking Authority (EBA), 2021; Sciarelli et al., 2021).

ESG principles characterizing socio-ecological and managerial risks are becoming increasingly dominant when making multi-level corporate decisions (primarily investment ones). Confirmation of this thesis is the appearance of regulations that consolidate the experience of ESG rating as one of the requirements for the verification system of sustainable (including green) development projects in the Russian Federation (Decree of the Government of the Russian Federation No. 1587, 2021), as well as the following facts. The value of the assets managed by organizations implementing the UN Principles of responsible investment (UNPRI) amounted to 86 trillion US dollars in 2019; the global issue of green securities in 2020 amounted to more than 258 billion US dollars (Stern, 2020; United Nations, 2021).

With regard to ESG standards, such an intangible benefit of the organization as its business reputation comes to the fore. Business reputation is not only a powerful intangible asset of an organization, but also provides an opportunity to assess its position in the so-called "reputation space", measured in three metrics—temporal, functional (actions) and its various aspects (Fig. 1) (Lazareva & Karaycheva, 2017).

The reputation space of an organization can be conditionally characterized by the situation in three zones—the so-called red zone (compliance with the norms of current legislation), the blue zone (corporate culture, ethics of doing business) and the green zone (socio-environmental projects, corporate management initiatives). A high level of business reputation of a business organization is achievable only if project initiatives are systematically implemented in all spatial zones.

The problem of ensuring the sustainability of economic trends based on ESG standards goes far beyond corporate policy, becoming a significant factor of national stability (Barnett & Salomon, 2002; Zhou et al., 2021). As a result, the number of ESG ratings of the development trajectories of corporations, regions, countries is growing, which allows assessing environmental, social risks, as well as the quality of management on a single scale, and making management decisions adequate to the current situation on this basis.

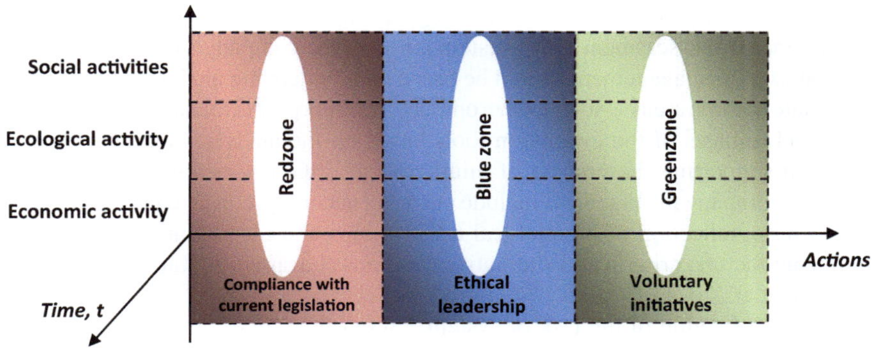

Fig. 1 Three-dimensional reputational space of an organization. *Source* Developed by the authors

Increasing the ESG transparency of companies by compiling ratings is associated with the development of this type of assessment by both foreign and Russian rating agencies. Currently, there are more than a hundred ESG agencies in the world, such a rating is often carried out on the basis of publicly available information, and not by the request of the company.

Nevertheless, the fragmentation of the indicator bases and evaluation methods used, the lack of a systematic approach to the design of ESG ratings significantly reduces the effectiveness of their application and, as a result, slows down the process of transition of economic agents to a sustainable development strategy. The lack of a unified methodology for compiling ESG ratings as a key tool for analyzing the degree of a company's orientation toward sustainable socio-environmental and economic development hinders the introduction of ESG standards into the corporate governance system and requires increased research to substantiate the priority directions of its ESG-oriented transformation (Gassmann et al., 2021; Geissdoerfer et al., 2018; Jílková, 2021).

The reputation-spatial assessment model of an organization creates the foundation for the development of system tools that provide a complete, objective and internally consistent multi-criteria analysis of environmental, social and managerial factors.

2 Methodology

The methodological basis of the approach used by the authors was the systemic innovation-cyclical paradigm of sustainable economic development, according to which the achievement of a certain level of well-being by modern and future generations is consistently determined by the quality of the accumulated resource base, structurally formed by conserving resources along with the productive (artificially created) potential of anthropo-social and ecological capital (Lazareva & Karaycheva, 2017).

Within the framework of this methodology, a unified methodology that allows for a comprehensive assessment of the sustainability of the company's development and the quality of its management should be based on a systematic analysis of indicators of the state of three areas—social, environmental and corporate management systems.

The advantages of the evaluation tools based on the analytic hierarchy process (AHP) in supporting the process of multi-criteria ESG assessment of the sustainability of company management include ensuring accuracy, consistency of the information base, reflection of hierarchical relationships and identification of the most significant factors: criteria and alternative solutions (Lazareva & Karaycheva, 2016; Lazareva et al., 2021).

The formalization of the task of system ESG evaluation of an organization as a multi-criteria hierarchical model is based on the principles of sustainable dynamic management and the following five-step procedure (Fig. 2):

1. Statement (type) of the problem characterizing the goals of decision-making. Solutions to problems in terms of goals are based on the axiom of "generating a supergoal". For example, an assessment of business reputation or the quality (sustainability) of the organization's management.
2. Formation of characteristics of the degree of achievement of the sub-goals of the established goal—criteria based on two basic principles—the principles of completeness and simplicity. According to the global model of sustainable development, the ESG assessment procedure should use indicators/criteria for the state of three subsystems—environmental, social and managerial.
3. Development of a set of rating scales (in expert or physical indicators).

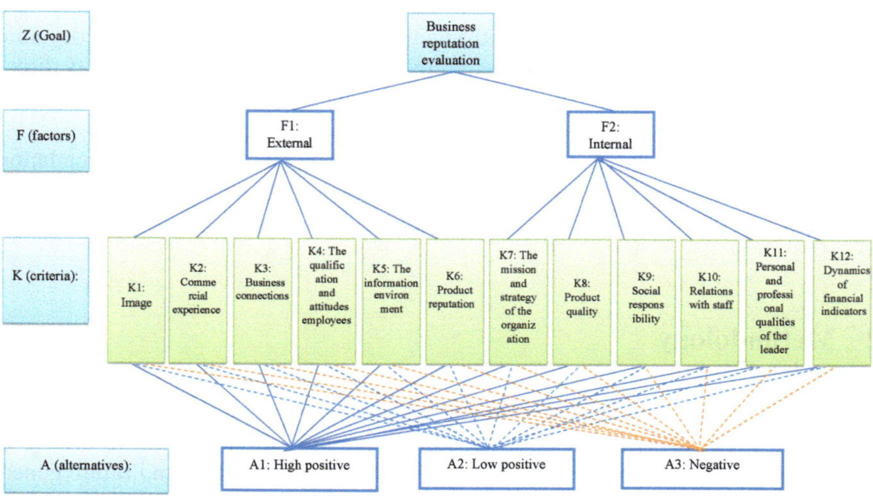

Fig. 2 MHI-hierarchy of business reputation assessment. *Source* Developed by the authors

4. Formation of ways to achieve the set goal—alternatives—satisfying certain requirements of assessments of the level of business reputation of the organization. The basic principles of forming alternatives are the quota rules (fixing the number of alternatives) and the rule of diversity of solutions.
5. Determination of ways to evaluate the results of solving the problem—the choice of the principle of comparison of estimates and determination of the most preferred of them—the decision rule. Two ways to evaluate the results are the assessment of the elasticity of the result depending on changes in factors and an absolute assessment based on the principle of "more–less".

The apparatus of the AHP method makes it possible to assess the business reputation and the quality of company management according to a set of criteria. When performing a multi-criteria comparative assessment of several alternative assessments, the classical principles of the AHP method are used: the principles of identity and decomposition, discrimination and comparative judgments, as well as synthesis. The first principle makes it possible to structure the problem in the form of a hierarchy by defining criteria and forming a set of alternatives, the second—to investigate the structures of the decision-maker's preferences by the paired comparison method, and the third—to determine the final priorities in accordance with the decision rule and the consistency of the hierarchy.

When applying the tools of the AHP method, evaluation criteria and factors were identified, a group of experts was formed, procedures for expert ESG assessment and calculation of integral evaluation indicators were implemented.

3 Results

The implementation of the ESG-evaluation procedure of an organization using the proposed tools of the AHP method, first of all, the identification (justification) of the hierarchical structure of interdependent endogenous and exogenous factors, as well as criteria for evaluating alternative solutions.

Endogenous factors include such G-factors-criteria as commercial experience (duration of operation, stability of the market position, relevance of the management structure, level and dynamics of profit), the image of the organization (stakeholders' assessment of the business qualities of a legal entity, defining its social status), the level of qualification and attitude of its employees, as well as the reputation of products (demand, volumes and dynamics of sales).

Significant endogenous S-factors are business relationships (number of counterparties, suppliers, contractors, credit history of the organization) and the information environment of the company (presence in the media space, access to accounting documents).

Relevant exogenous G&E&S factors of business reputation are such as the quality (reputation) of products/services, social responsibility (environmental projects, social initiatives, sponsorship), innovative strategy of sustainable development of the organization, personnel policy, corporate culture (climate), business qualities (personal reputation) of the head, dynamics of financial indicators.

Based on the results of the expert assessment of the level of business reputation, one of its three alternative integral assessments is formed—positive (high or low) or negative; measures are being developed to adjust the company's management decision system.

Thus, the results of comparing the main factors-criteria in the assessment of the business reputation of Danone JSC using the AHP method showed the highest significance of the criteria "product reputation" (0.257), "corporate image" (0.206) and "business experience" (0.133) (Table 1).

In the identified "coordinates", the A1 alternative (0.675) turned out to be the highest priority, which indicates a high positive level of the business reputation of Danone JSC (Table 2).

The advantage of the proposed evaluation procedure is the possibility of identifying reserves for improving the business reputation of the organization based on the analysis of private and generalizing estimates for each cluster and the introduction of the necessary control actions in the management system.

Table 1 Generalized expert assessments of the significance of factors-criteria of the organization's business reputation

Generalized expert assessments of the significance	Factors-criteria
0.206	Corporate image (К1)
0.133	Business experience (К2)
0.101	Business relations (К3)
0.084	The skill level and attitude of employees (К4)
0.049	Information environment (K5)
0.257	Product reputation (K6)
0.023	Strategy for sustainable development (K7)
0.058	Quality of products (K8)
0.028	Social responsibility (K9)
0.016	Personnel relations (K10)
0.010	The personality of the leader (K11)
0.036	Dynamics of financial indicators (K12)

Source Developed by the authors

Table 2 Generalized dominance vector relative to the goal of the three alternative assessments of the organization's business reputation

Alternatives	Specific weight of the alternative in achieving the goal
A1—a high positive assessment of the organization's business reputation	0.675
A2—a low positive assessment of the organization's business reputation	0.217
A3—a negative assessment of the organization's business reputation	0.092

Source Developed by the authors

4 Conclusion

The increasing importance of ESG factors in the modern knowledge economy serves as a prerequisite for the gradual transformation of the company's management system. The formation of an effective ESG-oriented management model must necessarily be systemic in these conditions.

The novelty and advantage of the proposed AHP-model consists in substantiating the algorithm of the system analysis of the business reputation of the organization and a detailed qualitative and quantitative assessment of its achieved level.

Completeness, objectivity and inter-level consistency of assessments using the AHP method creates a fundamental basis for the formation of unified ESG ratings and assessment of the quality of management of modern companies.

References

Barnett, M., & Salomon, R. (2002). Beyond dichotomy: The curvilinear relationship between social responsibility and financial performance. *Strategic Management Journal, 27*(11), 1101–1122.

Clementino, E., & Perkins, R. (2021). How do companies respond to environmental, social and governance (ESG) ratings? Evidence from Italy. *Journal of Business Ethics, 171*, 379–397.

Cogan, D. G. (2006). Corporate governance and climate change: Making the connection. Ceres. https://www.ceres.org. Data accessed: December 25, 2021.

Decree of the Government of the Russian Federation No. 1587 of 21.09.2021. On approval of the criteria for sustainable (including green) development projects in the Russian Federation and requirements for the verification system of sustainable (including green) development projects in the Russian Federation. Official internet portal of legal information. http://publication.pravo.gov.ru/Document/View/0001202109240043. Data accessed: December 25, 2021.

EBA Report on Management and Supervision of ESG Risks for Credit Institutions and Investment Firms EBA/REP/2021/18. European Banking Authority (EBA). https://www.eba.europa.eu. Data accessed: December 20, 2021.

Gassmann, P., Herman, C., & Kelly, C. (2021). Are you ready for the ESG revolution? Societal need and business opportunity are coming together to transform the way companies craft strategy, drive performance, and report results. *Strategy+Business*. PWC. https://www.pwc.com/gx/en/issues/esg/esg-revolution.html. Data accessed: November 29, 2021.

Geissdoerfer, M., Vladimirova, D., & Evans, S. (2018). Sustainable business model innovation: A review. *Journal of Cleaner Production, 198*, 401–416.

Jílková, P. (2021). Sustainable corporate strategy: The role of human capital in the time of COVID-19 crisis. *TEM Journal, 10*(2), 699–706.

Lazareva, E., & Karaycheva, O. (2016). Modern organizations' reputational capital' innovative management strategy specification in the international business integration network format. In *SGEM 2016 Conference Proceedings* (Vol. 1, pp. 419–426).

Lazareva, E., & Karaycheva, O. (2017). Human oriented reframing of the territories of innovative sustainable development system management model. In *SGEM 2017 Conference Proceedings* (pp. 467–474).

Lazareva, E., Karaycheva, O., Karaychev, G., & Frolova, I. (2021). The innovative blockchain technology in the sharing economy subjects' decision-making. In F. Gaol, N. Filimonova, & C. Acharya (Eds.), *Impact of disruptive technologies on the sharing economy* (pp. 129–150). Eurospan.

Sciarelli, M., Cosimato, S., Landi, G., & Iandolo, F. (2021). Socially responsible investment strategies for the transition towards sustainable development: The importance of integrating and communicating ESG. *The TQM Journal, 33*(7), 39–56.

Stern, H. J. (2020). Better bonus plans for ESG. Working Paper. SSRN. https://www.readcube.com. Data accessed: December 20, 2021.

United Nations, Inter-agency Task Force on Financing for Development. (2021). Financing for Sustainable Development Report 2021. United Nations. https://www.un.org/sites/un2.un.org/files/fsdr_2021.pdf. Data accessed: November 20, 2021.

Zhou, X., Caldecott, B., Harnett, E., & Schumacher, K. (2021). The effect of firm-level ESG practices on macroeconomic performance. Working Paper No. 20-03, University of Oxford. https://www.smithschool.ox.ac.uk. Data accessed: December 20, 2021.

Conceptual Approaches to Assessing the Effectiveness of Government and Business Cooperation Projects Implemented Within International Digital Integration

Natalya N. Yakovenko, Valentina N. Parakhina, Olga A. Boris, Galina V. Vorontsova, and Oksana N. Momotova

Abstract The article is devoted to the definition of the main conceptual approaches used for assessing the overall effectiveness of interaction between business and government, as well as the specifics of this process in the implementation of digital integration projects at the international level. The content analysis of dissertation and monographic materials, critical articles and the results of scientific research carried out by various teams of researchers made it possible to identify, and using the generalization method to summarize problems and contradictions, trends within the framework of the studied direction. The combination of general scientific methods of cognition with the tools of scientific search and comparative analysis of the theoretical views of the world scientific community contributed to the formation of the author's position, and then to the synthesis of their individual ideas in the results of the presented research. The authors' point of view was based on combining existing approaches to assessing the effectiveness of business and government cooperation from the standpoint of partnership, that is, equal representation and coordination of interests without domination by any of the parties. As a result, the authors managed to form an integrated criteria framework for assessing the effectiveness of interaction, reflecting the agreed positions of each of the interested parties. The fundamental basic principles of evaluating the effectiveness of interaction and the local principles from the point of view of every party interested in the project are formulated. The problems and contradictions in assessing the effectiveness of projects of business-government cooperation are identified and summarized. Approaches to the formation of a criteria framework for assessing effectiveness are proposed and the role of each of the participants in the interaction project is determined.

N. N. Yakovenko · V. N. Parakhina · O. A. Boris · G. V. Vorontsova (✉) · O. N. Momotova
North Caucasus Federal University, Stavropol, Russia
e-mail: vgv14@mail.ru

V. N. Parakhina
e-mail: vparakhina@ncfu.ru

O. A. Boris
e-mail: oboris@ncfu.ru

E. I. Lazareva et al. (eds.), *Innovative Trends in International Business and Sustainable Management*, Approaches to Global Sustainability, Markets, and Governance,
https://doi.org/10.1007/978-981-19-4005-7_15

Keywords Business · Government · Interaction projects · Coordination of interests · Effectiveness of interaction

JEL Classification M21 · H77

1 Introduction

The viability of implementing an interaction project between government and business should be determined, first of all, by evaluating its effectiveness for both participants, parties to interaction, and society as a whole. Conceptual approaches to evaluating effectiveness in the scientific literature are quite diverse. At the moment, there are no clearly defined criteria and methods for evaluating the effectiveness of interaction between business and government. Some authors use methodological approaches to this process by analogy with the evaluation of the performance of governmental entities, others consider the evaluation process only from the standpoint of efficiency for business processes.

Thus, Gabdullina (2012) suggests a comprehensive assessment based on the definition of public, budgetary, commercial, regional and sectoral effectiveness to assess the effectiveness of interaction. At the same time, she suggests using the following indicators in relation to regional or sectoral effectiveness: competitiveness of the enterprise participating in the interaction; income growth of related enterprises; international integration; environmental safety. Taking into account the positive aspects of such an integrated approach to solving the problem of efficiency, we note that it does not allow avoiding duplication in the assessment criteria and uncertainty of some indicators.

Chukhlomin (2011) focuses only on public, budgetary, commercial effectiveness, taking as a basis a comparison of all the actual benefits and costs arising from the implementation of the project from the point of view of each participant (budgetary, commercial) and society as a whole.

Polyanskaya and Naidanova (2015) considers the need to assess budgetary effectiveness for government and economic effectiveness for business, which in our opinion does not consider the assessment of the need for cooperation for society as a whole.

Smorgunov (2019) investigate only the social aspect of the government and business cooperation and propose to define social effectiveness as a function of minimizing transaction costs, which is directly related to the effective operation of the mechanism for coordinating social interactions.

Angelina and Roslavtseva (2016) suggest a methodology for assessing effectiveness by the criterion of "cash flows", which is based on a matrix of cash flows in the cooperation of government and business structures. In addition, the authors provide a set of indicators for determining budgetary, commercial and social effectiveness, as well as for assessing the overall effect of cooperation at the preparatory stage or at the project completion stage. We can agree with such an integrated approach, however, the use of absolute values in the formation of cash flows makes it possible to assess the absolute effect indicators at each step of the calculation horizon, but does not make it possible to assess the effectiveness considering the required costs at each level of cooperation.

In view of the diversity of authors' opinions in the scientific literature on the issue of assessing the effectiveness of cooperation and uncertainty in methodological assessment approaches, this study is devoted to the development of basic conceptual approaches to assessing the effectiveness of government and business cooperation in general and determining its features in the digital cooperation projects at the international level. Thus, the fundamental basic and local principles of assessing the cooperation effectiveness are defined, taking into account the positions of each participating party in the project. Problems and contradictions are identified and generalized, the effects of which must be taken into account when forming a methodology for assessing the effectiveness of projects of interaction between business and government. The participation of experts is proposed for an independent assessment of cooperation effectiveness starting at the stage of elaboration up to the stage of project completion.

2 Methodology

The article presents the results of a case study devoted to the following research problem: specific features of assessing the effectiveness of projects of interaction between government and business.

The objective of the study is to develop conceptual approaches and basic principles for assessing the effectiveness of government and business cooperation when implementing projects within the framework of international digital integration.

As the main research methods, the method of critical analysis of the opinions of various authors on the issues of evaluating the effectiveness of interaction between business and government, the method of classification analysis of performance evaluation criteria, taking into account the level of assessment, its implementation period, as well as the project stage, were used.

Dialectical analysis revealed the relationship between the causes of problems in assessing the effectiveness of interaction between business and government and the consequences of these problems in the form of contradictory and questionable assessment results.

Generalization and systematization of the analyzed provisions on the subject of study allowed to develop the main hypotheses of the study:

1. effectiveness assessment of government and business cooperation should be based on basic and local principles;
2. the need to build a hierarchy of criteria for assessing interaction, taking into account the participants in the process;

3. substantiation of the expediency of involving independent experts in assessing the effectiveness of interaction between business and government in international digital integration projects.

3 Results

Assessing the effectiveness of interaction between government and business structures is one of the most difficult problems in the implementation of any projects, this is especially important for projects implemented within the framework of international digital integration (Momotova et al., 2021).

This difficulty arises both because of the specifics of this type of relationship, which often does not allow us to define clear criteria for reliable value judgments, and because of the extreme lack of information in this area.

The effectiveness indicators of joint projects of government and business structures are affected by both objective and subjective factors and trends in the business environment. It is difficult to overestimate the negative impact that the ongoing coronavirus pandemic has on the effectiveness of international projects, including those characterized by high socio-economic significance (Shatskaya et al., 2020).

The results of interaction are often not obvious and unambiguous, and the process of interaction with authorities is a smooth and gradual process.

Achieving a visible result in the sphere of interaction between state and business may require many months of invisible painstaking work.

Moreover, there exists a certain paradox. With the well-established work on coordinating the interests of business and government, the results of interaction are more specific and, as a rule, yield tangible results not only to the activities of business and the implementation of government programs, but also clearly defined in terms of effectiveness for society as a whole.

In this case, there is no conflict between business and government, all issues are resolved promptly and in a timely manner.

In the absence or insufficient coordination of the interests of business and the state, there is a discrepancy in goals, which leads to difficulties in assessing the effectiveness of the projected and achieved results.

The methodological basis for assessing the effectiveness of cooperation between government and business should include certain principles that can be divided into basic and local ones.

The basic principles include:

1. the principle of goal-orientation (the interaction of business and government should lead to the achievement of the set goals, taking into account the effective use of the resources of all parties involved);
2. the principle of unity of economic, social and environmental goals (assessment of the effectiveness of interaction should be carried out from the position of unity, complementarity and coherence of economic, social and environmental goals. The project, which is cost-efficient, but having a negative impact on the

social sphere or the environment, should not be assessed as highly effective one);

3. the principle of scientific approach (assessment of effectiveness should be based on scientifically based assessment criteria, quantitative and qualitative, built into a certain assessment system, taking into account the hierarchy of importance and materiality);
4. the principle of objectivity (effectiveness assessment should be objective, taking into account the interests of all stakeholders and, above all, society as a whole).

Local effectiveness assessment principles define the basis of this process from the point of view of each of the parties involved:

1. for business
   - the principle of objectivity of effectiveness assessment for business structures;
   - the principle of ensuring development and profitability of the business;
   - the principle of responsibility for the planned results of effectiveness;
2. for public administration bodies
   - the principle of objectivity of effectiveness assessment for authorities;
   - the principle of ensuring not only the economic, but also the social and environmental orientation of the project;
   - the principle of assessment coherence from the point of view of the parties involved;
3. for society as a whole
   - the principle of consistency and comprehensiveness of assessment criteria;
   - the principle of openness of the assessment procedure and results;
   - the principle of priority of public interests in the assessment process.

The criteria and effectiveness indicators may differ for business and government, but the main point of their integration is effectiveness for society as a whole. That is, the main measure of the effectiveness of cooperation is the degree of sufficiency of the result or effect for society as a whole, that is, integral social effectiveness.

Almost all interaction projects involve certain financial investments, while three main financing options are possible: budgetary financing, financing from private capital, or project co-financing from both the budget and the business structure. In this case, the cost-effectiveness can depend on the indicators of the following investment effectiveness: payback period and discounted payback period (PP, DPP), net present value (NPV), profitability index (PI) and internal rate of return (IRR), calculated for each participant of the cooperation project.

However, in projects of interaction between the state and business, according to the listed assessment criteria, it is possible to obtain contradictory results, the project can provide positive and significant values of these indicators for business and negative or low effectiveness results for the budget.

Such a situation arises, for example, in projects where one party is represented by a business structure with a preferential taxation system (simplified taxation system, patent, etc.) or with benefits for one or more tax positions (for example, the VAT rate is 0% or 10%), or if the project provides for business on the territory of a technology park with a system of benefits provided for its residents. An example is the Nevinnomyssk Regional Industrial Park with an area of 725 ha, located on the territory of the Stavropol Territory, which specializes in industrial production, including processing production; disposal and recycling of household and industrial waste; transport and logistics services. Residents of the park have the following tax benefits:

- reduction of the corporate income tax rate by 4.5% for the payback period of the investment project and 2.5% after the payback of the investment project;
- exemption of organizations from property tax located within the territory of the regional industrial park;
- exemption from land tax;
- and other non-tax preferences.

As a result of the interaction on the creation and functioning of this technopark of the Stavropol Territory authorities and business structures, there is practically no direct budgetary effect, at the same time, business structures that are residents of this park show high effectiveness of interaction and ensure high rates of business development (Berezhnaya et al., 2018).

However, the opposite case is also possible, when the calculations of the project show high effectiveness for the budget, but the indicators for the business are not high enough to achieve their strategic goals or develop in the current period. In this case, business loses interest in cooperation and communication with state authorities.

However, it should be noted that there is always a third interested party in interaction projects—this is society as a whole and the assessment should be carried out primarily from the perspective of integral indicators of social effectiveness, and not only from an economic perspective, but also a social and environmental one.

Therefore, it is important to build a hierarchy of criteria and effectiveness indicators by the levels of participants involved: government, business and society as a whole (Table 1).

In addition to the main quantitative criteria indicated in the table, assessment of the effectiveness of government and business cooperation can apply qualitative criteria. For example, these include positive conflict-free relations of interaction participants, the relevance and timeliness of solving a key problem for current project, ensuring greater information openness in cooperation, reduction of corruption in business and government relations, and other criteria.

Determination of the level of both quantitative and qualitative criteria is subjective, therefore, an important aspect of the effectiveness assessment who and at what stage of interaction carries out such an assessment of the project.

It can be assumed that when assessing the effectiveness of interaction by government entities, there will be a certain subjectivity of assessments and there will be insufficient information about the activities of business structures, and vice versa,

Table 1 Possible assessment criteria

Criterion	Government	Business	Society
The main criteria for assessing the effectiveness of cooperation	Increase in gross domestic (regional) product	Growth of financial performance indicators and business development	The level of settling the socio-economic challenges
Validity of the goals and tasks of cooperation	Feasibility of the proposed goals and tasks	Compliance of the proposed goals and tasks with the interests of the company at the current moment and in future	Elaboration of the development scenario on a specific socio-economic challenge after achieving the set goal and implementing tasks
Achieving the set goals	Achieving the goals set by the government	Achieving business goals	Achieving the goals set by the society
Effective use of resources: labor, finance, industry	Effectiveness of budgetary funds	Effectiveness of labor, material and financial resources of the company	Comparison of all the relevant benefits and costs arising from the implementation of the project from the standpoint of society as a whole

Source Compiled by the authors

if the assessment is carried out by a business structure, then all the parameters and factors of interaction regarding authorities may not be taken into account. Therefore, it is extremely important in order to ensure the objectivity of the assessment, this process should be built on an independent basis with the involvement of regional infrastructure specialists who will have access to complete and reliable information about the interaction project.

Moreover, it is necessary to clearly determine at what stage of the project development it is advisable and possible to involve independent experts (Table 2) and what role all parties participating in this process play in the process of assessing the effectiveness of interaction.

Participation of independent experts in assessing the project effectiveness of government and business interaction in the form of public–private partnership is provided for by the Decree of the Government of the Russian Federation No. 1514 dated December 30, 2015 “On the procedure for the authorized body to assess the effectiveness of a public–private partnership project, a municipal-private partnership project and to determine their comparative advantage”. The objectivity of the assessment is ensured by the fact that the role of an independent expert is performed by the relevant authorized body. The results of this assessment and the methodology approved by this resolution affect the decision to approve or reject the public–private partnership project (Parakhina et al., 2019).

Table 2 The role of business and government participants at each stage of cooperation in assessing its effectiveness

Project stage	Government	Business	Society	Independent experts
Preparatory stage, coordination of goals and interests	Assessment of the goals and level of satisfaction of government interests	Assessment of goals and level of satisfaction of business interests	Assessment of the goals and level of satisfaction of the society's interests	–
Working out the details of the interaction project	Assessment of individual quantitative and qualitative parameters of the project from the viewpoint of the government	Assessment of individual quantitative and qualitative parameters of the project from a business point of view	Assessment of individual quantitative and qualitative parameters of the project from society's point of view	Option-based assessment of the effectiveness of interaction project implementation and determination of the most effective option
Implementation of interaction	Providing information about changes in project parameters to independent experts	Providing information about changes in project parameters to independent experts	Monitoring the progress of the project and public discussion of its intermediate results	Assessment of effectiveness indicators considering the progress of the project
Project completion	Assessment of the project results by the government	Assessment of the project results by business	Assessment of the project results by the society	Assessment of effectiveness indicators taking into account the progress of the project

Source Compiled by the authors

Undoubtedly, the engagement of an independent party to conduct an assessment is important for any project involving the interaction of the parties with differentiation in goal setting and resource provision, but the involvement of independent experts in the assessment of digital integration projects is of particular importance due to their specifics and the need to determine, in addition to standard criteria and indicators, parameters that take into account the specifics of integration and its consequences. Almost any integration IT project has its own unique features, and when assessing it, it is impossible to focus on individual functions (significant for both business and government), but it is necessary to assess the importance and effectiveness of integration as a whole.

The effectiveness of a digital project largely depends on how well an independent expert understands and assesses the entire process within which integration occurs. Moreover, this is important regardless of whether the digitalization of the entire process or only its individual parts is planned. It is also essential to assess the effectiveness of the distribution of information flows and their coordination in integration processes.

Thus, the evaluation of the effectiveness of the process of interaction between business and government should be carried out taking into account the proposed basic principles of goal-orientation, unity of economic, social and environmental goals, scientific approach and objectivity. But an important aspect is the respect of local principles, which take into account the specifics of their functioning and goal-setting in the implementation of interaction processes. Moreover, some local principles are the same for each participant, for example, the principle of objectivity of assessments, and some of them are strictly differentiated to cover the peculiarities of the participating party.

The participation of a third interested party, society as a whole, in projects of interaction, and the need for an integral assessment of social effectiveness, not only in economic terms, but also from a social and environmental point of view, should be emphasized. This concept is not always noted by researchers in this field due to the uncertainty of the criteria framework and the lack of a hierarchy of assessment criteria. The proposed evaluation criteria, arranged due to the levels in the hierarchy and the levels of participants, make it possible to form the consistency of the assessment and prioritize the individual results obtained.

An important aspect of the procedure for assessing the effectiveness of interaction is the definition of the subject of this procedure. Many authors, suggesting a list of assessment indicators, do not specify the methodology of their calculation and, moreover, do not determine by whom, when and at what stage of the project it should be carried out. We have proposed the participation of independent experts in assessing the effectiveness of interaction between business and government, armed with all the necessary information (received from all participants in the interaction process), competent in assessing effectiveness, taking into account the specifics of digital integration projects, as well as accompanying the project from the implementation stage to completion. An independent examination is designed to give an idea of the project on the part of society as a whole, with obligatory regard for the interests of interested parties.

4 Conclusion

In modern conditions of economic development, it is impossible to imagine the implementation of strategically important, large, socially oriented projects without the interaction of business and government. The existing variety of interaction forms and relevant results prove the feasibility and possibility of such partnership. The task of assessing the interaction effectiveness, considering the interests of each party involved and society as a whole, is currently unresolved.

The basic and local principles of the assessment process developed in this article make it possible to structure the assessment and differentiate criteria for individual participants in such interaction.

At the same time, the sorted list of criteria, arranged in a hierarchical order, will allow at the next stage of the study to develop a methodology for assessing the efficiency of government and business cooperation, which can be applied in evaluating relevant projects.

The methodology, first of all, will be proposed for assessing international business interaction projects within the framework of digital integration by independent experts to ensure the objectivity of the assessment and obtain reliable integral results.

Acknowledgements The research was carried out with the financial support of the RFBR within the framework of the RFBR research project "Development of the concept of building effective models of interaction between government and business structures at the regional level within the framework of digital integration of the Republic of Belarus and the Russian Federation", project No. 20-510-00025.

References

Angelina, I. A., & Roslavtseva, E. A. (2016). The efficiency analysis of interaction between business entities and public authorities. *Russian Journal of Entrepreneurship, 17*(18), 2301–2318. https://doi.org/10.18334/rp.17.18.365712317

Berezhnaya, O. V., Berezhnaya, E. V., Solovyova, N. V., Karapetyan, E. A., & Berezhnoy, V. I. (2018). Dynamics, peculiarities and financial factors for the industrial development of the South of Russia. *European Research Studies Journal, 21*(4), 533–544.

Chukhlomin, N. V. (2011). Evaluation of the effectiveness of public-private partnership in creation of special economic zones. Extended abstract of candidate's dissertation. Novosibirsk State University.

Gabdullina, E. I. (2012). Evaluation of projects as a mechanism of interaction PPP government and business in the region. *Modern Problems of Science and Education, 2*, 151.

Momotova, O. N., Vorontsova, G. V., Boris, O. A., Yakovenko, N. N., & Kharchenko, N. P. (2021). Tools for interaction between government and business structures in Russia and Belarus in the context of digitalization. In O. G. Shakirova, O. V. Bashkov, & A. A. Khusainov (Eds.), *Lecture Notes in Networks and Systems: Vol. 200. Current problems and ways of industry development: Equipment and technologies*. Springer. https://doi.org/10.1007/978-3-030-69421-0_113

Parakhina, V. N., Shalashaa, Z. I., & Ustaev, R. M. (2019). PPP as a tool of innovative-technological development of Russia and Abkhazia. Modern tools for sustainable development of territories (MTSDT 2019). Special topic: Project management in the regions of Russia. In *The European Proceedings of Social & Behavioural Sciences EpSBS* (pp. 731–738). https://doi.org/10.15405/epsbs.2019.12.05.89

Polyanskaya, N. M., & Naidanova, E. B. (2015). Assessing the efficiency of regional policy tools: Methodological aspects. *Economy of Region, 16*(2), 352–362.

Shatskaya, E., Kharchenko, N., Popovichenko, M., & Lukyanova, A. (2020). Modern instruments for joint management of international projects in a pandemic. *SHS Web of Conferences, 89*, 04005. https://doi.org/10.1051/shsconf/20208904005

Smorgunov, L. V. (2019). Efficiency of public administration. In *Public policy and management: Textbook in 2 parts. Part 1. Concepts and problems of public policy and management*. Yurayt.

Methodology (Methods) for Assessing Indicators of the Development of Economic Systems and the "Smart City" System Based on Information Theory

Sergey V. Iudin, Halina A. Shmarlouskaya, Tatiana N. Egorushkina, Oksana N. Mishchuk, and Maksim P. Kalynychenko

Abstract *Purpose* The purpose of the study is to solve the problem of numerical evaluation of integral indicators of the development of economic systems and the "smart city" system, as well as to develop an appropriate criterion. *Design/methodology/approach* The research methodology is based on a primary analysis of regulatory documents and current publications on the development of economic systems and the "smart city" system, as well as the methods of mathematical information theory. On the basis of this approach, the basic concepts of the "smart city" concept were considered, and the analysis of specialized literature was carried out. *Originality/value* The significant differences in the views of various scientists on the concept of "smart city" are revealed. Contradictions of interests among different groups of stakeholders of the "smart city" (citizens, businessmen, scientists, managers, politicians) can significantly reduce the effectiveness of the solutions being developed. Currently, the degree of the development of the structures of the "smart city" is assessed by formal indicators presented in the standards and guidelines. Considering the "smart city" not only as a system but also as a product, it is necessary to study it from the point of view of the interests of its consumers (stakeholders). Consumers can assess the product quality. To assess the quality of a smart city product, it is necessary to develop a numerical criterion showing the satisfaction of stakeholders' interests. It is shown that the criterion based on the mathematical apparatus of information theory and statistics "entropy" can be applied as an adequate, accurate, and reliable criterion. For this purpose, the relevant

S. V. Iudin · T. N. Egorushkina · O. N. Mishchuk · M. P. Kalynychenko (✉)
Tula Branch of Plekhanov Russian University of Economics, Tula, Russia
e-mail: mpk79@mail.ru

T. N. Egorushkina
e-mail: tegor@bk.ru

H. A. Shmarlouskaya
Belarus State Economic University, Minsk, Belarus

M. P. Kalynychenko
Northern (Arctic) Federal University named after M.V. Lomonosov, Arkhangelsk, Russia

E. I. Lazareva et al. (eds.), *Innovative Trends in International Business and Sustainable Management*, Approaches to Global Sustainability, Markets, and Governance,
https://doi.org/10.1007/978-981-19-4005-7_16

literature is considered, affirming the statements that this approach is universal. The developed criterion makes it possible, based on a sociological survey, to compare different stages of the city's development and determine the presence of trends toward improving the quality of life when building a "smart city". Some issues of the formation of a "smart city" in the example of Tula, Tula region, and the Russian Federation are considered. *Conclusions* It has been established that the main drawback is insufficient consideration of the opinion of the citizens, while the "smart city" should be considered as a product, which should be evaluated by the consumers—the citizens. For an objective assessment, an information criterion of the quality of a "smart city" and evaluation of the trends' development was created.

Keywords Economic systems · Smart city · Stakeholders · Trends · Quality · Theory of information · Entropy

JEL Classification C51 · C55 · L60 · M21 · M41 · P12 · P17

1 Introduction

"Smart city" is a newish definition of urban and municipal structure.

Deakin and Al Waer (2011) offer a list of four factors that determine the very concept of "smart city":

1. Applying electronic and digital technologies in society and cities;
2. Using information and communication technologies (ICTs) to transform the life and working environment within the region;
3. Introducing ICTs to public systems;
4. Combining ICTs and citizens to increase the innovative potential of the region and make the knowledge citizens have available to everyone.

Currently, the definition of "Smart city" is given as follows: "A smart sustainable city is an innovative city that uses information and communication technologies (ICTs) and other means to improve the quality of life, efficiency of urban operation and services, and competitiveness, while ensuring that it meets the needs of present and future generations concerning economic, social, cultural and environmental aspects". According to this proposed definition, a city is considered as an "integrated" system (The UNECE–ITU, 2015).

The main indicators of the development of "Smart city" are presented there. 72 indicators are classified along with the three prime areas: Economy; Environment; Society and Culture.

In 2019, based on the document (The UNECE–ITU, 2015), the international standard ISO/IEC 30146:2019 was developed (ISO/IEC 30146, 2019), which allows for objectively determining the maturity and development of urban settlement from the perspective of the "Smart city" concept.

In the light of the above-mentioned standard, the standard of the Ministry of Construction of Russia was developed (The Standard of the Ministry of Construction of the Russian Federation, 2019).

This article was written because of the active development of the Smart City program in Tula, Russian Federation (Projects of the Government of the Tula region on the development of a "smart city" and digital management, 2021; The passport of the project "Smart city of the Tula region", 2021).

Following the project "Smart Cities of the Tula region", by 2024 through the introduction of digital technologies in the management of urban infrastructure and the decision-making procedure for the development of cities, the goal of improving the quality of urban life should be achieved in Tula.

As a result of the project, the following tasks should be solved:

1. A digital platform for involving citizens in solving urban development issues is created.
2. A "Digital twin of the city" is created.
3. An intellectual center of city management is created.
4. Automated control over the operation of road and municipal equipment is introduced.
5. Intelligent transport models (systems) are introduced in pilot cities.

The number of funds of 1590.6028 million rubles should be contributed within 2021–2024.

Such solid investments for the region require serious monitoring and analysis of the results obtained.

2 Materials and Method

A lot of works have been devoted to the study of various aspects of the "Smart City" concept, for example, Bagloee et al. (2021), Blanck and Ribeiro (2021), Calzada (2020), Csukás and Szabó (2021), Delsing (2021), Dooley (2021), El Hilali and Azougagh (2021), Gary et al. (2021), Iudin et al. (2001), Katochkov et al. (2020), Kézai et al. (2020), Nakano and Washizu (2021), Odintsovo (2019), Patrão et al. (2020), Secinaro et al. (2021), Smart City (2019) and Syed et al. (2021).

Thus, in his work (Patrão et al., 2020) he notes that cities occupying 3% of the land produce 80% of the global GDP, generating 70% of greenhouse gas emissions. Population growth, environmental pollution, poor infrastructure, and other factors require a "Smart city" to solve these problems. This raises the question of evaluating "Smart Cities" that take into account the above.

Calzada (2020) showed that the concept of "smart city" has a large number of different views and approaches from the academic world, politicians, and businessmen. This complicates the construction of a "Smart city" model since there are contradictions among groups of citizens pursuing different goals.

In the work of Odintsovo (2019), based on the analysis of some documents, articles, and trends in the development and implementation of the "Smart city" concept, the following risks were identified: the growth of digital inequality and the emergence of a new rigid control tool; the risk of excluding citizens from the decision-making process; the risk of replacing the real agenda with the interests of elites; the risk of replacing the social and political agenda with technical issues; ignoring the peculiarities of each city; technical risks.

Iudin et al. (2001) note that the high complexity of the structure of new cities requires the use of big data analysis. It provides the possibility to make quicker, more reliable, and adequate management decisions in the system of "Smart Cities". At the same time, the authors have identified some problems that arise when analyzing rapidly changing factors, focusing on the necessity of further research.

Dooley (2021) has considered the issues of passive and active participation of city residents in the process of collecting and analyzing big data for various purposes. An example of studying the concept of direct passive participation in Helsinki is proposed.

Syed et al. (2021) have shown that the Internet of Things allows creating more "smart" cities, excluding routine, easily algorithmized work in various spheres of human life. However, IoT can lead to a violation of privacy and cybersecurity. SWOT analysis can reduce the risks in this area.

Dooley (2021) has noted that there are not enough specific engineering applications for the effective use of the "Smart City" concept. Their development is difficult both for technical reasons and due to the lack of highly qualified personnel. An original approach based on IoT, SOA, and SysML was proposed.

Kézai et al. (2020) using the example of a study of the dependence of startups on the belonging or non-belonging of cities to the group of smart cities, showed that there is no reason to say that the "Smart City" creates the best conditions for the emergence and development of startups.

In the review of trends in the digitalization of the urban economy (Smart City, 2019), a rating analysis of the TOP 10 "Smart cities of the world" was carried out, the standard of the "smart city" of the Ministry of Construction of Russia was considered. It is shown that the use of information and communication technologies (ICT) is not the main thing in the development of a "Smart city". The important difference between the Russian approach to building a "Smart city" was revealed. The fact is that great importance is attached to the development of "smart" housing and utilities infrastructure in the Russian Federation as one of the most important characteristics of the city.

The authors, based on the analysis of the literature and their own views, have concluded that the assessment of the development of a "Smart City" is currently based on technical indicators, while a "Smart City" is primarily created to improve the lives of citizens, therefore, they should give this assessment.

A "Smart city" can be considered as a kind of product, the quality of which is described by many parameters, but consumers-citizens should make the final decision.

It is noteworthy that some citizens are unable to assess the current level of development of a "Smart City" taking into account certain indicators of standards (ISO/IEC 30146, 2019; The Standard of the Ministry of Construction of the Russian Federation, 2019), but it is possible to assess the line of development (according to the "better-worse" principle) based on a survey of a representative sample of locals. At the same time, questions are asked on each indicator, "Do you see any improvement?" with the binary answer "Yes–No".

As a mathematical tool for assessing trends, it is proposed to use an entropy approach based on the methods of information theory.

Kullback (1978) in his monograph "Information Theory and Statistics", first published in 1968, showed the multipurposeness of the mathematical apparatus of information theory for solving problems of mathematical statistics, checking statistical estimates, and others.

The concept of information, as it is currently accepted, was first defined by Fisher (1925) in his work "Theory of statistical estimation" in 1925.

The further development of information theory is associated with the names of such scientists as Shennon (1948), Wiener (1948), who independently described the logarithmic measure of information in 1948. The mathematical expectation of information corresponds to the physical concept of entropy, considered as a measure of the uncertainty of the process.

Since the 70s of the twentieth century, entropy has been accepted as fundamental statistics used in modeling processes, testing hypotheses, building control systems, econometrics, and other scientific disciplines. Unique results with high accuracy and reliability were obtained.

A complete theoretical justification of the application of entropy in various fields is given in the work of Martin and James (1981) "Mathematical Theory of Entropy."

The scientific paper "Estimation of Entropy and Mutual Information" by Paninski (2003) is devoted to the application of entropy in cybernetics.

The fundamental issues of the modern approach to the use of statistics "entropy" are considered in the work of Gray (2011) "Entropy and Information Theory".

We can also note the works (Golan, 2006; Golan & Maasoumi, 2008) devoted to the application of entropy and information theory in econometrics.

The monograph of Iudin et al. (2001) showed the possibility of using information theory methods to solve problems of product quality management in mechanical engineering and the electronic industry.

The modern representation of the measure of the amount of information when observing one or another event has the form

$$I = -\ln p \tag{1}$$

p—the probability of observing the event of interest to us. If a stochastic process has a set of states,

$$E = \begin{vmatrix} E_1 \\ E_2 \\ E_3 \\ \dots \\ E_n \end{vmatrix} \quad (2)$$

observed with probabilities

$$P = \begin{vmatrix} p_1 \\ p_2 \\ p_3 \\ \dots \\ p_n \end{vmatrix} \quad (3)$$

then the information obtained by observing the *i*-event E_i ($i = 1 \dots n$) is determined from the formula (1). Entropy is equal to the mathematical expectation of information for all states, i.e.,

$$H = -\sum_{i=1}^{n} p_i * \ln p_i \quad (4)$$

Both information and entropy determined from formulas (1) and (4) are theoretical and defined only when the probabilities are known. At the same time, when conducting experimental studies, the probability distribution is usually unknown. The probabilities can only be estimated through estimation.

Suppose the probabilities for the event set (2) are calculated based on observations using the formula

$$p_i = \frac{k_i}{k}, \quad i = 1 \dots n \quad (5)$$

k_i—the number of observations of the event E_i, k—the total number of $\left(k = \sum_{i=1}^{n} k_i\right)$ observations.

Then the empirical entropy will be equal to

$$H = -\sum_{i=1}^{n} p_i * \ln p_i \quad (6)$$

Empirical entropy has a normal distribution (Gaussian distribution) with the following characteristics (Odintsovo, 2019; The UNECE–ITU, 2015):

$$\mathrm{MH} = H; \mathrm{DH} = \frac{a^2 - H^2}{k} \quad (7)$$

Here MN—Expected Value of empirical entropy; DH—its variance.

The parameter a^2 is determined from the formula

$$a^2 = \sum_{i=1}^{n} p_i * \ln^2 p_i \tag{8}$$

3 Results

In view of the above said, Iudin (2015), Iudin et al. (2001) has developed and widely applied an information criterion for identifying the type of distribution law in the study of random processes in mechanical engineering, electronic industry, and econometrics.

He has shown that the value of

$$J_c = \frac{h - H}{\sqrt{\frac{a^2 - h^2}{k}}} \tag{9}$$

where

$$\begin{cases} h = -\int\limits_{-\infty}^{\infty} w(x) \ln w(x) \mathrm{d}x \\ a^2 = -\int\limits_{-\infty}^{\infty} w(x) \ln^2 w(x) \mathrm{d}x \end{cases} \tag{10}$$

Here $w(x)$ is a normalized probability density function of a given class of distributions.

In our case, we are not dealing with the problem of identifying the distribution law, but with comparing the empirical distributions that arise during surveys to determine the existing trends.

In this regard, we are to use empirical entropies rather than theoretical, assumed parameters of distributions.

Based on the described J_c criterion, it is possible to create a trend criterion.

$$T_Y = \frac{H_1 - H_2}{\sqrt{\frac{a_1^2 - H_1^2}{k_1} + \frac{a_2^2 - H_2^2}{k_2}}} \tag{11}$$

Here are H_1, H_2—the empirical entropies calculated from the formula (6) at the first and second stages of the study, respectively;

$$a_m^2 = \sum_{i=1}^{k_m} p_{mi} \ln^2 p_{mi} \tag{12}$$

In (12) the following symbols are used: m—the survey number ($m = 1, \ldots, 2$); k_m—the total number of observations (questions asked) in the corresponding survey; p_{mi}—the estimation of the probability of observing the ith variant in the survey m.

This value has a Student's t-distribution with the number of degrees of freedom $r = k_1 + k_2 - 2$.

The probability density function of the Student's distribution is defined as follows:

$$f_k(x) = \frac{G\left(\frac{k+1}{2}\right)}{\sqrt{\pi k} G\left(\frac{k}{2}\right)} \left(1 + \frac{x^2}{k}\right)^{\frac{-k+1}{2}} \tag{13}$$

The gamma-function $G(z)$ is determined through an improper integral

$$G(z) = \int_0^{\infty} t^{z-1} e^{-t} dt \tag{14}$$

Let the confidence probability α be given, then the critical value of the criterion T_Y can be defined as the solution of the equation

$$T_Y(r, \alpha) : \int_{-T_{Y(r,\alpha)}}^{T_{Y(r,\alpha)}} f_r(x) dx = \alpha \tag{15}$$

The solution to Eq. (15) can be entrusted to the STUDENT.OBR.2X (T. SIN.2T) function in MS Excel®.

If the calculated value of the T_Y (11) criterion exceeds the table value (15), then the hypothesis of the presence of the trend is confirmed, otherwise, it is rejected.

The adequacy, accuracy, and reliability of this criterion are determined by the same for the J_c information criterion, which was studied in detail in the research (Iudin, 2015; Iudin et al., 2001), where it was proved that it was more accurate than standard criteria such as the Pearson criterion χ^2, requires a smaller sample size, and has narrower confidence limits.

The experimental study of the described criterion is planned to carry out in the middle or at the end of 2022. That time it will be possible to evaluate the work results of the construction of the "Tula Smart City" following the project passport (The passport of the project "Smart city of the Tula region", 2021).

4 Conclusions

The analysis of the literature devoted to the concept of "Smart city" has shown that, despite the general understanding of the importance of this problem, the assessment of the achievement of goals is carried out mechanically, hardly taking into account the opinion of citizens.

In essence, a "Smart city" can be considered as a kind of product, the quality of which is described by many parameters, but the final decision should be made by consumers-citizens.

To assess the trends in the development of "Smart city", the T_Y criterion was proposed, based on the methods of mathematical information theory and the concept of "entropy". Its adequacy, accuracy, and reliability correspond to an accurate and reliable information criterion for identifying the type of distribution law J_c.

In 2022 a sociological survey of Tula residents to obtain information on the assessment of the development of the "Smart city" will be carried out.

Acknowledgements The work was carried out with the financial support of Plekhanov Russian University of Economics.

References

Bagloee, S. A., Heshmati, M., Dia, H., Ghaderi, H., Pettit, C., & Asadi, M. (2021). Blockchain: The operating system of smart cities. *Cities, 112*, 103104. https://doi.org/10.1016/j.cities.2021.103104. Accessed: October 10, 2021.

Blanck, M., & Ribeiro, J. L. D. (2021). Smart cities financing system: An empirical modelling from the European context. *Cities, 116*, 103268. https://doi.org/10.1016/j.cities.2021.103268. Accessed: October 10, 2021.

Calzada, I. (2020). Democratising smart cities? Penta-Helix multistakeholder social innovation framework. *Smart Cities, 3*, 1145–1173. https://doi.org/10.3390/SMARTCITIES3040057

Csukás, M. S., & Szabó, R. Z. (2021). The many faces of the smart city: Differing value propositions in the activity portfolios of nine cities. *Cities, 112*, 103116. https://doi.org/10.1016/j.cities.2021.103116. Accessed: October 10, 2021.

Deakin, M., & Al Waer, H. (2011). From intelligent to smart cities. *Journal of Intelligent Buildings International, 3*(3), 140–152. https://doi.org/10.1080/17508975.2011.586671

Delsing, J. (2021). Smart city solution engineering. *Smart Cities, 4*, 643–661. https://doi.org/10.3390/smartcities4020033. Accessed: October 10, 2021.

Dooley, K. (2021). Direct passive participation: Aiming for accuracy and citizen safety in the era of big data and the smart city. *Smart Cities, 4*, 336–348. https://doi.org/10.3390/smartcities4010020. Accessed: October 10, 2021.

El Hilali, S., & Azougagh, A. (2021). A netnographic research on citizen's perception of a future smart city. *Cities, 115*, 103233. https://doi.org/10.1016/j.cities.2021.103233. Accessed: October 10, 2021.

Fisher, R. A. (1925). Theory of statistical estimation. *Proceedings of the Cambridge Philological Society, 22*, 700–725.

Gary, W., Zink, A., Codecá, L., & Clarke, S. (2021). A digital twin smart city for citizen feedback. *Cities, 110*, 103064. https://doi.org/10.1016/j.cities.2020.103064. Accessed: October 10, 2021.

Golan, A. (2006). Information and entropy econometrics—A review and synthesis. *Foundations and Trends® in Econometrics, 2*(1–2), 1–145.
Golan, A., & Maasoumi, E. (2008). Information theoretic and entropy methods: An overview. *Econometric Reviews, 27*(4–6), 317–328. https://doi.org/10.1080/07474930801959685. Accessed: October 10, 2021.
Gray, R. M. (2011). *Entropy and information theory* (328p). Springer. https://doi.org/10.1007/978-1-4419-7970-4
ISO/IEC 30146:2019. Information technology—Smart city ICT indicators. https://www.iso.org/standard/70302.html. Accessed: October 10, 2021.
Iudin, S. (2015). The informational criterion of identification of the distribution law. *Modern European Researches, 4*, 133–137. https://doaj.net/uploads/issue/issue_8.pdf. Accessed: October 10, 2021.
Iudin, S.V., Kozlova, N. O., & Childen, V. (2001). Information methods in quality management. *Moscow: RIA "Standards and Quality", 1*(10), 208.
Jiang, H. (2021). Smart urban governance in the 'smart' era: Why is it urgently needed? *Cities, 111*, 103004. https://doi.org/10.1016/j.cities.2020.103004. Accessed: October 10, 2021.
Kandt, J., & Batty, M. (2021). Smart cities, big data and urban policy: Towards urban analytics for the long run. *Cities, 109*, 102992. https://doi.org/10.1016/j.cities.2020.102992. Accessed: October 10, 2021.
Katochkov, V. M., Savin, G. V., & Toporkova, E. V. (2020). Current trends in the development of smart city in the world. *Bulletin of the Udmurt University, 30*(3), 340–345. https://doi.org/10.35634/2412-9593-2020-30-3-340-345
Kézai, P. K., Fischer, S., & Lados, M. (2020). Smart economy and startup enterprises in the Visegrád countries—A comparative analysis based on the crunchbase database. *Smart Cities, 3*, 1477–1494. https://doi.org/10.3390/smartcities3040070
Kullback, S. (1978). *Information theory and statistics* (399p). Peter Smith.
Martin, N. F. G., & James, W. (1981). *Mathematical theory of entropy* (257p). Addison-Wesley Publishing Company.
Nakano, S., & Washizu, A. (2021). Will smart cities enhance the social capital of residents? The importance of smart neighborhood management. *Cities, 115*(2021), 103244. https://doi.org/10.1016/j.cities.2021.103244. Accessed: October 10, 2021.
Odintsovo, A. V. (2019). The main risks of implementing the concept of "smart city". *Sociodynamics, 10*, 1–8. https://doi.org/10.25136/2409-7144.2019.10.30636.
Paninski, L. (2003). Estimation of entropy and mutual information. *Neural Computation, 15*, 1191–1253.
Patrão, C., Moura, P., & de Almeida, A. T. (2020). Review of smart city assessment tools. *Smart Cities, 3*, 1117–1132. https://doi.org/10.3390/SMARTCITIES3040055
Projects of the Government of the Tula region on the development of a "smart city" and digital management. https://digital71.ru/projects/gorodskoe-upravlenie/. Accessed: October 10, 2021.
Secinaro, S., Brescia, V., Calandra, D., & Biancone, P. (2021). Towards a hybrid model for the management of smart city initiatives. *Cities, 116*, 103278. https://doi.org/10.1016/j.cities.2021.103278. Accessed: October 10, 2021.
Shennon, C. E. (1948). A mathematical theory of communication. *Bell System Technological Journal, 27*, 379–423.
Smart City. (2019). Smart housing and communal services: An overview of trends in the digitalization of urban economy. Moscow. Foundation "Institute of City Economics", 74p. https://urbaneconomics.ru/sites/default/files/umnyy_gorod_avgust_2019_2_0.pdf. Accessed: October 10, 2021.
Syed, A. S., Sierra-Sosa, D., Kumar, A., & Elmaghraby, A. (2021). IoT in smart cities: A survey of technologies, practices and challenges. *Smart Cities, 4*, 429–475. https://doi.org/10.3390/smartcities4020024. Accessed: October 10, 2021.
The passport of the project "Smart city of the Tula region". https://econom.tularegion.ru/project/proekty/regionalnye-proekty/umnyy-gorod/. Accessed: October 10, 2021.

The Standard of the Ministry of Construction of the Russian Federation. (2019). Basic and additional requirements for smart cities (Smart City standard). https://minstroyrf.gov.ru/docs/18039/. Accessed: October 10, 2021.
The UNECE–ITU. (2015). The UNECE–ITU smart sustainable cities indicators. Economic and Social Council, Economic Commission for Europe. Committee on Housing and Land Management. https://unece.org/fileadmin/DAM/hlm/documents/2015/ECE_HBP_2015_4.en.pdf. Accessed: October 10, 2021.
Wiener, N. (1948). *Cybernetics*. Wiley.

Innovation System Management of the Trade-Export Organization in Business Digitalization Context: Modern Challenges and Solutions

Maksim Nozdrichev

Abstract Modern rapidly developing, complex and penetrating many industries and spheres digital transformation also affects business. Emerging challenges contain opportunities and threats that open up new ways to develop efficiency, stability and competitiveness. The study aims to propose the comprehensive structure of solutions for innovation system management, especially for trade-export organizations, in connection with modern challenges arising in the business digitalization context. In connection with this aim, business digitalization context is abstracted to specifics of trade-export organizations, and then analysed for challenges: phenomena groups as well as threats and opportunities contained therein. Further, solutions are proposed for each challenge in an abstract form. In addition, the empirical observation context and results are described. The study identifies 9 challenges and proposes solution groups for each of the challenges. The challenges and the solutions are to a certain degree conditioned and provided by business digitalization context and are intended for innovation system management, in particular, of trade-export organizations. The guide to the results practical use is proposed. An approach to strategy defining from viewpoint of cyclical, integrating, regenerating functions and focus on proactive thinking and behaviour renewal, as well as on maintaining the integrity and developing a corporate vision is proposed. Application features of project management as the most effective management technologies in innovation, the advantages and weaknesses that require management attention are also considered. As well as potential avenues for future research are proposed.

Keywords Innovation management · International trade business · Digital transformation · Business challenges

JEL Classification D22 · D83 · O32 · O33

M. Nozdrichev (✉)
Southern Federal University, Rostov-on-Don, Russia
e-mail: maksim.nozdrichev@yandex.ru

E. I. Lazareva et al. (eds.), *Innovative Trends in International Business and Sustainable Management*, Approaches to Global Sustainability, Markets, and Governance,
https://doi.org/10.1007/978-981-19-4005-7_17

1 Introduction

Modern environment of commercial organizations has many features, some of which are well defined and structured. Features of modernity, which this study focuses on, are based on the digital revolution as a driver. Such features contain opportunities and threats, which organizations need to manage to maintain efficiency, stability and competitiveness. The VUCA-world concept identifies four main factors: volatility, uncertainty, complexity and ambiguity. For example, volatility in technology manifests itself as the rate of technology change in terms of scale, scope, depth in the technological hierarchy and other aspects.

The Industry 4.0 concept describes forecasted transition to fully automated digital production, to control systems based on artificial intelligence. With the transition to the new industry, IT will move into the quality of an active subject of management, consulting, entrepreneurship.

The problem of the study is the lack of generally structured solutions for challenges, which are formed in business digitalization context and are relevant, in particular, for organizations engaged in export trade.

Various authors in the framework of their research raise certain aspects of this context and problem. For example, Ageev (2018) presents the structuring of highly probable and unlikely trends of the future. Chirumalla (2021) explores challenges regarding process innovations and ways of developing this type of innovation. Frolova (2017) describes some problems and obstacles in the technological development of the global economic field.

Revenko and Revenko (2019) describe the fact that the higher the innovative development of industry, the higher investment attractiveness; emphasize the available data amount raise a problem, and its processing capabilities. Martin et al. (2019) explore forms of interaction between main divisions and innovative ones. Bygstad and Øvrelid (2021) investigate the use of lightweight IT for testing and developing solutions.

This study aims to propose solutions for innovation system management of a trade-export organization in connection with modern challenges arising in the business digitalization context. The hypothesis is that the solutions proposed will allow organizations to take advantage of opportunities and counter threats contained in the relevant challenges.

2 Material and Methods

For theoretical, statistical and informational support of the study, the scientific works given in the references are used in the following areas: innovation management, IT management, digital business transformation, international trade.

The following research methodology is used, the main description of the methods of which is given in Edronova and Ovcharov (2013). By the abstraction method, the study limits analysed modernity within the framework of digital transformation problems inherent in trade-export organizations. At the first stage, a deductive analysis is carried out for phenomena that contain opportunities and threats.

At the second stage, for each of the phenomena, existing solutions are determined through deductive and system analysis. The solutions are given through the abstraction method, since a problematic of some particular solution, and hence its tool and methodological content, depends on the specifics of each organization as a user of the results.

At the third stage, according to the analogy method, the phenomena and the related solutions are grouped. Similarity criteria for phenomena are common causes or relationships between phenomena. Similarity criteria for solutions are relationships between solutions according to their sequence of application.

At the fourth stage, designation (name) for each challenge is formulated through the generalization method (if it was not done initially by other authors). A challenge in this study is an entity that unites grouped phenomena with a single alleged cause and its solutions group.

The main source of empirical information for realizing the monitoring method in the study was the Astra Alliance Group, namely, its structural division the Agro Zerno Yug LLC, engaged in export trade in the agricultural sector. The organization allocates funding for innovation activities, supporting the idea that technologies and innovation projects will allow achieving a competitive advantage in a technological plane.

3 Results

As a result of the study, the 9 challenges are identified, their significant phenomena are structurally described as specific factors, and then groups of the interrelated solutions for comprehensive response to each of the challenges are presented.

1. *Cyber-threats*

Sources were used to identify the challenge: Ageev (2018), Frolova (2017).

Firstly, information systems are becoming more and more complex. This can lead to data losses, damage or violation of intellectual property and other effects. Secondly, a human factor remains: users may mistakenly, for example, provide their data to third parties. Thirdly, even small organizations are exposed to a wide range of cyber threats, but they don't have appropriate resources to organize direct protective measures.

Solutions

Firstly, follow IT minimalism: minimize devices, storage and connections numbers. Secondly, within the financial opportunities framework, receive an ongoing external security audit and form necessary measures, which depend on particular infrastructure and business processes. Thirdly, develop IT literacy and staff qualifications,

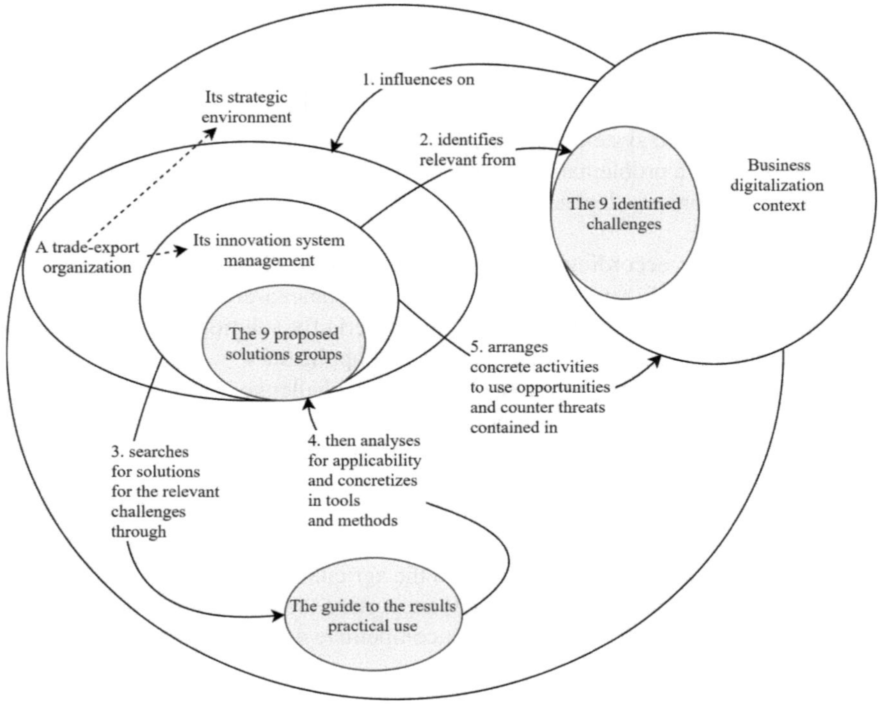

Fig. 1 5-stage process of using the study results by innovation system management. *Source* Developed and compiled by the author

including training and requirements for lawyers' and financiers' competence in IT, innovation, project management fields (Fig. 1).

2. *Degradation of natural intelligence*

Sources were used to identify the challenge: Ageev (2018).

The challenge manifests itself in such forms as intellectual dependence on technology, and a tendency to borrow values from digital templates. This leads to uncertainty in those areas of management that are more related to the human factor. In marketing, this is manifested in the inability of consumers to independently predict their preferences and decisions, as well as analyse their habits.

Marketing solutions

Predict consumer behaviour based on information content that they consume, as well as on data that they leave about themselves on the Internet. Data-driven marketing makes it possible to analyse and forecast consumer preferences more deeply than consumers themselves are capable of.

The challenge also manifests itself in the management of personnel, teams, in the development of leadership, cultural and professional identity. This forms the questions: are employees able to build long-term communications with a specific manager, organization and culture; how do they draw their boundaries of competence; are they capable to change their technological environment often?

Solutions for HR management

Firstly, inform employees about existing trends in thinking research fields, offer events and materials. Secondly, implement corporate IT solutions for cognitive abilities development. Thirdly, form a culture of intellectuality, scientific thinking.

3. *National borders transparency*

Sources were used to identify the challenge: Ageev (2018), Nikulina and Bugaeva (2016), Revenko and Revenko (2019), Sevostyanov (2021), Suprunovskiy et al. (2020).

The challenge is the effect of a high degree of digital innovation of organizations fighting for primacy in national markets and access to international markets. Anyway, it leads to one effect: mutual transparency of organizations and foreign markets, that is, universal access to the international information field, and therefore absolute cross-boundary competition.

Solutions

Firstly, assess competitiveness level by conducting benchmarking, trend watching and innovation monitoring on a global scale: proceed from the premise that all observed agents (also, non-commercial) are competitors. Secondly, develop and implement development strategy, initially relying on global, not local, experience. Thirdly, cooperate with consultants in IT, innovation, project management fields.

4. *Disunity amongst economic and other agents and, at the same time, a requirement by information technology for end-to-end access*

Sources were used to identify the challenge: Ageev (2018), Bygstad (2017), Distanont and Khongmalai (2020), Frolova (2017), Nikulina and Bugaeva (2016), Revenko and Revenko (2019), Suprunovskiy et al. (2020).

Lack of end-to-end access sets a certain limit for enterprises IT development. This means that agents should be strategically interested in the digital development of their environment. But firstly, the "insensitivity" of management to digital technologies emergence limits the development of IT already within organizations. Secondly, digital platforms (cross-organizational) during implementation face many cross-organizational problems.

Solutions

Firstly, assess the IT maturity of the industry and competitive environment. Secondly, develop an IT strategy. Thirdly, involve the organization in processes of industry IT infrastructure development. Fourthly, develop an IT culture. Fifthly, look for opportunities to connect to systems and interact with market counterparties, non-market institutions and non-industry technological enterprises.

5. *High demand from IT for financing and, at the same time, high uncertainty in results of implementation*

Sources were used to identify the challenge: Ageev (2018), Bygstad (2017), Bygstad and Øvrelid (2021), Chirumalla (2021), Distanont and Khongmalai (2020).

Compliance is necessary and a problem between objective results of an innovative IT project and, from another hand, subjective, sometimes intuitive, process in which the technology should be implemented. The increasing availability of IT and reduction of financing requirements for lightweight-IT projects open up opportunities for experiments and acquisition of technological competitive advantages even at the early stages of an organization's development.

Solutions

Firstly, develop talents who will be able to comprehensively solve the technological and organizational problems of IT implementation, including modern IT professions in organizational structure. Secondly, test digital hypotheses based on lightweight IT through business analysis; include in-house developers for implemented systems. Thirdly, develop process competence centres.

6. *Dependence of internal innovation activity results on order quality, first of all*

Sources were used to identify the challenge: Ageev (2018), Chirumalla (2021), Frolova (2017), Nambisan et al. (2019).

It is the project client's applied vision of opportunities in IT innovation that is what the success of innovative initiatives is based on. Thanks to the successful development of customers' capabilities to create high-quality IT orders, innovations will have greater potential to create competitiveness based on technology. In part, the lack of order quality is related to the perception of IT as providing processes, not as an organization development tool.

Solutions

Firstly, systematically develop digital skills amongst non-specialized customers and employees. Secondly, arrange presentations of innovation IT-projects business cases, where experts will develop clients' experience in this field. Thirdly, establish an IT culture as a tool for achieving competitiveness.

7. *Primitivization of knowledge*

Sources were used to identify the challenge: Ageev (2018).

Reproduction of universal concepts created earlier in simpler and narrowed representations leads to specializations separation, loss of universal integrating codes of thinking, and single conceptual apparatus. Against this background, barriers to interaction (both between departments and with external agents) and retraining are developing, which limit organizations' capabilities in innovation development.

Solutions

Firstly, develop an internal corporate aspiration for universalization of knowledge; identify commonalities between specializations and profile private. Secondly, be aware of modern specializations, develop profiles, explain roles of modern professions in processes, first of all, to managers. Thirdly, increase the transparency of requirements for candidates, manage employee development and develop cross-functional communications.

8. *Multiconceptuality*

Sources were used to identify the challenge: Ageev (2018), Chirumalla (2021).

Cultural gaps provided by IT lead to a low ability of enterprises to transform their processes, as well as to effective external interactions (for example, when predicting consumer behaviour). Each agent proceeds in his decisions from a unique set of cultural attitudes (values, patterns of interpretation, trust in information and authority), which makes it difficult to develop long-term commercial relations and productive cooperation.

Solutions

Firstly, identify cultural attitudes of employees, contractors, consumers to understand sources of their worldview and decision-making. And for this aim, analyse content from open data by using information technologies. Secondly, if necessary, inform participants about these procedures and comply with the legality of the use of personal data. And also consider solutions to challenge 2.

9. *Contradictions as a necessity*

Sources were used to identify the challenge: Alekseeva (2019), Bogatov (2018), Bourke and Roper (2017), Brazhnikova (2020), Martin et al. (2019), Nambisan et al. (2019), Sapelkin et al. (2017), Sergeeva (2020).

Consider the following contradictions.

(a) Strategic contradictions. Strategic management of the company strives for full manageability and transparency. Contradiction: for this, innovation management needs to develop creative IT departments, establish openness, take into account emotional intelligence, develop inter-level and cross-functional interaction.
(b) Contradictions in investment assessment and planning. It is necessary to combine a short-term (in profit and efficiency) and a long-term (in innovation productivity, modernization) approach to evaluating projects and processes.
(c) Contradictions in innovation management. It is necessary to combine regularity and consistency with creativity and iteration. Innovation processes require, in addition, continuous auditing and standardization, and also have high technological complexity.

(d) Contradictions in the interaction of core and innovation processes. It is necessary to create a competitive, productively conflicted and empathetic innovation environment along (in various forms) with a standardized, controlled, predictable, unambiguous environment of the core processes.

Solutions

Firstly, include an innovative component in strategy; develop strategic priorities or values.
Secondly, develop long-term planning and investments in the qualitative development of the organization.
Thirdly, develop standards of innovation activity; receive an external audit; introduce flexible management methodologies; develop tools for creative business problems solutions.
Fourthly, organizationally separate innovation processes in their main part; develop corporate standards. Involve key specialists in innovations in quantitative terms: in hours of working time, with reporting.
Fifthly, develop a culture of working with conflicting and counterintuitive ideas in innovation processes; encourage critical and objective thinking, as well as the ability to recognize the uncertainty of solutions and novelty of problems.

4 Conclusion

This study aimed to propose the comprehensive structure of solutions for innovation system management, especially for trade-export organizations, in connection with modern challenges arising in the business digitalization context. For this aim, the 9 modern challenges were identified and described, for each of which the solutions groups were proposed.

Here are some additions to the results.

Guide to the results practical use

For modern organizations, especially for trade-export, the results of this study provide a basic description of the challenges and solutions that arise in the business digitalization context and are planning sources for innovation management. We will propose the sequence of the following procedure for practical use of the results:

1. Through expert analysis, identify the challenges or their manifestations that are most relevant for user organization. The relevance is whether the organization can take advantage of opportunities and whether it is influenced by threats contained in the challenge. The expert analysis of the challenge is recommended to be carried out in cooperation with an expert who has specific competencies within a specific challenge.
2. After determining the actual challenges, it is necessary to analyse the degree of the organization's development in this direction. Next, choose and analyse

which of the solutions are relevant for the organization at this moment of its development.
3. After selecting the abstracted solutions, through expert analysis, determine the most effective tool and methodological content for the solutions within specific conditions of the organization.
4. Plan and implement the solution based on project methodologies by innovation management, and include the project product in the organization's system, manage the efficiency and lifecycle of the solution.

Strategy planning in the digital innovation context

Organization innovation system concerns issue of developing corporate vision along with strategy basic sources. Strategy innovation component comes into conflict—in the context of VUCA factors—with strategy definition in terms of overall long-term planning. It is necessary to approach strategy as a cyclical, integrative, regenerating process aimed at proactive thinking and behaviour renewal, as well as at maintaining the integrity and developing corporate vision.

Application features of project management in innovation

The main technologies of innovation management are project-based: aimed at research and implementation. This allows to flexibly manage teams, act iteratively, use an open approach to team formation, use part-time employment, the reward for results. The project approach will require managing risks such as weak interaction between development teams and users, inflexibility, conflict of real expectations, distrust, floating responsibility. Process and functional management technologies are effective for post-project services.

For future research purposes, the results of the study can be used: to investigate the manifestations of challenges and solutions for other objects, in other industries, contexts or areas of management. It is possible to propose other avenues for future research projects: to investigate in more depth and detail obstacles to the successful functioning of innovation systems inherent in enterprises, industries, spheres of activity.

References

Ageev, A. I. (2018). Managing the digital future. *The World of the New Economy, 12*(3), 6–23.

Alekseeva, N. V. (2019). Basic principles of construction and organization of the enterprise corporate innovative system. *Bulletin of the University, 2*, 35–38.

Bogatov, V. V. (2018). Conceptual model of the innovation process management system in the organization. *Management of Economic Systems: Electronic Scientific Journal, 6*(112), 16.

Bourke, J., & Roper, S. (2017). Innovation, quality management and learning: Short-term and longer-term effects. *Research Policy, 46*(8), 1505–1518.

Brazhnikova, N. B. (2020). Development of a system of motivation for employees providing innovative activities of the organization. *STAGE: Economic Theory, Analysis, Practice, 3*, 89–97.

Bygstad, B. (2017). Generative innovation: A comparison of lightweight and heavyweight IT. *Journal of Information Technology, 32*(2), 180–193.

Bygstad, B., & Øvrelid, E. (2021). Managing two-speed innovation for digital transformation. *Procedia Computer Science, 181*, 119–126.

Chirumalla, K. (2021). Building digitally-enabled process innovation in the process industries: A dynamic capabilities approach. *Technovation, 105*, 102256.

Distanont, A., & Khongmalai, O. (2020). The role of innovation in creating a competitive advantage. *Kasetsart Journal of Social Sciences, 41*(1), 15–21.

Edronova, V. N., & Ovcharov, A. O. (2013). System of methods in scientific research. *Economic Analysis: Theory and Practice, 10*, 313.

Frolova, N. S. (2017). Current trends in the development of international trade in the context of globalization. *Online Journal "Science Studies", 9*, 3.

Martin, A., Keller, A., & Fortwengel, J. (2019). Introducing conflict as the microfoundation of organizational ambidexterity. *Strategic Organization, 17*(1), 38–61.

Nambisan, S., Wright, M., & Feldman, M. (2019). The digital transformation of innovation and entrepreneurship: Progress, challenges and key themes. *Research Policy, 48*(8), 103773.

Nikulina, O. V., & Bugaeva, S. I. (2016). Introduction of innovative technologies to the international trading companies. *Practical Marketing, 1*(227).

Revenko, L. S., & Revenko, N. S. (2019). Digital information platforms as a driving force to increase agricultural markets transparency. *Russian Foreign Economic Bulletin, 7*, 21–33.

Sapelkin, R. S., Dumilse, S., & Da Silva, P. (2017). Modern approaches to the organization and planning of the system of innovative development of enterprises. *Economy. Innovation. Quality Management, 2*(19), 75–76.

Sergeeva, I. G. (2020). Evaluation of information technologies and systems usage for the innovative activity of organization. *Bulletin of St. Petersburg State University of Economics, 1*(121), 62–66.

Sevostyanov, A. L. (2021). Logistics concept of export and international trade of agricultural products. *Bulletin of Agrarian Science, 2*(89), 160–166.

Suprunovskiy, V. P., Klimov, A. A., & Gotz, I. G. (2020). Technologies of digital twins in transport corridors for sea and waterways in Russia. *International Journal of Open Information Technologies, 8*(12), 113–132.

Company's Management Information Systems for Solving the Tasks of Implementing Integrated Marketing Communications in the Conditions of Digitalization of the Economy

Irina Yu. Granovskaya

Abstract The relevance of the article's problems is determined by the fact that in the digital economy, technical and information capabilities actively stimulate the dynamics of marketing communications development, as well as the transformation of concepts and management strategies in marketing. The purpose of the study is to substantiate proposals for the implementation of the coordinating role of marketing information systems (MIS) when integrating them into corporate information systems (CIS) in order to solve the management task of implementing integrated marketing communications (IMC) in the conditions of digitalization of the economy. Research methods include: analysis of intra-organizational processes in the company, assessment of the marketing environment in which IMC is implemented, factor and strategic analysis, systematization of empirical and factual information, segmentation of the structure of marketing information systems. The results of the article consist of the author's analysis of the prospects for the development of MIS in the conditions of digitalization of the economy and informatization of society with the introduction of IMC. The interpretation of the issue of the introduction of MIS in the framework of intra-organizational events is new. An expanded list of elements of the IMC is proposed, the ideology and features of the functioning of marketing information systems in the implementation of the concept of integrated marketing communications are described. An expanded set of organizational solutions to improve the efficiency of communications using an integrated information system is proposed to optimize the company's management conditions and achieve a total positive result of the IMC in the digital economy.

Keywords Integrated marketing communications · Marketing information systems · Corporate information systems · Innovation management · Digitalization of the economy · Integrated marketing information systems · Transformation of marketing systems

JEL Classification M10 · M11 · M15 · M21 · M30 · G34 · O32

I. Yu. Granovskaya (✉)
Southern Federal University, Rostov-on-Don, Russia
e-mail: irinagran5@mail.ru

E. I. Lazareva et al. (eds.), *Innovative Trends in International Business and Sustainable Management*, Approaches to Global Sustainability, Markets, and Governance,
https://doi.org/10.1007/978-981-19-4005-7_18

1 Introduction

Relevance of the research issues. It is determined by the fact that the course toward digitalization of the economy in Russia is due to the increasing role of information technologies in the development of society. This process is directly related to the definition of the formats of communication channels in the economic sphere. The implementation of the information society development strategy in the Russian Federation stimulates an increase in the dynamics of changes in marketing management. The modern experience of Russian companies in the distribution of goods (services) is often determined by the intuitive application of marketing tools and methods. Transformations in the information field require the business community to develop and implement new principles, methods, and models of marketing communications management while maintaining a focus on budget savings for the promotion of goods and services. In these conditions, we should expect an increase in the interest of companies in the integrated marketing communications (IMC) system.

The problems of integrating companies' information systems into a single information field to solve the tasks of the IMC include the lack of development of new organizational and administrative management concepts that have not been fully implemented at the methodological level as part of the strategy for the digitalization of the economy.

The purpose of the study, the results of which are presented in the article, is to substantiate a set of proposals for the coordination of marketing information systems (MIS) when they are integrated into corporate information systems (CIS) of the company and to develop practical recommendations for solving management tasks for the functioning of CIS when implementing the IMC system in the digital economy.

Research objectives:

1. To evaluate the traditional management schemes of consolidation of various functional areas of the company.
2. To develop an alternative scheme for managing corporate information flows when implementing IMC in the conditions of digitalization.
3. To formulate algorithms for the formation of communications in the IMC system in the digital economy, taking into account the expanded integration of MIS into the corporate information system to achieve the overall goals of the company.
4. To substantiate the list of structural elements for the management of a corporate information system within the framework of the IMC.
5. To propose a list of organizational solutions to achieve effective communication using an integrated information system.

The scientific novelty of the results lies in the substantiation of the algorithm for integrating MIS into the company's information system, within which it is assigned the coordinating function of the corporate information environment in the conditions of the IMC. An expanded interpretation of the concept of integration for the functioning of corporate information systems in the conditions of digitalization of the economy is presented. In the organization of CIS not only the synthesis of marketing communications becomes available, but also individual communications arising through the work of each of the structural divisions of the company, embedded in the marketing policy and contributing to the achievement of the company's overall goals, are subject to integration.

2 Methodology

The modern concept of the IMC complex is based on methodologically verified approaches to cost optimization due to the synthesis of the company's existing communication environments and the formation of a single communication field to achieve internal and external integration when providing information about the company's policies, strategies and product range to the target audience. The IMC system is positioned as an effective marketing structure based on a combination of standard and innovative communication elements, the means and methods of which exceed the capabilities of traditional marketing techniques in the field of communications (Ketova & Granovskaya, 2020).

The assessment of the degree of knowledge of the company's information systems management experience indicates that the strategic focus of marketing management on the use of automation of marketing business processes was implemented in the form of marketing information systems (MIS), and took shape during the development of digital marketing systems. Under the influence of environmental factors, marketing information systems are integrated into corporate information systems (CIS). In the initial stage, the MIS is integrated and developed as an integral part of the CIS (Danko & Kitova, 2013; Stefanova & Gostev, 2019). At this stage of research, the objectives of the MIS functioning are presented as an internal information system and an analytical tool for the marketing department of the company (Charykova & Fedoseeva, 2017). Further, the integration processes of the marketing information system into the management system of MIS of companies are considered in terms of streamlining marketing information flows in accordance with the tasks of companies and are aimed at optimizing database structure. At the same time, the indicators of completeness of the information provided, labor and technical costs, software improvement, and data update frequency are taken into account, the principles of strategic focus on the integrated MIS are proposed, applicable for the use of data sets in order to predict future marketing environment trends. To assess the effectiveness of the use of automated systems, a profitable method is practiced based on profitability calculations (Hashimova, 2021).

There is an obvious need to study management processes when solving the problem of integrating MIS in the conditions of digitalization of the economy (Zhuravlev, 2018).

The instrumental and methodological apparatus of the research is formed in the context of a systemic-functional approach within the framework of the theories of communication and digitalization as the leading directions of modern economic development, marketing management, digital marketing, interaction marketing, goals and objectives of the IMC, as well as models of consumer behavior. The techniques of modern analysis, formation of innovative marketing systems are applied. The methods of studying the elements of the management system in the implementation of the IMC include factor and comparative analysis, the method of algorithm justification, methods of comparison, and systematization of practical and factual information.

3 Results

The solution to the problem of increasing the effectiveness of the promotion of goods (services) in the IMC system is based on the integration of all marketing capabilities of the company. In practice, understanding the concept of integration as a summation of the company's capabilities leads to management models of consolidation of various functional areas. The logical continuation of the direct interpretation of the concept of integration is the implementation of management schemes, according to the following principle—an IMC specialist should have knowledge in the field of advertising and sociology, management and marketing, psychology and economics. The functions of the marketing department in the company should include the task of coordinating all structural units to fulfill the tasks of communication policy formulated by marketers. The authority to coordinate, control and adjust the activities of various divisions of the company requires leadership at the level of the development director, who must have the ability to manage all departments of the structure—from production and human resources to the sales department. In the arsenal of the marketing manager, there should be organizational, administrative, legal, informational, and other means for the formation of communications at various levels (Kretova, 2008). Such an idea of the IMC as a system of intensive business development methods with functional centralization of the marketing department involves the implementation of the following management schemes:

- implementation of algorithms for managing the IMC system in the company on the basis of a single communication complex organized according to the principle of strategic subordination of the communication component in the activities of various functional zones of the company to the unified marketing policy of the company; solving communication problems using basic and synthetic marketing tools; ensuring and controlling integration;
- monitoring of the dominant factors of the local market and the internal environment that affect the functioning of the IMC management system in the company, namely: the external environment, the structure of the organization, and internal processes;
- development of communication efficiency management algorithms to achieve the company's marketing goals;

- selection and application of methods for evaluating the effectiveness of the reorganization of the integrated marketing communications management system, characterizing, on the one hand, the effectiveness of the new management system, and on the other hand, the effectiveness of communication integration;
- achieving financial integration, with the redistribution of a single communications budget between the available communication channels, taking into account the goals of the current moment of the company's communication policy.

The implementation of this concept of integration in the IMC system in the form of administration of actions to consolidate the work of various structural units to form a single communication message does not use the possibilities of digitalization; it may be labor-intensive, insufficiently flexible, and requires rethinking the basis of the administrative management system in the company.

According to the author, in the conditions of the course on digitalization of the economy, an alternative solution to the problem of functioning of the IMC management system, namely, on the basis of corporate information flow management, seems possible. The goal is the creation of a corporate information system, the algorithms for the formation of which assume the coordinating function of the marketing information system (MIS), in order to make tactical and strategic marketing decisions. To do this, the corporate information system should be formed taking into account the MIS and supplemented with an of up-to-date and reliable information, based on an analysis of external and internal factors. It is also important to substantiate strategies and carry out statistical analysis of the results of the implementation of current and strategic tasks, collected information about the positioning in the market, and the competitiveness of the company. The corporate information system should provide the target level of interconnection and interaction of the company with the market. Thus, most of the corporate messages sent on behalf of the company to the external environment will be able to be coordinated by the marketing communications system and integrated with the goals and objectives of the company's marketing policy.

In this case, the management of corporate information flows may include three main approaches to integration within the framework of the new communication policy:

1. Building an IMC management system in the company based on the administration of information flows, with the priority of data on marketing policy, namely: digitalization of algorithms and results of the company's activities based on the consolidation of databases of various structural units, with the inclusion in the database of updated information MIS data on the status of current and strategic goals of the company's activities, current trends in the development of the local market, the risks of negative impact of external factors, planned marketing activities currently being implemented. In addition, the principle of implementing the current tasks of developing relations with the target audience, the results and goals of the company's financial, economic, innovation, and investment activities, the tasks of strengthening various areas of the company's business reputation and competitiveness are relevant.

The integrated database is formed by creating a single database of the company, with indicators of the communication activity of each of the structural divisions of the organization (Lapshin, 2016). The consolidated database seems to be important for the purposes of coordinating solutions to current internal and external communication tasks by each structural element of the company, taking into account the proposed integrated data on the company's current tasks.

The integrated database should be structured by the company's management depending on the priorities of management tasks at each specific stage of its economic activity (Polyakova et al., 2019).

2. Building a management system of the IMC in the company on the basis of a unified organizational and methodological approach to the formation of integrated communication. The effectiveness of integrated communication of each structural unit of the company is achieved due to the requirements for the formation of communications:

   - based on the integrated information database of the company;
   - using innovative scientific achievements and modern technologies in the field of marketing;
   - ensuring the recognition of the company through the use of methods of differentiation of the source of communication;
   - providing for the multitasking of the message, taking into account the correct understanding of the segmentation of the company's target audience by the personnel of all its structural divisions;
   - selection and training of innovation-oriented personnel.

3. Building a complex of management of the IMC system in the company based on the idea of integration in its marketing policy as a combination of the information flows of the company's communications and the feedback message from each of the target audience segments. This approach corresponds to the classical idea of the factors of the consumer's choice of goods, according to which he chooses a product in accordance with his concepts of its value (quality, service, and price), information about which is presented to him in an understandable format and the quality of the product is associated with properties for which he is willing to pay (Smirnova, 2020). This approach is also applicable to other segments of the target audience, to which the socially-oriented part of communications is addressed. In the conditions of digitalization of the economy, the application of this integration algorithm becomes possible due to the introduction of digital technologies, neurotechnologies, and artificial intelligence.

According to the author, the algorithms for the functioning of the IMC management system in the digital economy can be built by taking into account the following representations of intra-organizational processes in the company:

- an expanded interpretation of the concept of integration seems appropriate, namely: not only marketing instruments and communication tools are integrated, but also individual communications formed as a result of the work of each of the company's structural divisions, which allows each of the target audience segments to send socially-oriented messages embedded in the marketing policy and contributing to the achievement of the company's overall goals.

- the subject of communications is determined by the need to move from transactional marketing activities to relationship marketing based on a combination of basic and synthetic marketing tools, consistent and coordinated messages that form a single favorable image of the company;
- tasks of the management of the IMC: a set of measures for the analysis, planning, organization, and control of the company's communications system in order to implement the appropriate level of contact with the target audience and solve the company's tasks, for which communications are formed taking into account the implementation of the product concept, the concept of orientation to consumer preferences, the concept of consumer motivation and the concept of social orientation of communications.

According to the author, the list of recommendations on the functioning of the IMC management system in the digital economy may include the construction of a corporate information system consisting of the following structural elements:

1. Formulation and justification of the algorithm for the implementation of the objectives of the activity and a unified strategy for the promotion of goods (services) of the company—for use by each structural unit in its line of work;
2. Collection and systematization of information about target audiences (direct and indirect contacts), entering into the database of consumers identified by such indicators as personal, social, and economic preferences, consumer activity, and activity in relation to certain brands;
3. Organization of the formation of a database with the results of publications in the media in relation to the company and its products;
4. Obtaining data for monitoring reviews of the quality of goods and services and the company as a whole on the Internet and from other sources, subject to verification of the authenticity of messages;
5. Maintaining a database with court decisions on financial and economic disputes of the company, collecting information on general judicial practice in the main areas of economic activity;
6. Updating the database with the results of inspections of regulatory authorities, recommendations, and measures taken to correct and eliminate weaknesses;
7. Collecting the level of business reputation, investment attractiveness, innovation activity, and planned activities to improve them;
8. Development and implementation of recommendations on the use of neuromarketing methods, techniques of psychotechnics, and other high-tech methods in solving communication problems;
9. Using the results of market research, competitors, analytical materials with the definition of risks, threats, and favorable opportunities in the main areas of activity, studying potential markets, consumer behavior of the company's customers, about the tasks of forming the target audience and communication resources of the company.

4 Conclusion

As the analysis showed, during the transition to the implementation of the IMC system in the company, it is advisable to apply the principle of integration in the form of administration of actions to consolidate the work of various structural divisions within the framework of administrative centralization of the role of marketing departments to form a single communication message of the company. This is largely determined by the possibilities of digitalization, may be labor-intensive, lack of flexibility, and will require rethinking the basics of the administrative management system.

Based on the results of the conducted research, an alternative scheme for managing corporate information flows during the implementation of the IMC in the conditions of digitalization is substantiated and structured, with the coordinating role of the MIS, in which most of the messages sent on behalf of the company to the external environment will be able to be coordinated by the marketing communications system and integrated with the goals and objectives of the company's marketing policy.

The algorithms of "immersion" of communications into IMC management systems in the digital economy are formulated, taking into account the expanded understanding of the integration of MIS into the CIS system, in which not only marketing instruments and communication tools are integrated, but individual communications are also subject to integration. They are formed along the lines of work of each of the company's structural divisions, which allows socially-oriented, consistent, and coordinated messages to be sent to each of the target audience segments. They can contribute to the formation of a single favorable image of the company in each segment of the target audience, despite the fact that such management elements can be organically integrated into the marketing policy and contribute to the achievement of the company's overall goals.

A systematic list of structural elements for managing the corporate information system within the framework of the IMC for the purposes of forming effective communication of the company in the digital economy is substantiated.

An expanded set of organizational and management solutions is proposed to improve the efficiency of communications using the integrated information system of the company, which will allow in practice to optimize management procedures with the achievement of a total positive result of the IMC.

References

Charykova, A. S., & Fedoseeva, E. A. (2017). Digital marketing in determining quality. *Young Scientist, 18*(152), 189–192.

Danko, T. P., & Kitova, O. V. (2013). Issues of digital marketing. *Problems of Modern Economics, 3*(47), 261–265.

Hashimova, D. P. (2021). Analysis and clarification of the basic principles of the formation of marketing information systems. *Economics and Business: Theory and Practice, 5–3*, 157–161.

Ketova, N. P., & Granovskaya, I. Yu. (2020). The opportunities for neuromarketing implementation to enhance the promotion of goods and services to consumers. *Creative Economy, 14*(1), 73–92.

Kretova, N. N. (2008). The use of integrated communications in modern enterprises. *Econominfo, 10*, 72–75.

Lapshin, V. S. (2016). Formation of a sustainable development management system based on an integrative approach. *Models, Systems, Networks in Economics, Technology, Nature and Society, 2*(18), 36–46.

Polyakova, N. V., Topolnyak, E. A., & Orlova, E. G. (2019). Problems of improving the marketing information system of a manufacturing enterprise. *Baikal State University, 2*, 74–81.

Smirnova, E. A. (2020). Trends in the development of marketing communications in 2020–2022. *Bulletin of ChelSU, 10*(444), 203–208.

Stefanova, N. A., & Gostev, D. V. (2019). Issues of development of digital marketing and integrated marketing information systems in the world and in Russia at the present stage. *Actual Issues of Modern Economics, 1*, 9–14.

Zhuravlev, V. A. (2018). Marketing information system of the enterprise in the conditions of digital economy. *Belarusian State University of Informatics and Radioelectronics, 4*(4), 7–8.

Application of Digital Technologies in Organization of Educational Activities During the Pandemic Period

Elena N. Galkina, Artem A. Sirotkin, Svetlana N. Kuznetsova, Elena P. Kozlova, and Olga A. Nemova

Abstract The article discusses the role of the use of digital technologies in educational activities that have developed during the pandemic. The author considered the transition of the education system to a distance learning format for the period 2020–2021. The aim of the study is to examine the stages of using digital technologies in the organization of educational activities during the pandemic, to consider the effectiveness of using digital technologies in the educational process of universities. The analysis of the theoretical study showed that the current situation in educational activities during the pandemic has largely changed the learning process and the preparation of the teacher for classes. Analysis of the data showed that the development of digitalization at this stage is inevitable, educational activities should enter a new stage in the development of digitalization of education. The author noted the development of network technologies in the education system, which create a sociocultural environment in human life, in which many participants interact with each other using a large number of devices, technologies and services, where digitalization is the basis. The conclusion that the development of digital technologies in educational activities today is necessary and is an effective process was made in the process of justification.

Keywords Digital technology · Distance learning · Pandemic · University · Efficiency

JEL Classification R11 · R12 · R 58 · Q13 · Q18

E. N. Galkina (✉)
Institute of Food Technologies and Design—A Branch of State University of Engineering and Economics, Nizhny Novgorod, Russia
e-mail: galkinaelena2205@gmail.com

A. A. Sirotkin
The Branch of the Samara State Transport University, Nizhny Novgorod, Russia

S. N. Kuznetsova · E. P. Kozlova · O. A. Nemova
Minin Nizhny Novgorod State Pedagogical University, Nizhny Novgorod, Russia

E. I. Lazareva et al. (eds.), *Innovative Trends in International Business and Sustainable Management*, Approaches to Global Sustainability, Markets, and Governance,
https://doi.org/10.1007/978-981-19-4005-7_19

1 Introduction

The educational system today in the period of the coronavirus is experiencing a great demand for an increase in the use of digital technologies and resources in the educational process (Andreev, 2013; Feskova, 2013; Lizunkov et al., 2021).

The transition of the education system to a distance learning format has become the most popular trend for the period 2020–2021. There is an increasing demand for the application and development of online courses. At the same time, the availability of electronic courses for mastering certain knowledge is not enough; it is necessary to develop new educational platforms using digital technologies (Garina et al., 2017, 2020a, 2020b, 2021; Gribanov & Shatrov, 2019; Kozlova et al., 2020).

The period of development of digitalization of educational activities during the pandemic can be attributed to a large-scale educational experiment in the history of the twenty-first century, which covered all educational structures: kindergartens, schools, colleges, universities and the system of additional education (Sedykh, 2019).

In this situation, the coronavirus demanded a massive transition from the digital transformation of educational institutions to the adaptation of classes in the online environment.

2 Methodology

The country's education system during the pandemic and the transition to online showed positive results, although the provision of digital technologies and the forced digital literacy of teachers were at low level.

The purpose of this study is to consider the stages of using digital technologies in the organization of educational activities during the pandemic, to consider the effectiveness of using digital technologies in the educational process of universities.

56 students from Nizhny Novgorod took part in this study. The survey on the effectiveness of the use of digital technologies in educational activities was conducted.

The situation associated with the pandemic will lead the education system to an increase in the growth of work on digital educational platforms, which have proven themselves well both on the part of the educator and on the part of the learners (Sirotkin, 2021).

It should be noted that the situation in 2020 gave, among other things, a serious impetus to the development of psychological and pedagogical science and the growth of its role in the development of the information technology industry. It became obvious that the further development of education is impossible without serious scientific research.

3 Results

Three main stages can be distinguished when examining the development of digital education in universities during the pandemic:

The first stage is spring 2020. At this stage, the education system was carried out by moving from a classroom-lesson form to a remote format using digital technologies such as Skype, Viber and a group in «VKontakte».

The second stage of the 2020–2021 academic year is characterized by more extensive use of digital technologies in educational activities, which provide a variety of interaction. Newer forms and types of activities of participants in educational relations began to be applied.

In this period, there is an increase in the development of information technologies that integrate traditional learning models into a new technological environment, and the purpose of such technologies is to improve the process and results of students through new technologies that make learning more accessible, high-quality, effective and comfortable for a person.

It would seem that mankind has passed on knowledge from generation to generation for many centuries. However, the field of education is still not perfect.

Many problems exist in many countries: insufficient efficiency, untimely updating of curricula and inaccessibility for students with disabilities.

New technologies have made it possible to find new solutions to these problems. The educational technology industry is looking for such solutions.

The third stage (2022–2023) is the stage of development and planning of the use of innovative digital technologies in educational activities, such as the introduction of robotic devices, the development of virtual information programs and, of course, the development of educational relations between the learning teacher and the family.

It is necessary to note the development of network technologies in the education system. Such technologies create a sociocultural environment in human life, in which many participants interact with each other using a large number of devices, technologies and services, where digitalization is the basis.

Network technologies include.

- comfortable communication, interaction at any convenient time and place, etc.
- obtaining any information and knowledge.

The development of digitalization leads to social changes in human psychological processes. Today, we observe that the development of network technologies has significantly changed the personality within the network process, and at the same time, we are just beginning to study the social, psychological environment of the network personality.

The demand in the development of a networked personality determines the state of the educational environment of the learning process: the formation of new requirements, methods and forms of learning, the application and development of information content using a network process that combines real and virtual space.

Such development requires a new approach to the organization of the educational process, reflecting the network development of the educational process: online learning and distance learning.

Based on the results of organizing the learning process at the first two stages, the following can be distinguished:

1. Online learning is becoming more and more possible and accessible in the educational environment of universities. Constant demands of the labor market are constantly increasing, while the need for continuous training is increasing.
2. The assessment of effectiveness in the educational process is being revised.
3. The new competence of the network personality is the ability to learn, self-organization and self-education.
4. One of the most important results, from our point of view, is a new format of interaction between educational organizations and families (this is directly related to the growth and new understanding of the social status of teachers).
5. Development of service systems, digital educational platforms as a tool for educational activities of the future.

As part of the study, we examined the effectiveness of the use of digital technologies in the educational process of universities in the process of research. The concept of training efficiency is considered as the concept of the quality of training in the process of organizing training activities during the pandemic. The process of effectiveness is associated with the achievement of educational and educative goals that require socioeconomic conditions in the organization of the learning process. The main criteria for the effectiveness of the use of digital technologies in universities are the following:

- differentiation of the learning process;
- the use of different organizational forms of training;
- completeness of content and teaching methods.

E-learning is one of the more widespread digital technologies during the pandemic. This training format is used in many universities. Electronic courses are being developed in disciplines using various information technologies. The following directions of the process can be distinguished for assessing the effectiveness of e-learning:

- achievement of educational results in accordance with the Federal State Educational Standard;
- increasing the motivation of students to the learning process;
- assessment of the impact of the developed courses on teaching methods and on the competitiveness of graduates.

The most common way to determine the effectiveness of training is a questionnaire. We have developed a number of questions on all aspects of the organization of the educational process in universities, such as.

- are teaching aids used effectively;

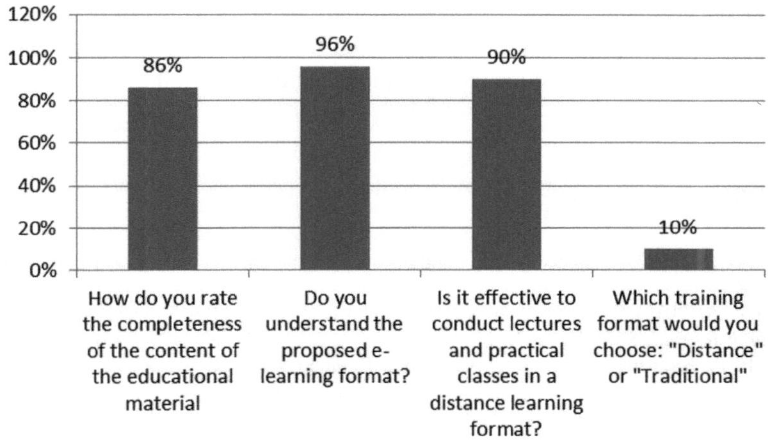

Fig. 1 Result of the survey of university students in Nizhny Novgorod. *Source* Compiled by the author

- how do you assess the quality of the e-course and the teaching methodology;
- the nature of the use of hardware and software.

Based on the results of the survey, the following conclusion can be drawn: Among most of the surveyed students, 86% noted the completeness of the content of the proposed educational material for all types of proposed tasks in the electronic course, for 96% of the surveyed students, the proposed material was clear and studied independently, 90% of students noted the effectiveness of lecture and practical training with the use of information technology, and 10% noted that the distance learning format is worse than the traditional form of education (Fig. 1).

The study was confirmed by the effectiveness of the use of digital technologies in educational activities during the pandemic.

4 Conclusion

Thus, today we see a strong growth in the use of digital technologies in educational activities. Research on the development of the digitalization process in universities has the highest rate, and this is obvious, because the situation associated with the pandemic gives us a chance in the development of education of the future—the introduction of new technologies, the development of new service programs and online learning without losing the quality of mastering knowledge. The educational activity of universities defines a new stage in the formation of a blended learning process or learning on demand.

After the pandemic, university teachers will be more active in mastering new digital educational platforms, and the demand for a teacher as a mentor who will teach and work on new solutions to educational activities will increase.

References

Andreev, A. A. (2013). Distance learning and distance educational technologies. *Open Education, 5*, 40–46.

Feskova, A. A. (2013). On the problem of increasing students' motivation for learning. *International Research Journal, 3–4*(23), 11–13.

Garina, E. P., Kuznetsov, V. P., Egorova, A. O., Romanovskaya, E. V., & Garin, A. P. (2017). Practice in the application of the production system tools at the enterprise during mastering of new products. In *Contributions to Economics* (No. 9783319606958, pp. 105–112).

Garina, E., Kuznetsov, V., Garin, A., Andryashina, N., & Romanovskaya, E. (2020a). Controlling as an instrument of industrial enterprise management in the conditions of modern economic activity. In *Lecture Notes in Networks and Systems* (T. 87, No. 11, p. 555).

Garina, E. P., Romanovskaya, E. V., Andryashina, N. S., Kuznetsov, V. P., & Shpilevskaya, E. V. (2020b). Organizational and economic foundations of the management of the investment programs at the stage of their implementation. In *Lecture Notes in Networks and Systems* (Vol. 91, pp. 163–169).

Garina, E. P., Romanovskaya, E. V., Andryashina, N. S., Kuznetsov, V. P., & Tsymbalov, S. D. (2021). Methodology for creating a product development system based on complexity management strategy. In: *Socio-economic Systems: Paradigms for the Future. Studies in Systems, Decision and Control* (pp. 1661–1669). Springer International Publishing.

Gribanov Yu, I., & Shatrov, A. A. (2019) Essence, content and role of digital transformation in the development of economic systems. *Bulletin of the Altai Academy of Economics and Law, 3*, 44–48.

Kozlova, E. P., Kuznetsov, V. P., Garina, E. P., Romanovskaya, E. V., & Andryashina, N. S. (2020). Methodological bases of the assessment of sustainable development of industrial enterprises (technological approach). In *The Century from the Positions of Modern Science: Intellectual, Digital and Innovative Aspects. Lecture Notes in Networks and Systems (LNNS 91)* (pp. 670–679).

Lizunkov, V. G., Morozova, M. V., Zakharova, A. A., & Malushko, E. Yu. (2021). *On the Issue of Criteria for the Effectiveness of Interaction Between Educational Organizations and Enterprises of the Real Sector of the Economy in the Conditions of Advanced Development Territories*. Vestnik of Minin University (Vol. 9, No. 1).

Sedykh, E. P. (2019). *System of Normative Legal Support of Project Management in Education*. Vestnik of Minin University (Vol. 7, No. 1, 26p).

Sirotkin, A. A. (2021). Master class «Digitalization of supply chain management». In *Actual Problems of Modern Economy: Materials of the IX International Scientific and Practical Conference: In 2 Parts. Omsk State University of Railway Transport. Omsk, Part 1* (pp. 253–259).

Modern Digital Communications as Pedagogical Tools in the Organization of Project Activities of the Educational Process

Zhanna V. Smirnova, Elena A. Kostyleva, Elena V. Romanovskaya, Natalia S. Andryashina, and Sergey D. Tsymbalov

Abstract This article discusses the organization of project activities of students using modern pedagogical tools. The author carried out a study in the field of organizing students' project activities using information platforms. The analysis of modern pedagogical tools for organizing the project activities of students was carried out. The criteria of modern educational resources are considered. A survey was conducted on the choice of a platform for placing an electronic course on the organization of project activities of students and for work in general. A brief description and possibilities of using the CORE educational platform were given. The conclusion of the study is that such an organization of project activities will allow diversifying the forms of education, will enable the student to independently study the material, to seek information and create a new product. The teacher needs to monitor the progress of the Lessons by the students and to monitor the percentage of correct answers that will affect the grade. The organization of project activities with the use of modern tools will diversify the forms of education, give the student the opportunity to independently study the material, search for information and create a new product.

Keywords Project activities · Pedagogical tools · Learner · Student · E-course · Platform

JEL Classification R11 · R12 · R58 · Q13 · Q18

Z. V. Smirnova (✉) · E. V. Romanovskaya · N. S. Andryashina · S. D. Tsymbalov
Minin Nizhny Novgorod State Pedagogical University, Nizhny Novgorod, Russia
e-mail: z.v.smirnova@mininuniver.ru

E. A. Kostyleva
Institute of Food Technologies and Design—A Branch of State University of Engineering and Economics, Nizhny Novgorod, Russia

E. I. Lazareva et al. (eds.), *Innovative Trends in International Business and Sustainable Management*, Approaches to Global Sustainability, Markets, and Governance,
https://doi.org/10.1007/978-981-19-4005-7_20

1 Introduction

The relevance of the topic is associated with trends in the socio-technical development of our country, an increase in the role of the human factor in all spheres of activity, the ability to show the acquired knowledge in the class in life. The use of modern pedagogical tools in the educational process allows to develop the cognitive activity of students in class and after school hours, allows to diversify the forms of work, to intensify the activities of students, to increase the attention and creative potential of the individual.

In modern society, where knowledge, the level of intellectual and creative potential is becoming a rather demanded resource and the most important factor in the successful development of an individual, the status of education is significantly increasing, new requirements are imposed on its level and quality. Each person needs certain thinking skills and personality traits, the ability to analyze, to compare, to highlight the main thing, to solve a problem, the ability for self-improvement and the ability to give adequate self-esteem, to be responsible, independent, to be able to create and cooperate.

2 Methodology

Trends in the improvement of educational technologies in accordance with the Federal State Educational Standard (hereinafter FSES) characterize the transition from learning as the assimilation of a set of knowledge to learning as a process of mental development aimed at using the acquired material (Federal State Educational Standard of Primary General Education, 2009). Therefore, it is very important to flexibly and effectively present educational material, especially to organize project work effectively, regardless of the form of organization of the educational process.

Future teachers need not only to tell and show everything in an accessible way, but also to teach pupils to think, to instill practical skills through electronic educational resources. The problem of using modern tools in teaching remains one of the urgent problems in pedagogical, psychological science and in educational practice. Such scientists as Kalitin (2013), Bayborodova (2016), Lazarev (2017), who consider a teaching tool—a computer, dealt with the use of modern teaching tools. It turns out that our topic is relevant.

Today, the issues of using an electronic educational resource in educational activities, the impact of EER on the quality of the formation of students' competencies are actively discussed in educational activities.

In this article, we also touch upon the issue of the use of EER as a modern tool for a teacher of the twenty-first century.

The scientific novelty of this article is due to the fact that the author theoretically substantiated the methodological development of organizing the learning process using the electronic platform of the CORE educational system (Bayborodova, 2016; Bykovsky et al., 2014).

The purpose of this article is a theoretical justification for the organization of project activities based on the CORE platform.

The main tasks are:

1. To study the theoretical foundations of the organization of project activities of students in educational institutions and to analyze modern pedagogical tools.
2. To consider the features of using the CORE electronic platform in the lesson.

The set research tasks are solved using the following methods:

1. theoretical: the study of literature, accompanied by the compilation of bibliography, abstracting, citing, as well as theoretical analysis using systematization, synthesis, generalization, classification;
2. practical: the study of the products of students' activities; analysis (graphics, works, drawings, abstracts), which gives information about the achieved level of knowledge and skills of students; the study of school documentation (class journals, student diaries, calendar-thematic plans), which gives data on the actual practice of organizing project activities.

The novelty of the work and the theoretical significance lie in the theoretical substantiation of the methodological foundations of organizing technology lessons using the electronic platform of the CORE educational system.

The practical significance lies in the development of the electronic course on organizing work on a project, methodological recommendations that can be used by a technology teacher when using electronic platforms to create courses.

The study involved 34 teachers from four schools in Nizhny Novgorod and 30 students of senior classes.

3 Results

The modern pedagogical tools of the teacher include technical teaching aids. Technical teaching aids are a system of means, consisting of two interrelated parts: specific teaching aids (information carriers) and equipment with the help of which information containing a certain didactic manual can be presented. Technical teaching aids are equipment and apparatus used in the educational process in order to increase its efficiency (Kulikova, 2015; Lazarev, 2017).

If we consider modern teaching aids, then the most effective impact on students is provided by audiovisual and multimedia teaching aids, which include electronic educational resources. In modern conditions, educational resources such as interactive whiteboards, electronic textbooks, educational websites and web quests are at the stage of development and application (Malushko & Lizunkov, 2020).

As a result of the study of the organization of project activities of students using modern pedagogical tools, a survey of school teachers in Nizhny Novgorod

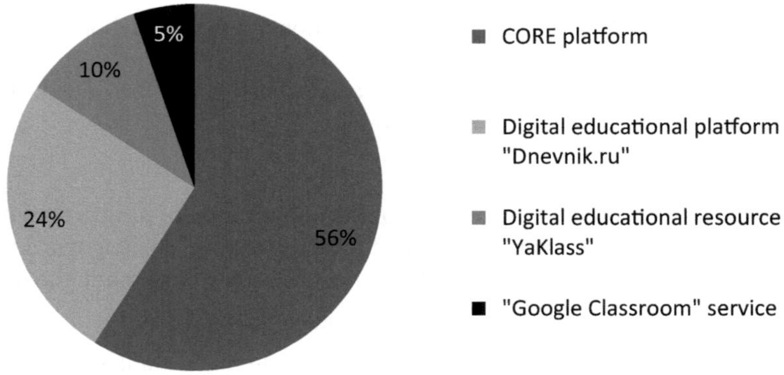

Fig. 1 The choice of platforms for organizing the project activities of students. *Source* Developed and compiled by the authors

on the choice of a platform for placing electronic courses as a pedagogical tool for conducting the educational process by discipline was carried out. Most of the respondents chose the CORE platform (Fig. 1).

The main advantage of the chosen CORE platform lies in the following indicators: fast communication speed, adaptability, an understandable constructor of online lessons, the possibility of automated assessment of students' work. The teacher can create any number of lessons using modern pedagogical approaches and use project-oriented forms of education (Gruzdeva & Tukenova, 2019; Kostyleva et al., 2021).

The main page of the CORE platform looks simple and concise. The main buttons are at the top. Getting to the home page, the developers focused on the phrase by which the user understands the purpose of the platform and the possibilities (creating webinars, courses, live lessons, conferences and special projects) (Deulina et al., 2021).

In the course of the research, instructions were developed for using the platform, starting with registration and ending with the creation of a course (Chaikina et al., 2021).

Research work on the organization of project activities of students using the CORE platform will consist in the formation of skills for mastering the project competencies of students working in the CORE platform.

The teachers of schools in Nizhny Novgorod developed the themes of design work in the subject area Technology for the preparation of testing the work of students. The usual subsections of the online course are created on the platform using available templates. Blanks for material placement are perfect as, for example, an information stage, diagnostics, final test, preliminary material before training, feedback from students on the results of the course, a platform for students to place homework and conduct test (Rudenko et al., 2021; Voronova et al., 2021).

Thus, the prepared material for the course will facilitate the teacher's work.

The result of the work on the project activities of students will be the formation of self-control skills of students of the senior classes (8–10) on the design of a presentation to present the result.

Self-esteem allows a person to see strengths and weaknesses and to build a program for further actions. The whole essence of evaluative activity, which the teacher sets out before evaluating it, should be disclosed to the student.

To evaluate the completed design work on one of the topics of the Technology lesson, assessment options were proposed:

1st level—the task was completed correctly, all conditions were taken into account.
2nd level—3 to 4 conditions were taken into account when completing the assignment.
3rd level—2 conditions were taken into account when completing the assignment.
4th level—no more than one condition was taken into account when completing the assignment.

Figure 2 shows the results of the levels of formation of the methods of educational activity.

Low level—the degree of the student's awareness of the importance and the need for control is manifested only if the teacher sets such a task—5 people (11%), medium level was shown by students, for whom the object of control (the result of the activity or its process) is extremely insignificant—11 people (61%), high level among students, the ratio of control in any situation requiring the purposefulness of its manifestation, as well as in cases where the task of control is not set—5 people (28%).

Thus, we can conclude that such an organization of project activities will diversify the forms of education, give a student the opportunity to independently study the material, to seek information and to create a new product. The teacher needs to

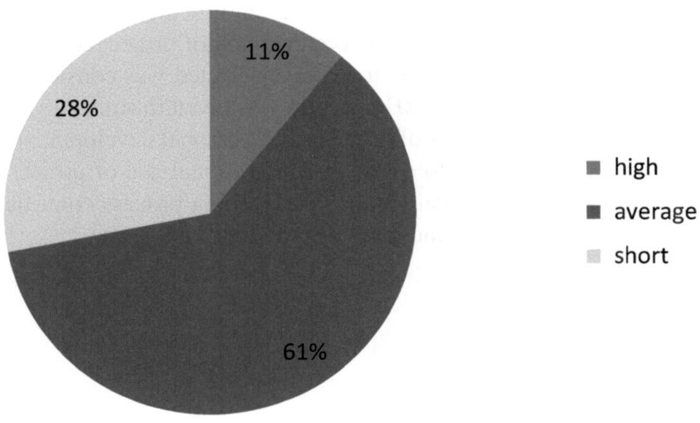

Fig. 2 Level of self-control skills formation. *Source* Developed and compiled by the authors

monitor the progress of the students in the lessons and to monitor the percentage of correct answers that will affect the grade.

4 Conclusion

The works of many scientists, teachers were studied in the process. Innovative pedagogical technologies can be combined in project activities, this increases the quality of knowledge, contributes to the formation of creative and cognitive abilities, prepares for real life conditions. Project activity in the subject «Technology» puts each student in the position of an active participant, makes it possible to realize individual creative ideas, and forms the ability to search for information.

The project method is a flexible model of the organization of the educational process, focused on the development of students and their self-realization in activities. It promotes the development of observation and the desire to find explanations for observations, teaches to ask questions and find answers to them, and then to check the correctness of answers by analyzing the information.

Using a computer as a modern tool provides teachers and students with new unique opportunities related to the interactivity of electronic learning platforms. The opportunity to save lesson time while increasing the amount of information and using visual material appears when a computer is operatively combined with other teaching aids.

Implementation of the project method in practice leads to a change in the teacher's position. He turns from a bearer of ready-made knowledge into a tutor in the cognitive activity of his students.

It was revealed that the CORE platform is a modern pedagogical toolkit that meets the latest requirements. In the course of the work, methodological recommendations on the preparation and placement of educational and methodological material for a technology teacher were developed, the organization of project activities of technology students according to the section we have selected was considered, and the approximate guide on using the CORE platform was given to students.

Thus, project activity is a means of learning and personal development. Learning using the project method allows to assert that the rational use of project activities with the use of modern pedagogical tools in the learning process contributes to the development of creative abilities and learning activity of students.

References

Bayborodova, L. V. (2016). *Project Activities of Schoolchildren in Different Age Groups: Guide for Teachers of Educational Organizations* (156 p).

Bykovsky, V. V., Mishchenko, E. S., Bykovskaya, E. V., et al. (2014). *Management of Innovative Projects and Programs: Tutorial*. Publishing House State Educational Institution of Higher Professional Education «Dagestan State Pedagogical University» (104 p)

Chaikina, Z. V., Mukhina, M. V., Kostylev, D. S., & Lukina, O. A. (2021). Integration of general and additional education as a factor in the successful vocational guidance of students. *Bulletin of Pedagogical Sciences, 1*, 193–198.

Deulina, S. A., Shvetsova Yu, V., & Chaikina, Z. V. (2021). Project management in the system of additional education for children. In *The Collection: Modern Approaches to the Transformation of the Concepts of State Regulation and Management in Socio-economic Systems. Collection of Scientific Papers of the 10th International Scientific and Practical Conference dedicated to the Year of Science and Technology in the Russian Federation, Kursk* (pp. 127–131).

Federal State Educational Standard of Primary General Education (approved by order of the Ministry of Education and Science of Russia dated October 6, 2009 No. 373, as amended by orders dated November 26, 2010 No. 1241, dated September 22, 2011 No. 2357).

Gruzdeva, M. L., & Tukenova, N. I. (2019). *Analysis of the Current State of Research and Development in the Field of Building Information and Educational Environments of Higher Educational Institutions*. Vestnik of Minin University (Vol. 7. No. 2 (27), p. 1).

Kalitin S. V. (2013). *Interactive Board. The Practice of Effective Use in Schools, Colleges and Universities: Tutorial*. Solon-Press (192 p).

Kostyleva, E. A., Smirnova, Z. V., & Kutepova, L. I. (2021). Organization of project activities of students in the system of additional education. *Problems of Modern Pedagogical Education, 70–4*, 195–198.

Kulikova, G. S. (2015). The influence of internet communications on other spheres of communication. *Problems of Speech Communication, 5*, 54–57.

Lazarev, V. S. (2017). *Project Activities at School: Textbook for Students in Grades 7–11*. Surgut, RIO SurGPU (135 p).

Malushko, E. Y., & Lizunkov, V. G. (2020). *The e-Education System as a Tool to Increase the Competitiveness of a Specialist in the Digital Economy*. Vestnik of Minin University (Vol. 8, No. 2).

Rudenko, I. V., Bystrova, N. V., Smirnova, Z. V., Vaganova, O. I., & Kutepov, M. M. (2021). Modern technologies in working with gifted students. *PROPOSITOS Y REPRESENTACIONES* (Vol. 9), January 2021. https://doi.org/10.20511/pyr2021.v9nSPE1.818

Voronova, E. M., Lapshova, A. V., Bystrova, N. V., Smirnova, Z. V., & Bulaeva, M. N. (2021). Organization of virtual interaction in the context of the coronavirus pandemic. *PROPOSITOS Y REPRESENTACIONES* (Vol. 9), January 2021. https://doi.org/10.20511/pyr2021.v9nSPE1.820

Priorities of Sustainable Smart Campus Management

Xiaowen Zhang

Abstract With the development of technology and network, the world has entered the era of big data. Smart education is the product of economic globalization, technological change, and knowledge explosion. It is also an inevitable stage of the development of educational informatization. Wisdom education is a new realm and demand for educational informatization. It needs to take the intelligent learning environment as the technical support, the intelligent learning as the fundamental cornerstone, and the intelligent teaching method as the catalyst. As an inevitable stage of the development of educational informatization, the construction of its sustainable development ability is an important means to promote the sustainable development ability of educational informatization. This paper focuses on the research and overview of the current situation and challenges of the sustainable development of smart campus management.

Keywords Smart campus management · Smart education · Education informatization · Sustainable development

JEL Classification R01 · F22 · F63

1 Introduction

Since the new century, while information technology is changing production and people's lifestyle, it is also causing more profound comprehensive reform and innovation of the education system (Anopchenko, 2016; Lazareva, 2013). Information technology has gradually changed the traditional teaching and learning mode, promoted the comprehensive reform of teaching ideas, methods, tools, contents, and evaluation, helped create a new learning environment, and promoted the comprehensive

X. Zhang (✉)
Henan University of Economics and Law, Henan, China
e-mail: skyof45_gg@qq.com

Southern Federal University, Rostov-on-Don, Russia

E. I. Lazareva et al. (eds.), *Innovative Trends in International Business and Sustainable Management*, Approaches to Global Sustainability, Markets, and Governance,
https://doi.org/10.1007/978-981-19-4005-7_21

innovation of education and teaching. Educational informatization has become the only way to realize educational modernization and build a learning society. With the initial scale of educational information infrastructure and the gradual formation of a digital educational resource system, the construction of educational informatization has entered the stage of application integration from the initial stage, and the development focus of educational informatization has shifted from building a basic platform to deepening application and promoting change. The status of the capacity for sustainable development of educational informatization has gradually become prominent and has become a core content of great significance in the construction of educational informatization.

In 2008, P. Mingsheng, President and CEO of IBM, in his speech entitled "The interpretation of the smart earth and the smart city," for the first time put forward the concept of "smart earth." Once the concept of "smart earth" was put forward, it attracted great attention from all walks of life in the world (Yongmin, 2010). After the concept of "smart earth" was put forward, many domestic and foreign scholars put forward the concept of "smart campus"; some scholars even pointed out the construction ideas of smart campus with advanced ideas (Ping et al., 2010). As an inevitable stage of the development of educational informatization, the construction of its sustainable development ability is an important means to promote the sustainable development ability of educational informatization. What are the deficiencies of constructing a smart campus at this stage, and how to rectify these deficiencies form the focus of this study?

2 Materials and Methods

In China, dozens of colleges and universities such as Southwest University, Chengdu University, and Tongji University gradually began planning and constructing a smart campus; the smart campus no longer stays at the conceptual level (Dongming, 2011). For example, the 12th Five Year Plan for informatization of Zhejiang University proposes to build an "exciting" smart campus, which supports ubiquitous network learning, integrated and innovative network scientific research, transparent and efficient school governance, rich and colorful campus culture, and convenient and thoughtful campus life (Yingjun, 2010). Nanjing University of Posts and Telecommunications has finished a relatively complete smart campus planning (Hongbo et al., 2011) and believes that the core characteristics of a smart campus are mainly reflected in three levels:

1. It provides a comprehensive intelligent perception environment and comprehensive information service platform for teachers and students and provides personalized role-based customized services;
2. It integrates the information service based on computer network into various application and service fields of the school to realize interconnection and cooperation;

3. Through an intelligent perception environment and comprehensive information service platform, it provides a mutual communication and perception interface between the school and the outside world.

This research studies and summarizes the current situation and challenges of the sustainable development of smart campus management through case analysis and literature analysis.

In terms of theoretical research, different scholars interpret the connotation of a smart campus from multiple angles. H. Ronghuai puts forward the "four generations" construction concept of a digital campus from the perspective of the construction process. He believes that the fourth-generation digital campus (smart campus) can effectively support teaching and learning, enrich the campus culture of the school, truly expand the space–time dimension of the school, take the service-oriented concept as the basis, and build business processes, resource sharing, and intelligent and flexible education and teaching environment (Ronghuai et al., 2012). Some researchers emphasize the role of Internet of Things technology in constructing a smart campus. For example, S. Jie and others believe that a smart campus is a unique campus system that organically integrates people, equipment, environment, resources, and social factors in the context of informatization. It is based on the Internet of Things and focuses on the relevance of information, provides a timely two-way communication platform through multiplatform information transmission means, in short, a more intelligent school (Jie & Yuxing, 2010). Z. Tong and others believe that a smart campus is an intelligent environment for integrating work, learning, and campus life based on the Internet of Things. This integration environment takes various application service systems as the carrier to fully integrate teaching, scientific research, management, and campus life (Tong & Wen, 2011). L. Chunruo believes that a smart campus is the specific application of the Internet of Things in school teaching management, public security, and logistics support, building an intelligent learning and living environment for the school (Chunruo, 2012).

Some researchers believe that a smart campus is a comprehensive application of various technologies. They believe that a smart campus is to make full use of information-related technologies, integrate various functional departments of the school, integrate and optimize existing resources, provide higher quality teaching and better services, and build a green environment and harmonious campus through monitoring, analysis, integration, and intelligent response to ensure the sustainable development of school education. Some researchers believe that the construction of a smart campus is not only the application of the Internet of Things but also a part of perception. We should give more consideration to the characteristics of technology and highlight applications and services (Yong, 2011).

To sum up, a smart campus is an artificial campus that makes full use of various high technologies. A smart campus refers to open education and teaching environment and a convenient and comfortable living environment with the concept of personalized service for teachers and students, which can fully perceive the physical environment, identify learners' individual characteristics and learning situations, provide seamless network communication, and effectively support teaching process analysis, evaluation, and intelligent decision-making (Ronghuai et al., 2012).

3 Results

A smart campus is the extension of educational informatization. Simultaneously, the sustainable development ability of a smart campus is regarded as an important support to ensure the sustainable and rapid development of educational informatization in China; it plays a supporting role in the whole system of development of educational informatization. Its composition mainly includes an educational technology training system, an educational informatization research support system, a reserve talent training system, and an educational informatization standard system. In the ten-year development plan for educational informatization (2011–2020) issued by the Ministry of Education in 2012, the content of capacity-building for sustainable development of educational informatization is clearly explained, including the following:

1. The implementation of educational ability and technical training for informatization personnel at all levels and in all types of schools. This is an important way to truly integrate information technology into the teaching process and promote educational reform.
2. Promote Yingchuan education informatization standard. Standardizing standard indicators such as technology, management, and evaluation, it will guide the construction of educational informatization in the future.
3. Establish the support system, research, and service system of an information-based campus, carry out innovative experimental research and technology development of independent intellectual property rights and provide technical support and sustainable development power for the innovative application.
4. Strengthen the training ability of reserve talents for educational informatization. By setting up a series of courses and building a special talent training base, we will cultivate a number of research teams and practical talents leading the development of the industry (Fig. 1).

Systematically identifying and evaluating the state of the sustainable development of a smart campus and correcting and improving the construction of a smart campus based on comprehensive evaluation became an important part of building a smart campus based on sustainability potential. Given the exploration of the sustainable development of a smart campus in colleges and universities, this paper takes South China Normal University and Jiangsu Business Vocational and Technical College as examples to explore and analyze the sustainable development of a smart campus in colleges and universities.

1. South China Normal University

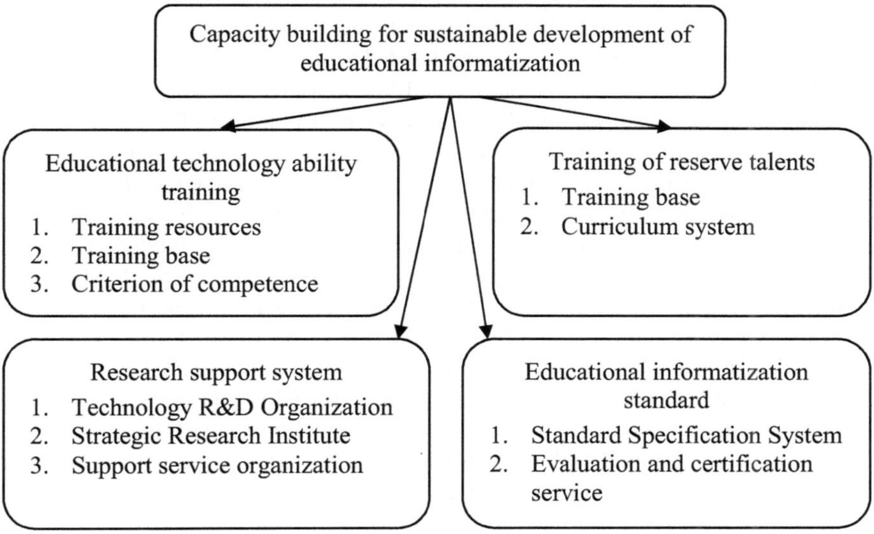

Fig. 1 Constituent elements of sustainable development ability of educational informatization. *Source* Developed by the author

From relevant research by H. Qintai and other scholars, it can be seen that South China Normal University independently developed various basic service platforms for applications, including an information portal, data center, and unified identity authentication, to ensure the overall construction of the project and the integrated service quality. Simultaneously, the school independently develops a campus service platform system composed of comprehensive services for teachers and students, campus mobile services and WeChat enterprise services, actively explores personal data services under the background of campus big data, takes service as the guidance, promotes the integration of management services, and provides strong support for promoting the modernization of campus governance. Additionally, the school has built a "one meter one" service platform, electronic identity registration center, and other systems to meet the increasingly personalized and diverse information service needs of teachers and students. The school develops a "cloud classroom" online teaching platform suitable for the actual teaching application of the school, providing "one-stop" services for teaching and learning resources and processes, focusing on the construction and application of the "cloud classroom," setting up teaching informatization development and maintenance team and support service team and constantly exploring the deep integration of information technology and education and teaching (Qintai et al., 2018).

After five years of exploration of educational informatization pilot work, the school has made many achievements. H. Qintai and others reported the changes in South China Normal University in recent five years. The basic conditions of the campus network have been updated, the export bandwidth of the campus network was expanded by 15g, more than 13,000 wireless hotspots were built, and the full coverage of the campus wireless network was completed. The information cloud platform has more than 1600 CPU cores, 7.3t memory, and 1362t storage, carrying more than 500 information applications. The basic software support platform of a smart campus has been developed systematically, seven basic software support platforms have been built, more than 30 information systems have been connected, and the amount of data integrated into the data center is nearly 500g. There are 300 courses on the teaching information platform, 271 online teachers, and 8236 students using the platform for online learning. It has three public information service platforms, 22 software development team members, 23 innovative applications, and 13 patents and software copyrights. It provides more than 150 "one-stop" information services. The network and information security system has been gradually established. Based on the independently developed website group, more than 130 campus websites have been transformed and relocated, and six security competition awards have been won. It has implemented more than 100 "National Training Plan" projects of the Ministry of Education, built more than 1600 "teacher workshops," benefited more than 100,000 teachers, and uploaded more than 30,000 micro-courses in various workshops and 15,000 mobile learning micro-courses.

2. Jiangsu Business Vocational and Technical College

Combined with the current diversified needs and future development trends, Jiangsu Business Vocational College aims to promote the construction of a new smart campus in colleges and universities. It has made remarkable achievements in constructing hardware infrastructure, a basic platform, and a business system (Xi, 2018).

In the report on the construction of the smart campus of Jiangsu Vocational College of Commerce and Trade, W. Xin pointed out that in addition to the upgrading of hardware infrastructure, the educational institution also vigorously promoted the full campus wireless coverage project to realize full wireless coverage of teaching and living areas (Xin, 2020). The newly built wireless networks are all pure 10 GB networks, meeting the future network development trend. It includes conference rooms, lecture halls, administrative office areas, classrooms, and other areas in the teaching area, and the living area includes a canteen, a playground, an outdoor leisure area, and other areas.

The university also promotes the construction of a campus unified information standard, a unified identity authentication platform, a unified information portal platform, a unified data center platform, and a unified communication platform. The data of the whole digital campus are encoded according to unified standards to realize the interconnection between school data and industry data. The information platform integrates distributed and heterogeneous information resources and provides an integrated environment that supports information access, transmission, and cooperation. Moreover, it ensures the standardization and unification of campus information, unifies the whole school based on code and basic information, and realizes the data interconnection of various business systems. This information platform allows building a safe, reliable, convenient, technologically advanced, standardized, unified, and flexible data center platform to provide more convenient and efficient services for school teaching, scientific research, and management, as well as building a more open digital living environment for school personnel, building a unified communication platform at the school level, fully implementing the summary of message reminders of various business systems, and sending relevant information to individuals through letters, SMS, e-mail, etc.

The report also covers the intellectual construction of a school to protect the environment. Based on the goal of building a paperless school office, it is necessary to integrate the office elements of various school departments and apply and approve all daily businesses and required forms in the OA system to realize the rapid construction and online use of businesses. The educational administration system covers all links of educational administration management, involving 12 aspects (teaching plan, schedule arrangement, teaching resources, elective courses, teaching management, textbook management, homework management, score management, examination management, evaluation management, student status management, and thesis management) to realize the interconnection between educational administration data and other business system data on campus. It provides a high-quality data basis for analyzing the overall school situation. The student work management system realizes many functions, such as student learning information management, orientation management, registration management, reward, punishment, loan assistance and attendance management, tuition fee reduction management, school departure management, "168" love student pairing, insurance management, comprehensive evaluation management, moral education practice course, dormitory management, pre-employment management, etc. Simultaneously, it provides services to users through the web and provides corresponding interfaces, seamless connection with the new smart campus platform, and data sharing with other business systems. The personnel research management system realizes the management of daily affairs, such as basic information management, further education, training management, contract management, recruitment management, and professional title declaration of the university staff. It implements many functions such as scientific research project declaration, online approval, expert review, and scientific research statistics.

With the advent of the era of "Internet + education," the traditional concept and mode of "Digital Campus" cannot meet the development needs of teachers and students for the rapid growth of information technology. The support and driving role of information technology in the various schools' work and education social services is difficult to highlight; the smart campus is the inevitable stage of the development of educational informatization. The construction of its sustainable development ability is an important means to promote the sustainable development ability of educational informatization. In the construction process, the smart campus still has problems such as low efficiency, low coordination, and low humanization in content construction, organization management, and user experience, which considerably affects the process of building the sustainable development capacity of the smart campus (Peng, 2016). It is mainly reflected in the following four aspects.

First, nowadays, there is a problem of insufficient information content in the construction of the smart campus in colleges and universities, and the information level needs to be improved. In recent years, colleges and universities in China have actively catered to the current development trend of the times and established a smart campus model based on big data and the Internet. However, due to the influence of factors such as a low level of science and technology and insufficient innovation ability, it is challenging to fundamentally improve the application and use of relevant data and improve the application efficiency of information. Simultaneously, in the process of information integration, processing, and transmission, it still focuses on the one-way operation mode, the accuracy of information is insufficient, and the "wisdom" feature of a smart campus is insufficient (Lin, 2007).

Second, there is a problem with building a closed campus network system at colleges and universities while creating a smart campus. It is necessary to strengthen the exchange of resources of different information, and the construction of the system lacks a certain openness. Colleges and universities are the highest level of education in China's education system. Due to the influence of many people, cumbersome institutions, cumbersome procedures, and other factors, the setting of management systems and service mechanisms at some colleges and universities is also relatively complex, such as all-in-one cards, score queries, and other contents, which need to log in to different platforms to realize the application. Simultaneously, due to the lack of due linkage and interaction between various systems, it is very easy to cause the repeated application of data and hinder the convenient development process of smart campus construction.

The next problem lies in the fact that the process of infrastructure construction lags behind the construction of a smart campus in colleges and universities. Due to the influence of insufficient funding, weak technical force, and imperfect system construction, it is difficult for colleges and universities to provide practical and solid scientific infrastructure for the construction of a smart campus, which further restricts the construction and development of a smart campus and gradually becomes the bottleneck of the development of most colleges and universities. For this reason, a smart campus plays a more important role in the use of most schools, but only the improvement of information management, which is not actually applied to the teaching process.

The last problem is the lack of a strong construction team in building a smart campus in colleges and universities, making it challenging to provide important talent support for constructing a smart campus in colleges and universities. At this stage, most educators and managers in colleges and universities focus on professional knowledge and lack a proper understanding of Internet technology, big data technology, and advanced technology. It is challenging to put forward targeted auxiliary opinions in constructing a smart campus in colleges and universities. Once there are problems in constructing a smart campus, there is no way to start; the construction team with a small number of technicians cannot meet the practical requirements of the current smart campus construction.

In view of these problems, as well as the new opportunities provided by the rapid development of network information technology for educational informatization, the reform of the education and teaching system needs to be deepened and developed continuously; efficient educational informatization also faces new challenges. The construction of a smart campus needs a very objective and rigorous construction strategy.

1. Building an open network system.

It is necessary to build an open characteristic network system and create a cloud-based platform for integrated information sharing for universities, and then promote the construction of a smart campus on the background of Internet Plus. On the one hand, colleges and universities should build an open network system and organically combine traditional media with new media, such as campus apps, WeChat communication platform, and interactive microblog community, so that students can interact online in the open system. Simultaneously, teachers can also use advanced digital information technology and methods to integrate various resources and management processes. The input and query of student test results and teachers' classroom activity are integrated into the network environment, and advanced multimedia technology is applied to build a computer platform that integrates lesson preparation, teaching, and students' listening to improve the quality and efficiency of teaching and save much time for teachers and students. In this way, under the condition of reforming the original teaching system, the personalized needs of students' teaching are greatly improved.

2. Accelerate the process of infrastructure construction.

Compared with other foreign countries, the construction and development of a smart campus in Chinese colleges and universities is relatively slow and started late. As a systemic project, the construction of a smart campus needs to invest a lot of human, financial, and material resources. Therefore, the government, enterprises, education departments, colleges, and universities should attach great importance to it and make important financial and policy support for the construction of a smart campus in colleges and universities, as well as to accelerate the construction of smart campus infrastructure in colleges and universities, and become a booster for innovation and reform in colleges and universities. To improve the level of talent training, we must renew educational ideas and improve educational methods. Educational informatization is a necessary means to promote lifelong education, realize personalized learning, and improve the level of talent training. A new challenge to educational informatization lies in the need to break through various restrictions of the traditional education model in terms of time and space, expand learning channels, innovate learning methods, form a talent training model with an open system, flexible mechanism, interconnected channels, and various choices, and let the learners carry out high-quality and guided learning anytime and anywhere.

3. Build a number of powerful information construction teams.

Colleges and universities should build a group of powerful information construction teams, provide important talent support for constructing a smart campus in the background of Internet Plus, and ensure the development of high-quality talents. As everyone knows, building a high-level smart campus requires matching personnel construction teams. Due to the lack of information talents at universities, universities should establish and improve the mechanism of personnel training and education and carry out publicity and education on information and Internet Plus knowledge for managers and educators (Ding, 2006). Simultaneously, colleges and universities can introduce IT talents with high quality to serve the construction of a smart campus to guide the construction of information teams in colleges and universities toward the direction of structural optimization.

4 Conclusion

Colleges and universities should take knowledge innovation and technological innovation as the core and improve the overall level of the school as the main goal, further strengthen scientific and technological work, and actively promote the transformation of achievements and the development of high-tech industries. With the development of scientific research, it is necessary to improve the quality of education and teaching, the academic level, and academic status, as well as to promote the comprehensive development of industry, university, and research, interactive and win–win. A smart campus is a dynamic process of promoting educational reform and innovation. It can use information technology to intelligentize, digitize, and network a series of teaching processes such as teaching concepts, teaching content, teaching means, teaching environment, and teaching evaluation to form a new teaching mode for realizing advanced educational reform. Then, it is necessary to realize the sustainable development of educational informatization supported by digital technology.

References

Anopchenko, T. Y., Lazareva, E. I., & Murzin, A. D. (2016). Network approach for innovation economy managers of international level education: Southern Federal University experience. In *SGEM 2016 Conference Proceedings* (pp. 917–922). Albena, Bulgaria.

Chunruo, L. (2012). The research of intelligent campus based on the Internet of Things. *Information and Computer (Theory), 2*, 91–92.

Ding, L. (2006). Exploration and practice of the road of sustainable development of local colleges and universities by increasing strength and contribution. *Chinese Higher Education Research, 2*, 54–55.

Dongming, L. (2011). Intelligent campus is not just an idea. *Chinese Educational Network, 11*, 29–35.

Hongbo, Z., Dengyin, Z., Longxiang, Y., Zhixin, S., & Ping, Z. (2011). Construction and planning of smart campus based on the Internet of Things technology. *China Education Network, 11*, 18–19.

Jie, S., & Yuxing, H. (2010). Smart campus and its construction. *Journal of Fujian Educational Institute, 6*, 122–125.

Lazareva, E. (2013). Features of national welfare innovative potential parametric indication information-analytical tools system in the globalization trends' context. In *CEUR Workshop Proceedings* (Vol. 1000, pp. 339–351). Retrieved from http://ceur-ws.org/Vol-1000/ICTERI-2013-p-339-351-ITER.pdf. Accessed August 15, 2021.

Lin, C. (2007). The tendency problem that Chinese education informatization must prevent. *Electrical Education Research, 4*, 18–21.
Peng, S. (2016). Discussion on the construction of university smart campus under the background of Internet +. *Journal of Jilin Radio and Television University, 000*(011), 134–135.
Ping, Z., Hongbo, Z., Gang, H., & Jianzhen, X. (2010). Research and design of smart campus based on Internet of Things. *Journal of Nanjing University of Posts and Telecommunications (Natural Science), 4*, 16–21.
Qintai, H., Nanhui, L., & Kai, Z., (2018). The exploration and practice of South China Normal University. *China Education Network, 7*, 2–5.
Ronghuai, H., Junfeng, Y., & Yongbin, H. (2012). From digital to smart: The evolution and trends of learning environment. *Open Education Research, 18*(1), 12–24.
Ronghuai, H., Jinbao, Z., Yongbin, H., et al. (2012). Smart campus: The inevitable trend of digital campus development. *Open Education Research, 18*(4), 6–9.
Tong, Z., & Wen, L. (2011). The research on construction on smart campus. *China Computer & Communication, 10*, 86–90.
Xi, Y. (2018). Research on new smart campus information service construction in higher vocational colleges. *Liaoning Higher Vocational College Journal, 5*, 103–105.
Xin, W. (2020). Research on the construction and practice of the new intelligent campus in colleges and universities: Taking Jiangsu Vocational College of Business as an Example. *Journal of Qingyuan Polytechnic, 13*(4), 5–10.
Yingjun, W. (2010). The smart campus-based "cloud." *China Education Network, 7*, 25–26.
Yong, M. (2011). Resources and application are significant to the smart campus. *Chinese Education Network, 11*, 29–33.
Yongmin, Z. (2010). The interpretation of the smart earth and the smart city. *China Information Times, 10*, 23–29.

Striving for Balance: An Analysis of China's Economic Policy Towards Ecologically Sustainable Development

Libin Ni

Abstract Economic policy plays an important role in the achievement of ecologically sustainable development. It is necessary to establish a complete management system to achieve sustainable economic and environmental development. The purpose of this article is to analyze the current development of sustainable economic policy in China and propose improvements. The main objective of this article is to investigate the economic policy in China. The author tries to analyze the development of economic policy by using the method of quantitative analysis, qualitative analysis and literature research. This article illustrates the basic concepts of sustainable economic development policy, further analyzes the policy from the aspects of the industry, finance, taxation, trade and other aspects and proposes improvements for the development of sustainable economic policies. It is shown that sustainable economic policies have achieved great results though there are still many problems in the development process.

Keywords Economic policy · Ecologically sustainable development · Industrial policy · Taxation policy · Trade policy · Financial policy

JEL Classification J24 · C54 · J64

1 Introduction

Ever since the Industrial Revolution, ecological pollution has been the haunted problem of the world. Many scholars attempted to solve the problem and put forward different solutions. In 1987, sustainable development was proposed for the first time. According to Brundtland Report, Sustainable development is defined as the development that meets the needs of the present without compromising the ability of future

L. Ni (✉)
Henan University of Economics and Law, Henan, China
e-mail: 871688596@qq.com

Southern Federal University, Rostov-on-Don, Russia

E. I. Lazareva et al. (eds.), *Innovative Trends in International Business and Sustainable Management*, Approaches to Global Sustainability, Markets, and Governance,
https://doi.org/10.1007/978-981-19-4005-7_22

generations to meet their own needs (Hanley, 1997). Economic policy eliminates the environmental problems in economic development by regulating the behaviour of economic activities. Sustainable economic development has to take into account the degradation of the environment, the depletion of natural resources, and all kinds of pollution of the land, water and air if economic growth is to remain sustainable. Hence the investigation of sustainable economic policies is of great significance (Anopchenko et al., 2019; Lazareva et al., 2020).

The investigation of the sustainable economic policy can be traced back to the 1990s. In recent years, a new theoretical system on resource economy including resource value theory, resource asset theory, resource industry theory and resource accounting theory was established. Theory of Resource Industry, Theory of Resource Accounting and New Theory of Resource Economy were published. The practice on pollution damage measurement has been conducted, with Economic Measurement and Research on Environmental Pollution Damage in China, Estimation, Forecasting and Result Analysis of National Environmental Pollution Damage in Recent Decades and Theory of Ecological Value being published. In recent years, green finance including green credit and green bond is also been a hot topic of research (Wu, 2019).

Based on the domestic and international research, this article analyzes the sustainable economic policy on the industry, finance, taxation, trade respectively and clarifies what has been achieved.

2 Materials and Methods

The investigation objective in this article is the sustainable economic development policy in China. Economic development serves as both the cause of environmental problems and the solution to environmental problems. Promoting sustainable economic development is the theme of today's era, the only way for China to achieve high-quality development.

This article tries to analyze the development of economic policy from the aspect of industry, taxation, trade and finance by using the method of quantitative analysis, qualitative and literature research.

3 Results

Industrial policy plays an indispensable role in the system of national economic development. Market forces are unable to reduce the detrimental effects of environmental degradation; various policies should therefore be used to internalize the social externalities (Joshua, 2017). The adjustment of industrial structure aims to achieve sustainable development by combining the optimization of the use of resources and environmental protection (Table 1) (Li & Zhou, 2021).

Table 1 The development of industrial policies in China from 1952

Time	Policies	The existing problems
1952–1978	Put the development of the heavy industry as the priority	A small share of primary and tertiary industry; an imbalance between light and heavy industry
1978–1992	Proportional development of three industries	The low proportion of the tertiary industry
1992–2002	Accelerate the development of the primary industry and the tertiary industry; environmental protection	Lack of core competence; low added value; backward production capacity
2002–2012	Develop high-tech industry and information industry; take the new path of industrialization	Environmental pollution; a high proportion of high-consuming industry
2012-	Place strategic emerging industries in a more prominent position in economic and social development; vigorously build a new modern industrial system; promote sustainable and healthy economic and social development	The conflict between the development of high-carbon and energy-consuming industries and environmental protection

Source Compiled by the author based on Zhang and Liu (2018)

According to Table 1, the development of industrial policy has a history of more than half a century. The development of environmental protection has been continuously completed. The industrial policy is adjusted according to the requirements of economic development, ecological preservation and social development.

Through the transformation and upgrading of industrial structure, traditional and backward industries are going to be eliminated, and the problems of overcapacity, resource consumption and environmental pollution can be solved. The development of the high-tech industry can not only reduce the damage to the ecological environment but also improve the quality of China's economic development.

Tax policy can also play an important role in environmental protection. Environmental tax policy can regulate the economic behaviour of enterprises and individuals, prevent environmental pollution and damage and protect the environment. Compared to developed countries, the theory and practice of environmental tax in China have been developed for a long time, and the road to legislation on environmental tax has taken many years of exploration (Fang, 2017).

Ever since the establishment of environmental tax law, China has been gradually formulating a series of tax policies on pollution, energy conservation, environmental protection, comprehensive utilization of resources and renewable energy. Some restrictive tax policies also force enterprises and the public to make adjustments to promote green development. For the air pollutants, water pollutants, solid waste and noise discharged by enterprises, the tax system design of "more discharge and

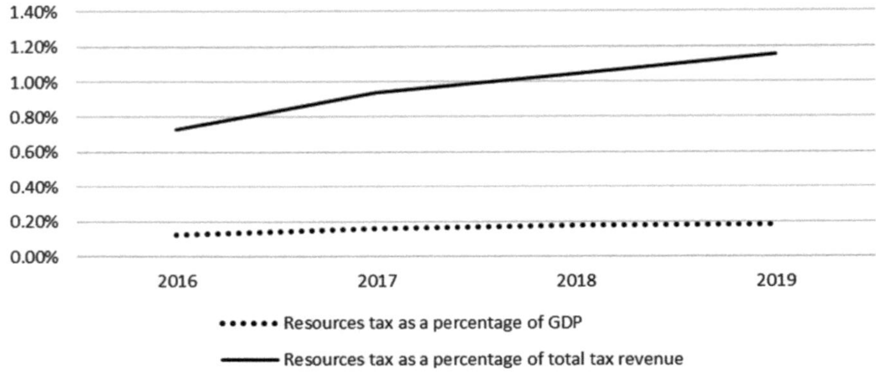

Fig. 1 The resources tax as a percentage of GDP and total tax revenue in China, 2016–2019. *Source* Compiled by the author based on National Statistics Bureau (2019)

more payment, less discharge and less payment, and no discharge and no payment" gives full play of tax. Other restrictive tax policies on environmental protection and resource conservation such as excise, resources tax and vehicle and ship tax have been completed gradually. As a result, the green tax system in China is taking shape (Guo, 2018).

Green taxes are technically designated environmental taxes, with environmentally friendly motivations. The "greening of a (national) tax system" is usually measured using two indicators: the revenues from environmentally-related taxes as a percentage of GDP, and the revenues from environmentally-related taxes as a percentage of the total tax revenues for a country (Fig. 1) (Kreiser, 2012).

According to Fig. 1, the proportion that resources take in GDP and total tax revenue is on the rise in the past four years, which indicates that the green tax system in China has already taken effect. In other words, green taxation provides an economic and legal instrument to economic and ecologically sustainable development.

For a long time, China's exports were dominated by primary raw material-based products with little or no consideration of the impact on resources and the environment. In recent years, although the structure of China's exports has been significantly optimized, the proportion of primary products that have a greater impact on the ecological environment and manufactured products that are highly polluting is still large.

The environmental problems brought about by the import trade are highlighted by the phenomenon of foreign polluting waste. There have been incidents where some industrialized countries attempted to export industrial waste, domestic waste and waste materials to China. Many countries have tried to transfer a large number of polluting industries to China using the excuse of exporting capital and technology (Wang, 2021).

The Chinese government has paid more attention to the establishment of the relevant trade policy to protect the environment in recent years. As the keywords of the environmental-related policies, transformation and upgrading are also frequently used by the government to coordinate the development of trade and the environment. It is generally believed that trade itself does not necessarily have a negative impact on the environment. The root cause of the negative impact is the market failure and the failure of the intervention in the process of trade. Only when environmental policy and trade liberalization develop together can trade have a positive impact on the environment.

Since President Xi announced to the world in 2020 that China would reach the carbon peak by 2030 and achieve carbon neutrality by 2060, the enthusiasm of all parties is very high. In this situation, green finance evokes heated discussion in China. Green finance refers to economic activities that support environmental improvement, resource conservation and efficient utilization. At present, China's green financial policy is advancing steadily and has made great progress in the fields of credit and bonds (Sachs et al., 2019).

As an important part of green finance, green credit is a financial instrument used by commercial banks and other financial institutions to provide loans at preferential interest rates to low-carbon, green and recycling enterprises (You et al., 2021). In 2007, the State Environmental Protection Administration and the People's Bank of China jointly proposed the relevant green credit policy to curb the blind expansion of high energy-consuming and high-polluting industries. This policy aims to build a new financial system and improve financial instruments for ecological protection and green finance (Table 2) (Liu, 2021).

In Table 2, it is obvious that China's green credit policy system has basically formed an institutional system with the statistical system and evaluation system as its focus since its construction in 2007. As the earliest, largest and most mature

Table 2 Development of green credit in China

Time	Document	The related policy
2012	"Green Credit Guidelines"	Financial institutions need to promote green credit strategically
2014	"Green Credit Implementation Key Evaluation Indicators"	It aims to promote green credit by banking financial institutions and develop key evaluation indicators for green credit implementation
2015	*General Programme for the Reform of the Ecological Civilisation System*	It proposes to establish a green financial system and promote green credit
2016	"Guidance on Building a Green Financial System"	The guidance points out the importance of building a green financial system and calls for the vigorous development of green credit
2020	"Proposal of the Central Committee of the Communist Party of China on Formulating the 14th Five-Year Plan for National Economic and Social Development and the Visionary Goals for 2035"	It states that the government should promote the balanced development of finance and the real economy and develop green finance in the next five years

Source Compiled by the author based on People's Bank of China (2021b)

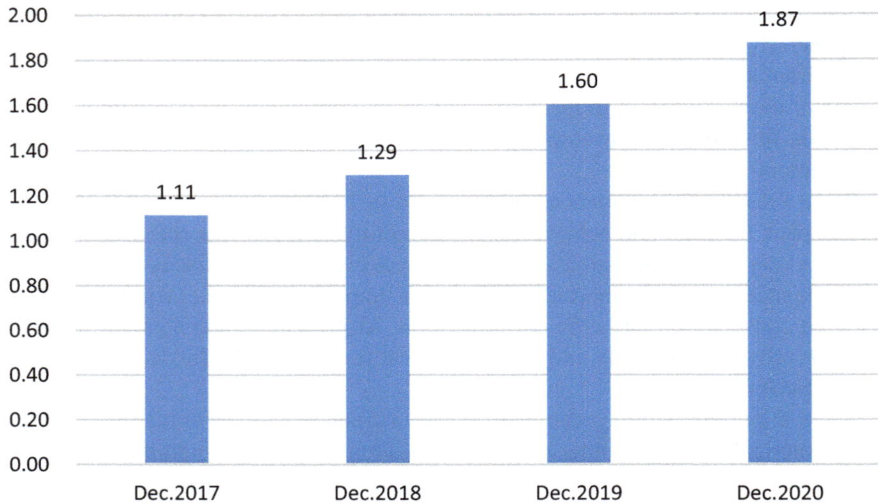

Fig. 2 Green loan balance of major financial institutions in China (trillion dollars), 2017–2020. *Source* Compiled by the author based on People's Bank of China (2021a)

product in China's green finance, green credit plays an important role in promoting green finance in China (Fig. 2).

According to Fig. 2, it is apparent that the balance of green loans keeps rising from 2017 to 2020, which helps to establish the green, circular and low-carbon economy and promote economic restructuring and the transformation and upgrading of the industrial structure.

China's green bond market officially was launched in 2016. Issuers receive funds to finance green projects and investors receive a fixed income in the form of interest by the way of a green bond. Green bonds are designed to finance projects with positive environmental or climate change benefits. Most of the green bonds or funds issued have a green purpose or are linked to green assets.

The relevant policies of the green bond have been completed gradually. China's green bond market has developed rapidly since its beginning in 2016. Up to now, China's green bond issuance venues cover both domestic and overseas, and the issuance volume has steadily increased, making it the second-largest green bond issuing country in the world.

The development of the green bond market has achieved remarkable results. The green bond market in China is on an upswing and the upward trend is expected to continue in the coming years. Meanwhile, a growing range of green bond products appears on the market. Carbon neutral bonds and sustainability-linked bonds have been launched in the interbank market since the beginning of 2021 (Wang & Li, 2021).

4 Conclusion

It is concluded that sustainable economic policies have achieved great results. According to Blue Book on Sustainable Development, China's sustainable development has been steadily improving, with overall indicators showing steady growth year on year over the past decade.

However, there are also problems in sustainable economic development. The imbalance of the governance structure caused by the unbalanced and inadequate development has led to the slowdown in economic growth. The contradiction between people's growing need for a better environment and ecological products and the overall fragile ecological environment is still very prominent.

It is recommended that institutional barriers should be broken down and dormant development potential should be activated with supply-side structural reform as the mainline through comprehensive economic system reform. Meanwhile, pollution prevention and ecological civilization should be strengthened to achieve sustainable economic and environmental development.

References

Anopchenko, T., Gorbaneva, O., Lazareva, E., Murzin, A., & Ougolnitsky, G. (2019). Modelling public-private partnerships in the innovative economy: A regional aspect. *Sustainability (Switzerland), 11*(20), 5588.

Fang, J. (2017). An analysis of the relationship between tax policy and sustainable economic development. *Business Economy, 12*(03), 51–53.

Guo, N. (2018). Study on the impact of resource tax reform on climate change. *Environmental Economy, 34*(01), 141–144.

Hanley, N. (1997). *Environmental Economics in Theory and Practice*. Macmillan Press Ltd.

Joshua, J. (2017). *China's Economic Growth: Towards Sustainable Economic Development and Social Justice*. Springer Nature.

Kreiser, L. A. (2012). *Green Taxation and Environmental Sustainability*. Edward Elgar Publishing Limited.

Lazareva, E., Gorbaneva, O., Murzin, A., & Roshchina, E. (2020). Socio-ecological potential increment in the system of innovation economy sustainable management. In *Proceedings—2020 2nd International Conference on Control Systems, Mathematical Modeling, Automation and Energy Efficiency, SUMMA 2020* (pp. 195–200).

Li, Z. Q., & Zhou, Q. Y. (2021). Does upgrading the industrial structure help to promote carbon reduction? *Ecological Economy, 37*(08), 34–40.

Liu, L. X. (2021). A study on the development of green finance in China—Review of green finance. *Environmental Economy, 37*(10), 230–231.

National Statistics Bureau. (2019). The data of resources tax, total tax and GDP. http://www.mof com.gov.cn. Accessed November 09, 2021.

People's Bank of China. (2021a). Green credit data. http://www.pbc.gov.cn. Accessed November 09, 2021.

People's Bank of China. (2021b). Green loan balance data. http://www.pbc.gov.cn. Accessed November 07, 2021.

Sachs, J. D., Woo, W. T., Yoshino, N., & Farhad, T. H. (2019). *Handbook of Green Finance*. Springer Nature Singapore Pte Ltd.

Wang, S. Q. (2021). Research on the sustainable development of China's foreign trade under WTO. *Economic Forum, 19*(08), 12–14.

Wang, Q., & Li, X. D. (2021). A study on the impact of green bonds on company value. *Economic Review Journal, 13*(09), 100–108.

Wu, S. Z. (2019). Processes, characteristics and prospects of environmental strategy and policy development in China. China Environment News. https://theory.gmw.cn. Accessed November 19, 2021

You, J., Zhang, B. S., & Zeng, M. L. (2021). Study on the countermeasures of green finance to support the construction of ecological civilization. *Chinese Market, 30*(28), 34–35.

Zhang, X. Y., & Liu, J. J. (2018). Retrospect and prospect of China's industrial structure policy over the past 40 years of reform and opening-up. *Reform, 12*(09), 42–54.

Prospects for the Implementation of Artificial Intelligence in Legal Proceedings

Arthur G. Bezverkhov, Andrew V. Yudin, Lydia A. Serzhantova, and Maria A. Agalarova

Abstract The paper aims to review the digital technologies involved in the area of legal proceedings in Russia, determining the prospects for the introduction of artificial intelligence as one of the most interesting and controversial examples of electronic litigation. The authors chose many research methods, including general scientific methods (synthesis, induction, deduction, analysis, system-structural method, hermeneutic method, and synergetic method) and special legal methods (comparative legal method). The study revealed a lack of unity in the understanding of the term "artificial intelligence." European standards for the development of information technology in the judicial sphere were identified. Moreover, the authors noted the importance of human control over all actions of artificial intelligence. Additionally, the authors identified areas of application of artificial intelligence in Russian legal proceedings and the prospects for further implementation of this legal phenomenon. The authors reached the following conclusions. The gradual introduction of digital technology helps optimize, simplify, and save financial, time, and labor costs in the process of conducting legal proceedings. Artificial intelligence will make it possible to free law enforcement officers and the court apparatus from the repetitive and routine processes typical of the various stages of the legal proceedings. Moreover, it will promote the implementation of transparency, openness, and accessibility of the judicial process. There is a clear auxiliary nature of the activities of artificial intelligence, which is not identical to the full implementation of justice by robots. An electronic system with artificial intelligence must be programmed so that its activities are based on the principles of limited, selective, and prioritized human decisions.

Keywords Artificial intelligence · Digitalization · Digital technology · Electronic legal proceedings · Electronic documents · Expert systems

JEL Classification K400 · K410

A. G. Bezverkhov · A. V. Yudin · L. A. Serzhantova (✉) · M. A. Agalarova
Samara National Research University Named After Academician S.P. Korolev, Samara, Russia
e-mail: lidia.yarigina@mail.ru

E. I. Lazareva et al. (eds.), *Innovative Trends in International Business and Sustainable Management*, Approaches to Global Sustainability, Markets, and Governance,
https://doi.org/10.1007/978-981-19-4005-7_23

1 Introduction

Digitalization is now gaining such momentum that it is unstoppable. Entering all areas of public life, it defines the vector of contemporary law. This was especially evident during the period of restrictive measures caused by COVID-19, when access to justice became possible, sometimes, only in electronic format. The nationwide economic recovery plan (June 2020) prepared by the Government of the Russian Federation, among other things, devotes considerable attention to the creation of legal conditions for court trials using digital technologies. The corresponding draft law was to be prepared by the Ministry of Justice of the Russian Federation in December 2020–June 2021.

Nevertheless, the issue of digitalization of the judicial process started to receive attention long before the restrictive measures related to COVID-19.

On April 19, 2000, the Supreme Court of the Russian Federation held the first hearing in the remote presence of the convicts (videoconferencing).

The federal program "Development of the judicial system of Russia for 2013–2020" outlined the areas of digitalization of justice, allowing to form an innovative approach, optimize and improve the delivery of justice, improve the quality and efficiency of research conducted by forensic institutions, and ensure the effective execution of court decisions (Government of the Russian Federation, 2012). During the implementation of this program, a considerable role was played by the foundation of the automated state system "Justice" in the courts of general jurisdiction. While the "Moi Arbitr" information system has been working effectively in arbitration proceedings for quite a long period, the electronic filing of documents in civil and criminal proceedings was not allowed for a long time. These innovations have become important in situations where citizens and legal entities do not have the opportunity to submit documents directly to the court, including in legal proceedings involving foreign persons located abroad. The filing of procedural documents in electronic form is accompanied by an electronic signature (simple or enhanced qualified). Electronic filing in criminal proceedings requires the electronic signature of a participant in criminal proceedings.

In 2016, amendments were made to the procedural codes regarding the use of electronic documents in courts (Article 35 of the Civil Procedure Code of the Russian Federation, Article 41 of the Arbitration Procedural Code of the Russian Federation, and Article 474.1 of the Civil Procedure Code of the Russian Federation).

Among others, courts operate such electronic systems as "Arbitration Case Files" and "Bank of Arbitration Court Decisions," which perform electronic circulation of documents in criminal, civil, arbitration, and administrative proceedings, thus implementing an integrated information field of federal courts of general jurisdiction and arbitration courts.

A new vector of digitalization of court proceedings is the development of a unified online platform "Justice Online." Its capabilities involve a continuous cycle of online litigation, from filing documents to participating in a court session and receiving court documents signed with an electronic signature. As indicated in the secondary literature, this service will rely on the methodology of "weak artificial intelligence" (Momotov, 2021).

The gradual introduction of various digital innovations has become so widespread that it has given rise to such a procedural concept as "electronic legal proceedings." There is no legal definition of this legal phenomenon in the legislation, which gives rise to many discussions and ambiguities in the understanding of the term by theorists and practitioners. We understand electronic proceedings as a statutory procedure for pre-trial and trial interactions between parties to legal relations with the help of information technology.

Today's technological advances allow the participants of legal proceedings to achieve the goals of justice more effectively. Informatization and automation significantly affect the current development of law, which, on the one hand, contributes to the development of these processes, providing them, but, on the other hand, is transformed under their influence. In this regard, the legislator and practitioners should be prepared for the manifestation of certain crises related to issues of information security, lack of standardization, the unpreparedness of some part of the population for the transition to the digital space. In particular, the courts are using outdated and incompatible technologies, where the e-justice system has no mechanism for internal document flow between courts at different levels. Despite the use of electronic justice systems, in practice, we have to duplicate standard procedures for the exchange of documents, taking them out of the digital format, with civil and criminal proceedings becoming more complicated and time-consuming. To make full use of e-justice tools, certain skills and knowledge of special terms are required. These skills and knowledge are not covered in the standard educational program. In this regard, it is worth thinking about the position of the so-called "technical officer of the court," who will solve the problems of judges and other court staff. In this case, the process of implementing electronic justice will go more smoothly. In this matter, we can also refer to foreign experience, in particular, the experience of the USA, where the development of electronic justice is at the proper level—the management of systems is decentralized; namely, the federal courts have their own servers. Moreover, access to judicial information through electronic systems is fee-based, and revenues from these fees go to maintain information systems and are used to offset other costs associated with e-justice.

To summarize, the introduction of information technology in court proceedings currently takes place in the following directions:

- Use of a qualified electronic signature in document flow;
- Holding a court session and certain investigative measures in a "remote" format, when the participants in the process are not in close proximity, communicating through various electronic technologies;
- Electronic recording of the course and results of investigative and other procedural actions;
- Development of a system of case management entirely in electronic form with its testing in some constituent entities of the Russian Federation;

- Uploading information to the Internet about the progress and procedural decisions on cases with the possibility of familiarization of the participants in the process;
- Application of certain capabilities of robotics (artificial intelligence) to assess the facts of the case, calculate the punishment for the crime committed, and make final decisions on cases.

Let us dwell in more detail on the last direction of digitalization of electronic justice—the introduction and use of artificial intelligence—as the least studied and ambiguous phenomenon.

2 Methodology

During the research, the authors applied general scientific methods (analysis, induction, deduction, synthesis, system-structural method, hermeneutic method, and synergetic method) and special legal methods (comparative-legal method).

3 Results

The term "artificial intelligence" is used in legal acts related to the use and development of digital technology. In particular, the Presidential Decree "On the development of artificial intelligence in the Russian Federation" (October 10, 2019 No. 490) states that artificial intelligence is a technical system aimed at the functional reproduction of human activity related to the search for answers to given questions, self-learning, and implementation of assigned tasks, comparable with human thinking activity (Presidential Executive Office, 2019).

The performance of various activities using artificial intelligence is becoming a reality of our lives. In 2020 in Moscow, a comprehensive global study was conducted on the introduction of robotics, the creation of all necessary conditions for its smooth operation, and the legal support of the use of the latest IT technologies (Russian Federation, 2020).

Another significant legal document in the field of artificial intelligence is the "European ethical Charter on the use of Artificial Intelligence in judicial systems and their environment" (December 3, 2018). The main idea of this legal document is a better implementation of advanced electronic technologies in legal proceedings (European Commission for the Efficiency of Justice (CEPEJ) 2018). It defines the following fundamental principles:

1. The development and implementation of artificial intelligence must consider and guarantee human rights and freedoms;
2. Human rights and freedoms may not be infringed based on a person's status;
3. Quality and safety control of the used IT technologies;

4. Digital justice must be transparent, impartial, reliable, and guarantee the availability of data processing methods;
5. User control of the systems used, which implies the rejection of the prescriptive approach.

These principles show that artificial intelligence cannot fully replace the judge. Any moral and ethical concepts and qualities are formed in a person in the process of socialization and upbringing. Obviously, these behavioral categories will not fit into the software algorithm. Separate attention should be paid to the principle associated with the control of the user.

Despite the high-tech process that should be used in the judicial system, humans must control all actions of artificial intelligence. In other words, control over the work of the artificial intelligence system is possible on the part of the participants in the proceedings and the court. In this case, a specialized artificial intelligence (auxiliary) is used, which works independently but under human control.

A retrospective analysis of the term "artificial intelligence" reveals the following points. Certain notions began to take shape in the second half of the twentieth century in the USA. However, initially, there was no unity in understanding; different synonymous concepts were used. A clearer terminology recognized by most experts formed gradually. The final stage of formation of the term is its unification and use in various dictionaries and encyclopedic reference books.

I. V. Ponkin and A. I. Redkina write that artificial intelligence is an artificial complex cybernetic computer-software-hardware system with a cognitive-functional architecture and its own or dedicated computing power of the necessary capacity and performance (Ponkin & Redkina, 2018). Morhat believes that artificial intelligence is a fully or partially autonomous self-organizing computer-hardware-software virtual or cyber-physical, including biocybernetic, system endowed with such abilities and capabilities as pattern recognition, symbolic systems and languages, reflection, reasoning, modeling, imaginative thinking, analysis, evaluation, self-maintenance in homeostasis, learning and self-learning, anthropomorphically intelligent independent decision-making, task performance, and problem identification" (Morhat, 2017). The author concludes that artificial intelligence has great potential applications—in addition to the creation of legal Internet portals, one can prepare legal documents, including the text of judicial decisions. Artificial intelligence is also capable of predicting (Morhat, 2018). The prediction will allow the parties to civil legal relations, using artificial intelligence, to find the most appropriate form of a contract of all found alternative forms.

The capabilities of robotics can be used to transcribe audio transcripts, autocomplete judicial practice, and analyze incoming court documents to sift out those that do not comply with legal requirements. The use of the capabilities of weak artificial intelligence in the court's document management activities will reduce the work of the court apparatus.

In addition to the above, artificial intelligence can be used to request and evaluate evidence in legal proceedings, but with certain conditions. Its use is possible to request and verify written, audio, and video evidence and various documents; such verification will be more objective and several times faster. For example, a handwriting expert examines the authenticity of receipts or signatures and spends a considerable amount of time analyzing documents, while the so-called human factor cannot be excluded (a small percentage of error, which may be significant for the further course of the trial and decision in the case), and if we use artificial intelligence, then the examination will be significantly reduced, and the percentage of errors will be reduced to zero. Nevertheless, the application of these technologies in civil litigation will lead to theoretical and practical problems, including the application of artificial intelligence on matters of evidence. In the course of the reclamation and evaluation of evidence in court proceedings with the help of artificial intelligence, the court will be able to investigate and verify the authenticity of written evidence. We think that such a request for the necessary documents and their subsequent evaluation will noticeably reduce the time of court proceedings. However, this entails the need to develop an electronic procedural form, which includes the transfer and recording of electronic information.

In criminal proceedings, expert systems that use elements of artificial intelligence have shown their effectiveness and have been quite successfully used since the second half of the twentieth century. Examples of such systems are "Narkoeks," "Balex," "Kortik," "Maniak," "Sprut," etc. These systems form the definition of possible directions of investigation, as well as providing further recommended actions (Afanasyev, 2018). However, the larger-scale use of expert systems in criminal proceedings involves the development of standard algorithms for implementing investigative and other procedural actions, normative regulation of the use of expert systems.

It would be useful to adopt foreign experience of pre-trial settlement of legal conflicts. The parties are invited to answer the questions posed by the system, after which options for dispute resolution are provided. This practice can be useful in criminal cases of private prosecution, where criminal prosecution depends on the victim's will (Kachalova, 2020).

These and other applications of artificial intelligence in criminal proceedings should continue to be created and used because an increasing number of crimes are committed with the use of advanced digital technology or the object of encroachment are computer and other electronic innovations.

Undoubtedly, the development of electronic justice requires a high level of technical equipment so that participants in the process can fully exercise their rights and obligations, and certain knowledge in this area is required. Additionally, the use of artificial intelligence is complicated by the fact that it is not properly provided by the international legal and domestic regulatory framework.

4 Conclusion

The use of electronic justice in Russian litigation can reduce the time required to perform repetitive, routine processes, typical of the various stages of legal proceedings. It contributes to the implementation of transparency, openness, and accessibility of legal proceedings. Artificial intelligence can definitely solve many current problems, but it is too early to talk about the implementation of justice by artificial intelligence. Such technology should be considered as an auxiliary element of law enforcement, which will facilitate the activities of law enforcement officials and the court apparatus and provide several procedural opportunities for participants in this process. In other words, artificial intelligence acts as an assistant that performs mundane paperwork that does not involve creativity. An electronic system with artificial intelligence must be programmed so that its activities are based on the principles of limited, selective, and prioritized human decisions. The introduction and application of artificial intelligence in the implementation of justice in civil and criminal cases, as well as in the implementation of work with documents, will ensure the implementation of more efficient and expeditious procedural activities of the court and other participants in the process. Undoubtedly, electronic justice is a promising direction of the development of the judicial system, which will provide additional accessibility and publicity for all participants of the judicial process and significantly accelerate judicial proceedings.

References

Afanasyev, A. Y. (2018). Artificial intelligence or intelligence of the subjects of crime identification, detection, and investigation: Which will win? *Library of criminalist. Scientific Journal, 3*(38), 28–34.

European Commission for the Efficiency of Justice (CEPEJ). (2018). European ethical Charter on the use of Artificial Intelligence in judicial systems and their environment. Strasbourg, France. Retrieved from https://rm.coe.int/ethical-charter-en-for-publication-4-december-2018/16808f699c. Accessed June 3, 2020.

Government of the Russian Federation. (2012). Decree "On the federal targeted program 'Development of the judicial system of Russia for 2013–2020'" (December 27, 2012 No. 1406). Moscow, Russia. Retrieved from http://government.ru/docs/all/85913/. Accessed June 3, 2020.

Kachalova, O. V. (2020). Artificial intelligence in justice—A bright future with reservations. *Criminal Procedure, 10*, 8.

Momotov, V. V. (2021). Artificial intelligence in litigation: State and prospects for use. *Courier of Kutafin Moscow State Law University (MSAL), 5*, 188–191. https://doi.org/10.17803/2311-5998.2021.81.5.188-191

Morhat, P. M. (2017). *Artificial Intelligence: A Legal Perspective.* Institute of State-Confessional Relations and Law.

Morhat, P. M. (2018). On the issue of the specifics of legal regulation artificial intelligence and some legal problems of its application in certain spheres. *Law & Legislation, 6*, 63–67. https://doi.org/10.24411/2073-3313-2018-10015

Ponkin, I. V., & Redkina, A. I. (2018). Artificial intelligence from the point of view of law. *RUDN Journal of Law, 22*(1), 91–109. https://doi.org/10.22363/2313-2337-2018-22-1-91-109

Presidential Executive Office. (2019). Decree "On the development of artificial intelligence in the Russian Federation" (together with the "National strategy for the development of artificial intelligence for the period up to 2030") (October 10, 2019 No. 490). Moscow, Russia. Retrieved from http://static.kremlin.ru/media/events/files/ru/AH4x6HgKWANwVtMOfPDhcbRpvd1HCCsv.pdf. Accessed June 3, 2020.

Russian Federation. (2020). Federal law "On conducting an experiment on the establishment of special regulation in order to create the necessary conditions for the development and implementation of artificial intelligence technology in the subject of the Russian Federation—The city of federal significance Moscow and amending articles 6 and 10 of the Federal Law 'On personal data'" (April 24, 2020 No. 123-FZ), Moscow, Russia. Retrieved from http://www.consultant.ru/document/cons_doc_LAW_351127/. Accessed June 3, 2020.

On the Trends of Subordination of Social Programming and Institutional Design of the Economic System in the Context of the Genesis of Noonomy

Anna V. Ipatova, Elena A. Strelchenko, Irina V. Movchan, Oksana A. Ishchenko-Padukova, and Marina G. Vaskina

Abstract *Purpose* Analysis of the functional role of institutional design in the system of social programming methods for building a socio-economic system transformed under the influence of digitalization processes. *Design/methodology/approach* The research is based on the use of institutional theory, development theory, research in the field of international economics and behavioral economics, which involves the use of both general scientific methods of cognition of economic phenomena and processes, and special tools presented by structural analysis, classification method, system approach. *Findings* A scientific heuristic analysis of the transformational consequences of the development of the economic system through social programming of the goals and results of its formation, which allows to propose the use in economic research of a differentiated approach to the implementation of institutional design regarding the design of public policy in the context of digital transformation. *Originality/value* The use of the methodological concept of institutional design, which makes it possible to formulate the achievement of social programming tasks in the implementation of state economic policy at the national and global levels in noonomy. In particular, the elements of scientific novelty are:

- formulation of the specifics of the regulation of socio-economic development within the new quality of the economic system, defined as "noonomy";

A. V. Ipatova (✉) · E. A. Strelchenko · I. V. Movchan · O. A. Ishchenko-Padukova · M. G. Vaskina
Southern Federal University, Rostov-on-Don, Russia
e-mail: avipatova@sfedu.ru

E. A. Strelchenko
e-mail: estrelchenko@sfedu.ru

I. V. Movchan
e-mail: ivmovchan@sfedu.ru

O. A. Ishchenko-Padukova
e-mail: oaishenko-padukova@sfedu.ru

M. G. Vaskina
e-mail: mvaskina@sfedu.ru

E. I. Lazareva et al. (eds.), *Innovative Trends in International Business and Sustainable Management*, Approaches to Global Sustainability, Markets, and Governance,
https://doi.org/10.1007/978-981-19-4005-7_24

- a systematic analysis of social programming that determines the elimination of negative effects of digitalization.

Keywords Macroeconomic policy · Institutional design · Social design · Globalization · Digitalization · Noonomy

JEL Classification E61 · J230 · F62

1 Introduction

The conditions of functioning of the majority of states during the coronavirus pandemic demonstrated both positive and negative consequences of the functioning of economic entities, and also revealed the specifics of the functions performed by the participants of the economic system, which indicates the need to consider the theory of institutional design for the development of socio-economic systems both in the sectoral context and at its global level. Currently, the problems of social programming are dealt with by Parikh (2002), Pacuit (2005), Tikhomirov and Frenkel (2017), Benthem (2014) and others. Also, the issues of institutional design are reflected in the studies of Tambovtsev (1997), Auzan (2007), Goodin (1996) and others. The problems of "noonomics" are presented in the studies of Aganbegyan (2020), Bodrunov (2019) and others. However, a complex mechanism for the formation of subordination of social programming and institutional design, taking into account the new quality of the development of economic systems—the genesis of noonomy, is absent in the proposed scientific developments.

Thus, the search for a solution to the problem of subordination of social programming and institutional design in economic development consists in the need to include modeling processes in scientific analysis, since the implementation of effective policy through the analyzed concept of institutional design will create a stable economic system that can be transformed taking into account the influence of its internal and external parameters.

2 Methodology

The methodological axiomatics of the research is based on clarifying the principles of the system approach in the context of the theory of institutional economics, behavioral economics and development theory.

The new quality of economic development, consisting in the transformation of the importance of key factors of economic growth, focused on the role of knowledge, information, the efficiency of production processes and, as a result, causing an increase in the importance of the non-material production sector, has led to an aggravation of the problem of socio-economic development. According to the concept of "noonomics", modern systemic interactions between individuals and the real sphere of production can often be characterized as non-existent. In other words, modern highly developed production imposes new requirements on the quality of human resources. The logical framework of their interrelation is changing, which is expressed in the full realization of the intellectual and creative individual abilities of participants in economic relations in the process of searching for innovative ways to meet the needs of society. Labor, acquiring a creative character, embodies new knowledge in the form of a unique result, providing innovative integration of research and production activities (Chandler, 2020), effective combinatoricity of technological and economic potential. Noonomic contours produce new attributive characteristics of labor resources, transforming, in turn, the system of values, incentives and motivation.

Global socio-economic processes determine the need for the development of intellectual production, a high-tech economic complex and the compliance of human resources with the needs of new high-tech markets. Therefore, the modern economic landscape in the coordinates of non-economic research acquires a new organizational structure based mainly on the formation and expansion of innovative ecosystems (McKeever, 2020) aimed at the development of reproduction institutions and the application of high-tech intellectual human capital, ensuring social and academic progress in society, which forms a new quality of traditional production conditions and established economic processes toward their socialization. Within the framework of the problem, the observed trends are:

- increasing the knowledge intensity and intellectualization of production, ensuring the intensification of economic growth;
- accumulation of intellectual human capital as the basis for the global development of the "post-industrial knowledge society";
- formation of new and noomization of established institutions that provide reproduction of human capital based on flexible adaptation mechanisms;
- increasing the economic return from the application of intellectual human capital and ensuring a high social effect, consisting in improving standards and quality of life.

These features of the development of productive forces initiate the modification of the guidelines of socio-economic development and forms of regulation of economic processes. The formation of an innovation-oriented economic policy requires the use of adequate tools, methodological support and mechanisms for its implementation. One of the productive instrumental concepts in terms of noonomics is the study of the subordination of social programming and institutional design.

It should be noted that the author of the idea of using "SocialSoftware" is Parikh (2002), the elements of which are modeling social situations, checking the correctness of social procedures and designing new ones. The development and implementation of social programming ideas can be compared with the transition from artisanal to industrial production, but this time in matters of social management (Shalak, 2016).

The system of social management technologies, including social programming in the new system of interaction between man and production, is undergoing evolution toward the formulation of effective tools for the implementation of the basic goals of socio-economic development. Raising the status of knowledge as a key factor in the economy involves focusing on the use of those elements that are aimed at achieving the stated goals. Thus, the chain of "interest—goal—problem formulation—choice of regulatory instrument" in the set of methods for managing socio-economic development is reduced to the need to use institutional design.

In modern research, the category "institutional design", proposed by the American scientist Ostrom in 2009, is often used (Ostrom, 1990). Moreover, Auzan's research focuses on the need to take into account "modernization cycles and path dependence problems" in modeling the reform of the economic system (Auzan, 2007). It should be noted that in both foreign and domestic literature, "institutional design" most often refers to the process of purposeful change of one or more structural elements of an institution (Tambovtsev, 1997), as well as the possibility of forming a fundamentally different institution (Goodin, 1996). Thus, economics most often uses the terminology "institutional project" and "institutional design" as synonyms. However, in our opinion, the semantics of the word "institutional project" most reflects the target orientation of the ongoing reforms, therefore, in the case of an analysis of the reform strategy, it is advisable to use this phrase. When analyzing the goal to emphasize the multidimensional nature of reforms, the combination of "institutional design" is the most successful.

3 Results

The modern era of noonomy demonstrates the absence of a clear systemic interaction between individuals and the sphere of "noonomic" production, or the technosphere. The implementation of subordination of regulation of the interests of individuals is carried out within the framework of institutional design, while the achievement of socio-economic development goals takes place within the framework of social programming. Therefore, it is advisable to consider the concept of subordination of social programming and institutional design, which is clearly presented in Fig. 1.

The process of inclusion of institutional design in the general mechanism of social programming makes it possible to determine the significance of the cognitive function of the formation of the educational environment in the economic system. Cognitive technologies in the field of education (Nozhichkina, 2021) form effective learning principles in order to improve academic performance, therefore, the use of a cognitive approach in education contributes to the development of learning models that seek to implement cognitive strategies in the context of specific academic content.

A comparison of traditional and cognitive approaches to learning is proposed in the research of Itinson, in which the creation of knowledge, the focus of the learning process on the student, as well as the predominance of an ideological approach in the learning process are highlighted as the basic characteristics of the cognitive approach;

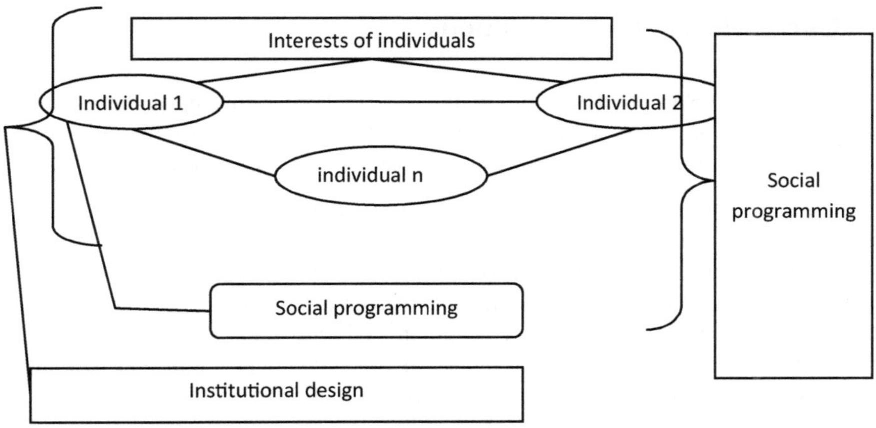

Fig. 1 Mechanism of subordination of social programming and institutional design in noonomics. *Source* Compiled by the authors

the following basic features of the traditional approach are analyzed: knowledge transfer, the primacy of the teacher in the learning process, as well as focus on facts (Itinson, 2020).

Scientists of Higher School of Economics conducted a study where they examined the totality of states represented on the one hand by a group of members from 32 so-called "rich" states, and the second group, which includes 59 developing countries with relatively low incomes, to which, in particular, Russia is attributed.

In Russia, the share of education spending (3.6%) is quite low even compared to poor countries (OECD member countries—5.3%; non-OECD countries—3.9%; Vietnam—4.2%; Colombia—4.5%; Brazil—6.2%) (Dashkovskaya, 2021). A number of domestic economists associate this picture with the underfunding of the domestic educational system. In addition, studies demonstrate the presence of a positive impact of gross domestic product on the level of spending on the education system, and moreover, the strongest correlation is observed in the long term for spending on secondary and vocational education. In addition, there is an economic attractiveness of both higher and secondary vocational education in Russia, which in the future will not significantly affect the desire of households to reduce the outflow to the economics of education on formal grounds, and if such a reduction is possible, it will occur not by reducing benefits, but by increasing costs. It must be admitted that in conditions of low and continuously decreasing returns from education, the policy of limiting the supply of educational services can be recognized as rational. However, "in conditions where returns remain consistently high, this can turn into serious losses for society in the long term" (Kapelyushnikov, 2021). Thus, the noonomic nature of the development of the economic system contributes to the increasing role of education in the context of its cognitive function, which actualizes the focus of research on the subordination of social programming and institutional design in modern economics.

4 Conclusion/Recommendations

The analysis of the problem of subordination of social programming and institutional design of the economic system in the context of the genesis of noonomy allowed us to conclude that there are the following elements of scientific novelty:

- the functioning of the economic system in noonomy is subject to the active use of cognitive technologies that incorporate methods and algorithms of behavior of subjects who focus their activities on interdisciplinarity and intersubjectivity, including data on the mechanisms of cognition, learning, communication, information processing, on the achievements of neuroscience, etc.;
- the study notes the high attractiveness of not only higher, but also secondary vocational education, which necessitates the formation of a strategy for the social design of the educational component through taking into account the totality of interests both at the state level and through satisfaction in the qualitative improvement of human capital.

Based on the elements of scientific novelty presented in the study, the authors proposed the following recommendations:

firstly, the focus of economic development on solving social problems requires, from a methodological point of view, the most active social programming with the inclusion of the concept of institutional design to achieve the set goals, which also provides for a focus on deepening the socially-oriented component in the regulation of socio-economic relations;

secondly, "the main advantages of social programming as a new area of research are revealed when we pay attention to the multi-subjectivity of social interactions" (Shalak, 2016), which increases the importance of interdisciplinary research in the field of sociology, economics, management, game theory, behavioral economics.

References

Aganbegyan, A. G. (2020). Crisis as a window of opportunities for socio-economic development. *Scientific Works of the Free Economic Society of Russia, 223*, 47–69. https://doi.org/10.38197/2072-2060-2020-223-3-47-69

Auzan, A. A. (2007). *Institutional Design of Reforms: Experience and an Attempt at Forecasting*. Higher School of Economics.

Benthem, J. (2014). *Logic in Games*. The MIT Press.

Bodrunov, S. D. (2019). Noonomics: Conceptual foundations of a new development paradigm. *Proceedings of the Ural State University of Economics, 20*(1), 5–12. https://doi.org/10.29141/2073-1019-2019-20-1-1

Chandler, S. (2020). Coronavirus turns Uber into gig platform for all work, Forbes. https://www.forbes.com/sites/simonchandler/2020/04/07/coronavirus-turns-uber-into-gig-platform-for-all-work/?sh=2ea1f7071db9. Data accessed: October 25, 2021.

Dashkovskaya, O. (2021). Investments in education: A contribution to the future or money for the wind? News of education. https://vogazeta.ru/articles/2021/10/25/analitycs/18377-investitsii_v_obrazovanie_vklad_v_buduschee_ili_dengi_na_veter. Accessed October 25, 2021.

Goodin, R. E. (1996). *The Theory of Institutional Design*. Cambridge University Press.
Itinson, K. S. (2020) Information and cognitive technologies: Modern educational trend. *Baltic Humanitarian Journal, 9*, 4(33), 84–86.
Kapelyushnikov, R. I. (2021) Returns to education in Russia: Nowhere below? *Voprosy Ekonomiki, 8*, 37–68. https://doi.org/10.32609/0042-8736-2021-8-37-68.
McKeever, V. (2020). Coronavirus lockdowns are making the working day longer for many. CNBC. https://www.cnbc.com/make-it/. Data accessed: October 25, 2021.
Nozhichkina, L. V. (2021). Cognitive research in education. https://ino.mgpu.ru/kognitivnye-issledovaniya-v-obrazovanii/. Data accessed: May 15, 2021.
Ostrom, E. (1990). *Governing the Commons: The Evolution of Institutions for Collective Actions* (pp. 149–153). Cambridge University Press.
Pacuit, E. (2005). Topics in Social Software: Information in Strategic Situations. PhD. thesis. City University of New York.
Parikh, R. (2002). Social software. *Synthese, 132*, 187–211.
Shalak, V. I. (2016). Social programming. *Social Time, 1*(5), 51–60.
Tambovtsev, V. L. (1997). Theoretical foundations of institutional design. *Economic Issues, 3*, 82–95.
Tikhomirov, B. I., & Frenkel, A. A. (2017). On unified socio-economic policy and strategic planning. *Economic Policy, 4*(12), 82–117. https://doi.org/10.18288/1994-5124-2017-4-04

Digital Technologies as a Factor in the Transformation of the Educational Process

Marina L. Gruzdeva, Victor P. Kuznetsov, Zhanna V. Smirnova, Evgeny A. Semakhin, and Elena V. Romanovskaya

Abstract In recent years, there has been a rapid penetration of digital technologies into the educational process of schools and universities. Due to the rapidity of this process, many educational institutions are guided not by rethinking and transforming the learning process into a format of interaction adapted to the digital environment, but by adapting the previous forms and methods of learning to the «digital format». The purpose of this article is to consider the transformation of the educational process under the influence of digital technologies. The authors considered the issues of using digital educational platforms in the learning process, new challenges, and tasks that pose the need for teachers and students to work with new digital tools. The article analyzes the experience of working with digital educational platforms of teachers in the period 2020–2021 in Nizhny Novgorod and the Nizhny Novgorod region. Technical and organizational issues that indicate the unreadiness of digital educational platforms for a complete transfer of the educational process to a distance format were identified on the basis of the study. At the same time, the teachers participating in the survey note the constant updating of the content of the existing digital educational platforms and the replenishment of their content and methodological components. The authors of the article, as educators, would like digital educational platforms to post more interactive tasks, educational games, and materials with feedback that can be used in the classroom, for example, for teamwork.

Keywords Digital technologies · Information educational environment · Student

JEL Classification I21 · I23

M. L. Gruzdeva (✉) · V. P. Kuznetsov · Z. V. Smirnova · E. A. Semakhin · E. V. Romanovskaya
Minin Nizhny Novgorod State Pedagogical University, Nizhny Novgorod, Russia
e-mail: gru1234@yandex.ru

Z. V. Smirnova
e-mail: z.v.smirnova@mininuniver.ru

E. V. Romanovskaya
e-mail: alenarom@list.ru

E. I. Lazareva et al. (eds.), *Innovative Trends in International Business and Sustainable Management*, Approaches to Global Sustainability, Markets, and Governance,
https://doi.org/10.1007/978-981-19-4005-7_25

1 Introduction

Modern education today functions in the context of the rapid transition of educational organizations to distance learning. In the context of the global informatization of the educational process, the question about the ability of digital technologies to ensure the completeness and quality of the educational process arises.

Information services to support the educational process have been used mainly in teaching children with disabilities and for additional preparation for classes over the past two decades. School teachers mostly used Dnevnik.ru, Uchi.ru services, and RES (Russian Electronic School) services were rarely used.

The rapid transition of a huge number of schools to «quarantine» at first did not force schools to search for and use digital educational platforms, but rather «led to the fact that most teachers began to use the simplest way of teaching according to the «provision of new material—control» scheme». They send students new educational material, links to a variety of educational resources, as well as homework, which they then check themselves (Karlov et al., 2020).

But it should be noted that the development of Russian digital educational platforms over the past two years, updating and filling the content of their subjects has led to the fact that more and more school teachers use educational resources (teaching materials, educational content, etc.) in their professional activities (Chelnokova et al., 2021; Garina et al., 2020).

2 Methodology

Digitalization is being introduced into various spheres of human activity, including educational activities. The education system is designed to «provide society with a confident transition to the digital era, focused on productivity growth, new types of work, human needs» (Nikulina & Starichenko, 2018). This is largely facilitated by digital educational platforms which have begun to develop rapidly in recent years and are increasingly used in the educational process of universities and schools.

«An information space that unites participants in the learning process, which provides an opportunity for remote education, provides access to teaching materials and information, and also allows testing to control the level of knowledge of students» is understood as a digital educational platform (Perelomov, 2021).

The use of digital educational platforms in the learning process expands the didactic learning opportunities: it increases the proportion of students' independent work, this provides them with such qualities as responsibility, organization, independence, and the ability to evaluate their strengths and capabilities in a balanced manner (Kuznetsov et al., 2019; Morozova et al., 2021).

The need to work with digital tools poses new challenges and tasks for teachers: the choice of technologies and methods of teaching in a digital environment, relying on the technical capabilities of students, writing methodological developments for working in a digital environment, building often individual educational trajectories with students (Romanovskaya et al., 2022; Smirnova et al., 2020, 2021).

So, today there is «an evolutionary path of development and rethinking of the educational process and the interaction of teachers and schoolchildren using digital tools» (Perelomov, 2021).

3 Results

This study is based on a survey conducted by Minin University teachers among school teachers in Nizhny Novgorod and the Nizhny Novgorod region during the Nizhny Novgorod Association of Technology Teachers.

The issues of using Russian digital educational platforms in 2019, 2020, and 2021 were discussed. Answers to the question «Have you used digital educational platforms?» from 2019 to 2021 were divided as follows (Fig. 1).

The following answers to the question «If Yes, what digital educational platforms do you use in the educational process?» were received: «Dnevnik.ru»—33 teachers, «Uchi.ru»—31 teachers, «RES» (Russian Electronic School) services—10 teachers, «Google Classroom»—5 teachers, «YaKlass»—2 school teachers in Nizhny Novgorod and the Nizhny Novgorod Region.

Teachers noted such a learning platform as «Yandex.Textbook». The platform has existed since 2018, and all this time it has been replenished with new interactive tasks in mathematics and the Russian language. The disadvantage of this platform is that it covers tasks from 1 to 5 grades. Due to the fact that the survey, organized by the authors of the article, was mainly attended by teachers of middle and senior classes, they did not use the digital platform «Yandex.Textbook» in their work. But they noted positive feedback from colleagues—primary school teachers, who often

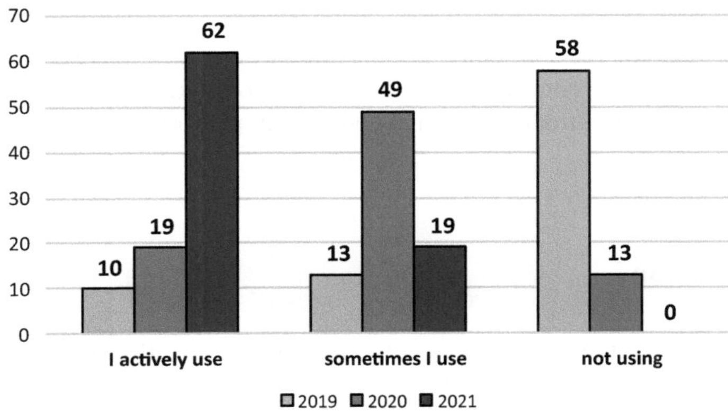

Fig. 1 Results of the teacher survey, answers to the question «Have you used digital educational platforms?». *Source* Compiled by the authors

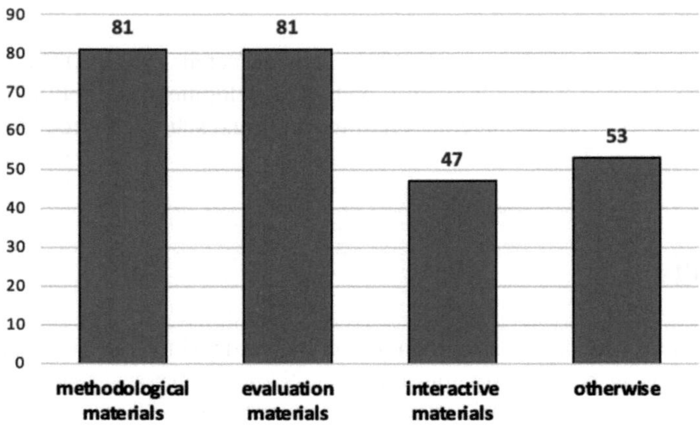

Fig. 2 Results of the teacher survey, answers to the question «What capabilities of digital educational platforms do you often use in the educational process?». *Source* Compiled by the authors

use the taskbook with automated knowledge testing. The developers of the digital content of the «Yandex.Textbook» platform note that it is planned to add content for 6–11 grades.

Teachers and students (target audience of the platform) use the «Foxford» digital educational platform, which contains distance learning courses in most subjects of the school curriculum (but not all), for additional preparation for Olympiads and final exams (both at 9 and 11 grades). The disadvantage of this platform is that most of the content is free of charge.

Teachers were also asked what features of digital educational platforms they often use in the educational process: teaching materials, assessment materials, and interactive materials. The answers were divided as follows (Fig. 2).

More than 80% of the respondents answered the question «Has the interest in the subject increased among students as a result of the use of digital educational platforms?» that middle and senior schoolchildren were most interested in the new format of education, younger students would like to return to full-time education but with elements of introducing digital educational platforms into the educational process.

4 Conclusion

The issue of using digital educational platforms in the educational process is especially acute when students are unable to attend educational institutions. Therefore, the rapid development of digital educational platforms took place precisely in 2020–2021, when all schools and universities were forced to transfer to a distance-learning format. But the pedagogical community, forced to use the digital environment in their work, notes that today the participants in the educational process (teachers and students) are not ready to completely switch to distance learning, no matter how rapid the growth of these digital services is. In addition to psychological factors that we will not consider in this article, there is a lack of readiness for this transition of the digital educational platforms themselves:

- technical capabilities (for example, a large number of students simultaneously studying on the platform slows down the work, sometimes it does not make it possible to complete the educational task by hanging);
- methodological possibilities (it is not always described how to use this or that content methodically in the classroom);
- «meaningful» opportunities (the content of the school curriculum from 1 to 11 grades is not fully laid out on any platform).

Today, it is absolutely clear that teaching using digital content requires teachers to take new approaches to organizing the educational process. The authors of the article, as educators, would like digital educational platforms to place more interactive tasks, educational games, and materials with feedback that can be used in the classroom, for example, for teamwork.

References

Chelnokova, E. A., Shobonova, L. Y., Romanovskaya, E. V., Andryashina, N. S., & Yashin, S. N. (2021). Educational robotics in practice of modern school. *Amazonia Investiga*, 238–246.

Garina, E., Kuznetsov, V., Garin, A., Andryashina, N., & Romanovskaya, E. (2020). Controlling as an instrument of industrial enterprise management in the conditions of modern economic activity. In *Lecture Notes in Networks and Systems* (Vol. 87. No. 11, p. 555).

Karlov, I. A., Kovalev, V. O., Kozhevnikov, N. A., Patarakin, E. D., Frumin, I. D., Shvindt, A. N., & Shonov, D. O. (2020). *Express-analysis of digital educational resources and services for organizing the educational process of schools in a distance form* (56p). National Research University Higher School of Economics, Institute of Education, M.: NRU HSE.

Kuznetsov, V. P., Kuznetsova, S. N., Romanovskaya, E. V., Andryashina, N. S., & Garina, E. P. (2019). Technological renewal of industrial sectors through creation of high-tech industrial eco-clusters. *Studies in Computational Intelligence, 826*, 1089–1095.

Morozova, G. A., Kuznetsov, V. P., Kozlova, E. P., Zaitseva, S. A., & Andryashina, N. S. (2021). The impact of artificial intelligence on the socio-economic development of society in modern conditions. In *Lecture Notes in Networks and Systems* (Vol. 200, pp. 406–414).

Nikulina, T. V., & Starichenko, E. B. (2018). Informatization and digitalization of education: concepts, technologies, management. *Pedagogical Education of Russia*, (8). http://journals.uspu.ru/attachments/article/2133/14.pdf. Data accessed: November 20, 2021.

Perelomov, S. V. (2021). The use of digital educational platforms in the educational process. *Informatics and ICT*. https://урок.рф/library/ispolzovanie_tcifrovih_obrazovatelnih_platform_v_202515.html. Data accessed: November 20, 2021.

Romanovskaya, E. V., Kozlova, E. P., Andryashina, N. S., Garina, E. P., & Smirnova, Z. V. (2022). The paradigm of economic development of the enterprise based on the mechanism of capital formation and distribution. In *Cooperation and Sustainable Development. Conference Proceedings* (pp. 1021–1029).

Smirnova, Z. V., Katkova, O. V., Golubeva, O. V., Romanovskaya, E. V., & Andryashina, N. S. (2021). Innovative technologies in the training of university specialists. In *Lecture Notes in Networks and Systems* (Vol. 155, pp. 352–359).

Smirnova, Z. V., Kutepova, L. I., Vaganova, O. I., Cherney, O. T., & Romanovskaya, E. V. (2020). Automatic submerged arc welding. *International Journal of Emerging Trends in Engineering Research*, *8*(7), 2989–2991.

Human Capital as the Main Factor of an Innovative Economy: New Managerial Guidelines

Human Capital as Economic Systems Competitiveness Increasing Factor in the Sustainable Development Context

Elena S. Shilets, Victoria A. Kravchenko, Liudmila V. Ganich, Andrei V. Hruzan, and Anna G. Turalina

Abstract The present article casts light upon the conceptual foundations and economics competitiveness increasing factors in the sustainable development context. Particular attention is paid to the human capital as determining increasing competitiveness and national economic growth factor in terms of the necessity of maintaining the stability of economic systems. The purpose of the study is human capital impact assessment on the stability of the economic system while increasing its competitiveness. The methodological basis of the study is made up of a set of general scientific and special methods of cognition. The research results can be used in the elaboration mechanism for increasing competitiveness in sustainable development. The present article is original research.

Keywords Human capital · Competitiveness · Sustainable development

JEL Classification O150 · D4 · O4

1 Introduction

At the present stage of international economic relations, developing during such pandemic impact as the economy stagnation, the closure of borders, the inertial decline in labor productivity and foreign economic activity of all countries of the world, the necessity of the innovative way of development, increasing the competitiveness and stability of the functioning of economic systems, i.e. all processes in the state, determines the relevance of the chosen topic of research. Regarding this, it is

E. S. Shilets · V. A. Kravchenko · L. V. Ganich · A. V. Hruzan (✉) · A. G. Turalina
Donetsk National University, Donetsk, Ukraine
e-mail: a.hruzan@donnu.ru

L. V. Ganich
e-mail: lud.ganich@yandex.ua

A. G. Turalina
e-mail: turalina.ana@yandex.ua

E. I. Lazareva et al. (eds.), *Innovative Trends in International Business and Sustainable Management*, Approaches to Global Sustainability, Markets, and Governance,
https://doi.org/10.1007/978-981-19-4005-7_26

necessary to identify the factors, shaping economic competitiveness. It is advisable to pay special attention to the study of human capital as a component of the innovative process of socioeconomic development, ensuring the rate of economic growth while preserving the environment.

The purpose of the study is human capital impact assessment on the stability of the economic system while increasing their competitiveness at the present stage.

The target of the work achievement necessitated the formulation and solution of the following tasks:

- to research the essence and factors that form the competitiveness of economic systems;
- to analyse the directions of competitiveness increasing in the context of the sustainable development;
- to assess the degree of human capital influence on the economy competitiveness increasing; to propose the priority areas for the economy sustainable competitiveness implementation, the central link of which is the human capital as the main innovations producer.

2 Materials and Method

The work is based on the scientific school's fundamental research and projects presented in the field of conceptual foundations of competitiveness, competitive advantages, sustainable development, and human capital. The methodological basis of the research is made up of dialectical methodology, general scientific methods of historical-logical, system-functional, comparative analysis, as well as methods of scientific abstraction, induction and deduction, and economic statistical methods of collecting information and its analysis.

In the present paper, educational and scientific publications of Russian and foreign researchers in the problem had been studied. As an analytical basis material of international scientific and practical conferences, research centers and international organizations data, data from the Federal State Statistics Service of the Russian Federation had been used.

Questions of theoretical understanding of the "competitiveness" concept were studied by foreign authors, among which are the works of Schumpeter (1942), Vernon (1974), and Russian scientists, including (Atkisson, 2015; Azoev, 1996; Fatkhutdinov, 2005; Karabanova et al., 2020; Magomedov & Alekseicheva, 2017; Mironov, 2004; Mokronosov & Mavrina, 2014; Rud, 2018; Zhukovskaya & Trofimova, 2008).

In practical models development, identification of factors and directions for the modernization of existing mechanisms for increasing the state's competitiveness were engaged such scientists as (Cho, 1994; Porter, 2005) and others.

Such foreign scientists of the economic school as (Akishin, 1995; Samuelson & Nordhaus, 1997) made a sustainable contribution to the study of sustainable development, the mechanism of its functioning.

Among Russian authors, one can note the works of Mirkin and Naumova (2018), Shlikhter (2020), Shumilov and Shumilova (2017), Ursul (2019).

Modern science trends indicate the human capital study from the point of view of an innovative economy formation and functioning, the competitive advantages of economic systems forming, based on innovative transformations, a high level of education, professionalism, qualifications, not just a set of competencies, but the use of personality traits. The works of Bendikov and Khrustalev (2007), Chevtaeva and Nikitina (2020), Egorova et al. (2015) and others are devoted to these issues.

At the same time, despite the economists numerous works on the scientific research topic, there is no comprehensive approach reflecting the general principles and model of human capital as economic systems competitiveness increasing factor in the sustainable development context utilization.

3 Results

At the present stage of the world economic relations development, competitiveness is the main determinant of ensuring the stability of economic systems, obtaining competitive advantages, contributing to accelerated growth in labour productivity, increasing the well-being of the population, more rational use of production factors, especially natural resources of a limited nature.

Considering modern approaches to the competitiveness interpretation, the variability in understanding this category is emphasized (Table 1). It is interpreted by various authors as a theoretical, multidimensional, and relative concept associated with the market mechanism. Among the subjects in the market, there are simultaneously high-, medium-, and low-competitive economic agents, and therefore, most likely the competitiveness concept should be defined as a set of object characteristics in relation to other comparable etalons in the market. Moreover, this category is used almost interchangeably with concepts such as productivity, innovation, market share, and development.

The main reason for the multiplicity of the competitiveness interpretations is the consistency of the term. It reflects the favourable position of the state's economy in the field of international trade and, at the same time, its ability to strengthen this position. That is, this term implies the occupation of a certain niche in the world arena and its subsequent retention, strengthening, ensuring *sustainable competitiveness* which is proposed to be interpreted as the actual and potential ability of a business entity to increase the efficiency of its activities and maintain the result of a positive trend on a long-term basis, providing the growing needs of society while maintaining the integrity of the environment with constant technological development. It should be borne in mind that in the globalization context, diversification risks have also become key by expanding the country's specialization (since narrow specialization determines dependence, limits) and differentiation of goods and services to strengthen competitive advantages.

Table 1 Competitiveness essence defining approaches

Author(s) source	Definition
T. Barker D. Kohler	A state's competitiveness is the degree to which a country can, in a free and fair market, produce goods or services that meet the requirements of international markets, *while maintaining and increasing the real incomes of its population in the long term*
European Commission	A nation's competitiveness is the ability of an economy to provide its population with a high and growing standard of living and *a high level of employment on a sustainable basis*
K. Outon J. Whittam	The competitiveness of a country implies *long-term productivity growth and the population standard of living increasing in line with an increase in employment or the maintenance of almost full employment*
IMD Global Competitiveness Yearbook	State competitiveness is the ability of a nation to create and sustain an environment that supports the creation of more value for its businesses and greater prosperity for its people

Source Compiled by the authors

Considering the definition from the management side, state's competitiveness is the ability of the country to achieve high rates of economic growth, to ensure a stable increase in real wages, to promote domestic firms to the world market, to promote the development of high-performance clusters that improve the quality of products and services, and also allow creating new jobs in the future. The key skill, in this case, is adaptability to changes in the market, based on various economic factors (such as the volume of investments, the availability of innovations and technologies, production capacities, etc.), social (the standard of living of the country's population, the availability and solvency of demand, level of education, qualification of human capital), and environmental (environmental friendliness, compliance with standards). Their combination and effectiveness must be complemented by public policies that promote competitive sustainability.

Human capital in this case is presented not only as an accumulated stock of knowledge, skills, and acquired skills but as the most important resource, which is an indicator of competitiveness forming the reproduction of national wealth, i.e. ensures the system stability.

The level of education, intellectualization of labour, individual abilities, personal characteristics, cultural, moral, entrepreneurial abilities, the degree of his activity, professionalism, focus on results, creativity, safety margin, and striving for new knowledge give a qualitatively new understanding of the characteristics of human capital—*qualifications*, forming the competitiveness of an individual, enterprise, and state.

The competitiveness models development had been facilitated by the work of world-renowned economists, such as Porter (2005) (the diamond of competitive advantage), in whose work the main determinants are the firm's strategy, demand parameters, and factor conditions that support the industry. Further development is presented in the model of "Double Diamond" by A. M. Rugman and J. D'Kruz, where the state's competitiveness is defined as the ability of firms engaged in value-added activities in a particular industry in a particular country to maintain it for long periods, despite international competition. In the generalized double diamond, the outer diamond represents global activity, and the inner diamond represents national activity. The size of the global diamond is fixed in the foreseeable future, while the size of the internal diamond varies depending on the competitiveness and country size.

More dynamic and comprehensive than M. Porter's "Competitive diamond" model is the "Nine Factor Model" by Cho (1994). This structure consists of the following elements:

- the human factor includes employees, politicians and officials, entrepreneurs, professionals, and specialists (including scientists, managers);
- the physical factor contains factor conditions, demand conditions, related and supporting industries, and business environment;
- an external factor, which includes random events, chance.

Thus, the nine factor model has some advantages over the competitive diamond model, namely:

- complexity in explaining the importance of the roles of various groups of people for their economic growth, as well as taking into account the different levels of economic development of countries and their comparison on this basis;
- dynamism, because human and physical factors interact to stimulate the development of the nation. It embodies M. Porter's idea that "national prosperity is created, not inherited";
- civil servants are endogenous (internal) factors in this model and have a direct impact on the competitiveness of the state.

Based on the analysis of the conceptual foundations of competitiveness, it can be argued that it is a fundamental determinant of economic growth. The constant growth of the competitiveness causes the sustainable development of economic systems (a set of processes occurring in an enterprise, organization, state, society). Among the factors that ensure the availability of competitive advantages of business entities, it is advisable to include human capital, which is directly involved in all processes of ensuring competitiveness in each of the blocks of the model, from the staffing of employees to effective demand. The presented models are confirmed by rating agencies research results, research institutes, surveys, and analytical reviews.

Thus, according to a business leader's survey, researchers from the International Institute for Management Development have identified the factors of the state's competitive advantages.

Among them, the largest share in Russia is held by a high level of education (72.2%), a skilled labour force (67%), and price competitiveness (46%). The disadvantages of the Russian economy are the weak structure of R&D (13.4%), incompetence of the government (8.2%), and an ineffective legal environment (3.1%) (Forecast of long-term socio-economic development of the Russian Federation for the period up to, 2030; Global Innovation Index, 2021).

It should also be noted that the Russian Federation economy needs a structural transition from the investment stage to the innovative stage of development, which can be carried out with coordinated government management. This transition was described in some programs adopted at the national level: "Forecast of the long-term socioeconomic development of the Russian Federation for the period up to 2030" (Forecast of long-term socio-economic development of the Russian Federation for the period up to, 2030); Decree of the President of the Russian Federation of July 21, 2020 No. 474 "On the national development goals of the Russian Federation for the period up to 2030" (Decree "On the National Development Goals of the Russian Federation for the period up to, 2030"). However, the goals and objectives described in the programs until 2020 have not been achieved and implemented. Let us study the strategic directions of the development of Russia for the implementation of the transition to the innovative stage of economic development (Fig. 1).

As the most important direction of the development of labour resources, human capital is understood, which is carried out by improving the education system functioning. Moreover, thanks to the implementation of an optimal educational program by the state, citizens are becoming aware of the importance of acquiring knowledge at every level of this system: from preschool to higher professional education.

Fig. 1 Strategic directions of the Russian economy's development. *Source* Compiled by the authors based on forecast of long-term socioeconomic development of the RF (Forecast of long-term socio-economic development of the Russian Federation for the period up to, 2030)

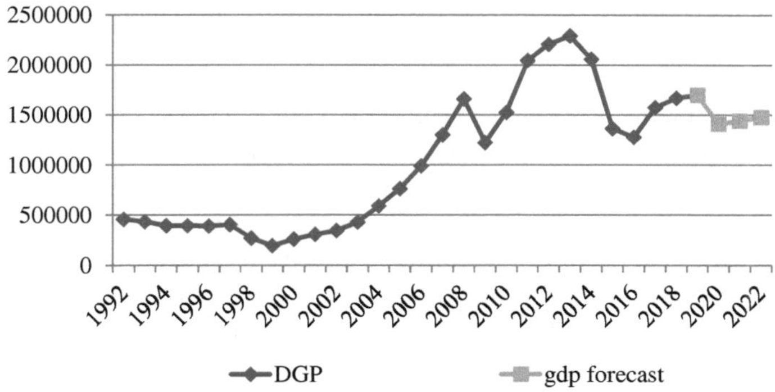

Fig. 2 Forecast of Russian Federation GDP, including model factors influence, thousand US dollars. *Source* Calculated and built by the authors

These areas are confirmed by the factors identified for the competitiveness analysis. Based on the available data, a GDP forecast for 2021–2022 had been built, taking into account changes in all model features (Fig. 2). In the calculation model, the indicators of the development of the Russian Federation economy had been used, and the most significant impact on the growth of the gross domestic product (GDP) was exerted by the dynamics of the results of foreign trade activities, the export of high-tech products, the inflow of foreign investment, as well as income from tourism activities.

Because the export of high-tech products is the result of a synergistic effect, which can be traced, for example, in the global innovation index, where Russia occupies high positions in terms of the generation of new knowledge (scientific publications, patents) and their acquisition (rights to the results of intellectual activity, saturation economy with highly qualified personnel) (Competitiveness Country Profiles, 2020; Decree "On the National Development Goals of the Russian Federation for the period up to, 2030"; Forecast of long-term socio-economic development of the Russian Federation for the period up to, 2030).

Despite the pandemic negative impact, the values are expected to increase in the future, demonstrating positive dynamics. Applying comprehensive measures for all vectors reflected in the study to restore the national economy will be expedient.

4 Conclusion

In the course of the study, the essence and models genesis had been characterized. The main factors of the competitiveness of the economic system had been highlighted. It has been determined that one of the key factors providing the factors of the economy's competitiveness is the human capital. The author's approach to understanding the essence of the concepts of competitive sustainability and qualification of human capital had been proposed.

The priority areas of the competitiveness of the economic system increasing in the sustainable development context had been highlighted, during the implementation of which it is necessary to reconfigure existing state programs and a package of national projects aimed at qualitatively strengthening and strengthening state support for the role of the knowledge economy, education, and human capital development.

Also, based on the 2020 pandemic crisis lessons and the growing trend of associated biosocial risks, priority should be given to the health and education sector, biotechnology and IT, as well as the training of highly qualified personnel to achieve and maintain sustainable economic growth with the preservation of biodiversity and the transition from resource towards an innovative way of development.

References

Akishin, V. V. (1995). *Competition: Modern trends, problems of formation* (153p). Kuzbass University Publishing House.

Atkisson, A. (2015). *How sustainable development can change the world* (432p). Binom. Laboratory of Knowledge.

Azoev, G. L. (1996). *Competition: Analysis, strategy and practice* (208p). Center for Economics and Marketing.

Bendikov, M. A., & Khrustalev, E. Y. (2007). Methodological bases of a research of the mechanism of innovative development in modern economy [Metodologicheskie osnovy issledovaniya mekhanizma innovatsionnogo razvitiya v sovremennoy ekonomike]. *Management in Russia and Abroad [menedzhment v Rossii i Za Rubezhom], 2*, 3–14.

Chevtaeva, N. G., & Nikitina, A. S. (2020). Human resource management in state and municipal management: Studies. In *Handbook for universities* (2nd ed., 187p). Yurayt. ISBN 978-5-534-12784-3.

Cho, D. (1994). A dynamic approach to international competitiveness: The case of Korea. *Journal of Far Eastern Business*, 17–36.

Competitiveness Country Profiles. (2020). IMD World Competitiveness Center. https://www.imd.org/wcc/world-competitiveness-center-rankings/competitiveness-country-profiles/. Accessed: September 15, 2021.

Decree "On the National Development Goals of the Russian Federation for the period up to 2030". Center for Legal Support of Environmental Management. https://www.ecours.ru/content/prezident-podpisal-ukaz-o-nacionalnyh-celyah-razvitiya-rossiyskoy-federacii-na-period-do. Accessed: April 27, 2021.

Egorova, M. S., Saltevskaya, E. E., & Monakhova, E. A. (2015). *Problems of human resource management. Text: direct* (Vol. 8, No. 88, pp. 521–523). Young Scientist. https://moluch.ru/archive/88/17537/. Accessed: January 15, 2020.

Fatkhutdinov, R. A. (2005). *Managing the competitiveness of an organization: A textbook* (544p). EKSMO.

Forecast of long-term socio-economic development of the Russian Federation for the period up to 2030. http://www.consultant.ru/document. Accessed: September 27, 2021.

Global Innovation Index. (2021). globalinnovationindex.org. Accessed: September 20, 2021.

Karabanova, O. V., Magomedov, M. D., & Sharapova, S. A. (2020). Competitiveness of a multicultural region's economy: Measuring and provision. In *Contributions to economics* (pp. 163–171). https://doi.org/10.1007/978-3-030-38497-5_19

Magomedov, M. D., & Alekseicheva, E. Y. (2017). The state and problems of managing the competitiveness of domestic enterprises. *Bulletin of the Moscow City Pedagogical University. Series: Economics, 2*, 30.

Mirkin, B. M., & Naumova, L. G. (2018). *Sustainable development: Introductory course: Studies manual* (312p). University Book.

Mironov, M. G. (2004). *Your competitiveness* (160p). Alfa-Press.

Mokronosov, A. G., & Mavrina, I. N. (2014). *Competition and competitiveness: A textbook* (194p). Ural University Publishing House.

Porter, M. (2005). *Competitive advantage: How to achieve a high result and ensure its sustainability: Trans. from English* (715p). Alpina Business Books.

Rud, A. E. (2018). Theoretical foundation of research of institutional regulation of the competitiveness of the organization. *Bulletin of Saratov University (N.S.), Series Economics Management Law, 18*(1), 81–86. https://doi.org/10.18500/1994-2540-2018-18-1-81-86

Samuelson, P. A., & Nordhaus, W. D. (1997). *Economics: Translated from English* (800p). "BINOM", "Laboratory of Basic Knowledge".

Schumpeter, J. A. (1942). *Capitalism, socialism and democracy* (381p). Harper & Row.

Shlikhter, A. (2020). Business strategies of companies in the context of sustainable development. *World Economy and International Relations [Mirovaya ekonomika i mezhdunarodnye otnosheniya], 4*(64), 37–44. https://doi.org/10.20542/0131-2227-2020-64-4-37-44

Shumilov, Y. V., & Shumilova, M. Y. (2017). On the concept of sustainable development in an unstable world. *Eurasian Scientific Association, 2*(24), 159–162.

Ursul, A. D. (2019). Conceptual problems of sustainable development. *Bulletin of the Russian Academy of Sciences Use and Protection of Natural Resources in Russia, 1*, 30–38.

Vernon, R. (1974). The location of economic activity. In J. H. Dunning (Ed.), *Economic analysis and the multinational enterprise* (pp. 89–114). George Allen & Unwin.

Zhukovskaya, V., & Trofimova, I. (2008). Competitiveness in micro-, meso- and macro-level dimensions. *Russian Economy Journal, 3*, 68.

Human Capital in the "Behavioral-Digital" Economics

Olga V. Evgrafova, Aleksei V. Bondarenko, Tatyana N. Vasilyuk, and Elena A. Kozlovskaya

Abstract The authors of the study aim to formulate the problem of the correlation of two innovative trends in the development of the modern economy that form its human capital—"behavioral" and "digital"; this is carried out within the framework of the methodology of interdisciplinary socio-humanitarian research. The first trend is considered as a theory, the provisions of which are related to the humanitarian factor of a significant form of human capital in economic culture in all the variety of its manifestations. The digital economy is interpreted not as a new type of economy, but as its total computerization in order to provide informational support for economic development; the formality of digitalization is emphasized, which has the potential to devalue the humanitarian component of economic development, deforming its human capital. The authors come to the conclusion that the trends considered are not antagonistic: "behavioral" with its economic culture emphasizes the socio-humanitarian content of economic activity, and "digital" marks the informational formality of a person's economic life in society; in their dialectical unity, they characterize the formation of a new quality of human capital, the originality of its author's consideration.

Keywords Economy · Capital · Behavior · Digitalization · Person · Culture · Interdisciplinarity

JEL Classification A12 · A13 · B41 · B52 · D13 · D83 · D91 · O15 · O30

O. V. Evgrafova (✉)
Rostov Branch of the Russian Customs Academy, Rostov-on-Don, Russia
e-mail: dia7@bk.ru

A. V. Bondarenko · T. N. Vasilyuk · E. A. Kozlovskaya
Odintsovo Branch of the Moscow State Institute of International Relations (University) of the Ministry of Foreign Affairs of Russia, Moscow, Russia
e-mail: a.bondarenko@odin.mgino.ru

T. N. Vasilyuk
e-mail: t.vasiluk@odin.mgino.ru

E. A. Kozlovskaya
e-mail: e.kozlovskaya@odin.mgino.ru

E. I. Lazareva et al. (eds.), *Innovative Trends in International Business and Sustainable Management*, Approaches to Global Sustainability, Markets, and Governance,
https://doi.org/10.1007/978-981-19-4005-7_27

1 Introduction

The modern economy is going through a complex and contradictory stage of its development: there is a search for new dominants of post-industrial growth. In this regard, the economic theory is increasingly asserting the position that its main condition is not just the introduction of organizational, technical, and technological innovations, but the modernization of the role of a person, traditionally represented by the concept of "human capital". It is regarded as the main resource of the "creative economy", the international year of which the UN has declared 2021. We should add that the winners of the Nobel Prize in Economics for this year were D. Card for "empirical contribution to labor economics", as well as J. Angrist and G. Imbens for "methodological contribution to the cause-and-effect relationships analysis in the labor market", identified in "natural" experiments. It is clear that human behavior in this market directly concerns the problems of human capital. All this justifies the relevance of the article.

In our study, we considered the problem of "combining" behavioral and digital trends of modern economic theory to modernize the interpretation of human capital. The purpose of the article is to analyze the hypothesis about the dialectic of these trends as a source of its modern development.

2 Methodology

Consideration of the problem of "behavioral-digital dualism" of human capital in the modern economy, its theoretical understanding is carried out within the framework of the methodology of interdisciplinary research (Kleiner, 2016). At the same time, we consider the "object" version of human capital, namely its behavioral and digital trends, from the standpoint of not only economic theory but also other social and humanitarian sciences: philosophy, psychology, history, and cultural studies. In addition, the methods of "pure consideration", analysis and synthesis are used.

There is an extensive literature on the subject of human capital, both foreign and domestic. Historically, this is due both to the analysis of the reasons for the superiority of "developed" countries and to the understanding of their transition to a post-industrial economy, which imposes new requirements for human participation in it.

The consideration of the phenomenon of man in the economy as a special "human capital" is associated with the name of T. Schultz, who studied the causes of economic underdevelopment of postcolonial countries (Shultz, 1968); at the psychological "micro level" it was justified by Becker (2003). Developing their ideas, many foreign scholars have considered various aspects of human capital, among which Denison (1978), Kuznets (1973), Lucas (1988), Myrdal (1978), Thurow (1970), Fogel (2003) and other Western scientists, economists, sociologists, historians, psychologists, culturologists laid the foundations of this interdisciplinary direction.

A sufficient number of domestic works that form the basis of our research are also devoted to various aspects of human capital. First of all, we rely on the works of Antonov and Ulupova (2012), Buzgalin and Kolganov (2006), Evgrafova (2013, 2016), Eliseev and Komarova (2013), Koritsky (2012), Korolev and Evgrafova (2019, 2020), Korchagin (2011), Kritsky (1991), Litvinenko (2016), Shchetinin (2001) and others.

The analysis of this literature shows that the majority of domestic publications, primarily of an economic nature, with all the depth of the analysis, leave gaps for understanding modern trends in the development of human capital, requiring an adequate interdisciplinary methodology of socio-humanitarian discourse.

3 Results

In order to adequately formulate the problem under consideration, it is necessary to determine the "working" ideas about the concepts that form it. It seems important to start by defining the concept of human capital. Without going into the depths of its special study, we note that by this capital we understand the state of the human "factor" of the economy (as its "driving force"), formed by the totality of all the qualities of a person involved in economic activity conditioned by a specific socio-cultural context. Thus, we are based on such an interpretation of human capital, which overcomes the traditional "resource" approach and complement it with the socio-humanitarian component of a person realizing all his "cultural" potential in economic activity (Evgrafova, 2013). It is obvious that the post-industrial society puts forward the need for such an understanding of modern human capital, its consideration in the light of two, in our opinion, the main innovative trends of modern economic theory, i.e., the concepts of "behavioral" and "digital" economics, noting the unity of irrational and rational components of the quality of human capital, forming the substantive and formal inconsistency of its development as an organic unity.

In order to conceptualize it, we consider it necessary to consider its constituent trends separately. Within the framework of behavioral economics, the consideration of human behavior in economic life has deep developments, as evidenced by the Nobel prizes for research on various aspects of this problem. Actually, "behavioral economics" caused a particularly strong resonance when the economist Richard H. Thaler won the 2017 Nobel Memorial Prize in Economic Sciences. He criticizes the "classics" of economic theory for trying to put all the variety of economic situations in which people find themselves within the framework of their rational understanding and behavior. He does not agree with the idea that the existing problems associated with the emotionally irrational aspects of their economic behavior are completely solvable on the basis of reason. In his works, Thaler emphasizes the importance of understanding the connection between economic and cultural-psychological practices of human decision-making and highlights the role of the irrational component of human behavior in economic life (Thaler, 2020). His supporter D. Kahneman also believes that in modern economic life, the behavioral paradigm with its irrational "riskiness" reduces the value of the classical theory with its objective and rational explanation of human economic behavior (Kahneman, 2017). In short, Thaler, like-minded scientists and his followers have shown that the absolute majority of people in the process of choosing their economic behavior do not act as rationally as it was commonly believed in the "classical" theory. As for management problems, it is important to note that "behavioral economics" is not just a new economic theory; it has a practical orientation, it is designed to adjust a person's economic life taking into account the role of the emotional and psychological component of his behavior, which now believed to be more important than previously thought. (In particular, Thaler (2020) introduce the concept of "libertarian paternalism", the practical implementation of which is designed to gently "push" people's economic behavior in the direction needed by the state, which is used in the implementation of the practices of appropriate management).

Thus, the questions arise:

1. How do these behavioral attitudes emerge in economic activity?
2. Is it possible to practically take into account the state of the human psyche in its characterization as "capital", manage the formation and functioning of the latter?

The traditional, "resource-based" approach to answering these questions has failed and cannot be used for this; we believe that a broader socio-humanitarian approach is needed here.

In its interdisciplinary implementation, in the consideration of a person as a multi-dimensional personality, not just capital, but a factor of the post-industrial economy, the concept of "economic culture", little studied in economic theory, appears. Relying on the interpretation given by one of the authors of the article (Evgrafova, 2016), as well as on the interdisciplinary consideration of the economic culture of human capital, we note that this culture, including the "psychology" of behavioral economics as one of its humanitarian factors, gives a broader understanding of the "ethos" of human participation in economic activity, taking into account its social, axiological and mental factors (Korolev & Evgrafova, 2020).

The study of the digital economy, due to its relative novelty, does not have such serious traditions; it has begun to be considered as a phenomenon of the information society (Castells (2000), Machlup (1962), etc.). In the domestic scientific literature, this concept is considered based on Western studies, but as a more multifaceted phenomenon (Dyachenko, 2019).

It is clear that we are primarily interested in publications that consider digitalization not a purely economic concept, but an interdisciplinary one. When analyzing its socio-humanitarian role, it is necessary to highlight the articles of the journal "Philosophy of Economics" by its head Osipov (2018), as well as Korolev and Evgrafova (2019, 2020), Kulkov (2017) and many other authors who consider the impact of digitalization on a person's entire life, and not only on its economic or social components.

How do the considered behavioral intentions correlate with the trend of the "digital economy"? It depends on its interpretation: we believe there are two of them—"Western" and Russian. In the West, the digital economy has become the subject of attention in connection with the formation of the so-called fourth technological order. At the major international economic summits of the G20 (2017 and 2019), special "Declarations on the Digital Economy" were adopted, in which digitalization is considered as a powerful means of increasing the efficiency of the economy, due to the rapid and accurate development of its growing masses of data (Big Data). But, we emphasize that such an interpretation of the "digital economy" does not have a paradigmatic novelty.

In Russia, this concept is considered more broadly and deeply: in the program "Digital Economy of the Russian Federation" adopted in 2017 (the year when R. Thaler won the Nobel Prize), two levels of its understanding and implementation can be identified. The first level can be called "information and communication", since the digital economy acts as a way of managing economic life based on the growing use of computer technologies, as a means of developing on their basis certain areas of technological progress that appear to be the "locomotives" of economic development. This level does not need a special theoretical justification, it is adequate to the well- and multilaterally elaborated Western interpretation of economic digitalization. At the same time, in our program, the digital economy has the potential to be considered from the perspective of the prospects for the progress of the state, the whole society, and the individual. It notes the "digital development of Russia", and not only its economy, which allows us to consider this concept at the second level—"socio-humanitarian" (Korolev & Evgrafova, 2019). (In particular, the importance of such an interpretation of digitalization is evidenced by the fact that a single digital platform is being created to provide operational support to Russians in the social sphere, on the basis of which it is planned to make all socially significant state and municipal services electronic by 2023, and in 2024 almost 80% of Russians will be able to receive federal assistance without paper documents).

But for this level, there is no special theory of the digital economics, digitalization has not yet been observed, the matter is limited to considering certain aspects of the impact of digitalization on the economy, as well as on society and man.

What are the prospects for this growing influence on the quality of human participation in economic activity, on its human capital? First of all, it should be noted the negative ones: with the rapid expansion of the scope of digital technologies, the growth of their impact on economic (and not only) life, there is a danger of separation of the digital computer form from the content of real (economic) processes, when the digital technologies do not just "present" this reality, but replace and even substitute it. And this is fundamentally important for the interpretation of human capital in the light of behavioral economics: can the "Digital technologies", having conquered the economy itself, conquer the person himself, his economic behavior (Osipov, 2018)? There are grounds for such alarm: digital technologies are increasingly creating limitations for a person of computer forms of relevant programs that do not directly allow interpreting economic realities in a way inherent to a person, not always rationally.

This narrows the possibilities of creative, "unformatted" human behavior (developed by answers to questions not only "how", but also "why", "for what"), reduces the potential of the necessary socio-cultural understanding of economic activity; in particular, situations where the economically profitable is not such in social and humanitarian terms (paid medicine, for example), and vice versa ("social responsibility of business") (Kulkov, 2017). This could lead to the devaluation of the substantial and axiological aspects of human economic behavior, its re-evaluation. In socio-humanitarian terms, this is so important because the digitalization of lifestyle increasingly affects a person, forms the mental, and ideological foundations of his behavior as a socio-cultural subject of economic activity.

After a brief description of the sides of the behavioral-digital unity of the human capital of the modern economy, we will characterize its dialectic. Can all of the above indicate a certain "antagonism" of the trends considered in it? How do they affect the quality of human capital and its development? We believe there is no essential contradiction between "behavioral" and "digital" trends if these approaches to economics are not viewed in the terms of abstraction. Each interpretation emphasizes its own: behavioral focus on the content aspect, digital—on the form of realization (economic culture) of human capital. The dialectic of intentions of "behavioral economics" and "digital economy" as dominant economic trends is a source of development of the theory of modernization of human capital: the behavioral component is designed to be formalized for its practical, managerial implementation, and the digital component is filled with humanitarian content.

4 Conclusion

1. The world economy, powerfully "stimulated" by overcoming the Covid crisis, intensively implements its reformatting, increases the importance of "inclusive capitalism", in the formation of which a special role is assigned to man, which no longer is considered as a classical, industrial "capital (resource)", but as a "capital (factor)" of post-industrial economic development, adequately represented by its economic culture.
2. The modernization of human capital can be worthy of its new role only if its behavioral and digital interpretations, embodying the unity of economic theory and practice, are combined. These interpretations have been shown not to be "antagonistic": they complement each other, forming a unity of irrational and rational in human economic activity, the source of which is post-industrial human capital.
3. The potential of this unity has not yet been revealed in Russia: the behavioral trend has remained an exotic innovation of economic theory, and the digital one is being implemented by the practice of computerization development, which has no special theoretical justification. The task of management is to develop a management model of practical unification of the considered trends for the

formation of modern human capital, which forms the prospect of its further research.

References

Antonov, A. D., & Ulupova, V. L. (2012). Human capital in Russian companies: The way to post-industrial economy. *Philosophy of Economy, 3*, 193–210.

Becker, G. (2003). Human behavior. Economical approach. In *Selected works on economic theory*. SU HSE.

Buzgalin, A. V., & Kolganov, A. I. (2006). Human being, market and capital in the 21st century economy. *Questions of Economics, 3*, 125–141. https://doi.org/10.32609/0042-8736-2006-3-125-141

Castells, M. (2000). *The information age: Economy, society and culture*. SU HSE.

Denison, E. F. (1978). The contribution of knowledge to economic growth: Cross-country analysis. *Soviet-American Symposium of Economists, 4*, 39–46.

Dyachenko, O. V. (2019). Categorical definition of digital economy in foreign and Russian economic theory. *Economic Revival of Russia, 1*(59), 86–97.

Eliseev, V. N., & Komarova, A. V. (2013). *The human dimension of economic development: Methodology and theory*. Publishing House Assistance—XXI century.

Evgrafova, O. V. (2013). *Human capital issues in socio-cultural discourse*. Russian Customs Academy Rostov Branch.

Evgrafova, O. V. (2016). *Economic culture*. Russian Customs Academy Rostov Branch.

Fogel, R. W. (2003). Secular trends in physiological capital: Implications for equity in health care. *Perspectives in Biology and Medicine, 46*(3), 24–38.

Kahneman, D. (2017). *Think slowly ... Decide quickly*. AST Publishing House.

Kleiner, G. B. (2016). Interdisciplinarity in modern socio-humanitarian knowledge. In *Proceedings of the All-Russian Scientific Conference*, Rostov-on-Don, June 22–23, 2016 (pp. 20–34). Southern Federal University Press.

Korchagin, Yu. A. (2011). *Human capital as an intensive socio-economic factor in the development of the individual, economy, society and statehood*. SU HSE.

Koritskiy, A. V. (2012) Assessment of the impact of human capital on economic growth. *Doctoral dissertation*. Novosibirsk.

Korolev, V. K., & Evgrafova, O. V. (2019). Digital economy and the "numerical world" (Pythagoreans): Updating the philosophy of economics. *Philosophy of Economy, 5*, 20–36.

Korolev, V. K., & Evgrafova, O. V. (2020). *Economic culture of human capital in the methodology of interdisciplinary discourse*. Southern Federal University Press.

Kritsky, M. M. (1991). *Human capital*. Publishing house of Leningrad State University.

Kulkov, V. M. (2017). The digital economy: Hopes and illusions. *Philosophy of Economy, 5*, 145–156.

Kuznets, S. (1973). *Population, capital and growth*. Norton.

Litvinenko, I. L. (2016). Human capital as the basis of an innovative economy. *Human Society Inclusion, 1*(25), 87.

Lucas, R. (1988). On the mechanism of economic development. *Journal of Monetary Economics, 22*, 3–42.

Machlup, F. (1962). *The production and distribution of knowledge in the United States*. Prinston University Press.

Myrdal, G. (1978). *Political and institutional economics*. Economic and Social Research Institute (ESRI).

Osipov, Yu. M. (2018). Economics and digital: Who wins? *Philosophy of Economy, 2*, 11–19.

Shchetinin, V. (2001). Human capital and the ambiguity of its interpretation. *World Economy and International Relations, 12*, 42–49.

Shultz, T. (1968). *Human capital in the international encyclopedia of the social sciences.*

Thaler, R. (2020). *New behavioral economics. Why people violate the rules of the traditional economy and how to make money on it*. Eksmo.

Thurow, L. (1970). *Investment in human capital.* Wadsworth Publishing House.

Social Trigger—A New Vector of Management in an Innovative Economy

Maria P. Pavlova

When I am motivated by a story about a frog in milk that knocked down butter with its paws, I always pay attention to, that she ended up in milk, and not in tar... Unknown author

Abstract Today, the large-scale diffusion of modern innovative technologies forms a new model of worldview, where the physical picture of the world is viewed through the prism of creativity, creating new types of creativity. The innovation space as a determinant of this new paradigm provides manifestations of a person's unique ability to creatively intervene in the course of society's development by generating and using their knowledge. A person acts as a translator of innovative culture, ensuring the formation of the human potential of the territory, capable of accumulation, reproduction of knowledge, their increment, self-development, and generating innovative transformations of the territory. Creative and innovative human activity shifts from the position of a spontaneous process and becomes a manageable resource for the development of the territory. Taking as a basis the socio-cultural theory of Vygotsky (Imagination and creativity in childhood. Perspektiva Publishing House, St. Petersburg, 125p, 2020) and the research of Ribot (Creative imagination: Trans. from the French Ed. 2-E. LENAND, Moscow, 328p, 2019), the author considers such managerial processes in the conditions of the initial formation of a comfortable socio-cultural space, where the interaction of individuals in the space of everyday life will be carried out in conditions of creativity and creativity. Here, the objects of management are an innovative personality (a new social type of personality, convenient for an innovative economy, capable of generating and introducing into economic circulation the results of intellectual activity) and a creative personality (self-creating, sufficiently contradictory, free, socially maladaptive). But it is worth noting that a creative person is not always an innovator. Social triggers for maximizing intellectual property objects and their commercialization in the territory ensure the participation of a creative person in the innovation economy, thereby changing the territorial management system of innovative development and its infrastructural support.

M. P. Pavlova (✉)
Togliatti State University, Togliatti, Russia
e-mail: levinamp@mail.ru

E. I. Lazareva et al. (eds.), *Innovative Trends in International Business and Sustainable Management*, Approaches to Global Sustainability, Markets, and Governance,
https://doi.org/10.1007/978-981-19-4005-7_28

Keywords Innovative economy · Innovation management · Creative personality · Social trigger · Creative creativity

JEL Classification J24 · O10 · O31 · O33 · P25

1 Introduction

The large-scale spread of modern innovative technologies is now becoming the main driving force of the economic and social processes of society. This innovativeness forms a new model of worldview, where the physical picture of the world is viewed through the prism of creativity, creating new types of creativity and changing the idea of creativity and its subject. Innovation space as a determinant of a new paradigm provides manifestations of a person's unique ability to creatively intervene in the course of society's development by generating and using their knowledge.

Creativity and creative and innovative human activity are increasingly shifting from the position of a spontaneous process and becoming a manageable resource for the development of territorial entities, so it is natural to assume that the trends that will contribute to their development and stimulation will become dominant in modern society, defining a new form of human existence, and the concept of a new socio-cultural paradigm.

Domestic and foreign scientists touch upon the issues of the formation of an innovation process management system in a territory where the main role belongs to the innovation environment/space, which is formed due to a harmonious combination of science, education, production and market, or a variable innovation infrastructure capable of ensuring the integrity and continuity of the innovation process, where every step throughout the process of creation, development and commercialization of innovations is provided with an infrastructure element represented as a resource or an economic entity. Thus, the environment/space and infrastructure form and activate innovative activity in the territory.

2 Materials and Method

Taking as a basis the socio-cultural theory of Vygotsky (2020) and the research of Ribot (2019), where the emphasis is on the development of cognitive abilities of an individual through social interaction, in his research the author considers the issue of activation of innovation activity 'from the opposite': the need for the formation of innovative infrastructure and/or innovative space/environment will be when the interaction of individuals in the space of everyday life will be carried out in a comfortable socio-cultural locum through the prism of creativity and creativity.

Creativity covers all spheres of human activity, it manifests itself wherever a person begins to imagine, change and create new things. Being in the creative process, a person is the creative beginning of a new reality. Heilman (2005) in his work 'Creativity and the brain' declares man to be the only organism on which creativity can be studied as the primary source of innovative transformations. At the heart of a person's creative activity is always an inability to adapt to the environment. Creative activity, for all its spontaneity and randomness, is an absolute historically continuous process that is carried out within the framework of the natural evolutionary processes of the territory, responds to the needs that are created in society now and rely on the opportunities that exist in the territory now.

Innovative world processes focus on the innovator as the only source of qualitative transformations in society, capable of creating, mastering and distributing innovations to the 'masses' that will provide a qualitative leap in the progressive development of society (Ivanova, 2014, 2017). It should also be noted that an innovator (a person who creates innovations) is not always a creative person, and a creative person is not always an innovator. A person with a high level of communicative potential, high motivation, management orientation, intellectual, possessing sufficient academic and functional knowledge, practical 'preparedness', capable of creating, reproducing and transmitting knowledge, motivated by a continuous process of intellectual perfection, ready to organize innovative activities, while this process is not always creative. An innovator is a 'convenient' tool for managing an innovative economy.

For a creative person with a 'different personality structure', these processes are 'too boring and monotonous', having satisfied the needs of internal motives, he loses interest in implementing his ideas. At the same time, the innovator involved in the innovation process does not always turn out to be creative, able to carry out creative activity (Lebedeva, 2003).

However, only a creative person has a creative activity—this is her life position (Makarova, 2008).

A person invents many times in everyday life, something that does not affect the progressive development of civilization but is related only to his everyday space. However, this is not enough for civilizational transformations. Yes, the results of individual creative activity are often insignificant in themselves, but if you scale this process, it is obvious that most of them were created by unknown people and remain nameless, although this is the result of individual creative activity.

Further developing this idea, we can talk about hidden innovations and missed opportunities for the qualitative development of the territory. There is an obvious correlation between the concentration of innovative products in the territory and the dynamics of the socio-economic potential of the territory, which increases the quality of life of the population. Innovations cause avalanche-like innovative changes in all spheres of human activity, which is further defined as the 'innovative way of development' of the country.

It is worth admitting that the results of creative activity are not always perceived by society immediately, a certain time lag is necessary for their acceptance—'… how many geniuses were burned at the stake of the Inquisition …'. The famous Russian scientist V. I. Vernadsky once said that 'the carriers of the new throughout the history of mankind have been outcasts of society' (Ushakov, 2011).

At the same time, a kind of avant-gardism of the creative personality makes its own adjustments to the relationship between the creative personality and society, which has existed since the emergence of civilization. The reduced adaptive potential of the creative personality and the complex motivational characteristics of creative activity do not allow us to consider the creative personality as an additional source that creates innovations.

3 Results

Based on the findings, the author introduces the concept of a social trigger—a person providing correlated, coordinated relationships, interactions and relationships between individuals in socio-economic processes aimed at innovative development of the territory, encouraging a creative person to perform a certain activity and creative behaviour, whose activities are focused on commercial success.

The phrase ‘social trigger’ used in this work increases the functional load on the term ‘trigger’, thus denoting the main focus of human activity, which provides correlated, coordinated relationships and interactions between individuals in socio-economic processes aimed at the innovative development of the territory.

The need for a social trigger appears when the result of creative activity is already known and represents a material/immaterial object. The social trigger acts as an adapter of a creative personality when interacting with economic entities to introduce into economic circulation his result of creative activity and with society to organize the process of ‘familiarization’ of innovations.

The related contours of interaction between a social trigger and a creative personality are shown in Fig. 1. The first contour of interaction is completed when the result of creative activity is transformed into innovation as a product that opens up new opportunities for the consumer to realize their needs. The second circuit characterizes the measures for the ‘familiarization’ of innovation in the territory and, as a result, the formation of a new social practice among the population. Coordinated actions in the first and second circuits of interaction make it possible to predict commercial success and determine the social effect of the implementation of the result of creative activity. As a result, a new everyday reality is being formed, the growth of innovative activity in the territory is registered, the innovative orientation of all socio-economic processes in the territory is ensured.

The synergy of the relationship between the social trigger and the creative personality in joint activities is aimed at encouraging the individual to creative activity and creative behaviour. The central construct in these social interactions and relationships is the social trigger itself, which actualizes the individuality of a creative person, ensures the integration of her individuality with the social environment, while maintaining her originality and non-standard in solving life tasks, and revealing the resources and potential of a creative person to increase the value of this person in society, thereby forming adequate positive reactions of society to the results of creative activity (Burzukova & Popova, 2015).

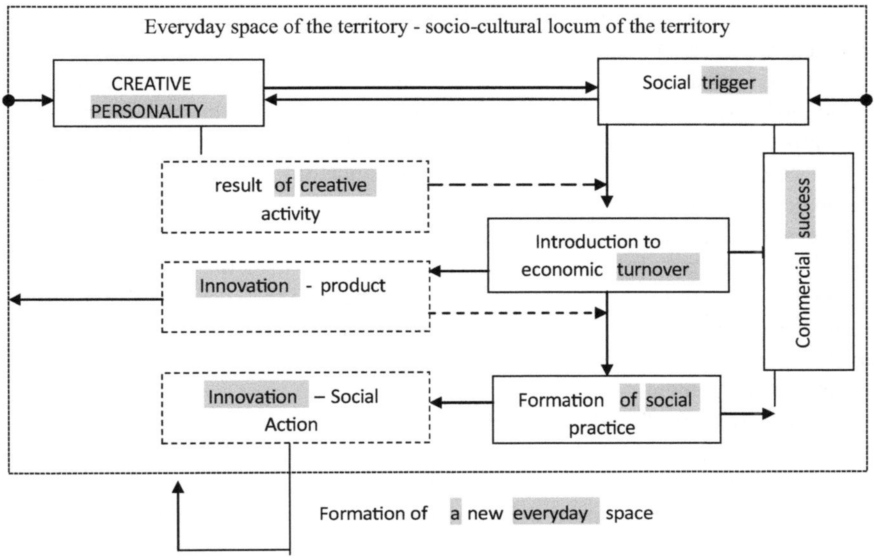

Fig. 1 Interaction of a social trigger and a creative personality on the territory. *Source* Compiled by the author

On the one hand, a social trigger enters into interpersonal relations with a creative person, and on the other hand, organizing the processes of converting ideas into a ready-made commercial product, implements managerial relations with socio-economic economic entities of the territory, which allows it to be considered as a participant in the management system of the innovative space of the territory.

Interpersonal relations between a social trigger and a creative personality are carried out in the socio-cultural locum of the territory, where the social roles and functions realized by the social actors of this territory are carried out taking into account the creative and intellectual components within the framework of cultural norms and traditions. Its influence on the formation of creative behaviour is carried out through reproductive processes that are aimed at preserving, activating, integrating, creating conditions for their self-realization and socialization.

The functional stages of the interpersonal relationship of a social trigger are represented by us in the form of an emotional connection, which acts as a basis for emotional support and mutual trust of individuals to each other; adaptive tactics, (for example: by organizing the participation of a creative personality in a social, multi-channel, decentralized network, which on the one hand can be considered as an intangible resource of adaptation of a creative personality to the social environment, on the other hand, are a resource that accumulates creative people to solve life problems); motivational techniques that encourage, guide and regulate creative activity and creative behaviour.

The managerial relations of a social trigger with independent economic entities represent socio-economic, socio-legal complex relations, which, ensuring the emergence of new areas of interaction in the management system of the innovative space of the territory, involve a full range of scientific, technical, industrial, financial and innovative potentials of the territory to solve management tasks assigned to the social trigger. Such connections ensure stable maintenance of the commercial potential of the object of creative activity at a certain level.

The main function of a social trigger in managerial relations is goal setting. Defining the purpose of the activity and the process of achieving it ensures the success of the activity, and determines the readiness of the social trigger to implement these relationships. The multilevel management activity of a social trigger involves the formation of a hierarchy of goals that will change depending on the object of management.

The involvement of intellectual property objects in economic turnover contributes to the ‘familiarization’ of innovations and the formation of new social practices among the population. In this process, management orientation is important for the social trigger, as there is a need to integrate the efforts of other people to implement production and economic stages to achieve commercial success. The communicative potential of the social trigger ensures the effectiveness of complex interactions and continuity of processes to achieve the goals. It should be noted that the social trigger in the process of involving intellectual property objects in economic turnover takes the position of the organizer of the process, who is responsible for the final result of his activities. At the same time, at each stage of the innovation life cycle, the social trigger enters into managerial relations with economic entities classified by different types of services, which, performing their functional duties in the innovation space management system, ensure the continuity of the process of achieving the goals of the social trigger.

At the same time, due to such local specialization, two types of infrastructural connections are formed between the participants of management relations, which will determine the effectiveness of the functioning of the management system for innovative development of the territory: internal communication–information communication that provides associations of participants of one type of service based on economic and legal relations to implement functional responsibilities in this management system; external communication–information communication that provides economic and legal relations between participants of different types of services to achieve maximum effect in managing the innovation process of the territory. Table 1 specifies the managerial relations of participants with a social trigger in the management system of innovative development of the territory.

4 Conclusion

The structure of the management system for the innovative development of the territory is considered by us from the point of view of systemic and cybernetic

Table 1 Managerial relations of participants with a social trigger in the management system of innovative development of the territory

Functional responsibilities of participants	The result of a managerial relationship with a social trigger
Implementation of effective direct and feedback communication between science, production, market	Information that contains appropriately ordered technical, economic, conjuncture-commercial and statistical data to identify the needs for a particular innovation Organization of promotional events and presentations of ITN and goods created based on OIC for the formation of a new social practice
Implementation of financing and crediting of processes of creation and replication of scientific and technical innovations	Organization of stability
Creation of a system for training specialists in the field of innovation and technological activities and innovative entrepreneurship	Maintaining the competence of a creative person
Increasing the impact on the intensity of the spread of innovative processes	Organization of production and economic processes related to the involvement in the economic turnover of the IIC

Source Compiled by the author

approaches and represents interacting blocks—the object of management and the subject of management, interconnected by direct, feedback, as well as links with the institutional network and resource provision of the territory, forming a hierarchy of interaction contours (Bir, 1996). The interaction of the management object with the socio-cultural locum, which participates in the construction of the inner world of a person as a reflection of the emotional, sensual and creative resources necessary for the organization of innovative activities in the territory, is considered as the first contour. This is where the realization of the creative vision and creative position of the individual in society takes place. Formations are formed here as the highest level of correlation of the creative process with the socio-economic and socio-cultural processes of the territory. The second circuit ensures the interaction of the management system with the resource provision. The instrumental component of the management process is represented by the institutions of economics, knowledge, society, and government formed in the territory. The third circuit reveals the management system in the territory through the influence of external factors on it, both at the meso- and macro-levels.

The input of the proposed management system receives information about the motivation for a new need of an individual of the territory, and at the output, the social practice of using innovative products in society is formed. The cyclical nature of the process is provided by a pattern in which a sense of inner comfort and balance is achieved in an individual through meeting the needs for financial and physical security.

The subject of management in the proposed management system is the administrative body of the territory. The object of management in the proposed management system is creativity/creative activity. In socio-economic systems, creativity management is carried out within the boundaries of social management and creativity management, where priority in managerial interactions is given to the socio-cultural context. In the life cycle of innovation, creativity is present at every stage of the cycle and the spontaneity of the creative process largely determines the uncertainty and unpredictability of the results of the achievement of the entire management system of the innovation space in the territory, therefore, the management of creativity is aimed at including creativity in the space of everyday life for effective dynamics of the achievement of the management system. At the same time, it should be understood that stimulating creative activity does not activate innovative activity and vice versa. To ensure this correlation, additional conditions, mechanisms of influence and methods of stimulation, designated by the author as a social trigger, are necessary.

Thus, the interaction in the management system of the innovative space of the territory, taking into account the above information, looks as follows in Fig. 2.

So, let's summarize. To maximize the objects of intellectual property in the territory, it is necessary to consider as sources of innovation the results of creative activity, which can be potential objects of intellectual property. The interaction of creative people with socio-economic objects to involve the results of creative activity in the economic turnover is corrected using the activity of a social trigger. In the management system of innovative socio-economic territories, a social trigger is considered as providing a human resource in a multilevel process of the innovation life cycle.

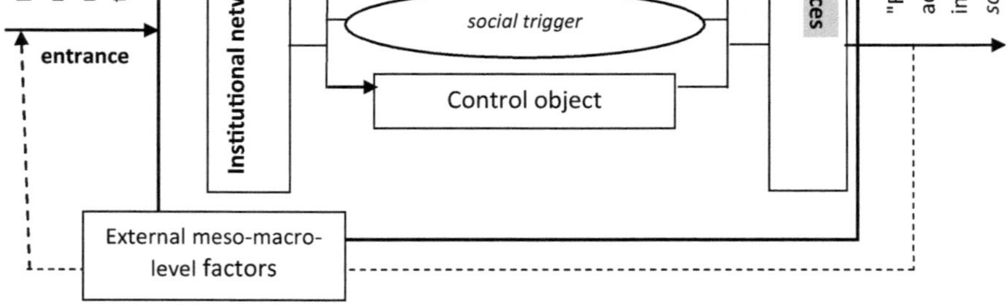

Fig. 2 Model of the innovation space management system in the territory. *Source* Compiled by the author

References

Bir, S. (1996). *Cybernetics and production management*. Fizmatgiz.

Burzukova, E. A., & Popova, N. V. (2015). Features of adaptive potential in adolescents with a high level of creativity and intelligence. *Theory and Practice of Social Development, 22*, 323–325.

Heilman, K. M. (2005). *Creativity and brain*. Psychology Press, Taylor and Fransic Group.

Ivanova, T. N. (2014). Innovative parameters of the conceptual model in the system of principles of the modern social and labor space of the Samara region. In the collection: Sorokin readings. In *Priority directions of the development of sociology in the XXI century: To the 25th anniversary of sociological education in Russia* (pp. 280–283).

Ivanova, T. N. (2017). On the socio-economic essence of the innovative regional model. *Actual Problems of Humanities and Socio-Economic Sciences, 11*(3), 119–121.

Lebedeva, I. L. (2003). Problems of abilities in domestic psychology. Actual problems of socio-humanitarian knowledge. In *A collection of scientific papers. Issue XX* (pp. 134–140). Prometheus.

Makarova, T. A. (2008). Creativity as a way and conditions of activity. *Analytics of Cultural Studies, 1*(10), 56–60.

Ribot, T. A. (2019). *Creative imagination: Trans. from the French Ed. 2-E* (328p). LENAND.

Ushakov, D. V. (Ed.). (2011). *Creativity: From biological foundations to social and cultural phenomena* (736p). Publishing House "Institute of Psychology of the Russian Academy of Sciences".

Vygotsky, L. S. (2020). *Imagination and creativity in childhood* (125p). Perspektiva Publishing House.

Digital Tools for the Export of Educational Services in the Post-soviet Space

Sergey V. Revunov, Svetlana M. Murzina, Alexander G. Oganyan, Vladimir A. Gubachev, and Chenxi Song

Abstract *Purpose* The purpose of the study is a comprehensive analysis of the main socio-economic mechanisms for ensuring the export of educational services to the world market, substantiation of a sustainable mechanism for the interaction of participants in the educational process in a digital environment based on the active use of information and communication technologies in the context of human capital development. *Methodology* The study uses a collection of empirical data reflecting the composition and dynamics of exports of Russian educational services. Based on analytical methods, an algorithm of digital interaction of participants in the educational process has been developed. *Findings* The considered problem of the study is the substantiation of approaches to the export-oriented model of Russian education with an analysis of the main socio-economic, information and communication tools for achieving the objectives. *The relevance of scientific research* is determined by the need to increase the competitiveness of Russian educational products on the world market in the context of digital transformation of the educational environment based on the development of remote access technologies. The factors influencing the competitive advantages of Russian educational products in the context of human capital development at the micro- and meso-economic levels are established. *Originality* The authors substantiate the tools for using the identified competitive advantages that allow the formation of high-tech educational clusters that contribute to the diversification of the Russian economy.

S. V. Revunov (✉) · V. A. Gubachev
Novocherkassk Engineering and Reclamation Institute Named After A. K. Kortunov, a branch of the Don State Agrarian University, Novocherkassk, Russia
e-mail: sergeirevunov25@gmail.com

S. V. Revunov · A. G. Oganyan · C. Song
Southern Federal University, Rostov-on-Don, Russia

S. M. Murzina
Don State Technical University, Rostov-on-Don, Russia
e-mail: merciana@inbox.ru

V. A. Gubachev
Platov South-Russian State Polytechnic University (NPI), Novocherkassk, Russia

E. I. Lazareva et al. (eds.), *Innovative Trends in International Business and Sustainable Management*, Approaches to Global Sustainability, Markets, and Governance,
https://doi.org/10.1007/978-981-19-4005-7_29

Keywords Export of education · Digital technologies · Distance education · Russian education · Educational technologies · Development paradigms

JEL Classification A22 · E24 · F15 · F16 · F22

1 Introduction

Currently, the issue of implementing the transition of the Russian economy to a non-primary segment is acute. The problem of increasing the prestige of domestic education urgently calls for a concept of exporting educational services to the world market based on foreign practice. Through preparation of the study, statistical data reflecting information on the dynamics of the export of educational services provided by higher educational institutions of the Russian Federation of various jurisdiction and form of ownership for the observation period from 1950 to 2018 were analyzed. According to the priorities of the Russian national project "Export of Education" for the period May 2017–November 2025, it is necessary to achieve a number of key goals, namely: to ensure the attractiveness of Russian educational programs for citizens of other states, to provide the quality and accessibility of living conditions for foreign students in the territory of the Russian Federation, to increase the prestige and brand awareness of Russian education abroad. According to the planned results of the implementation of all stages of the project, the total number of foreign citizens studying full-time educational programs in Russian universities should reach 220 thousand people in 2017 and 710 thousand in 2025, the total number of students from foreign countries studying under educational programs implemented by the exporting university using distance and online technologies should increase from 1 million 100 thousand people to 3 million 500 thousand people. The number of foreign citizens studying under the educational programs of primary, basic and secondary level should double in 2025 compared to 2016. In financial terms, the implementation of the project should bring over 373 billion rubles in 2025. However, in these studies, the main socio-economic, information and communication tools for exporting educational services outside the Russian Federation have not received sufficient scientific interpretation. The above facts determine the development of a strategy to increase the competitiveness of Russian education in the context of the model of export of educational services. The purpose of the study is to identify the main factors of improving the quality of educational services on the world market, to develop a sustainable algorithm for exporting education using information and communication technologies, to assess the role of human capital in the paradigm of education globalization.

2 Methodology

In the report of the United Nations (Concept note: Education in the COVID-19 era and beyond 2020), UNESCO (Education transforms people's lives, 2021), in the works of Lien and Miao (2018), in analytical reviews, the key priorities of eliminating inequality in the educational sphere are identified, the priority of education as a driving force of socio-economic development of society is determined, the impact of the globalization process in the educational segment of the Chinese economy is assessed. Paradigms of internationalization of educational technologies in transitional economic models are described in the work of Bennell and Pearce (1998). The work of John V. Winters is devoted to the prospects for the growth of social welfare within the framework of human capital development, improving the quality of life of citizens in the development of the model of accessibility and quality of education (Winters, 2011). Human capital as a factor of sustainable progressive development of socio-economic well-being is described in the studies of Li et al. (2021), Bosi et al. (2021), Dissou et al. (2016). The analysis of the expediency of using information and communication technologies in the context of increasing the development of human capital within the framework of the development of the export of educational services was studied in the work of Revunov et al. (2021). The relevance of the use of information and communication technologies for the purposes of progressive economic development is noted in the study of Pryadko et al. (2019).

3 Results

The Russian Federation is developing an education export strategy as part of a priority national project. The mechanism of implementation of the target model of the educational institution's work on issues related to the export of educational services, which includes the development of international services, whose work is aimed at the rapid adaptation of a foreign citizen in the educational system of the exporting country, contributes to increasing the attractiveness of the offered educational products. The implementation of the export model of education within the post-Soviet countries, as well as beyond their borders, provides for the development of joint programs in English, as well as an extensive online educational platform, interaction within which is carried out with digital tools. The study by Anopchenko et al. (2018) notes that the educational factor is an important component of human capital and affects the formation of many sectors of the economy. Financing of the costs associated with the promotion of Russian education to foreign markets within the framework of the main direction "Implementation of certain activities of the priority project "Development of the export potential of the Russian education system" takes place through the mechanism of subsidies distributed by the joint stock company "Russian Export Fund" in accordance with the procedure established by law (Passport of the priority project, 2017).

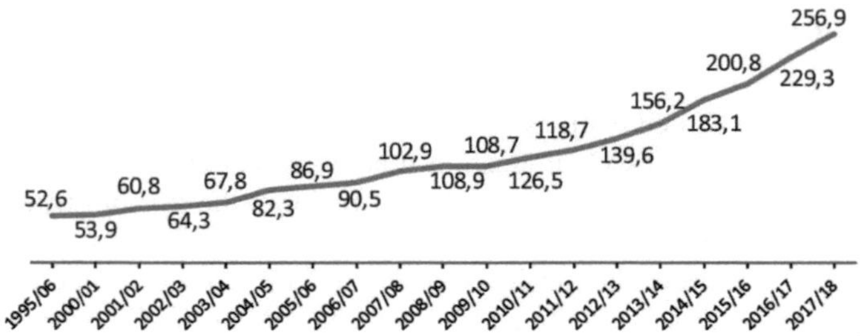

Fig. 1 Dynamics of the total number of foreign students enrolled in full-time programs at Russian universities in 1990/1991–2017/2018 academic years, thousands of people. *Source* Compiled by the authors based on Export of Russian educational services: A statistical collection (2019), Gokhberg et al. (2021)

Today, Russian education is very popular among the countries of the former Soviet Union. This trend can be associated with the demand of the labor market for highly qualified specialists capable of solving a wide range of scientific, practical and socio-economic issues. A graph illustrating the dynamics of the total number of foreign students enrolled in full-time programs at Russian universities in 1990/1991–2017/2018 academic years is shown in Fig. 1.

The analysis of the data presented in Fig. 1 shows a positive trend in the growth of the demand for full-time educational programs in Russian universities among foreign students: during the observation period 1995/1996–2017/2018 academic years, the number of students who arrived from abroad increased by 204.3 thousand people, the enrollment growth rate amounted to 79.5%. It should be noted that extrapolation into further years of observation of the above data on the dynamics of the growth of the contingent of foreign citizens who arrived for full-time training allows us to predict an exponential trend in the growth of the number of students. Table 1 shows information about foreigners arriving on the territory of the Russian Federation from the CIS countries, Georgia, Abkhazia and South Ossetia.

The analysis of the information presented in Table 1 shows a positive stable trend over the observation period. Thus, data on students from the Republic of Abkhazia show the following: an increase in the number of students by 594 people for the period 2008–2009 to 2014–2015 academic years (an increase of 51%); a decline in the period 2014–2015 to 2015–2016 academic years by 80 people (a decrease of 7%); an increase in the period 2015–2016 to 2017–2018 academic years (an increase of 26%). Data for the Republic of Azerbaijan show the dynamics of student growth for the period from 2008–2009 to 2014–2015 academic years is observed: an increase of 2882 people (an increase of 51%); a decrease in the period 2014–2015 to 2017–2018 academic years; a decrease in the contingent of 1069 people (a decrease of 19%). Negative growth rates are increasing for the period 2014–2015 to 2017–2018 academic years for the contingent from Azerbaijan. Armenia demonstrates an increase in the number of applicants for the period 2008–2009 to 2014–2015 academic years: the number of foreign students increased by 860 people (an

Table 1 The number of foreign citizens of the CIS countries, Georgia, Abkhazia and South Ossetia who studied at Russian universities in 2008/2009–2017/2018 academic years, by countries of origin, people

Country	Academic year									
	2008–2009	2009–2010	2010–2011	2011–2012	2012–2013	2013–2014	2014–2015	2015–2016	2016–2017	2017–2018
Abkhazia	568	677	811	852	924	995	1162	1082	1169	1454
Azerbaijan	2818	3345	4166	4411	4934	5479	5700	5327	4701	4631
Armenia	1871	1901	1964	2278	2058	2639	2731	2234	2160	2329
Belarus	3542	3837	4229	4480	4361	4695	4998	4621	5012	5482
Georgia	1169	956	903	907	936	977	997	812	767	991
Kazakhstan	13,720	14,294	16,616	19,189	23,656	27,524	33,730	35,111	39,757	41,285
Kyrgyzstan	1394	1516	2050	2564	2627	3591	3957	4541	5699	6896
Moldova, including Transnistria	1531	1753	2543	2889	2668	3398	3638	3960	3967	4088
Tajikistan	2226	2657	3556	4835	5660	6561	8789	11,284	13,672	16,291
Turkmenistan	2315	3783	5297	7661	10,954	12,114	12,192	14,004	17,264	22,093
Uzbekistan	3710	3289	3466	3996	5605	6288	8831	11,796	14,168	16,954
Ukraine	4236	4067	4919	4714	4737	6029	12,568	13,865	13,653	13,078
South Ossetia	168	351	466	468	569	620	635	525	519	518
Total	39,268	42,426	50,986	59,244	69,689	80,910	99,928	109,162	122,508	136,090

Source Compiled by the authors based on Export of Russian educational services: A statistical collection (2019), Gokhberg et al. (2021)

increase of 31%); in 2014–2015 to 2016–2017 academic years, there was a decline in the number of applicants by 74 people (a decrease of 3%); in the period from 2016–2017 to 2017–2018 academic years, the number of students from Armenia increased by 169 people (an increase of 7%). The number of students from Belarus as a whole shows a steady positive trend, since the number of students from Belarus increased by 1940 people during the observation period (35% student growth rate). The number of applicants from Georgia decreased by 178 people (the decrease in the contingent is 15%). The number of students from Kyrgyzstan has increased by 5502 people (an increase of 80%). The Republic of Moldova (including Transnistria) demonstrates an average stable growth of the contingent by 2557 people (an increase in the number of students by 63%). Steady enrollment rates of Tajikistan citizens are observed, indicating an increase in the number of students by 14,065 people (an increase of 86%). The number of students from Turkmenistan increased by 19,778 people (an increase of 89.5%). There were 13,244 more students from the Republic of Uzbekistan (an increase of 78.1%). The contingent of Ukrainian students increased by 8842 people (an increase of 67.6%). South Ossetia as a whole demonstrates an increase in the number of applicants to universities of the Russian Federation for the period 2008–2009 to 2014–2015 academic years by 467 people (an increase of 35.9%); however, for the period 2014–2015 to 2017–2018 academic years, the number of students decreased by 117 people (a decrease of 18.4%). Having analyzed the aggregate statistical data characterizing the number of foreign citizens who have mastered educational programs in Russian universities, we can come to the following conclusions: the number of foreign students increased by 96,822 people (an increase in the number of foreign students by 71.1%). The statistics shows that Russian education is especially popular in Central Asian countries: Tajikistan, Uzbekistan, Turkmenistan, etc. The generalized data confirm the fact that Russian education has sufficient export potential among post-Soviet countries to attract foreigners to enroll in full-time educational programs. Figure 2 shows a pie chart illustrating the share of income from full-time education of foreign citizens for the period 2017–2018 academic year in the structure of extra-budgetary income of the university. The distribution of interest is carried out by universities of various departmental subordination and forms of ownership.

Analyzing the information given in Fig. 2, it can be concluded that 53.7% of the structure of extra-budgetary income of higher educational institutions subordinate to the Ministry of Education and Science is income from the education of foreign citizens. Based on the above facts, it can be concluded that foreign citizens make a significant contribution to the income structure of higher education institutions (53.7% are universities of the Ministry of Science, 21.1% are universities of the Ministry of Health). Foreign students are ready to study in the Russian Federation, but the following circumstances may be barriers to access to Russian education in a full-time program: employment of a potential student at the place of residence, difficulties in overcoming the mechanisms of migration policy. The way out of this situation may be the use of digital software platforms and tools aimed at remote interaction of subjects of the educational process. The experience of combating the Covid-19 pandemic has shown the need for an integrated approach to the implementation of

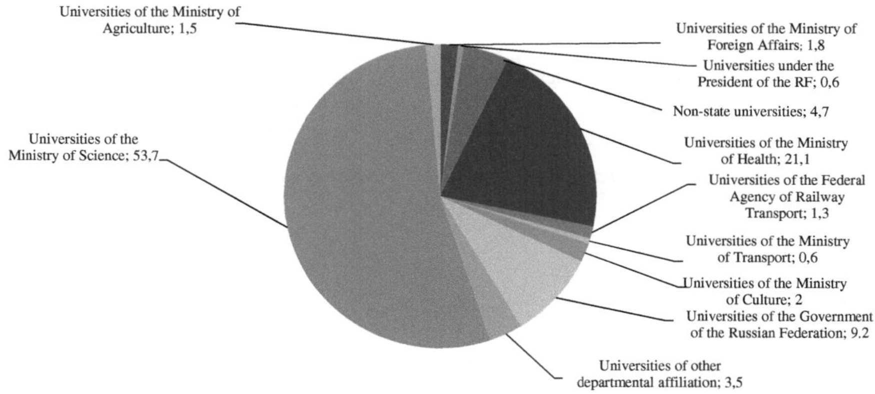

Fig. 2 The share of extra-budgetary income from full-time education of foreign citizens in the academic year 2017/2018, accounted for universities of various departmental subordination/form of ownership, %. *Source* Compiled by the authors based on Export of Russian educational services: A statistical collection (2019), Passport of the priority project (2017)

educational programs. The remote format of education has become in demand, and, as practice shows, many countries, including Russia, have been able to adapt to digital educational paradigms. Table 2 shows the trends in the number of students with whom the educational process is carried out through the use of e-learning and distance learning technologies.

The analysis of the data presented in Table 2 shows an increase in the number of students (including foreign ones) using e-learning technologies in the educational process for higher education programs by 854 thousand people, the percentage change from the total number during the observation period was 21.3%. The use of remote digital technologies used in the implementation of higher education programs for the period 2018–2019 to 2020–2021 academic years increased by 1402.5 thousand people, the percentage change was 36.2%. The dynamics of the use of information and communication technologies in all educational programs demonstrates steady growth. In the age group of potential applicants for higher education programs (15–24 years old), there is a fairly high percentage of mastering the skills of remote communication by e-mail (73.6% in the Republic of Azerbaijan); students from Uzbekistan have a minimum skill of remote work using messages—21.1%. 46.8% of young people from the Republic of Belarus are able to make reports on the completed task in electronic form, which is quite important when mastering natural sciences. Even minimal percentages of computer skills allow us to suggest that the realization of the export potential of Russian education is possible to some extent in these countries. The solution to the problem of diversification of educational services offered for export is the creation of sustainable mechanisms of interaction between participants in the educational process with digital technology tools. The investments of countries that are importers of Russian education in increasing the human capital index, in the structure of which an important place is occupied by the education of

Table 2 Number of students using e-learning and distance learning technologies (at the beginning of the academic year)

Indicators	Application of e-learning			Application of distance learning technologies		
	2018–2019	2019–2020	2020–2021	2018–2019	2019–2020	2020–2021
Educational programs of primary, basic general and secondary education						
Thousand people	2481.9	2694.8	3095.4	14.2	797.2	2621.1
As a percentage of the total number	15.4	16.3	18.3	3.8	4.8	15.5
Educational programs of secondary vocational education						
Thousand people	553.8	650.4	1075.8	179.8	215.5	1428.8
As a percentage of the total number	18.4	20.8	32.2	6.0	6.9	42.8
Educational programs of higher education						
Thousand people	676.9	839.9	1530.9	469.6	534.4	1936.9
As a percentage of the total number	16.2	20.5	37.5	11.2	13.0	47.4

Source Compiled by the authors based on Export of Russian educational services: A statistical collection (2019), Gokhberg et al. (2021)

their own citizens. This is the most important strategic task, the solution of which determines the positive socio-economic dynamics and the growth of the welfare of the population. The modern educational paradigm assumes ensuring the continuity of education throughout the entire life cycle of a citizen, its accessibility and quality. Information technologies make it possible to solve the problems of exporting educational services using remote learning. The stable mechanism of interaction of subjects of the educational process by means of digital technologies assumes the following key links:

1. The choice of an educational institution exporting educational services, an electronic platform within which students and teachers will interact. Currently, the most effective platforms for remote communication can be considered the Teams platform from the American developer Microsoft and the CMS-based distance learning system (CMS Management System) Moodle.
2. Development by educational institutions of effective strategies for conducting classes in a remote format using virtual laboratory experiment systems, provision of educational materials for courses in electronic form. The importance of this link of remote communication in the paradigm of exporting educational services is due to the fact that this model of training excludes the contact

method of conducting such an important segment of the educational process as laboratory work.

3. The problem of the language barrier can be solved by developing a system of pre-university linguistic training of potential applicants, as well as teachers implementing educational programs in the conditions of the export model, the main language to be used in educational activities. In order to expand the geography of the export of educational services, the priority of linguistic training should be shifted toward learning English.
4. Study of socio-cultural, as well as industrial and technological features of the countries importing Russian education. Such an approach will allow foreign students to effectively integrate into the educational system of the exporting country, to predict the results of educational activities in terms of its practical applicability.
5. Creation by the exporting university of exclusive multimedia educational content. The student will be able to reproduce the material at any time using a mobile phone or a personal computer.
6. Development of an electronic system for monitoring student progress. The development of tests is the most optimal method of knowledge control in terms of labor costs. Measures to develop the export potential of Russian education provide for financing from the federal budget. The largest amount of budget allocations is provided for 2021 in the amount of 894.6 million rubles (17.9%), the smallest is planned for the end of the cycle of implementation of the state program, i.e. for 2025 and provides 28.2 million rubles (0.5%). In the long term, there is a decrease in the share of state funding for the export of educational services.

4 Conclusions

Summing up the above, it is necessary to formulate the following main conclusions:

1. Russian education has a significant export potential. The number of foreign contingent in the structure of full-time students is growing. The following post-Soviet countries demonstrate positive dynamics of demand for Russian educational services: Abkhazia, Armenia, Belarus, Georgia, Kazakhstan, Kyrgyzstan, Moldova (including Transnistria), the countries of the Central Asian region: Tajikistan, Turkmenistan, Uzbekistan.
2. The widespread introduction of information and communication technologies in socio-economic activities leads to the transition to a new paradigm of the export of Russian educational services—digital transformation. Young people aged 15–24 years in one or another percentage have basic skills in the field of information and communication technologies necessary for the quality export of educational services. The adult population of the CIS countries, having to a lesser extent the above-mentioned skills, can be considered as part-time or full-time distance learning students.

3. The share of profits from full-time education of foreign citizens in the income structure of universities subordinated to the Ministry of Education and Science is more than half of the total amount of financial resources earned by an educational institution. Medical universities occupy the second place in terms of the share of income from the education of foreigners. It should be noted that the gap in the income level of universities according to the criterion of export of educational services is due to the requirements of the legislation of Russia regarding the areas of training, the implementation of which is possible with the use of information and communication technologies.
4. The main electronic platforms for the purpose of ensuring the export of educational services to post-Soviet countries include Microsoft Teams and electronic learning platforms based on CMS Moodle. The Teams platform includes the following remote communication tools: text messages, the ability to plan and conduct video and audio conferences. The screen demonstration mode makes it possible to carry out all types of educational work using the frontal method. Teams is distributed under a Microsoft license agreement with an educational institution on the use of the Microsoft Office software package and does not require additional financial investments. Electronic educational platforms based on CMS Moodle integrate highly customized communication tools for participants in the educational process, knowledge control is carried out using tests. Distance education systems based on CMS Moodle support the mechanism of mass registration and secure authentication of users and are focused on educational institutions with a large contingent. When using the Teams platform, the test system is developed in the Microsoft Forms application.
5. Financing of the export project of Russian education is carried out entirely at the expense of the state budget under the mechanism of granting subsidies to the joint stock company "Russian Export Center", which, in turn, distributes financial resources between exporting universities when they meet the requirements provided for in the decree of the Government of the Russian Federation. According to the authors, direct subsidization by the relevant Ministries of the universities subordinate to them seems to be optimal.
6. The active use of digital technologies in the paradigm of educational services export will have a significant impact on the dynamic development of educational clusters, remote communication means will allow combining domestic universities exporting educational services and foreign educational institutions into stable industry conglomerates on the Internet environment focused on the joint solution of strategic tasks of the economy. For the tasks of land reclamation and irrigation in countries with arid climates (Central Asian states), universities subordinated to the Ministry of Agriculture of Russia and students from Central Asian countries can unite to solve point tasks in an agricultural cluster.
7. The tools that encourage foreign citizens to make a choice in favor of Russian education include: the development of advanced training programs for foreign specialists, the provision of scholarship and grant support for foreign citizens for special achievements in academic and scientific activities, the creation of a

climate of harmonious relations between students of different ethnic, social and cultural backgrounds within the Russian educational system.

8. The high degree of competition with the educational systems of Western and Chinese countries requires export diversification taking into account the requirements imposed by the labor markets of the countries importing education, socio-economic and geopolitical development strategies, as well as entering the market with a proposal to integrate new forms of educational services at a faster pace. The competitive advantage of Russian education is the fact that citizens of the CIS countries speak Russian at a level sufficient for mastering educational programs offered for export.

References

Anopchenko, T. Y., Grinenko, S. V., Edalova, E. S., Zadorozhnyaya, E. K., & Murzin, A. D. (2018). Management of human capital reproduction processes in post-Soviet countries. *Espacios 39*(9).

Bennell, P., & Pearce, T. (1998). *The internationalisation of higher education: Exporting education to developing and transitional economies*. IDS Working Paper, 75. IDS.

Bosi, S., Lloyd-Braga, T., & Nishimura, K. (2021). Externalities of human capital. *Mathematical Social Sciences, 112*, 145–158. https://doi.org/10.1016/j.mathsocsci.2021.03.013

(2020). *Concept note: Education in the COVID-19 era and beyond*. The United Nations. https://www.un.org/sites/un2.un.org/files/policy_brief_-_education_during_covid-19_and_beyond_russian.pdf. Data accessed July 06, 2021.

Dissou, Y., Didic, S., & Yakautsava, T. (2016). Government spending on education, human capital accumulation, and growth. *Economic Modelling November, 58*, 9–21. https://doi.org/10.1016/j.econmod.2016.04.015

(2021). *Education transforms people's lives*. UNESCO official website. https://ru.unesco.org/themes/education. Data accessed: July 06, 2021.

(2019). *Export of Russian educational services: A statistical collection. Issue 9*. Center for Sociological Research. https://www.5top100.ru/upload/iblock/63a/Vyp.9_536_-p.2019_v-_1_.pdf. Data accessed: July 06, 2021.

Gokhberg, L. M., Ozerova, O. K., Sautina, E. V., Sutyrina, T. A., & Shugal, N. B. (2021). *Education in numbers: 2021: A brief statistical collection*. HSE.

Li, X., Guo, Y., Hou, J., & Liu, J. (2021). Human capital allocation and enterprise innovation performance: An example of China's knowledge-intensive service industry. *Research in International Business and Finance, 58*. https://doi.org/10.1016/j.ribaf.2021.101429

Lien, D., & Miao, L. (2018). Effects of Confucius Institutes on China's higher education exports: Evidence from Chinese Partner Universities. *International Review of Economics & Finance, 57*, 134–143. https://doi.org/10.1016/j.iref.2018.02.018

Passport of the priority project "Development of the export potential of the Russian education system". Approved by the Presidium of the Council under the President of the Russian Federation for Strategic Development and Priority Projects (Protocol No. 6 of May 30, 2017). http://static.government.ru/media/files/DkOXerfvAnLv0vFKJ59ZeqTC7ycla5HV.pdf. Data accessed: 06.07.2021.

Pryadko, I. A., Paytaeva, K. T., Revunov, R. V., Zelenova, G. V., & Evetskaya, S.V. (2019). Promotion of educational services in social networks. In E. Popkova & V. Ostrovskaya (Eds.), *Advances in Intelligent Systems and Computing: Vol. 726. Perspectives on the use of new Information and Communication Technology (ICT) in the modern economy*. ISC 2017. Springer. https://doi.org/10.1007/978-3-319-90835-9_104

Revunov, S. V., Rogova, T. M., Tutaeva, D. R., Murzin, A. D., & Plohotnikova, G. V. (2021). Modern information and communication technologies as a factor of human capital development. In E. G. Popkova, & B. S. Sergi (Eds.), *Lecture Notes in Networks and Systems: Vol. 198. Modern global economic system: Evolutional development versus revolutionary leap.* ISC 2019. Springer. https://doi.org/10.1007/978-3-030-69415-9_32

Winters, J. V. (2011). Human capital, higher education institutions, and quality of life. *Regional Science and Urban Economics September, 41*(5), 446–454.

Features of Human Resource Management as a Dominant Factor of Sustainable and Innovative Development

Natalya I. Khosroeva, Larisa G. Mamsurova, and Irina Kh. Kuchieva

Abstract The article is devoted to the problems of human resource management in the conditions of scientific, technical and technological development in accordance with the requirements of the market and society. This research develops the idea of an interconnected progressive development of science and technology, manifested in the constant impact of scientific discoveries and inventions on the level of development and use of human resources. The subject of this study defines scientific and technological progress as a complex category that has a functional organization in the structure of social reproduction. The authors highlight the fundamental characteristics of such a phenomenon as scientific and technological progress, pointing to its close relationship with the improvement of human resources, productive forces in general. These characteristics are interconnection and interdependence, because scientific and technological progress today is the main prerequisite for the development of human resources. The research is based on the position that the laws of technology development should be considered from the perspective of changing the structure of society's needs, improving productive forces, changing factors of economic modernization, as well as industrial relations at various levels of society's evolution. The authors substantiate the idea that today the progressive development of social and economic spheres is inseparable from the materialization of scientific and technological achievements, innovations. The results presented in the article can be used in forecasting technological trends, in the development of scientific and technical policy. The main provisions of the article may be in demand for the purposes of further theoretical and methodological substantiation and practical research on the problems of formation and development of human resources. The authors believe the fact that the modern mechanism of human resource management will be effective if it is based on the systemic interaction of scientific and technological progress, innovative processes and other factors described in the article. The main provisions

N. I. Khosroeva (✉) · L. G. Mamsurova · I. Kh. Kuchieva
North Ossetian State University Named After K.L. Khetagurov, Vladikavkaz, Russia
e-mail: khosroeva_n@rambler.ru

L. G. Mamsurova
e-mail: lg.mamsurova@nosu.ru

E. I. Lazareva et al. (eds.), *Innovative Trends in International Business and Sustainable Management*, Approaches to Global Sustainability, Markets, and Governance,
https://doi.org/10.1007/978-981-19-4005-7_30

of the article may be used for the purposes of further theoretical and methodological substantiation and practical developments on the problems of human resource management in the context of sustainable and innovative development.

Keywords Human resources · Technological progress · Sustainable innovative development · Priority system · Management mechanism

JEL Classification O15 · O33 · P00

1 Introduction

An important feature of human nature is that people's needs are endless, and therefore there is a constant need to satisfy them. This involves solving the problems that arise at each stage of development, and certain contradictions that arise between society and nature. The task, in our opinion, is to find a solution in which success would be as painless as possible, and economic activity would be conducted in the most rational and reasonable way (Lazareva, 2010; Lazareva & Khosroeva, 2020). This is possible only if the directions of the evolution of the development of human economic activity are correctly formed on the basis of an in-depth study of economic laws.

Considering the issues of economic reform in Russia, it should be noted that its strategy and tactics should be built in accordance with the scientific forecast of the development of society, as well as the adoption of a policy of changing the entire socio-economic structure (Akindinova et al., 2018). At the same time, the process of development of both the individual and society as a whole is a constant striving to meet emerging needs.

Summarizing the above, we can say that the progressive development of society, its productive forces in all diversity and unity ensures scientific and technological progress and sustainable innovation dynamics. The purpose of the study is to identify, and use adequate methods of human resource management at all levels in modern conditions of technology development.

2 Methodology

In a situation of increasing internal and external contradictions, which, as a result, generate uncertainty, it is difficult to predict the prospects for the socio-economic development of the country and its individual regions in Russia. The fact is that the lag of the Russian state from the leading economies in the field of scientific and technological development is observed, first of all, due to the lack of proper interest of public production in innovation. Today, Russian society is steadily progressing along the path of market development. No one doubts the need for market transformations anymore. What ways and forms should they have?

When forming and predicting the prospect of market development, one can, for example, draw up a picture of the "distribution of goods" on a global, state, regional, republican, municipal scale, identify consumer niches, predict the filling of existing niches and the emergence of new ones. It is important to monitor and regulate the harmony of such a picture, transform and modify it depending on changes in social needs, social preferences, depending on the development and growth of a complex social organism, and finally, the development of science. The transition to full-fledged market relations has affected the branch of science, which is also changing significantly due to the close relationship between the scientific system and the market economy. In the modern conditions of the formation of market relations, changes in the relationship "consumer–supplier" of scientific and technical products, different views are required on the problems of forecasting and organization of research and development, taking into account the specifics of the formation of human resources. In other words, it is necessary to build a modern effective mechanism for managing scientific and technological progress and innovative processes based on the systemic interaction of the factors described above. When analyzing the issues under study, it is necessary, in our opinion, to focus on the problem of determining the priority of scientific research. Recently, it has been emphasized in the economic literature devoted to scientific and technological progress and innovative development. It is necessary to identify priorities for fundamental and applied research (Martynova, 2017; Mindeli & Chernykh, 2016; Rogov, 2005; Supyan & Babich, 2015).

In this regard, a number of questions arise. Does it make sense to talk about progress, the development of science, technology, the consequences of development? What goals should we pursue? What priorities should be identified and formulated for technological or scientific and technological progress? For example, it may be the compatibility of technologies with humans in terms of ease of their application, or it may be compliance with environmental standards, economic alignment, the formation of a national digital economy, ensuring national interests and the implementation of national priorities (Decree of the President of the Russian Federation, 2016; Decree of the President of the Russian Federation, 2017). One way or another, the development of technology should be focused on the development of human resources. The problems of human resource management are closely related to the cycles of scientific and technological progress, require the development and implementation of a unified policy of regions, territories and the state as a whole (Molchan et al., 2016).

3 Results

Scientific and technological progress is, first of all, the process of various changes in the means of labor, equipment, technology and production. A special form of development of industrial relations is determined by the division of labor, the use of human resources (Begieva & Pashayeva, 2019; Khosroeva, 2019).

The management of scientific and technological progress and innovations should be based on the nature of the use of human resources in production relations, taking into account various methods of production, as well as various technological modes.

Another aspect of scientific and technological progress is the process of generating ideas, obtaining and accumulating knowledge, its appropriate use, the growth of the fund of knowledge, and all this leads to the emergence of new technological solutions, which, in turn, allow us to produce products with new unique characteristics (Rudtskaya et al., 2009).

The foundation of scientific and technological progress is the progress of science, i.e. we can talk about STP only when science turns into a direct productive force. "The productive development of society is not only the growing power of science, but also the scale in which it is already laid as fixed capital, the size of the breadth of its implementation and the scope of its entire production" (Marx & Engels, 1960).

In other words, if we consider technology as a broad field of purposeful application of sciences of all fields of knowledge with all their material part, then scientific and technological progress, in our opinion, is the development and movement of technology in socio-economic systems.

The criteria for choosing certain areas of scientific research, determining their "socio-economic cost", socio-economic consequences are the basis for the development of a motivational mechanism that should work to achieve certain goals set for various areas of development of science and technology. In other words, it is necessary to focus on the final result, on the economic and social effect. Today, first of all, we must be based on socio-economic needs that result from the natural process of historical development, as well as on the objective stage of changing contradictions that need to be solved with the help of scientific and technological progress.

There can be many priorities, depending on what goals we pursue, what scope of problems we solve. Determining priorities is also a difficult task because the value orientations of society are not amenable to accurate quantitative analysis and measurement. In determining priorities, no less difficult, in our opinion, is the question of the criteria used in their assessment. Every study has intermediate results, final results, immediate effect, indirect effect. There are many cases described in the literature when scientific developments in agriculture, construction, mining, chemical industry, etc., having, at first glance, brilliant results, lead to environmental disasters of various scales.

An example of determining priorities is the data of the National Science Foundation on the expenditures of the US Federal Budget on R&D for national purposes. Fundamental research in the field of healthcare is ahead of many budget items. The expenses under this article are 2.5 times higher than the costs of space exploration (this ratio is quite stable), more than 10 times higher than the articles "energy" and "natural resources". In other developed countries and regions, health research has also a growing position (Table 1).

The table shows that in the USA, the European Union and China, the number of published research results on biological, medical and engineering topics is growing. In the period from 2003 to 2018, there are changes in the disciplinary structure of

Table 1 Publications of relevant topics, (thousands)

Years	Engineering publications			Biological and medical publications		
	USA	European Union	China	USA	European Union	China
2003	40	42	26	157	186	23
2004	43	46	37	167	195	30
2005	51	57	51	174	205	40
2006	49	59	59	178	212	46
2007	49	67	67	181	218	52
2008	48	70	78	184	225	59
2009	50	75	85	189	230	64
2010	54	79	92	191	232	66
2011	54	80	100	201	242	70
2012	53	88	94	209	255	79
2013	54	85	101	212	259	94
2014	51	91	107	217	265	109
2015	51	91	114	213	259	115
2018	46	87	148	211	255	148

Source Compiled by the authors based on Science and Engineering Indicators (2018), Since and Engineering Indicators (2020)

science, the importance of biology, genetics, medicine, biochemistry, biophysics—the whole complex of sciences "about life" is increasing. Interdisciplinary research is being conducted, creating fundamentally new areas of application.

The domestic expenses on research and development for socio-economic purposes in the Russian Federation are as follows (Table 2).

As can be seen from the table above that the structure of domestic expenses on research in Russia did not change dramatically during this period. By 2020, relative to 2006, the expenditure under "public health" has almost doubled (1.8%), the expenditure under "general science" and "environment" has reduced in roughly equal proportions.

4 Conclusion

Defining short- and long-term priorities of scientific and technical policy in accordance with the goals of sustainable and innovative development, management structures at various levels should initiate the creation of multi-purpose research programs aimed at discovering new knowledge, ensuring the development of new technologies in the twenty-first century. The relevant structures need to determine legislative

Table 2 Domestic expenses on research and development for socio-economic purposes, RF, (%)

Years	Economics	Energy	Social goals, including		General science	Space
			Environment	Public health		
2006	35.5	4.1	0.9	2.0	21.0	4.8
2010	36.6	4.8	1.1	2.7	19.9	5.2
2012	44.0	4.7	1.1	2.8	16.8	5.4
2013	43.2	5.3	0.8	3.0	17.4	6.9
2014	35.4	5.3	0.9	3.2	16.1	5.8
2015	30.9	5.2	0.8	3.0	15.9	6.3
2016	29.6	5.6	0.7	3.6	14.8	4.9
2017	39.8	10.2	0.6	3.0	13.7	4.0
2018	39.8	9.7	0.7	3.1	16.5	4.2
2019	38.9	9.7	0.6	3.4	17.2	5.3
2020	38.1	10.6	0.6	3.8	19.0	4.1

Source Compiled by the authors based on Federal State Statistics Service (2022)

measures to directly and indirectly stimulate their implementation and the introduction of the results of developments in the social and economic sphere, including production.

Direct methods of state regulation of scientific, technical and social progress are carried out, as a rule, in two ways: administrative-departmental and program-targeted (Khosroeva & Khosroeva, 2015). For all industrially developed countries, the state scientific and technical policy aimed at creating new technologies and the policy in the field of human resources are the basis of socio-economic national policy.

Modern features of human resource management as a dominant factor of sustainable and innovative development require a radical revision of the national development strategy.

In conclusion, it should be noted that at the present stage of scientific and technological progress, there is a large-scale movement and development of technologies. It is necessary to use world experience in determining priorities and shaping the needs of society, to update the experience of domestic prognostics and theoretical developments in the field of STP. It is necessary to choose adequate tools and mechanisms for the development and implementation of scientific and technological development programs in order to follow the "technological vector" of the modern world. At the same time, the structure of scientific research should meet the current and future needs of socio-economic growth, determine trends in the formation of human resources.

References

Akindinova, N. V., Bessonov, V. A., & Yasin, E. G. (2018). *The Russian economy: From transformation to development*. Publishing House of the Higher School of Economics. https://publications.hse.ru/books/218065150. Data accessed: January 02, 2022.

Begieva, A. S., & Pashayeva, Z. S. (2019). Actual directions of the effective use of labor resources of the enterprise. *Economics and Entrepreneurship, 8*(109), 735–738.

Decree of the President of the Russian Federation No. 642 of December, 01, 2016. *On the strategy of scientific and technological development of Russia until 2035*. http://static.kremlin.ru/media/events/files/ru/uZiATIOJiq5tZsJgqcZLY9YyL8PWTXQb.pdf. Data accessed: January 02, 2022.

Decree of the President of the Russian Federation No. 203 of 09.05.2017. *On the strategy for the development of the information society in the Russian Federation for 2017–2030*. http://docs.cntd.ru/document/420397755. Data accessed: January 02, 2022.

Federal State Statistics Service. https://rosstat.gov.ru›mediabank›nauka_5. Data accessed: January 02, 2022.

Khosroeva, N. I. (2019). Human capital and labor as components of production relations. *Economics and Entrepreneurship, 8*(109), 290–292.

Khosroeva, N. I., & Khosroeva, O. T. (2015). *Program-targeted methods of innovative development planning. Management of the economic and social systems of the region, VI* (pp. 248–252). Publishing house of North Ossetian State University named after K. L. Khetagurov.

Lazareva, E. I. (2010). National welfare as an integrated resource of innovation-oriented economic development: Theory, methodology and research tools. *Doctoral dissertation.*

Lazareva, E. I., & Khosroeva, N. I. (2020). Innovative management of human development trends in Russian regions through the prism of global Sustainable Development Goals. *Bulletin of North Ossetian State University named after K L. Khetagurov, 3*, 167–177. https://doi.org/10.29025/1994-7720-2020-3-167-177

Martynova, E. A. (2017). Monitoring of budget financing of scientific research and development for 2010–2015. *Science Management and Sceitometrics, 2*(24), 134–156. https://sie-journal.ru/assets/uploads/issues/2017/2(24)_07.pdf. Data accessed: January 02, 2022.

Marx, K., & Engels, F. (1960). *Full collection of works* (2nd ed., Vol. 46, part II). https://informaxinc.ru/marx/46-2.html. Data accessed: January 02, 2022.

Mindeli, L. E., & Chernykh, S. I. (2016). Financing of fundamental research in Russia: Modern realities and the formation of predictive estimates. *Forecasting Problems, 3*(156), 111–122.

Molchan, A. S., Pogrebnaya, N. V., & Surnina, Y. V. (2016). Russian sphere of research and development: Modern investment realities. *KubGAU Scientific Journal—Scientific Journal of KubSAU, 123*, 1544–1554.

Rogov, S. M. (2005). *The state and the public good: Global trends and the Russian way*. Institute of the USA and Canada of the Russian Academy of Sciences.

Rudtskaya, E. R., Khrustalev, E. Y., & Tsyganov, S. A. (2009). Methods of accumulation of scientific knowledge for innovative development of the Russian economy (RFBR experience). *Forecasting Problems, 3*, 134–139.

Science and Engineering Indicators. (2018). *Recent trends in U.S. R&D performance*. National Science Board. National Science Foundation. https://www.nsf.gov/statistics/2018/nsb20181/assets/nsb20181.pdf. Data accessed: January 02, 2022.

Science and Engineering Indicators. (2020). *The state of U.S. science and engineering 2020*. National Science Foundation. https://ncses.nsf.gov/pubs/nsb20201/. Data accessed: January 02, 2022.

Supyan, V. B., & Babich, S. N. (2015). *Scientific and technical potential of the USA: The role and place of the National Science Foundation and National Academies*. Russia and America in the XXI century, 1. http://www.rusus.ru. Data accessed: January 02, 2022.

The Use of Human Resources to Drive Business Transformation Through Digital Evolution

Yulia S. Chernysheva, Zhanna V. Gornostaeva, and Andrey B. Mikhailov

Abstract The article examines the mechanisms for assessing the scale of development of the digital economy, analyzes the data of digitalization of Russian society in comparison with other countries. A hypothesis is put forward that there is a relationship between the level of human development and the level of digital intelligence which is tested using regression analysis tools. Human potential is a unique resource that determines the success of initiatives to digitalize the economy and the level of public confidence in digital technologies in general. Therefore, it needs increased attention and responsible management on the part of the state. Recommendations on the use of human resources for business development in the Digital Evolution are offered. As a result of the study, it was proved that the level of human development largely determines the level of digital intelligence in the study area. Consequently, the rate of development of the digital economy and the level of public confidence in digital technologies depend on the duration and quality of life, the duration of education and the gross national income.

Keywords Human resources · Business · Transformation · Digital evolution · Digital economy

JEL Classification E24 · J24 · M21 · O15 · O31 · O32 · O33 · O38

1 Introduction

The active development of digital technologies has launched a digital transformation of the business, affecting various aspects of the company's activities including personnel management. In the process of transforming the ways of interaction have changed and new roles of human resources in the creation of digital intelligence have been identified (Cozzolino et al., 2021).

Y. S. Chernysheva (✉) · Z. V. Gornostaeva · A. B. Mikhailov
Institute of Service and Entrepreneurship, Shakhty, Russia
e-mail: Julia_chern@mail.ru

E. I. Lazareva et al. (eds.), *Innovative Trends in International Business and Sustainable Management*, Approaches to Global Sustainability, Markets, and Governance,
https://doi.org/10.1007/978-981-19-4005-7_31

Today digital intelligence is a brand that forms the competitive advantages of business structures. Having digital intelligence is not just about collecting data, it is important to use the information obtained for the improvements that are needed by the company's customers. The development of digital intelligence is particularly relevant at a time when the global economy is recovering from the large-scale crisis caused by the SARS-CoV-2 coronavirus pandemic.

Digital transformation is a complex process and it is important to take into account all resources to realize its full potential including human resources. First of all, this concerns the experience of implementing a digital strategy introducing a culture of innovation in society, etc. (Jesse, 2018).

This article puts forward a working hypothesis that the level of human development determines the success of initiatives to digitalize the state's economy and the level of public confidence in digital technologies. This study is intended to test the hypothesis put forward.

2 Materials and Methods

Today one of the key factors in the development of the digital economy is human resources which are the objects of research in the works of various authors (Fischer et al., 2020). The theoretical basis of the research was formed by the works of specialists on aspects of the development of the digital economy and human potential including publications of (Assa, 2021; Cozzolino et al., 2021; Fischer et al., 2020; Hanafizadeh & Kim, 2020; Hussain, 2021; Popkova et al., 2020).

The working hypothesis suggests that there is a link between the level of human development and the level of digitalization of the economy. In this situation, one of the indicators under consideration is the Global Human Development Indicators (HDI). This indicator allows us to assess the key characteristics of the human potential in the study area: the standard of living, literacy, education and longevity of the population. To increase the objectivity of the assessment, the Human Development Index adjusted for socio-economic inequality (IHDI), the Gender Inequality Index (GII) and the Gender Development Index (GDI) are also used (Hanafizadeh & Kim, 2020).

The Human Development Report 2020 provided data on the level of human development in 189 countries around the world. In 2019, the Russian Federation ranked 52nd in terms of human development (HDI = 0.824 points). The ratio of human development indices in Russia and the world (UNDP, 2020) shows that in 2019, the human development index in Russia was higher than the average value in the whole world. The calculation of the global human development index for Russia was carried out taking into account the following data:

- life expectancy at birth-72.6 years;
- the expected period of study-15 years;
- the gross national income (GNI) per capita is 26,157 rubles.

For the period from 1990 to 2019, the HDI value in Russia increased by 1.12 times.

Russia is an important participant on the world stage and is a member of various international organizations. In 2019 Russia was one of the leaders among developing countries in terms of human development. The average value of this indicator for developing countries was 0.740 points while for Russia this indicator was 0.824 points.

The situation is completely different in advanced economies. In these countries, the level of human development is much higher than in Russia (UNDP, 2021).

Without the use of modern technologies, it is not possible to ensure the development of the state's economy. To assess the level of development of the digital economy, the Digital Intelligence Index is used, which combines more than 358 indicators in two evaluation tables: the state of digital evolution (Digital Evolution) and digital trust (Digital Trust) (Sites, 2021).

The central hypothesis of digital evolution is that the digitalization of the economy is regulated by equally significant factors: supply conditions, demand conditions, the institutional environment and innovations, changes (Popkova et al., 2021).

According to the Digital Intelligence Index, all countries are divided into four categories:

1. STAND OUT—countries with highly developed economies (USA, Singapore, Hong Kong, etc.), have a high level of digital technology development and demonstrate high growth rates of the digital economy.
2. STALL OUT—countries with a stable economy (Finland, Denmark, Norway, Japan, etc.), have an average level of development of digital technologies and a minimum increase in the rate of development of the digital economy.
3. BREAKT OUT—countries with progressively developing economies (China, Poland, Uruguay, etc.), have a lower level of digital technology development, but demonstrate high growth rates of the digital economy.
4. WHATH OUT—countries with unstable developing economies (Peru, Tunisia, Nigeria, etc.) have a minimal level of development of digital technologies and demonstrate a lack of growth rates of the digital economy.

According to the Digital Intelligence Index, Russia takes 49th in the world ranking, significantly inferior to countries with developed economies (Popkova et al., 2020). The main factors hindering the digital transformation of business in Russia are the low level of public confidence in digital technologies, without which the development of e-commerce and online commerce is impossible, digital inequality among various categories of citizens, the lack of necessary conditions for attracting investment in the development of digital enterprises, etc. (Hussain, 2021).

3 Results

This study hypothesizes that the level of human development determines the success of initiatives to digitalize the economy and the level of public confidence in digital technologies. To test the proposed hypothesis, the regression analysis method was used (Assa, 2021). The initial data for testing the hypothesis was taken from the Human Development Report 2020, as well as from the evaluation maps of Digital Evolution and Digital Trust, 2020. The results of the regression analysis are presented in Table 1.

The obtained values of the sample correlation coefficients for all the groups indicate that there is a significant relationship between the values of the Human Development Indicators and the Digital Intelligence Index. Most of all, this relationship can be traced in countries with stable economies of STALL OUT.

The average approximation error did not exceed 10%, which indicates the satisfactory quality of the regression models. The reliability of the regression models was evaluated based on the Fisher F-test with a significance level of 0.05. For all the studied groups of countries, the value $F_{\text{fact}} > F_{\text{tabl}}$, therefore, all the obtained regression models can be considered statically reliable, and the working hypothesis can be proved.

Table 1 Regression analysis of the dependence of the human development index on the digital intelligence index

Index	Groups of countries by level of digital intelligence			
	STALL OUT	WHATH OUT	STAND OUT	BREAKT OUT
Average value of the level of human development	0.930	0.739	0.905	0.766
Average value	79.308	45.431	78.33	52.00
Regression equation	$y = 262.12x$ -164.56	$y = 81.348x$ -14.756	$y = 168.32x$ -74.158	$y = 66.955x$ $+0.7223$
Coefficient of determination R^2	0.72	0.80	0.54	0.61
Standard error	3.83	4.79	5.53	5.44
Average approximation error $\overline{A}$, %	3.82	6.73	9.00	8.52
Correlation coefficient, r	0.85	0.9	0.73	0.78
T_{obs}	6.61	9.22	3.59	5.71
t (0.05, n−2)	2.11	2.07	2.2	2.07
F_{fact}	43.74	85.13	12.92	32.68
F_{tabl} (0.05, 1, n−2)	4.45	4.32	4.84	4.32
Coefficient of elasticity	3.07	1.32	1.94	0.98

Source Calculated by the authors

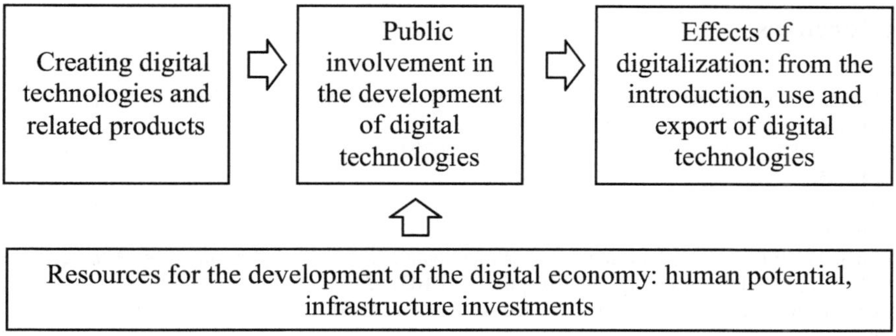

Fig. 1 A model for measuring the level of development of the digital economy, taking into account the key characteristics of human potential *Source* Calculated by the authors

4 Discussion

The relevance of digital transformation of business makes it necessary to assess the processes of digitalization both at the level of economic entities and the state as a whole (Mangaraj & Aparajita, 2020). This is evidenced by a significant number of scientific studies aimed at assessing the digital economy and identifying the factors that determine the level of development of digital intelligence in a particular region of the world. As a rule, such an assessment is limited to formal indicators that are associated with the assessment of the intensity of the use of digital technologies (Achmad & Hamzani, 2015; Yakunina & Bychkov, 2015).

Despite the high degree of scientific elaboration of the research problem, the question of the influence of human potential on the level of digitalization of the economy is not clearly defined (Verma et al., 2021). To eliminate this imbalance, a model for measuring the level of development of the digital economy was proposed, taking into account the key characteristics of human potential (Fig. 1).

Human potential is a unique resource that determines the success of initiatives to digitalize the economy and the level of public confidence in digital technologies in general. Therefore, it needs increased attention and responsible management on the part of the state.

5 Conclusion

As a result of the study, it was proved that the level of human development largely determines the level of digital intelligence in the study area. Consequently, the rate of development of the digital economy and the level of public confidence in digital technologies depend on the duration and quality of life, the duration of education and the gross national income.

References

Achmad, D., & Hamzani, U. (2015). *Procedia—Social and Behavioral Sciences, 211*, 953–959. https://doi.org/10.1016/j.sbspro.2015.11.126

Assa, J. (2021). *Ecological Economics, 185*, 107045. https://doi.org/10.1016/j.ecolecon.2021.107045

Cozzolino, A., Corbo, L., & Aversa, P. (2021). *Journal of Business Research, 126*, 385–400. https://doi.org/10.1016/j.jbusres.2020.12.058

Fischer, M., Imgrund, F., Janiesch, C., & Winkelmann, A. (2020). *Information and Management, 57–5*, 103262. https://doi.org/10.1016/j.im.2019.103262

Hanafizadeh, P., & Kim, S. (2020). *Digital Business, 1*, 100006. https://doi.org/10.1016/j.digbus.2021.100006

Hussain, Z. (2021). *Digital Applications in Archaeology and Cultural Heritage*, e00182. https://doi.org/10.1016/j.daach.2021.e00182

Jesse, N. (2018). *IFAC PapersOnLine, 30*, 486–491. https://doi.org/10.1016/j.ifacol.2018.11.310

Mangaraj, B. K., & Aparajita, U. (2020). *Socio-Economic Planning Sciences, 70*, 100778. https://doi.org/10.1016/j.seps.2019.100778

Popkova, E. D., Alekseev, A. N., Lobova, S. V., & Sergi, B. S. (2020). *Technology in Society, 63*, 101390. https://doi.org/10.1016/j.techsoc.2020.101390

Popkova, E. G., DeLo, P., & Sergi, B. S. (2021). *Research in International Business and Finance, 55*, 101315. https://doi.org/10.1016/j.ribaf.2020.101315

Sites. (2021). Digital technologies in the time of COVID. The Fletcher School at Tufts University. https://sites.tufts.edu/digitalplanet/digitalintelligence/ Accessed 11 April 2021.

UNDP. (2020). Human development index (HDI) ranking. From the 2020 Human Development Report. http://hdr.undp.org/en/content/latest-human-development-index-ranking Accessed 11 April 2021

UNDP. (2021). Human development reports. United Nations Development Program. https://report.hdr.undp.org/ Accessed 11 April 2021

Verma, S., Sharma, R., Deb, S., & Maitra, D. (2021). *International Journal of Information Management Data Insights, 1*, 100002. https://doi.org/10.1016/j.jjimei.2020.100002

Yakunina, R. P., & Bychkov, G.A. (2015). *Procedia Economics and Finance, 24*, 766–771. https://doi.org/10.1016/S2212-5671(15)00692-9

Modeling of the Unified Educational Space of Eurasian States

Sergey V. Revunov, Roman V. Revunov, Alexander G. Oganyan, Galina V. Plokhotnikova, and Chenxi Song

Abstract *Purpose* The purpose of this study is to analyze the strategic directions of personnel training for the economy of the Russian Federation, the development of human capital by increasing the competitiveness of Russian education, identification of factors to stimulate the export of educational services. *Design/methodology/approach* The achievement of the goals set by the study is based on the analysis of the main measures for the introduction of progressive digital tools into the export model of education, the formation of conditions for the effective self-realization of participants in the educational process, regardless of their territorial location. We used such methods of scientific cognition as: synthesis, analysis, identification of trends in the development of social processes. *Findings* Analysis of the main trends in the global labor market shows that the basic requirements for educational and professional qualifications of applicants are constantly increasing. The relevance of the work is connected with the need to create attractive and favorable socio-economic conditions for the study and residence of foreign citizens on the territory of the Russian Federation, as well as for the application of knowledge gained in the Russian education system to meet the needs of the labor market for qualified personnel, both in Russia and in their own countries. One of the primary tasks is to find a universal and effective mechanism for managing human capital by modern means of infocommunications in the context of an export educational model. The analysis of empirical data shows that at the present stage the Russian Federation, the Republic of Uzbekistan, the Republic of Belarus, the Republic of Kazakhstan have the potential for integration in the educational space, which allows, with the help of digital tools, to form an effective environment for the training of highly

S. V. Revunov · G. V. Plokhotnikova
Novocherkassk Engineering and Reclamation Institute named after A. K. Kortunov, a branch of the Don State Agrarian University, Novocherkassk, Russia
e-mail: g409zx@yandex.ru

S. V. Revunov · R. V. Revunov (✉) · A. G. Oganyan · C. Song
Southern Federal University, Rostov-on-Don, Russia
e-mail: rrevunov@mail.ru

C. Song
e-mail: 471906597@qq.com

E. I. Lazareva et al. (eds.), *Innovative Trends in International Business and Sustainable Management*, Approaches to Global Sustainability, Markets, and Governance,
https://doi.org/10.1007/978-981-19-4005-7_32

qualified specialists for various sectors of national economies. *Originality/value* The results of our research can be considered the development of a set of socio-economic, organizational and technological recommendations aimed at increasing the human capital index and, as a result, the quality of life for all participants in the educational system (both in the export model and for an effective strategy for the development of education within the country).

Keywords Human capital · Export of education · Unified educational space · Digital education · Information and communication technologies · Global labor market

JEL Classification A22 · E24 · F15 · F16 · F22

1 Introduction

Current trends in the development of the world labor market are the reason for the search for optimal solutions in the field of improving the level of education of citizens in order to achieve enhanced efficiency and productivity. Researchers Anopchenko et al. (2018) note that the development of human capital (and education, if evaluated from the point of view of investment in a person) provides such effects as economic growth, reduction of social tension, development of mutually beneficial cooperation between states. The problem of strengthening the family as an institution, issues of upbringing, accessibility of quality education for young people and, as a result, increasing labor productivity by the next generations of workers is studied in the work of Anopchenko et al. (2019). The constant readiness of a citizen for innovation, professional and educational mobility, continuous learning is a requirement imposed by the digital age, the problems of professional self-identification, the criteria for employee motivation are highlighted in the scientific article Murzina et al. (2018). At the present stage of the development of information and communication technologies, there is a problem of reformatting socio-economic mechanisms toward the development of non-resource sectors, in particular the export model of education, and the creation of a single educational space for cooperation between Russia, as an exporter of educational services, and other CIS countries. The influence of the human capital factor on socio-economic dynamics, the level of education and the quality of life are reflected in the works of Bosi et al. (2021), Usman et al. (2021), Bäker et al. (2021), Zhang and Wang (2021), Rahim et al. (2021), Gillman (2021). However, in these studies, the development of an effective mechanism for managing human capital using information and communication technology tools in the context of an export educational model has not found an exhaustive interpretation.

2 Methodology

The study used an extensive set of empirical data reflecting the dynamics of the total number of foreign citizens enrolled in Russian educational programs for the period from 1995–1996 to 2017–2018 academic years. This made it possible to assess the place of Russian education in the growth dynamics of the global human capital index. The methodology of the study is based on the concept of commonality of post-Soviet countries according to certain criteria: geographical (territorial proximity), economic and social. Socio-economic interconnectedness is caused by the trends of labor migration between Russia and the CIS countries. The close interrelation of the educational spaces of these countries is connected with the classical system of mass education, which has been preserved since Soviet times. One of the objectives of the implementation of the export educational strategy is the development of social and behavioral skills of participants in the educational process, including the ability to work in a team, understanding the emotional state of another person, conflict resolution and partnership skills. All these factors contribute to the increase in the human capital index. Thus, the world economy with a high level of automation of technical processes begins to appreciate human abilities that cannot be fully reproduced by machines.

3 Results

It is important to consider the age structure of the population of the CIS countries for the purpose of identifying the main consumers of export educational services. The age composition of the CIS population is given in Table 1.

If we consider young people as the main consumers of export educational services, out of 286 million people in the CIS structure, about 52 million are the age group of 15–29 years. Of these, the proportion of the population aged 15–29 years is 18%, the age group of 30–64 years –48%. Despite the fact that the total population of the CIS countries is increasing, there is a steady trend toward aging of the population and a decrease in the proportion of young people. During the observation period of 20 years, this indicator decreased from 24 to 18%. The quality improvement in healthcare system in the structure of the human capital index of the countries under consideration has affected the increase in life expectancy. However, a decrease in the proportion of young people in the structure of educated people of working age may have negative socio-economic consequences for the CIS countries in the context of the stability of the labor market and pension provision.

There is a demand for Russian education among foreign citizens. Table 2 presents data characterizing the dynamics of the number of foreign citizens who have completed full-time and part-time education in Russian higher educational institutions and their share in the overall structure of the contingent.

Table 1 Age structure of the CIS population at the beginning of 2020

Country	The entire population as of 1.01.2020, thousand people	In % by 2000	The proportion of young people, in %, 2020	The change in the proportion of young people compared to 2000, percentage points
Azerbaijan	1,00,671	124.1	22.4	−3.6
Armenia	29,597	91.7	19.5	−5.9
Belarus	94,134	93.7	16.1	−5.7
Kazakhstan	1,86,318	125.0	20.5	−5.2
Kyrgyzstan	65,235	132.5	24.5	−3.1
Moldova	26,404	–	17.6	–
Russia	1,467,486	99.9	16.0	−6.7
Tajikistan	93,138	148.7	27.3	−0.3
Uzbekistan	3,39,052	136.6	25.5	−2.9
Ukraine	4,17,328	85.8	16.0	−6.0

Source Compiled by the authors based on (Pryadko et al., 2019; Youth in the Commonwealth of Independent States and the Sustainable Development Goals 2021)

The analysis of the data presented in Table 2 shows an increase in the number of foreign citizens by 329.3 thousand people during the observation period (+80.7%), an increase in the proportion of foreigners in the structure of the contingent of higher educational institutions was 73%. The high demand for Russian educational products is due to the following qualities: fundamental nature, accessibility, practical orientation to the needs of the labor market. The self-identification of young people in the labor market is determined by a set of indicators: the level of education, the gender aspect, the probability of loss of professional skills due to a long period of forced unemployment, the trend in the number of young people who are currently not working and not studying. The dynamics of recent years illustrates that the labor force, determined by the sum of employed and unemployed, is estimated at 135 million people in the Commonwealth of Independent States as a whole. The share of young foreign citizens of the CIS countries aged 15–29 years in its structure decreased over the decade from 26 to 19%, which amounted to 25 million people according to 2019 data (excluding data for Turkmenistan and Uzbekistan). The steady pace of automation of production, the development of information and communication technologies—the combination of these factors determines the trend of reformatting educational approaches toward the creation of a single educational space with the leading role of Russia as an exporter of educational services. Labor migration of the population of the CIS countries leads to the search for socio-economic and technological solutions in the field of ensuring the inclusiveness, speed, accessibility and quality of educational services provided. Extrapolating this logic to other countries of the Commonwealth, it can be concluded that youth migration occurs mainly within the CIS, the proportion of migrants from the Commonwealth countries ranges

Table 2 Dynamics of the number of foreign citizens who have completed full-time and part-time education in Russian higher educational institutions and their share in the overall structure of the contingent

Years	The number of foreign citizens who studied at universities RSFSR/RF, thousand people	The total number of students in universities of the RSFSR/RF, thousand people	The proportion of foreign citizens in the composition of the student population of Russian universities,%
1950–1951	5.2	796.7	0.65
1960–1961	10.9	14,967	0.73
1970–1971	20.7	26,717	0.77
1980–1981	64.5	30,458	2.12
1990–1991	89.6	28,245	3.17
2000–2001	72.4	47,414	1.53
2005–2006	113.8	70,646	1.61
2006–2007	126.2	73,414	1.72
2007–2008	147.6	74,613	1.97
2008–2009	166.4	75,131	2.21
2009–2010	175.6	74,190	2.36
2010–2011	187.3	70,498	2.65
2011–2012	198.5	64,900	3.05
2012–2013	225.0	60,750	3.70
2013–2014	250.2	56,470	4.43
2014–2015	282.9	52,090	5.43
2015–2016	296.2	47,665	6.21
2016–2017	313.1	43,995	7.11
2017–2018	334.5	42,459	7.88

Source Compiled by the authors based on (Murzina et al., 2018; Youth in the Commonwealth of Independent States and the Sustainable Development Goals (2021)

from 20 to 40% of the total. Free competitive markets and active migration of young people determine the demand for educational services without departing from the basic kind of activity. There is a need for a qualitative revision of the paradigms of the development of domestic education in the field of information and communication technologies. In their study, Revunov et al. (2021) identified the main factors determining the trend of the transition of the export model of education to the digital model, assessed the impact of the use of information and communication technologies as a factor in improving the quality of education in the context of human capital development. Young people of the CIS countries are motivated to improve the quality of life through receiving educational services that will be in demand in their future work. The Russian Federation implements the export of educational services within the framework of the priority project "Export of Education", the main objectives of which are: to increase the number of full-time foreign students by 69% (from 220 thousand people in 2017 to 710 thousand in 2025), the number of foreign citizens who have completed online training in additional education programs should increase by 68.5% (from 1 million 100 thousand people to 3 million 500 thousand people). The revenue from the project should amount to more than 373 billion rubles in 2025. The construction of a centralized digital environment was implemented within the framework of the state priority project in the field of digital education development "Modern digital educational environment in the Russian Federation". This project was approved by the Government of the Russian Federation on October 25, 2016 as part of the implementation of the state program "Development of Education" for 2013–2020 One of the goals of this project was an attempt to create a single digital educational platform within which it would be possible to combine online training courses of leading universities in Russia. Such an approach would ensure the monopolization of the market for the export of educational services by large educational institutions, while provincial universities are full and valuable participants in this market, ensuring a steady influx of foreign students.

Potential consumers of export educational services of different levels of training (secondary vocational education, bachelor's degree, master's degree) in the age range of 15–19 years and 20–24 years are mostly confident users of the global network. Russia and Belarus show the largest share of Internet users among the studied age groups. When choosing the optimal information and communication tools for interaction within a single educational model, it is necessary to take into account the high percentage of users of the World Wide Web as a factor of rapid adaptation to the transition to a new, digital format of interaction between participants in the educational process. The choice of methods and means of remote communication presupposes the availability of technical capabilities and the geographical areas of coverage of the global network. High-quality export of educational services in the conditions of modeling a single educational space is possible only if there is a stable Internet connection. Broadband Internet access will allow the use of video and audio communications for educational purposes. The data given below demonstrate the possibility of exchanging information by e-mail between subjects of the educational process aged 15–24 years in the following CIS countries, which are the main consumers of export educational services: Azerbaijan—73.6%, Belarus—66.4%, Kazakhstan—61.9% (Pryadko et al., 2019; Revunov et al., 2021). It is also possible to achieve positive results of interaction for educational purposes in the adult population of the CIS countries within the framework of building a unified educational space. The leading positions in the level of e-mail skills as a means of remote communication are occupied by: Azerbaijan—42.2%, Kazakhstan—55.1%, Russia—42.6%. To a greater or lesser extent, young people of the CIS countries have the necessary information and communication skills to choose the type of interaction with the university exporting of educational services.

4 Discussion

Currently, one of the segments of the economy is a modern branch of this science—the knowledge economy, which determines the relationship of information received by a person and professional skills. The value of investments in the development of the knowledge economy and human capital is investigated in the work of Boris et al. (2019). Human capital is part of a more general concept—social-anthropological capital. It includes human, productive and natural capital. The importance of education in the structure of human capital as a factor of sustainable development of urbanized territories is noted in the study of Lazareva et al. (2020).

The study by Pryadko et al. (2019) proves the expediency of using social networks for the purpose of promoting educational services within the framework of marketing strategies. In our opinion, the potential of social media users among a large number of young people not only in Russia, but also in the CIS countries can be used for educational purposes: the creation of thematic groups, the exchange of information, tools available in this social network. One of the main policy priorities of the CIS countries and the Russian Federation is the development and implementation of effective socio-economic and technical tools to support distance learning and inclusive education programs. Further development of the export potential of Russian education expands opportunities for CIS youth living in remote areas and in rural areas, as well as young people with health disabilities to receive quality education. The implementation of such tasks in practice requires a wider introduction of modern technologies and equipment for online communication, stable access to high-speed Internet.

To build a unified digital educational space, it is necessary to choose electronic platforms that integrate the necessary means of remote communication: video communication, chat and personal messages, the ability to support a large number of simultaneously active online users by the servers of an educational organization. For small and medium-sized educational institutions, it is possible to use the MS Teams platform, for large universities with a large number of students, it is advisable to use a distance learning system based on CMS Moodle.

5 Conclusion

Summing up the above, it is necessary to formulate the following main conclusions:

1. Economic instruments for stimulating the export of educational services include a reduction in the tax rate on profits received by an educational institution from the export of educational services, the development and implementation of a set of tax preferences—tax holidays for a certain period of time, a mechanism for fiscal or financial incentives for an educational institution in case of achieving the set targets for the export of educational services: enrollment of a certain

number of foreign students with a projected increase in this indicator, as well as sustainable development of international relations.

2. Young people of the CIS countries have a fairly high level of education: 30–80% have vocational education of different levels. However, the share of young people with higher education in the structure of unemployment in the Commonwealth countries is quite large. This fact forces young people to engage in less qualified work, which leads to a loss of qualifications and, as a result, to ineffective government expenditure on education. The creation of international educational clusters focused on solving specific problems of the economy of the country importing educational services as a system of multilevel and multicomponent training of specialists will also ensure recognition of the importance of postgraduate education by foreign citizens. Within the framework of a cluster system (for example, a land reclamation cluster, an alternative energy cluster), students' education is continuous and comprehensive, taking into account the demands of the labor market and the economic characteristics of the importing state. The development of the system of educational clusters diversifies regional and country strategies for the export of educational services provided by the Russian Federation, according to the criterion of compliance with the needs of the labor market of the country importing educational services, as well as taking into account a complex of socio-economic, historical, cultural and geopolitical factors.
3. In our opinion, in order to fully transition to a single digital educational system, it is necessary to provide a comprehensive replacement with virtual analogues of installations used by educational institutions as laboratories.
4. The disadvantage of the digital model of education can be attributed to the lack of practical skills in the study of technical and natural science disciplines. The educational institution has the right to conduct practical and laboratory work as separate modules and, as a result, the personal presence of the student will be necessary for the qualitative development of educational material in practice. Within the framework of the educational model of digital export, one of the effective tools for socio-economic stimulation of a student's personal attendance for the period of practical and laboratory classes is the development by educational institutions of a mechanism for additional financial benefits when providing places of residence to foreign students.
5. The concept of educational clusters implies the development of a long-term strategy to attract a foreign contingent. The implementation of partnership relations between the states which are subjects of the educational process provides for the implementation of a number of measures: informing a potential foreign applicant about modern educational products, updating information on measures of socio-economic stimulation of a foreign citizen participating in the export model.
6. There is a noticeable imbalance in the labor market of the CIS countries between the need for highly qualified personnel and the supply from educational institutions. When developing a strategy for the export of educational services, it is

necessary to consider the issues of increasing the attractiveness of basic vocational training. The acquisition of a trade qualification that are currently in demand means the basis for further career growth of a foreign citizen by determining, in accordance with a combination of factors, an educational institution with higher-level educational programs.

7. A complete transition to the digital model of education at this stage of historical development is possible only in humanitarian areas. The problem of building a unified educational space using information and communication technologies has not been fully solved due to the impossibility of working with real equipment, which is an important factor affecting the practical training to develop a competent workforce.

References

Anopchenko, T. Y., Grinenko, S. V., Edalova, E. S., Zadorozhnyaya, E. K., & Murzin, A. D. (2018). Management of human capital reproduction processes in Post-Soviet Countries. *Espacios 39*(9).

Anopchenko, T. Y., Murzin, A. D., & Murzina, S. M. (2019). Human capital gender structure as a factor of socio-economic regional development. *European Proceedings of Social and Behavioural Sciences, 59*, 777–784. https://doi.org/10.15405/epsbs.2019.04.84

Bäker, A., Breuninger, S., & Pull, K. (2021). Pushing performance by building bridges: Human and social capital as mechanisms behind the mobility-performance link. *Journal of Vocational Behavior, 129*, 1–16. https://doi.org/10.1016/j.jvb.2021.103613

Boris, O. A., Gyyazov, A. T., Kuzmenko, I. I., & Anopchenko, T. Y. (2019). Strategic features of investing in human capital in the era of innovation. In *The Proceedings of the International Scientific and Practical Conference "Contemporary Issues of Economic Development of Russia: Challenges and Opportunities". The European Proceedings of Social and Behavioural Sciences*, (Vol. 59, pp. 759–766). https://doi.org/10.15405/epsbs.2018.02.113

Bosi, S., Lloyd-Braga, T., & Nishimura, K. (2021). Externalities of human capital. *Mathematical Social Sciences, 112*(C), 145–158. https://doi.org/10.1016/j.mathsocsci.2021.03.013

Gillman, M. (2021). Steps in industrial development through human capital deepening. *Economic Modelling, 99*. https://doi.org/10.1016/j.econmod.2021.02.011

Lazareva, E., Anopchenko, T., & Murzin, A. (2020). Human capital in the system of urban territory sustainable development management. In V. Vasenev, E. Dovletyarova, Z. Cheng, R. Valentini & C. Calfapietra (Eds.), *Green Technologies and Infrastructure to Enhance Urban Ecosystem Services. Conference Proceedings SSC 2018* (pp. 269–277). Springer Geography. https://doi.org/10.1007/978-3-030-16091-3_28

Murzina, S. M., Murzin, A. D., & Rogova, T. M. (2018). Economic identity as factor of formation of human capital institutions. *European Proceedings of Social and Behavioural Sciences, 35*, 961–971. https://doi.org/10.15405/epsbs.2018.02.113

Pryadko, I. A., Paytaeva, K. T., Revunov, R. V., Zelenova, G. V., & Evetskaya, S.V. (2019). Promotion of educational services in social networks. In E. Popkova & V. Ostrovskaya (Eds.), *Perspectives on the use of new information and communication technology (ICT) in the modern economy*. ISC 2017. Advances in Intelligent Systems and Computing (Vol. 726). Springer. https://doi.org/10.1007/978-3-319-90835-9_104

Rahim, S., Murshed, M., Umarbeyli, S., Kirikkaleli, D., Ahmad, M., Tufail, M., & Wahab, S. (2021). Do natural resources abundance and human capital development promote economic growth? A study on the resource curse hypothesis in Next Eleven countries. *Resources, Environment and Sustainability, 4*. https://doi.org/10.1016/j.resenv.2021.100018

Revunov, S. V., Rogova, T. M., Tutaeva, D. R., Murzin, A. D., & Plohotnikova, G. V. (2021). Modern information and communication technologies as a factor of human capital development. In Popkova E. G., & Sergi B. S. (Eds.), *Modern global economic system: Evolutional development versus revolutionary leap*. ISC 2019. Lecture Notes in Networks and Systems, (Vol. 198). Springer. https://doi.org/10.1007/978-3-030-69415-9_32

Usman, A., Wirawan, H., & Zulkifli. (2021). The effect of human capital and physical capital on regional financial condition: the moderating effect of management control system. *Heliyon, 7*(5). https://doi.org/10.1016/j.heliyon.2021.e06945

Youth in the Commonwealth of Independent States and the Sustainable Development Goals. (2021). The CIS Statistical Committee, UNFPA.

Zhang, X., & Wang, X. (2021). Measures of human capital and the mechanics of economic growth. *China Economic Review, 68*. https://doi.org/10.1016/j.chieco.2021.101641

Place and Role of the Discipline 'Foreign Language' in the Formation and Development of Human Capital at University

Ellina A. Sidelnik, Leila K. Salnaia, and Natalia S. Lutsenko

Abstract *Purpose* This paper aims at determining the place and role of the course 'Foreign Language' in the formation and development of human capital at university. Human capital has become the key factor in modern society. In this paper, we define human capital, its description and analysis. The level of human capital development can be evaluated with the Human Development Index taking into account life expectancy, education level, the standard of living and others. *Design/methodology/approach* Interdisciplinary approach is chosen and defined as one of the most effective means to increase the Human Development Index for Russia. *Findings* It is stated that universities are to take the leading role and apply an interdisciplinary approach to university education and work out some tools for the student's professional development. Such an approach will contribute to their successful socialization in the professional community. The academic discipline 'Foreign Language' at university is a means of professional communicative competence formation. It enables specialists to be more competitive in the international labour market and more productive in the workplace. Communicative competence is achieved by working with specially designed course books, using such methods as content-language integrated learning—CLIL, dealing with tasks aimed at developing soft skills. Foreign languages in the modern educational process are at the forefront of the student's professional growth, they retain a leading position in the development of human capital in the context of digitalization of the world community and the use of online learning opportunities. *Originality/value* Interdisciplinary approach is applied while designing the forms and tasks for miscellaneous ESP courses developed at the Foreign Languages Departments both in Moscow Institute of Physics and Technology and Southern Federal University. The classification of tasks for soft skills and, consequently, human capital development is presented in the article.

E. A. Sidelnik · L. K. Salnaia (✉)
Southern Federal University, Taganrog, Russia
e-mail: lksalnaya@rambler.ru

N. S. Lutsenko
Moscow Institute of Physics and Technology, Moscow, Russia
e-mail: nataly.1@inbox.ru

E. I. Lazareva et al. (eds.), *Innovative Trends in International Business and Sustainable Management*, Approaches to Global Sustainability, Markets, and Governance,
https://doi.org/10.1007/978-981-19-4005-7_33

Keywords Human capital · Interdisciplinary approach · Soft skills · Socialization · Professional community · Communicative competence

JEL Classification I210 · J24 · I230 · I250

1 Introduction

Today, the competitiveness of any country depends not only and not so much on the number of natural resources, which, unfortunately, are gradually depleted but on the level of human capital development. Human capital plays a crucial role in the stable economic, political and technological development of any society and state. To evaluate the level of human capital development, Human Development Index is used, which takes into account such indicators as life expectancy, education level, the standard of living and others. This index is calculated annually by the United Nations and is used to conduct a comparative analysis of the level of human capital development in different countries of the world. As it is stated in the annual report 'On Human Development 2020' of the United Nations Development Programme (UNDP) (Report of the United Nations Development Programme (UNDP) 2020) the human capital development index in the Russian Federation is 0.824. This value allows Russia to be classified as a country with a relatively high level of human development. However, taking the 52nd position out of 189, Russia lags far behind the most prosperous countries, such as Norway, Switzerland, Ireland, Germany, Hong Kong, Australia, Iceland, Sweden, Singapore and the Netherlands, which are among the top ten countries according to the human development index in 2020 (Report of the United Nations Development Programme (UNDP) On Human Development 2020), with values from 0.954 to 0.933.

One of the main parameters taken into account when calculating the human development index is the level of education of the population. On this basis, we believe that institutions of higher professional education can and should play a leading role not only in the formation and development of human capital but should also create conditions for its application at universities and after graduation. We define human capital as a set of intellectual abilities and practical skills acquired in the process of learning, socialization and professional activity. The development of human capital, in our opinion, also implies the formation and development of soft skills, namely, emotional intelligence, personal qualities and communicative competence (Salnaia, 2019). Thus, communicative competence, namely foreign language communicative competence contributes to student's professional development and increases the level of human capital development.

We believe that the discipline 'Foreign Language' within the framework of an interdisciplinary approach to university education has several tools for the student's professional development and contributes to their successful socialization in the professional community. Introduction to professional information in a foreign language, acquaintance and participation in activities of international professional communities, presentation of the results of their professional and scientific activities at international conferences, professional and informal communication contribute to the socialization of students not only in society, but also give them opportunities to increase their competitiveness in the labour market, identify personal career goals, trajectories of professional growth and, therefore, significantly improve the quality of life, thereby developing human capital. The purpose of this study is to select the most effective mechanisms for the development of student's human capital through the academic discipline 'Foreign Language' at university.

2 Methodology

Representatives of the classical economic theory (Petty, 1940; Ricardo, 1993; Smith, 1956) were the first who began to study the correlation between the level of education, health and abilities of a person with the level of economic development of the country and laid the foundations of the concept of human capital.

The theory of human capital as an independent scientific direction was formed due to certain socio-economic conditions that developed in the second half of the twentieth century:

- scientific and technological progress that stimulated the development of innovative production;
- increasing the importance of intellectual and highly professional labour costs in the production process;
- humanization of socio-economic relations in the society.

American economists, Nobel laureates (Becker, 1962; Schultz, 1960) conduced to the development of the contemporary concept of human capital. Theodor Schultz paid special attention to the power of education used to enhance human capital (Schultz, 1971). He claimed that to ensure a person's well-being and economic growth it is vitally important to invest in education. Developing the concept of human capital, (Becker, 2003) emphasized the importance of education and proved the economic feasibility and necessity of public and private investments in the 'human factor', namely in education. Heine (2000, p. 360) also speaks about the importance and role of education in the accumulation and development of human capital.

Russian researcher (Korotkov 2010, pp. 374–375), analyzing the 'human capital', points out the direct correlation of the competence level, creative potential and the desire for constant professional and personal development of employees with the level of education they received.

We cannot but agree with (Shirinkina & Baksheev 2016, p. 223), who believe that the level of education is a leading factor in the formation of human capital.

Considering fundamental competencies formed in the process of studying at institutions of higher professional education, scientists single out communicative competence as one of the basic ones in the process of forming human capital (Silkin, 2013).

Communicative competence can significantly increase the value of human capital, as it makes it possible not only to perceive but also to create speech utterances following the norms of the language and achieve the desired communicative results (Sturikova, 2015). Hence, if we want to expand our graduate's human capital in the domestic as well as in the international markets, then at universities special attention should be paid to the formation of foreign-language professional communicative competence.

We support the definition of foreign-language professional communicative competence given in (Sergeeva & Bushmanova 2011, pp. 241–242). Foreign-language professional communicative competence enables specialists to be more competitive in the international labour market and more productive in the workplace.

We consider foreign-language professional communicative competence as one of the basic interdisciplinary competencies formed in the process of studying at institutions of higher professional education. Therefore, as (Sidelnik & Lutsenko, 2021) notes, the most complete development and formation of this competence are possible only within the framework of an interdisciplinary approach that ensures integrative learning. The interdisciplinary approach creates an opportunity to synthesize scientific knowledge obtained during the study of various courses at university. It is achieved through the use of research methods of one field of scientific knowledge in other ones (Boruha & Verzunova, 2012).

There is a variety of university courses aimed at the formation and development of foreign-language professional communicative competence. As for Southern federal university, we can mention Foreign Language for Professional Communication, Foreign Language for Special Purposes and Foreign Language for Business Communication. We believe that it is the interdisciplinary approach that should be used to efficiently organize training in the above-mentioned courses. The interdisciplinary format of teaching foreign languages increases the motivation and interest of students, develops their critical scientific and professional thinking, as it creates conditions for the synthesis of professional knowledge and foreign-language skills while modelling their future professional activities (Vakhrusheva & Masharova, 2017). We share the point of view of (Popova and Stepanova, 2010) who speaks about the benefits of an interdisciplinary approach at universities.

Considering the requirements of teaching foreign languages according to an interdisciplinary approach, (Sleserenko, 2007) highlights the following ones: the focus of courses on the integrated development of professional foreign-language communicative competence and critical professional thinking; a foreign language as a means of developing professional foreign-language competence.

To implement an interdisciplinary approach in teaching foreign languages, a great variety of textbooks for the course 'Foreign Language for Professional Communication' has been developed at the Department of Foreign Languages of Southern federal university. They are Computer Engineering, Electronic Engineering, English for Information Security, Get Ready for Scientific Communication, English for Mathematics and others (Bondarev et al., 2015; Salnaia & Ovcharenko, 2017; Salnaia & Sidelnik, 2020).

Quite a large number of interesting and productive, active and interactive teaching methods have been developed at the present stage of development of the methodology of teaching foreign languages. However, not all of them can be applied for an interdisciplinary approach. The main aim of this paper is to select the most effective methods and means of teaching foreign languages which will form and develop professional foreign-language competence, soft skills and, as a result, human capital.

Undoubtedly, in this context, the most productive method of teaching foreign languages for professional communication is the method of subject-language integrated learning (content-language integrated learning—CLIL), which allows you to build the learning process on an interdisciplinary integrative basis.

We believe content-language integrated learning (CLIL) to be the most effective method of teaching foreign languages for professional communication as it allows us to organize the process of study on an interdisciplinary integrative basis. The advantages and problems of applying this method are analyzed in the works of (Salnaia,2017; Sidelnik & Lutsenko, 2021).

3 Results

The textbooks developed at the Department of Foreign languages SFedU are intended to develop the professional foreign-language competence and soft skills of students in their 3rd–4th years. The teaching aids have some creative, communicative tasks that help students to prepare for work in the international professional community. Since a foreign language is considered as a means of obtaining professionally valuable information, all text, audio and video materials of the textbooks have practical value for students. The tasks of the textbooks improve the ability to perform logical thinking operations, work with various sources of information, think outside the box, communicate productively while performing tasks and present the results of work. It is worth mentioning that the developed tasks include various types of speech activity, require an integrated approach when performing them (for example, watching a video, analyzing it, presenting the results of the analysis, etc.).

For instance, one of the popular tasks among students from vocabulary sections of the textbook 'Replace the words/terms in bold by their synonym's aims at vocabulary enrichment, the ability to apply and define terms in various professional communication situations. Rewriting sentences using Passive Voice or expressing ideas through gerunds, various types of infinitives or participles leads to activation of grammatical structures characteristic of professional communication. Role plays, presentations, brainstorming topics like 'Study the current situation with blockchain technology, point out the advantages and problems of its application and present your opinion about its use in the future' result in the development of skills of professional monologue and dialogic speech in different styles (formal, informal, scientific, popular science), abilities to achieve a communicative goal. Tasks in reading sections teach students to determine the style and communicative purposes of the text, highlight the main ideas, find the necessary information and use it for further work and discussion in the classroom. Such writing tasks as 'Study the diagram and the table given below. Complete the sentences illustrating data protection in the Internet of Things. Write an abstract of your course paper' develop the skills to understand and interpret graphic, textual information, multimodal texts as well as to enrich the knowledge of the features of written professional and scientific foreign-language papers. Listening or watching tasks followed by completing summaries or adding figures or details allow students to learn and distinguish key and valuable information, important details, to understand the opinion of an interlocutor and purposes of communication. In general, the complex of tasks in the textbooks encourages students to use the studied professional textbook material for their professional purposes and, conversely, to use personal experience for professional development. These exercises also inspire students to solve tasks creatively, to collaborate, form the qualities necessary for a modern specialist such as independence, initiative, responsibility, provide joining of the learning process and professional activity. Besides, the educational process can be and is partially performed online via TEAMS.

More detailed information about the types of tasks for developing soft skills is presented in the textbooks of the Department of Foreign languages of the Southern Federal Univesity and available at https://figshare.com/ with the identifier https://figshare.com/s/f0a9549bbaa5a1d56c2a.

Getting a master's degree at the Moscow Institute of Physics and Technology is an example of a successful 'business plan' for students. For instance, young people with a bachelor's or specialist's degree and work experience in their speciality became masters of technological entrepreneurship major last year. These are successful people of 30 years old on average who have a pragmatic approach to life and for whom education as a whole is an integrated part of their life. The decision to continue the educational process was made due to the need to acquire additional skills related to human capital, the opportunity to get useful acquaintances for a joint or collaborative business, communicate with people who have similar interests and supplement their scientific base with the latest technological innovations. Masters in this field are people living in countries such as Russia, Luxembourg, Estonia, Kazakhstan, the United Arab Emirates and others. Such communication during classes contributes to the development of international business, helps to get to a new level in business, share experiences, work with colleagues from different countries and become an adviser or advisee. Classes of English are held online and give a practical opportunity for young people to use the language to solve their business problems: to write a competent resume in English, prepare and conduct a presentation of their business project, present their idea to potential investors (the so-called elevator pitches), prepare a template of a white paper for their project to present for stakeholders, answer questions from the targeted audience and, possibly, find a business partner.

4 Conclusion

Nowadays learning a foreign language is not a goal in itself, it is much more useful to apply the language to other pragmatic goals and objectives. For example, in the context of modern globalization and an increasingly 'shrinking' world, language learning helps to join the world professional community and become competitive in the international labour market. Investments into the human capital, namely into education, education, development—and now as well as many years ago are expensive, however, these investments pay off in the long term. Human capital today can be considered a successful business project, and the more thoughtful the 'business plan' is, the more significant the return on 'investment's will be.

Under today's economic conditions in our society, a person must be flexible, mobile, able to adapt to the requirements of the market. That is why students understand the value of education in the digital community: you need to constantly move in the professional field, develop, try, search and experiment. Thus, human capital is developing, its rational use leads to an increase in worker's incomes and, as a result, people invest in health, self-development and self-improvement. Our human capital is the only outlay that is more likely to guarantee future success. In the future, we can talk about an increase in the quality of life and life expectancy. Investments in education in the long term will certainly pay off both on the scale of the individual and on the scale of the country as a whole. Teaching a foreign language as a practical discipline retains a leading position in the development of human capital in the context of the digitalization of the world community and the use of online learning opportunities. Using an interdisciplinary approach, CLIL and specially developed teaching aid as well as taking advantage of online learning contribute to the development of soft skills and human capital.

Data Depository

Department of Foreign languages Southern Federal University. URL: https://figshare.com/ with the identifier https://figshare.com/s/f0a9549bbaa5a1d56c2a.

References

Becker, G. S. (1962). Investment in human capital: A theoretical analysis. *Journal of Political Economy, 70*, 9. https://doi.org/10.1086/258724

Becker, G. S. (2003). *Human behaviour: An economic approach* (pp. 592–594). Selected Works on Economic Theory. Higher School of Economics.

Bondarev, M. G., Andrienko, A. S., Burenko, L. V., Mel'nik, O. G., & Sidel'nik, E. A. (2015). *Computer engineering*. Flinta Nauka.

Boruha, S. Yu., & Verzunova, L. V. (2012). The technology of interdisciplinary advanced training of professional personnel in the conditions of integration of education, science and production [Tekhnologiya mezhdisciplinarnoj operezhayushchej podgotovki professional'nyh kadrov v usloviyah integracii obrazovaniya, nauki i proizvodstva]. *Modern Problems of Science and*

Education [Sovremennye problemy nauki i obrazovaniya], *4*. https://science-education.ru/ru/article/view?id=6904 Accessed 15 October 2021.
Heyne, P. T. (2000). In *The economic way of thinking*. Pearson.
Korotkov, E. M. (2010). Management.
Petty, V. (1940). *Economic and statistical works*. Sotsekgiz.
Popova, N. V., & Stepanova, M. M. (2010). Interdisciplinary approach to teaching a foreign language in a non-core Master's degree program [Mezhdisciplinarnyj podhod k prepodavaniyu inostrannogo yazyka v neprofil'noj magistrature]. *Papers of the IInd International Scientific Conference Actual Problems of Science and Education* [Aktual'nye Problemy Nauki i Obrazovaniya], (pp. 76–81) North Caucasus Federal University.
Report of the United Nations Development Programme (UNDP) "On Human Development 2020" (2020). http://hdr.undp.org/sites/default/files/hdr2020_ru.pdf Accessed 15 October 2021.
Ricardo, D. (1993). In *Anthology of economic classics*, (Vol. 1, pp. 308)
Salnaia, L. K. (2017). Improving the professional competence of the university teaching staff in the field of content and language integrated learning [Sovershenstvovanie professional'noj kompetentnosti professorsko-prepodavatel'skogo sostava universiteta v oblasti predmetno-yazykovogo integrirovannogo obucheniya]. *Philological Sciences. Issues of Theory and Practice* [Filologicheskie Nauki. Voprosy Teorii i Praktiki], Gramota, Tambov, *12*(4), 206–208.
Salnaia, L. K. (2019). *English for information security*. Southern Federal University Publishing.
Salnaia, L. K., & Ovcharenko, V. P. (2017). The formation of soft skills of engineering university students by means of the discipline "Foreign language" [O formirovanii universal'nyh kompetencij studentov inzhenernogo vuza sredstvami discipliny «Inostrannyj yazyk»]. *Gramota, Tambov, 6*(72), 199–202.
Salnaia, L. K., & Sidelnik, E. A. (2020). *Get ready for scientific communication*. Southern Federal University Publishing.
Schultz, T. W. (1960). Capital formation by education. *Journal of Political Economy, 68*, 571. https://doi.org/10.1086/258393
Schultz, T. W. (1971). *Investment in human capital: The role of education and research*. The Free Press.
Sergeeva, N. N., & Bushmanova, Y. A. (2011). Professionally oriented foreign language communicative competence of a technical university student [Professional'no orientirovannaya inoyazychnaya kommunikativnaya kompetentnost' studenta tekhnicheskogo vuza]. *Kazan Science [kazanskaya Nauka], 8*, 241–242.
Shirinkina, E. V., & Baksheev, S. L. (2016). The role of higher education in the formation of human capital [Rol' vysshego obrazovaniya v formirovanii chelovecheskogo kapitala]. *Fundamental Research* [Fundamental'nye Issledovaniya], *10*, 1. https://fundamental-research.ru/ru/article/view?id=40837 Accessed 17 October 2021.
Sidelnik, E. A., & Lutsenko, N. C. (2021). On the issue of using the method of subject-language integrated learning in a non-linguistic university (within the framework of the interdisciplinary method) [K voprosu ispol'zovaniya metoda predmetnogo-yazykovogo integrirovannogo obucheniya v neyazykovom vuze (v ramkah mezhdisciplinarnogo metoda)]. *Baltic Humanitarian Journal* [Baltijskij Gumanitarnyj Zhurnal], *1* (34). https://cyberleninka.ru/article/n/k-voprosu-ispolzovaniya-metoda-predmetnogo-yazykovogo-integrirovannogo-obucheniya-v-neyazykovom-vuze-v-ramkah-mezhdistsiplinarnogo Accessed 17 October 2021. https://doi.org/10.26140/bgz3-2021-1001-0058
Silkin, V. V. (2013). Communicative competence in the development of human capital [Kommunikativnaya kompetentnost' v razvitii chelovecheskogo kapitala]. *Public Service* [Gosudarstvennaya Sluzhba], *6*, 86. https://cyberleninka.ru/article/n/kommunikativnaya-kompetentnost-v-razvitii-chelovecheskogo-kapitala Accessed 17 October 2021.
Sleserenko, I. V. (2007). Goal-setting in teaching a foreign language at a technical university: An interdisciplinary approach [Celepolaganie pri obuchenii inostrannomu yazyku v tekhnicheskom vuze: Mezhdisciplinarnyj podhod]. *Bulletin of Tomsk State University, 296*, 59–61.
Smith, A. (1956). *Research on the nature and causes of the wealth of nations*. Sotsekgiz.

Sturikova, M. V. (2015). Communicative competence: on the question of definition and structure [Kommunikativnaya kompetenciya: k voprosu o definicii i strukture]. *Innovative Projects and Programs in Education* [Innovacionnye Proekty i Programmy v Obrazovanii], *6*. https://cyberleninka.ru/article/n/kommunikativnaya-kompetentsiya-k-voprosu-o-definitsii-i-strukture Accessed 17 October 2021.

Vakhrusheva, S. N., & Masharova, T. V. (2017). Interdisciplinary integration of the educational process in the training of a lawyer [Mezhdisciplinarnaya integraciya obrazovatel'nogo processa v podgotovke yurista]. *Bulletin of Kostroma State University, 4*, 107–110.

Internet Corporate Social Responsibility as a Factor of Corporate Sustainability: Issues and Solutions in Management

Yang Yang

Abstract After the COVID-19 epidemic Internet companies have become the main organization of global economic recovery. While pursuing profits, Internet enterprises must take up more social responsibilities and make greater contributions in product quality, technological innovation, environmental protection and protection of stakeholders' rights and interests. It is found that CSR plays an important role in the path of sustainable development of enterprises. Social responsibility is not only an obligation due to a company, but most importantly, it is related to the survival and development of a company. This paper combines the relevant stakeholder theory, considers the realistic characteristics of Internet enterprises, analyzes the problems and current situation of fulfilling the social responsibility of representative Internet enterprises in China, and proposes to fulfil social responsibility in six dimensions: economic responsibility, legal responsibility, moral responsibility, charitable responsibility, economic responsibility and innovation responsibility to solve social problems and promote the sustainable development of enterprises and society.

Keywords Corporate social responsibility · Internet corporate · Corporate sustainability · Environment · Issues

JEL Classification R01 · F22 · F63

1 Introduction

The current research on CSR is mostly in traditional industries such as the food industry, construction industry and medicine. The Internet industry belongs to the emerging industry in China and has certain industry specificity, and the research on social responsibility activities carried out by Internet enterprises has made a useful exploration of this field. In addition, the existing CSR dimensions still follow Archie

Y. Yang (✉)
Southern Federal University, Rostov-on-Don, Russia
e-mail: 393567991@qq.com

E. I. Lazareva et al. (eds.), *Innovative Trends in International Business and Sustainable Management*, Approaches to Global Sustainability, Markets, and Governance,
https://doi.org/10.1007/978-981-19-4005-7_34

Carroll's CSR model and do not innovate according to social and economic changes. The era of the digital economy has come, and Internet CSR should expand the scope of social responsibility according to the changes of the times so that enterprises, the economy, society and the environment can develop harmoniously.

2 Materials and Methods

According to stakeholder theory and sustainable development theory, the stakeholders of an enterprise should include at least shareholders, creditors, employees, community and society, government and the public. Shareholders, creditors and employees are the internal stakeholders of the Internet enterprise, while the community, society, government, public and customers are the external stakeholders of the Internet enterprise (Jiang & He, 2015). In addition, according to sustainability theory, Internet platform stakeholders are constantly changing and updating, while Internet enterprises have two special objects - Internet users and network environment.

This paper selects representative Internet companies in China, such as Alibaba, Tencent, Jingdong, etc., uses the CSR pyramid model of American management scientist Archie B. Carroll to classify social responsibility into economic responsibility, legal responsibility, moral responsibility, and philanthropic responsibility, follows the basic idea of "identifying problems, analyzing problems, and solving problems", analyzes the current situation and problems of CSR of Internet companies in detail, and concludes that Internet companies must perform social responsibility from six dimensions to fulfil social responsibility and promote sustainable development of enterprises.

3 Results

The social responsibility of Internet enterprises includes the responsibility of the enterprises themselves, but also the responsibility to stakeholders, such as the responsibility to the environment, the responsibility to consumers and the responsibility to economic growth (Lam & Li, 2018). The issues and situations of Internet enterprises' social responsibility fulfilment are as follows. In 2021, Southern Weekend officially released the "China Internet Industry Social Responsibility Watch Report (2020–2021)" (Ou, 2020). Compared with the previous year, this year's Internet industry social responsibility has the following performance.

First, Internet enterprises resisted the impact of the epidemic and the market scale continued to grow. 64% of the enterprises achieved profit growth, and 42% of the enterprises with revenue over 10 billion yuan (Chen & Wen, 2021). According to the report on the business income of 41 SMEs in Hubei in the first quarter of 2020 published by Hubei Province, the average business income of enterprises in the first quarter of 2020 was RMB312814771.78, a decrease of RMB131668972.44.

The higher turnover growth is in medical enterprises and Internet enterprises, and the largest decrease in turnover is in small and medium-sized enterprises (Southern Weekend Magazine).

Second, Internet enterprises' energy consumption has caused huge carbon emissions, and the "Green Cloud 2021" released on April 21, 2021, comprehensively compares the response speed and implementation efforts of China's Internet technology industry for "carbon peaking by 2030 and carbon neutral by 2060", and is based on renewable energy performance, energy disclosure, energy-saving and carbon reduction performance, and influences ranked 7 leading Internet cloud service and data centre companies based on four dimensions. From these four perspectives, analyzing the carbon emission standards of 7 Internet companies from these four perspectives, Tencent's score is 61 points, just passing, and the other six companies such as Alibaba, Jingdong, Huawei, Baidu, Jinshan, and wave group failed the carbon emission standards. In general, most of my country's leading Internet technology companies have made progress in terms of energy information disclosure, energy-saving and carbon reduction, and renewable energy. However, the overall carbon neutralization progress is lagging (Wangmao, 2017). Only Qinhuai data proposes to achieve group scope one and scope two by 2030. Net-zero emissions and a 100% renewable energy target. Tencent announced the launch of its carbon–neutral plan but did not clarify the timeline and implementation path (Xu & Liu, 2018).

Third, Internet companies have irregularities and monopolistic tendencies. Many large Internet companies exploit regulatory loopholes, including counterfeiting, tax evasion and vicious price dumping (Kraiczy et al., 2015), and many online stores hire employees to buy first and then return to boost sales in order to gain a false brand effect and guide users to place orders. Some online stores evade taxes and fees, and some platforms force merchants to choose applications, but they also deprive merchants and consumers of free choice and compete viciously with competitors, causing stock prices to plummet by 1.6% (Ballou et al., 2012).

Fourth, consumer's rights were damaged and the online ecosystem became more chaotic (Li, 2016). Among the 150 CSR alerts collected by the Southern Weekend in May 2021, the Internet information service industry accounted for about 21%, involving various areas such as consumer rights, compliance management, responsible governance, safety and health, etc. Among them, consumer rights issues dominate and the issues cross each other (Zhang, 2019). The main areas of lack of Internet corporate social responsibility include responsible governance, consumer rights, employee responsibility, environmental protection and so on (Wangmao, 2017). Problems such as an illegal collection of user's personal information, false propaganda to induce consumption, and substandard food quality are highlighted as the reasons behind the weak responsibility of Internet enterprises and disregard for consumer rights protection (Li & Yang, 2016), and there is an urgent need to create a good network ecological environment.

Fifth, Internet enterprises lack corporate social responsibility culture and the social responsibility system is not perfect (Wang & Shen, 2018). After a literature survey, many Internet enterprises do not have a clear understanding of social responsibility (Jiang, 2019). They are lack scientific social responsibility culture and evaluation mechanism and only passively fulfil their social responsibility, individual large Internet enterprises fulfil their social responsibility just to promote themselves and do not fulfil their promises, which eventually lead to the loss of consumer trust.

4 Conclusion

In order to make Internet enterprises better fulfil their social responsibility and participate in social governance, CSR has become an important factor in promoting corporate competitiveness and improving corporate performance. This paper proposes that Internet enterprises social responsibility should fulfil social responsibility from six dimensions to improve the sustainable development of enterprises.

1. Economic responsibility - Internet companies promote economic recovery, on-site sales of goods to promote consumption.
2. Legal responsibility - prohibits monopolistic behaviour, eliminate counterfeiting and protect patents.
3. Moral responsibility - cares for employees, uses the platform to enhance materials.
4. Charity responsibility - sets up special funds and provides a reliable charity platform.
5. Environmental responsibility - protects internal network environment and external ecological environment.
6. Innovation responsibility - participates in social responsibility through technological innovation, shares quality resources and provide life-friendly applications.

Acknowledgements I would like to thank Professor Lazareva Elena Iosifovnar. In addition to my busy work schedule, my teacher spared no effort to give me patient guidance on direction of my topic. I was given patient guidance on direction of my topic, the structure of my dissertation and the research methodology of the materials required for my dissertation.

References

Ballou, B., Casey, R. J., Grenier, J. H., & Heitger, D. L. (2012). Exploring the strategic integration of sustainability initiatives: Opportunities for accounting research. *Accounting Horizons, 26*(2), 265–288.

Carcello, J. V., Hermanson, D. R., & Ye, Z. (2015). Corporate governance research in accounting and auditing: Insights, practices, implications, and future research. *Auditing. A Journal of Practice and Theory, 30*(3), 1–31.

Chen, W., & Wen, M. (2021). Sustainable development and corporate social responsibility based on triple bottom line. *Business Management, 10*, 105–201.

Jiang, Q., & He, W. (2015). Strategic choice of corporate social responsibility and sustainable development of private enterprises. *Business Economy and Management, 11*, 51–56.

Jiang, Y. (2019). Research on corporate social responsibility report assurance based on sustainable development governance. *Journal of South China University*, 215–220.

Kraiczy, N. D., Hack, A., & Kellermanns, F. W. (2015). What makes a family firm innovative? CEO risk-taking propensity and the organizational context of family firms. *Journal of Product Innovation Management, 32*(3), 334–348.

Lam, K., & Li, Y. (2018). Does corporate governance matter? The case of environmental and social responsibility committees on the board. *Working Paper, 16*, 356–362.

Li, J. W. (2019). Effects of different dimensions of corporate social responsibility on corporate financial performance in tourism-related industries. *Tourism Management, 32*(4), 790–804.

Li, P. (2016). On corporate social responsibility and sustainable development. Modern finance and economics. *Journal of Tianjin University of Finance and Economics, 10*, 11–15.

Li, X., & Yang, J. (2016). Think about sustainable development and corporate social responsibility. *Indusry Survey, 7*(3), 5–47.

Ou, L. (2020). Study on the impact of COVID-19 on small and medium-sized enterprises in Hubei Province and Countermeasures. *Journal of Hubei College of Economics (Humanities and Social Sciences Edition), 10*, 255–263.

Southern Weekend Magazine https://www.haotougao.com/nanfangzhoumo/ Accessed 12 May 2019.

Wang, Q., & Shen, J. (2018). Corporate social responsibility culture promotes sustainable development of enterprises. *Human Resources Development in China, 35*(3), 149–153.

Wangmao, X. (2017). Research on the relationship between corporate social responsibility and sustainable development. *Reform and Strategy, 5*, 179–180.

Xu, Z. L., & Liu, N. (2018). Research on the integration of corporate social responsibility and corporate strategic objective management based on sustainable development. *China Industrial Economy, 24*, 130–132.

Zhang, H. (2019). Sustainability assurance and internal auditing in emerging markets. *Corporate Governance, 11*(4), 475–488.

Education Digitalization as a Factor in Human Capital Asset's Development: Modern Challenges and Development Prospects

Svetlana M. Murzina, Sergey V. Revunov, Elena N. Lavrinenko, Roman V. Revunov, and Anton D. Murzin

Abstract The study aims to scientifically search the optimal socio-economic and technical solutions in the field of educational process digitalization in the context of human capital asset's development. The scientific novelty is predetermined by the goals of minimizing the options for choosing between a wide variety of software products presented at this technical development stage, the use of which involves the transfer of some educational process elements into the virtual space. On the example of natural scientific disciplines, the possibility of transferring the educational process to virtual space is considered. The working hypothesis is due to an intensive search for the methods to reduce financial costs by the educational institution while ensuring the goal of quality education achievement with the intensive use of information and communication technologies. The research methods include a comprehensive analysis of the digital education elements, the selection of effective tools for implementing the transition to a digital model, an assessment of the potential prospects for the development of a mixed traditional-digital approach in education, a scientific study of the distance learning concept as one of the promising trajectories for the further educational development and one of the main components of the digital learning. The current state of education in the context of a market economic model is assessed in research methodology development. The result of the study is the substantiation of the strategic directions for increasing the education system functioning efficiency using digital technologies in the context of human capital development.

S. M. Murzina · A. D. Murzin (✉)
Don State Technical University, Rostov-on-Don, Russia
e-mail: admurzin@sfedu.ru

S. M. Murzina
e-mail: merciana@inbox.ru

S. V. Revunov
Novocherkassk Engineering and Reclamation Institute named after A. K. Kortunov—a Branch of the Don State Agrarian University, Novocherkassk, Russia

S. V. Revunov · E. N. Lavrinenko · R. V. Revunov · A. D. Murzin
Southern Federal University, Rostov-on-Don, Russia
e-mail: enlavrinenko@sfedu.ru

E. I. Lazareva et al. (eds.), *Innovative Trends in International Business and Sustainable Management*, Approaches to Global Sustainability, Markets, and Governance,
https://doi.org/10.1007/978-981-19-4005-7_35

Keywords Education · Digitalization · Human capital · Modern challenges · Development prospects

JEL Classification E24 · I24 · J24

1 Introduction

Modern education is in the stage of transition from the traditional model, focused on the central role of the teacher in the learning process, to a more modern one, focused on the practicable competencie's development in students. According to such authors as (Habibi et al., 2020; Iivari et al., 2020; Martinengo et al., 2020; Velez et al., 2021; Zhao et al., 2021) a large number of disciplines, focused on general engineering training, are studied. The competency-based approach is focused on a clear understanding of the goals of studying a particular discipline. Even before the start of mastering the course, the student has an idea of the tasks of its acquisition. At the technology development present stage many processes are actualized by the task of digitalization: the provision of public services, all educational institutions, including schools and universities, have their own electronic educational environment—a set of digital and technical means of unhindered communication between the educational process subjects, remote interaction and knowledge control methods. The processes of transition to digital technologies have a certain chaotic nature at this historical stage in the main segment of educational institutions in the Russian Federation. There are precedents due to the introduction of domestic and international experience, as well as experimental scientific research on the use of digital technologies in the processes taking place in a general educational organization. The education system has a clear goal of digital transformation, the new concept formation of a "digital" educational organization with progressive tools for the implementation of activities, basic and auxiliary processes, innovative mechanisms for interactive communication of participants in the educational process, and new digital tools.

The factors of analyzing the potential for digital technologie's use in education, the step-by-step condition's implementation for their effective use, taking into account the rapidity of changes in technological processes at the present stage of development, as well as the need to form the competencies of students that meet the modern trends of the Information Age, are actualized in the current conditions. Special attention of the scientific community is paid to the identification, formation, and transfer of digital transformation positive practices experience.

Researched in the scientific works of (Bowyer & Kahne,2020; Çetin, 2021; Fleaca & Stanciu, 2019; Ivanov et al., 2020; Nortvig et al., 2020; Wharrad et al., 2021) on the transformation of the educational paradigm, determined by the introduction of digital technologies, is global dynamics of improving the quality of educational systems and the transition to building personalized educational trajectories. This factor determines the basic difference between the digital educational format and classical educational approaches. The digitalization process does not set itself the task of replacing the routine professional and pedagogical operations (for example, filling out educational journals and diaries in secondary school, creating work programs for disciplines, a fund of assessment tools in higher education). The digitalization process puts the teacher in a position that is both directed toward the past accumulated experience and focused on modern science and technology achievements. Thus, the teacher transforms personal identity, constantly asking himself what the essence of his professional activity is; according to what criteria it can be transformed to the Information Age, is it possible to integrate the digital tools into the practice of educational activities, and assess the feasibility of including the instrumentarium to achieve the goals and objectives of educational activities.

2 Materials and Methods

Such researchers as (Brevik et al., 2019; Failed, 2017; Limani et al., 2019; Zain, 2021) were engaged in the process of solving the problems of transforming the educational process in the context of digitalization, taking into account the need to develop human capital. Such methods of scientific knowledge as observation, analysis, synthesis, and scientific forecasting, which made it possible to ensure a high level of the conclusions and research result's reliability were used by the authors for the presented survey.

3 Results

Digital educational technologies predetermine the direction of social values for transformation, provoke the Internet identification of a biological individual, giving rise to a new type of student—able to independently build the educational trajectories based on personal preferences.

Digital formation specialists focus their own intellectual resources on self-development and self-determination, integrating learning processes into work. The digital concept of education development should provide a rapid breakthrough in the era of active use of information and communication technologies, characterized by the rapid development of economic systems and the development of new strategies for the interaction between the employer and the employee. Digital intelligence, which ensures the implementation of certain routine actions, may appear in the labor market through digital technologies.

The focus of the education system's attention, in our opinion, should be shifted to the development of such a set of professional competencies for modern specialists, which should be developed to implement the non-standard solutions, a creative approach to work, and the communication skills development. The presence of digital literacy must be considered as the basic element of the transition to a digital education model. By a combination of factors, digital literacy is one of the top priorities in education. This term can be understood as a whole range of such skills as the ability to work in automatic design systems, reproduce any kind of content using digital technologies, a program in modern languages, develop multimedia educational online courses, and have basic skills in processing graphic material.

The state provides financial support for the education digitalization development (Table 1).

Due to the lack of financial resources and their uneven distribution, low qualifications of employees, the trend of educational institution's digitalization is unevenly distributed, showing the ineffectiveness of the socio-economic reforms carried out in this area. It should be noted that the inertia of socio-economic transformations, which is also applied to the education system, causes some risks in the transition to digital models.

Table 2 systematizes the negative factors of the modern technologie's introduction in the educational process.

Table 1 National action plan to ensure the employment and incomes recovery of the population, economic growth, and long-term structural changes in the economy

Measure	Beginning	End	Responsible executor	Budget, RUB bln	
				2020	2021
1. Implementation of the program for financial and methodological support of educational institutions of higher education digitalization	September 2020	December 2021	Ministry of education, Ministry of digital science, Russia	0.915	2.79
2. Digital educational environment development and implementation	October 2020	December 2021	Ministry of education, Russia	14.8	14.8
3. Determination of the procedure for the free use of works for educational and scientific purposes in electronic form stored in libraries, without the need for physical presence in the library premises	November 2021	Not limited in time	Ministry of culture, Russia	–	–

Source Developed and compiled by the authors based on source (Failed, 2017; Ivanov et al., 2020)

Table 2 Negative factors of the digital technologie's introduction into the educational process

Qualitative improvements in the use of digital technologies	Potential socio-economic and educational risks	Changes in the traditional education system
Ability to process large data bulk	Lack of stably working domestic software	Decreased (lost) cognitive function
Almost instant communications, remote payments	Possible personal data breach, security vulnerability	The digital image of the teacher may not correspond to his real psychological state
Development of a human digital identification system, biometrics	Difficulties in creating private space, great psychological attachment to digital images	Decrease in the level of personal interaction of students, difficulties in an objective assessment of the student's knowledge
Massively available information technology services. Building automation control from a mobile device	Market monopolization by large multinational companies	Additional investments by the educational institutions in technical teaching aids
Automation of production processes, increase in labor productivity	Growing social tension due to job loss	Decrease in the teaching staff share of universities, decrease in the share of intellectual work
Standardization of many sectors of the national economy, including education	The imperfection of the regulatory framework in the field of digitalization	Professional development of a teacher as a manager in the field of education, a shift in the training vector toward the provision of educational services, a decrease in the level of education quality
Development of startups, investment in high-tech technologies, development of the cryptocurrency market	Leaving the market of domestic companies due to technological lag	Reducing the number of students in educational institutions. A modern student is focused on skills development at the expense of fundamental scientific knowledge

Source Developed and compiled by the authors

The key role in the rather slow response of educational institutions to modern challenges of the time can be played by the lack of high-performance personal computers, the lack of financial resources for the purchase of specialized programs, and the unavailability of comprehensive provision of the educational process with digitized educational and methodological publications. Young people more often give preference to the development of so-called skills—highly specialized abilities in a certain area, developed in a relatively short time, most often in the areas of programming and Internet technologies in the digital technologie's widespread introduction era in many sectors of the national economy (Fig. 1). There are enough commercial projects on the educational services market providing such services.

Hard skills	Soft skills
foreign language proficiency	communication skills
professional skills	teamwork skills
computer programs knowledge	conflict resolution skills
programming skills	punctuality and organization
speed of typing on a keyboard	ability to learn, complete assignments
speed of information perception	tranquillity and stress resistance
basic knowledge of mathematical operations	public speaking skills

Fig. 1 Basic skills (professional abilities) of a modern specialist *Source* Developed and compiled by the authors

4 Discussion

It is necessary to develop a stable mechanism for the effective digitalization process implementation, taking into account the following main elements: the presence of an electronic educational environment, which includes the necessary communication tools between the subjects of educational relations, virtual platforms for setting up a laboratory experiment for the natural science disciplines, the development of a remote knowledge control system (interim assessment) in the form of testing.

The criteria for choosing software products include:

- financial costs minimization;
- the possibility of distribution between the educational process subjects;
- stable operation under heavy load on servers;
- intuitive software interface;
- work on mobile and stationary platforms.

The aforementioned selection criteria correspond to the electronic platforms based on the Moodle learning management system and the teams platform from Microsoft. The advantages of online learning systems based on Moodle include a rich toolkit for interaction between the educational process actors: a flexibly customizable system for building a curriculum, an integrated environment for testing, a forum for communication between a teacher and a student. Educational materials are presented on the platform in the following formats familiar to the user: .pdf, .pptx, .doc. The educational process within this site is focused on the independent study of educational material in the format of presentations or text. In this case, the discussion on the topic takes place in chat mode on the forum. Moodle-based platforms are targeted at large universities with a large number of students. Open-source code makes it possible to customize this electronic educational environment for the required tasks. The structure of the training course, built on the Moodle basis, has several common features, namely: the laid-out annotation of the discipline introduces the key goals and objectives of its study, the developed competencies, the topics studied during the semester with a description of their content, files with lectures and presentations, a glossary, tests for each topic and final testing at the end of the semester to the students.

The platform allows working on mobile phones. All this information (except for transitions to external resources using a system of hyperlinks) is organically integrated into the platform, without requiring a transition to other sites. Tools for analyzing statistics on class attendance and passing tests make it possible to monitor the material assimilation quality. The disadvantages of online courses based on Moodle include lack of professional user support, a fairly high threshold for mastering the system, and unstable work with a large number of users simultaneously working on the platform.

An alternative solution for the educational process of digitalization can be the use of the teams platform. This digital environment can be provided free of charge as a part of a Microsoft software subscription. It should be noted that most educational institutions in the Russian Federation use the Microsoft Office programs pack, therefore, using the teams platform for educational purposes does not require additional financial investments. The platform has the following tools for user communication: voice and video conference system, streaming services from the developer company, connected as additional application modules. The platform work is based on the creation of teams, which are the study groups. Educational content can be uploaded to designated places (for example, the "educational materials" section) and made available for download either to the team members or to the users with appropriate access rights. Teams provide technical ability to demonstrate actions on a monitor screen. This allows a front-end laboratory experiment for the entire team. The platform allows creating a calendar of classes, notifications about which the users receive on their work platforms—computers or mobile phones, since teams, like Moodle, has a mobile version. The platform works stably for the contingent of small universities, it is advisable to conduct research on peak load during the period of simultaneous connection for a large number of users. The disadvantages of using teams in the educational process can be attributed to the resource requirements of hardware platforms; for testing, an external Microsoft Forms resource should be used. According to the criterion of flexibility in testing settings, the use of online courses on Moodle seems to be more promising. With a systematic approach to the educational process digitalization, the question of the laboratory work implementation in a remote format arises. In the absence of the possibility of installing programs on the student's personal computer for the experiment implementation, the teacher should carry out these works frontally, using screen demonstration technologies. According to the consistency criterion of the material accumulated within one digital environment, the Open Physics digital environment from the Russian company "Fizikon" can be noted. The program is not demanding on computer resources, it allows to remotely carry out a wide range of laboratory work in the course of general physics in the screen sharing mode.

The question of the appropriateness of using a particular electronic platform is considered based on the needs and capabilities of the educational organization, taking into account the format of the educational programs being implemented. A complete transition to the use of exclusively digital technologies is impossible for some reasons, including the fact that industrial production has not fully switched to "smart" processes automation. The labor market requires specialists with the skills to repair and operate the installations. However, software virtualization of certain elements of industrial production can make it possible to train highly qualified workers already at the training stage. An example of positive practices for using virtual models can be the simulators for training pilots and vehicle drivers.

5 Conclusion

The study analyzed the current state of education, the advantages, and disadvantages of using electronic educational platforms, substantiated the methodology for implementing educational communication using an exclusively remote format. The experience of combating the COVID-19 epidemic spread threat has shown that the Russian education system is capable of quickly restructuring in line with the challenges of the time. IT products market offers a wide range of tools both for virtualizing experiments and for building individual educational trajectories for students. Progressive educational institutions use the applications from National Instruments, Fizikon, PTC, etc. However, such an educational model may entail a restructuring of the student's thinking paradigm, since idealized virtual models may not fully reflect the entire variety of processes in many respects, which is especially important for the natural science disciplines. At the same time, the organic combination in the educational process of digital, remote tools, together with the field experiments (if possible), gives a possibility to increase the efficiency of training engineering personnel, which favorably affects the human capital development at the micro- and meso- economic levels. Digital technologies in education are a future development stage that makes it possible to train a specialist with flexible creative thinking, being able to creatively solve professional problems for the labor market.

References

Bowyer, B., & Kahne, J. (2020). The digital dimensions of civic education: Assessing the effects of learning opportunities. *Journal of Applied Developmental Psychology, 69*, 101162.

Brevik, L. M., Guðmundsdóttir, G., Lund, A., & Strømme, T. (2019). Transformative agency in teacher education: Fostering professional digital competence. *Teaching and Teacher Education: An International Journal of Research and Studies, 86*.

Çetin, E. (2021). Digital storytelling in teacher education and its effect on the digital literacy of pre-service teachers. *Thinking Skills and Creativity, 39*, 100760.

Fleaca, E., & Stanciu, R. D. (2019). Digital-age learning and business engineering education–A pilot study on student's E-skills. *Procedia Manufacturing, 32*, 1051–1057.

Habibi, A., Mukminin, A., & Hadisaputra, P. (2020). Science teacher's integration of digital resources in education: A survey in rural areas of one Indonesian Province. *Heliyon, 6*(8), e04631.

Iivari, N., Sharma, S., & Ventä-Olkkonen, L. (2020). Digital transformation of everyday life–How COVID-19 pandemic transformed the basic education of the young generation and why information management research should care? *International Journal of Information Management, 55*, 102183.

Ivanov, I., Cobo, J. C., & Kosonogova, M. (2020). Implementation of developmental education in the digital learning environment. *Procedia Computer Science, 172*, 517–522.

Limani, Y., Stapleton, L., Hajrizi, E., & Retkoceri, M. (2019). Digital transformation readiness in higher education institutions (HEI): The case of Kosovo. *IFAC-PapersOnLine, 52*(25), 52–57.

Martinengo, L., Ying Yeo, N. J., Markandran, K. D/O., Olsson, M., Kyaw, B. M., & Tudor Car, L. (2020). Digital health professions education on chronic wound management: A systematic review. *International Journal of Nursing Studies, 104*, 103512

Nortvig, A.–M., Petersen, A. K., Helsinghof, H., & Braender, B. (2020). Digital expansions of physical learning spaces in practice-based subjects-blended learning in art and craft and design in teacher education. *Computers and Education, 159*, 104020.

Pryadko, I. A. (2017). Promotion of educational services in social networks. In *Perspectives on the use of new information and communication technology (ICT) in the modern economy*, Springer.

Velez, J. A., Keene, J. R., Corwin, M., Elko, S., Potter, & R. F. (2021). A visual interactive narrative intervention (VINI) for aphasia education: Can digital applications administer augmented input to educate stroke survivors with Aphasia? *Patient Education and Counseling.*

Wharrad, H., Windle, R., & Taylor, M. (2021). Designing digital education and training for health. In *Digital innovations in healthcare education and training* (pp. 31–45). Academic Press.

Zain, S. (2021). Digital transformation trends in education. In *Future directions in digital information.* (pp. 223–234). Chandos Publishing.

Zhao, Y., Pinto Llorente, A. M., & Sánchez Gómez, M. C. (2021). Digital competence in higher education research: A systematic literature review. *Computers and Education*, 104212.

Transformation of the Higher Education Services Market: Comparative Analysis by OECD Countries

Nadezhda V. Pilipchuk, Tatiana D. Strelnikova, Olga V. Batova, Alisher Sh. Subkhonberdiev, and Alexander V. Lyalyuk

Abstract The research hypothesis consists in the scientific assumption that in modern conditions there is a transformation of the market of higher education services in terms of increasing openness, globality and expanding online accessibility due to the raised dynamics of society and technology development, as well as under the influence of the COVID-19 pandemic. The research is aimed at conducting a comparative analysis of the higher education services market in the OECD countries, as well as identifying its transformational trends and determining the directions of state educational policy that contribute to adaptation to new requirements. The authors identified transformational trends in the market of higher education: an increase in the educational level of the population and the demand for higher education services; increased dynamics of the development of society and technology, requiring regular updates and additions to basic higher education; expansion of requirements for educational services in terms of content, volume, forms and methods of obtaining knowledge following changing needs of society. It is determined that during the pandemic, the higher education system of the OECD countries faced challenges related to the organization of remote online exams; unequal technological equipment of participants in the learning process; risks of technical failure; lack of effective forms of e-learning for the training of specialists of a narrow profile. The state policy measures proposed

N. V. Pilipchuk (✉)
Tver State University, Tver, Russia
e-mail: economresearch@mail.ru; nadezda.pilipchuk@gmail.com

T. D. Strelnikova
Lipetsk Branch of the Financial University under the Government of the Russian Federation, Lipetsk, Russia

O. V. Batova
Saint-Petersburg Mining University, Saint-Petersburg, Russia

A. Sh. Subkhonberdiev
Voronezh State University of Forestry and Technologies named after G.F. Morozov, Voronezh, Russia

A. V. Lyalyuk
Kuban State Technological University, Krasnodar, Russia

E. I. Lazareva et al. (eds.), *Innovative Trends in International Business and Sustainable Management*, Approaches to Global Sustainability, Markets, and Governance,
https://doi.org/10.1007/978-981-19-4005-7_36

by the authors can be used to overcome the difficulties of the transformational and pandemic period in the higher education of the OECD countries.

Keywords Higher education · Educational services market · OECD · Transformation · Digitalization · Knowledge society · Pandemic

JEL Classification I21 · I23 · I25

1 Introduction

The sphere of education is fundamental for the development of the national economy and society. The training of highly qualified specialists to ensure activities in the sectors of the economy, taking into account changing requirements, is entirely the prerogative of the higher education system. The global market of higher education services is actively developing. According to experts, its volume was 600–800 billion US dollars by 2030. The leading positions in the global market of higher education services are traditionally occupied by the OECD member countries: USA, UK, Australia and Canada.

The development of scientific and technological progress and the ongoing changes of a socio-mental nature impose new requirements on specialists with higher education, and as a result, transformational processes are launched in the higher education system itself. Today, more than ever, universities and the entire system of training personnel of the highest category must quickly adapt to the increased dynamics of the development of society and technology and provide educational services of new quality. For example, intensive generation and use of digital technologies are possible if there is a reliable basis in the form of a competitive education system, high-quality educational services that ensure the formation of specialists required for the digital economy, as well as the expansion of educational opportunities (Konovalova et al., 2020; Maksaev et al., 2020). The processes of globalization, liberalization and internationalization occupy a significant place among the factors of the development of higher education in the world.

Of course, the impact of the coronavirus pandemic on the organization of educational activities should not be ignored. In 2020, the COVID-19 pandemic affected more than one and a half billion students in 191 countries around the world. In most countries, educational institutions have been completely or partially closed, and many students have been transferred to distance learning. The emergency transition to distance learning of higher education institutions is associated with obvious problems, mainly due to the unavailability of the infrastructure of mass distance education, the lack or poor training of teachers to work in new conditions (IAU, 2020; Malee Bassett & Arnhold, 2020). These and other problems challenge the higher education system in a transformational period. Therefore, the analysis of emerging trends and existing difficulties in the development of educational organizations in the OECD countries is especially relevant currently.

2 Literature Review

Current trends in the development of the market of higher education services are reflected in the studies of (Astratova, 2016; Bhandari et al., 2011; Vlasova & Molokova, 2016). The authors note that higher education is becoming one of the largest sectors of the world trade in services (Galichin, 2015). Researchers name various reasons for the intensification of the development of higher education. In particular, Tatarkin and Pilipenko note that the massive desire of the population to obtain higher education was a consequence of the formation of the knowledge economy (Tatarkin & Pilipenko, 2007). Wachstein et al. (Pilipchuk et al., 2021) point to the strengthening of employer's requirements for the higher education of employees as a necessary initial stage for mastering the profession. This explains the desire of people to obtain higher education, as well as the priorities of the educational policy of economically developed countries. In the digital age, the process of obtaining higher education goes beyond the previously established restrictions. With technological development and the formation of a knowledge society, there is rapid obsolescence of knowledge, which causes changes in the labour market and the need for their continuous updating (Makarova, 2020). Digital technologies come to the rescue to implement online learning (Konovalova et al., 2020; Maksaev et al., 2020). Digital technologies have helped to relieve tension in the higher education system due to the spread of coronavirus infection. The applied digital learning formats have helped universities, teachers, students and managers to see new opportunities and gain new positive experiences (Shtykhno et al., 2020).

3 Methodology

The purpose of the study is to conduct a comparative analysis of the higher education services market in the OECD countries, to systematize the factors determining its transformation, as well as to determine the directions of state educational policy that contribute to adaptation to new requirements.

Research objectives: (1) to identify transformational trends in the market of higher education services in modern conditions; (2) to conduct a comparative analysis of the state of the higher education services market in the OECD countries, including during the pandemic; (3) to determine the directions of the state educational policy as the basis for the successful transformation of the market of educational services of higher education.

Research methods: theoretical analysis, comparative analysis, graphical method, economic analysis and system approach.

4 Results

Let us highlight the transformational trends in the market of higher education services.

1. *Mass aspiration and growing demand for higher education.* The massive desire of the population to obtain higher education has become a global trend that manifests itself in most economically developed countries of the world. Worldwide, the demand for people with a broader knowledge base and more specialized skills continues to grow (OECD, 2021a). The population with higher education includes persons who have received higher education both as part of the development of theoretical programs leading to advanced research or highly qualified professions (e.g., medicine) and more professional programs that allow them to occupy their niche in the labour market. According to the OECD, in 1997 about 14% of Europeans aged 25–34 had a higher education, and in 2002, this percentage was already 18% (Vakhstein et al., 2005). In 2019, the proportion of the adult population aged 25–64 years with higher education (ISCED 6, 7 and 8) in its total population was 37.2% in the UK, 29.3% in Germany, 19.6% in Italy, 33.2% in Canada, 36.1% in the Republic of Korea, 37.6% in the USA, 23.3% in France, 33.9% in Sweden and 31.3% in Japan. If we consider the proportion of the population aged 25–34 years, the values of the indicators will be even higher: 69.8% in the Republic of Korea, 63% in Canada and 61.5% in Japan (Gokhberg et al., 2021). On average, in the OECD countries in this age group, there was an increase in the percentage of people with higher education in the period 1997–2020 (Fig. 1).

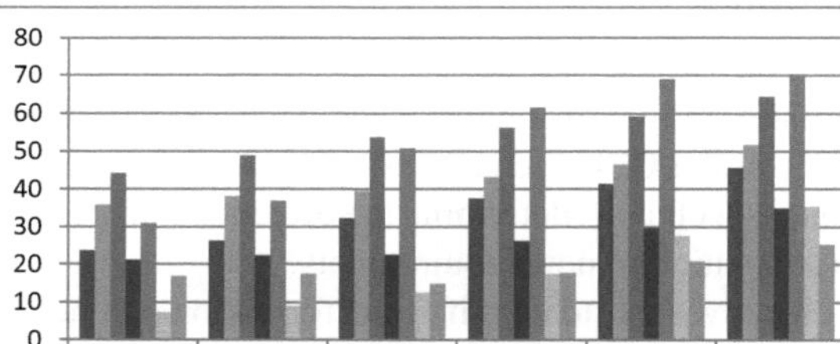

	1997	2000	2005	2010	2015	2020
OECD-Average	23.56	26.1	32.15	37.36	41.31	45.51
USA	35.7	38.08	39.36	43.13	46.52	51.58
Canada	44.17	48.8	53.69	56.17	59.18	64.39
Germany	21.04	22.25	22.49	26.13	29.59	34.88
Korea Republic	30.87	36.81	50.86	61.45	68.86	69.81
Turkey	7.32	8.88	12.51	17.45	27.52	35.33
Mexico	16.73	17.45	14.92	17.7	20.81	25.29

Fig. 1 Population with higher education aged 25–34 years, % of this age group, 1997–2020. *Source* Compiled by the authors according to (OECD, 2021a)

The data show that in the period 1997–2020, the share of the population with higher education aged 25–34 in the OECD countries increased by 93%. Meanwhile, there are significant differences in the level of education of the population. In particular, the dynamics of this indicator in Germany is positive during the study period, but the values of the indicator lag far behind, for example, the USA and Canada. The fact that Germany has a relatively low percentage of higher education compared to other countries is explained by the fact that its educational centre is focused not so much on higher academic education, as, for example, on apprenticeships, technical and vocational training, etc. Indeed, this is usually seen as the main reason for Germany's economic success. Turkey seems to be completely unprepared for the technological age, since its citizens are far behind in knowledge of key technical skills, and the proportion of the population with higher education is 1/3 of the age group of 25–34 years. This is a consequence of the systemic contradiction of professional education in Turkey, consisting of the divergence of key-value foundations, in particular, the desire for European values and the installation of Islamic traditions (Pleshakova, 2019).

The demands of the labour market and the idea of higher education as a "social elevator" that guarantees a certain rise in the material level and quality of life contributed to the increase in the educational level of the population (Vakhstein et al., 2005). In European countries, the share of jobs for specialists with higher education reaches 30–40% (OECD, 2004). On average, in OECD countries, full-time workers with higher education earn 54% more than those with secondary education (OECD, 2020a). Adults with higher education are more resistant to long-term unemployment. For example, in 2018, their employment rate was 9 percentage points higher than that of adults with a full secondary education. Their advantage grows with age: 25–34-year-old adults with tertiary education earn 38% more than their peers with a full secondary education, and upon reaching 45–54 years, the difference in earnings is 70% (OECD, 2019).

In Estonia, Hungary and Iceland, 50% or more of students receive higher education in engineering, manufacturing and construction. By contrast, higher education programs in business, administration and law are the most popular fields in Luxembourg and Switzerland. In Ireland, the Netherlands, Spain and the United Kingdom, the field of health and social security is the most popular of the selected areas (Economic Research Institute, 2020).

2. *Increased dynamics of society and technology development, requiring regular updating and addition of "basic" higher education.* Some sectors of the OECD economies are experiencing difficulties in finding the skilled workers they need. Although such areas as engineering, industrial production and construction, as well as the direction of information and communication technologies are most often associated with the best results in the labour market, in 2017, only 14% of graduates received a diploma in the first direction, and 4% received a diploma in the second direction (OECD, 2019). In addition, the introduction of digital technologies in various fields of activity of enterprises requires updating

knowledge and obtaining digital skills of employees, as well as professional retraining.

The existence of demand for qualified employees with higher education leads to an increase in professional training and retraining programs at universities, as well as to the expansion of the non-university sector of higher education. However, two problems are relevant in this aspect: ensuring the financial efficiency of higher education and the quality of non-university higher education.

In the first case, we are talking about finding a balance between state funding of universities and their extra-budgetary income from the provision of paid educational services. For example, government spending on higher education (ISCED 6, 7 and 8) in OECD countries is distributed as follows: In Sweden, they account for 1.4% of gross domestic product, followed by Germany (1%), France (0.9%), Canada (0.9%), USA (0.9%), Republic of Korea (0.6%), UK (0.5%), Italy (0.5%) and Japan (0.4%) (Gokhberg et al., 2021). At the same time, the share of private investments in higher education varies in different OECD countries. In particular, the amount of private spending on higher education in China, the United Kingdom, Japan, The United States and South Korea reaches 75% of total education spending. A feature of Finland, Denmark and Norway is the financing of most of the higher education costs from budgetary sources (up to 95%). On average, the share of private spending on higher education in GDP in OECD countries is 1.7–1.9%, and in Chile, South Korea and the United States it is the highest (Nedospasova et al., 2016). The average value of public spending on higher education in the OECD countries in 2018 amounted to 66.16% of total education spending, while since 2010 there has been a trend of their reduction. The average value of private spending on higher education in the OECD countries in 2018 reached 30.1% of total spending on education, and the increase in the value of the indicator compared to 2010 was 12% (Fig. 2a, b).

a

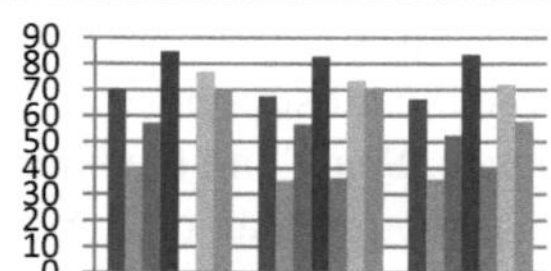

	2010	2015	2018
■ OECD-Average	70.17	67.45	66.16
■ USA	39.99	35.2	35.64
■ Canada	57.15	56.58	52.34
■ Germany	84.64	82.72	83.37
■ Korea Republic		36.13	39.74
■ Turkey	76.9	73.41	72.03
■ Mexico	69.88	70.86	57.57

b

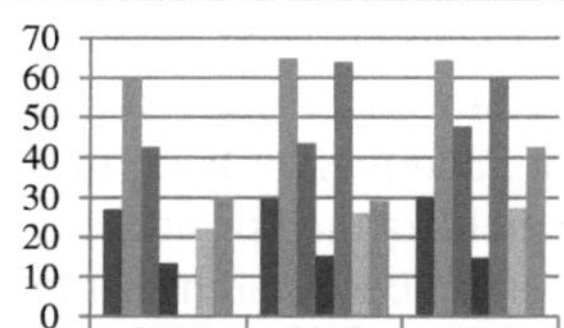

	2010	2015	2018
■ OECD-Average	26.86	29.63	30.1
■ USA	60.01	64.8	64.36
■ Canada	42.47	43.42	47.66
■ Germany	13.39	15.29	14.84
■ Korea Republic		63.87	60.26
■ Turkey	22.06	25.98	27.18
■ Mexico	30.12	29.14	42.43

Fig. 2 **a** Government spending on higher education in OECD countries, % of total education spending, 2010–2018; **b** Private sector spending on higher education in OECD countries, % of total education spending, 2010–2018. *Source* Compiled by the authors based on (OECD, 2021)

The provision of financial support mechanisms also contributes to making higher education more accessible to more people. In the OECD countries with the highest tuition fees, more than 70% of students receive grants or loans (OECD, 2019).

The requirement of constantly updating the skills of a specialist who can quickly assimilate and apply new knowledge in practice as well as the desire to expand the availability and increase the financial efficiency of higher education often forces universities in OECD countries to follow the path of autonomy or choose an extensive direction of development. The first direction is connected with obtaining broad powers in choosing financial and educational strategies for their development and determining the vector of international cooperation (Larionova & Gorbunova, 2010). The second direction implies that universities that do not have the status of a university or are affiliated organizations of universities aim to meet the broad demand for higher education following the needs of the labour market. As a rule, such universities provide educational services of an applied nature, but at a lower level while minimizing costs, ensuring the growth of students and employment of graduates. For example, colleges in England, vocational training schools in Germany and Switzerland and institutes in France acquire the status of universities to perform these functions. However, such a non-university higher education is devoid of fundamentals, primarily in terms of conducting scientific research and generating new knowledge.

3. *Expanding the requirements for educational services in terms of content, volume, forms, methods of obtaining knowledge following the changing needs of society.* The key trends determining the requirements for educational services of the higher education system are the globalization of socioeconomic processes and the associated internationalization of the educational services market, as well as digitalization and the development of innovative educational technologies. The globalization of higher education is associated with a continuous historical process, the universalization and homogenization of the world, as well as the openness of national borders (Larionova & Gorbunova, 2010). It has an impact on the higher education system both directly (an increase in funding for education and science, e.g., in the USA, causes the need for additional investments in these areas in European countries) and indirectly (the need to match the knowledge and skills acquired by students to the needs of technological and economic changes in the labour market) (Commission of the European Communities, 2003).

The concept of internationalization of higher education in the global context includes internationalization within the country and education abroad (cross-border education) (Larionova & Gorbunova, 2010). The internationalization of higher education is connected both with the individual mobility of students and teachers, the mobility of educational programs and with the formation of international standards of educational programs and the development of strategic educational alliances. All forms of internationalization contribute to increasing the accessibility of higher education, the universalization of knowledge, the emergence of international quality standards and increasing the innovativeness of higher education, the expansion and

Table 1 Dynamics of the number of foreign students in universities of OECD countries, 1997–2016

Country	Number of international students, person		Difference, %	The share of international students in the total number of students, %	
	1997	2016		1997	2016
USA	582,996	1,043,839	+79	3.7	5.2
Canada	40,033	563,855	+1308	3.0	12.9
United Kingdom	225,722	496,690	+120	10.1	21.1
France	147,402	399,642	+171	10.0	10.8
Australia	120,987	292,352	+142	17.7	20.7
Germany	219,039	235,858	+8	10.1	8.7
Japan	74,892	152,062	+103	1.9	4.2
Spain	44,860	76,057	+70	2.4	4.9

Source Compiled by the authors based on (Eurostat, 2021; Ryazantsev et al., 2019)

strengthening of international cooperation and the activation of academic and student mobility.

The number of international students in the OECD member countries increased from 1997 to 2016 (Table 1).

The USA, Canada, Great Britain, France, Australia and Germany are the most active countries in terms of providing educational services, and they account for 73% of all international students studying in OECD countries. Canada, France and Australia are characterized by positive dynamics of the growth of the contingent of foreign students, especially in the period 1997–2016. In all the OECD countries analysed, except for Germany, the share of foreign students in the total number of university students increased during this period. For example, in Canada in 1997–2016, it increased 4.3 times, in the UK, Japan and Spain more than 2 times. The involvement of scientists and teachers is also an important factor in the development of national higher education systems in the OECD countries. In particular, the United States is actively attracting scientists and professors from developing and European countries (Ryazantsev et al., 2019). Thus, the statistics confirm the strengthening of the trend of internationalization in higher education in the OECD countries.

The transformation of requirements for educational services is determined by the growing demand for distance higher education programs implemented by foreign universities in their country of residence (OECD, 2009). The leaders in the implementation of cross-border higher education programs are the United Kingdom and Australia, and they accept up to 300 thousand foreign students per year (Ryazantsev et al., 2019).

Universities in most developed OECD countries have proved to be well prepared for the challenges of digitalization (Karpunina et al., 2021a, b). This concerns the management of research data from the collection of raw data to archiving, creating a creative digital environment for teaching and learning and improving workflows in administration (Konstantinova et al., 2021).

In particular, in the USA, the policy of digitalization of higher education provides for the expansion of learning opportunities using digital technologies, including providing high-speed Internet access, the implementation of individual training programs and blended learning using new technologies (virtual learning laboratories, simulators and augmented reality technologies), bridging the gap in the use of digital technologies. An important aspect of digitalization here is the training of teachers using innovative educational technologies, as well as continuous professional training. The launch of open educational resources has become an integral part of the digitalization of universities (Konstantinova et al., 2021). The practice of using mass open online courses is typical not only for the USA but also for other OECD countries. Since 2012, the largest platforms Coursera, Udacity, FutureLearn, Openclassroom and OpenLearning have been launched. Coursera offers access to two thousand courses, and the number of registered users reaches 25 million people. In Germany, the strategy of digitalization of the higher education system is based on the development of digital competencies, improvement of the digital environment and creation of digital architecture (online administration of digital educational data and individual learning opportunities). Japan is implementing the concept of digitalization of higher education, based on the promotion of measures to employ advanced technologies to support learning in a new era, the use of achievements in the field of robotics, big data, AR/VR, artificial intelligence in the learning process, promoting individual learning and improving the IT environment and the effective use of electronic textbooks and didactic materials.

Despite the active digitalization of universities in the OECD countries, the pandemic provoked an extreme transition of higher education to a distance mode. Higher education institutions around the world have closed their campuses, which affected about 99% of the global number of students of higher education institutions (Malee Bassett & Arnhold, 2020).

Let us highlight the main difficulties faced by the higher education system of the OECD countries during the pandemic:

(1) Organization of remote online exams: the transfer of student's exams to online led to an increase in the number of cases of dishonest behaviour of students, which required the development of a strategy for evaluating and certifying practical knowledge and skills of students.
(2) Unequal attitude towards the participants of the training in terms of the availability of different levels of conditions and technological equipment (screen sizes, computer speed, connection bandwidth, etc.).
(3) Risk of technical failure. An adequate and stable technical infrastructure that provides students and teachers with high-quality access to the Internet and the necessary equipment is a key condition for organizing online training and conducting exams. However, even with advanced technological infrastructure, the occurrence of technical failures remains possible (OECD, 2020b).

(4) The development of narrow professional skills requires the search for new forms of e-learning that allow students to develop their competencies, unlike academic education, where it is possible to use more flexible options for distance learning educational programs (Shtykhno et al., 2020).

Overcoming the existing difficulties in the field of higher education in the OECD countries requires the implementation of the following measures: (1) increasing the use of online and virtual platforms to ensure continuity of training; (2) financing breaks in training or extension of training; (3) providing financial support for salaries for the maintenance of students in order to maintain contact with employers; (4) offering flexible assessment of skills and the assignment of qualifications; since in many sectors, especially in health care, it may be necessary to quickly create a direct path to obtaining qualifications in response to the COVID-19 crisis; (5) investing in higher education programs to mitigate future skills shortages and minimize the negative consequences caused by the crisis (Economic Research Institute, 2020); (6) combining the preferences of students and employers in educational programs, ensuring the transfer of skills to support professional mobility; (7) support for teaching staff, including the development of partnerships with various industries, encouraging part-time work, flexibility in recruiting, pedagogical training of masters of industrial training; (8) development of on-the-job training programs and creating conditions to meet the growing demand for full-fledged vocational education and training. The authors justified the need to implement a set of measures of state educational policy in the OECD countries to overcome the difficulties of adapting higher education systems to new conditions.

5 Conclusion

Thus, the article highlights the following transformational trends in the market of educational services in the field of higher education: increasing the educational level of the population; raised dynamics of the development of society and technology, requiring regular updates and additions to basic higher education; expanding the requirements for educational services in terms of content, volume, forms and methods of obtaining knowledge following changing needs of society. The difficulties faced by the higher education system of the OECD countries during the pandemic are systematized. They include the organization of remote online exams; unequal treatment of participants in terms of the availability of different levels of conditions and technological equipment; the risk of technical failure; the lack of effective forms of e-learning for the development of narrow professional skills of students.

References

Astratova, G. (2016). Modern trends in the development of the higher education services market. *Science Studies, 8*(4). http://naukovedenie.ru/PDF/95EVN416.pdf. Accessed 12 December 2021.

Bhandari, R., Belyavina, R., & Gutierrez, R. (2011). *Student and the internationalization of higher education: National policies and strategies from six world regions*. Institute of International Education.

Commission of the European Communities. (2003). Communication from the commission. *Investing efficiency in education and training: An imperative for Europe*, Commission of the European Communities.

Economic Research Institute. (2020). A brief overview of education 2020. https://economy.kz/ru/OESR/Sobytija_OESR/id=889. Accessed 12 December 2021.

Eurostat. (2021). Share of mobile students from abroad enrolled by education level, sex and country of origin. https://ec.europa.eu/eurostat/databrowser/view/educ_uoe_mobs03/default/table?lang=en. Accessed 12 December 2021.

Galichin, V. (2015). *International market of educational services: Main characteristics and development trends*. Publishing House Delo RANEPA.

Gokhberg, L., Ozerova, O., & Sautina, E. (2021). *Education in numbers: 2021: A brief statistical collection*. HSE.

IAU (2020). The impact of Covid-19 on higher education around the World, International Association of Universities, Paris. https://www.iauaiu.net/IMG/pdf/iau_covid19_and_he_survey_report_final_may_2020.pdf Accessed 12 December 2021.

Karpunina, E., Galieva, G., Andryiashka, M., Vorobyeva, A., & Bakulin, O. (2021a). Country risk assessment as a tool for improving the quality of state economic security management (on the example of Germany). *Quality—Access to Success, 22*(183), 136–142.

Karpunina, E., Kosorukova, I., Dubovitski, A., Galieva, G., & Chernenko, E. (2021b). State policy of transition to Society 5.0: Identification and assessment of digitalisation risks. *International Journal of Public Law and Policy, 7*(4), 334–350.

Konovalova, M., Tavbulatova, Z., Bogomolova, A., Shakhvatova, S., & Karpunina, E. (2020). Digitalization of Russian universities: problems and prospects. In *Proceeding of the 36th IBIMA Conference*, 4–5 November 2020, Granada, Spain (pp. 7800–7808).

Konstantinova, L., Gagiev, N., Smirnova, E., Petrov, A., & Nikonova, O. (2021). The main trends of digitalization of higher education. https://www.rea.ru/ru/org/managements/Nauchno-issledovatelskijj-institut-razvitija-obrazovanija/Documents/Мониторинг%20Выпуск%201.%20ЦИФРОВИЗАЦИЯ.pdf. Accessed 12 December 2021.

Larionova, M., & Gorbunova, E. (2010). Internationalization of higher education in OECD countries. OECD—HSE Center. https://globalcentre.hse.ru/data/2010/03/05/1231450871/IN_education.pdf Accessed 12 December 2021.

Makarova, M. (2020). Prospects of online education in Russia. *Modern Education, 2*, 59–70.

Maksaev, A., Surakatov, N., Sobolevskaya, T., Lebedeva, S., & Karpunina, E. (2020). Online education in developing countries: a comparative analysis of the development of the sector in Russia, China and Brazil. In *Proceedings of the 36th IBIMA Conference*, 4–5 November 2020, Granada, Spain (pp. 2266–2277).

Malee Bassett, R., & Arnhold, N. (2020). COVID-19's immense impact on equity in tertiary education. World Bank Blogs. https://blogs.worldbank.org/education/covid-19s-immense-impact-equity-tertiary-education Accessed 12 December 2021.

Nedospasova, O., Kaida, A., & Nedospasov, A. (2016). Financing of higher education in conditions of economic instability: General and private for OECD countries. *National Interests: Priorities and Security, 7*, 78–191.

OECD. (2004). *Trade-offs in restructuring tertiary education: The roles of tertiary institutes and colleges*. OECD Publishing.

OECD. (2009). *Higher Education to 2030. Vol. 3, Technology, Forthcoming*. OECD Publishing.

OECD. (2019). OECD multilingual summaries. Education at a Glance 2019. OECD Indicators. https://www.oecd-ilibrary.org/sites/594fed61-ru/index.html?itemId=/content/component/594fed61-ru Accessed 12 December 2021
OECD. (2020a). *Education at a glance 2020: OECD indicators*. OECD Publishing.
OECD (2020b). Remote online exams in higher education during the COVID-19 crisis. https://www.oecd.org/education/remote-online-exams-in-higher-education-during-the-covid-19-crisis-f53e2177-en.htm Accessed 12 December 2021.
OECD. (2021a). Population with tertiary education (indicator). https://doi.org/10.1787/0b8f90e9-en Accessed 16 December 2021a
OECD. (2021b). Spending on tertiary education (indicator). https://doi.org/10.1787/a3523185-en Accessed 16 December 2021b
Pilipchuk, N., Beilina, A., Udovik, E., Orlovtseva, O., & Karpunina, E. (2021). The development of digital competences of teachers in the higher education system. In *Proceeding of the 37th IBIMA Conference*, 1–2 April 2021, Cordoba, Spain, (pp. 517–527).
Pleshakova, A. (2019). Vocational education and training in turkey: Traditions and global challenges. *Contemporary Higher Education: Innovative Aspects, 11*(2), 108–114.
Ryazantsev, S., Rostovskaya, T., Skorobogatova, V., & Bezverbny, V. (2019). International academic mobility in Russia. *Trends, Types, Government Incentives. The Economy of the Region, 15*(2), 420–435.
Shtykhno, D., Konstantinova, L., & Gagiev, N. (2020). Transition of universities to remote mode during a pandemic: Problems and possible risks. *Open Education, 24*(5), 72–81.
Tatarkin, A., & Pilipenko, E. (2007). Economics of knowledge: Problems of theory and methodology. Institute of Economics, Ural Branch of the Russian Academy of Sciences.
Vakhstein, V., Zhelezov, B., & Meshkova, T. (2005). The main trends of state policy in higher education in the OECD Countries. *Questions of Education, 2*, 32–46.
Vlasova, N., & Molokova, E. (2016). Models of higher education in conditions of combination of market and state regulators. *Bulletin of Ural State University of Economics, 3*(65), 26–38.

The Strategies for the Sustainability of China's Basic Pension Insurance System in the Digital Economy

Zhang Xiaran

Abstract With the aggravation of China's ageing population and the slowdown of economic growth, the sustainability of the basic pension insurance system has become an important issue that needs to be paid more attention to. At the same time, the vigorous development of the digital economy has not only profoundly changed the way of human production and life but also affected the labour market and workers' rights and interests. The emergence of new employment forms a great challenge to the current social security system based on the registered residence system and labour relations. The weakening of the function of pension insurance is a prominent problem. Therefore, the sustainability of the pension insurance system is not only related to the imbalance of revenue and expenditure of insurance funds but also connected with the background of population development, economic performance, institutional changes and digital economy. This paper discussed four aspects that affect the sustainability of the basic pension insurance systems: acceleration of population ageing, rising old-age dependency ratio and delayed retirement; co-development of three pillars' pension insurance; revenue and expenditure gap, new employment forms and new resources of pension fund from the digital economy; maintaining and increasing the value of pension insurance fund. It also puts forward suggestions to support the sustainable development of the basic insurance system.

Keywords Basic pension insurance system · Revenue and expenditure gap of pension fund · Sustainable development · Digital economy

JEL Classification R01 · J14 · J18 · J21 · J26 · I38 · P36

Z. Xiaran (✉)
Southern Federal University, Rostov-on-Don, Russia
e-mail: zhangxiaran722@126.com

E. I. Lazareva et al. (eds.), *Innovative Trends in International Business and Sustainable Management*, Approaches to Global Sustainability, Markets, and Governance,
https://doi.org/10.1007/978-981-19-4005-7_37

1 Introduction

Since the 1990s, China's pension insurance system has been established for nearly 30 years. Nowadays, in the background of the digital economy, for the pension insurance system, the continuous guarantee and challenge of reforms coexist. The State Council's Decision to Improve the Basic Pension Insurance System of Enterprise Employees (State Council document 2005 No. 38) proposed that the goal of the pension insurance system reform is to establish a basic pension insurance system suitable for China's national conditions and achieve sustainable development. According to Zheng (2019) released by the world social security research centre of the Chinese Academy of social sciences on April 10, 2019, although the current balance of the basic pension insurance fund for urban employees in 2019 is 106.29 billion yuan, it may be negative for the first time in 2028, which is negative 118.13 billion yuan. By 2035, it is possible to exhaust the accumulated balance. Therefore, it is of great practical significance to study the sustainability of pension insurance in the digital economy.

2 Materials and Methods

Faced with the severe population ageing trend and financial burden, the goal of pension insurance reform is to solve the future pension insurance fund gap and establish a sustainable, robust and risk-resistant pension security system. Grech (Grech, 2013) took ten European countries such as France and Germany as examples and established a comprehensive framework system for evaluating the sustainability of pension insurance system reforms. He believed that studying the sustainability of pension insurance is rather important. In terms of sustainability factors, (Elize, 2003) believed that the sustainability of the pension system will be affected by factors such as economic development, management level, and demographic structure. The pension system cannot rely solely on the government's financial support. The intensified population ageing will greatly increase the possibility that fiscal revenue will not cover expenditures. Blake and Mayhew (2006) pointed out that population ageing is closely related to the sustainable development of social pension insurance funds. The government can take measures to promote economic development, increase fertility, delay retirement age and other measures to enhance the payment ability of the social pension insurance fund. In China, (Feng & Zheng, 2019) discussed the four dimensions that affect the sustainable development of basic pension insurance based on a macroperspective and believed that the sustainable development of pension insurance should be carried out in all-around coordination of population, economy and society.

It is a critical issue to assess Pension Reserve Funds' sustainability over the long run. Moreover, the sustainability analysis is particularly complex, due to the interaction between the macroeconomic environment, financial performance and the labour market (Pablo et al., 2021). This article collects and analyses the trend of population ageing, the old-age dependency ratio, the three-pillar model of China's basic pension insurance, the revenue and expenditure balance of basic pension insurance fund over the years, the investment return of the pension fund and other data, using the urban residents' pension fund revenue and expenditure ratio to measure the financial sustainability of pension insurance, that is, the ratio of pension insurance fund income to expenditure in that year, if the ratio is greater than 1 for many consecutive years, it indicates that the financial sustainability of pension insurance is relatively positive, and vice versa, it indicates the lack of financial sustainability.

The data of revenue, expenditure, balance and other relevant information of basic pension insurance funds of the whole country and provinces (municipalities, autonomous regions) are derived from the 2011–2021 China Statistical Yearbook (Ministry of Human Resources & Social Security of the People's Republic of China, 2021; National Bureau of Statistics of the People's Republic of China, 2021).

3 Results

3.1 The Acceleration of Population Ageing, Rising Old-Age Dependency Ratio and Delayed Retirement

China's ageing process is faster than that of developed countries, but there is little preparation time to deal with it. In 2020, there are 190 million people aged 65 and over, accounting for 13.5% of the total population (National Bureau of Statistics of China, 2019). It is estimated that China will enter a stage of deep ageing in 2025 (China Industry Research, 2019). By 2055, the proportion of the population over 65 will exceed 20% (Li, 2017). With the acceleration of population ageing, the substantial growth of the number of people receiving benefits is increasingly enhanced in the financial dependence. In some areas, especially some provinces and cities in central and western regions, the current income of the basic pension insurance for employees cannot offset the expenditure, so it is necessary to rely on the financial subsidy funds or use fund accumulation to ensure that pensions are issued on time, of which financial subsidies have been 300 billion per year. Around, central financial subsidies account for more than 90% (China Association of Aging, 2019).

In 2020, the old-age dependency ratio (China National Health Commission's Department of Aging Health, 2020) has reached 19.70%, and ageing has greatly increased the payment burden and pension pressure of the young generation. The influence of population ageing on the economy is decreasing the savings rate and insufficient investment. It also manifests a decline in corporate competitiveness after low-cost advantages, and the economic recession will continue to face greater difficulties. In the case of an increasingly severe old-age dependency ratio, to maintain the operation of the pension insurance system, the insurance contribution rate will face upward pressure. It is worrying that although the coverage of pension insurance is expanding, there are still some cities with negative growth in the number of urban workers participating in the basic pension insurance system, and the phenomenon of insufficient payment of insured personnel has begun to highlight.

Extended life expectancy, low fertility rate, high old-age dependency ratio and premature retirement age have a direct negative impact on the financial sustainability of pension funds. In the case of a continuous rise in the old-age dependency ratio, in order to maintain the operation of the pension insurance system, the contribution rate should not be reduced but should be further increased. With the increase of life expectancy, the deepening of ageing and the reduction of the employed population, the risk of pension payment gap increases. Delaying the legal retirement age has become a worldwide trend. Delayed retirement can significantly reduce the old-age dependency ratio, the ratio of pension to GDP, increase contribution income and reduce pension expenditure. It can have a two-way positive impact on the financial situation of the system and also is an inevitable choice in the case of population ageing. At the same time, it can increase the supply of the labour force.

The co-development of three-pillar-model pension insurance. The three pillars of China's pension insurance are basic pension insurance, enterprise supplementary pension insurance (enterprise annuity), personal savings pension insurance or commercial pension insurance. At present, China's pension insurance system mostly relies on the first pillar. According to the data of China's National Bureau of statistics, before 1999, the replacement rate of pension for Chinese enterprise employees (the proportion of pension in pre-retirement wage income) was generally maintained at more than 75%. By 2018, the replacement rate of pension for urban employees showed a downward trend year by year, and now, it is below 40%. More than 90% of employees fail to enjoy the enterprise annuity, and its insured personnel are mainly employees of state-owned enterprises in monopoly industries. The three pillars do not give full play to their respective roles and form a tripartite situation. The excessive contribution rate of the first pillar has occupied the development space of the second and third pillars. If the proportion of the social overall planning part is reduced and increased to other parts, it will be beneficial to enterprises and employees and can promote the rapid development of enterprise annuity and commercial pension insurance.

Given the severe situation governments of China have begun to start the corresponding measures, the Measures of Professional Annuity in Organization Institutions, adopted on March 27, 2015, clarify the mandatory establishment of the professional annuities of the second pillar in order to change the unbalanced pattern of excessive relying on basic pension insurance. The Measures of Enterprise Annuity were jointly issued by the Ministry of Human Resources and Social Security and the Ministry of Finance, which officially implemented from February 1, 2018—as long as the employer and its employees who have participated in the basic pension insurance for enterprise employees can establish an enterprise annuity system. On November 20, 2020, the Insurance Association of China released the Research Report on the Third Pillar of China Pension (Insurance Association of China, 2020). Report forecasting, in the next 5–10 years, China is expected to have a pension gap of 8–10 trillion yuan, and this gap will further expand over time. In the digital economic background, scientific and technological methods such as the Internet are introduced to create a popular, online pension distribution and account management system. Recently, Internet technology has had a unique role in covering the underwriting customers, considering the introduction of such technical means to expand the coverage of the people. At the same time, it also encourages marketized distribution model to meet the needs of multi-level pension savings in different regions and different income levels.

3.2 *The Revenue and Expenditure Gap, New Employment Forms and New Resources of Pension Funds from the Digital Economy*

From 2011 to 2020, China's social insurance fund and pension insurance fund revenue and expenditure ratios have basically shown a downward trend (Table 1). The pension insurance fund revenue and expenditure ratios have been between 1–1.5 in most years over the past ten years, indicating that the sustainability of current Chinese residents' pension insurance finances is relatively good. However, in 2019, the pension insurance fund revenue and expenditure ratio was only 1.07, showing that the expenditure was offset by the source of revenue and there was not much pension insurance fund balance accumulated in the same period. In 2020, the social insurance fund and

Table 1 2011–2020 China's social insurance fund and pension insurance fund revenue and expenditure ratio

	Social insurance fund			Basic pension insurance fund		
	Revenue (100 million yuan)	Expenditure (100 million yuan)	Ratio	Revenue (100 million yuan)	Expenditure (100 million yuan)	Ratio
2011	25,153.3	18,652.9	1.35	16,894.7	12,764.9	1.32
2012	30,738.8	23,331.3	1.32	20,001	15,561.8	1.29
2013	35,252.9	27,916.3	1.26	22,680.4	18,470.4	1.23
2014	39,827.7	33,002.7	1.21	25,309.7	21,754.7	1.16
2015	46,012.1	38,988.1	1.18	29,340.9	25,812.7	1.14
2016	53,562.7	46,888.4	1.14	35,057.5	31,853.8	1.10
2017	67,154.5	57,145.6	1.18	43,309.6	38,051.5	1.14
2018	79,254.8	67,792.7	1.17	51,167.6	44,644.9	1.15
2019	83,550.4	75,346.6	1.11	52,918.8	49,228	1.07
2020	75,512.5	78,611.8	0.96	44,375.7	51,301.4	0.86

Source Compiled and calculated by the author based on (National Bureau of Statistics of China, 2019; National Bureau of Statistics of the People's Republic of China 2021)

pension insurance fund revenue and expenditure ratios are both less than 1, especially the insurance fund revenue and expenditure ratio of 0.86, meaning that the sustainability of China's pension insurance fund is already facing a certain degree of pressure.

By the end of 2020, the accumulated balance of China's pension insurance fund was 4.5 trillion yuan. Although the state raises the social security fund by allocating state-owned capital and other means, according to the data of China Pension Actuarial Report 2019–2050 released by the Academy of Social Sciences, under the condition that the enterprise contribution rate is 16%, even if the current government financial subsidy mechanism is retained, there will be a gap in the current pension revenue and expenditure in 2028, and the income will not offset the expenditure. It is expected that the accumulated pension surplus will be exhausted in 2035.

The central pension adjustment system was implemented in 2018, and the pension has entered the era of national overall planning. All provinces pay a certain proportion of pensions, which are transferred to all localities through allocation. From the perspective of areal distribution, in 2020, only seven provinces in China achieved net pension contributions. Guangdong, Beijing, Zhejiang, Jiangsu, Shanghai, Fujian and Shandong contributed a total of 176.7 billion yuan. Only Guangdong Province contributed more than one-third, meanwhile Guangdong and Beijing together contributed more than 60%, becoming the largest financial source for central pension adjustment. On the contrary, the ageing degree of the three northeastern provinces is serious, and the pension in some provinces has long been out of pocket (Fig. 1) (Ma & Zhao, 2015).

The income growth of pension insurance funds has slowed down significantly, which is mainly affected by two factors: the number or the coverage of insured employees and the contribution bases or wage level. The sustained and rapid growth of pension fund expenditure is also affected by two factors: first, the number of retirees or system alimony rate and retirement age; second, the level of pension substitution rate and growth mechanism. Nowadays, the rapid growth of financial subsidies for pension funds not only affects the structure of financial expenditure but also profoundly affects the operation of the national economy. As an important source of income for pension funds, financial subsidies are also facing the dilemma of difficulty to increase significantly—because in recent years, the growth rate of national financial revenue has been reduced from the previous 20% to below 10%.

In recent years, the digital economy, network economy and platform economy have attracted a large number of young people for employment. Many of them have an income higher than the social average and hope to have basic pension insurance. However, because there is no employer for insurance payment and they are unwilling to bear the full amount of personal burden for themselves, they have departed from pension security. It is feasible to take these people as the target group of the personal pension system. The personal pension is account management, and the property right belongs to individuals, supported by the government, incentive and attractive to young employees of new business forms. It is necessary to re-understand the role of the individual pension system in social security. It is not only a supplement to pension, but also can become the main pillar of pension security for flexible employees. During

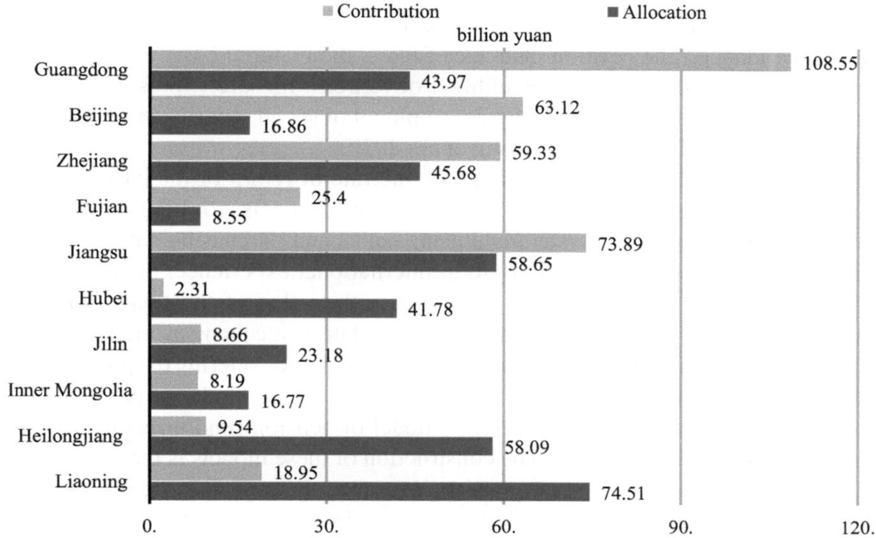

Fig. 1 Top five and the bottom five provinces in the balance of contribution and allocation adjusted by the central government (2020). *Source* Compiled by the author based on (National Bureau of Statistics of China, 2019; National Bureau of Statistics of the People's Republic of China 2021)

the 14th Five Year Plan period, it is necessary to explore various mechanisms that give equal attention to tax incentives and subsidies, and combine voluntary insurance with automatic participation, so as to expand the individual pension system.

3.3 *The Value Maintenance and Increase of the Pension Insurance Fund*

On September 14, 2021, the Annual Report on Entrusted Operation of Basic Pension Insurance Fund issued by the National Social Security Fund Council (Ministry of Human Resources & Social Security of the People's Republic of China, 2021) shows that the return on equity investment of basic pension insurance fund in 2020 is 113.577 billion yuan, an increase of 47.191 billion yuan compared with 66.386 billion yuan in 2019. Meanwhile, the return on investment of the pension fund reached 10.95% in 2020, which not only outperformed the inflation rate in the same period (CPI in 2020 was 2.5%), higher than the yield of national debt (the yield of the 10-year national debt at the end of December 2020 was 3.14%) but also exceeded the average annual return on investment since the entrusted operation of the pension fund (6.89%), a new high since 2017. Although allowing pension insurance funds to operate in the capital market may improve the return on investment of insurance funds, there are still huge risks in the market-oriented operation of pension insurance funds, because the nature of pension insurance funds is relatively special and there are certain requirements for risk avoidance. The pension insurance fund is the material basis of the pension insurance system, the source of livelihood of retirees. Its safety, preservation and appreciation are related to the healthy development of social security and even to the harmony and stability of society (Dong et al., 2020).

The main ways to maintain and improve the rate of return of the basic pension insurance fund include broadening the investment channels, forming an effective market-oriented investment system and using banks and purchasing national bonds to make value-added. From the long-term international experience, the investment capital market can better maintain and increase the value of the fund. Build the optimal investment strategy and reasonable regulatory mechanism models of the pension fund, such as the dynamic asset allocation model considering the profitability, risk and liquidity of pension fund, the regulatory incentive model of pension fund investment managers and the risk reserve model of pension fund investment based on embedded income guarantee. The construction of these models is the enrichment and improvement of the existing pension insurance theoretical system. Applying portfolio theory and optimal decision theory, it can be proved that there is an optimal investment strategy for pension in theory, and the risk and income are balanced at the same time.

4 Conclusion

First, the population ageing, digital economy, sustainable development, these macrobackgrounds are directly related to the operation of the pension insurance system, and the constraints cannot be changed can only be adopted, which requires the need to comply with historical trends to find sustainable strategies for maintaining the pension insurance system. From the perspective of national strategy, China should establish a scientific and effective population fertility management and service mechanism, improve the government's subsidy level for the cost of family childcare, reduce the burden of family parenting, improve the family's fertility will, fertility level and population quality and deal with the impact of the crisis of population ageing on the pension payment system.

Secondly, in order to respond to the unbalanced problems of the pension insurance fund, China has started to trial the elastic retirement method and establish a scientific long-term mechanism for fiscal investment. In terms of fund savings, the fund's sustainability should be "broaden sources of income and reduce expenditure". Delayed retirement has increased the time of paying pension insurance and reduces the time to receive pensions, increase labour supply and increase production. The three-pillar co-development of the pension insurance system guarantees multiple channels of pension supplies. And lowering the growth rate of pension is a measure to reduce expenditure, and enriching the social security fund with state-owned capital has filled the arrears left over by history. In terms of reducing expenditure, the sustainable development of the pension insurance system is mainly realized by raising the

Table 2 Measures to maintain the basic pension insurance fund

Measures of increasing income	Measures of reducing expenditure
• Expand the coverage of basic pension insurance to increase the number of contributors • Delayed retirement • Co-development of three pillars' pension insurance • Government subsidies • Fund market-oriented operation and value-added • Population policy to promote fertility	• Delayed retirement • Slowing pension growth

Source Compiled and summarized by the author based on the results of this paper

retirement age and controlling the excessive growth of pension benefits. When raising the retirement age, it is necessary to introduce employment support, income assistance and other comprehensive supporting measures for the elderly, insist on the principle of fundamentals and control the growth of pensions (Table 2).

Finally, China should deal with the contradiction between the levels of pension insurance and labour cost according to the principle of affordability. In terms of China's national conditions of the new forms of economy and rapid and deep ageing problems, it is necessary to weigh the possible contradiction between the degree of old-age security and economic growth. Improving labour productivity while ensuring economic growth is the fundamental way to deal with ageing and realize the sustainability of basic pension insurance.

References

Blake, D., & Mayhew, L. (2006). On the sustainability of the UK state pension system in the light of population ageing and declining fertility. *Economic Journal, 512*, 286–305. https://doi.org/10.1111/j.1468-0297.2006.01100.x

China Industry Research: 2020–2026 China's elderly care industry market research and development trend research report, Sept. 2019. Retrieved from https://www.chyxx.com/research/201702/493919.html. Accessed December 15, 2021.

China National Health Commission's Department of Aging Health: National Development Bulletin on Aging in 2020, Oct. 2021. URL: http://www.cncaprc.gov.cn/llxw/192690.jhtml. Accessed December 15, 2021.

Dong, K., Yao, Y., & Sun, B. (2020). China pension finance 50 people forum. In *Annual Report on The Development of China's Aging Finance*. Beijing: Social Sciences Literature Press, September 2020.

Edited by the Office of the National Working Committee on Aging, China Association of Aging: China's Aging Career in Progress, 2019.

Elize, V. Z. (2003). The old age pension system in South Africa. In *Paper presented at the Globalization & Social Protection Research Conference*. Switzerland: Chateau de Coppet, February 26, 2003.

Feng, J., & Zheng, C. (2019). Research on the sustainable problem of basic endowment insurance system in China. *Financial Science, 4*.

Grech, A. (2013). Assessing the sustainability of pension reforms in Europe. *Journal of International and Comparative Social Policy, 29*(2), 143–162. https://doi.org/10.1080/21699763.2013.836980

Insurance Association of China: Research Report on the Third Pillar of China Pension, Nov. 2020. URL: http://www.iachina.cn/art/2020/11/20/art_22_104724.html. Accessed December 15, 2021.

Li, Z. (2017). *Social Security Theory* (4th ed.). China Labor and Social Security Press.

Ma, G., & Zhao, L. (2015). Study on the sustainability of basic endowment insurance in China and Its influencing factors—based on provincial wire data. *Economic Wail, 32*(04), 155–160.

Ministry of Human Resources and Social Security of the People's Republic of China. URL: http://www.mohrss.gov.cn. Accessed December 15, 2021.

National Bureau of Statistics of China: China Statistical Yearbook for 2019, China Statistics Press, 2019. URL: http://www.stats.gov.cn/tjsj/ndsj/2019/indexch.htm. Accessed December 15, 2021.

National Bureau of Statistics of the People's Republic of China. URL: http://www.stats.gov.cn. Accessed December 15, 2021.

Pablo, C., Ruben, C., Eduardo, F., Juan, P. M., & Felix, V. (2021). Saving for the future: evaluating the sustainability and design of pension reserve funds. *Pacific-Basin Finance Journal*. https://doi.org/10.1016/j.pacfin.2020.101335

Zheng, B. (2019). Actuarial Report of China Pension 2019–2050. China Labor and Social Security Press, April 2019. URL: http://www.cisscass.org/yanjiucginfo.aspx?ids=26&fl=1. Accessed December 15, 2021.

Contemporary Metropolitan Language: The Case of the Republic of Tatarstan

Elena V. Volkova, Sazida V. Viugina, and Alla Yu. Filkova

Abstract The research studies the changes in the language of a metropolis occurring in today's world. It is revealed from the point of view of complex social processes that support the continuity, reproduction, and development of the urban environment. The development of the language of the metropolis is considered a factor of sustainable development, especially in the Muslim republics. It ensures the security and stability of the region. The communicative activity of an individual is presented as the cooperation of human qualities, developing new objectivity of the language as a means for the implementation of successful mutual understanding, cooperation, and sustainable development of the region. The relevance of the research is related to the fact that changes in language cause changes in human consciousness, impact personalities of people, form their culture, contribute to stability in relationships, and reduce conflicts. The methods of observation and survey used within the framework of the interdisciplinary social approach show that the linguistic personality of a person is formed under the influence of the environment and the human habitat environment of the individual. A person, who absorbs the culture, becomes a part of this linguistic culture, its traditions, and a language. Manipulations in language cause a change in a person's consciousness and a change in their speech behavior. What our language of intercultural communication will be in the future, such will be the society of the future.

Keywords Language standard · Unique lexical units · Internet slangs · Lexicalization · Verbal environment · New communicative spaces · Language depersonification · Factor of sustainable development

JEL Classification I20 · R11 · R58 · R190 · Z11 · Z18 · Z19

E. V. Volkova (✉) · S. V. Viugina
Kazan National Research Technological University, Kazan, Russia
e-mail: wolfkova@mail.ru

A. Yu. Filkova
Kazan Cooperative Institute (Branch) of the Russian University of Cooperation, Kazan, Russia
e-mail: Fikova_alla@bk.ru

E. I. Lazareva et al. (eds.), *Innovative Trends in International Business and Sustainable Management*, Approaches to Global Sustainability, Markets, and Governance,
https://doi.org/10.1007/978-981-19-4005-7_38

1 Introduction

Sustainable development of the Republic of Tatarstan is primarily a process of stabilizing the economic and social development of the region aimed at ensuring the quality of life of people, human needs, and aspirations. The issues of change in today's language are becoming most popular, especially in large metropolitan areas and million cities of Muslim republics with the prevailing mixed population. Many young people with their culture, traditions, and native languages come to the cities searching for work and life success, to satisfy their ambitions, and these factors cannot but affect the language of the metropolis. Nowadays, linguistic issues are raised in contemporary literature from the perspective of sustainable development in large cities. An interesting overview of the language of a metropolis, using Moscow as an example, and the influence of the social situation in society on language development is presented in the collective monograph "A townsman: What do we know about an inhabitant of a big city." Scholars such as V. Kurennoy, E. Shulman, A. Novikov, Yu. Grigoryan, M. Alekseevskiy, G. Yudin, and M. Krongauz raise issues related to the formation of an urban personality type in their collective monograph "The Citizen," where one of the important points of discussion is the language component of the person (Kurennoy et al., 2017).

Indicators of "literary-centric language in a metropolis" are more important than ever because they unite the population of large cities, make it equal, create a kind of basis for the life of a metropolis, a large country (Krongauz & Furman, 2017), thereby acting as stabilizers of society and factors in the sustainable development of the region. When there is mass unrest for various reasons in large cities, language issues are the first concern because, through language, it is possible to manipulate the public consciousness and conduct a certain ideology. These issues are discussed in monographic studies by Ch. Bally, B. A. Serebryanikov, E. Kubtyakova, V. Postovalova, V. Teliya, A. Ufimtseva, V. I. Karasik, N. D. Galskova, and N. I. Gez (Bally, 2003; Galskova & Gez, 2008; Karasik, 2002; Krongauz & Furman, 2017; Kurennoy et al., 2017; Puzanova et al., 2015; Serebryanikov et al., 1988). Aggressive advertising and aggressive communicative behavior of citizens, in some cases, caused by the high rhythm of life, can provoke a conflict, the resolution of which does not always end peacefully, breaking the usual rhythm of life and a stable equilibrium in society. Therefore, the relevance of the research is dictated, first of all, by the current sustainable development of society in cities. It is also relevant for a person living in large metropolitan areas, a migrant who came to the city in search of a better life, to absorb the right language, form the right culture of speech behavior and education, contributing to personal development, the development of society, and security in general.

2 Methodology

The authors conducted our research at the university site of Kazan National Research Technological University and the Russian University of Cooperation. The study was conducted within the framework of an interdisciplinary social approach aimed at studying changes in the language of the metropolis as a factor of sustainable development within society. The authors analyzed theoretical problems of language and their impact on the development of human personality and the environment of the metropolis. Within the framework of the socio-interdisciplinary approach, the researchers used three main methods: analysis, method of observation and description, and interviewing (Puzanova et al., 2015). The use of methodological techniques of analysis allowed the authors to study the foreign and Russian literature on the research topic. Theoretical analysis of the data contributed to the definition of the range of studied issues. This study analyzes the problems of the interpenetration of the Tatar and Russian languages, the development of digitalization and its impact on the linguistic personality of citizens, and the role of language in the informational and communicative space of the metropolis as a factor of sustainable development. In this research, the authors used the method of non-involved, informalized observation, with the help of which they were able to involve students in the implementation of this method in practice. The collected information showed changes in the language culture of the metropolis in the following directions: literary language, jargonisms, depersonalization of language under the influence of digitalization, and semiotic direction in the language. The method of observation allowed the authors to focus on the key points in the research, and, on this basis, to proceed to the method of survey, forming a questionnaire (see Appendix), which allowed the authors to identify key control points in the research, the experimental data on which proved changes in the language and identified vectors in the sustainable development of the region influenced by these linguistic changes.

3 Results and Discussion

As a factor in the sustainable development of the Republic of Tatarstan, the language of the metropolis, using the example of Kazan, the capital of the republic, forms its own special linguistic standard, in which a certain dialect is present. The literary language in the Republic of Tatarstan was formed under the influence of Muslim culture. The interpenetration of languages has had a positive impact on the political, economic, and social stability of the region.

For example, comparing the languages of Moscow and Kazan allows establishing the place of residence of the speaker. Thus, in Tatarstan, the following words are used that are not typical to other regions: "sarai" instead of "khlev" [both words meaning shed], "bazar" [Bazar] instead of "rynok" [both words meaning market], "bashka" from the Tatar word "bash"—head, "ajda" instead of "let's go," "babai"—grandfather. Such comparative projects are gaining popularity among linguists. The Russian language in Tatarstan is still slightly different from the Russian language in Moscow. On the one hand, it is some deep age-old differences, that is, the influence of dialects and the intonation of the language. On the other hand, there are current differences, the emergence of new words and the interpenetration of languages, which contribute to the sustainable development of the region.

When we talk about the language of a city, we can simply talk about a literary language or a standard language. Nevertheless, in reality, there are many languages living in big cities: these are the many jargons and possible dialects of the territorial area whose center is a metropolis. For example, the influence of English on the Russian language is more noticeable in large cities, with the maximum degree observed in the capital. Moscow is the place of maximum influence of English as the language of the global world on Russian. The language of the Russian provinces is more conservative and more independent of outside influences. Nevertheless, the influence of English is also observed in Tatarstan. For example, the following signs can be seen in Kazan: Ikea, where all products are listed in Swedish in large letters, and the translation is given in Russian in small print. In this case, we encounter the popularization and influence of a foreign language on the Russian language. In metropolises, including Kazan, in entertainment venues, one can sometimes see signs of words—sexisms in the name of hot drinks aimed at attracting young people and increasing aggressive sales of alcohol.

Different language variants are called "lexes": there are dialects and sociolects. A dialect is a regional version of a language. A sociolect is a social version of a language. Since dialects have acquired the meaning of not just a regional variant but precisely a rural variant, the term "regiolects" emerged. Regiolects are different urban languages that differ in a small set of vocabulary.

How do languages get along in the same city, and do they fight over who will be in charge? It is not necessary at all. For example, in the twenty-first century, digitalization has created its own language, mostly the language of urban culture. There is a kind of jargon in the youth environment, professional jargon of brokers at the stock exchanges, in sports. Nevertheless, they all exist in certain communities with their own clear boundaries. It brings young people closer, but they understand that they need to switch to literary language with their parents.

The reconstruction and the digitalization of society led to the fact that these boundaries were torn down—the usual prohibitions began to be violated. People have come to realize freedom, including freedom of speech. Freedom of speech is realized not only as political freedom but also as cultural freedom, that is, freedom from cultural rules, without realizing that freedom does not mean permissiveness. The 1990s saw the expansion of swearing into the common speech of city-dwellers and into the cultural space—on the pages of newspapers and magazines, the stage, and in movies. Apparently, no sustainable development in society was out of the question in those years. One of the most important processes of that time was precisely the destruction of the boundaries between the literary language and the numerous jargon. Jargons and elements of colloquialism began to be used in common speech. In the 1990s, youth slang became prestigious. Often, expressing a desire to be closer to their children, parents switched to youth slang to fit the spirit of the times.

The years of social restructuring have played a considerable role in breaking down linguistic boundaries. During this period, there the competition emerged between jargon, and then the influential jargon of representatives of criminal structures appeared. For almost ten years, it actively influenced the common language of the urban citizens; it was fashionable to use it in speech. The criminal language, reflected in various literary, theatrical, and film productions and the media, did not correlate with the thieves' slang of previous eras. On the contrary, it took shape precisely in the 1990s, representing a new phenomenon in language.

However, in the early 2000s, the position of state power strengthened, as evidenced by the many high-profile criminal cases, including those involving organized crime groups in Kazan. Nowadays, we do not observe jargon in the speech of citizens. Although, generally speaking, criminal subjects have not disappeared. There was a stratification of society: somebody went to power, others stayed in their places; most of the generation of 1970s in Russia has already passed away under the conditions of the collapse of the country, unemployment, the destruction of moral values of society, the war in Afghanistan, Chechnya, and drugs and alcohol addiction. Thus, they ceased to be an important social phenomenon, and we no longer find these words in the common language.

Digitalization has enabled the emergence of a new digital type of person, confidently navigating the space of the Internet and social networks with its language, speech behavior, and knowledge of digital culture (Volkova et al., 2021). Youth slang and industry words have moved beyond the confines of their respective communities. Computerspeak spreads extremely quickly. In the 2000s, the fashion for Internet jargon spread beyond the Internet. The invention of the Internet and new communication spaces (the blogosphere and social networks) within the Internet was a huge technological breakthrough in the life of society and every individual. People communicate differently; communication is performed more in writing than verbally, which significantly affects the language. The Internet provides unique opportunities to spread new words: some words thrown into the language, no matter where, no matter from whose computer, become known worldwide. The global network can add something to the language. Nevertheless, it will not lead to an absolute identity of the vocabulary of people living in Kazan or Moscow. We will give examples of the language of gamers from different countries who use their vocabulary to organize game activities (Volkova, 2017). For example, In the language of gamers, "tp" means to teleport; "dmg" means "damage, harm, injury"; "khasanit"—drive fast with danger and risk, break the rules; "spalitsya"—to be discovered, to be caught; "kranty" means "the end" to someone or something; "loose streak"—several losses in a row.

If there is any social group that is now imposing its jargon, it is most likely the "sentimental language of middle-aged girls with average education," with all sorts of words like "xoxo"—kiss, "awww"—cute, "kawaii"—adorable, "freaks," "sorry." Many people who run their blogs today are teenage girls, unusually dressed and thinking outside the box. Their language of speech communication is now quite popular among young people, especially among teenagers and 18-year-old boys and girls. Thus, the new jargons replace the old ones. We may often hear words like "izi"—from English "easy"; "crush"—in love at first sight; "zhiza"—really, vitally; "cringe"—an embarrassing situation; "sharit"—to understand; "ROFL"—a joke; "really"—true, truth; "chill"—to relax; "facts"; "lol"—funny.

Despite the fact that migrant workers and quite a few visiting merchants have appeared in major cities, their languages have little effect on Russian, at least in public space. We do not have words from Tajik, Kyrgyz, and other languages. These words did not appear in other languages of metropolises either. This is most likely because migrants and emigrants do not socialize well in other countries, preferring to communicate exclusively in their diaspora. However, it is possible that this influence is just not yet noticeable. In this case, the most crucial factor will be the school and the joint education of children with different native languages.

Since the 2000s, Kazan, the capital of the Republic of Tatarstan, has become a multicultural metropolis. Nowadays, there is a maximum concentration of interesting changes in the language, which spreads to other regions of Russia, as talented young people in Tatarstan seek to participate in various innovative international projects.

Speaking of lexical innovations, we mean, primarily, borrowing, when we simply borrow a foreign word. The second important mechanism is the emergence of a new meaning under the influence of a foreign language. In Russian, a word takes on meaning because a similar meaning exists in another language. For example, the word "bug" is now used by programmers to define an error in a computer program, meaning something small that interferes with the smooth operation.

However, there is the language of the city as a semiotic system. When villagers enter the capital of Tatarstan, Kazan, they inevitably see many different words around them: on signboards, in shop windows, in newspapers, on road signs. Generally speaking, this language is organized differently in each city. In Soviet times, everything was organized in an extremely uncomfortable and unfriendly way to a person, especially a tourist, especially a foreigner. Nowadays, a tourist in the capital of Tatarstan gets into a completely different linguistic environment of the metropolis and can navigate in it freely, even without knowing a foreign language.

The phrase "metropolitan language" can be interpreted not only as the language that is usually spoken by city dwellers but also as the "invisible" language affecting people through signboards and product labels. It is partly devoid of a speaker and depersonalized, but the city speaks to us with advertisements and names. For example, in Kazan, one is influenced by such word-signs as "Lakomka"—gourmet, "Ekiyat"—tale, "Tatarskaya Usadba"—Tatar estate; "Bakhhetle"—happy. These names have their own meaning. They are associated with the national cuisine and Tatar culture and traditions. Moreover, they have already gained a certain popularity among the capital's tourists, positioning Kazan as the gastronomic capital of Russia. In these cases, there are definitely cooperative merger techniques, a strategy that contributes to the sustainable development of the region.

An interesting question for the linguist is how the semiotic structure of language coincides with the territorial boundaries of the city. The authors will consider the linguistic relationship of the name, its meaning, the symbol, and its localization.

Moving away from the conditional center of Kazan, we encounter some other appearance of the city, including the language. Stylistic techniques in the names used in one territory do not work in a completely different linguistic environment. If we come with a sign or cafe name used in Kazan to a small town in Tatarstan or even a suburb or village, it can cause shock and rejection.

In general, the choice of a name is a relevant problem in the city. An example of this is the scandal with the name of the restaurant "Kresty" [Crosses] on Kosmonavtov Street, which popularized the prison subculture, although the younger generation of Kazan residents does not remember this story. This name was forbidden in Kazan; the citizens did not want any reminders of the lawlessness and organized crime in the 1990s. The result of this confrontation between the owners of the restaurant and the city authorities was the renaming of the restaurant and, subsequently, its closure. Residents generally do not like renaming. The older generation remembers how the residents of Naberezhnye Chelny expressed their dissatisfaction with the renaming of their city to Brezhnev. Although the new name was in honor of the General Secretary of the Soviet Union, it did not take root among the residents of the city of Naberezhnye Chelny. The residents who were dissatisfied with the renaming of the city were not opponents of the Communist regime and supported this policy, but they were used to living in this city, and this toponym became meaningful to them (Krongauz & Furman, 2017). In this regard, we can also recall Nursultan Nazarbayev Street in Kazan. Over the past three decades, this street has changed three names: Zhdanova Street, Esperanto Street, and the current one. However, there were no serious issues with the residents of this street because the appearance of this street has changed, as well as the category of citizens living on it. This area of Kazan was rebuilt; dilapidated housing was demolished. If people have lived all their lives on Bolshaya Krasnaya Street in Kazan, they may not want to live on Gorbachev Street, even if they admire the leader's talent and have a negative attitude toward communist ideology.

A name begins to take on its own images and its aura, if it exists for a long time and is associated with an interesting and important phenomenon. A person who arrived on Bolshaya Krasnaya Street yesterday may well prefer the new name, but those who have lived on it all their lives prefer the old one. For the majority, it is a matter of habit, nothing more, but habit plays almost a major role in language. It turns out to be a significant urban problem. On the one hand, the city's landscape is formed based on some ideology and politics: for example, an abnormal number of Lenin and Karl Marx streets that can be found in every major city of the Russian Federation. On the other hand, when we start renaming them and replacing them with either the old names or new, neutral names, we encounter the rejection of the people who grew up in this space, causing conflicts, intolerance, and, thereby, disrupting the sustainable development of the region. The new name does not immediately take root in urban culture; first, the generation that got used to the old name must leave.

4 Conclusion

Based on the survey of students (see Appendix), we can conclude the following:

1. Observance of speech etiquette by inhabitants of a metropolis contributes to stabilization in the development of society and reduces the degree of conflict between people;
2. The digitalization of society creates the conditions for the emergence of a new digital personality type, with its own language and slang which are understandable to young people. This factor destroys interethnic discord and unites young people in the information and communication space;
3. Language interpenetration in a metropolis promotes the development of small businesses and, consequently, the sustainable prosperity of the region;
4. The obscene and aggressive language used by citizens can be a destabilizing factor in the management of the sustainable development of the region.

Thus, entering the current linguistic environment of a metropolis, a person learns to speak the "right" language, mastering this language through his or her environment, through the profession. A person does not read textbooks; no one teaches them this new information and communication space as a special subject; people learn and master a new language during intercultural communication (Volkova, 2013). This is the transition from someone else's to one's own. This is fusion and cooperation in the philosophical sense of the word. A person becomes an "insider" as he or she enters this community, including assimilation of the language used in this community. A person begins to dress like other members of this community. He or she begins to behave as members of this community behave, and he or she begins to speak as members of this community. It is one of the ways of mastering a foreign language. One can read textbooks and dictionaries, listen to recordings of foreign language lessons, or he or she can dive into a foreign environment and assimilate into it. Nowadays, our society needs qualified professionals who are competent to solve important practical tasks and professional problems. Knowledge of the language of the metropolis is a key factor in achieving this goal and ensuring sustainable development (Volkova et al., 2015).

Appendix

A questionnaire on speech culture for students living in metropolitan areas.

1. Are you familiar with the concept of literary language?
2. Do you consider the problem of speech etiquette which is, relevant in terms of the sustainable development of the region?
3. How can speech etiquette affect the stability of everyday life?
4. Do you follow speech etiquette in your speech when talking on the phone, on the Internet?

5. If you give a positive answer to a peer's question on the Internet, what lexical form will you follow?
6. What greetings do you use when communicating with your peers on the Internet?
7. What form of farewell do you take when communicating with your peers on the Internet?
8. Do you use obscene language in your speech?
9. Do you think that obscene language can provoke interethnic, and religious conflicts?
10. Do you use slang words in your speech?
11. How often do you use slang words?
12. Do you think that the abundance of recently borrowed words "litter the Russian language" and can provoke conflicts in interpersonal and interethnic communication?
13. Do you consider insufficient knowledge of a second language as an obstacle to employment and socialization in society?
14. For what purpose do you use slang words?
15. What slang words do you use in your everyday speech?
16. Do teachers correct your speech?
17. How do your parents feel about your speech?
18. Which language is the benchmark for you?
19. Do you think jargonisms will supplant the words of literary Russian?
20. Do you consider today's youth slang the norm?
21. How do negative changes in language culture affect the sustainable development of society?

References

Bally, C. (2003). *A language and a life* (I. I. Chelysheva & E. A. Velmezova Transl. from French). Moscow, Russia: "URSS" Publisher (Original work published 1952).

Galskova, N., & Gez, N. (2008). The theory of foreign language teaching. In *Linguodidactics and methods*. "Academy" Publisher.

Karasik, V. (2002). *A language of a social status*. "Gnosis" Publisher.

Krongauz, M. (2017). Words geography: What language townspeople speak. In J. Furman (Ed.), *A townsman: What do we know about an inhabitant of a big city?* (pp. 138–149). Strelka Press.

Kurennoy, V., Shulman, E., Novikov, A., Grigoryan, Y., Alekseevskiy, M., Yudin, G., & Krongauz, M. (2017). In J. Furman (Ed.), *A townsman: What do we know about an inhabitant of a big city?* (pp. 198–211). Strelka Press.

Puzanova, Z. H., Trotsuk, I. V., & Vitkovskaya, M. I. (2015). *Practical course of "Methodology and methods of sociological researches"*. Publishing house "Higher Education and Science"

Serebryanikov, B., Kubtyakova, E., Postovalova, V., Teliya, V., & Ufimtseva, A. (1988). *A role of a human factor in a language: A language and a worldview*. Nauka.

Volkova, E. V. (2013). Different approaches to the problems of intercultural communicative competence. In *Proceedings of the ICL 2013: International Conference on Interactive Collaborative Learning* (pp. 444–445). https://doi.org/10.1109/ICL.2013.6644621

Volkova, E. V. (2017). Foreign languages: Forming secondary linguistic personality. *Scientific Survey: Humanitarian Researches, 10–11*, 54–62.

Volkova, E., Semushina, E., & Tsareva, E. (2021). Developing cross-cultural communicative competence of university students in the globalized world. In M. E. Auer, & T. Rüütmann (Eds.), *Educating engineers for future industrial revolutions* (pp. 405–416). Springer. https://doi.org/10.1007/978-3-030-68198-2_38

Volkova, E., Zinurova, R., & Tuzikov, A. (2015). Formation experience of sociocultural competence in the system of additional foreign education. In *Proceedings of the ICSSS 2015: 4th International Conference on Social Sciences and Society* (pp. 144–147). Paris, France. Retrieved from https://www.researchgate.net/profile/Katarzyna-Szymczyk/publication/317057301_IT_Authorisation_of_the_Process_of_Knowledge_Management/links/5a8888a2aca272017e5f5cc2/IT-Authorisation-of-the-Process-of-Knowledge-Management.pdf. Accessed January 1, 2022.

Digitalization: Experience of Using Online Platforms in Teacher's Preparation for Classes

Zhanna V. Smirnova, Nelli G. Perevozchikova, Sergey D. Tsymbalov, Svetlana N. Kuznetsova, and Svetlana V. Bulganina

Abstract This article discusses the issue of using online platforms in the educational activities of a teacher. There are a huge number of different online resources where teachers can plan their activities. In modern conditions, the use of online platforms in the educational environment is gaining momentum. The author analyzes scientific and methodological literature, notes that the global Internet network and the development of various communication services contribute to the opening of a cultural and educational environment with open access, which ultimately can facilitate the preparation of a teacher for his studies. The education system evolves from a chalkboard to computer-based teaching programs. The main learning objectives that online platforms are aimed at are considered. The positive results of using online platforms in preparation for the lesson are noted. As a result of the study of the use of online platforms in educational activities, a survey was conducted among school teachers. The conclusion was made on the basis of the study.

Keywords Online platform · Information technology · Teacher · Educational process · Modern technologies

JEL Classification R11 · R12 · R 58 · Q13

Z. V. Smirnova (✉) · S. D. Tsymbalov · S. N. Kuznetsova · S. V. Bulganina
Minin Nizhny Novgorod State Pedagogical University, Nizhny Novgorod, Russia
e-mail: z.v.smirnova@mininuniver.ru

S. N. Kuznetsova
e-mail: dens@52.ru

S. V. Bulganina
e-mail: bulganina_sv@mininuniver.ru

N. G. Perevozchikova
Institute of Food Technologies and Design—a branch of State University of Engineering and Economics, Nizhny Novgorod, Russia

E. I. Lazareva et al. (eds.), *Innovative Trends in International Business and Sustainable Management*, Approaches to Global Sustainability, Markets, and Governance,
https://doi.org/10.1007/978-981-19-4005-7_39

1 Introduction

Relevance of the topic. Significant changes in the field of education associated with the introduction of new federal state educational standards (FSES) and the adoption of the new Federal Law of the Russian Federation «On Education in the Russian Federation» orient the pedagogical process of general education organizations toward improving the quality of education (Federal State Educational Standard of Basic General Education, 2010). Accordingly, the level of teachers' preparation for classes should only grow. At the moment, there are a huge number of different online platforms that help teachers to create lessons at a new, higher level.

A teacher is a profession in which there are a large number of different types of planning: planning of educational work, planning of educational work in a children's team, planning of work with students' parents, planning of participation in innovative activities, planning of work on self-education, advanced training, generalization and dissemination of own work experience.

The education system has been evolving from a chalkboard to computer-based teaching programs.

We touch upon the issue of the teacher's level of preparation for lessons, which, accordingly, should only grow when we investigate the topic of the problem of the application and modernization of information technologies in educational activities. At the moment, there are a huge number of different online platforms that help teachers to create lessons at a new, higher level.

2 Methodology

The modern educational process cannot be represented without the search for new, more effective technologies used by teachers in their work.

The global Internet and the development of various communication services contribute to the opening of a cultural and educational environment with open access, which ultimately can facilitate the preparation of teachers for their studies. The education system has been evolving from a chalkboard to computer-based teaching programs, it's the same with teacher's planning (Polat, 2007).

V. A. Sukhomlinsky said: «Whatever education, whatever category, whatever length of service a teacher has, he still needs to prepare for lessons» (Tiunova, 2016). Online platforms come to help teachers. There are a huge number of different online resources where teachers can plan their activities. In modern conditions, the use of online platforms in the educational environment is gaining momentum.

The stated goal of the research is to study the process of preparing and developing a lesson by a teacher using modern online platforms. The use of online sites in teacher's preparation for classes in «Technology» increases the quality of the lesson in the «Technology» subject area.

The research uses theoretical and empirical methods. Literature study, theoretical analysis using synthesis, generalization and classification—all this refers to theoretical research methods. Conducting a survey among teachers, analyzing didactic material, analyzing lecture notes for lessons in the «Technology» subject area, talking with teachers and a teacher-mentor, researching their experience are carried out.

The use of online platforms in preparation for Technology lessons by teachers in Nizhny Novgorod is considered for the first time in the study.

The research participants are Technology teachers (3 people) and students (20 people) of School No. 124 in Nizhny Novgorod.

Before composing lessons using online platforms, it is necessary to find out which platforms are used by Technology teachers in preparing for their classes. Initially, a conversation with teachers was conducted, on the basis of which the first conclusions about their use of online platforms in their preparation for lessons were formulated. Then a Google survey, which would help to organize and record the information that was heard, was compiled.

The purpose of the survey is to find out which online platforms teachers use to prepare for their lessons.

The applied research methods are a questionnaire survey of teachers, analysis of Technology teachers' plans-abstracts, research of teachers' experience, observation, analysis of didactic support for lessons, conversation with teachers.

The questions of the questionnaire, consisting of 5 questions, are devoted to the topics of the use of computer technologies in the learning process, access to the Internet in an educational institution, what online platforms do you own and use in your work.

The following conclusions were formulated when the results were analyzed:

1. The most popular online platform used by Technology teachers is «Dnevnik.ru». However, teachers do not know about all the capabilities of this resource and use it as a CTP.
2. 30% of teachers do not use any online platforms in their training, they attribute this to a lack of awareness of the systems or simply to the presence of vast teaching experience. The teacher-mentor of Secondary School No. 124 also does not use any online platforms to prepare for lessons in his practice, with the exception of «Dnevnik.ru».
3. Online educational platforms are actively used by teachers between the ages of 23 and 30. There is a tendency: the older the age, the less teachers turn to various educational resources for help. This can be explained by the fact that the older generation has difficulty while working with online platforms. They also have enough experience to prepare for lessons without resorting to the help of electronic resources.
4. The respondents have not heard of the existence of such online platforms as «CORE», «Learn from Home», «Yandex.school», «Foxford». Accordingly, no one uses them in their work.
5. All teachers who voted that they do not use any online platform in their preparation for lessons in their questionnaires are over 45 years old.

6. Based on the results of the study, it was found that some teachers find online platforms difficult to understand and even complicate the teacher's work.
7. Such platforms as «Uchi.ru», «RESH», «YAKLASS» are considered by teachers from 23 to 25 years old to be excellent assistants when creating their lessons. This is because they contain a huge number of examples of ready-made lessons.

3 Results

According to N.N. Tiunova's definition, an educational platform is «a limited, personality-oriented Internet resource dedicated to education and self-development issues and containing educational materials that are provided to users on certain conditions» (Rudenko et al., 2021; Russian electronic school, 2021).

There are several basic learning challenges that online platforms aim to address:

(1) control of knowledge of students in an educational institution and implementation of distance learning;
(2) automation of the process of professional development and training of employees of various organizations;
(3) organization of training in different areas of education.

All educational platforms have something in common—the tasks that they allow to solve. Platforms can only be distinguished by their interface, tariff plan, method of presenting the material and the information content itself (Petrovskiy et al., 2018; Sedykh, 2019).

Benefits of educational platforms:

1. The ability to acquire knowledge by a student at any convenient time, regardless of location.
2. The use of modern technology and multimedia.
3. Studying the educational material in an accessible, visual and interesting way for the student.
4. The access to all necessary educational materials during training based on the online platform.
5. The development of self-organization and discipline in the process of independent work on assignments.
6. The opportunity to receive education for people with disabilities.

Despite the huge number of advantages, online platforms also have disadvantages:

1. The use of an online platform provokes a shortage of live communication and decreases emotional involvement in the learning process.
2. Control over discipline becomes more difficult when working with online platforms (Smirnova et al., 2017).

The processes of informatization, introduction of new scientific discoveries, rapid renewal of knowledge and professions put forward the requirements for increased professional mobility and lifelong education. The formation of set of key competencies has been and will be for a long time one of the most important tasks of the modern education system. These competencies are considered as the ability of students to use the acquired knowledge, skills, methods of activity in real life to solve practical problems. Possession of these key competencies allows a person to become more successful, mobile and in demand in society.

In the course of the study, the pedagogical experiment was conducted, the results of which will reveal how the use of online platforms in preparation for a Technology teacher's classes and how their use affects the effectiveness of Technology lessons.

The purpose of this experiment is to check how the use of online platforms affects the increase in the cognitive activity of students.

The methods used: conducting a survey among teachers, analyzing didactic material, analyzing lecture notes for the Technology lessons, talking with teachers and researching their experience.

Participants in the experiment: female students of the 5th grade. Number: 56 people.

The pedagogical experiment was carried out on the basis of secondary school No. 124 among pupils of the 5th grade. This experiment consisted of two Technology lessons. The first one is conducted using such an online platform as the Russian Electronic School (RESH). Before that, this kind of activity had never been used in the lessons. The second lesson was held in a traditional manner. The teacher voices new material, the children write down definitions from the textbook, then they do practical work from the textbook in the same way. At the end of the second lesson, the children were asked to go through a small survey, according to the results of which the attitude of children to the lessons with the use of educational platforms would be clarified (Arkhipova et al., 2017; Ibatova, 2017).

According to the results of the survey, the following data were established in Fig. 1.

According to the students' answers, they liked how the teacher explained the material most of all in the lesson, 44 people said that they like to listen to the new

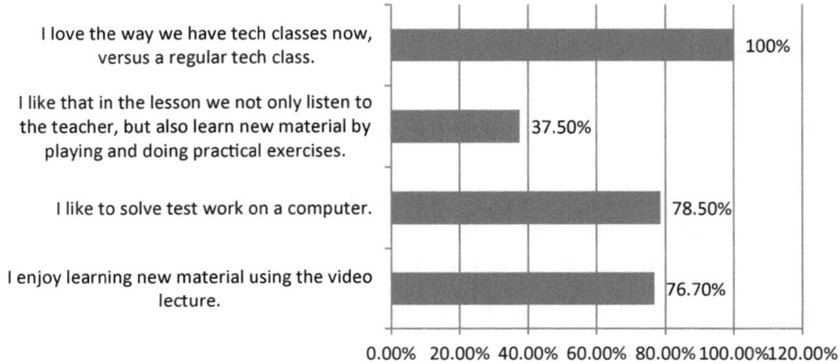

Fig. 1 Results of student surveys. *Source* Developed and compiled by the authors

material on the video lecture. 12 students do not like to study new material using video materials, 21 students like to take tests using RESH, 45 students do not, but this is not surprising, because students have less opportunity to cheat or peep. And if you clicked to confirm the answer, you cannot change it. All 56 people noted that they enjoy learning new material through games and practical exercises. All 56 people said that they like the lessons of this format.

Thus, as a result of the experiment, it was revealed that the students prefer the learning format using online platforms more. There was a significant difference in the activity of children in the traditional lesson and in the lesson with the use of new electronic resources.

In the traditional lesson, some of the children were looking at their phones, there was a lower activity of children, compared to the lesson in the educational platform. During lessons with the use of RESH, the children did not have time to sit on their phones, they were always involved and enthusiastic, it was clear that this lesson format was new for students, and it was interesting for them to learn and try to study in this format. As additional evidence of the effectiveness of the use of online platforms by teachers in preparation for classes, the time for developing a lesson using the RESH online platform was recorded. The elapsed time was 47 min. It took 1 h 44 min to prepare for the lesson without using educational platforms, but using more traditional methods of preparing for classes. It took me much less time to prepare a lesson using the online platform «Russian Electronic School» than to prepare using electronic resources, a paragraph of a textbook, self-compilation of tests and practical materials (Dnevnik.ru—digital educational platform, 2021; Gorbunkova, 2016, Mazurenko & Pavlova, 2020).

The use of online platforms by technology teachers in their preparation for lessons is at a low level at school No. 124. Only a small percentage of teachers use this resource in their teaching activities. Many people have not even heard of the opportunities that online platforms open up to teachers.

The use of online platforms in the technology lesson increases the cognitive activity of students.

4 Conclusion

The aim of the research was to study the process of preparing and developing a technology lesson by a teacher using modern online platforms.

In the process of this study, it was possible to implement all the tasks set to achieve the goal and to make certain conclusions about the use of modern online platforms by teachers in preparation for technology lessons:

1. The analysis of scientific, pedagogical and methodological literature on the research problem made it possible to clarify the definition of educational online platforms. The educational platform is a limited, person-centered Internet resource dedicated to education and self-development issues and containing

educational materials that are provided to users on certain terms. The tasks of educational online platforms, their structure, advantages and disadvantages were highlighted, described and concretized.
2. In the course of the work, it was found out which online platforms a technology teacher can use in his work, and which platforms can be used at various stages of the teacher's preparation for his classes.
3. As a result of the survey among technology teachers in Nizhny Novgorod, the level of using online platforms in teachers' prepation for their classes was determined.
4. An experimental study made it possible to find out how the use of educational platforms affects the cognitive activity of students in a technology lesson. Also, as a result, the hypothesis that the use of online platforms improves the quality of teacher preparation for classes, saves him time spent on developing a lesson was confirmed.
5. The results obtained thanks to this research can be used and adapted for any teacher.

It can be concluded that the knowledge obtained in the course of the research will be useful and necessary in the course of further work as a technology teacher, will help to competently organize the learning process of schoolchildren with the maintenance of high motivation and cognitive activity.

References

Arkhipova, M. V., Belova, E. E., Gavrikova, Y. A., Lyulyaeva, N. A., & Shapiro, E. D. (2017). Blended learning in teaching EFL to different age groups. In *International conference on Humans as an Object of Study by Modern Science Springer, Cham* (pp. 380–386). https://link.springer.com/chapter/https://doi.org/10.1007/978-3-319-75383-6_49. Data accessed December 20, 2021.

Dnevnik.ru—digital educational platform. (2021). https://dnevnik.ru. Data accessed December 20, 2021.

Federal state educational standard of basic general education. (2010). [Electronic resource]: dated December 17, 2010, No. 1879. http://window.edu.ru/resource/768/72768/files/FGOS_OO.pdf. Data accessed December 20, 2021.

Gorbunkova, L. A. (2016). Qualitative preparation of the teacher for the lesson. *School pedagogy*, 2, 1–3. https://moluch.ru/th/2/archive/27/729/. Data accessed December 20, 2021.

Ibatova, A. Z. (2017). The conference as an effective form of organizing the evaluation of students' project and research activities. *Revista ESPACIOS*, 38(55). http://www.revistaespacios.com/a17v38n55/17385504.html. Data accessed December 20, 2021.

Mazurenko, E. V., & Pavlova, I. N. (2020). Analysis of the application of various online platforms for distance learning. https://cyberleninka.ru/article/n/analiz-primeneniya-razlichnyh-internet-platform-dlya-distantsionnogo-obucheniya/viewer. Data accessed December 20, 2021.

Petrovskiy, A. M., Smirnova, Z. V., & Vaganova, O. I. (2018). Formation of professional competencies of university students in the course of practical training. *Problems of Modern Pedagogical Education, 58*(3), 213–216. https://elibrary.ru/item.asp?id=32636555. Data accessed December 20, 2021.

Polat, E. S. (2007). *Modern pedagogical and information technologies in the education system* (p. 42). Academy.

Rudenko, I. V., Bystrova, N. V., Smirnova, Z. V., Vaganova, O. I., & Kutepov, M. M. (2021). Modern technologies in working with gifted students. *PROPOSITOS Y REPRESENTACIONES, 9*. https://doi.org/10.20511/pyr2021.v9nSPE1.818. Published: January 2021

Russian electronic school. (2021). https://resh.edu.ru. Data accessed December 20, 2021.

Sedykh, E. P. (2019). Normative legal support system of project management in education. *Vestnik of Minin University 7*(1) (26), 1.

Smirnova, Z. V., Vaganova, O. I., & Trutanova, A. V. (2017). Prospects for the use of cloud technologies in the educational process of the university. *Baltic Humanitarian Journal, 6*(3), 284–286. https://elibrary.ru/item.asp?id=30381940. Data accessed December 20, 2021.

Tiunova, N. N. (2016). Educational platforms as a means of intensifying the professional training of college students. Professional education in Russia and abroad, pp. 103–108.

Sustainability and Innovation Management

Evolutionary Management in Managing Economic Growth and Sustainable Development

Evgeny M. Martishin, Svetlana V. Gladkaya, Alexey N. Yeletsky, Tatyana A. Zotova, and Ashkhyen B. Yatsenko

Abstract *Purpose* The purpose of this article is to develop the content of new concepts—evolutionary management, etc. and the use of their tools in the analysis of the management of economic growth and sustainable strategic development of the economic system. *Design/methodology/approach* Definitions of growth and sustainable development, other basic evolutionary and genetic methodological terminology of the sphere of management of these processes are given. The article substantiates the interdisciplinary and systemic methodology that determines economic growth and development, the principles of its use, the logical and semiotic nature of economic genes and genotypes, the genotypic matrix that determines economic growth and development. The block-modular and logical-structural methodology are used. *Findings* In this paper, synthesizing intermediate and final economic results are distinguished, affecting the growth and development of the economic genotype management units of the system with its structure of genotypic concepts, economic genes that. Genotypic concepts form conservative and liberal management mechanisms, their dynamics, unfolding into stages, stages, stages and cycles of world economic evolution with corresponding models of management and management. Genotypic content forms strategic goals at the macro and micro levels of development, mechanisms of strategic directed development and economic growth. Thus, the foundations of economic growth and development are hidden in the content of the economic genotype. *Originality/value* This article shows the relationship of economic growth and sustainable development with economic evolution and genetics, mechanisms for managing new sources and driving forces of growth. This paper also reveals the logical and semiotic content of economic genes and their carriers of genotypic concepts, the directions of management of these processes.

E. M. Martishin (✉)
South Russian State Polytechnic University, Novocherkassk, Russia
e-mail: martishin@bk.ru

S. V. Gladkaya · A. N. Yeletsky · T. A. Zotova · A. B. Yatsenko
Southern Federal University, Rostov-on-Don, Russia
e-mail: tazotova@sfedu.ru

A. B. Yatsenko
e-mail: abyacenko@sfedu.ru

E. I. Lazareva et al. (eds.), *Innovative Trends in International Business and Sustainable Management*, Approaches to Global Sustainability, Markets, and Governance,
https://doi.org/10.1007/978-981-19-4005-7_40

Keywords Evolutionary management · Economic genetics · Economic growth · Sustainable development

JEL Classification B52 · O10 · O11 · O20 · O43

1 Introduction

Economic growth and development (ERID) express the efficiency of the country's economy, characterize sustainable sources of improving the welfare and standard of living of the population, promote employment and social protection, scientific and technological development of the country and its economic security, solving demographic issues, protecting the environment. Of particular relevance is the search for new driving forces and stable growth resources, the identification of effective development strategies and the management of these processes.

ERIR by their nature are complementary to evolutionary processes, economic genetics, which is an integral component of evolution. Some authors of this article actively use evolutionary and DNA management for the analysis and strategic management of the regional economy of the Rostov Region. The basic blocks of DNA management—structural relationships, information support, decision-making mechanisms, motivation determine the specifics of both corporate and regional management.

At the same time, the literature poorly studies the potential of these management areas in the management of ERIR, which is due to insufficient theoretical knowledge of economic evolution and genetics processes. Economic growth in the specialized literature is mainly studied as direct analysis of the factors that causes an increase/decrease in GDP, for example, capital accumulation, STP, etc., but these components are located in the economic system, hence the systemic interaction of ERR mechanisms becomes essential. It is necessary to understand the internal processes that control the economic system in the ERIR mechanisms. The global economic crisis of 2020, including the crisis of the Russian economy, further actualizes the problem under consideration.

Our article identifies essential evolutionary-genetic and institutional patterns, principles and problems of ERIR management. The article aims to develop the content of a new concept of evolutionary genetic management and the use of its tools in managing economic growth and sustainable strategic development of the economic system, the allocation of motivational and institutional mechanisms of influence on the processes of ERR. Achieving this goal involves setting and solving the following interrelated tasks:

- Disclosure of the basic laws governing the evolution of heredity and variability of economic systems, mechanisms synthesizing the results of management;
- Identification and analysis of economic genes and genotype as factors of ERIR management;

- Identification of evolutionary and genetic tools and mechanisms of strategic management in the implementation of socio-economic development goals and priorities of socio-economic policy.

2 Materials and Method

Let us highlight the initial evolutionary-genetic methodological tools. *Economic evolution* is the irreversibility of development processes, the communicativeness of economic agents, the formation of a new one, self-organization and self-regulation, the unity of continuity and discontinuity, choice in development. *Economic genetics* studies the laws of heredity (succession) and variability (formation of a new one) in the economy. *Sustainable economic development* is associated with the genotypic mechanisms of stadial and intrastate variability that cause economic growth. Factors, mechanisms and results of growth characterize the quality of economic growth. *The economic genotype (EG)* is a set of economic genes that determines the economic system and its orientation. *The genotypic matrix (GM)* assumes a logical-structural approach in which the elements of the matrix are connected into a single structure through logical interactions. In the development of development strategies and project management, a logical-structured approach is applied.

The works of neoclassicists and Keynesians are devoted to theories of economic growth, supplemented by directions of optimization and empirical research. Modern research focuses on endogenous ERIR factors, as opposed to exogenous ones. In terms of genetic mechanisms, ERIR concepts are classified according to the nature of needs and motivation in society, industry structure, social groups, institutions, types of interactions (conservative and liberal) between enterprises (entrepreneurship), the market (competition), the state (state policy in the field of economic growth), households, etc. (Argyrous et al., 2004; Barro & Sala-i-Martin, 2010; Easterly, 2006; Lucas, 2013; Nelson et al., 2018; North, 1993; Solow, 1996; Todaro, 1997).

The evolutionary approach assumes a general scientific system methodology, since the integrity, the system evolves. The application of interdisciplinary evolutionary-genetic methodology presupposes the transformation of biological sciences into universal ideological and epistemological models of economic research.

According to research, economic genes are semantic communications, images of memory, instructions, memes (imitations), routines (rules), etc. (Arifovic, 1994; Mayevsky, 2005; Riechmann, 1999). In Mayevsky (2005), "the genotype of macro generations (a set of macro branches) is transmitted 'by inheritance' from old macro generations to young ones".

Our article substantiates the logical-semiotic nature of economic genes and genotypes. Semiotics is an interdisciplinary science that integrates natural sciences and humanities, studies the patterns of information transmission through sign structures. It is possible to build a "chain" of formation and management of iconic structures: an economic object (denotation, spheres of production-exchange-distribution-consumption)—a word (designation)—a term—systematization of terms based on a logical valence relationship—genotypic concepts—terms systematized by genotypic concepts—economic categories.

Our study also uses a *block-modular management methodology*, which assumes the grouping of processes with the allocation of control flowcharts. The block-modular approach depends on the external and internal consistency of the modules and their components, which contributes to the understanding of the structure and mechanisms of the object. Modules are relatively autonomous in the functioning and evolution of the object. The GM is based on a *logical-structural* approach, in which the elements of the matrix are connected through logical interactions in a single structure.

3 Results

From the standpoint of evolutionary and genetic management, the management of ERIR involves an active impact on genotypic structures and economic genes. The economic system consists of two EG modules. The first is the most "deep, essential timeless" level of EG, which forms genotypic concepts and their primary economic genes-categories that determine economic growth and the direction of development. The primary module of EG forms a secondary module of "long-term" economic secondary genes—economic concepts, logical judgments and conclusions, decision-making (all three logical forms are defined in the literature as concepts in a broad sense). These concepts constitute a genotypic matrix (GM) synthesizing intermediate and final economic results, social wealth.

The concepts of the primary EG module are relations:

(1) *Reproductions* that ensure reproduction and heritability of the "production–consumption" spheres. Reproduction of the production–consumption spheres is realized through genes-categories- needs-goals-means (factors of production)-etc. elements-the results of production and consumption, acting as ERR factors, which can be subject to regulation. These categories act as descriptors—key factors and mechanisms of the semantic content and structure of the concept. Concepts are forms of storage of interrelated categories. Categories are signs, models of economic processes; they store, transmit, and then "deploy" and use the primary economic information of concepts, become category genes.

(2) The *equilibrium* relations of economic actors (individual subjects and society) in the "exchange-distribution" spheres. The concept of equilibrium is the balance of power, stability, conditions and the result of the economic process. The conditions of equilibrium are the social division of labor (branch structure) with its social groups, other genes-categories of this concept, forming a social functional system of organization and regulation. Equilibrium is realized through distribution in the country's fiscal system and the mechanism of

equality in market exchange. Equilibrium (equality, socio-economic justice) is the most important condition for economic growth and development.

(3) Harmonization and optimization are formed by superposition (superimposition) of reproductive and equilibrium concepts.

The superposition (superimposition) of the reproductive and equilibrium concepts allows the superimposed processes to be simultaneously in opposite component states, produce different effects and obtain different results in activating growth and development. Heterogeneous systems are diversified and efficient. Sapir (Nelson et al., 2018). Harmonization is a binding mechanism of unity (identity) of opposites. Each named concept contributes by increasing the effect of EG, with the exclusion of one or another way, for example, because of mutations or modifications, the final effect decreases.

The mechanisms of individual reproduction form mainly conservative forms of EG with the dominance of public institutions over economic entities. Reproduction mechanisms depend on society, which provides the production with resources, norms and rules of management, contribute to the reimbursement of socially necessary costs and income generation by the producer, ensure market conditions and the development of consumer spheres, etc.

In the "old" institutionalism, a conservative system dominated by public institutions is considered. There are also some theories of conservative incentives and management, the development of production–consumption spheres—McGregor, McClelland, Herzberg, etc.

The subsequent liberal form of EG is the result of the implementation of the equilibrium concept, where public institutions are formed by economic entities and are dependent on the latter. In functional and procedural theories, theories of justice, etc., free individuals interact with equality of opportunity, competition, civil society, and control over the state. Neo-institutional theory, like liberal theories, applies the principle of methodological individualism: "individuals are primary, institutions are secondary".

The concept of harmonization and optimization of management emergently combines conservative and liberal forms—the ways that underlie the basic models of the welfare state, the principles of social justice of society. Emergent patterns theoretically coincide in content with the new institutional economic theory (NIET), which is different from the neo-institutional economic theory. The NIE combines the neo-institutional direction and the traditional (old) institutionalism of Khudokormov (2012). In terms of content, the optimization level of EG includes the meanings of modern "old" and "new" institutionalism of Brendeleva (2006). Structural functionalism presupposes the unity of structural and functional approaches, the reproduction of socio-economic elements and their functioning in a stable interaction. Porter and Lawler developed a complex theory of motivation. Thus, reproduction, balance, optimization of genotypic concepts ensures the harmonization of the interests of economic entities and society, creating incentives for development and growth, mechanisms for managing these processes.

Development management is implemented through strategic forecasting and planning, while it is important not to unambiguously or probabilistically anticipate development scenarios, but to establish, first, a logical sequence of economic events. Strategic management involves the implementation of socio-economic development goals and priorities (preferences) of socio-economic policy. Such goals at the macro and micro levels are the content of genotypic concepts—the mechanisms of reproduction, balance, harmonization and optimization of the content of the evolutionary system.

The institutions and content of genotypic concepts are deployed in stages, stages, stages and cycles of world economic evolution, setting the evolutionary and genetic orientation of countries. For example, in the process of evolution, the conservatism of primitive society replaces the liberal stage based on an equilibrium concept, relations between subjects—classes and estates. Because of the changeability of genotypic content, intra-stage stages, stages, patterns as subsystems are also determined. Thus, the "multilevel" ("multilayered", "fan") stages, stages and stages of world economic evolution are distinguished.

Genotypic concepts define economic paradigms—cost, utility, alternative-cost, as well as the corresponding business models. The logic of genotypic concepts defines three main stages of the evolution of economic doctrines:

(1) Classical political economy based on the cost paradigm of the dominant spheres of production–consumption and their reproduction;
(2) The theory of marginalism based on the utility paradigm of the dominant spheres of exchange-distribution of the equilibrium concept;
(3) The content of the directions of modern economic theory.

GM is the second systemic economic block, formed through the mechanisms of economic morphogenesis, replication, transcription and translation, through economic paradigms. Let us single out the following properties of the GM, which determine the effective control of the analyzed processes. The appendix presents the first level of the GM. The first two digits of the designation of concepts mean the numbers of levels and rows in the matrix, the subsequent digits are the numbers of columns.

The first property of GM. Economic concepts (in a broad sense) GM are formed by concepts and categories of EG. For example, the concept of use-value (quality of goods). The value paradigm is formed by the norms and rules (technological and institutional) of the production–consumption spheres of the reproductive concept. First of all, needs, goals, means, values-results determine quality. Market relations, the activities of the equilibrium concept state, as well as the industry structure (industries are producers and consumers of products), the structure of social groups with their incomes, institutions, influence the quality of goods. The quality-cost (cost) ratio plays an important role.

The second property of GM. In GM, there is a periodicity of the formation of economic values, their logical forms following the logic of economic paradigms. Every third group of logical forms represents unity with the two preceding ones. For example, the optimum of consumer choice (1.9.1.9) is the unity of budget constraints

(1.7.1.7) and indifference curves (1.8.1.8). Hence, the GM has some properties of a fan matrix.

The third property of GM. There are "horizontal" interrelations and interactions of economic processes. First, a "horizontal" increment is created. Let us take this as an example of the formation of GDP. At the first level of the GM, qualitative and quantitative characteristics of public wealth are distinguished, their measure in the form of money. The use-value (1.2.1.2) in interaction with the value (1.2.2.2) determines the function of money as a means of circulation (1.2.3.2)—the initial factor in the formation of GDP (4.2.3.2). At the second level of the GM, consumption and accumulation funds are formed (2.2.3.2)—the most important components of GDP, which depend primarily on property institutions (2.2.1.2) and capital volumes (2.2.2.2). At the 3rd level of the GM, functional forms of capital (monetary, productive and commodity) (3.2.1.2), real capital turnover—full reimbursement of capital at cost and in a kind, completion of the cycle of turnover of invested capital (3.2.2.2) form the conditions for the realization of the total social product (3.2.3.2) carried out intersectoral balance, the "input–output" method. At the 4th level of the GM, GDP, national income and personal disposable income (4.2.3.2) are horizontally directly determined by income generation mechanisms in the factor markets (4.2.1.2) and income redistribution (4.2.2.2).

The fourth property of GM. There are "vertical" interrelations of economic processes in GM. The LM can represent the interaction of the first and second levels of the GM-IS model, which reflects the relationship of equilibrium money and commodity markets. Money market: L is the demand for money at income Y; M is the supply of money. Equilibrium in commodity markets: equality of aggregate supply (Y) to aggregate demand (private sector consumption (C), private investment (I), public spending (G)). In the unity of these markets and taking into account the MOB, an equilibrium volume of output/income (Y) is formed in the form of SOP with the structure of consumption (C), investment (I), government spending (G), net exports (Xn).

Thus, the function of money as a means of circulation (1.2.3.2) of the first level of GM in unity with the funds of consumption and accumulation (2.2.3.2) of the second level of GM form the conditions for the realization of the aggregate social product (3.2.3.2) of the third level. Moreover, the funds of consumption and accumulation (2.2.3.2) of the second level of GM in unity with the conditions for the realization of the aggregate social product (3.2.3.2) of the third level form GDP, other concepts (4.2.3.2). Economic processes and their logical-genetic forms act in interrelation and development. As we have seen, the matrix mechanisms identify the systemic factors that most affect GDP growth. At the same time, GDP and all its named growth factors belong to the value paradigm with the dominance of production–consumption spheres, which implies the need to develop new indicators of economic growth following subsequent economic paradigms of evolutionary management.

4 Conclusion

From the standpoint of evolutionary management, the management of economic growth and sustainable development involves the activation and stimulation of genotypic structures and economic genes, the elimination of socio-economic negative mutations, if any. Genotypic concepts and their primary economic genes-categories define secondary factors and mechanisms of economic growth and directed development. Genotypic concepts through value, utility, alternative-value paradigms and genetic mechanisms form logical signs—economic concepts, logical judgments and conclusions, decision-making reflecting GM processes, synthesizing intermediate and final economic results, "chains" of social wealth, their growth. The foundations of economic growth and development are hidden in the content of the EG. The formation of social wealth, its logical and semiotic forms is carried out in the GM horizontally and vertically because of the progressive and cumulative effect, sequencing of economic genes—their logical sequence affecting the productivity and dynamics of economic systems. In addition to GDP, it is necessary to move to new indicators of economic growth and development following evolutionary and genetic patterns and mechanisms.

Application

Genotypic matrix of the economic system (first level)

* 1.1.1.1—commodity wealth (value); 1.2.1.2—use value; 1.3.1.3—exchange value; 1.4.1.4—economic benefits (usefulness); 1.5.1.5—General 1.6.1.6—marginal utility; 1.7.1.7—budget restriction (alternative cost); 1.8.1.8—indifference curves; 1.9.1.9—optimum consumer choice;
* 1.1.2.1—quantity and 1.2.2.2—value; 1.3.2.3—quantitative value relations; 1.4.2.4—demand and 1.5.2.5—supply; 1.6.2.6—their equilibrium; 1.7.2.7—individual demand (effects); 1.8.2.8—market demand and elasticity; 1.9.2.9—consumer surplus;
* 1.1.3.1—money as a measure of value; 1.2.3.2—means of circulation and 1.3.3.3—preservation of value; 1.4.3.4—quantities of demand for money and 1.5.3.5—money supply; 1.6.3.6—equilibrium of quantities of demand and supply of money; 1.7.3.7—partial demand for cash balances (effects); 1.8.3.8—total demand for cash balances and monetary aggregates; 1.9.3.9—optimum of cash reserves.

Acknowledgements The chapter was prepared with the financial support of the Russian Fund for Fundamental Research. Grant of the RFFR 20-010-00323-A.

References

Argyrous, G., Forstater, M., & Mongiovi, G. (2004). *Growth, distribution, and effective demand.*

Arifovic, J. (1994). Genetic algorithm learning and the cobweb model. *Journal of Economic Dynamics and Control, 18*(1), 3–28.

Barro, R., & Sala-i-Martin, H. (2010). *Economic growth.* Binom. Laboratory of knowledge.

Brendeleva, E. (2006). *Neoinstitutional economic theory* (pp. 20–23). Business and Service.

Easterly, W. (2006). *In search of growth: The adventures and misadventures of economists in the tropics.* Institute for Integrated Strategic Studies.

Khudokormov, A. (2012). *Economic theory: The latest trends of the West* (255 pp). INFRA-M.

Lucas, R. (2013). *Lectures on economic growth.* Gaidar Institute Publishing House.

Mayevsky, V. (2005). Evolutionary macroeconomic theory. In D. S. Lviv (Ed.), Introduction to Institutional Economics (618 pp). Ekonomika.

North, D. (1993). *Institutions and economic growth: A historical introduction* (Thesis) 1(2)

Nelson, R., Dosi, G., Helfat, C., Pyka, A., Winter, S., Saviotti, P., Lee, K., Malerba, F., & Dopfer, K. (2018). Modern evolutionary economics: An overview Cambridge (282 pp). Cambridge University Press.

Riechmann, T. (1999). Learning and behavioural stability an economic interpretation of genetic algorithms. *Journal of Evolutionary Economics, 9*(2), 225–242.

Sapir, J. (2001). *On the economic theory of heterogeneous systems: Experience in the study of a decentralized economy* (pp. 119–121). Higher School of Economics.

Solow, R. M. (1996). Prospects of the theory of growth. *The world economy and international relations, 8.*

Todaro, M. (1997). *Economic development.* MSU, UNITY.

Open Innovations in Modern Radical Innovation Activity

Irina N. Shvetsova, Irina S. Zinovyeva, Sergei N. Yashin, Oksana V. Pliusnina, and Natalya Y. Veselova

Abstract The article is devoted to the study of the features of the modern innovation process and the identification of key factors that ensure successful breakthrough innovation activity. The main focus of the research is aimed at identifying the role of open innovations in the activities of large and small organizations, as well as analyzing modern types of organizational structures for generating various types of innovations. The purpose of the article is to identify the optimal parameters of the activities of organizations that correspond to the features of the modern radical innovation process. As a result of the conducted research, the authors determined that the main share of breakthrough innovations falls on small and medium-sized enterprises, and also identified the main reasons for this pattern. The role of the concept of open innovation in innovation activity at the level of startups and mature enterprises is investigated. It is concluded that it is necessary to use it in the implementation of breakthrough projects. For supporting activities, the implementation of the provisions of this concept is not so important. A new type of matrix organizational structure, optimal for radical innovation activity, is presented. It is based on the synthesis of the provisions of open innovations and well-known types of organizational structures, including network and matrix structures.

I. N. Shvetsova (✉)
Pitirim Sorokin Syktyvkar State University, Syktyvkar, Russia
e-mail: economresearch@mail.ru; irshv@mail.ru

I. S. Zinovyeva
Voronezh State University of Forestry and Technologies Named After G.F. Morozov, Voronezh, Russia

S. N. Yashin
Lobachevsky State University Nizhny Novgorod, Nizhny Novgorod, Russia

O. V. Pliusnina
Ukhta State Technical University, Ukhta, Republic of Komi, Russia

N. Y. Veselova
Kuban State Technological University, Krasnodar, Russia
e-mail: veselova111@inbox.ru

E. I. Lazareva et al. (eds.), *Innovative Trends in International Business and Sustainable Management*, Approaches to Global Sustainability, Markets, and Governance,
https://doi.org/10.1007/978-981-19-4005-7_41

Keywords Radical innovation · Incremental innovation · Network structure · Open innovation · Matrix organizational structure

JEL Classification O31 · O32

1 Introduction

Incremental and breakthrough (radical) innovations have pronounced differences like their impact on the market. If incremental innovations are aimed at improving and developing existing markets, then breakthrough innovations by their appearance destroy markets and create new ones in their place. The processes of their implementation are also quite different, manifested at all stages of development and commercialization. For example, breakthrough products and services are aimed at creating new markets, respectively, at developing new market needs. Consequently, forecasting demand is a more complex task that cannot be solved with the help of traditional marketing tools.

The leaders of most innovative organizations understand this problem and try to develop specialized approaches and practices for managing breakthrough developments. For example, XEROX Corporation has founded a separate PARC laboratory to generate breakthrough innovations, where the development and commercialization processes are radically different from those that were established in the main structure. Many other companies have followed the same path. It is noteworthy that the key technologies and products in the laboratory were developed more than 20 years ago, but since then the generation of radical innovations in the laboratory has stopped. Also, companies are increasingly applying the concept of open innovation to achieve disruptive business changes (Stefik & Stefik, 2004; Vinokurova & Kapoor, 2020).

In the field of innovation, there is a tendency to slow down breakthrough activities carried out by large enterprises. Today, most of the transformational innovations are implemented by small teams of scientists and innovators in the form of startups. At the same time, many of the large companies demonstrate success in incremental innovations. Thus, the importance of finding and applying new management approaches to breakthrough innovations is becoming more and more obvious.

The nature of innovation activity has also undergone significant changes during the development of digital technologies. Innovative enterprises, both large and small, are increasingly cooperating to jointly implement innovative projects, which has led to the formation of the concept of open innovation.

2 Theoretical Foundations of the Study

Davila, Epstein and Shelton (Beugelsdijk & Jindra, 2018) developed a typology of innovations based on two parameters: novelty in technology and novelty in the business model. This approach is a priority in the article for designating breakthrough innovations.

Amaral and Uzzi (Amaral & Uzzi, 2007) conducted a study on the potential of management based on achievements in the theory of complex networks. The potential of network and virtual structures in the context of innovation was studied by Pouwels and Koster (2017). The assumption that most organizations will be created based on network and virtual structures is justified by Vecchi et al. (2021).

A significant contribution to the addition of the concept of network and virtual organizations was made by Gummesson. The researcher noted the inevitability of the transition of the corporate world to new organizational structures due to the slowness and "clumsiness" of the traditional ones. The trend is clearly manifested in the practice of modern business, which is demonstrated in this work (Gummesson, 2011).

The role of digital transformation in changing modern organizational structures was studied by Mirković et al. (2019). The lean startup methodology developed by Ries (2011), supplemented by Maurya (2012), plays an important role in modern innovative business, allowing to significantly reduce resource costs for development. The work of Yordanova (2018) explores the possibilities of applying the methodology in radical innovation.

3 Methodology

The purpose of the research is to identify optimal structural and other parameters of organizations' activities that correspond to the features of the modern radical innovation process.

Research objectives:

1. Testing the hypothesis that the main contribution to the creation and implementation of radical innovations in the modern innovation environment is made by small groups of developers (startups);
2. Determination of the causes of the revealed regularity;
3. Identification of the role of open innovation in radical innovation;
4. Drawing up a new organizational structure scheme that is optimal for the systematic implementation of radical innovative projects by large enterprises.

4 Methods

The authors selected a list of key innovations for the period since 2000 to test the hypothesis. The ratio of innovations developed by startups and mature innovative enterprises has been calculated. The reasons for this pattern are revealed based on analytical methods and a review of the relevant literature.

The authors reveal the role of open innovations in the activities of small and large enterprises.

The differences between radical and incremental innovations are outlined, the role of open innovations in the modern radical innovation process is investigated. This aspect of the research is implemented mainly on the basis of the comparative method of cognition.

At the final stage, a new type of organizational structure has been created that best meets the goals of radical innovation. It is based on the synthesis of existing organizational structures and provisions of the open innovation concept.

5 Results

The Independent journal has compiled a list of 20 innovative technologies and products that have determined the further development of innovations since the 2000s. In robotics, BigDog became the first walking robots used for practical purposes, and SmartThings introduced the first full-fledged automation system for household devices with voice control (Cuthbertson & Griffin, 2021; Xu et al., 2019). We have indicated the most breakthrough products for this period developed within the framework of these technologies (Table 1).

The following items are not presented in the table from this list: quantum computers, as they have unproven efficiency; Bitcoin (not subject to commercialization); and many different companies and scientific groups took an equal part in the development of 3G/4G/5G technologies, artificial intelligence and biometrics. It should be noted that the scale of development companies during the creation of breakthrough products is taken into account. For example, Amazon Corporation was just starting its activities in 2001 (Bruer & Brake, 2021).

Table 1 shows that only 3 out of 15 innovations were developed by large corporations (20% of the total). The remaining 12 were created by small and medium-sized companies. Half of them were subsequently absorbed by corporations. Startups that have not undergone acquisitions have subsequently grown to the scale of large companies. Thus, large innovative organizations occupy an ever-smaller share in radical innovation activities. This may be due to the following reasons:

- Intensive horizontal connections, opportunities for researchers to find like-minded people in startup communities;
- Availability of a variety of programs for startups: incubators, accelerators and others;
- Simplified access to financing, including venture capital and crowdfunding;
- High demand for innovation from business;
- A significant share of innovation activity in the modern world is concentrated in the field of programming. Mastering this area of knowledge does not require specialized education, which makes it more accessible to potential innovators;

Table 1 Key innovations over the past 20 years and development companies

Year	Technology (product)	Developers	Corporation/SME	Has it undergone a takeover?	The buyer company
2001	Online marketplace (amazon.com)	Amazon	SME	✖	
2001	Wikipedia	Wikimedia foundation	SME	✖	
2002	Online gaming (Xbox)	Microsoft	Corporation		
2003	Skype	Skype	SME	✔	Microsoft
2004	Social media (Facebook.com)	Facebook	SME	✖	
2004	Always-available maps (Google Maps)	Lars & Jens Rasmussen	SME	✔	Google
2005	YouTube	YouTube	SME	✔	Google
2005	Robotics (BigDog)	Boston dynamics	SME	✔	Google, Hyundai
2007	iPhone	Apple	Corporation		
2007	Streaming (Netflix)	Netflix	SME	✖	
2009	Gig economy (Uber)	Uber Technologies	SME	✖	
2008	Electric cars (Tesla Roadster)	Tesla	SME	✖	
2012	Smart home (SmartThings)	SmartThings	SME	✔	Samsung
2012	VR and AR (Oculus Rift)	Oculus	SME	✔	Meta
2012	Reusable rockets (Starship)	SpaceX	Corporation		

Source Compiled by the authors

- Popularization of the practice of "lean startup" based on the methodology of introducing new products with minimal resource costs. The practice is based on systematic testing of minimally viable products (MVP) to determine market needs and allows small groups with limited resources to compete with corporations;
- In the field of innovation, there is a pronounced specialization in various industries. For the development and production of complex products, there is no need to produce each component independently, since most components are developed by specialized firms. This greatly simplifies the product development process

but requires more intensive inter-organizational interaction (Andergassen et al., 2018).

Product development is becoming an increasingly complex task in terms of technology, requiring the participation of many different institutional players. Large organizations are in a much more vulnerable position today than they were a few decades ago when identifying potential threats to business was not such a difficult task. The data from the report on corporate innovations in the digital age confirm this. According to the report, the life cycle of the largest companies is shrinking over time. Thus, the average life cycle of organizations listed in the S&P500 index was more than 50 years in 1960, more than 30 years in 1980, and only about 20 years in 2010. The trend continues to this day (Thompson et al., 2018).

To adapt to changing business conditions, modern companies are increasingly adhering to the strategy of open innovation. Open innovations represent a new business paradigm, which consists in active interaction and information exchange between various participants in the innovation process. Open innovations imply the rejection of established approaches to development, which have traditionally been conducted within individual companies in conditions of high secrecy. Marais and Shute (2009) distinguish the following models of open innovation:

- Product platforming. The idea is to create a partially completed product in order to provide a framework and a set of tools for various users. Thus, the task of product development is solved by expanding its functionality;
- Contests of ideas. Involvement of participants outside the organization in the process of generating ideas, including by crowdsourcing. In addition to accumulating promising innovative ideas, such a measure allows a deeper understanding of the needs of the market;
- Active interaction and information exchange with suppliers and buyers;
- Joint research and development with other participants in the field of innovation. This model, unlike product platforming, assumes the controlling role of the organization that initiates the project. This model occupies an important place in the practice of inter-company interaction;
- Innovative networks. The organization creates a network of participants in the innovation process, offering rewards for solving various tasks. The task of the participants is to solve specific research or design tasks, unlike the idea contest, and not to initiate a new project.

More and more organizations are using these tools to overcome the challenges faced by the innovation sector as a whole. The development of digital technologies, as well as the accumulated experience of implementing open innovation models in practice, allow organizations to attract carriers of missing competencies and knowledge to implement new innovative projects.

Small and medium-sized enterprises are the most active followers of the open innovation strategy. Due to the limited set of competencies of the staff, they are forced to interact with other participants in the field of innovation. The advantage of small enterprises is greater mobility and flexibility of organizational structures. The introduction of open innovation practices for large companies is fraught with certain difficulties, and a significant proportion of modern corporations implement closed innovation strategies.

Business theorists and practitioners do not give an unambiguous answer to the question of the most effective innovation strategy for large companies—open, closed or hybrid. For example, Apple, which is one of the innovative leaders, adheres to the strategy of closed innovation. It is known that the development processes in the company proceed in conditions of high secrecy. By contrast, the rival company Xiaomi actively applies the practice of open innovation. The company demonstrates success in the field of electronics manufacturing, expanding its presence in the market (Lajoso et al., 2020).

Incremental and radical innovation processes have significant differences. High performance in supportive activities is poorly correlated with performance in radical innovations. Accordingly, the assessment of the role of open innovation in radical activity requires the study of these differences (Deffains-Crapsky & Sudolska, 2014).

The main features of incremental innovation:

- new to the firm;
- builds upon existing knowledge and resources;
- exploits existing technology, utilizes existing competencies and processes;
- enhances existing organizational competencies;
- low uncertainty and risk;
- operates within the existing business model;
- a relatively small change in performance;
- improves competitiveness within current markets or industries;
- perpetuates existing social practices;
- is the lifeblood of innovation.

The main features of radical innovation:

- new to the world;
- requires new knowledge and resources;
- explores new technology, requires new competencies, skills or expertise;
- destroys existing organizational competencies that lose their value;
- high uncertainty and risk;
- requires a change in the business model;
- step-change in performance;
- creates a dramatic change that transforms existing markets or industries, or creates new ones;
- necessitates social and systemic change;
- appears relatively rare.

Radical innovations require new organizational competencies and skills while existing competencies are destroyed. Incremental innovations are created based on existing knowledge and processes. The traditional approach to solving the problem of developing new competencies lies in the policy of mergers and acquisitions, as well as the formation of additional divisions with the involvement of a large number of relevant specialists. This approach most often leads to an increase in the centralization of management and the formalization of management procedures.

Incremental innovations are created based on existing processes and knowledge, which indicates a lesser role of the open innovation strategy in this activity (Farhana & Swietlicki, 2020). Peris-Ortiz et al. (2018) confirm this thesis, noting a more pronounced positive impact of open innovations on radical innovations than on incremental ones.

A radical innovation process is characterized by high uncertainty, and its development is associated with high risks. It is obvious that standardized R&D processes created for innovations with high planning and predictability of final results cannot meet the goals of radical innovations. For the implementation of such projects, the factors of excessive centralization and bureaucratization of management are disastrous. For this reason, project teams should have a high level of independence and flexible work processes. This is confirmed by the studies of (Beugelsdijk & Jindra, 2018; Jugend et al., 2018; Ladikas et al., 2019).

Thus, large innovative organizations should ensure high independence of research units in order to preserve the ability to radically innovate. Each of the research units should be a carrier of certain competencies. This implies a transition to the network principle of organizational activity. Divisions should act as independent companies, have the authority to initiate their own projects and establish horizontal links with other companies, both inside and outside the parent organization (startups, universities, corporations). New project groups are formed through such interaction.

Such an approach to the organization of interaction forms a network organizational structure. These structures are divided into two types: the first type involves the interaction of independent units within a single corporation; the second type of independent units establishes interaction with other firms and universities. Given that radical innovative projects require new knowledge and competencies, the second type of structure is more suitable for their implementation on a systematic basis (Fig. 1).

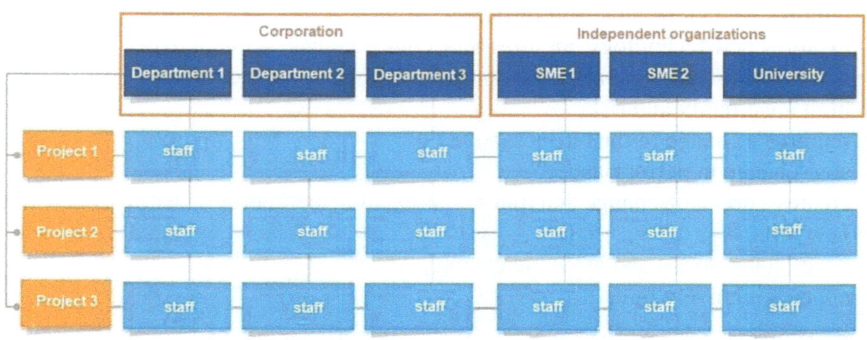

Fig. 1 Matrix organizational structure based on the network principle of inter-company interaction. *Source* Compiled by the authors

This form of inter-company interaction develops into a new format of a matrix organizational structure, which has three distinctive features, in comparison with traditional matrix structures:

- It includes not only divisions of one organization, but a wide network of enterprises of various sizes, research centers and universities operating based on the principle of open innovation;
- These divisions and organizations are allocated mainly not on a functional basis, but the principle of specialization in a certain part of the innovations being created;
- These business units are not directly subordinate to the top management of corporations but act as independent structures cooperating based on agreements.

An example of a structure based on the network principle of work and implementing an open innovation strategy is the 3 M company. The scope of its activities covers many industries, including electronics, transport, consumer goods and many others. At the same time, each of the divisions acts as independent structure. Chief Technical Director, Palenski describes the scheme of their interaction on the example of creating a new type of sandpaper. He notes that of the seven technologies that were required to create it, only two were developed in the abrasive materials division. He emphasizes the company's commitment to open innovation: corporate laboratories constantly attract new employees and technologies from universities and other sources, and the company itself works closely with customers (Coster, 2017; Palensky, 2011).

6 Conclusions

The authors have established that open innovations are an integral component of modern breakthrough innovation. The complexity of the innovation process has led to the fact that small and medium-sized enterprises are forced to cooperate with many other participants in the innovation sphere to implement complex projects and use various models of open innovation. Their main advantage is the pronounced mobility and flexibility of the organizational structure.

Less mobile and more susceptible to bureaucratization, innovative corporations are experiencing difficulties with the implementation of such projects. The authors concluded that when creating a network of decentralized enterprises, divided based on industry specialization, and not according to the principles of functional or divisional division, corporations can establish the implementation of breakthrough projects on a systematic basis. The practice of open innovation is no less important for large companies than for startups since each breakthrough project requires new competencies for the organization.

The analysis of business practice shows that the application of the described provisions takes place in the activities of individual large companies. The authors described the scheme of inter-organizational interaction of these enterprises using the example of an improved version of the matrix organizational structure. Such a scheme should serve as a model for conducting breakthrough activities in the modern corporate world.

The results of the study should be taken into account by the management of both large and small enterprises. The authors determined that successful startups, as a rule, grow to the scale of corporations. At the first stages of the existence of these companies, the principles of developing a network organizational structure should be laid down. Carrying out appropriate transformations in mature organizations is a much more complex task that requires structural and cultural changes. This is fraught with the loss of many strengths of these enterprises that affect the generation of incremental innovations, or other aspects of their activities.

Management should be aware that each type of organizational structure has its own advantages in innovation. However, an additional advantage of network structures is a more pronounced diversification by industry activity. The absence of a pronounced monolithic structure makes it possible to compensate for failures occurring within one of the autonomous business units, due to the successful activities of others. This is an important factor in the sustainability of the entire organization in the long term.

References

Amaral, L., & Uzzi, B. (2007). Complex systems—a new paradigm for the integrative study of management, physical, and technological systems. *Management Science, 53*(7), 1033–1035.

Andergassen, R., Nardini, F., & Ricottilli, M. (2018). Innovation, specialization and growth in a model of structural change. *The BE Journal of Macroeconomics, 18*(2). https://doi.org/10.1515/bejm-2017-0095

Beugelsdijk, S., & Jindra, B. (2018). Product innovation and decision-making autonomy in subsidiaries of multinational companies. *Journal of World Business, 53*(4), 529–539.

Bruer, A., & Brake, D. (2021). Mapping the 5G Leadership Landscape: The Impact of Global Telecommunications Standard Setting on US Strategy and Policy. https://papers.ssrn.com/sol3/papers.cfm?abstract_id=3898242. Accessed November 19, 2021.

Coster, J. (2017). Lessons from 3M Corporation: managing innovation over time and overcoming the innovator's dilemma. https://www.semanticscholar.org/paper/Lessons-from-3M-Corporation%3A-managing-innovation-Coster/2a4804458373b20175cbfcc8bc01a94597b461b2. Accessed November 19, 2021.

Cuthbertson, A., & Griffin, A. (2021). The 20 Technologies That Defined the First 20 Years of the 21st Century. https://www.independent.co.uk/life-style/gadgets-and-tech/features/technology-bitcoin-iphone-tesla-ai-b1821678.html. Accessed November 19, 2021.

Deffains-Crapsky, C., & Sudolska, A. (2014). Radical innovation and early-stage financing gaps: Equity-based crowdfunding challenges. *Journal of Positive Management, 5*(2), 3–19.

Farhana, M., & Swietlicki, D. (2020). Dynamic capabilities impact on innovation: Niche market and startups. *Journal of Technology Management & Innovation, 15*(3), 83–96.

Gummesson, E. (2011). *Total relationship marketing*. Routledge.

Jugend, D., Pimenta, M., Gobbo, J., Jr., & Ribeiro de Araujo, T. (2018). The role of cross-functional integration in new product development: Differences between incremental and radical innovation projects. *Innovation, 20*(1), 42–60.

Ladikas, M., Hennen, L., Hahn, J., & Kulakov, P. (2019). Responsible research and innovation in Germany–between sustainability and autonomy. *Journal of Responsible Innovation, 6*(3), 346–352.

Lajoso, J., Albuquerque, J., Sousa, A., & Mineiro, R. (2020). Closed against open innovation: A comparison between Apple and Xiaomi. In *World conference on Information Systems And Technologies* (pp. 436–448). Springer.

Marais, S., & Schutte, C. (2009). The development of open innovation models to assist the innovation process. In *Proceedings of the 23rd Annual SAIIE Conference* (Vol. 96). Roodevallei.

Maurya, A. (2012). Running lean: iterate from plan A to a plan that works. O'Reilly Media, Inc. https://www.oreilly.com/pub/pr/2988. Accessed November 19, 2021.

Mirković, V., Lazarević, S., Lukić, J., & Vojinovic, Z. (2019). Key characteristics of organizational structure that supports digital transformation. In *Proceedings of the International Scientific Conference Strategic Management and Decision Support Systems in Strategic Management* (pp. 256–261). Faculty of Economics, Subotica.

Palensky, F. (2011). 3M's Open Innovation. https://www.strategy-business.com/article/00078. Accessed November 19, 2021.

Peris-Ortiz, M., Devece-Carañana, C., & Navarro-Garcia, A. (2018). Organizational learning capability and open innovation. *Management Decision.* https://doi.org/10.1108/MD-02-2017-0173

Pouwels, I., Koster, F. (2017). Inter-organizational cooperation and organizational innovativeness. A comparative study. *International Journal of Innovation Science, 9*(2). https://doi.org/10.1108/IJIS-01-2017-0003

Ries, E. (2011). *The lean startup: How today's entrepreneurs use continuous innovation to create radically successful businesses.* Crown Publishing Group.

Stefik, M., & Stefik, B. (2004). *Breakthrough: Stories and strategies of radical innovation.* MIT Press.

Thompson, N., Bonnet, D., & Ye, I. (2018). *The foundations of corporate innovation in the digital age.* MIT Press.

Vecchi, A., Feola, R., Crudele, Ch., & DellaPiana, B. (2021). Talent management processes and outcomes in a virtual organization. *Business Process Management Journal.* https://doi.org/10.1108/BPMJ-06-2019-0227

Vinokurova, N., & Kapoor, R. (2020). Converting inventions into innovations in large firms: How inventors at Xerox navigated the innovation process to commercialize their ideas. *Strategic Management Journal, 41*(13), 2372–2399.

Xu, Z., Wang, A., Zhao, A., & Zhai, B. (2019). Comparative studies of robot navigation. In *Proceedings of the International Conference on Natural Computation, Fuzzy Systems and Knowledge Discovery* (pp. 301–310). Springer, Cham.

Yordanova, Z. (2018). Lean Startup method hampers breakthrough innovations and company's innovativeness. *International Journal of Innovation and Technology Management*, 15(2). https://doi.org/10.1142/S0219877018500128

The Introduction of a Value-Oriented Approach to the Management of Modern Universities in the Formation of Human Capital in an Innovative Economy

Elena Y. Polyakova

Abstract Modern universities have a significant impact on the formation of human capital. Human capital, on the one hand, is a reflection of accumulated knowledge, social and personality attributes, labor skills that are necessary for participation in social and economic activities, on the other hand, it is the result of continuous self-development and vocational training. The dynamic development of society and the economy puts forward new requirements for knowledge, skills and abilities, which gives a powerful impetus to the development of universities themselves. The introduction of a value-oriented approach to the management of modern universities makes it possible to establish a new holistic university environment aimed at the formation of intellectual abilities and practical skills in the innovative economy.

Keywords Target audience · Values · Value-oriented management · Human capital

JEL Classification M31 · L31 · O15 · O35

1 Introduction

Human capital is the basis for the formation and development of an innovative economy. The transformation of the economic system is impossible without a complex of knowledge, skills, and skills of professionals in various industries and fields of activity. Undoubtedly, the main role in the formation of a new generation of qualified personnel is played by modern universities. In turn, universities, in a rapidly changing reality, must provide a timely response to historically justified socio-cultural changes and demands, that is, apply a value-based approach when forming the mission, strategic objectives and priorities for the development of higher education.

E. Y. Polyakova (✉)
Southern Federal University, Rostov-on-Don, Russia
e-mail: epolyakova@sfedu.ru

E. I. Lazareva et al. (eds.), *Innovative Trends in International Business and Sustainable Management*, Approaches to Global Sustainability, Markets, and Governance,
https://doi.org/10.1007/978-981-19-4005-7_42

Effective management plays a very important role in solving this problem and is considered as a key factor in the strategic development of the university. The introduction of a value-oriented approach to the management of modern universities will allow solving in more detail the issues of training graduates of a new generation, meeting the qualification requirements for the teaching staff, interaction with professional and educational communities, etc.

2 Methodology

The value-oriented approach to the consideration of the issue of marketing interaction in the management of modern universities is quite new.

Value orientation to the needs and demands of the target audience, that is, an assessment of the situation from the perspective of consumers, becomes possible when referring to the 4C model (Cost; Customer wants and needs; Communication; Convenience). This model was first proposed by Robert F. Lauterborn in 1990 (Schullz et al., 1993). As part of this approach, the focus of marketing efforts is shifted to the consumer. In our opinion, this method of building marketing relations makes it possible to consider consumer value as a central link in the management models of modern universities.

A modern university forms its mission, unique offer and unique position based on the values of the target audience.

It should be borne in mind that modern universities have a wide range of contact audiences, which also need to be studied in order to form a value proposition for them.

At the same time, it is necessary to take into account the specifics of the educational service itself, which is a product of intellectual labor aimed at the formation of socially significant benefits. This means that it includes not only learning, but also the formation of a human personality within the socio-cultural development of society at a given historical moment. According to this, universities, on the one hand, are a platform for the formation of social values and norms, and on the other hand, universities should rely on the values of target groups and contact audiences.

Taking into account D. Keller's "ARCS" model (Keller, 2000), according to which the educational process should be based on such components as Attention, Relevance, Confidence, Satisfaction, as well as the so-called "Awareness Ladder" invented by B. Hunt, which is a marketing tool that allows analyzing the client's path by levels of awareness about solving his problem, it is possible to determine points of contact with target groups at various stages of interaction using a value-oriented approach to the management of modern universities. The system of interaction between the university and its contact groups and target audiences will allow to determine their possible "points of contact", and will also allow to create value propositions, to respond to ongoing demands, thereby forming a flexible ecosystem.

To clarify professional and personal values, it is proposed to use the method "Value orientations", developed by the American psychologist Milton Rokeach, aimed at studying the value-motivational sphere of personality (Rokeach, 1973). The results obtained are a reflection of the most powerful motivation and engagement, and this determines their significance within the framework of the value approach and management of the educational organization.

In addition, these results should be taken into account when building a new management paradigm, according to which universities should act as a knowledge center for innovation and reproduction of human capital for an innovative economy.

3 Results

In the university management complex, quality is characterized by a number of indicators:

- goal setting;
- versatility;
- the quality of decision-making;
- monitoring the implementation of decisions;
- motivation and stimulation system;
- speed of information exchange;
- delegation of authority;
- personnel policy;
- communication;
- marketing thinking;
- partnership and cooperation, etc.

The value-oriented management is based on the values of the consumer, that is, a web of values is formed. Intertwining the values of the participants of this organism forms the core of the values of the organization, reflected in the mission and strategic goal of the university.

Marketing research to identify existing needs, trend analysis and identification of emerging needs, analysis of the marketing environment provide value coordinates of development and determine the range of contact groups and target audiences interested in cooperation and promotion of the university, their key needs and demands. Stakeholders are flows of values that are formed in the university itself (internal environment) and external to the university (external environment) (Freeman, 1984).

The internal structure of the university includes:

- students of all levels and forms of education and their parents (legal representatives);
- teaching staff;
- administrative staff;
- research staff;
- training and support staff.

The external environment of the university covers all socio-economic spheres involved in the formation of human capital:

- the state that regulates the normative and legal activities of the university, establishes the order for the training of specialists and quotas of admission to state-financed places;
- regional executive authorities and local self-government bodies;
- employers interested in obtaining competent specialists;
- students, applicants and their parents who are at the stage of choosing an educational institution;
- educational institutions;
- public organizations and associations.

A value-oriented approach to university management should take into account the values of both employees and stakeholders in order to prevent a gap in value perception when the most important values are ignored by groups interested in interacting with the university, participating in the formation of human capital.

As part of the marketing research conducted in 2020 on the perception of brand values of the Faculty of Management, a survey was conducted with the participation of undergraduate students and teaching staff of the Southern Federal University (SFU), representatives of the business community, applicants (Bozhenko & Polyakova, 2020). Proportional sampling was used. The working tool was a questionnaire. A total of 138 people were interviewed. The questionnaire, along with other questions, included a question on identifying the respondents' value orientations: "In your opinion, what are the priority values of modern higher education (no more than three)?".

According to the answers, the main common values of university education characteristic of all groups of respondents are: knowledge in the professional field, the ability to solve professional problems (89.8%), qualified teaching staff (71.4%), employment opportunities for graduates (53.1%), material and technical base and infrastructure (42.9%), the level of organization of university student life (42.9%), flexible organization of the educational process (40.8%).

Based on the results obtained, it is possible to form a value proposition, focusing marketing efforts on the key values of the main interested groups of interaction.

To strengthen the position of the university, it is obvious that this gap should be minimal, i.e. the perception of employees and the perception of stakeholders of the image of the corporate brand of the structural unit should coincide.

To do this, close attention must be paid to:

- the marketing analysis and monitoring of stakeholders' positions, covering the internal and external environment of the university;
- the communications and PR—interaction with stakeholders;
- the interests and values of stakeholders when planning the activities of the university;
- cooperation and co-creation, including at the decision-making level.

4 Conclusion

A modern university forms its mission based on the values of the target audience, forms a unique offer and unique positioning based on the key values of stakeholders.

A value-oriented approach in university management ensures that the behavior of employees and stakeholders corresponds to the brand values, which provides the dominant role of the brand and marketing thinking in the strategy of the organization.

Marketing interaction allows us to consider value as a central link in the management models of modern universities, while the focus of marketing efforts shifts to the consumer.

The introduction of a value-oriented approach to the management of modern universities makes it possible to establish a new holistic university environment aimed at the formation of intellectual abilities and practical skills in the innovative economy.

References

Bozhenko, E. S., & Polyakova, E. Y. (2020). Internal branding and self-identification of an organization in the market (on the example of higher education). *Economics and Entrepreneurship, 12*(125), 1169–1174. https://doi.org/10.34925/EIP.2021.125.12.234

Freeman, R. E. (1984). *Strategic management: A stakeholder approach*. Cambridge University Press.

Keller, J. M. (2000). How to integrate learner motivation planning into lesson planning: The ARCS model approach. In H. D. Stolovitch & E. J. Keeps (Eds.), *Handbook of human performance technology* (2nd ed.). Jossey-Bass Pfeiffer.

Rokeach, M. (1973). *The nature of human values*. The Free Press.

Schullz, D. E., Tannenbaum, S. I., & Lauterborn, R. F. (1993). *The new marketing paradigm: Integrated marketing communications*. NTC Business Books.

Impact of Unethical Behaviour on the Value of Firms in the Real Sector

Njoroge Parmenas, Nina Szczygiel, Dmitry A. Shevchenko, and Gor A. Abramyan

Abstract Firms in the manufacturing sector are faced with tough decisions when trying to maximize profits and use environment-friendly methods of production. In the recent past, investors have been using ethical standards, corporate social responsibility rating, and environmental protection standards, to choose investment portfolios. In the age of social media, reports of unethical behaviour spread very fast, and this can have a very drastic negative effect on share prices. In this article, we seek to understand to what extent the publication of news of unethical behaviour by firms listed on the stock exchange influences stock prices. Results confirm that stock prices respond to news on unethical behaviour. Six of the eight firms record negative abnormal returns for all days after the event day. Adopting a comprehensive corporate strategy would not only address company reputation among investors but also promote trust and confidence with stakeholders, increase future profits and shareholders' wealth.

Keywords AAR · Abnormal returns · CAR · CSR · Corporate news · Corporate social responsibility · Ethics · Event study · Stock prices · Unethical behaviour

JEL Classification G14 · G32 · D22

N. Parmenas · D. A. Shevchenko · G. A. Abramyan (✉)
Southern Federal University, Rostov-on-Don, Russia
e-mail: gorabramyan@sfedu.ru

N. Parmenas
e-mail: ndzhoroge@sfedu.ru

D. A. Shevchenko
e-mail: dashevchenko@sfedu.ru

N. Szczygiel
University of Aveiro, Aveiro, Portugal
e-mail: nina.szczygiel@ua.pt

E. I. Lazareva et al. (eds.), *Innovative Trends in International Business and Sustainable Management*, Approaches to Global Sustainability, Markets, and Governance,
https://doi.org/10.1007/978-981-19-4005-7_43

1 Introduction

Although many jurisdictions have created laws regulating business ethics, there are various definitions of what business ethics is. Business ethics is a set of rules, standards, and codes, which guide the correct conduct in different professional situations (Lewis, 1985). According to (Erwin, 2011), many firms have a written code of ethics that guides how the business should operate in order to ensure smooth operations. Ethical issues have a lot to do with the perception of whether the firm has followed due diligence. Even if no law has been broken, the perception of management negligence can move investors away from the stock leading to a fall in price.

In modern financial management, the main goal of the firm is shareholders' wealth maximization. The value of a firm's stock in the capital market is one of the methods that can be used to access the increase or decrease in shareholders' value. To increase the intrinsic value of the firm, firms seek to achieve a high growth rate, increase market share, attain technological leadership, promote employees' welfare, etc. Environmental, social, and governance factors should be taken into consideration while pursuing these goals.

While issues such as environmental protection, human rights, transparency, giving back to society, and sound financial management are important areas in today's corporate world, it is important to understand how each of these factors affects shareholder's value. Investors' reactions to allegations of financial fraud may differ from allegations of polluting the environment. In the recent past, investors have been using ethical standards, corporate social responsibility ratings, and environmental protection standards to choose investment portfolios. As a result, some firms have developed well-outlined corporate social responsibility policies, to guide them on how to deal with issues such as environmental protection, human rights, corruption, fraud, and transparency.

2 Methodology

A growing number of investors are paying attention to corporate behaviour, either to reduce the risk of exposure to corporate scandal or to assess long-term corporate value (Scalet & Kelly, 2010). Research shows that there is a positive significant relationship between corporate governance attributes and the firm's performance (Allouche & Laroche, 2005; Laallam et al., 2017).

However, the existing literature shows that different markets respond differently to different types of news. Cellier et al. (2016) find that human rights and business behaviour significantly influence investors' choices whereas environmental risk does not have a significant impact on stock prices. Landi and Sciarelli (2019) do not find any significant impact of ethics on stock prices meaning that Italian listed companies cannot gain a market premium due to high standards of corporate social responsibility.

They, however, find that the Italian market responds to environmental information. Thus, investors react differently to different issues of ethical concern.

Several studies confirm that stock prices respond to environmental information, by penalizing the firms with poor environmental records (Beatty & Shimshack, 2010; Clarkson et al., 2011). Choosing environmental friendly production methods may be costly, but they result in increased efficiency and reduced waste, which can improve the firm's performance. Firms in the manufacturing sector are faced with tough decisions when trying to maximize profits and minimize production costs. These investment decisions need a long-term approach, due to the high capital investment involved. Therefore, managers need to know whether such decisions bring added value to the firm.

Given that different markets react differently to the news of certain unethical behaviour and that this reaction is likely to vary within industries or firms, it is important to understand the impact of corporate ethical lapses on firm value. We also explore prospects of sustainable value creation for firms in the real sector.

The objective of this research is to examine the behaviour of stock prices around the publication of news of unethical behaviour by listed firms. We set up the following hypotheses that will be tested with different kinds of statistical tests:

H0: There are no abnormal returns surrounding the publication of news of a firm's unethical behaviour.
H1: There exist abnormal returns on the publication of news of a firm's unethical behaviour.

In this paper, we investigate corporate news on unethical behaviour for eight companies that have experienced ethical lapses in the past. A summarized information on the studied events is provided in Table 1.

We obtain daily stock prices from Yahoo finance and obtain Fama French global factors for the corresponding period in the Fama French Website (Fama & French, 2019). To calculate abnormal returns on publication of unethical news, we use the advanced abnormal return calculator (aARC), which is an analysis tool for conducting sophisticated event studies with multiple event types (Schimmer et al., 2014). To employ the Fama French three-factor model on the aARC app, we prepare an 'analysis request file' that specifies our analysis parameters, a 'firm data file' that holds the firm financial data required for our analysis, and a 'market data file' that holds the respective capital market data. We upload these files in comma-separated values (CSV) format. We obtain a comprehensive set of statistics that include abnormal returns (AR) for each event, aggregated abnormal returns (AAR) for all the events, cumulative abnormal returns (CAR) for each event, and cumulative aggregated abnormal returns (CAAR) for all the events. The aARC app also performs several statistical tests including AR T-tests, CAR T-tests, and standardized residual test, developed by Scalet and Kelly (2010), to test the null hypothesis.

The actual day of when the event happens is defined as the $t = 0$. Day $t = -1$ is the trading day immediately preceding the event day. Day $t = +1$ is defined as the trading day immediately following the event day. The period to be examined in detail

Table 1 Summary of studied unethical events

Firm	Event date	Even description
Apple	20.10.2017	Apple admits to using software updates to slow down old models of iPhone in order to prevent sudden shut down due to old batteries
Boeing	10.03.2019	The Boeing 737 MAX 8 heading from Addis Ababa to Nairobi crushes a few minutes after take-off. Several airlines ground the aircraft model citing safety concerns
BP	20.04.2010	Devastating oil leak in the Gulf of Mexico after a marine well spilt over into the sea
Equifax credit bureau	08.09 2017	Equifax credit bureau announces a security breach that could have resulted in identity theft
Facebook	17.03.2018	The Guardian and the New York Times report that data of around 50 million Facebook users was harvested and used to send personalized political advertisements to influence voting
Kobe Steel	8.10. 2017	Kobe Steel admits to supplying products with falsified specifications to about 500 customers
Siemens	15.10. 2006	Prosecutors raid offices and homes of Siemen staff in investigation of misuse of funds
Volkswagen	18.09.2018	480,000 vehicles sold in the USA are recalled after it was established that they had installed devices to provide dishonest information about emission compliance

Source Developed and compiled by the author

for the purpose of the study is 21 days in length, consisting of the event day (day $t = 0$), the 10 days immediately preceding the event day (day $t = 0$), and 10 days immediately following it. The event window consists of 21 days ($t-10$ to $t + 10$), and the estimation period consists of 120 days ($t-130$ to $t-11$).

We use the standardized residual test, developed by Patell (1976) which tests the null hypothesis that the cumulative average abnormal return is equal to zero. Under the assumption that abnormal returns are uncorrelated, variance is constant over time, each abnormal return is standardized by its estimated standard deviation:

$$\mathrm{SAR}_{i,T} = \frac{\mathrm{AR}_{i,T}}{S\left(\mathrm{AR}_{i,T}\right)}$$

The standard deviation is estimated from the time-series of abnormal returns of the estimation window:

$$\hat{\delta}^2 \mathrm{AR}_i = \frac{1}{m_1 - d} \sum_{\mathrm{Est_{min}}}^{\mathrm{Est_{max}}} \left(\mathrm{AR}_{i,t}\right)^2$$

where m_1 is the number of non-missing returns and d the degrees of freedom. Simple abnormal returns, the standardized version can be cumulated over time:

$$\text{CSAR}_{i,(T_1,T_2)} = \sum_{T=T_1}^{T_2} \frac{\text{AR}_{i,t}}{S(\text{AR}_{i,})}$$

Under the null hypothesis, the distribution of SAR_i is a student's t-distribution with $M_i - d$ degrees of freedom (for further discussion see (MacKinlay, 1997)). It directly follows that the expected value of CSAR_i is zero and the standard deviation is

$$S(\text{CSAR}_i) = \sqrt{(T_2 - T_1 + 1)\frac{m^1 - d}{m^1 - 2d}}$$

The test statistic for the null hypothesis, that the cumulative average abnormal return is equal to zero, is

$$T_{\text{Patell}} = \frac{1}{\sqrt{N}} \sum_{i=1}^{N} \frac{\text{CSAR}_{i,(T_1,T_2)}}{S(\text{CSAR}_i)}$$

3 Results

The results of cumulative abnormal returns of the eight firms along the event window are presented in Table 2.

The results show that four of the firms: BP, Equifax Credit Bureau, Boeing, and Kobe steel have the CAR t-test value greater than ±2 (the generally accepted degree

Table 2 Summary of cumulative abnormal returns and the corresponding t-test

Firm	Window	CAR value	BHAR value	CAR t-test
Apple	(−10, 10)	−0.0464	−0.0492	−1.0438
Boeing	(−10, 10)	−0.2121	−0.2101	−3.4032
BP	(−10, 10)	−0.118	−0.1145	−2.6823
Equifax credit bureau	(−10, 10)	−0.3259	−0.3118	−10.6145
Facebook	(−10, 10)	−0.0842	−0.0819	−1.4468
Kobe steel	(−10, 10)	−0.4267	−0.3989	−4.2518
Siemens	(−10, 10)	0.0074	0.0065	0.1114
Volkswagen	(−10, 10)	0.1232	0.1238	1.6698

Source Developed and compiled by the author

of freedom for a small N) meaning that the p-value is less than 0.05. The results are therefore significant. This means that the news significantly affected the cumulative abnormal returns of these firms.

Figure 1 shows the plots of AR and CAR against the event window for each firm to analyse the behaviour of abnormal returns and cumulative abnormal returns against the event window. For six of the eight firms, cumulative abnormal returns drop to negative after the event day and remain negative for the remaining period under analysis.

Although the graphs for Apple and Facebook show drop-in share prices after the publication of news of ethical lapses, the results are not significant. Further research is needed to investigate stock prices reaction to ethical lapses for firms in the ICT sector. Two firms (Volkswagen and Siemens) record positive CAR after the event day meaning that the news did not affect stock returns negatively. However, in the case of these two firms, the results are not statistically significant.

Table 3 shows the aggregated abnormal returns for the eight studied firms.

As illustrated in Table 3, CAAR has a Patell Z-value of -7.5305, which is lower than ± 2 (the generally accepted degree of freedom for a small N) meaning that the p-value is less than 0.05. The results are therefore significant. We, therefore, reject H0, which stated that there were no abnormal returns surrounding the publication of news of a firm's unethical behaviour.

Our results show that stock prices negatively react to the publication of news of unethical behaviour. We can observe two different reactions to the publication of such news. Firstly, in six of the eight firms, CAR is negative for all the days in the event window after the event day. This is inconsistent with the efficient market hypothesis which states that stock prices adjust quickly to reflect all the information in the market (Fama, 1970). Statistical tests confirm that CAR figures for four of these firms are statistically significant.

The second reaction involves two remaining firms, which demonstrate positive CAR figures even after the event day. However, CAR figures for these firms are not statistically significant. The cumulative aggregated abnormal returns for the eight firms across the event window are negative. Statistical tests have confirmed that stock prices respond to the publication of news of unethical behaviour of firms. These results are consistent with those of (Allouche and Laroche, 2005; Cellier et al., 2016). On the other hand, the results contradict the findings of (Landi and Sciarelli, 2019; Schimmer et al., 2014) who do not find any significant impact of ethics on stock prices.

A firm's policies on issues of ethical concern are an important part of corporate management since they inform and shape investors' attitudes towards a firm. For sustainable shareholders value creation, this study underscores the importance of a corporate plan (strategy) that sets out organizational ethics, values, and culture and ensures effective risk management. A sound corporate plan:

- analyses future risks and recommends strategies for risk management;
- sets out organizational values and ethics, which is essential in establishing a sound corporate culture;

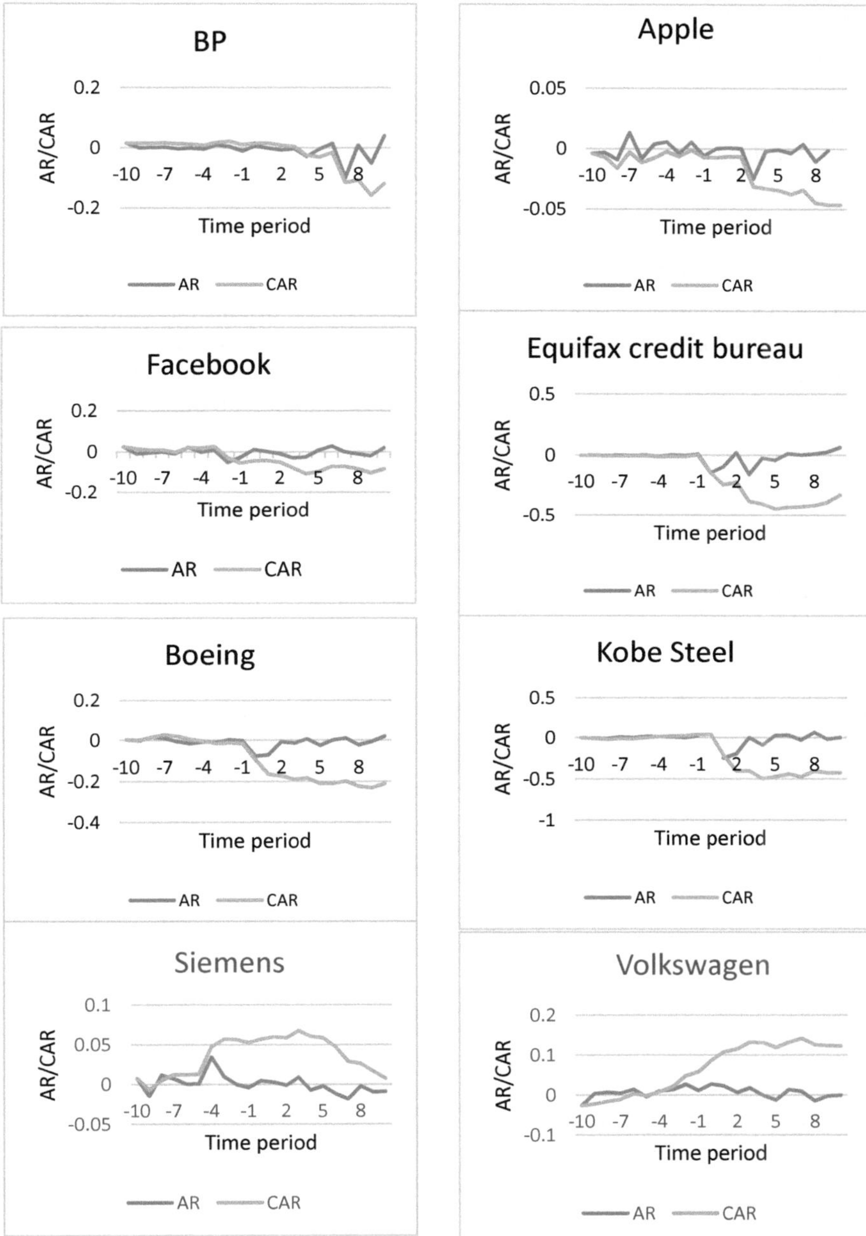

Fig. 1 Plots of AR and CAR against the event window for respective firms. *Source* Developed and compiled by the author

Table 3 Summary of cumulative aggregated abnormal returns and the corresponding *t*-test

CAAR value	ABHAR	*N*	Patell Z	Csect t	Generalized Sign Z	StdCSectZ	Rank Z
−0.1353	−0.1295	8	−7.5305	−2.1344	−1.3673	−2.0583	−0.6445

Source Developed and compiled by the author

- lays out a cost–benefit analysis for the adoption of new technologies;
- outlines the firm's strategy with regards to ESG factors;

A sound corporate strategy is an important tool for sustainable value addition. Although it is costly to implement environmental-friendly means of production, this decision can have a significant impact on the firm value in the long run. A case of firms in the automobile industry provides a good example. Figure 2 shows market capitalization (in million dollars) for four firms in the automobile industry from 2010 to 2020.

Figure 3 clearly shows a significant increase in Tesla's market capitalization with a sharp increase towards the end of 2019. Considering that Tesla specializes in the manufacturing of environmental-friendly electric vehicles, the success underscores the importance of integrating ESG factors in the business model, for sustainable value addition.

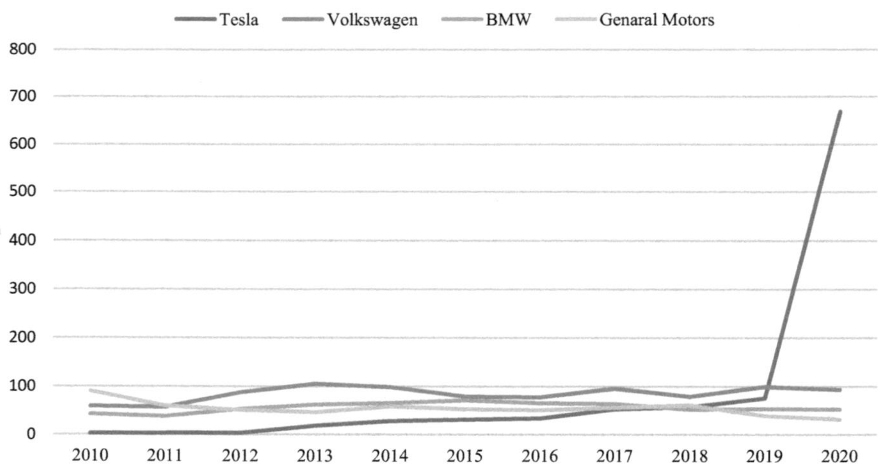

Fig. 2 Market capitalization for four firms in the automobile industry from 2010 to 2020. *Source* Compiled by the authors based on (Companiesmarketcap.com, 2021)

4 Conclusion

Our results show that CAR for six firms is negative for all the days in the event window after the event day (four of these CAR are statistically significant). The aggregated cumulative abnormal returns for the eight firms across the event window are negative. Statistical tests have confirmed that stock prices respond to the publication of news of unethical behaviour of firms.

Consequently, it is critical for a company to have a solid corporate plan that outlines organizational values and ethics, a risk management strategy, the viability of adopting new technologies, and a strategy for incorporating ESG factors into the business model. A comprehensive corporate strategy would not only address company reputation among investors but also promote trust and confidence with stakeholders, increase future profits and shareholders' wealth, and avoid litigation costs. Although our findings show that abnormal returns on the publication of news of ethical lapses for firms in the ICT sector are not statistically significant, our sample is not large enough to conclude that these firms are less impacted by ethical lapses. Thus, more research on this area is necessary.

References

Allouche, J., & Laroche, P., (2005). A meta-analytical investigation of the relationship between corporate social and financial performance. *Revue de Gestion des Ressources Humaines*, July–Sep, 18–41.

Beatty, T., & Shimshack, J. (2010). The impact of smoking bans on the hospitality industry: New evidence from stock market returns. *The B.E. Journal of Economic Analysis & Policy*, *10*(1), 1–29 .

Cellier, A., Chollet, P., & Gajewski, J. F. (2016). Do investors trade around social rating announcements? *European Financial Management, 22*(3), 484–515. https://doi.org/10.1111/eufm.12066

Clarkson, P. M., Li, Y., Richardson, G. D., & Vasvari, F. P. (2011). Does it really pay to be green? Determinants and consequences of proactive environmental strategies. *Journal of Accounting and Public Policy, 30*(2), 122–144. https://doi.org/10.1016/j.jaccpubpol.2010.09.013

Companiesmarketcap.com (2021). *Market capitalization of Tesla (TSLA)*. https://companiesmarketcap.com/tesla/marketcap/. Accessed November 21, 2021.

Erwin, P. M. (2011). Corporate codes of conduct: The effects of code content and quality on ethical performance. *Journal of Business Ethics, 99*(4), 535–548. https://doi.org/10.1007/s10551-010-0667-y

Fama, E. F. (1970). Efficient capital markets: A review of theory and empirical work. *Jstor, 25*(2), 383–417. https://doi.org/10.1684/bdc.2014.1986

Fama, E., & French, K. (2019). *Current research returns*. https://mba.tuck.dartmouth.edu/pages/faculty/ken.french/data_library.html. Accessed September 28, 2019.

Laallam, A., Alom, F., & Mohamad, A. (2017). The effects of corporate governance attributes and code amendments on the performance of Malaysian trading and services firms. *International Journal of Economics and Business Research, 13*(1), 72–94. https://doi.org/10.1504/IJEBR.2017.081772

Landi, G., & Sciarelli, M. (2019). Towards a more ethical market: The impact of ESG rating on corporate financial performance. *Social Responsibility Journal, 15*(1), 11–27. https://doi.org/10.1108/SRJ-11-2017-0254

Lewis, P. V. (1985). Defining "business ethics": Like nailing jello to a wall. *Journal of Business Ethics, 4*(5), 377–383. https://doi.org/10.1007/BF02388590

MacKinlay, C. A. (1997). Finance event studies are used to assess damages. *Journal of Economic Literature, 35*(1), 13–39. https://doi.org/10.2307/2729691

Patell, J. M. (1976). Per share of earnings forecasts corporate tests empirical and stock price behaviour. *Journal of Accounting Research, 14*(2), 246–276.

Scalet, S., & Kelly, T. F. (2010). CSR rating agencies: What is their global impact? *Journal of Business Ethics, 94*(1), 69–88. https://doi.org/10.1007/sl0551-009-0250-6

Schimmer, M., Levchenko, A., & Müller, S. (2014). *EventStudyTools (Research Apps)*, St.Gallen. www.eventstudytools.com. Accessed September 13, 2019.

Digital Transformation as a Driver of Oilfield Services Industry Development

Alexey V. Beloshitskiy and Vera V. Biryukova

Abstract The paper focuses on national oilfield services as a leader in the progress of the oil and gas industry. Moreover, the paper discusses the dependence of oilfield services on imported technologies in the current development period. The authors note a negative influence of the depending factor on the development of new hard-to-reach oil and gas fields. Digital transformation of oilfield service companies is proposed as a good option for developing oilfield service businesses under sanction conditions. It is noted that digital transformation can provide a good economic result due to its relatively low cost compared with technological innovations and its ability to change the business structure, the principles of the company's work, and the business culture. The basic terms of digital transformation are considered. Digital transformation is defined as introducing advanced IT technologies into business processes and adaptive management of changes in forms of doing business, corporate culture, internal relations, and external communications. The high level of education of employees and their inner willingness to structure changes and permanent improvement is taken as a key factor in providing a necessary level of "digital maturity" of oilfield services, which confirms its willingness to the digital transformation. The connection between technological development and digital transformation is noted, as well as its ability to provide a continuous process of improvement and search for the most effective options for the organization of the oilfield service process to achieve high economic results.

Keywords Oilfield services industry · Foreign technologies · Sanctions · Digital transformation · Technological development · Digital maturity · Business process · Corporate culture · Economic results

JEL Classification 125 · 123 · 124

A. V. Beloshitskiy
Luzin Institute for Economy Studies of the Kola Science Centre of RAS, Apatity, Russia
e-mail: bel@bngf.ru

V. V. Biryukova (✉)
Ufa State Petroleum Technological University, Ufa, Russia
e-mail: v.birukova@yandex.ru

E. I. Lazareva et al. (eds.), *Innovative Trends in International Business and Sustainable Management*, Approaches to Global Sustainability, Markets, and Governance,
https://doi.org/10.1007/978-981-19-4005-7_44

1 Introduction

As in the whole world, the Russian oil service has always been a leader in implementing advanced scientific developments in the national oil industry. It continued the previously formed engineering school while being more and more different from it. Thus, the Soviet oilfield service, almost based on domestic scientific developments, sold well abroad. In the twentieth century, our experts in drilling, geophysics, hydrocarbon field development, and intensification of oil production significantly contributed to the national budget of the union state, assisting in the development of African, the Middle East, and Southeast Asia countries. Nowadays, one of the characteristic features of the development of the Russian oilfield services industry is a significant dependence on foreign technologies in the search, exploration, and exploitation of hydrocarbon deposits.

Currently, when many of the well-known oil and gas fields are at a late stage of development, the issues of maintaining the appropriate levels of hydrocarbons and the reproduction of the necessary mineral resources are more urgent than ever to ensure economic sovereignty of Russia. The solution to the problem largely depends on the state of the oilfield services industry. Indeed, the development of hydrocarbons from hard-to-recover deposits, the development of production on the shelf and in transit fields, offshore fields of deep occurrence is not a complete list of objects, the commercial exploitation of which is possible only with the use of the most advanced oilfield services currently available in the world. This should also include the processes of enhanced oil recovery in mature oil and gas fields (Beloshitskiy & Garayshin, 2020).

That is why the sanctions restrictions of recent years have significantly complicated the situation in the oilfield services industry, where the share of imports is as follows: in horizontal drilling—more than 85%, hydraulic fracturing—90%, logging while drilling—90%, high-density seismology—almost 100%, and the list goes on (Iliinsky et al., 2019). As a result, many promising subsoil development projects have been temporarily suspended ("frozen") or significantly slowed down, such as, for example, the development of the Arctic shelf in the adjacent seas of the Arctic Ocean, the development of shale from the Achimov and Bazhenov formations in Western Siberia, the Russkoye field in the Yamal-Nenets Autonomous Area, Kharasaveyskoye and Yuzhno-Tambeyskoye gas condensate fields, and several others. The import substitution policy announced and supported by the Government of Russia plays a positive role; a certain effect has already been obtained, including in the oil industry. However, the development and implementation of oilfield service technologies and equipment into production is slow, extremely expensive, and complicated by the collapse of the world's oil quotations and a subsequent reduction in production based on the OPEC + agreements to stabilize the market, as well as the general economic crisis caused by the COVID-19 pandemic.

According to the authors of this research, the digital transformation of the industry is one of the options for the successful development of the oil service business in the current environment, which is generally characteristic of the domestic industry.

It can lead to impressive results because of its technological and organizational leadership in the oil industry and the "low start" effect (Adieva et al., 2020). The research by experts from the KMDA analytical company showed that, over the past two years, Russian business has realized the importance and recognized the need for the digital transformation of the national economy (Trends, 2021). In 2018, only 33% of company representatives called digital transformation necessary for business; in 2020, their number almost doubled to 64%. Enterprise owners of various types of activity are ready to invest considerable sums in transformation and related changes—according to statistics, from 3 to 10% of the proceeds (Trends, 2021).

2 Materials and Methods

2.1 Research Methodology

Terms and concepts such as "digitalization," "digital transformation," "the fourth industrial revolution," or "Industry 4.0," "Internet of Things"—are part of a chain; they are currently known to every manager in the oil and gas industry, most of whom anyway have encountered the elements of the named processes in practice in one way or another (Afanasiev et al., 2019). It is important to understand that digital transformation is not just a digitization of the main production processes and support services but also the result of the collision and subsequent symbiosis of the wave of the latest information technologies, industrial automation, and scientific organization of production processes. The above-mentioned components of digital transformation previously developed relatively independently and only supplemented each other; today, their integration has caused a significant synergistic effect and has led to high economic results.

Let us analyze the difference between concepts. According to interviews with KMDA analysts, a third of respondents see digital transformation as a new name for automation, an incomprehensible or artificially created term, and the definition is often equated with digitalization or even digitization of processes. At first glance, these phenomena may seem similar or even identical, but there is a significant difference between them in the scale and depth of changes:

- **Digitization of business processes** is the translation of processes into digital format;
- **Digitalization** is the next level of change, where data and processes translated into digital format can already be used to simplify and optimize operations;
- **Digital transformation** is a deeper and larger-scale process of complex transformation of an enterprise using digital solutions and technologies, the purpose of which is to enter new markets, create new sales channels and solutions that can generate additional net revenue, and increase the value of the company.

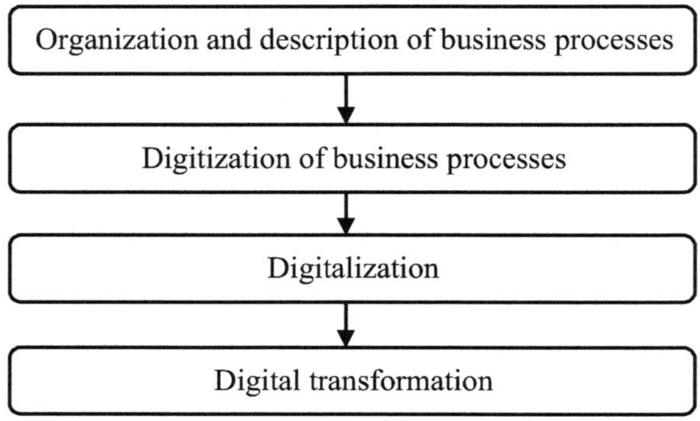

Fig. 1 Stages of digital transformation. *Source* Created by the authors

The sequence of stages of the transition to digital transformation is graphically presented in Fig. 1.

As we can see, the transformation is based on **the description and organization** of production processes, the implementation project of which allows using any available and well-known tools such as, for example, a quality management system (ISO 9000 and others), a balanced scorecard, kaizen management systems, 5S, and other solutions, the result of the implementation of which is the formalization of the business processes of oil and gas services as a single interconnected system capable of control and change.

Digitization of business processes based on the results of project implementation allows providing modeling of technological oil service operations to find possible solutions for optimizing the value chain, reducing production costs, and increasing business margins.

At the stage of **digitalization**, it is already possible to create software products that combine all previously digitized processes, data, and service applications. The efficiency of the oilfield service business increases by several percent and, depending on the scale, brings good money. However, it does not allow significantly breaking away from competitors, leaving the enterprise with traditional service products, unchanged production process, and familiar customers. The author's experience in implementing such solutions shows that, in the situation of "customer-contractor" (this is how the relationship between the vertically integrated oil company (customer) and the oil service company (contractor) is built), an additional economic effect from the implementation of this stage arises with the mutual trust of partners and, as a result, mutual admission to the monitoring of production operations in real-time.

The final stage of **digital transformation** implies a very deep and large-scale introduction of digital solutions into traditional methods of providing oilfield services, considerably increasing business efficiency and providing a gap from competitors. The quality of service cannot be compared to the usual market product because it is much more interesting for the oil customer company. Achieving such an effect requires the oilfield service company to constantly update current production processes, improve technological operations, and be flexible in strategic thinking, which means constant monitoring of the service package offered to the customer to ensure that it matches the current business model of the oil and gas company. Such a model, in turn, should meet the current needs of the oil and gas industry and stimulate the contractor to expand the range of oilfield services, open up opportunities for the creation and implementation of fundamentally new oilfield service strategies that can bring more value to customers and the contractor, assuming subsequent adaptation, integration, and optimization of production processes.

Based on the above, the following definition of digital transformation can be formulated. Digital transformation is the introduction of advanced information technologies for data exchange in the business processes of an enterprise to promptly respond to external challenges and adaptive management of drastic changes in methods and forms of doing business, corporate culture, internal relations, and external communications.

2.2 Theoretical Fundamentals

Let us make a reservation: in its specificity, the oilfield service business belongs to the service sector, also belonging to the B2B category. It has powerful production and technological resources and highly qualified trained personnel, significantly different from the average level of a service worker. In other words, workers employed in the oilfield services industry have high educational qualifications (Musina et al., 2020; Okorokov et al., 2019).

In fact, this is where the strategic potential of the vector for the development of the oilfield service business, proposed by the authors, lies. Without minimizing the importance of technological innovations, the implementation of a digital transformation project for the oilfield services industry is "much more than just an introduction of new technologies" (Laptev, 2020). Moreover, as already mentioned, at the stage of restrictions on accessing advanced high-performance technologies and a shortage of financial and time resources, for the development and even "survival" of enterprises, "in addition to using new technologies, there is a need for new ways of thinking, new roles and skills, new organizational structures and operating models for doing business, and adapting to a much faster pace of change" (Weiss, 2017).

Technological superiority in the oilfield services industry allows us to achieve a competitive advantage due to the high quality of the service and the speed of its provision. Simultaneously, the cost of services rendered using high-tech foreign equipment is generally significantly higher than its domestic counterparts. The crisis events of recent years, including the COVID-19 pandemic, force oil companies to limit the costs of expensive services of international oil service corporations in favor of Russian companies, in the process reducing the current levels of hydrocarbon production in accordance with the OPEC+ protocols, which led to a temporary oversupply of oil service capacities in the Russian market, thus causing a "buyer's market" situation, which resulted in the "freezing" of prices for the services of domestic oilfield services companies.

Simultaneously, the desire of the owners of the oilfield services business and top managers to make more profits remains, for which it is necessary to increase the margins of services, which, in the conditions of decreasing price pressure from customers (oil companies and the temporary absence of technological improvements), can only be ensured by a decrease in current production costs. In this situation, the practical implementation of available digital technologies and the latest management methods is highly possible to lead to a significant increase in the profitability of the oilfield services business.

Indeed, the introduction of new industrial technologies when they appear and become available usually does not change the principles and structure of the business processes that have been developed at the oilfield service enterprise. Moreover, technological renewal is always associated with significant or capital investments, which are generally provided by loan capital. Given the exchange rate volatility, this is another challenge for the oilfield service company in choosing the latest rational solution to technological development.

Unlike technological innovations, digital transformation insignificantly increases the assets of an oilfield service company and is much cheaper compared with basic production assets. Nevertheless, it can radically change the business structure and the principles of the enterprise and improve the business culture. Transformation stimulates innovative activity in the formation of business strategies and business models of an oilfield service enterprise, the structure of products and services offered to the customer, internal business processes, human capital management, and external relations (Schreibfeder, 2019).

3 Results

A key factor in the success of the digital transformation of an oilfield service company is the previously mentioned high educational qualification of industry workers, who, based on the author's experience, are well aware of structural changes and are ready for them. It is necessary to note the readiness of the staff for continuous improvement. The basic oilfield service enterprise where the study is conducted has been organizing, digitalizing, and improving business processes for a relatively long time; it has sufficient experience in implementing best production management practices and a relatively high level of "digital maturity." The latter term is the main indicator for determining the readiness of an organization to implement digital solutions in business processes. The Ministry of Digital Development of Russia has already presented a general methodology for calculating this indicator. It is expected that indicators for particular industries and areas of activity will appear for the subsequent formation of a model of digital maturity of the state to assess the possibility of its digital transformation. In approaching the digital transformation, enterprises must represent their level of maturity and willingness to change business processes and approaches to business process management.

In general, the Russian oil and gas industry, including oilfield services, is in a "rudimentary" process of digital transformation. Therefore, the digital potential of the industry can develop rapidly and grow in various innovative directions. In world studies, when assessing the digital potential of countries, the following criteria are considered:

- Availability of digital drivers (human potential—employees of generation Z; technologies and new developments, know-how; infrastructure; the ability to participate in foreign economic activity and access to investments; reliable, continuous provision of resources, domestic demand);
- Industrial and economic potential (the scale and complexity of production, structural connectivity of economic sectors).

According to experts in the field of oil and gas consulting, Russian oil and oil service companies are part of the so-called Industrial Heritage group. The name reflects the continuity of the industry compared to the so-called pre-market development period of the oil and gas industry in the era of state-planned regulation in the 1960–1980s. This period witnessed the main development of the oil and gas industry, associated primarily with the discovery of the largest oil and gas fields in Western Siberia. The development of fields and their subsequent exploitation, together with the formation of a domestic oil engineering school, ensured the production potential that has survived to this day, despite the relatively outdated (by today's standards) methods of developing oil deposits. A feature of this group is that such companies have a fairly high level of economic development and significant potential for industrial growth but provide medium drivers of digital development. Some enterprises even give low scores of digital maturities, being located closer to the Outsiders group (the latter includes companies that have lost their growth opportunities and economic potential, as well as those who are just starting to lose their positions).

To correctly evaluate and place a company according to its readiness for digital transformation, there are such evaluation criteria as the International Digital Economy and Society Index (I-DESI) (Galieva, 2020). Based on the I-DESI, the authors propose the following indicators:

- Provision of digital technologies;
- Availability and degree of development of communication services, storage and transmission of information related to business;
- Availability of qualified human capital;
- Digitalization of business, including the level of automation of internal processes;
- Information security;
- Government control, tax regulators, and the presence or absence of barriers to the development of digital technologies.

Oilfield service companies, which can be classified as "mature," digitally transform existing processes following new requirements, operate much easier, and grow in an ever-changing current environment. Meanwhile, time resources and financial costs are used much more productively, which ultimately brings the oilfield services business to a new, more successful level of operational productivity. In the current format, digital transformation is about ensuring sustainability, maintaining and increasing the number of customers and partners, competent analysis, and selection and creation of new business models for the production activities of oilfield service companies, where concern for the safety and comfort of employees is among the priorities of the transformation.

4 Discussion

Considering that digital transformation processes are a relatively new phenomenon, it is challenging to name the number of enterprises in the oilfield services industry, in respect of which it is possible to draw a conclusion on the completion of digital transformation projects. Nevertheless, already now, it is necessary to be ready to assess the results of such transformations, which, due to the novelty of the processes, can be difficult. It should be noted that at the state level, in accordance with the Order of the Government of the Russian Federation "On the approval of the program 'Digital economy of the Russian Federation'" (July 28, 2017 No. 1632-r) (Government of the Russian Federation, 2017), criteria for evaluating innovative companies have been prepared, and, as mentioned before, industry indicators are expected to appear for the possibility of assessing the results of digital transformations. Nevertheless, there is no basis for a practical analysis of the scale of the results (Maklakov, 2019). In this regard, a logical continuation of this study can be the development of methodological applications that allow for a practical objective assessment of the results of the effectiveness of business models of enterprises in the oil and gas industry after the completion of digital transformation projects. In this case, the authors believe that one of the main problems to be solved is the study of the possibility of using classical methods for assessing the effectiveness of economic activities of companies in the oil and gas industry, such as key performance indicators (KPI) and margin of safety (MOS).

5 Conclusion

In conclusion, the authors would like to note that under the ongoing conditions of sanctions pressure on the Russian Federation, which is constantly growing, the digital transformation of the oilfield services industry is a reasonable, affordable, and relatively inexpensive solution to achieve success in a market environment for doing business. This is a difficult path that requires concentration and a full dedication from all participants in the transformation process. Moreover, according to the authors, a key factor in the success of digital technologies in business process management should be the internal readiness of personnel involved in transformations to make constant changes. However, psychologically it is very difficult, especially for the middle-aged and older generation, who constitute the main productive human capital in the oilfield services industry. However, there is no alternative to digitalization processes. Another thing is that the plan for this work should be based on an understanding of the changing digital environment and a willingness to constantly adjust this plan as information about new, increasingly impressive digital technologies becomes available. Digital transformation is a process of technological development. However, as already noted by the authors, it is affordable and relatively inexpensive and also has a very important feature—digitalization provides a continuous process of constant improvement. It searches for the most convenient and effective methods of organizing production processes of oilfield services, the introduction of progressive, innovative solutions and ideas, and, as a result, the transformation of the oilfield service business to achieve high economic results in the future.

References

Adieva, O. A., Beloshitskiy, A. V., Biryukova, V. V., & Garayshin, S. G. (2020). Some problems of cooperation between a classic education and a corporate training. *Journal of Oil Industry, 9*, 78–82. https://doi.org/10.24887/0028-2448-2020-9-78-82

Afanasiev, M., Rachenko, I., & Arbuzov, M. (2019). Role and significance of mobile technologies in digitalization of procurement systems in oil and gas companies. *IOP Conference Series: Materials Science and Engineering, 497*, 012021. https://doi.org/10.1088/1757-899X/497/1/012021

Beloshitskiy, A. V., & Garayshin, S. G. (2020). Forming of the corporate training at JSC "Bashneftegeofizika." *Problems of Economics and Management to Oil and Gas Complex, 9*(189), 38–43. https://doi.org/10.33285/1999-6942-2020-9(189)-38-43

Galieva, D. (2020, December 07). *"Digital" is being analyzed for maturity threshold*. Kommersant. Retrieved from https://www.kommersant.ru/doc/4602997. Accessed 20 April, 2021.

Government of the Russian Federation. (2017). *Order "On approval of the program 'Digital economy of the Russian Federation'" (July 28, 2017 No. 1632-r)*. Retrieved from https://www.garant.ru/products/ipo/prime/doc/71634878/. Accessed 25 April, 2021.

Iliinsky, A., Afanasiev, M., & Metkin, D. (2019). Digital technologies of investment analysis of projects for the development of oil fields of unallocated subsoil reserve fund. *IOP Conference Series: Materials Science and Engineering, 497*, 012028. https://doi.org/10.1088/1757-899X/497/1/012028

Laptev, V. V. (2020). Russian geophysics at a new stage of development. *Journal of Drilling and Oil, 2*, 3–8.

Maklakov, G. V. (2019). The influence of time on the efficiency of commodity circulation. *Journal of CITISE, 3*(7), 2.

Musina, D. R., Yangirov, A. V., & Nasyrova, S. I. (2020). Dependence of a country's competitiveness on its information infrastructure. In *European Proceedings of Social and Behavioural Sciences EpSBS*, (Vol. 80). https://doi.org/10.15405/epsbs(2357-1330).2020.3.2

Okorokov, R., Timofeeva, A., & Kharlamova, T. (2019). Building intellectual capital of specialists in the context of digital transformation of the Russian economy. *IOP Conference Series: Materials Science and Engineering, 497*, 012015. https://doi.org/10.1088/1757-899X/497/1/012015

RBC Trends. (2021, April 08). *How to distinguish digital transformation from digitalization*. Retrieved from https://trends.rbc.ru/trends/industry/cmrm/606ae4c49a794754627d6161. Accessed 25 April, 2021.

Schreibfeder, J. (2019). *Achieving effective inventory management* (Yu. Orlova Transl. from English). Alpina Publisher. (Original work published 2005).

Weiss, E. S. (2017). Planning in the enterprise (organization): A textbook. KnoRus.

The Role of Transaction Costs in the Concept of Sustainable Enterprise Development

Yuliya N. Marakulina and Anton D. Murzin

Abstract The article analyzes the concept of "sustainability", identifies groups of factors that have a direct impact on the sustainability of the enterprise, among which the authors propose to consider, in addition to the well-known, such a factor as the presence of transaction costs. The main purpose of the article is to analyze the essence of the concept of "sustainability" and assess the impact of transaction costs on it as an internal impact factor. The study revealed the direct impact of transaction costs on the sustainability of the enterprise and its further development.

Keywords Sustainability · External and internal factors affecting the sustainability of the enterprise · Transaction costs

JEL Classification G31 · L14 · M21

1 Introduction

Currently, the global economy needs to actively recover from the impact of the COVID-19 coronavirus pandemic. The condition for returning to the pandemic indicators of the development of economic entities is both measures of state support and the organizations' own potential to maximize sustainability. The organization's own potential should be considered as its own sources of financing or, in other words, its own financial resources. The size of these funds is directly related to the stability of the company, its financial independence and growth prospects.

Y. N. Marakulina · A. D. Murzin (✉)
Southern Federal University, Rostov-on-Don, Russia
e-mail: admurzin@sfedu.ru

Y. N. Marakulina
e-mail: ymarakulina@sfedu.ru

A. D. Murzin
Don State Technical University, Rostov-on-Don, Russia

Plekhanov Russian University of Economics, Moscow, Russia

E. I. Lazareva et al. (eds.), *Innovative Trends in International Business and Sustainable Management*, Approaches to Global Sustainability, Markets, and Governance,
https://doi.org/10.1007/978-981-19-4005-7_45

2 Methodology

The works of Russian scientists on a given topic were studied using meaningful analysis as the main method of our research. This method made it possible to determine the general characteristics of the concept of "sustainable development" from the point of view of Russian scientists, to identify various aspects and formulate authors' definitions that take into account the specifics of the phenomena under consideration. The works of domestic economists were chosen as the information base of the study due to the fact that the sustainable development of the enterprise is based on certain aspects, including the regulatory framework, accounting procedures and other factors that are not considered by foreign scientists.

At the first stage of the analysis, it is necessary to determine the essence of the very concept of "sustainability of enterprise development" in order to further identify the resource base and justify the adequacy of the measures developed to achieve it.

3 Results

The study and analysis of the works of modern Russian authors on this topic allowed us to conclude that this category is extremely multifaceted and has no well-established definition. The latter may be related to the fact that different groups of economists focus on one or another aspect, depending on the specifics of the functioning of economic entities.

Thus, some researchers associate sustainability with the production activity of an enterprise, defining it as "synthesis of a set of properties of the most important components of the economic system: production activity, management, material and technical base, resource provision, human and intellectual potentials that determine the integrated quality of the economic system in relation to complex factors of the external environment, 'market relations', as well as in relation to similar systems of another level" (Litvinenko, 1996). G. N. Zakharov considers sustainability as "such a state of the material and cost structure of production and sales of products, which ensures a consistently high result of the functioning of the enterprise" (Zakharov, 2020). E. V. Shevrina defines economic sustainability as "the ability of an enterprise to maintain and increase its own production potential for a relatively long period of time in order to preserve its position in its market segment" (Shevrina, 2000). The presented definitions reflect the authors' opinions that the main source of enterprise sustainability is the internal environment of the organization, namely the production and organizational structure. However, in this case, the impact on the stability of the external environment is not considered, although any organization is an open system. It has a complex internal structure of interrelated and interdependent elements and constantly interacts with elements of the external environment.

Another group of authors defines sustainability as the ability of an enterprise to respond in a timely manner to changes in both internal and external factors. T. V.

Kolosova believes that the sustainability of enterprise development is "a continuous process of bringing the economic system of the enterprise in line with the requirements of the market, expressed in ensuring competitiveness based on increasing innovation potential" (Kolosova, 2011). D. V. Lavrushin believes that sustainable development is "the status of functioning of an enterprise characterized by a constant or positive change in stability formed under the influence of a system of external and internal factors for certain reporting periods" (Lavrushin, 1999). D. N. Klepikov considers the sustainable development of an enterprise as "a set of tools capable of ensuring the competitiveness of products and production, flexibility to respond to changing market conditions, innovation and investment activity, environmental friendliness of production" (Klepikov, 2007).

The analysis of the definitions discussed above suggests that the sustainable development of the organization is based on elements of both the internal and external environment.

Other economists further expand the scope of the concept of "sustainability". According to Yu. M. Suleymanova, "economic sustainability is the ability to maintain a certain level of values of economic parameters, which ensures its cost-effective functioning and stable development" (Suleymanova, 2013). V. A. Medvedev notes that sustainability is reduced to "an equilibrium of economic resources, which ensures stable profitability and normal conditions for extended reproduction in the long term, taking into account the most important external and internal factors" (Medvedev, 2001).

This group of authors introduces the financial and economic component of the functioning of enterprises into the concept of "sustainability", which undoubtedly makes it possible to evaluate the category in question more comprehensively. Financial stability itself acts as the basis of the overall sustainability of the enterprise and plays one of the most important roles due to the fact that it allows an economic entity to ensure an optimal structure of sources of asset financing, balance of its financial flows, solvency and profitability.

Based on all of the above, we can conclude that the concept of "sustainability" is extremely multifaceted and can reveal various aspects of the activity of an economic entity. These aspects are reduced to the goal of achieving sustainability: ensuring the balance of the elements of the economic system, maintaining a consistently high result of the functioning of the enterprise or the ability of the enterprise to respond in a timely manner to changes in internal and external factors.

We propose to consider the sustainability of an enterprise as a condition in which key economic performance indicators are maintained at a given level regardless of various impact factors.

In this case, the volume of production and sales of products, profit, liquidity and solvency should be considered as key economic indicators. As for the impact factors, the analysis of scientific sources suggests that all the factors affecting the sustainability of the enterprise can be divided into two groups: external factors that the enterprise cannot change and is forced only to adjust its management decisions to minimize the consequences and internal factors that the business entity can directly manage.

Political and legal, economic, technological, social and cultural factors can be attributed to external factors affecting sustainability, while organizational and managerial, production and financial and economic factors are internal ones (Kuchinskaya & Maidanevich, 2016). Due to the fact that the degree of influence of internal factors directly depends on the company's management decisions, they are a matter of close examination.

As one of the internal factors affecting the sustainable development of the enterprise within the group of financial and economic factors, in our opinion, it is advisable to single out transaction costs in the structure of the organization's expenses. They directly affect the process of formation and use of own funds and, consequently, the majority of financial and economic factors: the level of financial stability and solvency, the share of own and borrowed capital, the level of financial risks and others.

Back in the twentieth century, economic scientists suggested the presence of "hidden" transaction costs in addition to the overall cost structure of enterprise, the methodology of accounting and quantitative measurement of which has not been definitively determined yet. Another point complicating the procedure for accounting for these costs is the absence of the concept of "transaction costs" in our accounting, and, consequently, this makes it impossible to attribute this or that type of costs to the type of transaction ones. The above reasons prevent the accounting and assessment of the degree of influence of transaction costs on the formation of own funds and the sustainable development of the enterprise: the more internal funds the company has, the higher its financial independence and, as a result, its overall sustainability.

In order to determine the impact of transaction costs on the stability of the enterprise, it is advisable to divide them into two groups, based on the possibility of forming an inflow or outflow of funds into the company's own funds (Marakulina, 2012):

1. Transaction costs that contribute to the formation of cash inflow into own financial funds. The enterprise spends financial resources in the process of its economic activity, reducing the amount of its own funds; however, the cost outlay generates an inflow of funds in absolute terms exceeding the outflow, which contributes to the formation of reserves for expanding production, modernizing funds, improving product quality through the use of new technologies, etc.
2. Transaction costs that contribute to the formation of cash outflow from own financial funds. These are expenses attributed to the group of transactional ones that form the outflow of the company's own funds; however, their presence in the overall cost structure contributes to ensuring the rhythmic and efficient operation of the enterprise (operating costs, logistics), competent and timely adjustment of management decisions depending on changes in the external environment (company management).

Table 1 shows the impact on the sustainable development of the enterprise of transaction costs that contribute to the formation of cash inflows.

Table 1 Transaction costs that contribute to the formation of the inflow of own funds

Type of costs	The essence of costs	The nature of the impact on the sustainability of the enterprise
Marketing costs	Collecting and processing information about customers, conducting promotion campaigns, evaluating sales markets, maintaining the company's image and business reputation	These expenses contribute to the promotion of goods on the market, an increase in sales volumes, an increase in profits and the amount of its own financing sources, which forms the economic basis for the diversification of activities, expansion of the assortment and modernization of productive capital stock
Bargaining costs	Representation expenses	
Transportation costs	This type of cost gives a competitive advantage to the company, due to the fact that additional services for transporting the purchased goods to the customer's warehouse contribute to the growth of the loyalty of counterparties to the enterprise, provided that products of similar quality and price are offered on the market	
Costs related to legal registration and transaction support	These costs include the expenses of legal services for formation contracts and other documentation, which further protects the rights of the company and provides the possibility of collecting funds in case of opportunistic behavior of counterparties	This type of expenditure contributes to ensuring the inflow of financial resources within the framework of the contract or the application of penalties for non-compliance with it, which makes it possible to form reserves for the modernization of funds, improvement of production technology, etc
Insurance	The conclusion of an insurance contract, on the one hand, entails additional costs for insurance contributions, and on the other hand, it acts as a guarantee of maintaining the stability of the enterprise in the event of force majeure and the possibility of compensation for losses incurred	The inflow of financial resources during the payment of insurance compensation provides an opportunity for the company to restore or modernize funds, re-equip or restore lost assets

Source Compiled by the authors on the basis of Marakulina (2012)

To understand the data presented in Table 1, the following logic should be used: Within the group of transaction costs that contribute to the formation of the inflow of own funds, we select, for example, marketing costs. This type of expenditure is designed to ensure the maximum possible volume of product sales, which entails both compensation for all production costs, sales (well-planned marketing activities pay off), and the formation of own funds that can be spent on new modern technologies, expansion of the retail network and staff training. All these measures will have a beneficial effect on the overall sustainability of the enterprise and will allow you to maintain key performance indicators not only at a given level, but also to improve them.

Within the group of transaction costs (Table 2), which form the outflow of the company's own funds, it is advisable to focus on the "costs of interaction with the external environment", by which we mean the amount of bad debts associated with the opportunistic behavior of counterparties. The most striking illustration can be the overdue accounts receivable: The company enters into a contract for the supply of products to its counterparty, thereby waiting for the fulfillment of the terms of the contract; that is, receiving funds within the specified period that would compensate for all production and sales costs would form a profit fund. However, there is no transfer of funds, and we are forced to compensate for our expenses either from our own funds, or, alternatively, at the expense of credit funds, which implies an additional fee for their use. In other words, in this situation, we significantly reduce the amount of our own resources or even use borrowed sources of financing, thereby making the company dependent on an external lender. Considering the economic concept of "sustainability", we can emphasize that with the loss of funds, it is extremely problematic to ensure a balanced state of economic resources and normal conditions for expanded reproduction, as well as to increase one's own production potential. Currently, bad debts are increasingly becoming the cause of bankruptcy of enterprises, and the appearance of outstanding receivable is the first signal indicating possible future financial losses and a decrease in the economic stability of the business in general. To confirm the growth rate of overdue accounts receivable at Russian enterprises (except small businesses), we can cite data from Rosstat of the Russian Federation: Since 2018, there has been a gradual increase in the amount of accounts receivable from 46,669 billion rubles to 61,156 billion rubles in 2020 (Dynamics of accounts receivable of organizations (excluding small businesses) of the Russian Federation, 2021). On the one hand, the increase in the absolute value of this indicator should not be considered as a negative phenomenon; however, on the other hand, the analysis of the quality of accounts receivable suggests the danger of loss of stability due to the growth of overdue accounts receivable in its composition from 2647 billion rubles in 2018 to 2661 billion rubles in 2019 and further to 2926 billion rubles in 2020. Most of the overdue accounts receivable relate to the debt of buyers and customers (2018–1822 billion rubles, 2019–1897 billion rubles, 2020–2115 billion rubles), which indicates that the contractors of enterprises do not fulfill their obligations, do not pay for the delivered products on time this means that the contractors of the enterprises do not fulfill their obligations and do not pay for the products delivered on time. Accordingly, enterprises find themselves in a situation of lower revenues,

Table 2 Transaction costs that form the outflow of own funds

Type of costs	The essence of costs	The nature of the impact on the sustainability of the enterprise
Operating costs of technical means	These are the costs of installation, integration into a common system, technical support of various information systems, the costs of service and repair of office equipment and the use of various types of communication. The main purpose of using information systems is to provide access to a single internal personnel database of different departments	The reduction of search and information costs allows you to save money, form your own funds necessary to broaden the assortment and improve the quality of products
Company management	Costs for the organization of the business as a whole and for the remuneration of the company's managers	These types of costs contribute to the efficient operation of the enterprise, the growth of profits, from which managers will be able to form a financial base for expanding production, etc
Material and technical support	The costs in this area make it possible to ensure the smooth operation of the enterprise both in terms of the availability of resources and in terms of the state of fixed assets	
Security	Payment for the services of units engaged in the protection of facilities	
Costs of interaction with the external environment	The amount of bad debts associated with the opportunistic behavior of counterparties	Reduces the amount of own funds, forms the item of expenditure "bad debts", which are subsequently covered from the company's own funds. The smaller the value of these costs, the more stable the company is

Source Compiled by the authors on the basis of Suleymanova (2013)

which may negatively affect the overall stability of the company during the period under review. In order to avoid such cash gaps, it is advisable for the company's management to form reserves for bad debts. Accounting and management of this type of transaction costs will allow the company to ensure overall sustainability.

4 Conclusion

Thus, the following main results were obtained during the study:

1. The concept of "sustainability" characterizes the condition of an enterprise in which key indicators of economic activity are maintained at a given level regardless of various impact factors.
2. It is advisable to divide all factors affecting the sustainability of the enterprise into two large groups: external and internal factors. Among the internal factors, we propose to single out transaction costs, dividing them into transaction costs that contribute to the formation of inflow and outflow of funds to/from own financial funds.
3. The impact of transaction costs on the process of formation and use of own funds and, consequently, on most financial and economic factors is logically justified. These include the level of financial stability and solvency, the share of equity and debt capital, the level of financial risks and others.

The analysis carried out in the article gives us every reason to believe that transaction costs contribute to the formation of company's own funds, which, with proper management, can be used to maintain the sustainability of the enterprise and its development. The formation of additional funds is extremely important for enterprises in difficult economic realities, since it is the funds saved with proper management that allows for sustainability at a certain stage of development.

References

Dynamics of accounts receivable of organizations (excluding small businesses) of the Russian Federation (2021). https://rosstat.gov.ru/storage/mediabank/PYOkMyBC/Din_deb.pdf. Data Accessed November 07, 2021.

Klepikov, D. N. (2007). *Improvement of the mechanism of sustainable development of the chemical fiber industry*. Extended abstract of candidate's dissertation. Moscow.

Kolosova, T. V. (2011). *Ensuring the sustainable development of an enterprise based on increasing its innovative potential*. Candidate's dissertation. Nizhny Novgorod.

Kuchinskaya, P. V., Maidanevich, Y. P. (2016). Analysis of internal and external factors affecting the economic stability of the enterprise. Scientific periodical "CETERIS PARIBUS", (Vol. 5), (pp. 47–51).

Lavrushin, D. B. (1999). *Management of sustainable development of the enterprise (on the example of machine-building enterprises)*. Candidate's dissertation. Saratov: SGSEU.

Litvinenko, I. A. (1996). *Economic stability of corporate economic systems in Russia*. Candidate's dissertation. Moscow: Russian Academy of Public Administration.

Marakulina, Yu. N. (2012). The influence of transaction costs on the distribution of cash flows of the enterprise. *Financial Research, 1*(34), 209–215.

Medvedev, V. A. (2001). *Sustainable development of society: Models, strategy*. Academy.

Shevrina, E. V. (2000). *Assessment of the economic sustainability of agricultural enterprises*. Candidate's dissertation. Chelyabinsk.

Suleymanova, Y. M. (2013). *Management of innovative development of an industrial enterprise according to the criterion of economic sustainability*. Extended abstract of candidate's dissertation. Chelyabinsk.

Zakharov, G. N. (2020). *Formation of an economic mechanism for the sustainable development of a petrochemical enterprise*. Candidate's dissertation. St. Petersburg.

Stability of the Functioning of Credit Institutions as a Factor in the Development of Information Technologies in the Context of the Digitization of the Economy

Nadezhda I. Yashina, Olga I. Kuryleva, Elena P. Kozlova, Svetlana N. Kuznetsova, and Natalia S. Andryashina

Abstract The future development of IT technologies could easily lead to the fact that an increasing number of credit institutions will switch to the digital bank business model digital banks will be able to completely oust traditional banking institutions from the market by 2025, this will lead to cardinal transformations in the financial system. The basis of the methodology for assessing the stability of the functioning of credit institutions is the choice of a system of indicators, their regulation, standardization, and taking into account volatility. The object of the research is credit institutions in the banking services market in the regions of Russia. The subject of the research is the stability of the functioning of credit institutions. The research methodology is based on general scientific and specific scientific methods: grouping, ranking, probabilistic assessment, analysis of volume indicators, variation series, and construction of integral indicators. The rating assessment based on complex normalized indicators showing the bank's reliability characterizes the relative opportunities for the growth of industrial production in a particular region. According to the results of the study, classes of stability in the functioning of credit institutions that are ready to move to digital transformation in the face of volatility in the economy have been established. The complex nature of assessing the reliability of a bank, determining the stability class of credit institutions based on the stability indicator, which allows assessing the possibilities of digital transformation of the bank and digitalization of the banking sector, is a distinctive feature of the study.

N. I. Yashina (✉)
Lobachevsky State University of Nizhny Novgorod, Nizhny Novgorod, Russia
e-mail: sitnicof@mail.ru

O. I. Kuryleva · E. P. Kozlova · S. N. Kuznetsova · N. S. Andryashina
Minin Nizhny Novgorod State Pedagogical University, Nizhny Novgorod, Russia
e-mail: dens@52.ru

N. S. Andryashina
e-mail: natali_andr@bk.ru

E. I. Lazareva et al. (eds.), *Innovative Trends in International Business and Sustainable Management*, Approaches to Global Sustainability, Markets, and Governance,
https://doi.org/10.1007/978-981-19-4005-7_46

Keywords Digital transformation · Banking sector · Digitalization risks · Reliability and stability of functioning · Credit institution

JEL Classification H61 · H7 · R11 · L5

1 Introduction

Russia entered the top countries in the digitalization of banks due to the achievements of major market players. But other financial organizations are also following this path. The foreground is the dialogue of the client not with the operator, but with the remote assistant, the provision of services online.

The digitalization of credit institutions is heterogeneous, and large banks provide services more widely. This is not typical for other markets, where, on the contrary, the leaders in innovation are medium-sized or even small financial organizations (Garina et al., 2021). This reflects the position of the Russian banking market in relation to innovation and digitalization on a global scale, which has long been denied, especially by foreign experts.

Most banks realized the urgent need for digitalization only this year, when the pandemic divided them into those: who are truly digital and can provide services without the help of their branches or call centers; who have just started the process, this is the majority of medium-sized credit organizations. In order to develop digitalization of credit institutions in the regions, it is important to assess their reliability and stability of functioning, because these are the factors that are the basis for investments in digital technologies (Tolstykh et al., 2020a).

According to experts, more than 30–50% of the GDP of most countries that have entered the information era will be realized within the ecosystem of the digital economy by 2025, which means that the bulk of all economic and business processes will be implemented using the latest information tools and virtual platforms (Tolstykh et al., 2020b).

In the face of crises, increased interbank competition, an assessment of the reliability and stability of the functioning of credit institutions will contribute to their digital transformation, improving the services provided and increasing the security of user data, because the client's comfort always comes first.

Authors Tan, and Floros tested the relationship between risk, competition, and performance in the Chinese banking sector from 2003 to 2013 using the Lerner index, adjusted for effectiveness and ineffectiveness of stability as indicators of competition and risk of insolvency (Tan and Floros, 2018). The results show that Chinese commercial banks with higher efficiency have higher credit and insolvency risks, but lower liquidity and capital risks. Increased competition reduces credit and insolvency risk, but increases liquidity risk. Credit risk and insolvency risk are significantly and positively related to efficiency, while liquidity risk and capital risk are significantly and negatively related to it. Finally, lower liquidity risk reduces competition (Kozlova et al., 2021a).

In assessing the stability of the bank's functioning, it is important to consider the compression limits of the capital base of credit institutions—the lower limit of the «subsidence» of the capital adequacy ratio, which is critical from the point of view of not only compliance with the Central Bank of the Russian Federation standards but also the ability of banks to perform the function of creditors of the Russian economy. The complexity of the transition to Basel requirements is due to the relatively low quality of capital, its significant dependence on «subordinated» injections, as well as the low quality of assets, taking into account the increased requirements for the state of liquidity (Kozlova et al., 2021b).

2 Methodology

The methodological toolkit is based on the indicators of the CAMEL methodology, which determine the reliability of credit institutions: capital adequacy, asset quality, and earnings.

At the end of the calculations characterizing the reliability of credit institutions, the quantitative ones are normalized, which ensures their typification. Normalization of indicators leads, on the one hand, to a loss of dimension, however, on the other hand, the structure of changes in individual coefficients is preserved. Indicators are heterogeneous, for example, an increase in some of them contributes to a decrease in the level of reliability of credit institutions, while an increase in others causes an increase in the level of reliability of credit institutions. Further, the indicators using formula (1) are standardized considering the volatility of the credit system as a whole or the group under consideration

$$\mathrm{KK}_{ijv} = \frac{\mathrm{KK}_{ij}}{\sigma_i}, \tag{1}$$

where KK_{ijv}—standardized coefficient of the ith bank considering volatility,
σ_i—standard deviation of the normalized coefficient of the ith bank.

$$\mathrm{KKK}_{iv} = \sum_{j=1}^{m} \mathrm{KK}_{ijv}, \tag{2}$$

where KKK_{iv}—complex standardized indicator of the ith bank considering volatility.

The final conclusion is formed by summing up all standardized indicators calculated considering the risk of the credit system as a whole or the group under consideration.

The complex standardized indicator KKK_{iv} of the bank's reliability is interpreted as: the lower the KKK_{iv}, the better. Subsequently, banks are classified according to the levels of reliability (Romanovskaya et al., 2021).

The stability class of credit institutions is determined based on the stability indicator. Calculation of the stability indicator:

1. Credit institutions are ranked, the rank is determined by the value of the complex standardized indicator of the bank considering volatility.
2. The bank with the lowest value of the complex standardized indicator of the bank considering volatility is assigned the first place or one point.
3. All ranks of all banks are summed up.
4. The stability indicator is defined as the ratio of the rank of a particular bank to the average value obtained for all ranks.

The stability indicator from 0.5 to 1.0 indicates the bank's high stability class.

The value of the stability indicator up to 0.5 indicates effective performance of banks, and above 1.0 indicates a possible crisis situation in the bank.

3 Results

The rating based on the bank's comprehensive standardized indicator considering volatility is presented in Table 2. To determine the ranks, we assume that the bank with the highest value of the bank's reliability has the first rank.

Determination of the stability class based on the stability indicator is based on the calculations shown in Table 1.

Banks belonging to the first and second classes of stability are highly likely to use innovative technologies and move to new digital platforms.

4 Conclusion

The presented methodology based on a comprehensive standardized indicator of reliability considering volatility will make it possible to see banks capable of implementing digital platforms.

The digital transformation of the banking sector, being a tool for the development of the modern economy, will allow it to turn into an independent developing economic sector (Yakushenko and Shimanskaya, 2017).

This «trend» was formed long before the COVID-19 pandemic, but, undoubtedly, this situation with the pandemic has accelerated the process of digitalization of the financial sector. Now the priority is the safety and health of people, therefore, in order to remain competitive on this «battlefield», the leaders of the financial market should be «digital» and keep up with modern trends in the introduction of the latest technologies into the banking system (Zumakulova, 2019). To do this, first of all,

Table 1 System of indicators of bank reliability

No	Indicator name	Interpretation of indicators	Interpretation of indicator change
1	Equity (capital) adequacy indicators (PC1); the indicator of total capital adequacy (PC2) and the indicator for assessing the quality of capital (PC3)	The PC1 indicator characterizes the adequacy of the absolute amount of equity (capital) of a credit institution to cover the risks of balance sheet and off-balance sheet transactions accepted by it The indicator of total capital adequacy PC2 characterizes the adequacy of the absolute amount of capital in relation to the volume of risky balance sheet assets The criterion for the quality of equity capital is expressed by one indicator PC3, which characterizes the ratio of additional and fixed capital	Maximization of indicators
2	Assets valuation indicators: loan quality (PA1), asset quality (PA2), as well as the share of overdue loans (PA3)	Indicator PA1 is the share of bad loans in the total volume of loans The risk of loss indicator (PA2) is defined as the percentage of assets not covered by reserves, reserves for possible losses, for which should be more than 20 percent, to the bank's own funds (capital). The indicator of the share of overdue loans (PA3) is the share of overdue loans in the total volume of loans	Maximization of indicators
3	Indicators for assessing profitability: return on assets (PD1), return on equity (PD2), and the indicator of net interest margin (PD5)	Return on assets (PD1)—the percentage change in the financial result to the average value of assets, the optimal value of the indicator should exceed 1.5%. Return on equity (PD2)—the percentage change in the financial result to the average capital. The optimal return on equity is considered to be at least 8%, the maximum value of additional capital is 30%. Net interest margin (PD5)—the percentage change in net interest income to the average asset value, the indicator must exceed 5%	Maximization of indicators

(continued)

Table 1 (continued)

No	Indicator name	Interpretation of indicators	Interpretation of indicator change
4	Indicators from the liquidity group: the ratio of highly liquid assets and borrowed funds (PL1), indicators of instant liquidity (PL2) and current liquidity (PL3)	The ratio of highly liquid assets to borrowed funds (PL1)—the optimal value should exceed 12%. Instant liquidity (PN2) is determined in accordance with the procedure established for calculating the mandatory current liquidity ratio The bank's instant liquidity ratio (PL2) regulates the risk of the bank losing liquidity within one operating day and determines the minimum ratio of the amount of the bank's highly liquid assets to the amount of the bank's liabilities on demand accounts, the optimal value being 17% The current liquidity indicator (PL3) is determined in accordance with the procedure established for calculating the mandatory ratio of the bank's current liquidity indicator The bank's current liquidity ratio (PL3) regulates the risk of the bank losing liquidity and determines the minimum ratio of the amount of the bank's liquid assets to the amount of the bank's liabilities on demand accounts, the optimal value should exceed 55%	Maximization of indicators

Source Compiled by the authors

financial organizations need to focus their main efforts on IT infrastructures and to abandon outdated mechanics.

Table 2 Bank ratings based on a comprehensive standardized reliability indicator considering the bank's volatility for 2020

Name	Comprehensive standardized bank indicator considering volatility	Reliability grade	Stability indicator	Stability class
JSC «Togliattikhimbank»	33.09	1	0.045	Second
class 1 standard—effect	33.76	2	0.091	Second
JSC CB «NIB»	34.86	3	0.136	Second
JSC «Databank»	37.82	4	0.182	Second
PJSC «BystroBank»	37.89	5	0.227	Second
JSCB «Energobank» (JSC)	38.44	6	0.273	Second
«ALTYNBANK» LLC	39.09	7	0.318	Second
JSC Bank «Venets»	39.14	8	0.364	Second
PJSC «Norvik Bank»	39.99	9	0.409	Second
JSC «IC Bank»	40.17	10	0.455	Second
JSC «Econombank»	42.36	11	0.500	Second
JSC «TATSOTSBANK»	42.59	12	0.545	Second
class 2 standard	43.45	13	0.591	First
PJSC «NBD-Bank»	43.52	14	0.636	First
«Bank Zarechye» (JSC)	43.64	15	0.682	First
LLC «AutoCreditBank»	44.22	16	0.727	First
LLC «Bank 131»	44.36	17	0.773	First
JSC CB «Arzamas»	44.52	18	0.818	First
JSC «KS BANK»	46.43	19	0.864	First
LLC Bank «Avers»	46.55	20	0.909	First
JSC «BALAKOVO-BANK»	46.89	21	0.955	First
LLC Bank «Saratov»	46.98	22	1.000	First
JSC «First Dortransbank»	47.20	23	1.045	Third
JSC CB «Solidarity»	48.22	24	1.091	Third
CB «Sputnik» (PJSC)	48.26	25	1.136	Third
JSC «KOSHELEV-BANK»	48.50	26	1.182	Third
JSC «SAROVBUSINESSBANK»	48.55	27	1.227	Third
JSC «Avtogradbank»	48.57	28	1.273	Third
LLC «Kamkombank»	48.71	29	1.318	Third
PJSC CB «Khimik»	48.95	30	1.364	Third
LLC «Zemsky Bank»	49.28	31	1.409	Third
Bank «Yoshkar-Ola» (PJSC)	49.31	32	1.455	Third

(continued)

Table 2 (continued)

Name	Comprehensive standardized bank indicator considering volatility	Reliability grade	Stability indicator	Stability class
PJSC «AKIBANK»	49.41	33	1.500	Third
JSC CB «Khlynov»	49.55	34	1.545	Third
CB «OBR» (LLC)	49.59	35	1.591	Third
LLC CBED «Bank of Kazan»	50.09	36	1.636	Third
JSC «AKTIV BANK»	50.39	37	1.682	Third
PJSC Bank «Kuznetskiy»	50.57	38	1.727	Third
JSC «Bank «Agroros»	52.49	39	1.773	Third
Standard—3 class crit	54.26	40	1.818	Third
JSC «Gazneftbank»	54.84	41	1.864	Third
PJSC «AK BARS» BANK	60.49	42	1.909	Third

Source Authors' calculations based on open data from the Bank of Russia and the Federal State Statistics Service of the Russian Federation (2019)

References

Federal State Statistics Service of the Russian Federation (2019). https://rosstat.gov.ru/. Data accessed December 20, 2021.

Garina, E. P., Romanovskaya, E. V., Andryashina, N. S., Potashnik, Y. S., Garin, A. P. (2021). The product development system category: Components and modeling approaches. *Studies in Systems, Decision and Control, 314*(c), 465–471.

Kozlova, E. P., Kuznetsova, S. N., Garina, E. P., Romanovskaya, E. V., & Andryashina, N. S. (2021a). The concept interpretation of sustainable development mechanism in the conditions of technological transformation of industrial enterprises. *Studies in Systems, Decision and Control, 314*, 729–736.

Kozlova, E. P., Morozova, G. A., Kuznetsov, V. P., Romanovskaya, E. V., & Andryashina, N. S. (2021b). Interaction of human and smart technologies in modern conditions. *Lecture Notes in Networks and Systems, 155*, 609–618.

Romanovskaya, E. V., Andryashina, N. S., Kuznetsova, S. N., Smirnova, Z. V., & Ivonina, O. G. (2021). Digital technologies in Russia: Trends, place and role in economy. *Lecture Notes in Networks and Systems, 155*, 344–351.

Tan, Y., & Floros, C. (2018). Risk, competition and efficiency in banking: Evidence from China. *Global Finance Journal, 35*(C), 223–236.

Tolstykh, T. O., Shkarupeta, E. V., Kostuhin, Y. Y., Zhaglovskaya, A. V., & Andryashina, N. S. (2020a). Formation of the ecosystem as a factor in the development of industrial enterprises in the digital economy. *Lecture Notes in Networks and Systems, 73*, 1247–1254.

Tolstykh, T. O., Shkarupeta, E. V., Kostuhin, Y. Y., Zhaglovskaya, A. V., & Garin, A. P. (2020b). Scenarios for the development of industrial complexes in the digital economy. *Lecture Notes in Networks and Systems, 73*, 1255–1261.

Yakushenko, K. V., & Shimanskaya, A. V. (2017). Digital transformation of information support for economic management of the EAEU member states. *Science and Technology News (Minsk), 2*(42), 11–20.

Zumakulova, F. S. (2019). Digitalization of the banking sector. In *Materials of the international scientific and practical conference* (pp. 356–380). Federal State Budgetary Educational Institution of Higher Education «Kabardino-Balkarian State Agrarian University named after V.M. Kokov» (Nalchik), Russia.

Assessment of the Stakeholders' Contribution to Enterprise Value of the Russian Metallurgical Industry

Maksim P. Kalynychenko, Tatiana V. Voronina, Ashkhyen B. Yatsenko, and Irina V. Savenkova

Abstract *Purpose* The purpose of this paper is to develop an approach that makes it possible to assess the contribution of individual groups of stakeholders to the increment in the capitalization of the Russian metallurgical enterprises. *Design/methodology/approach* The research methodology includes econometric methods. Based on econometric methods using the EViews 9.0 software package, the contribution of certain groups of stakeholders to the increase in capitalization of the Russian metallurgical enterprises has been assessed. *Findings* The existing scientific and methodological approaches of monetary and non-monetary assessments of stakeholder groups' contribution to the increment of the enterprise value have been systematized, which enabled to conclude the dominance of integrated approaches using quantitative and qualitative indicators. It has been found that among the methods for assessing stakeholders' contribution, the following ones are most frequently used: a survey in the form of a questionnaire or interview, expert assessments and their varieties. In exceptional cases, econometric analysis tools and multiple regression methods are used. *Originality/value* It has been explored that of all groups of stakeholders, the largest contribution to the capitalization of the Russian metallurgical enterprises is made by non-financial stakeholders (personnel) and financial stakeholders (shareholders and creditors).

Keywords Capitalization · Stakeholders · Stakeholder contribution · Stakeholder value · Enterprise

JEL Classification C51 · C55 · L60 · M21 · M41 · P12 · P17

M. P. Kalynychenko (✉)
Northern (Arctic) Federal University named after M.V. Lomonosov, Arkhangelsk, Russia
e-mail: mpk79@mail.ru

Tula branch of Plekhanov Russian University of Economics, Tula, Russia

T. V. Voronina · A. B. Yatsenko · I. V. Savenkova
Southern Federal University, Rostov-on-Don, Russia
e-mail: abyacenko@sfedu.ru

E. I. Lazareva et al. (eds.), *Innovative Trends in International Business and Sustainable Management*, Approaches to Global Sustainability, Markets, and Governance,
https://doi.org/10.1007/978-981-19-4005-7_47

1 Introduction

Stakeholders' welfare maximization depends on their goals and interests. Each stakeholder chooses an enterprise as a way to achieve their goals and interests. When implementing the mechanism for harmonizing interests, it is necessary to understand not only their expectations for obtaining results but also their contribution to the activities of the enterprise.

The success of the harmonization of the various stakeholders' mutual interests depends on the centres of responsibility or profit as elements of the market management system of an enterprise, which can build order of consistent and subordinate interests between the respective stakeholders. The harmony of interests between the enterprise and its stakeholders will be marked by the following conditions: the amount of demand for a product (commodity market) or resource (resource market) will be levelled by supply; in the course of harmonization of interests, the well-being of the parties increases, and the main goal of the enterprise is achieved. Then, in an economic sense, interests will be balanced, existing conflicts will be resolved, and additional organizational and managerial decisions will only enhance the achieved effect.

The objective of the article is to develop an approach that makes it possible to assess the contribution of individual groups of stakeholders to the increment in the capitalization of the Russian metallurgical enterprises.

2 Materials and Method

The volume of scientific publications within the framework of the stakeholder approach continues to grow, while there are still no single methodological principles for assessing the stakeholders' contribution to the value of an enterprise. Our theoretical generalizations show that a lot of researchers emphasize the need to harmonize the mutual interests of stakeholders with the interests of the enterprise (Akulinin & Chernova, 2019; Cosmulese et al., 2019; Lutz & Bodendorf, 2020). At the same time, there are much fewer publications that offer specific scientific and methodological approaches to assessing the contribution of stakeholders and benefits they obtain from interaction with the enterprise (Ivashkovskaya, 2012, 2019; Mints et al., 2020; Novozhilova, 2017). Currently, integrated approaches based on monetary and non-monetary assessments of the contribution of stakeholders' contribution to the increment of the enterprise value, using quantitative and qualitative indicators, dominate.

The question of stakeholders' classification remains open, and it does not allow to solve the problem of ranking them effectively. The method of theoretical generalizations made it possible to establish the existing variety of approaches to the classification of stakeholders (Bocharov, 2015; Clarkson, 1995; Fassin, 2009; Mitchell et al., 1997). The common component of all approaches to the classification of stakeholders is understanding that the relative importance of groups for the enterprise should be reflected in management priorities: formalization of the main goal, the hierarchy of goals, as well as strategies for interaction with stakeholders and the results achieved.

The stakeholder approach requires taking into account the interests and contributions of all owners of both financial and non-financial capital involved in active and passive forms of participation in the activities of the enterprise in order to get economic benefits from interaction with it. Within the framework of the format of this work, emphasis should be placed on the fact that until recently, in theory, and practice, the shareholder business model has dominated, prioritizing the interests of owners and maximizing value for shareholders (founders). Among the latest theoretical and applied research results, it is especially worth highlighting those works which indicate that the concept of stakeholder value is replacing the concept of value-based management (Ivashkovskaya, 2019). If we go beyond the VBM concept, then the stakeholder value model is focused on "achieving an intellectual, social, financial balance of the capital structure". In accordance with this, it is proposed to develop stakeholders' contribution indices to reflect the contribution of stakeholders to the formation of the enterprise value, aimed at assessing the ratio of the accumulated flow of economic profit of the enterprise and the costs of building relationships with stakeholders (Felício et al., 2014; Kalynychenko, 2013). However, when developing a corporate strategy, the search for a balance of stakeholders' interests comes into conflict with the target criterion for maximizing the value of a business for shareholders, in particular the market value of shares. Among the methods for assessing the contribution of stakeholders, the following are most often used: a survey in the form of a questionnaire or interview, expert assessments and their varieties. In exceptional cases, econometric analysis tools and multiple regression methods are used.

3 Results

It is possible to assess the stakeholders' contribution to the value of an enterprise within the framework of the monetary approach through the sources of financing of the enterprise that they form, which is consistent with the items of the liability balance at the time of its compilation. Analysis of the balance sheet liabilities of PJSC "Trubnaya Metallurgicheskaya Kompaniya" (TMK) allows us to present the contribution of stakeholders in terms of financing the enterprise (Table 1).

As we can see from Table 1 the largest share belongs to such key stakeholders as accounts payable (62.4%), shareholders (13.2%) and customers (12.2%). As a result, this is reflected in the financial model of the company and the financing source structure for PJSC "TMK".

The analysis of the financial statements of some metallurgical enterprises enables the identification of the contribution and benefits of their financial and non-financial stakeholders. When forming the statistical base of the study, the sample included

Table 1 Assessment of the stakeholders' contribution to the liability of the balance sheet of PJSC "TMK", %

Stakeholders	Liabilities and shareholders' equity (line code)	2019	2018	2017
Creditors	Borrowed funds (p. 1410 F1); Borrowed funds (p. 1510 F1)	59.3	61.6	66.2
Shareholders	Authorized capital (p. 1310 F1); Own shares (p. 1320 F1); Revaluation of non-current assets (p. 1340); Additional capital (p. 1350 F1); Reserve capital (p. 1360 F1); Retained earnings/uncovered loss (p. 1370 F1)	11.1	14.7	13.7
Customers	Advances received (p. 1526 F1)	13.3	11.3	11.9
Suppliers	Accounts payable to suppliers and contractors (p. 1521 F1)	15.2	11.9	7.6
State	Deferred tax liabilities (p. 1420 F1); Accounts payable to state extra-budgetary funds (p. 1523 F1); Tax arrears (p. 1524 F1)	0.97	0.4	0.5
Personnel	Accounts payable to employees (p. 1522 F1)	0.05	0.04	0.05

Source Developed and compiled by the authors

nine enterprises of the Russian metallurgical industry: PJSC "Ashinsky Metallurgicheskiy Zavod" (AMET), PJSC "Uralskaya Kuznitsa" (USP), PJSC "Novolipetskiy Metallurgicheskiy Kombinat" (NLMK), PJSC "Magnitogorskiy Metallurgicheskiy Kombinat" (MMK), PJSC "Mechel", JSC "Obyedinennaya Metallurgicheskaya Kompaniya" (OMK), PJSC "Severstal" (SS), PJSC "Trubnaya Metallurgicheskaya Kompaniya" (TMK), PJSC "Chelyabinskiy Metallurgicheskiy Kombinat" (ChMK). The observation period is 7 yr. JSC "OMK", PJSC "MMK", PJSC "TMK" and PJSC "NLMK" show negative individual effects. After conducting the correlation analysis and checking for the multicolarity of independent variables, the indicators that have the greatest influence on the dependent variable KAP (capitalization) were identified. These are AKC (i.e. shareholders' contribution), KR (i.e. creditors' contribution) and PER (i.e. personnel's contribution).

Using the pooled least squares method, the parameters of the linear exponential, power, logarithmic and other models were estimated from the combined observations of panel data. The study was carried out using the EViews 9.0 software package. As a result, a power-law model was chosen as the most reliable one with all significant regression coefficients (Table 2).

Thus, the constructed power-law model in terms of stakeholder contributions is.

$$\log \mathrm{KAP} = 14.746 + 0.407 \cdot \log \mathrm{AKC} - 0.467 \cdot \log \mathrm{KR} + 0.4396 \cdot \log \mathrm{PER} \text{ or}$$
$$\mathrm{KAP} = 2535749.977 \cdot \mathrm{AKC}^{0.407} \cdot \mathrm{KR}^{-0.467} \cdot \mathrm{PER}^{0.4396} \quad (1)$$

Table 2 Assessment of the pooled model with panel data on stakeholders' contributions

Dependent variable: LOGKAP?				
Method: Pooled least squares				
Variable	Coefficient	Std. Error	*t*-Statistic	Prob.
LOGAKC?	0.406961	0.125089	3.253375	0.0019
LOGKR?	−0.466767	0.149420	−3.123864	0.0028
LOGPER?	0.439607	0.211545	2.078079	0.0421
C	14.74558	2.755501	5.351327	0.0000
R-squared	0.889274	Mean dependent var		20.22451
Adjusted *R*-squared	0.790808	S.D. dependent var		1.941527
S.E. of regression	1.677893	Akaike info criterion		3.934341
Sum squared resid	166.1041	Schwarz criterion		4.070413
Log likelihood	−119.9317	Hannan-Quinn criter		3.987859
F-statistic	8.004583	Durbin-Watson stat		1.640729
Prob(*F*-statistic)	0.000146			

Source Developed and compiled by the authors

The value of the coefficient of determination shows the significance of the model as a whole and indicates that 88.93% of the variation in capitalization is explained by variation in the contributions of shareholders, creditors and personnel. The value of the Durbin-Watson statistic is in the range between the lower $d_L = 1.48$ and the upper $d_U = 1.69$ boundaries, which indicates the absence of autocorrelation of residuals in the original specification. Checking the model for heteroscedasticity using the Breusch-Pagan-Godfrey test showed that the Fisher statistic is F-statistic $= 2.057466$ with the Prob. F (3.59) $= 0.1156$. This means that the hypothesis of homoscedasticity of the residues cannot be rejected.

However, this model (1) is the most restrictive of all the possible ones, since it assigns the same behaviour to all objects in the sample at all times, therefore, it is necessary to evaluate the regression by including random individual effects, which may allow taking into account the heterogeneity of the sample in the covariance matrix of random errors. Let's first check the hypothesis about the absence of individual effects:

$$H_0 : \{\gamma_i = 0\}, \quad i = 1, \ldots, 9$$

To test the hypothesis, we will use the F-test: Cross-section F-statistic $= 88.13$, Prob (F-statistic) $= 0.00$. The hypothesis of the absence of individual fixed effects is rejected at any level of significance. Thus, the most appropriate way would be to use a fixed-effects panel data model, which can be broadly written as follows:

$$\text{KAP} = \gamma_1 \cdot d_1 + \gamma_2 \cdot d_2 + \cdots + \gamma_9 \cdot d_9 + c + \beta_1 \cdot \text{AKC} + \beta_2 \cdot \text{KR} + \beta_3 \cdot \text{PER},$$

where γ_i is the PLS estimates of the model parameters before the dummy filter variables d_i for the i enterprise ($i = \overline{1, 9}$), β_j is the PLS estimates of the model parameters before the independent variable j ($j = \overline{1, 3}$). The obtained estimates of the coefficients of this model are presented in Table 3.

We obtain a panel data model for stakeholders' contributions with fixed effects:

$$\begin{aligned}\log \text{KAP} = {} & 1.703 \cdot d_{\text{AM}} + 0.321 \cdot d_M - 2.019 \cdot d_{\text{MMK}} - 1.312 \cdot d_{\text{NDMK}} \\ & - 2.453 \cdot d_{\text{OMK}} + 1.099 \cdot d_{\text{SS}} + 1.928 \cdot d_{\text{TCHMK}} - 1.422 \cdot d_{\text{TMK}} \\ & + 2.155 \cdot d_{\text{UK}} + 10,500 + 0.0322 \cdot \log \text{AKC} - 0.138 \cdot \log \text{KR} \\ & + 0.765 \cdot \log \text{PER}\end{aligned} \quad (2)$$

Table 3 Fixed effects model

Dependent variable: LOGKAP?				
Variable	Coefficient	Std. Error	*t*-Statistic	Prob.
LOGAKC?	0.032204	0.013996	2.300900	0.0147
LOGKR?	−0.138990	0.075652	−1.837218	0.0320
LOGPER?	0.764613	0.208967	3.659008	0.0006
C	10.50040	3.760473	2.792307	0.0073
Fixed effects (Cross)				
_AMET–C	1.703118			
_Mechel–C	0.321196			
_MMK–C	−2.018824			
_NLMK–C	−1.311533			
_OMK–C	−2.452901			
_SS–C	1.098667			
_ChMK–C	1.927603			
_TMK–C	−1.422436			
_USP–C	2.155110			
	Effects Specification			
Cross-section fixed (dummy variables)				
R-squared	0.950022	Mean dependent var		20.22451
Adjusted R-squared	0.939242	S.D. dependent var		1.941527
S.E. of regression	0.478569	Akaike info criterion		1.533610
Sum squared resid	11.68043	Schwarz criterion		1.941826
Log likelihood	−36.30871	Hannan-Quinn criter.		1.694163
F-statistic	88.13137	Durbin-Watson stat		1.401337
Prob(*F*-statistic)	0.000000			

Source Developed and compiled by the authors

As we can see from Table 3 the estimates of all the coefficients of the model with individual fixed coefficients (2) according to the Student's *t*-statistic (Prob. < 0.05) are considered significant. The quality of the fit in the model should be judged by the coefficient of determination, which is 0.9500, which indicates a sufficiently high quality of the model fit to the original data. The analysis has shown that the model with individual fixed coefficients is advisable to use for forecast purposes. An increase in the shareholders' contribution ratio of 1% will lead to an increase in capitalization of 0.032%. The largest contribution to capitalization is made by personnel, with an increase of 1%, capitalization will rise by 0.76%. The individual effects identified in the model for stakeholders' contributions reflect the impact on the capitalization level that is individual for each enterprise. These may be factors related to the properties of each enterprise, which are considered by stakeholders, as well as the nature of organizational and economic relations with stakeholders and the level of harmony of mutual interests at the "input of the system", the quality of management, the position of the enterprise in the commodity and related resource markets, etc. At the same time, the greater the individual fixed effect is, the more opportunities the company has to increase the level of capitalization due to factors not included in the model. As a result of building a model for the contribution of stakeholders, enterprises were ranked according to the size of the individual effect. The greatest positive effects are observed at the next enterprises: USP, ChMK, AMET, Severstal. The negative individual effects are demonstrated by OMK, MMK, NLMK and TMK. Negative effects at the above-motioned enterprises may mean the presence of unfavourable factors that reduce capitalization in the direction of "stakeholders' contribution".

4 Conclusion

The assessment of key stakeholders' contribution to the value of the enterprise within the framework of the monetary approach through the sources of the enterprise financing formed by them has been carried out. Econometric analysis based on panel data using the EViews 9.0 software package has enabled us to assess the contribution of certain groups of stakeholders to the increment in the capitalization of the Russian metallurgical enterprises. A distinctive feature of the author's approach is the formalization of econometric models for contributions, which can be used as a tool for measuring, on the one hand, the value created by stakeholders for the enterprise, and, on the other hand, the value created for the stakeholders by metallurgical companies. The individual effects identified in the panel data models on stakeholders' contributions should be evaluated for a specific enterprise based on non-monetary indicators through surveys of each group of stakeholders.

References

Akulinin, F. V., & Chernova, P. S. (2019). Motives and incentives in the work of stakeholders in the corporate governance system. *Rationing and Wages in the Industry, 11*, 74–78.

Bocharov, N. A. (2015). Stakeholders as a tool for social interaction of companies. *Bulletin of the University, 10*, 250–254.

Clarkson, M. A. (1995). A stakeholder framework for analyzing and evaluating corporate social performance. *Academy of Management Review, 20*(1), 92–117.

Cosmulese, C. G., Socoliuc, M., Ciubotariu, M. S., Grosu, V., & Mihaila, S. (2019). An empirical analysis of stakeholders' expectations and integrated reporting quality. *Ekonomska Istrazivanja, 1*, 3963–3986. https://doi.org/10.1080/1331677X.2019.1680303

Fassin, Y. (2009). The stakeholder model refined. *Journal of Business Ethics, 84*(1), 113–135.

Felício, J. A., Ivashkovskaya, I., Rodrigues, R., & Stepanova, A. (2014). Corporate governance and performance in the largest European listed banks during the financial crisis. *Innovar, 53*, 83–98.

Ivashkovskaya, I. V. (2012). *A stakeholder approach to management focused on the increment of the company's value*. Corporate Finance, 1(21), 59–70. http://ecsocman.hse.ru. Accessed May 30, 2021.

Ivashkovskaya, I. V. (2019). *Modelling company value*. Strategic responsibility of the board of directors: monograph. Moscow, INFRA-M.

Kalynychenko, M. (2013). Harmonization of social and labour relations in the marketing management system of an enterprise. *Economic Journal, XXI*(11-12-1), 54–57.

Lutz, C. J., & Bodendorf, F. (2020). Analyzing industry stakeholders using open-source competitive intelligence—a case study in the automotive supply industry. *The Journal of Enterprise Information Management, 3*, 579–599. https://doi.org/10.1108/JEIM-08-2019-0234

Mints, A., Schumann, A., Kamyshnykova, E. (2020). Stakeholders' rank of reflexion diagnostics in a corporate social responsibility system. *Economic Annals-XXI*(1–2), 92–104. https://doi.org/10.21003/ea.V181-08

Mitchell, R. K., Agle, B. R., & Wood, D. J. (1997). Toward a theory of stakeholder identification and salience: Defining the principle of who and what really counts. *The Academy of Management Review, 4*, 853–886.

Novozhilova, Yu. V. (2017). Information and analytical support of integrated reporting: Assessing the impact of stakeholders on the change in value created. *Statistics and Economics, 1*, 43–50.

Public-Law Institute of Civil Services and the Fourth Industrial Revolution

Vladimir E. Berezko

Abstract Under the conditions of the new technological revolution, understanding the role and significance of the public-law model of civil services becomes especially relevant. If the state is understood as a republic and the basis of stability and prosperity, then the achievement of social peace is possible only with a proper understanding of the public-law institution of public services. The public authorities and the public-law institution of the civil services will be able to resist other problems of the twenty-first century effectively. Moreover, scientists have called the activities leading to climate change as the biggest threat of this century. In this regard, the paper aims to form a well-founded understanding of the public-law institution of civil services in the context of the fourth industrial revolution. The research used systemic methods, methods of comparative jurisprudence, and logical analysis. A significant place is given to the methods of exegesis and hermeneutics. During the analysis, the value and significance of the public-law institution of civil services in the new conditions were substantiated. Realizing the people's collective will, civil servants ensure the proper solution of "common affairs," which is the essence of the state as the "trinity" of territory, population, and power. Together with the public interest, private interest is fully realized. The central role in solving the associated problems of climate change will be played by the public authorities and the public-law institution of the civil services. As a result of the study, it was found that in the context of the fourth industrial revolution, the public-law institution of civil services acquires particular importance for ensuring the stable development of a modern state and solving both internal and global problems.

Keywords Fourth industrial revolution · State · Executive power · Public service · Law · Public-law institute of public service · Climate change

JEL Classification K10

V. E. Berezko (✉)
MGIMO University, Moscow, Russia
e-mail: vberezko@yandex.ru

E. I. Lazareva et al. (eds.), *Innovative Trends in International Business and Sustainable Management*, Approaches to Global Sustainability, Markets, and Governance,
https://doi.org/10.1007/978-981-19-4005-7_48

1 Introduction

The founder and President of the World Economic Forum in Davos, Klaus Martin Schwab, quite rightly speaks of the "crossroads" faced by today's world (Schwab & Davis, 2019). In his opinion, current "social and political systems" are no longer capable of coping with the challenges they face. However, is it really so?

2 Methodology

The research used the systemic method, the method of comparative jurisprudence, and logical analysis, besides the methods of exegesis and hermeneutics.

3 Results and Discussion

Before answering the question posed in the introduction, I believe that it is necessary to quote the opinion of Immanuel Kant. The great philosopher noted precisely that, in reality, the state is governed by the one who holds the executive power in his hands—the potestas executoria (Kant, 1994).

Let me emphasize that the philosophical understanding of the essence of the state and public service in the context of the fourth industrial revolution is acquiring special relevance. Finding the correct and objectively correct answers to the questions posed by the development of today's civilization determine, without exaggeration, the entire existence of humankind, not just specific sovereign states. In the desire to ascribe to the state (understood as the "trinity" of territory, population, and power), some contemporary publicists see an inability to effectively respond to emerging challenges, an ordinary desire to replace public state power with corporate power of transnational companies. Contemporary legal scholars find a certain justification for this. For example, professor G. V. Atamanchuk quite rightly noted that the ideology of management penetrates the system of public administration not as disinterestedly as it may seem at first glance. On the contrary, this ideology contains the interests of the largest corporations in the world: "The ideology of transnational corporations is reduced to bringing almost to zero everything related to state with its national borders, citizenship (instead, people of the world), national interests, customs, national currency, state language, other national attributes, ideals, values, and goals of life. They—the rulers of the planet's economy—do not need anything from the state: it interferes with the freedom of their domination" (Atamanchuk, 2008).

Simultaneously, it should be noted that the problems of corporate governance in Russia arouse the unflagging interest of researchers (Dementieva & Zavyalova, 2020).

It should be noted that the philosophical understanding of the substance of the state and state institutions is acquiring more and more importance and relevance in today's world. The Israeli historian Yuval Noah Harari, speaking about the challenges that the world faces in the era of the fourth industrial revolution, quite rightly notes the apparent fact that the existence of humanity is impossible without a philosophical understanding of the challenges facing humanity. Harari clearly sees the fact that ignoring such an understanding can ultimately lead to the dominance of a primitive form of private interest of small shopkeepers—"How much did I earn today?" (Harari, 2019). The problem of objectifying ethics in the digital age not only prevents anachronism but also gives a new impetus to human development, "… when designing an unmanned vehicle Toyota or Tesla, the theoretical problem of philosophical ethics turns into a practical engineering problem" (Harari, 2019). The conceptual aspects of legal regulation of digital assets are of great scientific interest to modern scientists (Zavyalova et al., 2020).

Kant's categorical imperative may well be organically woven into a computer program. Yuval Noah Harari finds a vivid and easy-to-understand description for such a synthesis, "… then each car would be controlled by an algorithm consisting simultaneously of Michael Schumacher and Immanuel Kant" (Harari, 2019). Surely, after reading these lines, many owners of the collected works of the great German philosopher will look at the dusty books and realize that the light Ratio is eternal.

For this reason, in the digital age, one of the most demanded professions, surprisingly enough, can become the profession of a philosopher, which in the twenty-first century was hastily declared nearly dead.

The skills of philosophers will represent a rather tangible market value (Harari, 2019). The philosophical knowledge will help people ensure a decent life in new conditions.

What will happen to the institution of public services under these conditions? The public-law model of the civil services, which presupposes the consideration of the activities of civil servants as the realization of the collective will of people, the division into public offices and civil services positions, the implementation of a "common cause" and public interest, which, in turn, guarantees the realization of private, special interest, and also requires philosophical understanding and an objective answer to the question of its relevance in the context of the digital revolution.

Yuval Noah Harari, in his reasoning on how to make the coming "new world" happy and wonderful and not blanketed by unprecedented discrimination (which, in principle, in my opinion, will not allow talking about any "globalization," since the inferiority of any discrimination is quite apparent), believes that the regulation of ownership of data and information is the "main political issue" of the era experienced by humankind. Even representatives of the poetry workshop can help in answering it (Harari, 2019). This thesis confirms the interconnection of various types of cognition—scientific and artistic.

The apparent fact should be noted—it is necessary to regulate not only the possession of information, which is extremely important for the post-industrial information society, but also to regulate the ownership of manufactured products. In this regard, the most important aspect is the distribution of the goods produced. The key question,

"Who will own the wealth and power?", has not lost its relevance since the time of Marx and Engels. The question of power—algorithms or people—also continues to gain relevance with the development of algorithms. In this situation, the importance and role of public authorities and the public-law institution of the civil services as an institution for the practical implementation of "common affairs" are probably difficult to overestimate. According to the famous French jurist Maurice Hauriou, the essential bit of public service is serving people, serving the common good (Hauriou, 2013).

Against this background, judgment about replacing professional civil servants with volunteers appears quite naive. I think it is hardly possible to dispute the fact that a professional in any field—from sports to the system of public administration—will always be more effective in protecting and implementing a "common cause," a public interest, which objectively presupposes the realization of private interest and protection of rights and freedoms of people and citizens. In this regard, the liberal idea preserves its significance, filling the fourth industrial revolution era with new content—the struggle for freedom in new conditions.

The public authority and the public-law institution of the civil services can quite effectively confront the pressing problems of the twenty-first century. According to Harari, the biggest threat is the processes leading to climate change—"the reality in which we live" (Harari, 2019).

According to Klaus Schwab, "Climate change, in fact, is already undermining national economies and affecting living conditions. They wreak havoc on people, communities, and systems, causing uncertainty and instability" (Schwab & Davis, 2019).

The salvation from this reality can be geoengineering, which involves intervention in the natural system and counteracting climate change (Schwab & Davis, 2019). Geoengineering can also use new approaches based on the technologies of the fourth industrial revolution. According to the supporters of this approach, geoengineering can achieve unprecedented success in neutralizing harmful emissions in the atmosphere (Schwab & Davis, 2019). However, it is not a panacea.

The large-scale use of geoengineering presupposes a well-coordinated management system at the intergovernmental level. Such projects can only be implemented by the public authorities, not by corporate ones. What makes us look in a new way at the future of the public-law institution of civil services? The orientation of the state and public authorities toward solving "common affairs" and the realization of public interest, which presupposes the realization of private interest, remains unchanged. As Klaus Schwab wrote, "A human-centered approach also requires the protection and promotion of human rights within states and in the international space, especially the rights of the least influential citizens who occupy the lowest positions in society" (Schwab & Davis, 2019).

The achievements of the fourth industrial revolution will help to cope with the consequences of climate change and, above all, with carbon dioxide emissions (Schwab, 2016).

The practical implementation of "mitigating the consequences" will be dealt with by the public authorities, which are carried out by professionals. The executive authorities will play the primary role.

Potestas executoria is the main carrier in public administration (Atamanchuk, 2010). Prominent statespersons from Stalin to Luzhkov have spoken about this more than once. In a fundamental sense, power is explored in the writings of Machiavelli.

The executive branch establishes an administrative regime governing civil society (Hauriou, 2013).

Joseph Stiglitz, an excellent economist, and Nobel Prize laureate, is convinced that public authorities should take an active part in eliminating environmental problems. It is quite apparent to him that the market system cannot solve them on its own. Speaking of teamwork, "government is one of the most important forms of teamwork. … Since in modern society we have many opportunities to help and harm each other, the government inevitably becomes large and complex" (Stiglitz, 2019).

According to the famous American scientist, the public authority objectifies the idea of good: "The creation of public institutions that increase the likelihood of government becoming an effective force for good has been the task of democracies from the very beginning. This is precisely the challenge facing the United States today" (Stiglitz, 2019).

It should be emphasized that government-business cooperation may well play a role in mitigating the effects of climate change. There are interesting scientific works on this topic (Zavyalova et al., 2021).

The understanding of the state as a "trinity" of territory, population, and power, an instrument of universal harmony, an "effective force of good" dictates the corresponding idea of the institution of public service. Sizable Russian legal scholars do not doubt the position that the institution of public service is public-law. It is the public-legal paradigm of the civil services that contributes to the objectification of the state as a national, general social institution: "The state becomes a national institution only through the formation of the public service as an actual service to the people, their right and the law, i.e., as a public service to the common good and the public interest of conducting public affairs" (Kazantsev, 1999).

Famous pre-revolutionary lawyers, N. M. Korkunov and N. S. Tagantsev, also wrote about the nature of civil services as public-law (Korkunov, 1909; Tagantsev, 1902).

This approach defines the meaning of the main activities of a civil servant that the activity of an official is not so much a service as "how much service." In one of the messages, V. V. Putin said this idea very accurately, "The meaning, the mission of the civil services is precisely in the service … Our task is to ensure high living standards, equal opportunities for every person, and throughout the country" (Presidential Executive Office, 2020).

I would like to emphasize that service to the Russian people and their state is understood as a "trinity" of territory, population, and power. The right of the people to govern their own state is manifested in the institution of public service (Kazantsev, 1999).

It is precisely the negative theory of the state that kindles the corresponding negative attitude toward the institution of public services when the imperative to reduce the staff becomes main (Kazantsev, 1999).

This does not correspond to the real state of affairs at all. Moreover, as practitioners note, such a position can do nothing but harm (Luzhkov, 2002).

Understanding the institution of civil services as a public one, there is a division into politics and administration, which, according to professor Kazantsev, allows for increasing the efficiency of public administration. The main significance of such a division is that officials serve only one desire—the law: "The division of the public-legal system of the state into political and administrative public service is the basis of their mutual control over the legality and efficiency of functioning of state power and public service" (Kazantsev, 1999). It should be noted that Max Weber wrote about the separation of politics and administration and the service of an official only to the law (Weber, 1990).

Only serving the law can lead to a proper solution to environmental and many other problems.

According to professor Kazantsev, the difference between an official and a politician lies in the following—political intellectuals are looking for "new entities," but a government official "is not called to be a free-thinking intellectual, but a cog in a system that automatically, administratively executes the law, regardless of the person, like Themis blindfolded" (Kazantsev, 1999).

The official carries out the public interest precisely for the "common cause." This is, by the way, the real meaning of public service and public administration. With the realization of public interest, the private interest gets the opportunity to be objectified.

As a public-legal institution, public service objectifies in practice and embodies state power in real life so that it can be felt and almost touched. It is civil servants who ensure the stability of state power. This context was noticed by Machiavelli in his work "The sovereign."

It is thanks to the officials—who, according to Machiavelli, should not be "bad"—that the state administration is realized and objectified in reality. The civil services embody the functions of the state and objectify them to the population.

This requires an organizational structure. The main purpose of the organizational structure is the effective and systemic functioning of the state (Atamanchuk, 2010).

Civil services should become a public institution. The institutionalization of the civil services is the most important condition for the functioning of a constitutional state, its power mechanism, and functioning for the common good.

Additionally, no state can do without bureaucracy. To dream about it is naive and absolutely incorrect from a scientific point of view.

Professor Obolonskiy believes that the criticism of the shortcomings of the bureaucracy does not at all eliminate its absolute necessity for the state and society. (Obolonskiy, 2002).

The outstanding Russian state scientist B. N. Chicherin discussed this aspect. In his opinion, the bureaucracy strengthens the state and ensures the implementation of political and strategic decisions (Chicherin, 2002).

For civil services to fulfill the high mission assigned to it, it must acquire the character of an institutional phenomenon that has a constitutional and legal expression (Atamanchuk, 2008).

It is clear that civil servants can fulfill their duties only if they have high qualifications (Kant, 1994).

The well-known expert on Kant, professor of state law B. N. Chicherin rightly believed that a systemic approach based on scientific knowledge is needed in public administration. "Here, you need a systematic and serious study. The state is a polysyllabic organism that contains an infinite variety of relationships. The science of the state includes philosophy, history, jurisprudence, living conditions, and economic issues. All this must be studied to form a complete understanding of the subject" (Chicherin, (2002)). Unfortunately, our great Russian literature gives images of officials that are not entirely captivating. This is—to put it mildly. Relevant examples can be found in the works of Chekhov, Zoshchenko, and other writers.

Professor Obolonskiy notes that there has always been enough criticism of civil servants in Russia. He writes about this with a certain irony, "'Our Tsar is kind, but the boyars are evil'—the eternal Russian way of explaining all troubles" (Obolonskiy, 2002).

In times of disturbances and revolutions, the attitude toward officials was sharply negative. This was especially evident in the long-suffering year for Russia in 1917. "In a sickly dizziness, the Provisional Government hastily destroyed every administration throughout Russia" (Solzhenitsyn, 1999).

Professor Kazantsev emphasizes the most important point of the public-law paradigm of civil services—the legal protection of officials from unjustified dismissals at anyone's request. In all fairness, it should be noted that I. Kant spoke on this topic in his famous Metaphysics of Morals. "As for the civil services, the question arises here: does the sovereign have the right at his discretion to take away a position from someone to whom he himself granted it (at the same time the official did not commit any crime)? I say no!" (Kant, 1994).

In other words, an official in the public-law model of civil services should enjoy special legal protection. Ideally, appointments and dismissals should be carried out not by a new team in a specific ministry (which is typical for Russian conditions) but by a specially created national department. According to professor Kazantsev, "being a purely administrative body and a functional department, it should operate on the territory of the entire Russian Federation, being subordinate to the President of Russia" (Kazantsev, 1999).

The message is simple: without the knowledge of the President of the Russian Federation, when the department is directly subordinate to him, the newly appointed team in the ministry will not be able to change its "supporting basis"—the apparatus, consisting of professional civil servants. Often, we observe a different picture with the arrival of a new political appointee; there is a "change of team," which also entails huge material costs—payments for dismissal and so on. As professional officials leave and newcomers come in their place, the damage is done to the public administration system as a whole. The mechanism of effective activity of the federal executive body is simply destroyed for some time. This is associated with huge material costs that drain the coffers without giving any positive results—just like water flowing into the sand of the desert. Sands remain sands, without green shoots.

Being protected by the law from arbitrary and random executive decisions, civil servants will become even more zealous in fulfilling the law, thereby fulfilling their essential and substantial purpose. Therefore, professor Kazantsev noted, "In the United States, for example, the fourth power is not called the media, as in our country, but the civil services" (Kazantsev, 1999).

By the way, the reforms in Great Britain showed that market principles take root rather poorly in the state apparatus (Obolonskiy, 2002).

In my opinion, the reason is not that the state apparatus is "cumbersome" and "stagnant," as the adherents of the "pure" market and "pure" capitalism would gladly say. The fact is that a civil servant, realizing his or her competence, symbolizes public interest in reality. A civil servant serves the whole society. How to measure the profitability of the actions of a civil servant if economic benefits from large national projects may appear not tomorrow but decades later? In the short term, these are only large investments. However, profit will definitely appear. Failure to understand this seemingly apparent fact bring out the lack of a strategic style of thinking which can distinguish between strategic gain and benefit from tactical, momentary advantages. Speaking at the level of mundane, routine knowledge—they do not waste their time on trifles. They win from a strategic perspective.

The modernization of the market economy into a socially-oriented system aimed at serving people, not just making profits, finds more and more followers. In their opinion, the effectiveness of such a system becomes much higher, especially "from the point of view of the long-term perspective" (Lannon & Lannon, 2012). "Selfishness" in business, the inability to see public interest, leads to various kinds of crises. In a sense, the authors follow the precepts of the famous industrialist Henry Ford.

It is necessary to note one more important point. The office of a minister in Russia is a political one—a public office but not a public service office. A number of influential scientists quite rightly believe that the post of the minister should be attributed not to politics but to the administration (Hauriou, 2013). This does not mean that civil servants should be viewed exclusively as cogs of the state machinery—completely "metallic" and soulless.

Today's researchers of the problems of civil services give an example of the unique personality traits of M. M. Speransky, which helped him make a career in civil services. "To make a successful career path, Mikhail Mikhailovich was forced to turn every new boss into his patron" (Okhotskiy, 2011).

How did this happen? Professor Okhotsky reveals that the secret of Speransky's charm was "…to catch the thought from a half-word and skillfully transform your own thought, if necessary, into the thought of your boss. Simultaneously, he remained in the shadows, and the boss looked smarter and stronger. In this regard, M. M. Speransky had no competitors. This was also the main secret of the management's goodwill towards him" (Okhotskiy, 2011).

By the way, other researchers also wrote about similar methods, not applying them to Speransky. For example, the English military historian Basil Liddell Garth (2017) and Robert Green (2008).

The unity of state power of the Russian Federation, constitutionally enshrined as one of the foundations of the constitutional system, urgently requires a detailed consideration of the problem of organizing public services in a federal state. Additionally, the urgent requirement of scientific analysis and practical activities of the state is the development of a strategy for the development of civil services in a country with a federal form of the state structure. The key point is that civil services should be viewed as an integral system, a single service to the state (Atamanchuk, 2010).

Military service is one of the most important types of service for the country. It cannot disappear in the foreseeable future. Or rather, it will never disappear "unless the whole planet unites in a pacifist impulse" (Atamanchuk, 2008). In this regard, the remark of the famous French lawyer Maurice Hauriou is very interesting. In his opinion, military service is a special type of tax paid in a special currency: "The state regime requires… equal and compulsory military service for all—'blood tax'" (Hauriou, 2013).

The great German philosopher Georg Wilhelm Friedrich Hegel also vividly wrote about military service. He called it "the estate of courage" (Hegel, 1990).

According to Hegel, the main difference between military personnel and other civil servants lies in the ability to sacrifice their own lives. "The military estate is the estate of universality, which should protect the state and whose duty is to realize the quality of being ideal in themselves, that is, to sacrifice themselves" (Hegel, 1990).

British Prime Minister Margaret Thatcher's assessment of the differences between the types of public service is of particular interest. "The most necessary quality for him is, first of all, courage. For those whose lives are subject to discipline, the focus is on responsibilities, not rights. That is why military service is considered a noble occupation" (Thatcher, 2012).

It should be emphasized that the departure of the civil services from the public-law paradigm is fraught with serious problems in practice. All of them are associated with the use of public power in private interests, which completely contradicts its substantial meaning.

If we talk about other models of public service, then it should be specially recognized that models that are based not on public service but on private interest cannot fully concentrate on fulfilling their substantial purpose of serving people and solution of the problems that are vital for the people. Professor Kazantsev says that the service model of the civil services has several shortcomings (Kazantsev, 1999). The same applies to the labor model of civil services. According to professor Kazantsev, the latter considers not the general but the special (Kazantsev, 1999).

It is very difficult to disagree with the opinion of professor Atamanchuk that the motivation of civil servants should have a completely different state, public character. "Money-lovers, money-grubbingers, bourgeois (by orientation), hucksters will never serve the state" (Atamanchuk, 2008).

Simultaneously, it should be noted that the public-law institution of public service may well absorb all elements useful for the realization of public interest contained in other models of public service. Its foundation will always be the service to the whole society and the implementation of public interests.

The dispute between adherents of different models of public service does take place, and proponents of various concepts continue to find more and more positive aspects of their theories. However, we must admit that the subtleties of this dispute are not at all interesting to ordinary citizens of the country, whose rights, freedoms, and interests are designed to ensure the institution of public services. They must work "… all 24 h a day" (Atamanchuk, 2008), and the digital revolution only contributes to this. Contemporary researchers attach decisive importance to using digital strategies on a global scale (Konina, 2021).

One of the most essential conditions for the competent functioning of public-law institutions of civil services is the professionalism of civil servants. The pace of changes in the course of the fourth industrial revolution gives rise to many challenges for the public, state power, and public service. First, they are dictated by the speed of the occurring changes (Schwab & Davis, 2019). In turn, this imposes special requirements on the qualifications of managers and the continuity of professional development. In this case, Harari rightly refers to the change as "the only constant" (Harari, 2019).

To improve professionalism, each official should pay more attention to his or her own development (Okhotskiy, 2011). Otherwise, the life of an official as a "Man in a box" is consequently like the "Death of an official," if we understand public service in a public-legal sense, talking not about physical death, like Chekhov's, but about professional oblivion and inability to respond to rapidly emerging challenges.

It is no secret that the low level of professionalism leads to various kinds of accidents and problems in public administration. This is how the famous Russian scientist, professor Ye. V. Okhotskiy wrote about it in historical retrospect, "The events at the Chernobyl nuclear power plant, the death of the Kursk submarine, fires at factories and museums, collapses of water parks and stadiums, explosions on gas pipelines, and the destruction of the Sayano-Shushenskaya hydroelectric power station are not only a chain of tragic coincidences. This is not a technical but a purely "human" factor" (Okhotskiy, 2011). Unqualified use of geoengineering, for example, can only lead to new catastrophes and not to the improvement in the ecological situation.

Reforming civil services is one of the most problematic aspects of the life of today's Russia. They have been trying to solve this difficult task for many years, but the emergence of new reform programs makes us still think about the incompleteness of reforms. What lies ahead?

The institutionalization of the civil services is the most important task of public administration and civil services reforms. The creation of an efficiently operating institution of public service, independent of personal influence or as independent as possible, leads to the consolidation of freedom in practice and the effective functioning of the general social state, which guarantees the observance of human and civil rights and freedom. The state apparatus should have "an intellectual core that meets the already known paradigms of the twenty-first century and is ready to face new challenges" (Atamanchuk, 2008).

Professor Kazantsev quite rightly emphasized that the formula for the sustainable development of the state is hidden in the public-law model of the civil services and in the officials that implement the "common cause" (Kazantsev, 1999). The public-law institute of public service can ensure the real capacity of the authorities. The authorities are not fake, stupidly obeying developed algorithms. Civil servants make power a reality, objectifying authoritative words into practical deeds; citizens perceive power exactly as it appears to them in the form of an institution of public service.

The institution of civil services manifests itself in practice in the form of state bodies. The famous German state scientist Georg Jellinek quite rightly believed that the state simply could not be realized if there were no state bodies (Jellinek, 2004).

The well-known Russian lawyer, professor Elistratov spoke out remarkably on this issue. He quite rightly noted that the state, understood not as an instrument of oppression, acts as the bearer and implementer of a very special mission—one might even call it sacred. The significance of this mission is very difficult to overestimate if we talk about its significance for each individual and member of society. "State activity, since it is imbued with the beginning of public service, differs from other forms of human activity by the property of an obligatory public mission. Officials are distinguished from among ordinary citizens by the legally binding nature of their public service" (Elistratov, 1915). Professor Elistratov rightly noted that it is the state bodies, the authorities, that serve as the backbone of the legal order. The latter is simply unthinkable without them.

A fundamental feature of the public-law paradigm of public service is that an employee is viewed exclusively as a person implementing the power of the people, fulfilling the will of the people, and not his own interests. In this sense, a civil servant is in a special position compared to managers of private corporations; if the latter realize private interests, strive for profit, and the opportunity to earn as much as possible, then the civil servant fulfills a higher purpose—realizing the public mission. Mitigating climate change is the most important public mission. As an example of the implementation of potestas executoria of such a public mission, one should cite the order of the Government of the Russian Federation "On approval of the goals and main directions of sustainable (including green) development of the Russian Federation" (July 14, 2021 No. 1912-r) (Government of the Russian Federation, 2021).

A healthy sense of justice is the foundation on which the service of officials is built—not to themselves, as a private corporation, or to private interests, but to the people and their country. It is quite apparent that the public-legal model of civil services is inconceivable without a healthy sense of justice, and creating an effective institution of civil services without a healthy sense of justice is inconceivable.

The public-law institution of civil services realizes an old Russian dream. After Griboyedov, professor Kazantsev also wrote about it, "The old dream of Russian bureaucracy, to serve the cause and not the people, cannot be realized otherwise than through the institutional public-law regulation of the civil services as a service to the Russian state" (Kazantsev, 1999).

Civil services are about enforcing the law, not about power struggles. The execution of the position is based on a legal procedure. The procedural implementation of the civil services makes it independent of momentary hobbies and passions. This is a precise, pedantic process of implementing the Constitution of the Russian Federation in practice. The presence of a legal procedure turns civil services into an instrument providing the rule of law (Kazantsev, 1999). In fact, it is the legal process that makes law real and objectifies it in reality.

In my opinion, a subjective legal institution regarding civil services cannot be legal. In this case, it loses its characteristic because it is no longer aimed at ensuring the existence of law but at satisfying narrow corporate interests. It should be added that then the institution of public service begins to degenerate from public-law into a kind of corporation of officials, and the state, in full accordance with the precepts of the classics of Marxism, turns into a "state machine," "instrument," and "special club," losing its own essence as a "trinity" of territory, population, and power. The population cannot respect such a state corporation because it will inevitably be against the population. Instead of protecting and guaranteeing its rights, it will violate them with impunity. In this case, is it worth being surprised at the "Renaissance" of the Marxist teaching?

The public speeches of certain Russian politicians and officials give a very depressive answer to this question. Publicists write about this aspect with irony and bitterness, "Surprisingly, the last verbal pearls of our managers illustrate the phrase of the antipode of Thatcher—Karl Marx, who believed that the state is the property of the bureaucracy. I am afraid that, unlike 50-year-old Artamonov, Olga Glatskikh no longer studies Marx, but all their views and manner of doing business leave no doubt that the thesis of the classic for them is just something like the bureaucratic 'Lord's Prayer'" (Shchipanov, 2018).

4 Conclusion

The analysis allows us to conclude about the relevance of the public-law institution of civil services in the context of the fourth industrial revolution. The understanding of the state as a "trinity," an instrument of universal harmony, dictates the idea of the institution of public service as a public institution.

Public authority and the public-law institution of the civil services are capable of fully ensuring the objectification of the idea of good and the solution to pressing state and global problems. These include the problem of eliminating the consequences of climate change. The market system cannot solve these problems on its own.

The public-law institution of the civil services presupposes a division into politics and administration—between political power and the public administration system. The main point of this division is that officials serve only one passion—the law.

The significance of public service is in the realization of the public interest. Through this, the possibility of objectification and private interest materialize.

The institutionalization of the civil services is the most important condition for the functioning of a constitutional state and its power mechanism. Institutionalization and organization make it possible for freedom to exist objectively and for the citizens to feel the state.

An official in the public-law model of the civil services should enjoy special legal protection—to have a lifetime jurisdictional status.

The presence of a procedural form for implementing public service makes the legal existence of the Constitution of Russia and laws possible.

The presence of a legal procedure makes civil services a tool to ensure the rule of law.

References

Atamanchuk, G. V. (2008). *The essence of public service: History, theory, law, practice.* Moscow, Russia: Publishing House of the Russian Presidential Academy of National Economy and Public Administration.

Atamanchuk, G. V. (2010). *The theory of public administration.* Moscow, Russia: Omega-L.

Chicherin, B. N. (2002). What are protective principles? In B. N. Chicherin (Ed.), *Several contemporary questions.* State Public Historical Library of Russia.

Chicherin, B. N. (2002). Introductory lecture on state law, read at Moscow University on October 28, 1861. In B. N. Chicherin (Ed.), *Several contemporary questions.* State Public Historical Library of Russia.

Dementieva, A., & Zavyalova, E. (2020). *Corporate governance in Russia: Quo vadis?* De Gruyter. https://doi.org/10.1515/9783110695816

Elistratov, A. I. (1915). *Essay on state law (constitutional law).* Moscow, Russian Empire: Mysl.

Government of the Russian Federation. (2021). *Order "On approval of the goals and main directions of sustainable (including green) development of the Russian Federation" (July 14, 2021 No. 1912-r).* Moscow, Russia. Retrieved from https://base.garant.ru/401509630/. Accessed 21 June, 2021.

Green, R. (2008). *The 48 laws of power* (E. Ya. Migunnova Transl. from English). Moscow, Russia: Ripol Classic. (Original work published 1999).

Harari, Y. N. (2019). *21 lessons for the 21st century.* Sinbad. (Original work published 2018).

Hauriou, M. (2013). *Fundamentals of public law. Moscow: Infra-M.* (Original work published 1910).

Hegel, G. V. F. (1990). *Philosophy of law* (Transl. from German). Moscow, Russia: Mysl.

Jellinek, G. (2004). *General doctrine of the state.* Legal Center Press.

Kant, I. (1994). Metaphysics of morals. In V. F. Asmus. A. V. Guliga, & T. I. Oizerman (Eds.), *Kant I. Works (Vol. 6).* Mysl.

Kazantsev, N. M. (1999). *Public law regulation of civil service: Institutional and functional analysis.* Moscow, Russia: Publishing House of the Russian Presidential Academy of National Economy and Public Administration.

Konina, N. (Ed.). (2021). *Digital strategies in a global market: Navigating the fourth industrial revolution.* Palgrave Macmillan. https://doi.org/10.1007/978-3-030-58267-8

Korkunov, N. M. (1909). *Russian state law (Vol. 1).* St. Petersburg, Russian Empire.

Lannon, J., & Lannon, L. (2012). *The social capitalism.* RDA Press.

Liddell Hart, B. H. (2017). *Strategy: The indirect approach.* AST. (Original work published 1941).

Luzhkov, Yu. M. (2002). *The path to an effective state.* Moscow University Press.

Obolonskiy, A. V. (2002). *Bureaucracy for the 21st century?* Civil service models: Russia, USA, England, Australia. Moscow, Russia: Delo.

Okhotskiy, E. V. (2011). *Civil servant: status, profession, vocation*. Moscow, Russia: Economy.
Presidential Executive Office. (2020, January 15). *Message of the President of the Russian Federation to the Federal Assembly*. Retrieved from http://www.consultant.ru/document/cons_doc_LAW_342959/. Accessed 21 June, 2021.
Schwab, K. (2016). *The fourth indusrial revolution*. Eksmo. (Original work published 2016).
Schwab, K., & Davis, N. (2019). *Shaping the fourth industrial revolution* (K. Akhmetov, A. Vrublevsky, V. Karpyuk, & A. Kozlov Transl. from English.). Moscow, Russia: Eksmo. (Original work published 2018).
Shchipanov, M. (2018, November 17). *The Glatskikh case lives on and shocks*. Retrieved from https://news.ru/mnenie/delo-glackih-zhivet-i-shokiruet/. Accessed 21 June, 2021.
Solzhenitsyn, A. I. (1999). Reflections on the February revolution. In *Lenin in Zurich: Stories; Krokhotki; Publicism* (pp. 591–634). Yekaterinburg, Russia: U-Factoria. Retrieved from http://lib.ru/PROZA/SOLZHENICYN/fevral.txt. Accessed 21 June, 2021.
Stiglitz, J. (2019). *People, power, and profits: Progressive capitalism for an age of discontent*. Alpina Publisher. (Original work published 2019).
Tagantsev, N. S. (1902). *Russian criminal law*. Lectures (Vol. 1). St. Petersburg, Russian Empire.
Thatcher, M. (2012). *Statecraft: Strategies for a changing world* (V. Ionov Transl. from English). Moscow, Russia: Alpina Publisher. (Original work published 2002).
Weber, M. (1990). Politics as a vocation and profession. In Yu. N. Davydov (Ed), Weber, M. Selected Works. Progress.
Zavyalova, E. B., Shumskaia, E. I., & Kuzmin, M. D. (2020). Smart contracts in the Russian transaction regulation. In E. G. Popkova, & B. S. Sergi, (Eds.), *Scientific and technical revolution: Yesterday, today and tomorrow* (pp. 205–212). Springer. https://doi.org/10.1007/978-3-030-47945-9_22
Zavyalova, E. B., Pichkova, L. S., & Krotova, T. G. (2021). The role of business and government cooperation in preventing and mitigating global biogenic challenges. In E. G. Popkova, & B. S. Sergi (Eds.), *Modern global economic system: Evolutional development vs. revolutionary leap* (pp. 2229–2244). Springer. https://doi.org/10.1007/978-3-030-69415-9_244

Assessment of the Efficiency of Implementation and Forecasting of Innovative Processes in the Region

Shamil I. Nigmatullin

Abstract Based on the conducted analysis of forecasting trends of long-term development of innovation processes in the regions based on current provisions and normative documentation defining the state strategy of long-term innovation development, the author substantiates the necessity of further development of the structural-logical procedure of forecasting of development of innovation processes in the region, including adequate econometric and mathematical models in interrelation with analytical-expert methods of judgment. In the context of designing directions of development of innovation processes in the region, the methodological provisions for determining the types of development of innovation processes in the region were supplemented. These methodological provisions are based on the models reflecting the receipt of 5D-effects from the implementation of projects of innovation transformations in the region, the need for which arose in response to the identified 5D-deficiencies of the progressive development of innovation processes in the region. These violations were fixed as a result of the negative dynamics of the direct-directed indicators and the positive dynamics of the reverse-directed indicators.

Keywords Innovative processes · Innovative development · Evaluation system · Region · Innovative activities · Forecasting

JEL Classification O18 · O31 · O29 · O32

1 Introduction

The study of the issues of assessing the development of innovation processes in the region is carried out in various aspects. It includes private problems such as the formation of an adequate and realistic innovation and technological development strategy of enterprises and organizations (Starikova et al., 2012) and assessment of

S. I. Nigmatullin (✉)
Ufa State Petroleum Technological University, Ufa, Russia
e-mail: shamilnigmatullin@mail.ru

E. I. Lazareva et al. (eds.), *Innovative Trends in International Business and Sustainable Management*, Approaches to Global Sustainability, Markets, and Governance,
https://doi.org/10.1007/978-981-19-4005-7_49

economic efficiency of creation and implementation of innovation (Davydov, 2010). It also includes global problems concerning the formation of a unified system of indicators and criteria for assessing innovation activity for further rating and monitoring of regions. Analyzing current trends in the development of society, we can note its large-scale transformation under the influence of innovative transformations, mediated by the influence of scientific, technological, and socio-economic progress, which have covered all areas of activity. At the current stage, priorities for the development of socio-economic relations are associated with digitalization, informatization of knowledge, and its impact on economic growth, as well as structural changes in society in the direction of the predominance of human capital, resetting social needs in favor of innovative technologies. Simultaneously, along with positive trends in socio-economic development, society faces global problems and crises, the probability of which is currently increasing, including in connection with the threat caused by COVID-19.

Regarding the development of innovative processes, the region is an integrative set of economic, industrial, and social relations between organizations, institutions of different forms of ownership and industries, and public authorities aimed at improving the scientific level, business activity, and innovative development of education based on the existing potential.

The problem of methodological support of projecting directions of development of innovation processes in the region demonstrates general theoretical and applied interest because the identification and use of effective methods and tools of forecasting the development of innovation processes in the region is an effective way to increase innovation activity of socio-economic systems in society.

Summarizing the basic requirements for designing the directions of development of innovation processes in the region, it is necessary to form a conceptual and methodological approach to forecasting the development of innovation processes using the system of processing large amounts of data and the base of scientific analytics. These platform tools represent efficient, combined communications and integrate predictive analytics and products to create new data mining processes to guide the development of innovation processes.

2 Materials and Methods

The current development of industry in society shows that the emerging conditions of technological innovations necessarily impose certain requirements for the application and practical implementation of these innovations. The main requirement becomes the creation of a certain environment in society, in which new technologies based on the achievements of scientific and technological progress will be introduced, developed, commercialized, and, ultimately, exist. It follows that the methods, techniques, procedures, and operations that constitute technology exist in the plane of society and cannot exist outside of public space, becoming a reflection of social relations.

Meanwhile, new ideas are generated, reflecting, on the one hand, the high level of achieved results of innovative activity and setting new directions in the development of technology, and, on the other hand, the vices in the development of society, acquiring the character of irreversible phenomena.

In the face of this systemic phenomenon, a solution is required in the interest of further joint development of the provisions of the theory of innovation and the theory of forecasting. In this direction, it is important to form systemic knowledge in the development of methods for designing innovative transformations and forecasting the development of innovative processes, which, in addition to promoting the implementation of scientific and technological progress, will encourage the processes of technology management by society, setting an algorithm for creating a high-tech space safe for humans.

The analysis of scientific publications on the indicated problem showed that the contemporary studies do not reflect the development of the theory of innovation, associating the parallel analogy of the spread of innovation with the spread of viruses.

Thus, the works of Baudrillard (2015) show the identified analogy in the socio-economic processes of development of society and the destructive processes occurring in the human body under the influence of viruses. Shiller (2019) offers a new perspective on economics and economic change. He provides a groundbreaking account of how stories help drive economic events and why financial panics can spread like epidemic viruses.

There are sporadic studies based on the development of ideas of innovative behavior similar to viruses. Thus, the main idea of the concept of Shewhart (1924) is that "we should not look for fault, but, involving all those involved, look for the causes of discrepancies and eliminate them," thereby improving quality by reducing the variability of the production process. Shewhart's research revealed the influence of the variability virus on the quality of the results of the production process. According to him, if the source of variability at each production stage is eliminated, the result becomes more predictable, and production becomes more manageable due to the reduced downtime and costs. Thus, the basic idea is to eliminate the variability virus and thus improve the reproducibility of production.

American scholar Juran (1964) continued research on Shewhart's theory and captured the essence of virus spread in a statement known as "Juran's rule." In his opinion, 85% of the problem is caused by the existing management system and 15% by the employees. He associates the causes of variability with viruses, believing that variability infects every process where it occurs, like viruses.

The scientific works of Russian scientists (Valinurova et al., 2020; Vanchukhina et al., 2018, 2020) identified current trends in Russian practice of implementing innovative approaches to management in various business systems, as well as promising areas of innovation development in the industrial revolution. Belenkova et al. (2018) reveal different approaches to the study of categories of innovative development and innovative transformations.

However, given the current realities, the ideas of the above authors require reflection, a thorough systematization, and modernization, considering the needs arising from the course of Russia on the innovative transformation in society.

The observed negative dynamics of transformational development of innovation processes in the region can be summarized as D—violations of the progressive development of innovation processes in the region, which are fixed by the relative dynamics of changes in the indicators of innovation activity level, innovation productivity, innovation intensity, innovation dynamism, innovation cost capacity, and return on the use of innovation potential in the regions. The study of the causes of the emergence of such phenomena in the relationship at the regional level is important to identify the 5D-deficiencies of the development of innovation processes in the region and fixation of the so-called 5D-effects of projects of development of innovation processes in the region in the context of designing directions of the development of innovation processes in the region in conditions of innovation economy as an economic system, withstanding external challenges and internal threats.

The author presents the 5D-deficiencies in the development of innovation processes in the region formulated by him:

- 1D—Economic and political crises, global epidemics, the economy's focus on resource-based development, a decline in the competitiveness of the national economy, and a decline in the quality of life contribute to the destabilization of socio-economic and innovative systems.
- 2D—Disintegration of scientific, technical, industrial, and educational policies is manifested in the dissociation of organizational, regulatory, legislative, personnel, and financial mechanism to ensure the convergence of these policies, followed by the identification of breakthrough research and promising areas of reform of models of organization to create and promote innovation.
- 3D—The imbalance between the financial support and the results of scientific and innovative activities is manifested, first, in violation of the pace correlation between the amount of funding for basic and applied research and the volume of gross domestic product and gross regional product. Second, it is manifested in financing venture investments at the expense of the budget system of the Russian Federation rather than at the expense of private investors. Third, it is manifested in the imbalance between the financial state resources allocated to the creation of innovation and the results obtained from the implementation and commercialization of innovative developments, products, methods, and techniques.
- 4D—Decyclization of innovative processes is associated with a change in the cyclical trajectory of innovative processes, which has a cascading structure. Decyclization is caused by the uneven duration of phase intervals of different types of cycles (revival-growth-maturity-crisis, depression), in which different types of innovation and stages of the innovation process (emergence of innovation, creation of innovation, and implementation and commercialization of innovation) prevail. Violation of the cyclic nature of innovation processes leads to difficulties in the design and implementation of strategic directions of innovative development of regions and industries, as well as changes in the pace of change of technological modes.

- 5D—Disaggregation of the system of reproduction of human capital and personnel training is manifested in the low level of staffing of scientific, research, and innovation activities, the concentration of human capital in high-tech areas, and reduction of the pace and scale of updating of human capital based on innovations in accordance with the objectives of development of innovation processes in the region.

A general system of design provisions for the directions of development of innovation processes in the region and forecasting the development of innovation processes in the region is presented based on the basic concepts of forecasting and design, virulence assessment methodology, and traditional and alternative methods of quantifying the influence of factors.

Because of the dominant need for innovative transformations in society, including the digitalization of all processes, the use of D-deficiencies of the progressive development of innovative processes in the region in the context of designing directions of development of innovative processes makes it necessary to build predictions on the type of mechanism of viral spread with the identification of the so-called 5D-effects.

Based on the conducted research of different approaches to the study of categories of innovation development, innovation transformations, development of viral economy concepts, and innovation efficiency, it is established that the drivers of technological development and economic growth are building projects of innovation transformations and evaluation of integration impact of 5D-effects, caused by the influence of D-deficiencies of the progressive development of innovation processes in the region on the rate of economic growth in the global innovation.

This approach will allow analyzing the current state of innovation processes in the region and identifying the prerequisites for designing and forecasting the development of innovation processes in the region, considering the factors of influence on the forecasting of the development of innovative processes in regions that determine the level of stability, integration, balance, cyclicality, and aggregation of phenomena and processes.

To assess the 5D-deficiencies and identify the potential for design and forecasting of innovative processes in the region, it is necessary to develop methodological provisions, supplementing the existing logically structured groups of indicators, the calculation of which considers the diversity, variability, and effectiveness. Table 1 systematizes the indicators to determine the 5D-deficiencies in the regions, considering the factors of influence on the forecasting of the development of innovative processes in the region.

In our opinion, to identify predictive trends in the long-term development of innovation processes in the region and predictive evaluation of the development of innovation processes in the region, these methodological provisions should be supplemented by the definition of types of development of innovation processes in the region based on models reflecting the 5D-effects of innovative transformation projects in the region, the need for which arose in response to the identified 5D-deficiencies, fixed by the negative dynamics of straightforward indicative indicators and the positive dynamics of inversely directed indicators.

Table 1 Systematization of indicators to determine the 5D-deficiencies in the regions, considering the factors of influence on the forecasting of the development of innovative processes in the region

Types of 5D-deficiences	Serial number of the indicator	Indicator	Description of the indicator
1. Destabilization of socio-economic and innovation systems	I1	The level of innovation activity in the region, %	The share of enterprises, implementing innovations in the total number of operating enterprises in the region
	I2	The level of innovative productivity of enterprises in the region, %	The ratio of the output of innovative products to the number of employees-researchers
	I3	The level of return on innovation in the region, %	The ratio of the output of innovative products to the cost of innovation activities
	I4	The level of high-tech industries in the region, %	The share of gross value added of high-tech products to the gross regional product
2. Disintegration of science, technology, industry, and education policies	I5	The level of intensity of R&D costs, %	The ratio of domestic spending on R&D to total GRP
	I6	The level of intensity of cooperation between science and business, %	The share of organizations that participated in joint R&D projects in the total number of organizations
	I7	The level of dynamism in the development of advanced technologies, %	The relative growth rate of the number of developed advanced production technologies in the region
	I8	The level of productivity and manufacturability of workplaces, %	The relative growth rate of high-productive jobs in the region, %
3. The imbalance between financial support and the results of scientific and innovative activity	I9	The ratio of the level of funding of R&D costs from different sources, %	The ratio of budgetary and non-budgetary funding of R&D
	I10	The level of intensity of high-tech production, %	The share of high-tech products in the total volume of shipped products

(continued)

Table 1 (continued)

Types of 5D-deficiences	Serial number of the indicator	Indicator	Description of the indicator
	I11	The level of cost capacity for innovation activities, %	The ratio of expenditures on innovative activity to the volume of released innovative products
	I12	The level of patent activity in the region, %	The ratio of the number of issued patents to the number of enterprises engaged in innovative activity in the region
4. Decyclization of innovation processes	I13	Relative change in investment in the innovative activity, %	The growth rate of the ratio of expenditures on innovation to the volume of investment
	I14	The ratio of the relative dynamics of investment in innovation and GRP, %	The ratio of GRP growth rate to the growth rate of investment in innovation
	I15	The ratio of the relative dynamics of domestic spending on R&D and GRP, %	The ratio of the growth rate of GRP to the growth rate of domestic spending on R&D
	I16	The level of return on the use of intellectual potential in the region	The ratio of the number of developed advanced innovative technologies per 1000 researchers, ‰
5. Disaggregation of the system the reproduction and training of human capital	I17	The level of intensity of scientific potential in the region	The number of researchers with a degree per 1000 permanent residents in the region, ‰
	I18	The level of research activity in the region	The ratio of the number of researchers to the total number of personnel at enterprises in the region, %
	I19	The ratio of remuneration of researchers in the region and in Russia as a whole	The ratio of the level of salaries of researchers in the region to the level of salaries of the same category of employees in Russia, %
	I20	The level of regional wages compared to the national average, %	The ratio of wages in the region and in Russia as a whole

Source Compiled by the authors

Obtaining 5D-effects from the implementation of projects of innovative transformations in the region, which means achieving the goal and obtaining the final result, in general, is based on the ratio of benefits received and costs incurred in connection with it. The following 5D-effects should be highlighted:

1. The functional and technological effect is manifested in an increase in the level of innovation activity of the region and small business entities located in its territory, an increase in product quality, and a decrease in costs.
2. The scientific and technical effect is connected with the usefulness, breadth, and depth of dissemination of innovations, as a result of which the level of intensity of R&D costs will increase, the level of intensity of cooperation of science and technology will increase, advanced technologies will be introduced more dynamically, and the number of highly productive jobs will increase.
3. The financial effect is caused by the increase of the efficiency of the implementation of innovative projects with the subsequent reflection in the growth of the intensity of high-tech productions and the growth of regional patent activity.
4. Resource and production effect is manifested in the increase of the dynamism of implementation of innovation processes, which is caused by the growth of the volume of funds allocated to the innovation component in investments and the increase in the rate of investment in modernization processes.
5. The socio-economic effect is manifested in the saving of human capital with innovative thinking, the improvement of the quality of life, the improvement of working conditions, and the increase in productivity of the intellectual potential of the region.

Innovative transformations carried out to develop innovation processes in the region predetermine the need to forecast the long-term nature of innovative development with the receipt of these 5D-effects using the mechanisms of diffusion of innovation.

The set of evaluative indicators can include indicators of directed action, the dynamic increase of which indicates the absence of D-deficiencies, the dynamic decrease of which fixes certain D-deficiencies and indicates the need for innovative transformations to obtain a certain D-effect. The set of evaluative indicators can also include inverse indicators, the dynamic decrease of which indicates the absence of D-deficiencies, the dynamic increase of which captures certain D-deficiencies and indicates the need for innovative transformations to obtain a certain D-effect.

In this regard, based on the initial data on the values of indicative indicators, a matrix of estimates is formed, the elements of which take the value (0) in the absence of D-deficiencies, fixed based on the obtained values of indicative indicators in the dynamics, and the value (1) in the presence of D-deficiencies, fixed based on the obtained values of indicative indicators in the dynamics.

Then, based on the resulting matrix, the range of assessment of the level of development of innovative processes in the region is set with an indication of the need to implement innovative transformations to achieve each of the 5D-effects using a discrete scale on the interval $[0, 4]$. The upper limit of the scale has a quantitative value of 4 (based on the maximum number of indicative indicators for each D-deficiency).

The lower limit of the scale has a value of 0 (based on the minimum number of deficiencies for all indicative indicators characterizing a particular D-deficiency).

To assess the achievement of the cumulative effect of innovative transformations, the range of assessment of the level of development of innovative processes in the region is set with an indication of the need to implement innovative transformations to achieve a set of 5D-effects using a discrete scale on the interval [0, 20]. The upper boundary of the scale has a quantitative value of 20 (based on the maximum number of indicative indicators, fixing all 5D-deficiencies in the aggregate). The lower boundary of the scale has a value of 0 (based on the minimum number of violations for all indicative indicators, characterizing the entire set of D-deficiencies).

Next, the author provides a general characteristic of the assessment range for compliance with the type of effectiveness of the development of innovative processes in the region, which can characterize the achieved result for all D-effects.

- 16/20–20/20—weak development of innovative processes in the region: low activity and low results of the development of innovative processes in the region. When designing an innovation development strategy for this type, regional authorities should, first of all, develop measures aimed at improving innovation capacity, in connection with which large-scale innovative transformations are required with the achievement of D-effect;
- 10/20–15/20—low efficiency of development of innovation processes in the region: high innovation activity and a low result of innovation activity. This type tends to characterize regions where innovation potential has already been created but has not yet manifested itself in the form of innovative activity, which requires significant innovative transformation to achieve the D-effect;
- 5/20–9/20—an optimal type of development of innovative processes: low innovative activity and a high result. This type indicates the presence of a universal high-tech innovation system in the region, in view of which a slight innovative transformation to achieve the D-effect is currently required;
- 0/20–4/20—a highly efficient development of innovation processes in the region: with high innovative activity, high efficiency was achieved; there is currently no need for radical innovative changes.

3 Results

Table 2 summarizes the indicators on the example of the Republic of Bashkortostan in accordance with the 5D-deficiencies and the range, characterizing the innovative activity of the region.

According to Table 2, the total final score of 5D-deficiencies in the Republic of Bashkortostan was 9 out of 20 over the past decade, which shows the presence of just over 50% of deficiencies of the development of innovative processes in the region, as evidenced by the obtained values of the indicators. In this case, the implementation of even minor innovative transformations will allow getting D-effects, providing a

Table 2 Final assessments characterizing the 5D-deficiencies and the type of innovative development of the Republic of Bashkortostan

Type of D-effect	Serial number of the indicator	The value of the assessment characterizing the D-deficiency	The final score, reflecting the type of innovative development of the region
Republic of Bashkortostan			
Functional and technological effect	I1	1	4/4
	I2	1	
	I3	1	
	I4	1	
Scientific and technological effect	I5	0	0/4
	I6	0	
	I7	0	
	I8	0	
Financial effect	I9	0	1/4
	I10	0	
	I11	1	
	I12	0	
Resource and production effect	I13	0	1/4
	I14	1	
	I15	0	
	I16	0	
Disaggregation of the system of human capital reproduction and training	I17	1	3/4
	I18	0	
	I19	1	
	I20	1	
Final score			9/20

Source Compiled by the authors

dynamic innovative development of the region and confirming the presence of highly effective development of innovative processes in the region.

4 Conclusion

Thus, existing approaches to the management of innovative processes in society consider only separate aspects and directions (such as management of processes of creation of new knowledge, management of creative potential, management of mastering of innovations) connected with the development of the purpose of receiving high profit and competitive advantages due to constant updating of production and increase of its innovativeness.

New realities and trends in development are associated with the formation of policies aimed at initiating changes that ensure progressive changes in society. This circumstance does not allow the full use of existing methods of design of innovative transformations and necessitates the justification of new approaches to the construction of the system and models for the development of innovative processes in the region.

Acknowledgements The reported study was funded by the Russian Foundation for Basic Research under Scientific Project No. 19-310-90037/19.

References

Baudrillard, J. (2015). *Simulacra and Simulation* (A. KAchcalova, Trans. from English). Moscow, Russia: Publishing house "POSTUM." (Original work published 1981).

Belenkova, O. A., Vanchukhina, L. I., & Leybert, T. B. (2018). Innovative culture: Nature, structure, implementation. In *Proceedings of the SGEM 2018: 5th International Multidisciplinary Scientific Conference on Social Sciences and Arts* (pp. 531–538). Sofia, Bulgaria. https://doi.org/10.5593/sgemsocial2018/2.2/S09.067

Davydov, A. A. (2010). The correlation between Global Innovation Index BCG, Innovation Capacity Index, and Global Innovation Index INSEAD. Retrieved from https://ssa-rss.ru/files/File/info/Index.pdf. Accessed October 16, 2021.

Juran, J. M. (1964). *Managerial Breakthrough.* McGraw-Hill.

Shewhart, W. A. (1924). *Statistical method from the viewpoint of quality control.* The Graduate School, the Department of Agriculture.

Shiller, R. J. (2019). *Narrative economics: How stories go viral and drive major economic events.* Princeton University Press.

Starikova, M. S., Mikalut, S. M., & Reznichenko, A. A. (2012). Approaches to ensuring effective innovative development of corporations. *Innovative Newsletter Region, 3*, 81–86.

Valinurova, L. S., Leibert, T. B., & Khalikova, E. A. (2020). Innovative approaches to corporate financial management in business systems. In E. Popkova, & B. Sergi (Eds.), *The 21st century from the positions of modern science: Intellectual, digital and innovative aspects* (pp. 83–95). Springer. https://doi.org/10.1007/978-3-030-32015-7_11

Vanchukhina, L. I., Leybert, T. B., Khalikova, E. A., & Luneva, N. N. (2018). Modern approaches to operational planning in oil refinery using the PIMS software product. *Quality—Access to Success, 19*(S2), 123–129.

Vanchukhina, L. I., Leybert, T. B., Khalikova, E. A., Rudneva, Y. R., & Kantor, O. G. (2020). Methodological foundations of measuring the effectiveness of implementation of the circular economy in the economic systems' practice. In E. G. Popkova, & A. V. Bogoviz (Eds.), *Circular economy in developed and developing countries: Perspective, methods and examples* (pp. 67–85). Emerald Publishing Limited. https://doi.org/10.1108/978-1-78973-981-720201011

Management of Institutional Transformation of Higher Education Identified as a Resource-Factor of Innovative Development of the Economic System of Russia

Alexander G. Oganyan

Abstract *Purpose* The purpose of the article is the process of managing the institutional transformation of higher education, defined as a resource-factor of innovative development of the economic system of Russia. *Methodology* The research is based on an integral scientific and ideological platform, which provides for the possibility of complementary use of the heuristic potential of system-functional, institutional, and evolutionary approaches to achieving the goal. The theoretical and methodological basis of this research is the fundamental works of domestic and foreign scientists on the problems of managing the institutional transformation of higher education. *Results* The features of the management of the institutional transformation of higher education, which is determined by the imperatives of the process of innovative development of the economic system of Russia, are revealed. The causal relationship of systemic changes in the organizational and economic mechanism of the entities of the institutional structure of higher education, combining the imperatives of strategic and innovative approaches in its functionality, has been identified, which has a significant impact on the innovative and transformational nature of the development of a new type of national economy. *Scientific novelty* In the paradigm of the dialectics of cause-and-effect mutual transitions, it is established that the management of transformational processes implemented at all levels of the Russian economic system naturally leads to changes in its various subsystems, including the institutional modernization of higher education. Understanding the interdependence of the studied processes allows us to form an objective idea of the target orientation of the management of the institutional transformation of higher education as a resource-factor of the innovative development of the economic system of Russia.

Keywords Target orientation · Higher school · Management of Institutional transformation · Innovative economy · Innovative transformation · Innovation process · Innovation environment · National economic system

JEL Classification B15 · B41 · O34

A. G. Oganyan (✉)
Southern Federal University, Rostov-on-Don, Russia
e-mail: alexsander.oganyan@yandex.ru

E. I. Lazareva et al. (eds.), *Innovative Trends in International Business and Sustainable Management*, Approaches to Global Sustainability, Markets, and Governance,
https://doi.org/10.1007/978-981-19-4005-7_50

1 Introduction

The development of the national economic system in modern conditions is aimed at the widespread introduction of innovations, both in the process of transformation of production technologies and in the field of management. At the same time, it should be noted that the vector of innovation policy in Russia is actually a set of narrowly targeted measures, which indicates a lack of consistency in approaches aimed at implementing innovative transformation of the national economy (Prazdnichnykh, 2013, p. 108).

As the influence of innovations on the development of the entities of the institutional structure of higher education grows, which are collectives of these institutions, research institutes of the higher education system, experimental productions and small enterprises at universities, interuniversity innovation and research centers, and specialized clusters, innovative ideas and solutions in management approaches are becoming even more imperative (Kovalchuk, 2018, p. 95). The effectiveness of the management of the institutional transformation of higher education should be based on the development and implementation of a strategy based on knowledge and generating intellectual potential as a resource for the innovative development of the economic system of Russia (Kazakova, 2015, p. 248).

The entities of the institutional structure should create innovations by forming joint experimental productions with small innovative businesses to commercialize the results of intellectual activity (Milner & Orlov, 2010, p. 325), providing the necessary regularity and dynamism in comparison with existing and potential competitors in the market. That is, the innovation process in the system of Russian higher education should have a systematic and highly dynamic character, allowing the use of an innovative growth strategy as a tool to increase the activity of entities of the institutional structure of higher education.

The process of managing their innovative activity is identified as a prerequisite for economic and innovative growth (Dereli, 2015, p. 367), when there are practically no targets regulating the mechanism of strategic decision-making on managing the institutional transformation of higher education as a resource-factor of innovative development of the economic system of Russia.

Today, there is a need to form effective mechanisms and models for managing the institutional transformation of higher education that fully realize its potential as a resource-factor for the innovative development of the Russian economic system. In order to develop a system to identify the latest state of innovation activity of entities of the institutional structure of higher education and choosing a promising strategy for their innovative growth, it is necessary to formalize an integration model of interaction between the processes of managing the institutional transformation of higher education and the innovative development of the economic system of Russia.

The solution to these tasks will make it possible to qualitatively improve the process of managing the institutional transformation of higher education and increase the competitiveness of the entities of its institutional structure, identify the points of growth of innovation activity in the national economic system (Dmytryshyn & Zvarych, 2018, p. 70).

2 Methodology

The research was carried out on an integral scientific and ideological platform, which provides for the possibility of complementary use of the heuristic potential of system-functional, institutional and evolutionary approaches. In addition, general scientific and private methods reflecting the specific features of innovation management were used, including methods of system analysis, process and project-based approaches to innovation management, design, and modeling of innovative processes of entities of the institutional structure of the Russian higher school.

3 Results

In the context of the formation of new management mechanisms inherent in the innovative economy, the target orientation of the management process of the institutional transformation of higher education as a resource-factor of innovative development of the economic system of Russia becomes an important issue. As an indicative criterion characterizing the development of the entity of the institutional structure of higher education in the context of increasing the effectiveness of its innovation activity, it is advisable to use the apparatus of metric measurement of the level of its innovative development (Courvisanos & Mackenzie, 2014, pp. 42–43).

Innovative development of the entity of institutional structure of higher education is a long-term and sustainable increase in the efficiency of its functioning based on the intensification of innovative processes in all areas of its activities using new approaches to the functioning of the organizational and economic mechanism, as well as to management decisions taken in research, educational, financial, commercial or administrative matters (Oganyan, 2021, p. 115). Innovative development is the basic determinant of the formation of competitive entities of the institutional structure of higher education, acting as a resource-factor in the innovative development of the economic system of Russia (Ovchinnikov & Oganyan, 2019, p. 120).

The definition of the innovation development strategy should be identified as the choice of the optimal vector of innovation activity of the entities of the institutional structure of higher education, which determines the complexity of managerial decisions on the most effective usage of the intellectual potential as a resource for institutional transformation of higher education (Makarov, 2019, p. 56).

The study of the features of the process of strategic and innovative management of the institutional transformation of higher education allowed us to identify two main indicative indicators of its efficiency: the dynamics of the innovative potential of the entities of the institutional structure of higher education, ensuring the achievement of the goals in the strategic perspective; the dynamics of their innovative activity, which is an indicator of the timeliness of the entities' response to the requirements of the innovation-oriented institutional transformation of higher school.

In the course of the study, a modular structure of the process of developing and implementing the strategy of innovative development of the entities of the institutional structure of higher education is proposed (Fig. 1), providing for the need for their effective adaptation to the macro environment (Caetano & Amaral, 2011, p. 333).

Based on the approach according to which economic targets should be part of any strategy (Matei & Aldea, 2012, p. 968), in relation to the higher school system, four main target economic targets can be distinguished in the strategy of innovative management of the entities of its institutional structure: the strategy of extensive innovative development (formation by the higher school system of more competitive entities of its institutional structure); the strategy of intensive innovative development (creation of new organizational and economic mechanisms for the functioning of the entities of the institutional structure of higher education and qualitative improvement of the technologies used for their external and internal interaction in the process of generating innovations) (Mahroum & Al-Saleh, 2013, p. 320); the strategy of adaptive innovative development (development of promising areas of innovation and technology); the strategy of progressive innovative development (development and

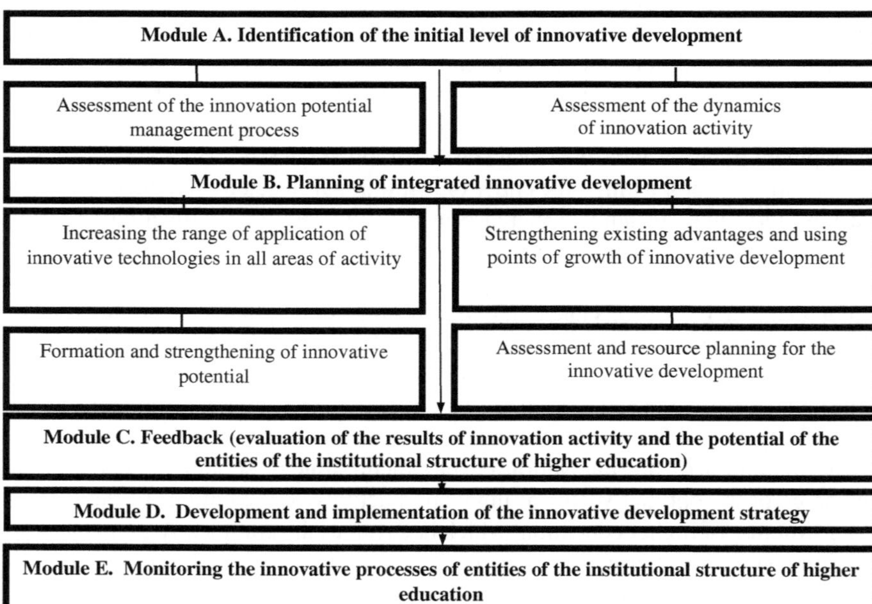

Fig. 1 Modular structure of the study of the process of developing and implementing the strategy of innovative development of entities of the institutional structure of higher education. *Source* Developed by the authors

implementation of a more effective organizational architecture of the entities of the institutional structure of higher education and improving the process of managing the institutional transformation of higher education as a whole).

The process of managing the innovative activity of the entities of the institutional structure of higher education is provided through the use of various methods, in particular: a method based on the strategy of extensive innovative development (creation by the higher school system of more competitive entities of its institutional structure) (Lu et al., 2014, p. 208); a method based on the strategy of adaptive innovative development (development of promising areas of innovation and technology) (Eggink, 2013, p. 4); a method based on the strategy of progressive innovative development (development and implementation of a more effective organizational architecture of the entities of the institutional structure of higher education and improving the process of managing the institutional transformation of higher education as a whole).

Thus, the choice of strategy is based on the formation of targets, the analysis of the state of the entities of the institutional structure of higher education and the macro environment, the analysis of innovation potential and innovation activity (Knyazev & Drantusova, 2013, p. 10; Gunay & Kazazoglu, p. 157).

The calculation of the integral indicator of innovative development of the entities of the institutional structure of higher education is proposed according to the following formula:

$$n\mathrm{ID} = \sum_{i=1} \mathrm{Ii}_w \times \mathrm{Ii}_c, \quad (1)$$

where:

Ii_w the weight coefficients for indicative indicators;
Ii_c the calculated value of the indicative indicator.

Indicative indicators of innovative development of entities of the institutional structure of higher education include (Gokhberg et al., 2020, p. 337).

- the growth of intangible assets;
- the increase in net (retained) profit;
- the flexibility indicator, i.e., the ability of the entity of the institutional structure of higher education to reallocate resources from one type of activity to another to produce new products and services;
- the share of R&D expenditures in the total costs of the entity of the institutional structure of higher education;
- the level of motivation of staff to conduct innovative activities;
- changes in the educational level and professional qualifications of employees.

Table 1 The level of innovative development of the entity of the institutional structure of higher education

Characteristics of the level of innovative development	The corridor of values of innovative development	Direction of the innovation development strategy
High level of innovative development	ID > 2	Strategy of intensive innovative development
Middle level of innovative development	1 < ID ≤ 2	Strategy of extensive innovative development
Low level of innovative development	0 < ID ≤ 1	Strategy of adaptive innovative development
Lack of innovative development	ID ≤ 0	Strategy of stagnant innovative development

Source Developed by the authors

Indicative "corridors" of the value of the integral indicator of innovative development of the entities of the institutional structure of higher education are presented in Table 1. The result of the complex calculation of the integral indicator is a generalizing indicative assessment, focusing on the key problems of innovative development of the higher school system.

Figure 2 shows a formalized scheme of the formation of the innovative potential of the entity of the institutional structure of higher education.

In accordance with the results of the analysis, a formula for assessing the innovative potential of the entities of the institutional structure of higher education (IP) is proposed, which has the following form:

$$\text{IP} = 0,4\ \text{Ii}_1 + 0,7\ \text{Ii}_2 + \text{Ii}_3 + 1,2\ \text{Ii}_4 + 0,7\ \text{Ii}_5 + 0,4\ \text{Ii}_6, \quad (2)$$

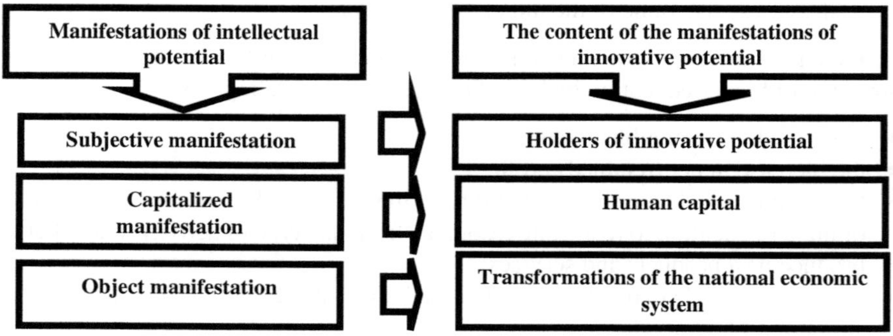

Fig. 2 Scheme of formation of the innovative potential of the entity of the institutional structure of higher education *Source* Developed by the authors

where: Ii_w—the possibility of introducing innovations, Ii_2—quality of the personnel training and retraining system, Ii_3—financial stability, Ii_4—willingness to innovate, Ii_5—intellectual property management, Ii_6—ability to successfully carry out innovative activities.

The innovative potential of the entity of the institutional structure of higher education should be understood as the ability to quickly and accurately identify the essence and substantive aspects of the dynamics of innovative changes (Leydesdorff et al., 2014, p. 33), as well as to use the available resources (financial, human, etc.) in a timely manner to improve the efficiency of the innovation process (Milner, 2018, p. 541).

The innovative activity of the entities of the institutional structure of higher education (IA) can be represented by the following formula:

$$IA = (IA_{GI} + IA_{TT} + IA_{IAS} + IA_{IC})/4, \quad (3)$$

where: IA_{GI}—institutional innovation activity; IA_{TT}—innovative activity of technological transformation; IA_{IAS}—innovative activity of individual groups of entities of the institutional structure; IA_{IC}—innovative activity in the field of intellectual capital generation.

Indicative indicators of the studied entities of the institutional structure of higher education can be aggregated into three corridors of values of innovation activity:

1. The range of scores from 1 to 2 (Middle);
2. The range of scores from 2 to 5 (Low);
3. The range of scores from 5 to 7 (High).

The use of modular organization of scientific research based on a systematic approach allowed us to reveal the components of the studied process of managing the institutional transformation of higher education as a resource-factor of innovative development of the economic system of Russia (Table 2).

4 Conclusion

The ability to effectively implement the strategy of innovative development and the practical use of innovations by the entities of the institutional structure of higher education in modern conditions becomes a necessary factor in the intensification of economic development, as well as innovative transformation and the growth of competitiveness of entities in the market.

Methodological tools of innovation management of entities of the institutional structure of higher education are proposed. They are based on the formation of an innovative development strategy combining the following strategies:

- the strategy of extensive innovative development;
- the strategy of intensive innovative development;

Table 2 Components of the studied process of managing the institutional transformation of higher education as a resource-factor of innovative development of the economic system of Russia

Systematic formation of innovative potential of higher education			
Subject component	Object component	Process component	Environmental component
Holders of the innovative potential of higher education, entities of the institutional structure of higher education, personnel potential	Institutional structure, innovative technologies, resource support of the innovation process, intellectual capital, investment resources directly involved in the innovation process	Generation, distribution, circulation, and use of the creative potential of the economy, capital movement of educational organizations, transfer of investment funds to the market of educational products, competition in this market	Current norms of the institutional environment of higher education, partnership, internal and external communications

Source Developed by the authors

- the strategy of adaptive innovative development;
- the strategy of stagnant innovative development.

A number of indicative indicators have been developed to assess the innovative development of the subjects of the institutional structure of higher education. They include: analysis of algorithms for the interaction of economic, scientific, educational, personnel, and innovative resource factors that determine the key problems of innovative development and act as an operational basis for aggregating an integral indicator as a tool for choosing methods of innovation management.

The algorithm of selection and implementation of the strategy of innovative development of the entity of the institutional structure of higher education is substantiated. It is based on: economic targets for the formation of an innovative development strategy, indicative indicators of innovative development, assessment of innovation activity, which together make it possible to increase the innovative potential of the entities of the institutional structure of higher education.

References

Caetano, M., & Amaral, D. C. (2011). Roadmapping for technology push and partnership: A contribution for open innovation environments. *Technovation, 31*(7), 320–335.

Courvisanos, J., & Mackenzie, S. (2014). Innovation economics and the role of the innovative entrepreneur in economic theory. *Journal of Innovation Economics, 2*(14), 41–61.

Dereli, D. D. (2015). Innovation management in global competition and competitive advantage. *Procedia—Social and Behavioral Sciences, 195*, 365–1370.

Dmytryshyn, L., & Zvarych, O. (2018). Innovations as a priority factor of the regional economic development. *Baltic Journal of Economic Studies, 4*(2), 70–77.

Eggink, M. (2013). The components of an innovation system: A conceptual innovation system framework. *Journal of Innovation and Business Best Practices*, 1–12. https://doi.org/10.5171/2013.768378

Gokhberg, L. M., Ditkovskiy, K. A., Evnevich, E. I., Kuznetsova, I. A., Martynova, S. V., Ratay, T. V., Rosovetskaya, L. A., & Fridlyanova, SYu. (2020). *Indicators of innovation activity: 2020.* HSE: Data Book. National Research University Higher School of Economics.

Gunay, E. N., & Kazazoglu, G. N., National innovation efficiency during the global crisis: A cross-country analysis. Springer Nature.

Kazakova, O. B. (2015). *Institutional conditions of innovative development of the economy*. KnoRus.

Knyazev, E. A., & Drantusova, N. V. (2013). Institutional dynamics in Russian higher education: Mechinary and trajectory. *University Administration, 1*, 6–17.

Kovalchuk, O. V. (2018). Modernization and problems of innovation management of educational systems development. *Man and Education, 3*(36), 92–97.

Leydesdorff, L., Park, H. W., & Lengyel, B. (2014). A routine for measuring synergy in university-industry-government relations: Mutual information as a Triple-Helix and Quadruple-Helix indicator. *Scientometrics, 99*(1), 27–35.

Lu, W. M., Kweh, Q. L., & Huang, C. L. (2014). Intellectual capital and national innovation systems performance. *Knowledge-Based Systems, 71*, 201–210.

Mahroum, S., & Al-Saleh, Y. (2013). Towards a functional framework for measuring national innovation efficacy. *Technovation, 33*(10–11), 320–332.

Makarov, V. L. (2019). Horizons of innovative economy in Russia. Law, institutions, models. Moscow: Lights.

Matei, M. M., & Aldea, A. (2012). Ranking national innovation systems according to their technical efficiency. *Procedia—Social and Behavioral Sciences, 62*, 968–974.

Milner, B. Z. (2018). *Innovative development: Economics, intellectual resources, knowledge management*. INFRA-M.

Milner, B. Z., & Orlov, T. M. (Eds.). (2010). *Innovative development: Economics, intellectual resources, knowledge management*. INFRA-M.

Oganyan, A. G. (2021). Predictive potential of project activities as a tool for institutional modernization of the higher education system: Domestic and foreign experience. In E. G. Popkova, & B. S. Sergi (Eds.), *Economic problems of social entrepreneurship* (pp. 113–124). Palgrave Macmillan. https://doi.org/10.1007/978-3-030-77291-8_11

Ovchinnikov, V. N., & Oganyan, A. G. (2019). Conceptual (structural—functional) model of the organizational-economic mechanism of institutional modernization of higher education as a driver of innovative transformation of the economic system of Russia. *Bulletin of the University, 6*, 115–123.

Prazdnichnykh, A. N. (2013). Building an innovation nation for future prosperity. *Russian Journal of Management, 11*(2), 107–150.

Digitalization of the Oil Refining Business Sector and Assessment of Its Effectiveness

Marat R. Usmanov

Abstract The article proposes a methodology for assessing the digitalization of an engineering project. The digitalization tools used in the project are grouped by blocks of the knowledge management system, digitalization tools at the stage of development of «product-production» systems, digitalization tools at the stages of implementation in production and operation. The methodology involves the construction of a coordinate matrix with the subsequent decision-making regarding the use of tools for digitalization of projects. The resulting effects of the implemented solutions include a comprehensive increase in operational efficiency, implemented within the framework of the engineering project under study: formation of a basket of effective projects; reduction in operating costs; increasing the efficiency of facilities operation; maintenance of major repairs; general design; system digitalization; knowledge management.

Keywords Digital transformation · Digitalization · Digitalization tools · Methodology for assessing digitalization

JEL Classification D22 · L23 · O21

1 Introduction

Digitalization of projects in the oil refining industry within the framework of the «Industry 4.0» paradigm is a condition for increasing the competitiveness of domestic companies in the global energy market. The digitalization tools of vertically integrated companies are engineering projects using technologies of «artificial intelligence», «machine learning», etc. The effects of implemented decisions include:

M. R. Usmanov (✉)
LINK LLC, Nizhny Novgorod, Russia
e-mail: usmanovmr@bk.ru

E. I. Lazareva et al. (eds.), *Innovative Trends in International Business and Sustainable Management*, Approaches to Global Sustainability, Markets, and Governance,
https://doi.org/10.1007/978-981-19-4005-7_51

reduction of the time for making and executing decisions; increasing labor and equipment productivity, product quality; improvement of production systems, their logistics support and maintenance. This necessitates active promotion of digitalization in the industry and the study of the issue both at the level of theory and in its practical aspect.

The purpose of the study is to evaluate the digitalization indicators achieved by a business unit using the example of a separate engineering project, to propose solutions regarding the use of project digitalization tools: replication of best practices in other projects; intensification of the use of digitalization tools; refusal to use tools.

The object of the study is the oil and gas engineering center LINK LLC (formerly LUKOIL-Nizhegorodniinefteproekt LLC).

The subject of the research is the digitalization of operating activities implemented as part of an engineering project.

The following methods of analyzing digitalization at the enterprise level can be distinguished: Digital quotient—DQ, «Index of maturity of Industry 4.0», RoCPS (Return on cyber-physical systems), ODM3 (model of maturity of a digital manufacturing company), «Index of digitalization of Russian energy companies», TPRL (TechnologyProjectReadinessLevel) (Gileva, 2019). Digitalization tools, often implemented by the business sector, are blockchain, internet banking, ebilling, ecommerce (Armashova-Telnik, 2020).

Comparison of the methods with the specifics of their implementation in industry projects made it possible to determine the following:

- the historical prevalence of the functional approach to management over the process approach limits the practical application of classical methods of informatization;
- there is a need to develop original approaches to the digitalization of business operations for certain sectors of the economy;
- the trend toward increased digitalization of projects requires business to evaluate the digitalization tools used in the project with the subsequent prolongation of the results obtained (Merzlov et al., 2020).

In practice, ongoing digital transformations require business to develop approaches to reorganizing individual business processes or in a system with the formation of an accompanying monitoring system, process controlling, which determines the relevance of the study (Akberdina, 2019; Babkin & Pestova, 2019; Kupriyanova, 2019).

2 Methodology

In this regard, in the business sector of oil refining, petrochemistry, gas processing of the object of study, there is a need to develop a unique methodology for assessing the digitalization of an engineering project, that is being tested in a pilot form under the name «Methodology for analyzing the digitalization of engineering projects», developed on the basis of an approach to assessing the maturity of a digital manufacturing company «Organizational Digital Manufacturing Maturity Model—ODM3», developed by the NTI Center of SPbPU «New Production Technologies» and «Skolkovo») (Energy Bulletin, 2020). At the same time, adaptation required tools that were irrelevant for engineering projects of oil refining, the logic of their grouping, indicators of selection and evaluation of the effectiveness of using digital tools. And the assessment algorithm included 3 stages.

Stage 1. Expert assessment of the digitalization tools used in the project, incl. grouped by blocks:

- knowledge management systems in the course of: improving processes and products, building a knowledge base, accumulated experience (books of knowledge, handbooks)»; the use of data centers, computing clusters, internal cloud storage and information architecture of the enterprise and project partners; corporate scientific, technical and industrial library; instrumental technology repositories, banks of 3D models; digital reverse engineering during project implementation; electronic bank of prototypes with the results of their tests;
- digitalization tools for the development stage of «product-production» systems, including: FEA/CFD/CAE; productivity systems, production and business processes (systems, tools and process mining technologies) (Garina et al., 2020); predictive analytics technologies for the service of digital twins during the project implementation; CAD; PLM-MES-ERP; the use of additive technologies in the project; SCADA systems during project implementation;
- digitalization tools at the stages of implementation in production and operation: feedback from the product at the stage of its operation; practice of remote service support, implementation of installation supervision and commissioning; analysis of 3D models to select the optimal production process and means of production (DFM, design-for-manufacturability); automated technological preparation (CAM); automated production process control systems (MES); resources (ERP) (Usmanov, 2019).

Stage 2. Construction of a coordinate matrix for analyzing the use of digitalization tools with the allocation of the «Quandrant of best practices», «Strategic quadrant», «Non-strategic quadrant», «Quadrant of false practices».

An example of constructing a coordinate matrix for the project is shown in Fig. 1.

Stage 3. Making decisions regarding the use of project digitalization tools: replicating best practices in other projects; intensification of the use of digitalization tools; refusal to use tools.

3 Results

Comprehensive improvement of the operating efficiency of a refinery, implemented as part of the engineering project, involves a number of solutions: formation of a

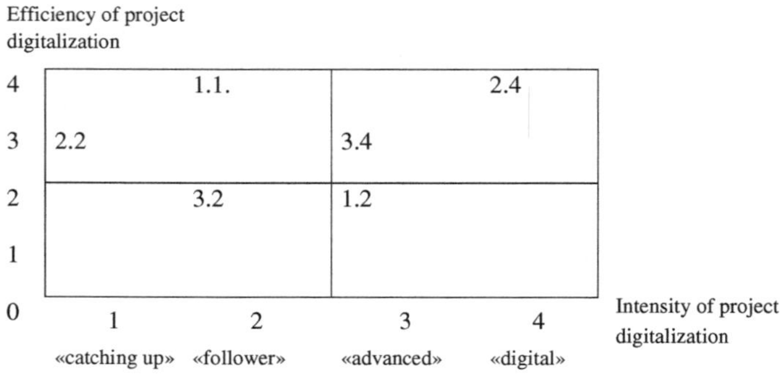

Fig. 1 Example of building a matrix «efficiency—intensity of project digitalization». *Source* Developed and compiled by the authors

basket of effective projects; reduction in operating costs; increasing the efficiency of facilities operation; maintenance of major repairs; general design; PMC, PCE, EPC; digitalization; knowledge management.

The instrument of digitalization of the oil refining business sector is the engineering project using «machine learning» technology. The groundwork for the project can be considered as described below. In 2018, the first pilot projects in the field of machine learning appeared in the company. In 2019, approaches and methods were studied in solving problems using artificial intelligence of the company's contractors. In 2020, the center has assembled a unique team of specialists with cross-competencies for all stages of creating and implementing machine learning models. As the first independent project, a plant with one of the most complex processes in oil refining (H-Oil), which cannot be simulated using classical methods, was chosen. A native tool for working with machine learning models has been created. In 2020, the approaches of mathematicians and technologists in building machine learning models were combined. The previous projects were: formation of an integration platform with APC and DCS; implementation of a storage of technological information (data lake), taking into account the requirements of machine learning; development of the unique tool for visualization, research and understanding from the point of view of technologists of machine learning models; development of the universal visualization platform successfully applied in the «PRORIV» and «Mobile Supervisor» projects.

Expert assessment of the digitalization tools used in the bitumen production digitalization project, including grouped by blocks, systematized in tabular form (Table 1).

Expected technical and economic characteristics of the project: the total effect of the implementation of the efficiency improvement program for complex refineries reaches 10% EBITDA; 60% of activities have a payback period of up to 1 year; program implementation period—up to three years (Shushkin et al., 2020).

Table 1 Example of an assessment of production digitalization project

Digitalization tools	Intensity of tool use	Tool efficiency
Knowledge management		
1.1 Information banks for proposals for improving processes and products	1.9	2.8
1.2 Systems «Knowledge base, collections of accumulated experience (books of knowledge, handbooks)»	2.1	3.2
1.3 Use of data centers, computing clusters, internal cloud storage and information architecture	2.2	3.0
1.4 Instrumental technology repositories (banks of 3D models)	2.4	2.5
1.5 Digital reverse engineering of the project implementation (3D scan libraries)	3.5	2.0
1.6 Electronic bank of prototypes with the results of their tests	2.0	3.1
1.7 Corporate science and technology library	3.1	2.4
Digitalization tools for the development stage of «product-production» systems		
2.1 Enterprise hardware capacity (FEA/CFD/CAE)	1.9	1.8
2.2 Automation systems for performance analysis and optimization of production and business processes (systems, tools and process mining technologies)	2.3	2.2
2.3 Additive technologies in the project	1.8	1.5
2.4 Predictive analytics technologies for the service of digital twins	3.5	2.3
2.5 Computer-aided design (CAD)	2.5	2.5
2.6 Integration of PLM-MES-ERP (data transfer between automation systems) in the enterprise	3.2	3.8
2.7 Data collection during equipment testing using a SCADA system	3.5	3.6
Digitalization tools at the stages of implementation in production and operation		
3.1 Using the possibilities of digital feedback from the product at the stage of its operation	1.8	3.5
3.2 Augmented reality technologies	2.1	1.8
3.3 Practices of remote service support, implementation of installation supervision and commissioning through augmented reality headsets	3.5	3.2
3.4 Automated analysis of 3D models to select the optimal manufacturing process and capital goods (DFM, design-for-manufacturability)	2.8	2.2
3.5 Computer aided manufacturing (CAM)	3.2	2.2
3.6 Manufacturing execution systems (MES)	3.4	3.4

(continued)

Table 1 (continued)

Digitalization tools	Intensity of tool use	Tool efficiency
3.7 Enterprise resource planning (ERP)	2.8	3.4

Source Developed and compiled by the authors

4 Conclusion

The methodology allows identifying in which of the digitalization blocks there are certain problems or maximum efficiency has been achieved, as well as making management decisions regarding the optimization of the use of various digitalization tools as part of the implementation of an engineering project. In the considered project of digitalization of production, thanks to the author's methodology, tools for digitalization of the stage of development of «product-production» systems, which require either adaptation to the declared strategy of the business unit, or improvement, have been identified: 2.1. Enterprise hardware capacity (FEA/CFD/CAE) and 2.3. Additive technologies in the project, as well as inappropriate use of a digitalization tool within the framework of the project's specifics at the stages of implementation in production and operation in part 3.2. The use of augmented reality technologies during the implementation of the production digitalization project. Approbation of the author's methodology in the practice of the engineering project allows us to note its feasibility and the possibility of its prolongation in subsequent projects of the engineering center.

References

Akberdina, V. V. (2019). Digital transformation of the industrial complex of Russia. Collection of reports of the St. Petersburg International Economic 2394 *Journal of Economics*, Entrepreneurship and Law # 9'2020 (September) Congress (SPEC-2018) «Foresight «Russia»: a new industrial society. Future». St. Petersburg, pp. 11–24.

Armashova-Telnik, G. S. (2020). On the issue of digital economy tools. Vestnik VGUIT. *Proceedings of VSUET, 82*(2), 243–250. (in Russian). https://doi.org/10.20914/2310-1202-2020-2-243-250

Babkin, A. V., Pestova, A. Yu. (2019). Algorithm for assessing the level of digitalization of an industrial enterprise. In A. V. Babkina (Eds.), *Digital transformation of the economy and industry: a collection of proceedings of a scientific and practical conference with foreign participation* (pp. 683–680), June 20–22, POLITECH-PRESS, SPB.

Energy Bulletin «Gas Routes to Europe» (2020). *Analytical Center for the Government of the Russian Federation.* https://ac.gov.ru/uploads/2-Publications/energo_feb_2020.pdf. Data accessed December 01, 2021.

Garina, E. P., Romanovskaya, E. V., Andryashina, N. S., Kuznetsov, V. P., Shpilevskaya, E. V. (2020). Organizational and economic foundations of the management of the investment programs at the stage of their implementation. *Lecture Notes in Networks and Systems, 91*, 163–169.

Gileva, T. A. (2019). Enterprise digital maturity: assessment and management methods. *Bulletin USPTU Science, Education, Economy Series Economy, 1*(27), 38–52.

Kupriyanova, M. V. (2019). Methodological approaches to assessing the level of digitalization of industrial production. In *Law, Economics and Management: Topical Issues: Collection of Materials of the All-Russian Scientific and Practical Conference with International Participation* (pp. 28–34).

Merzlov, I. Y., Shilova, E. V., Sannikova, E. A., & Sedinin, M. A. (2020). Comprehensive methodology for assessing the level of digitalization in the organizations. *Economics, Entrepreneurship and Law, 10*(9), 2379–2396.

Shushkin, M. A., Fomenkov, D. A., & Usmanov, M. R. (2020). Analysis of digitalization of engineering projects on the example of the oil and gas sector. *Information Technologies, 26*(12), 688–696.

Usmanov, M. R. (2019). Assessment of the potential of a system of continuous improvement as a condition for innovative technological development of «product-production» systems. *Scientific Review: Theory and Practice 9*(10(66)), 1496–151.

Valuation of Intangible Assets of the Brand of a Medical Institution

Natalia P. Ketova and Maxim A. Kuznetsov

Abstract Modern conditions determine the need for effective use of the resources of medical institutions, including the intangible assets of the brand, as their intangible nature makes it difficult to measure them. *The purpose* of this article is to develop and substantiate a methodology for evaluating the effectiveness of intangible brand assets, including indicators such as the frequency with which a medical institution is mentioned in the information space, the number and nature of contacts with stakeholders, the number of repeated requests to the organization and the number of company activities. *The methodological basis* of the article is the dialectical method, as well as methods of comparative, correlation and regression analysis, which provide the possibility of establishing the degree and nature of the interdependence of the proposed criteria for evaluating intangible assets of the brand. Among *the main results of the study*, it is worth highlighting the creation of a methodology for assessing the intangible assets of the brand of a medical institution, which allows to establish the strengths and weaknesses of the organization in interaction with the external environment. *The originality* of the conducted research lies in the combination of generally accepted scientific methods and research tools for integrating quantitative indicators into the structural area of branding in order to develop an effective tool for evaluating the effectiveness of a medical institution to attract new consumers and retain the regular customers.

Keywords Branding · Intangible assets · Brand evaluation · Marketing in healthcare · Medical services · Promotion of services

JEL Classification I11 · L84 · M21 · M31 · M37

N. P. Ketova (✉) · M. A. Kuznetsov
Southern Federal University, Rostov-on-Don, Russia
e-mail: nketova@sfedu.ru

E. I. Lazareva et al. (eds.), *Innovative Trends in International Business and Sustainable Management*, Approaches to Global Sustainability, Markets, and Governance,
https://doi.org/10.1007/978-981-19-4005-7_52

1 Introduction

In the conditions of oversaturation of modern markets of goods and services, as well as a high level of uncertainty associated with the current level of epidemiological tension in Russia and the world, the effective use of intangible assets of the company's brand is particularly important and relevant.

Their use is of particular importance in the context of the current state of the paid medical services market in Russia, as it contributes to saving money by ensuring an appropriate level of resilience of companies operating in the market to the crisis caused by the COVID-19 pandemic.

The distinctive features of the brand's intangible assets, the evaluation criteria of which are the frequency of mentioning a medical institution in the information space, the number and nature of contacts with interested parties, the number of repeated visits to the organization and the number of company events (promotions, events, open days, etc.), are their impalpability and, as a consequence, the complexities in measurement. However, together with the originality of the visual embodiment of the proposals of medical companies, which ensures better memorability of the advertising message, the intangible brand assets can become an effective qualitative indicator of the activity of a medical institution in the field of forming consumer loyalty.

Thus, the purpose of this article is to create and substantiate a methodology for evaluating the effectiveness of intangible brand assets of a medical institution.

2 Methodology

The peculiarities of the influence of intangible assets on the promotion of medical services are actively studied in the works of such authors as Anopchenko (2020), Bekturganov (2015), Gorodnova et al. (2019), Dyatlova (2018), Ketova (2021), Lyadova (2018), Malakhova (2018), Sagidov (2012), Sertakova (2020), Tarasenko and Dvoryashina (2019).

As for the intangible assets of the brand as a whole, the great merit in their study belongs to Aaker (2016), Barden (2020), Zyman (2017), Kahneman (2020), Kotler (2021), Miller (2020), Osterwalder et al. (2020), Raymond (2020).

However, despite the high degree of development, the problem of using intangible brand assets to promote medical services remains relevant, since in modern science and practice there is no unified approach to their use for marketing purposes.

To study the relationship between the level of recognition of a medical institution in the information space and the number of events of the organization, contacts with stakeholders, as well as repeated visits to a medical institution, along with the dialectical method, methods of correlation and regression analysis are used.

In addition, methods of comparative and plan-fact analysis, as well as benchmarking, are used to study the level of deviation of the indicators of the frequency of mentioning a medical institution in the information space from the desired values established on the basis of key indicators of competitors.

3 Results

The object of the study is the medical center "Resonance", located in Rostov-on-Don. The results obtained as part of the analysis of the marketing activity of this medical institution can be extrapolated to any company representing the paid medical services market in the region, since the key characteristics of paid medical services, such as price, service and quality are equally perceived by consumers in the selected territory.

The proposed system for assessing the intangible brand assets is based on a cumulative assessment of the following indicators:

- the frequency of mentioning a medical institution in the information space;
- the number and nature of contacts with stakeholders;
- the number of repeated visits to the organization;
- the number of company activities (promotions, events, open days, etc.).

These evaluation criteria were chosen because they are quite easy to calculate with a high degree of accuracy of the final result, identify intangible factors directly related to the brand of the institution, and also provide the opportunity to establish a correlation between each other and between the conditions of their implementation and the final result.

The purpose of creating this system is to provide the possibility of a primary assessment of the intangible brand assets, contributing to the establishment of intangible brand characteristics that have the greatest impact on the implementation of the company's marketing strategy.

It is reasonable to consider each of the proposed elements of the evaluation system in more detail. The frequency of mentioning a medical institution in the information space is an evaluation criterion that characterizes the number of publications about a company in the media over a certain period of time. Modern technologies allow measuring this value with a high degree of accuracy. To do this, various information platforms are used that perform an advanced search for mentions of an institution on the Internet using Big Data.

An example of such a platform is Integrum. Interactions with it are carried out by going to the site www.integrum.ru and further registration.

The next indicator for evaluation is the number and nature of interaction with stakeholders. Its calculation makes it possible to determine the level of brand activity in relations with partners and suppliers, and also provides the possibility of forming a general scheme of interaction with counterparties.

The complexity of such calculations lies in the presence of a qualitative component, expressed in the nature of interaction with stakeholders. However, this task can be solved already at the stage of organizing the counting of the number of contacts with counterparties for a certain time by introducing plus/minus columns into the table characterizing interaction with stakeholders.

For example, if contact with a counterparty led to the termination of the contract, had a negative impact on their interpersonal relations, worsened the conditions of cooperation for a medical organization, etc., such interaction should be characterized by a minus sign, while in the case of opposite effects as a result of communication with a partner, a plus sign should be used.

Another criterion for assessing the intangible assets of the brand is the number of repeated patient visits to the medical center. This indicator characterizes the quality of medical services of the institution, as well as the overall patient satisfaction with the company.

Its calculation can be carried out, for example, on the basis of feedback questionnaires at the reception. The disadvantage of this method is that it is impossible to provide an accurate calculation, since patients may fill out the questionnaire incorrectly, or not fill it out at all. Nevertheless, at the initial stage, even this method of calculating this indicator contributes to the formation of a primary idea about the quality of medical institution services and the level of customer loyalty.

Finally, the last evaluation criterion used in this system is the number of activities of a medical institution for a certain period of time. At the same time, activities are understood as promotions used to promote the company's services, and events organized by a medical institution to attract new consumers and maintain the loyalty level of existing ones.

The calculation of this indicator is the simplest of all presented, since in this case there is no need to use special software, additional involvement of customers and taking into account the nature of interaction, since any such activity is a priori positive for both consumers and the medical center.

In order to be able to evaluate this indicator, it is only necessary to organize a record of the number of activities carried out by a medical institution for a certain period of time.

Thus, as a result of the use of the proposed system for evaluating the intangible brand assets, an integrated view of the effectiveness and efficiency of the brand of a medical institution is formed in the following areas:

- brand for the public;
- brand for stakeholders;
- brand for consumers.

As for the time period for which it is necessary to calculate the selected indicators, it is proposed to use a year as an objective time period for assessing intangible brand assets of a medical institution, since it is long enough for an objective assessment, but at the same time does not lead to the formation of blurred time boundaries that may hinder the effectively measuring performance of the designated indicators.

As shown in Fig. 1, the average value of the frequency of mentioning well-known competitors in the information space (1500 times per year based on data from the Integrum information and analytical system www.integrum.ru) was taken as a planned indicator per year; the plan of contacts with stakeholders and activities (promotions)

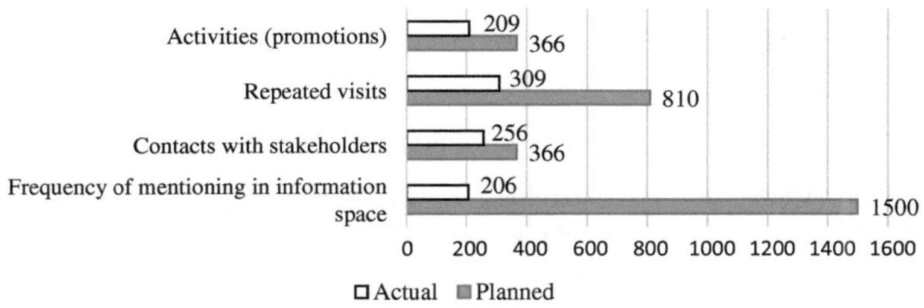

Fig. 1 The ratio of actual and planned indicators of the criteria for assessing the intangible assets of the Resonance Medical Center. *Source* compiled by the authors on the basis of data from the Resonance Medical Center

was formed at the rate of 1 promotion (contact) per day, so the planned indicator is 366. At the same time, the plan for the number of repeated visits was 810 (the number of clean feedback questionnaires filled out by consumers).

At the same time, actually, during the year, the medical institution implemented 209 promotions, the basis of which were sales promotion activities carried out in accordance with various holidays related to health care; out of 810 consumers ready to re-contact with the medical center, 309 people actually revisited, and 256 contacts with stakeholders were made within the framework of the market functioning of the organization. The final index of mentions in the media was 206 mentions out of the planned 1500, which indicates the potential for an increase in the activity of the medical institution in this direction.

Calculate the degree of achievement of each indicator by dividing the actual value by the planned value. As a result, we get the following data: the indicator for activities (promotions) was fulfilled by 57%, the indicator of repeated visits was fulfilled by 38%, the indicator of contacts with stakeholders was fulfilled by 70%, the indicator of media activity was fulfilled by 14%.

For illustrative purposes, we will construct a petal diagram containing four designated indicators in order to identify the most developed areas and, on the contrary, problematic ones of activity of the Resonance Medical Center related to the formation and use of intangible assets of the organization's brand (see Fig. 2).

Thus, the proposed system for assessing intangible brand assets of a medical institution made it possible to calculate four indicators of the activity of the Resonance Medical Center related to the formation and use of the intangible brand assets of the organization.

4 Conclusion

As a result of the calculation, it was found that the number and nature of contacts with stakeholders (business activity indicators) are at an acceptable level, the number

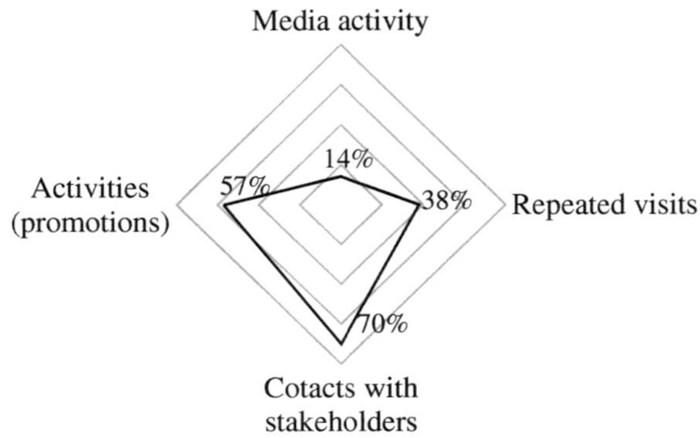

Fig. 2 Assessment of intangible brand assets of the medical center "Resonance" for 2020. *Source* compiled by the authors on the basis of data from the Resonance Medical Center

of activities and promotions carried out by the medical center is also quite high for a crisis year.

As for media activity and the number of repeated visits, these areas are definitely potential growth areas of the institution. To correct the situation with the level of activity in the information field, it is proposed to hire a PR specialist, form a clear media plan, and also increase the activity of the institution in social networks (Instagram, VKontakte, Facebook, etc.).

Nevertheless, for its implementation, the management should think about a number of factors, such as improving infrastructure and saving clients' time by introducing simultaneous admission of patients where possible (for example, one patient is undergoing a medical procedure, and the doctor is consulting another patient at this time).

At the same time, it should be noted that achieving the benchmark of this indicator is impossible for objective reasons. Moreover, the requirement that only regular customers visit the institution is irrational, because although this indicates a high level of patient loyalty, it may limit the activity of attracting new customers, which is no less important than retaining existing ones.

Thus, the establishment of four criteria within the framework of the assessment system for intangible brand assets, expressed in the frequency of mentioning of the institution in the information space, the number and nature of contacts with stakeholders, the number of repeated visits to the organization, the number of company activities, provided the opportunity to conduct both qualitative and quantitative research based on the achievement of the designated KPIs, and to determine the level of completeness of the intangible assets of the brand in the market space.

At the same time, the calculation of quantitative values within the framework of the proposed system for assessing intangible brand assets made it possible to determine the degree of achievement of key performance indicators based on the ratio of actually obtained and reference values, as well as to identify the relationship between them and the conditions of their implementation.

References

Aaker, D. (2016). *Aaker about branding: 20 principles that drive success.* Eksmo.
Anopchenko, T. Y. (2020). *Marketing in healthcare.* Dashkov & K.
Barden, P. (2020). *Decorded: The science Bihind why we buy.* Mann, Ivanov and Ferber.
Bekturganov, Z. Z. (2015). Consumer demand for commercial medicine services as a factor of medical education development in the region. *Russian Entrepreneurship, 2*(272), 347–358. https://doi.org/10.18334/rp.16.2.64.
Dyatlova, M. I. (2018). Perspectives and world market trends of medical products, Russian manufacturing competitiveness level of medical products. Bulletin of the RUDN. *Journal of Economics, 26*(2), 296–305. https://doi.org/10.22363/2313-2329-2018-26-2-296-305.
Gorodnova, N. V., Klevtsov, V. V., & Ovchinnikov, E. N. (2019). Prospects of telemedicine development in the context of digitalization of the Russian economy. *Issues of Innovative Economy, 9*(3), 1049–1066.
Kahneman, D. (2020). *Think slowly... Decide quickly.* AST.
Ketova, N. P. (2021). *Modern marketing mix: Traditional solutions and innovative technologies: Monograph.* Southern Federal University Press.
Kotler, P. (2021). *Marketing insights from A to Z. 80 concepts every manager needs to know.* Alpina Publisher.
Lyadova, A. V. (2018). Digital health: Myth or reality. In *Proceedings of the XXI international conference in memory of Professor L. N. Kogans "Culture, identity and society in the modern world: methodology, empirical studies"* (March 22–23, 2018, Yekaterinburg) (pp. 1451–1461). Ural Federal University Press.
Malakhova, N. G. (2018). *Marketing of health services.* Knizhnyy Mir.
Miller, D. (2020). *Building a story brand: Clarify your message so customers will listen.* Alpina Publisher.
Osterwalder, A., Pigneur, Y., Smith, A., Bernarda, G., & Papadakos, P. (2020). *Value proposition design: How to create products and services customers want.* Alpina Publisher.
Raymond, M. (2020). *Trend research. Practical guide.* MYTH.
Sagidov, A. K. (2012). Marketing in health care as the main factor in the promotion of paid medical services. *Issues of Structuring the Economy, 1*, 69–71.
Sertakova, O. V. (2020). Digital medicine as a platform for improving the quality of medical care and rehabilitation of the population in cities and remote places of residence. *Economy and Society: Modern Models of Development, 10*(3), 299–308.
Tarasenko, E. A., & Dvoryashina, M. M. (2019). Pivate healthcare market in Russia: A marketologist view. *ECO, 6*(540), 43–61.
Zyman, S. (2017). *The end of marketing as we know it.* Potpourri Publishing House.

The Phenomenon of the Background in Solving the Problem of the Intentionality of Future Graduates for the Hospitality Industry in the Context of a Dynamically Developing Sphere of Economic Activity

Larisa Kh. Gazgireeva, Olga L. Zaitseva, Marina G. Gadzhimuradova, Marina V. Vilyeva, and Tatyana A. Tsybina

Abstract The approach to considering the issue of training future specialists for the Horeca sector is to comprehend it from the perspective of existential philosophy, the intentionality of a modern personality in order to accumulate positive experience—the background. The article analyzes the main types of activities that perform an existential-value role in the formation of future specialists in the hospitality industry and tourism, as well as competencies that contribute to the accumulation of the background, are formulated. On the basis of certain competencies, a "roadmap of the educational route for the formation of a professional background" has been developed. The idea is that certain types of social and scientific activities in higher educational institutions orient future specialists of the Horeca sector toward the development of professional identity, as well as creative constructive, spiritual, and moral initiative. Currently, there is an increasing emphasis on taking measures to develop public–private partnerships, create a favorable economic climate, introduce effective mechanisms and motivations for investors, provide guarantees for the safety and repayment of their funds, and expand business.

Keywords Background · Intentionality · Graduate student · Personnel potential · Hospitality industry · Tourism · Existential philosophy · Personal self-realization · Economic climate

JEL Classification Z30 · Z31 · Z32 · Z33

L. Kh. Gazgireeva (✉)
Russian State University of Tourism and Service, Moscow, Russia
e-mail: amor-lora@mail.ru

O. L. Zaitseva · M. G. Gadzhimuradova · T. A. Tsybina
Pyatigorsk State University, Pyatigorsk, Russia

M. V. Vilyeva
Moscow Aviation Institute (National Research University), Moscow, Russia

E. I. Lazareva et al. (eds.), *Innovative Trends in International Business and Sustainable Management*, Approaches to Global Sustainability, Markets, and Governance,
https://doi.org/10.1007/978-981-19-4005-7_53

1 Introduction

Today, the hotel business is a rapidly developing and promising area of the economy. At the same time, business processes in tourism and the hospitality industry are increasingly moving into the digital space (Nikolskaya et al., 2019, p. 1197). The hospitality industry can become a significant source of revenue to regional budgets, which will be useful for the country's economy as a whole (Gorbunov et al., 2018, p. 64). The number of hotels of various price categories is growing in cities and towns. The number of hotels of various price categories is growing in cities and towns. As for Moscow and St. Petersburg, the housing supply ratio is increasing every day (Lepeshkin et al., 2017, p. 57).

According to the Federal Agency for Tourism (Rostourism), "measures have been planned and are being implemented in Russia to dramatically increase the capital construction of new hotels and other collective accommodation facilities, reconstruction and restoration of the existing room capacity of hotels and sanatoriums" (International Forum "Security of the Hospitality industry", 2021). It is planned to attract over 1.7 trillion rubles of budget funds and private investments in the development of tourism infrastructure by 2035. Taking into account the implementation of the National Project "Tourism and the Hospitality Industry", it is planned to build 298 hotels and sanatoriums, as well as 284 projects of tourist complexes. The number of collective accommodation facilities in Russia should increase by 51,000 units (International Forum "Security of the Hospitality industry", 2021). In this regard, there is a need to train professional personnel in the field of tourism and hospitality.

The problem of training future specialists in the field of tourism and the hospitality industry is an integral part of the dynamically developing sphere of the economy because it is the human potential that determines the achievement of certain goals for the long-term development of enterprises in this sector (Gorbunov et al., 2021, p. 48). In this article, the object of economic research is the *labor potential of an individual*.

Moreover, the development of personal and professional qualities of future specialists should be based on mastering certain competencies.

Many graduates of higher educational institutions face difficulties in finding a job. Lack of practical work experience; excessive demands on one's own personality (a kind of "impostor syndrome"); unrealistic expectations from work; an imbalance between "investing" in oneself as a specialist and providing basic needs (A. Maslow); stress of the transition period; lack of understanding of the need for a progressive career trajectory (the desire to achieve all goals quickly and immediately)—all these are existential manifestations of personality in the conditions of modern social reality. Philosophers regard this phenomenon as a "departure from reality", where "an individual does not have a specific goal in the activity itself." Such a "departure", according to the authors of the article, should not be confused with the manifestation of his spiritual essence—the desire to acquire a professional background (Gazgireeva, 2014, p. 4).

Consideration of this problem is an interdisciplinary study. The issue of training human resources for Horeca is a complex process and can be considered from different perspectives:

- the formation of a harmonious personality occurs in the process of developing life skills and intellectual abilities, cultural training, education, and upbringing, obtaining professional experience (pedagogy);
- the solution of the problem of intentionality, the central property of human consciousness ("something different from oneself"—the Arab philosophers of the XII and XIII centuries; "the concept of the subjective component"—Franz Brentano; consciously directed to some kind of activity, event, subject—Edmund Husserl), can be considered in the aspect of the study of speech acts (modern analytical philosophy: "naturalization of intentionality" —John Searle) (Martynov, 2007, p. 12), philosophical anthropology, in particular existential philosophy, although the origin of this term is usually attributed to medieval philosophy (history of philosophy, social philosophy);
- representing the interests of companies, a future specialist should learn how to work in a team, develop stress tolerance, the ability to overcome certain obstacles regarding the achievement of goals related to self-development (psychology of personal growth);
- the analysis of the development of the labor potential of an individual cannot be carried out without understanding the structure of the image of the ego; E. Erickson considered such a dynamically developing structure in accordance with the social identification or self-identification of a personality under the influence of significant others; in the concept of ego identity, it is interpreted as a phenomenon of formation, development, crises, and connection with the self-image of a personality and other processes and phenomena (E. Erickson, H. Tegefel, U.P. Belinskaya) (Kolinichenko et al., 2019);
- the study of the basics of human resource management by students will contribute to the improvement of tourism and hospitality industry enterprises, since it is necessary to understand that the current staff is focused on performing basic production operations, and the strategic staff is focused on solving strategic tasks in the development of enterprises that should generate a stable income (management, economics, personnel technologies in the hospitality industry);
- the development of the speech culture of the future specialist is associated with the ability to build a dialogue with a potential consumer of services, to take into account his mental characteristics, lifestyle, temperament, level of education, awareness of the guest/tourist, belonging to a certain type of client (culture of speech, rhetoric, psychology), etc.

Having outlined the main directions of the problem of developing the personal and professional potential of employees of the tourism and hospitality industry, it is necessary to consider such a capacious modern concept as the background, the lexical meaning of which reflects all its multidimensional nature and complexity.

2 Methodology

The theoretical and methodological basis of the research was the works of well-known domestic and foreign scientists in the field of the theory of providing hotel and tourist services in the conditions of transformation of socio-economic systems in the modern period of society development.

The methodological basis of the research was the fundamental provisions of the scientific direction—the economics of the sphere of hotel and tourist services. This scientific research is carried out from the standpoint of systematic views, taking into account the structural, functional, and managerial aspects, as well as the principles of determinism, complexity, and consistency.

Revealing the essence of the problem from the standpoint of social philosophy, the authors of the article, firstly, rely on *the general scientific principle of objectivity, or the principle of evidence* (E. Husserl), according to which cultural, political, and socio-economic factors of the development of the hotel industry and tourism are taken into account. The significance of transformational processes in these fields of activity dictates a "new paradigm in training and education" (Adolf & Ilyina, 2010, p. 83) of the future generation of modern Horeca specialists. Secondly, the authors of the article emphasize that the interpretation of the question of intentionality requires the use of *a phenomenological method*, or *the method of intentional analysis* (E. Husserl, M. Heidegger), that is, the definition of the vector of consciousness on a particular problem /subject. In other words, "understanding of the essence of this problem/thing in the process of experiencing it" leads to a reassessment of values, one's own attitude to oneself, and one's accumulated experience, that is, the level of mastery of one's own background. Thirdly, the question of the background phenomenon provides for the use of *the existential method of substantiating the problem* of the status of the future specialist of the Horeca sector in the system of existential-value relations (M. Heidegger) (Gazgireeva, 2014, p. 13).

3 Results

Background is a term denoting "backdrop", "preparation" (if we are talking about design). In relation to a person, the background is his entire past, some backstory; this is all that relates to "life, education, connections, human experience; this is the intellectual level, cultural training, degree of education, life and professional experience" (Background, 2021). This term has appeared in the Russian language relatively recently. In 1953, a film with the same name directed by Daniel Birt on the play by Warren Chetham Strode was released in the UK. Many people liked the film because it showed the transformation of the personality of the main character, who returns from the war after 20 years and works hard to succeed in his profession.

The value of the background phenomenon is emphasized in many works of famous scientists. However, it was called differently. E.N. Shiyanov, for example, considered "the development of a student's subjective position through the experience of his activity" (Shiyanov, 1991, p. 33).

It should be noted that within the framework of this scientific research, the concept of "intentionality", introduced by Arab scientists in the XII–XIII centuries, is of particular interest. In the Middle Ages, intentionality in the development of personality was considered as "something different from oneself" (Intentionality, 2021).

The phenomenon of intentionality was considered from the standpoint of phenomenology by such philosophers as Franz Brentano and Edmund Husserl. The phenomenon of intentionality was viewed from the standpoint of phenomenology by such philosophers as Franz Brentano and Edmund Husserl. F. Brentano, who elaborated a novel concept of consciousness, tried to prove that acts of consciousness are characterized by intentionality, that is, *desirability*/attempt; *selectivity*/choice; *aspectuality*/focus on a certain object; *interest*/experience. E. Husserl stressed that intentionality is an act of consciousness that dominates the subconscious (Intentionality, 2021).

John Searle in his book "Intentionality" outlined the essence of this concept from the perspective of modern analytical philosophy, linking it with the theory of speech acts. Thus, J. Searle tried to combine the concepts of "intentionality" (attempt) and "qualia" (the central element of the theory of consciousness). Consequently, intentionality is considered by the scientist as a kind of interest in the object (Intentionality, 2021). From these positions, it is possible to emphasize the need for students to comply with the basic characteristics of intentionality in order to have an effective background.

The participation of students of Russian State University of Tourism and Service in activities of various levels contributes to the development of universal, general professional, obligatory professional competencies and professional competencies established by the university, necessary for future career development. Such experience confirms the professional-competence approach not only to education within the Alma mater but also to the training of future specialists for the Horeca sector. On the basis of these competencies, a "*roadmap of the educational route for the formation of a professional background*" has been developed, which has been introduced into the educational process of students of the "Hotel business" direction (bachelor's degree level).

In accordance with the implementation of the "roadmap", students of the 43.03.03 direction "Hotel Business" of Russian State University of Tourism and Service (Moscow) actively participate in such events as: National Project "Tourism and the hospitality industry: a vector for increasing industry's human resources potential" (strategic sessions of RSUTS, Moscow); Hospitality Online Expo (Moscow); Clean Expo (Moscow); International Forum-Exhibition on tourism "Leisure" (Central Exhibition Complex "Expocentre", Moscow); "Russian Investment Forum"; International exhibition "Intourmarket"; International Tourism Exhibition MITT (Moscow); Russian Tourism Forum "Travel!"; St. Petersburg International Economic Forum; "Eastern Economic Forum"; International Exhibition of the hospitality industry "Pir Expo" (Moscow); International Conference "Innovative management technologies and strategies for territorial development of tourism and Hospitality" (Moscow); student scientific conference "Business technologies in Tourism and Hospitality" (Moscow); expert session "Boiling point" RSUTS (Moscow); competition "Masters of Hospitality" (Moscow); "Forum of country hoteliers" (Moscow); competition of final qualifying works, "Geographical dictation", "Big ethnographic dictation"; International online seminar (for example, "Features of business development in post-capitalism: new realities and challenges" (Bulgaria) and others (Russian State University of Tourism and Service, 2021).

In order to obtain information about the prospects for the development of their own self-image, "Educational intensive courses" are held annually at the RSUTS (Moscow) for graduates of higher educational institutions. They help them determine their goals for the future, choose a career development strategy, and master the necessary competencies in the field of professional activity.

Moreover, future graduates of the direction of training 43.03.03 "Hotel business":

- participate in student projects;
- conduct active social activities;
- implement ideas related to traineeships and various types of practice;
- are engaged in volunteering;
- perform functions related to work at the university;
- conduct research independently or under someone's guidance (teachers-mentors of the higher school/institute);
- are fond of something (have 1–3 hobbies);
- are involved in activities aimed at attracting an audience through engaging/immersive content (blogging), etc.

The above suggests that students gain valuable experience by constantly improving their backgrounds.

The graduate needs to keep in mind that it is necessary to constantly improve his background level, which will help to create a curriculum vitae (biography, resume), taking into account competently presented information related to the professional background (OGOGO Media, 2021). Moreover, future specialists in the service sector will acquire psychological stability, i.e., confidence that they have a sufficient level of professionalism to start their career.

4 Conclusion

On the basis of the above, we can draw the following conclusion that mastering the content of an educational program is aimed at building of the following competencies of future graduates:

- the ability to consciously and purposefully master the basic skills necessary in future professional activity;
- constant desire to acquire knowledge, to learn something;

- the desire to think globally;
- the ability to self-reflection;
- the ability to find the "golden mean"/"existential equilibrium" (a term introduced by Gazgireeva (2014) in solving vital issues;
- the ability to apply the law of synergy in the organization of their activities ("the ability of a person to perceive people and consider various phenomena of socio-cultural reality in a holistic picture of the world, to realize the existence of opposites/antinomies of ambivalence in it." (Andrienko, 2002, p. 165);
- willingness to participate in various international and domestic conferences in order to understand the choice of speakers of certain topics for discussion, taking into account their way of activity, preferences, abilities, interests, upbringing and education, nationality, ethnicity, mentality, etc.

Subsequently, having an impressive background, graduates of higher educational institutions will be able to confidently move up the career ladder and have the prospect of taking a leadership position. Job search trajectories can be: university career centers, digital career environment/platform "Faculty", networking, websites, social networks of companies, career, and specialized exhibitions, internships, such large portals as hh.ru, superjob.ru, rabota.ru, worki.ru, etc., print media, recruiting agencies, district centers for employment assistance, applications from candidates, etc.

In order to obtain professional training among students of higher educational institutions, they must participate in *research, project, and volunteer activities*, since these types of social and scientific activities contribute to the development of creative, constructive, spiritual, and moral initiatives among future specialists of the Horeca sector, as well as assist in mastering the humanistic strategy of understanding, self-realization, self-improvement and creative self-expression (Gazgireeva et al., 2018, p. 45).

Thus, it can be concluded that the background is the basis /solid foundation for mastering basic knowledge, skills, and abilities. A person with a background has good knowledge and skills in any field, or he is a recognized professional who knows how to realize his potential and achieve high results. A personality/Homo sapiens/Homo aestheticus/Homo ludens/Homo festivus/Homo creativus, existentially worried about his own "self" during life, will always be far ahead of the competition. And the developed "roadmap of the educational route for the formation of a professional background" will allow students to master the necessary competencies in the course of their studies.

References

Adolf, V. A., & Ilyina, N. F. (2010). Innovative activity in education: Problems of formation. *Higher Education in Russia, 1*, 81–87.

Andrienko, E. V. (2002). *Psychological and pedagogical foundations of the formation of professional maturity of a teacher*. Doctoral dissertation. Novosibirsk.

Background. (2021). *HR-Portal*. https://hr-portal.ru/varticle/bekgraund. Data accessed November 20, 2021.

Gazgireeva, L. Hk. (2014). *The spiritual life of modern Russian society in the existential-value dimension*. Abstract of the doctoral dissertation. North Caucasus Federal University Publishing House.

Gazgireeva, L. Hk., Burnyasheva, L. A., & Nyrova, N. I. (2018). Pedagogical requirements for the development of competitiveness in the context of modernizing higher professional education: organizational and value-based aspect. *Bulletin of the Voronezh State University. Series: Problems of Higher Education, 1*, 43–47.

Gorbunov, A. P., Kolyadin, A. P., Burnyasheva, L. A., Gazgireeva, L. Kh., & Kosenko, O. Y. (2018). Tourist and recreational clusters as organizational and economic mechanism of control of formation and development of innovative capacity of the North Caucasus Federal District. *Amazonia Investiga. University of the Amazon, 7*(17), 60–71. https://amazoniainvestiga.info/index.php/amazonia/article/view/326

Gorbunov, A. P., Kolyadin, A. P., Gazgireeva, L. Kh., & Burnyasheva, L. A. (2021). Man, his spiritual and moral potential and the limitless nature of postmodern hedonism in the provision of hotel and tourist services in the context of the transformation of socio-economic systems. In E. G. Popkova, B. S. Sergi (Eds.), *Modern global economic system: Evolutional development vs. revolutionary leap*. ISC 2019. Lecture Notes in Networks and Systems (Vol. 198). Springer. https://doi.org/10.1007/978-3-030-69415-9_6

How to write about your professional background. (2021). OGOGO Media. URL: https://ogogo.media/copywriting/kak-napisat-pro-svoj-professionalnyj-bekgraund/. Data accessed November 20, 2021.

Intentionality. (2021). *Free encyclopedia "Wikipedia"*. https://en.wikipedia.org/wiki/Intentionality. Data accessed November 20, 2021.

International Forum "Security of the Hospitality industry". (2021). *Association for the safety of tourist industry facilities*. Safety of tourism. https://www.tourismsafety.ru/news_one_5564.html. Data accessed November 20, 2021.

Kolinichenko, I. A., Nikulina, S. A., Basanova, E. E., Kosenko, O. Y., & Asrieva, E. N. (2019). Studying the professional identity of preschool teachers as a prospect for their mastering of new information technologies. In E. Popkova, & V. Ostrovskaya (Eds.), *Perspectives on the use of new Information and Communication Technology (ICT) in the modern economy*. ISC 2017. Advances in Intelligent Systems and Computing (Vol 726, pp. 1109–1115). Springer. https://doi.org/10.1007/978-3-319-90835-9_125

Lepeshkin, V. A., Kulgachev, I. P., Blinova, E. A., Manteifel, E. A., & Romanyuk, A. V. (2017). Business activity in the field of tour operator services in Russia and development of the national tourism. *International Journal of Applied Business and Economic Research, 15*(8), 53–70.

Martynov, K. K. (2007). *Intentionality as a single problem field of analytical philosophy of consciousness and phenomenology. Abstract of the doctoral dissertation*. Lomonosov Moscow State University.

Nikolskaya, E. Y., Lepeshkin, V. A., Blinova, E. A., Kulgachev, I. P., & Ilkevich, S. V. (2019). Improvement of digital technology in the tourism sector. *Journal of Environmental Management and Tourism, 10*, 6 (38), 1197–1201.

Russian State University of Tourism and Service. (2021). *Official website of the university*. https://rguts.ru/en. Data accessed November 20, 2021.

Shiyanov, E. N. (1991). *Theoretical foundations of humanization of pedagogical education. Abstract of the doctoral dissertation*. Moscow Pedagogical State University.

Blue Economy and Nature Saving Management of Sustainable Development

Methodology for the Definition of the National Blue Growth Priority Targets in the Context of International Policy Initiatives. Case of the Black Sea Region

Andrei D. Lappo, Larisa V. Danilova, Galina V. Baturova, Alexey M. Konovalov, and Polina O. Krupysheva

Abstract On May 31, 2018, in Burgas (Bulgaria), the Ministerial Declaration "Towards a Common Maritime Agenda for the Black Sea" was signed. A Vision Paper for an SRIA was proposed on European Maritime Day 2018. As a follow-up to its provisions, the implementation of the Strategic Research and Innovation Agenda for the Black Sea started in May 2019. It requires each participating country to define national SRIA's priority targets. This study proposes the methodology for this prioritization based on the key national priorities, regional marine policy, and national and sectoral strategies.

Keywords Black Sea · Black Sea Region · Blue economy · Blue Growth · Circular economy · Marine spatial planning · Sustainable development · Ecosystem-based approach · Ecosystem-based management

JEL Classification Q56 · Q01 · A12 · C18 · D85 · Q25 · Q20 · C8

1 Introduction

The Strategic Research and Innovation Agenda for the Black Sea (SRIA) is aimed at shaping a common vision of a favorable, safe, and sustainable development of the Black Sea by 2030, taking into account the peculiarities and uniqueness of its ecosystem, biodiversity, cultural heritage sites, and other factors. SRIA focuses on four key pillars:

A. D. Lappo · L. V. Danilova (✉)
Scientific and Research Institute of Maritime Spatial Planning Ermak NorthWest, St. Petersburg, Russia
e-mail: l.danilova@ermaknw.ru

G. V. Baturova · A. M. Konovalov · P. O. Krupysheva
Institute for Integrated Studies of National Maritime Policy MIREA—Russian Technological University, Moscow, Russia
e-mail: bagalina@bk.ru

E. I. Lazareva et al. (eds.), *Innovative Trends in International Business and Sustainable Management*, Approaches to Global Sustainability, Markets, and Governance,
https://doi.org/10.1007/978-981-19-4005-7_54

- Pillar 1. Black Sea Knowledge Bridge—addressing fundamental Black Sea research challenges;
- Pillar 2. Black Sea Blue Economy—developing products, solutions, and clusters underpinning Black Sea Blue Growth;
- Pillar 3. Key infrastructure and Policy enablers—the building of critical support systems and research infrastructures for the benefit of Black Sea communities;
- Pillar 4. Empowered Citizens and Enhanced Blue Workforce – education and capacity building (SRIA, 2019).

In 2020–2021 national SRIA consultation workshops have been organized by the Black Sea countries to undertake prioritization activities for various groups of stakeholders, including policymakers, regulatory authorities, researchers, and marine sectors. In these workshops, SRIA actions were ranked according to national priorities; in addition, each country was called upon to conduct prioritization of national SRIA targets.

Such a task presents significant methodological complexity, since the prioritization should be based on the analysis of the positions and ambitions of various stakeholders and national priorities in extremely diverse research areas, pressing challenges as well as taking into account the resources and capacity to fulfill the actions assigned. It should be borne in mind that SRIA actions were identified over a five-year dialogue. All of them are of high importance and require further implementation.

2 Methodology for Identifying Russian National Priorities for International Blue Growth Actions

With regard to SRIA, it should be noted that the list of actions selected by this study is preliminary and must be clarified. The selection of a few (ten in this case) priority actions from a set of equal importance requires breaking down SRIA into its unrelated components. The achievement of a comprehensive outcome requires the inclusion of all actions. At the same time, these actions themselves, despite their importance and relevance, are not complete. In some cases, actions are assigned to different pillars and goals according to their expected outcomes. This study, therefore, allows for the redefinition of certain actions following the "private to general" principle (UK Commission for Employment and Skills, 2011). In order to select preliminary national SRIA priorities, we examined the state science and higher education policy as well as the National Maritime Policy (NMP), strategic goals, and key tasks of the other national strategies. Among these are:

- Basic principles of the state strategic planning policy of the Russian Federation (SSPP) (President of the Russian Federation, 2021);
- Strategy for Scientific and Technological Development of the Russian Federation (SSTD) (President of the Russian Federation, 2021);

- State program "Scientific and technological development of the Russian Federation" (Government of the Russian Federation, 2019);
- Long-term program for fundamental scientific research (Government of the Russian Federation. Order, 2020);
- Maritime Doctrine of the Russian Federation (MD) (President of the Russian Federation, 2015);
- Strategy for the development of maritime activities of the Russian Federation until 2030 (SDMA) (Government of the Russian Federation, 2030);
- National projects "Education" (Praesidium of the Presidental Council for Strategic Development & National Projects, 2018a), "Science and Universities" (Praesidium of the Presidental Council for Strategic Development & National Projects, 2018b), "Digital Economy" (Praesidium of the Presidental Council for Strategic Development & National Projects, 2018c), "Ecology" (Praesidium of the Presidental Council for Strategic Development & National Projects, 2018d), "Tourism and the hospitality industry" (Praesidium of the Presidental Council for Strategic Development & National Projects, 2018d).

Under the documents related to science, higher education, and maritime strategy priority are given to comprehensive, intersectoral (interdepartmental) areas that form the backbone of state policy.

While defining Russian national SRIA priorities, the following principles were proposed:

- the priority should correspond to the main directions of state science and higher education strategy, the NMP and strategic goals, and key tasks as defined in related strategic planning documents;
- the priority should be given to actions that are comprehensive in defining backbone systems of an institutional nature, focused on creating conditions for the sustainable development of both traditional and innovative industries that complement the development of the "blue economy";
- the actions selected should have high multiplier effects in various spheres (scientific, international, social, environmental, etc.);
- when selecting actions, stakeholder concerns should be taken into account;
- actions should be focused on the implementation of fundamental research outcomes in real sectors of the economy and the establishment of management processes that increase applied value and contribute to the integration of findings from science and high education. These actions should allow for the development of decision-making processes (Barca, 2009), public awareness, and the introduction of new technologies for sustainable development in the "blue economy" through various forms of public–private partnerships (Baturova, 2013).

In general terms, the methodology can be graphically represented as a triad (Fig. 1).

Fig. 1 Graphical presentation of the methodology for defining national priorities modeled as a triad. Overlapping of two or more different priorities creates areas that are highly effective and serve as a "litmus test" for targeting joint actions. *Source* Developed by authors

3 Results

As an example of the prioritization of actions based on the proposed study methodology is considered national clarification of ten SRIA priorities for the Black Sea international strategies, programs, and projects with the provision of appropriate justifications for the SRIA. The publication details the prioritization for Pillar 3 (five actions).

In the first stage, independent experts with different areas of expertise evaluated the actions of SRIA on the three integrated indicators defined by the proposed methodology: 1. Compliance with the challenges of national public policy; 2. Multiplier effect; 3. Expectations of stakeholders on a 10-point scale. The scores obtained for each indicator were summed. The final quantitative assessment was done by adding up the score for each indicator. Actions that received the maximum points amount got the highest priority. Quantitative assessment results are presented in Fig. 2.

Following the quantitative assessment, a qualitative assessment was carried out which demonstrated the high reliability of the proposed methodology as most experts agreed with the results of the evaluation and confirmed the qualitative justification presented below.

(3.1.2) Produce, collect and make available compatible high-quality data sets (the FAIR principles and open data access) (Short/Medium Term). All decisions and actions for the management of marine activities are based on data that must be of high quality that fully reflect the ongoing process. The bulk of Black Sea data should be collected in publicly accessible databases. This action should include fundamental research together with accumulated data specified in actions *(1.1.1) Address eutrophication, deoxygenation, pollution, (1.1.2) Enhance food systems research, (1.1.5)*

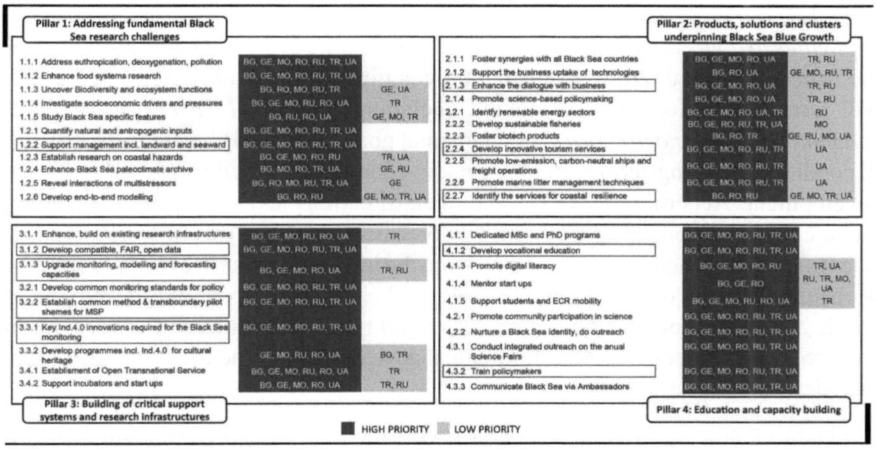

Fig. 2 Priority-setting activities based on national SRIA consultations conducted by the project Black Sea Connect with ten Russian priorities for the international strategies, programs, and projects identified (marked with frames). *Source* Developed by authors

Study Black Sea specific features, (1.2.3) Establish research on coastal hazards, (1.2.4) Enhance Black Sea paleoclimatic archive. One of the most comprehensive issues of this action is the development of a national MSDI compatible with the already extant national SDI, sectoral, and regional GIS services. In addition, it should automatically upload validated data to the regional databases and GIS services. Another area is an improvement in the international exchange of open scientific data. Such data is agglomerated, for example, on the EMODnet data portal which presents archived and current observational data and uses modern visualization and data transmission technologies. EMODnet is a part of GOOS–EuroGOOS project and the regional observing and data exchange system (Black Sea ROOS). National principles and mechanisms for the international transfer of scientific data have not yet been established. According to SSTD, the main directions and measures for the implementation of its policy include:

- provision of access for research groups to national and international information resources;
- transition to modern models of statistical observation, analysis, and assessment of the economic and social efficiency of scientific, technical and innovation activities, new industries, and markets.

In accordance with the MD, information management of maritime activities forms the basis for decision-making in the study, development, and use of resources and spaces of the World Ocean at all levels and areas of NMP implementation. According to the SDMA, the main national priorities for the development of maritime activities over the long term include improving the information management of maritime activities to increase their efficiency and security.

(3.1.3) Integrate, strengthen and upgrade monitoring, modeling, and forecasting capacities to address societal challenges (Short/Medium Term). The analysis showed the expediency required to supplement the action with socio-economic issues that will form a basis for decision-making, including action *(1.1.4) Investigate socio-economic drivers and pressures.* Fundamental goals of the SSPP include the creation of conditions for long-term sustainable socio-economic, scientific, and technological development. According to SSTD, the main directions and measures of the policy include the development of a system for forecasting and analysis of world trends in scientific development, as well as improving the quality of expertise to make effective decisions in areas of scientific, technological, and socio-economic development, public administration and the rational use of all types of resources. The tasks of the state program "Scientific and technological development of the Russian Federation" include:

- obtaining new knowledge through the development and support of fundamental research that ensures the country's readiness for major challenges and timely assessment of risks caused by scientific and technological developments;
- support for all stages of the "life cycle" of knowledge through the effective communication of the science, technology, and innovation system thereby increasing the adoption of innovation within society and the economy;
- creation of conditions for the development of science-intensive business.

The first task of the Program for Fundamental Scientific Research in the Russian Federation in the long term (2021–2030) is to form an effective management system for fundamental and exploratory scientific research to ensure an increase in the effectiveness, significance, and relevance of scientific research results for the development of the national economy and society.

(3.2.2) Establish a common methodology and transboundary pilot schemes for marine spatial planning at national and regional levels based on the ecosystem approach (Short Term). Although the action was approved in principle and highly rated, the comprehensive analysis showed that it can feasibly be reformulated as follows: *Development of common approaches to the methodology of transboundary pilot marine spatial planning.* The experience in maritime spatial planning (MSP) in the Baltic Sea has shown that countries may have different MSP methodologies as well as different key priorities (Baklanov, 2018; Blinovskaya et al., 2021; Erbach, 2013; Gopnik et al., 2012; Lappo & Danilova, 2015). All national methodologies must conform to general regional principles to enable the development of coherent transboundary marine spatial plans. MSP acts as a spatial basis for management decisions reflected in strategic planning documents at national and regional levels (Mikhailichenko, 2004).

In the SDMA, the transition to integrated planning for the development of coastal and marine areas is referred to as one of the main priorities for the development of maritime activities over the long term. At the same time, the overall strategic goal associated with the transition to an integrated approach will require that specific country coasts are each managed by their single body of state management that will enable the implementation of integrated management programs for natural resources in coastal and marine areas. The goal is to ensure sustainable development of the Black Sea Region and this cannot be achieved through the actions of one country alone. Regional integration of maritime activities, the spread of pollution, eutrophication, and other common challenges experienced by all countries require coordinated efforts based on the justified spatial distribution of anthropogenic pressures through cross-border MSP.

(3.3.1) Identify and promote key technologies and innovations required for the Black Sea monitoring and research in close interaction with solution providers and best practices (Short/Medium Term). Identifying and promoting key technologies and innovations is the foundation for the successful development of coastal communities. The action is fully consistent with *(2.1.2) Support the business uptake of technologies, (2.2.2) Develop sustainable fisheries, (2.2.3) Foster biotech products, (2.2.4) Develop innovative tourism services, (2.2.5) Promote low-emission, carbon–neutral ships,* and is also in line with developing MSP *(3.2.2).*

In accordance with SSTD, the main directions and measures for its implementation include the creation of conditions that ensure the mutual influence of the scientific community and society by encouraging society to request the dissemination of results from research activities.

The goals of the state program "Scientific and technological development of the Russian Federation" include scientific and technological development and intellectual support of structural changes in the economy; efficient organization and technological renewal of scientific, technical, and innovative (high-tech) activities.

The List of Critical Technologies of the Russian Federation (President of the Russian Federation, 2011) includes technologies that directly and indirectly affect maritime activities. Technologies directly related to the study, development, and exploitation of resources and spaces of the World Ocean include renewable energy; monitoring and forecasting the state of the environment; search, exploration, mining, and extraction; prevention and elimination of natural and man-made emergencies; creation of high-speed vehicles and intelligent control systems for new types of transport, etc. Technologies that have an indirect impact on maritime activities include nano-, bio-, information, cognitive technologies; biosensors, biomedical and genomic technologies; bioengineering; information and control systems; nanodevices and microsystems, etc.

Considerable attention is paid to certain areas of maritime activities in the Forecast of Scientific and Technological Development until 2030 (Government of the Russian Federation, 2030). This paper identifies the following promising areas of scientific and technological support of maritime activities:

- systems of hydrometeorological observations and forecasts;
- systems of ecological monitoring of the hydrosphere integrated monitoring of hazardous natural phenomena;
- new materials and nanotechnologies in shipbuilding;
- systems for early detection and forecasting of emergencies;
- software for systems and complexes for modeling to predict events and phenomena (technogenic, climatic, seismic, geophysical, etc.);

- cellular, genomic, and post-genomic technologies for the conservation of biological resources of the World Ocean;
- complexes for cleaning inland and sea waters from hydrocarbon (oil) pollution, as well as for carrying out rescue operations and remediating the consequences of emergencies;
- aquabioculture, etc.

4 Conclusion

The methodology presented makes it possible to determine the preliminary national priorities of the Russian Federation for the implementation of SRIA in the international strategies, programs, and projects. By its universality, this methodology can also be used for the prioritization of actions in the fields of Blue Growth, blue economy, and the integrated development of coastal and marine areas (Fetisov et al., 2012). In addition, it can be used to check and verify compliance with the national priorities of international projects of a close topic. A broader study will follow the same principles and methodology, but with a significant increase in the number of recipients (Blue Growth experts and stakeholders). The number of estimates is sufficient, but may be increased after the presentation of the study and the next round of SRIA international consultations.

Acknowledgements This research was performed in the framework of the state assignment of the Ministry of Education and Science of the Russian Federation (theme No.730000Ф.99.1.БВ16АА02001) for the Russian implementation of the project Black Sea Connect CSA.

References

Baklanov, P. Ya. (2018). Marine spatial planning: Theoretical aspects. *The Baltic region, 10*(2).

Barca, F. (2009). *An agenda for a reformed cohesion policy. A place-based approach to meeting European Union challenges and expectations.* Independent Report prepared at the request of Danuta Hübner, Commissioner for Regional Policy. – DG Regio, Brussels. OECD.

Baturova, G. V. (2013). *Approaches to the formation of quantitative indicators of complex development.* Tr. conf. Strategic planning in regions and cities of Russia: potential for integration (pp. 123–126).

Blinovskaya, Ya. Yu., Mazlova, E. A., Lappo, A. D., Zemlyanov, I. V., Shilin, M. B., & Danilova, L. V. (2021). *Geological and ecological aspects of marine spatial planning: Theory, practice, perspective.* Publishing Center of the Gubkin Russian State University of Oil and Gas.

Erbach, G. (2013). *Spatial planning for the "blue economy": Maritime spatial planning and integrated coastal management.* Library Briefing. Library of the European Parliament.

Fetisov, G. G., Granberg, A. G., S. Yu., Glazyev, Vashanov, V. A., Konovalov, A. M., Mikheeva, N. N., Razbegin, V. N., & Pilyasov, A. N. (2012). *Spatial development problems: Research methodology and practice.* SOPS.

Gopnik, M., Fieseler, C., Cantral, L., McClellan, K., Pendleton, L., & Crowder, L. (2012). Coming to the table: Early stakeholder engagement in marine spatial planning. *Marine Policy, 36*(5), 1139–1149. https://doi.org/10.1016/j.marpol.2012.02.012.

Government of the Russian Federation. Decree No. 377. *On approval of the state program of the Russian Federation "Scientific and technological development of the Russian Federation"*. March 29, 2019.

Government of the Russian Federation. Order No. 1930-r. *On approval of the Strategy for the development of maritime activities of the Russian Federation until 2030*. August 30, 2019.

Government of the Russian Federation. *On approval of the Forecast of scientific and technological development of the Russian Federation for the period up to 2030*. January 3, 2014.

Government of the Russian Federation. Order No. 3684-r. *On approval of the Long-term program for fundamental scientific research in the Russian Federation (2021–2030)*. December 31, 2020.

Lappo, A., & Danilova, L. (2015). Pilot projects on maritime spatial planning in the Russian Federation. *Bulletin of the Maritime Institute in Gdansk, 30*(1), 23–40. https://doi.org/10.5604/12307424.1158321.

Mikhailichenko, Yu. G. (2004). Adaptation and development of world experience in integrated management of coastal zones of the seas. *Izvestiya RAN. Geographic Series, 6*, 31–40.

Praesidium of the Presidental Council for Strategic Development and National Projects. Protocol No. 16. *On approval of the National project "Education"*. December 24, 2018a (last amended on September 1, 2021).

Praesidium of the Presidental Council for Strategic Development and National Projects. Protocol No. 16. *On approval of the National project "Science and Universities"*. December 24, 2018b (last amended on September 1, 2021).

Praesidium of the Presidental Council for Strategic Development and National Projects. Protocol No. 16. *On approval of the National programme "Digital Economy of the Russian Federation"*. December 24, 2018c (last amended on September 1, 2021).

Praesidium of the Presidental Council for Strategic Development and National Projects. *Protocol No. 16. On approval of the National project "Ecology"*. December 24, 2018d (last amended on September 1, 2021).

Praesidium of the Presidental Council for Strategic Development and National Projects. Protocol No. 16. *On approval of the National project "Tourism and the hospitality industry"*. December 24, 2018e (last amended on September 1, 2021).

President of the Russian Federation. Decree No. 143. *On approval of the Strategy for scientific and technological development of the Russian Federation*. March 15, 2021.

President of the Russian Federation. Decree of the No. 899. *On approval of the List of Critical Technologies of the Russian Federation*. July 7, 2011.

President of the Russian Federation. *On approval of the Maritime Doctrine of the Russian Federation*. July 26, 2015.

President of the Russian Federation. Decree No. 633. *On approval of the Basic Principles of the State strategic planning policy of the Russian Federation*. November 8, 2021.

Strategic Research and Innovation Agenda for the Black Sea (SRIA). April 2019.

UK Commission for Employment and Skills. *Rebalancing the economy sectorally and spatially: An evidence review*. Volume 1 Main report. Evidence Report 33, August 2011.

Regulatory Functions of Ecological Imperatives in Environmental Management

Victor N. Ovchinnikov and Natalia P. Ketova

Abstract The purpose of the article is to identify the role of environmental imperatives in the regulation of human economic activity, taking into account the natural living conditions, and their use as natural resources or consumption as environmental goods. Disrupting the natural homeostasis of the natural environment, this activity is antientropic in nature, since it destroys the connections of the elements of geobiocenosis that have been formed for centuries, and, consequently, negatively affects the stable equilibrium of the natural ecosystem, weakening its carrying and regenerative capacity. This makes it necessary to use the methodology of modeling the reproduction of a stable equilibrium when developing an environmental management strategy and assessing the fixed costs of various types of resources to maintain the reproductive mode of functioning of an artificially created environmental management system. The imbalance between the consumption of natural resources and environmental benefits is fraught with serious, and sometimes irreversible negative consequences, as clearly evidenced by the example of the loss of the Aral Sea. Negative externalities are increasingly manifested at the planetary level, which increases the importance of the problem of systematic consideration of the ecological imperative in the management strategy of natural ecosystems. Based on the results of the study, reasonable recommendations have been developed on the use of nature-like agricultural technologies and renewable sources of energy. The content and text of the article are based on the results of the authors' research.

Keywords Ecosystem · Environmental management system · Natural resources · Environmental benefits · Nature-like technologies · Sustainable equilibrium · Environmental management

JEL Classification Q50 · Q56 · Q57

V. N. Ovchinnikov (✉) · N. P. Ketova
Southern Federal University, Rostov-on-Don, Russia
e-mail: vovchinnikov@sfedu.ru

N. P. Ketova
e-mail: nketova@sfedu.ru

E. I. Lazareva et al. (eds.), *Innovative Trends in International Business and Sustainable Management*, Approaches to Global Sustainability, Markets, and Governance,
https://doi.org/10.1007/978-981-19-4005-7_55

1 Introduction

Relevance. Among the global problems of a planetary scale affecting the interests of all mankind, the impact of human activity on climate change occupies a special place due to its significance for the fate of civilization and relevance in the time dimension. *The research problem.* The article attempts to determine the nature and extent of the impact of human activity on the natural ecosystem, as well as to substantiate the functionality of the ecological imperative as an instrument of environmental management policy using nature-like technologies in accordance with the criteria of resource conservation and preservation of a clean environment. *The purpose and objectives of the study.* The purpose of the article is to identify the principles and environmental imperatives of the organization of human reproductive and sustainable environmental management. The achievement of this goal is realized in the process of solving three tasks: consideration of environmental management activities in the format of the functioning of natural ecosystems, illustration of the negative experience of violation of sound principles and imperatives on the example of the natural ecosystem of the Aral Sea basin, and identification of solutions to the problem of climate change on a planetary scale.

2 Methodology

The research is conducted in the paradigm of substantiating the principles and imperatives of the implementation of the reproductive approach to the design and functioning of natural ecosystems.

3 Results

1. Consideration of environmental management activities in the format of the functioning of natural ecosystems

Natural–economic systems are ecosystems artificially created by human production and economic activity in the natural environment. Based on the idea of entropy as a measure of stability (equilibrium) of any system, it should be recognized that in relation to naturally formed balanced sustainable natural biogeocenoses (ecosystems), any human activity for their production and economic development and use has an antientropic (lowering entropy) character.

Indeed, invading the natural ecosystem, a person tries to adapt it to his production and economic activities (land clearance or surface mining). This leads to the disruption of the connections formed over the centuries between the elements of the biogeocenosis, thereby reducing the stability of the artificially created ecosystem and, consequently, lowering its entropy.

In environmental management, it is important to be guided by the generally recognized principle of "sustainability through diversity", which explains the phenomenon of sustainability of natural and biogeocenotic ecosystems due to the diversity of its organic elements (living organisms of flora and fauna) and the system-forming links between them, generating the effect of emergence and synergy (in this case, organicity). At the same time, it should be borne in mind that carrying and regenerative capacity of the ecosystem retains its functionality when less than 10% of the links formed in it are broken ("the ten percent principle").

In such a situation (when creating ecosystems), the destruction of part of its system-forming links, which weakens the stability of the natural ecosystem, can be partially compensated by duplicating the system-forming functions of the preserved links, as well as the resource potential of the ecosystem's reproduction.

The ecosystem artificially created by human activity, being by definition unstable, constantly needs to support the reproductive regime of its functioning by the permanent involvement of additional resources: labor (weeding, control of pests, weeds and diseases, soil fertilization, increasing resistance, yield and productivity, breeding and genetic activities, etc.), techno-energy, organic and mineral fertilizers, biosecurity of plants and animals, etc.

Since the nature-economic system is formed in order to ensure a long period of its productive functioning, it is important to use tools that correspond to this guideline of project thinking. The fact is that the management of this process involves not only the difficulties associated with the inclusion of the nature-economic system in the formed homeostasis of the naturally formed ecosystem, but also the foresight of long-term consequences and socio-ecological externalities.

It seems that an adequate tool for the program-planned development of such large-scale environmental projects is strategic management with an emphasis on its ecological mission. When developing a strategy for environmental management, it is important to be guided by the principle of generic homogeneity of functionally specified resource factors of the natural ecosystem: Natural resources are potential factors of material production that affect the living conditions of society and environmental benefits—the natural provision of a favorable habitat for people as elements of a single "repository" of natural conditions for the reproduction of the socio-ecosystem.

At the same time, it is necessary to take into account its capacity and the limitations of non-renewable resource factors, many of which can alternately perform the function of natural resources or environmental benefits while preserving the overall capacity. This means that the same resource factor of a natural ecosystem can be used in a functional or other functional role. Being used as a natural resource, it is lost in the potential role of an environmental good. This situation creates the problem of ensuring a rational balance between the needs of the economy and the preservation of a clean environment for human life.

An ecosystem is a socioeconomic system, and, according to James Moore, "Any socio-economic system is open, that is, it gives and receives resources (energy) by interacting with the external environment" (Moore, 1993). This circumstance determines the ecological principle of integration of natural and economic systems into the natural environment (Astvatsaturov, 2006; Doroshenko & Shelomentsev, 2017).

These principles determine the ecological imperatives to ensure the harmony of human environmental management with the principles of stability of the functioning of natural biogeocenoses (ecosystems), in the format (area) of which they are located (Ecosystems in the Space of the New Economy, 2020). These requirements are equally applied to natural ecosystems of meso-, macro- and mega-levels (Ovchinnikov, 2020).

2. The origins and causes of the ecological catastrophe of the natural ecosystem of the Aral Sea.

Today, the scale of human economic activity, its impact on the natural environment and climate are of reasonable concern. In this context, it seems appropriate to consider an example of such an impact on the ecosystem of the meso-level. For meso-level ecosystems, a naturally emerging taxonomic unit that is often used is the area of the river basin. Using this approach, it is possible to illustrate the negative externalities of the impact of human economic activity on the well-known example of the ecological catastrophe of the Aral Sea basin and the Syr-Darya and Amu-Darya rivers. Chronologically, the origins of the current plight of the Aral ecosystem date back to the middle of the twentieth century, when there were significant changes in the world cotton market due to the fact that a number of leading exporting countries, primarily the United States, limited supplies, considering it a strategic raw material. The situation with import restrictions gave impetus to a significant expansion of the cultivation of this crop, and accordingly, the total area of crops increased in a number of countries, including the USSR.

The older generation remembers those times when cotton was tried to be grown on the Don and Kuban, where climatic conditions were not favorable enough. Naturally, cotton plantations were developed in the Soviet Union in the republics of Central Asia, which have favorable climatic conditions for this. Large-scale economic development of semi-desert and dry-steppe territories for cotton cultivation has begun and especially intensively in Uzbekistan in the Aral Sea basin and the Syr Darya and Amu Darya rivers (The Aral Sea. Consequences of the drying up of the Aral Sea, 2021).

The sources (with tributaries) of these longest rivers in Central Asia, whose freshwater flows into the salty Aral Sea, originate from the snow-capped peaks and glaciers of the Pamir, Tien Shan and Hindu Kush mountain ranges. Nothing foreshadowed environmental threats in the initial period of expansion of agricultural land for cotton cultivation, but a large volume of ploughing and stripping works (for the construction of hydro-reclamation systems: canals and water gangs) caused serious pollution of the atmosphere by suspended atmospheric dust.

Dust storms, along with a huge amount of earthworks and the construction of asphalt plants for the large-scale development of road transport infrastructure in the construction zone of the Great Turkmen Canal, caused significant and irreversible pollution of snow peaks and glaciers, which are sources the rivers of the Aral Sea basin.

This led to a sharp increase in their glaciological coefficient (by 22 times—from 2 to 44%), which characterizes the ratio of absorbed and reflected radiant energy of the Sun and conventional heat flows. Due to the multiple increase in heat, polluted high-altitude snow and glaciers began to melt more intensively and, no less importantly, earlier than the previous climatic regime (term).

Such a shift in the thermal seasons of the year caused earlier floods on the rivers of the Aral Sea. This, in turn, led to a discrepancy between the timing and measures of seasonal and agrotechnical support for the established growing season of cotton, on the one hand, and the possibility of using excess flood waters, on the other. Earlier periods of flooding coincided with the period of irrigation of cotton plantations, when young plants take root in the soil in 2–3 weeks and are ready for watering.

Thus, flood waters were used for irrigation of cotton, so the peak of the flood did not pose a threat to the spontaneous destructive force of nature for hydraulic structures and coastal settlements, and the water regime of the rivers was close to the ordinary and maintained the laminar nature of the flow. But this balance in the stable-reproductive mode of functioning of the formed nature-economic system was disrupted by the above-mentioned environmental factors and externalities.

Now, the time of the destructive and turbulent peak of the flood on the Aral rivers, which is useless for irrigation, falls on the period of cotton sowing, when irrigation is impossible, and by the time of irrigation, the floodwaters recede, and water has to be taken from the ordinary-laminar flow of the rivers. This situation leads to their dehydration to such a state that rivers can no longer maintain the water balance of the Aral Sea due to the intense evaporation of water from a once large area of the sea, and the dried riverbeds are lost in the sands before reaching the Aral Sea.

The remains of former fishing ships half-buried in sand a few kilometers from today's shore of the "lake", which had a home port of Nukus, look sad, the view of the capital of Kara-Kalpakia, Takhia-Tasha, does not inspire optimism. Even more pessimism is caused by the view of today's dried-up water area of the Aral Sea, which has turned from the sea into a large shallow salt puddle.

The situation is worsened by the fact that the wind picks up the smallest salt crystals from its dried-up shores and saturates the atmosphere of the region with them, causing upper respiratory tract diseases in people. Unlike silicosis, an occupational disease of miners whose lungs are damaged by coal dust, the aggressive environment of the air saturated with salt suspended particles damages the alveoli of the lungs. This disease covers 85% of the adult population of the autonomy and 92% of less protected organisms of children, acquiring the features of an ecological disaster.

These are the results of economic decisions that are ill-considered from the standpoint of strategic management and environmental criteria, sometimes leading to the destruction of seemingly stable meso-level natural ecosystems.

It is also extremely important to analyze the situation with the impact of human economic activity on a mega-level ecosystem of a planetary scale.

3. Planetary environmental challenges to humanity and imperatives for environmental management.

There is a growing body of scientifically confirmed evidence of anthropogenic and technogenic impact of social development on the natural environment in the mass media. This is a general warming of the climate, an increase in the temperature of the World Ocean by 1 °C over the previous two centuries, the collapse of glaciers of Antarctica and Greenland, the melting of permafrost, high-altitude snow and glaciers, the expansion of the ozone hole area over Antarctica, the greenhouse effect and much more.

The concern of the world community about climate change and its consequences, as well as the search to overcome this global environmental threat, has been adequately reflected in the United Nations Framework Convention on Climate Change, the Paris Agreement and the outcome of the Climate Summit in Glasgow.

It is proposed to develop cooperation between the countries in three main areas: reduction of polluting emissions, adaptation to the climate change and financing of necessary measures to adapt and prevent pollution of the atmosphere, lithosphere and hydrosphere of the planet (What is climate change, 2021).

With regard to the reduction of polluting emissions, the target for achieving net zero emissions by 2050 assumes the implementation of half of the planned measures by 2030. And this means that during this period, the production of fossil energy resources should be reduced by 6% annually.

The solution to the problem of adaptation to the climate change provides for the implementation of a system of measures to protect the population, people's homes, their habitat, sources of livelihood, enterprises and infrastructure facilities from the negative externalities of this process. Financing of the necessary measures for the implementation of such a project on a global scale is impossible without providing developing countries that do not have their own resources for this, annual assistance of $ 100 billion.

The urgent need for a constructive response of society to these challenges on a planetary scale dictates environmental imperatives to human economic activity. Priority among them are: the transition to the use of nature-like technologies in production and economic practice (Ovchinnikov et al., 2019), the widespread use of low-carbon production methods in the real sector of the economy, intensive development of hydrogen energy and electricity resources for a paradigm shift in the design and technology of new types of mobile engines for transport, significant expansion of the range of use of renewable energy sources: wind, solar, geothermal, tidal and biofuels. At the same time, nature-like technologies, for example, are fundamentally new technologies that do not cause damage to the surrounding world, but coexist with it in complete harmony and allow restoring the balance between the biosphere and the technosphere disturbed by man (Nature-like technologies as a response to new global challenges, 2019).

Only with a real balance of economic and environmental interests of society in the rational use of natural conditions of human activity as natural resources (for production) and environmental benefits (to ensure a favorable habitat), sustainable reproduction of ecosystems in the noosphere of human civilization development is possible.

4 Conclusion

The conducted research allowed us to draw the following conclusions.

1. Environmental management should be based on an understanding of its antientropic nature, which requires constant efforts to maintain the reproductive and sustainable regime of artificially created ecosystems included in the natural conditions of human life.
2. Violation of the principles and environmental imperatives of the ecosystem management of the Aral basin led to its death and the emergence of an ecological disaster zone on the former site of the lake.
3. The problem of overcoming the negative consequences of climate change under the influence of external factors of human environmental management implies the need to solve three interrelated tasks by 2050: the complete cessation of emissions polluting the planet, the adaptation of mankind to the ongoing climate change and the mobilization of necessary financial resources, including the annual provision of $ 100 billion to developing countries for the transition to a "green" economy (Taking urgent measures to combat climate change and its consequences, 2021).

References

Astvatsaturov, A. E. (2006). Engineering ecology. Ecologist. Ecology and environmental safety. https://ekolog.org/books/18/. Data accessed 3 November 2021.

Doroshenko, S. V., & Shelomentsev, A. G. (2017). The entrepreneurial ecosystem in the contemporary socio-economic studies. *Journal of Economic Theory, 4*, 212–221.

Ecosystems in the Space of the New Economy. (2020). *Collective monograph* (pp. 540–541). SFU Publishing House.

Moore, J. F. (1993). Predators and prey: A new ecology of competition. *Harvard Business Review, 71*(3), 75–86.

Nature-like technologies as a response to new global challenges. (2019). ROSCONGRESS. The space of trust. https://roscongress.org/news/nature-inspired-technologies-as-a-response-to-global-challenges-and-basis-for-a-new-industrial-revolution/. Data accessed 14 November 2021.

Ovchinnikov, V. N. (2020). *Dialectics of the interdependence of rational consumption of natural resources and environmental benefits in the use of natural conditions of the regional society* (p. 151). Monograph. SFU Publishing House.

Ovchinnikov, V., Ketova, N., & Lysochenko, A. (2019). Nature management imperatives in the system of ensuring food security in Russia. *Quality—Access to Success, 20*(173), 131–134.

Taking urgent measures to combat climate change and its consequences. (2021). The United Nations. Sustainable Development Goals. https://www.un.org/sustainabledevelopment/ru/climate-change/. Data accessed 14 November 2021.

The Aral Sea. Consequences of the drying up of the Aral Sea. (2021). UN Mmulti-Partner Human Security Trust Fund for the Aral Sea Region in Uzbekistan. https://aral.mptf.uz/site/aralsea.html. Data accessed 23 December 2021.

What is climate change? (2021). The United Nations. Measures to combat climate change. https://www.un.org/ru/climatechange/what-is-climate-change. Data accessed 9 November 2021.

The Blue Economy and the Black Sea: Research Trends and Prospects for Scientific Cooperation in the Black Sea Region

Anton A. Afanasyev, Stavros Kalognomos, Andrei D. Lappo, Larisa V. Danilova, and Alexey M. Konovalov

Abstract *Purpose* This paper identifies the current state and prospects for scientific cooperation in the field of the Blue Economy in the Black Sea Region. *Design/methodology/approach* We conducted a bibliometric analysis of scientific publications indexed in one of the largest international citation databases of peer-reviewed literature (Scopus) for the past 5 years. The following terms were selected: Blue Economy, Ocean Economy, Blue Growth, Ecosystem-Based Management and Marine Spatial Planning. For the detailed search query, we adopted the classification of the traditional and emerging sectors of the Ocean Economy, developed by the OECD, and integrated relevant keywords (equivalents) from the marine economy framework classification of the EU, US and China Blue Economy sectors. *Findings* The results show that non-regional actors (like the United States, the United Kingdom, Australia, Canada) have been actively involved in the research agenda in the field of the Blue Economy, inter alia in the Black Sea Region, while the representation of the regional stakeholders (in particular, the BSEC Member States) is relatively low. The majority of the countries in the Black Sea Region are involved in the common scientific research agenda related to the Blue/Ocean Economy, including its traditional and emerging marine (ocean-based) sectors. Ecosystem-Based Management is underrepresented as a research area. The Black Sea Region significantly

A. A. Afanasyev (✉)
Southern Federal University, Rostov-on-Don, Russia
e-mail: afanasyev.anton@mail.ru

S. Kalognomos
The Balkan and Black Sea Commission (BBSC), Brussels, Belgium
e-mail: stavros.kalognomos@crpm.org

A. D. Lappo · L. V. Danilova
Scientific and Research Institute of Maritime Spatial Planning Ermak NorthWest, St. Petersburg, Russia
e-mail: l.danilova@ermaknw.ru

A. M. Konovalov
Institute for Integrated Studies of National Maritime Policy MIREA—Russian Technological University, Moscow, Russia

E. I. Lazareva et al. (eds.), *Innovative Trends in International Business and Sustainable Management*, Approaches to Global Sustainability, Markets, and Governance,
https://doi.org/10.1007/978-981-19-4005-7_56

lacks academic-corporate collaboration in the field of the Blue Economy. *Originality/value* The current studies related to the development of the Blue Economy as a scientific area of research specifically in the Black Sea Region are underrepresented in the academic literature. The study allowed us to identify the countries from the Black Sea Region that are leading in terms of the research related to the Blue/Ocean Economy, as well as determine research trends for international cooperation related to the development of Blue/Ocean Economy in the Black Sea Region.

Keywords Blue Economy · Black Sea Region · International cooperation · Research areas · Bibliometric analysis · Marine Spatial Planning · Ecosystem-Based Management

JEL Classification Q56 · Q01 · A12 · C18 · D85 · Q25 · Q20 · C8

1 Introduction

The Blue Economy as a concept experienced rapid development in recent years. The main stakeholders around the world recognize the increasing need to develop sustainable marine or ocean management and to foster innovative international partnerships, that become the essential element of achieving the Sustainable Development Goals (especially, 14—Life Below Water and 17—Revitalize the global partnership for sustainable development). The Decade of Ocean Science for Sustainable Development (2021–2030), proclaimed by the United Nations, emphasizes the relevance of the availability of the common science and research agenda. There are several ongoing initiatives in the Black Sea Region related to the development of research, innovation, marine management and the Blue Growth, in particular, the Black Sea Strategic Research and Innovation Agenda (SRIA) and Common Maritime Agenda for the Black Sea (CMA), as well as specific coordination and support actions for the implementation of these initiatives—the Black Sea CONNECT and the Black Sea Assistance Mechanism (BSAM).

Regional scientific organizations and universities usually serve as main participants of such projects, while international organizations in the Black Sea Region, like the Black Sea Economic Cooperation (BSEC), the Commission on the Protection of the Black Sea against Pollution (BSC) and the Balkan and Black Sea Commission (BBSC) may initiate and/or coordinate the development and implementation of such projects. Despite the active development of interaction and communication between stakeholders in the field of the Blue Economy from the Black Sea Region, inter alia within recently introduced multilateral projects with the extensive support of the European Union, like the BRIDGE-BS (Advancing Black Sea Research and Innovation to Co-Develop Blue Growth within Resilient Ecosystems) and the DOORS (Developing Optimal and Open Research Support for the Black Sea), the overall level of the involvement of key regional stakeholders in the common agenda, in particular, research or scientific agenda, is still relatively low. However, the understanding of the necessity of efficient sustainable development based on science, knowledge, data and strong international cooperation is recognized among all countries in the Black Sea Region. In this regard, the study is aimed to identify the current state and prospects for scientific cooperation in the field of the Blue Economy in the Black Sea Region based on the scientometric approach.

2 Materials and Methods

The approaches to the concept of the Blue Economy, Ocean Economy and Blue Growth, as well as to the terminology related to this notion have been actively discussed in the academic literature (Brears, 2021; Cristiani, 2017; Martínez-Vázquez et al., 2021), including the conduction of a bibliometric analysis of the coastal tourism as a part of the Blue Economy (Kabil et al., 2021), as well as the transdisciplinary analysis of this area in general (Spalding et al., 2021). The Blue Economy is widely recognized as a driver of economic growth, although the research and technological activities toward the revitalization of the established marine and ocean industries are still limited (Sousa et al., 2020). Meanwhile, sustainable management, integrated ecosystems management or ecosystem-based management are considered essential elements of the Blue Economy (Konovalov et al., 2019; Sumaila et al., 2021). The necessity of the development of the Common maritime agenda and Marine spatial planning has been also recently viewed as an integral part of the Blue Economy (Frazão Santos et al., 2019; Lappo & Danilova, 2015). However, the studies related to the development of the Blue Economy as a scientific area of research in the Black Sea Region are underrepresented in the academic literature.

In order to identify the current state and prospects for the development of joint scientific research in the area of the Blue Economy in the Black Sea Region, we conducted a bibliometric analysis of scientific publications indexed in one of the largest international citation databases of peer-reviewed literature for the past 5 years (from 2016 to 2020). Initially, the Scopus, WoS and Dimensions databases were considered as a source of data. However, in the framework of this study the analysis was limited to the one database, in particular, Scopus, due to the highest coverage of articles in natural sciences, engineering and technology disciplines and to the similar representation of the results in other databases (Singh et al., 2021). Nevertheless, to guarantee the data integrity we carried out a test search query in the WoS and Dimensions databases using the same keywords and criteria, and received similar results. It should be noted that the analysis of the national databases is of particular interest for further research.

For the general search query, the following terms were selected: Blue Economy, Ocean Economy, Blue Growth, Ecosystem-Based Management and Marine Spatial Planning. It should be noted that the Marine Spatial Planning, Maritime Spatial Planning and Integrated Sea/Ocean Management planning reflect the nature of national planning systems and the methodological approaches to the development of this area, inter alia focusing more on earth and ocean sciences, flora and fauna of oceans and seas or technologies and efficient exploitation of sea and ocean resources. The term Marine Spatial Planning is used further in this study.

To carry out the detailed search query, we adopted the classification of the traditional and emerging sectors of the Ocean Economy, developed by the OECD (2016), and integrated relevant keywords (equivalents) from the marine economy framework classification of the EU, US and China Blue Economy sectors (European Commission, 2021). Carbon capture and storage, and Marine monitoring were separately included in the search query within the emerging marine (ocean-based) industries, as they have been considered key research trends in the field of carbon balance calculation systems to reduce the carbon footprint and Artificial Intelligence-based monitoring systems, as well as sustainable development in general.

The Black Sea Region and the BSEC Member States, in particular, are considered the key objects of this study. The averages for Europe and the BSEC Region are provided for comparison. The top 10 countries of the world are identified, as well as the top countries of the Black Sea Region in terms of the number of publications on the considered topics and the share of the relevant publications related to the Black Sea. The data obtained during the study is visualized for further analysis and interpretation.

3 Results

The results of the bibliometric analysis show that the United Kingdom, the United States and Italy have the highest publication activity related to the scientific research in the field of the Blue Economy, Ocean Economy or Blue Growth conducted for the past 5 years. Although, Italy and Spain have the highest share of the research in the respective scientific areas related to the Black Sea, the average numbers of the relevant publications for European countries and the BSEC Region, in general, are relatively low.

As shown in Fig. 1, for the past 5 years Greece, Russia, Turkey, Romania and Bulgaria have been actively conducting scientific research in the field of the Blue Economy, Ocean Economy or Blue Growth in the Black Sea Region. Georgia, Romania, Serbia, Bulgaria and Ukraine have the highest share of the research in the respective scientific areas related specifically to the Black Sea. Of all BSEC Member States, Greece has the highest number of scientific publications in the field of Ecosystem-Based Management, although, the highest share of the research in the respective scientific area related specifically to the Black Sea belongs to Ukraine (50%), Turkey (40%) and Russia (20%). Ecosystem-Based Management as a research subject area is underrepresented in the Black Sea Region. For the past 5 years, eight countries from the Black Sea Region (out of 13 BSEC Member States) have been actively involved in scientific research, related to Marine Spatial Planning. The highest share of the research in the respective scientific area, related specifically to the Black Sea, belongs to Romania (87%), Bulgaria (75%) and Turkey (57%). It is noteworthy that despite having relatively low publication activity, all scientific

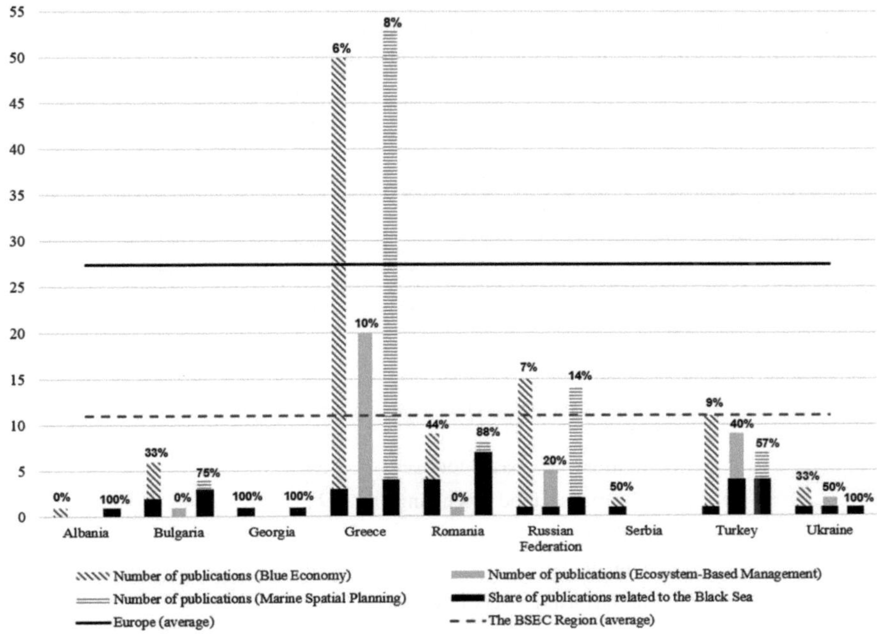

Fig. 1 The BSEC member states that conduct scientific research on the Blue Economy, the Ecosystem-Based Management, the Marine Spatial Planning including the share of publications related to the Black Sea (by the number of publications). *Source* Authors'

publications from Albania, Georgia and Ukraine in this research area are dedicated specifically to the Black Sea.

As shown in Table 1, the most represented research areas in the traditional marine (ocean-based) industries/sectors in the Black Sea Region (13 BSEC Member States) are Marine manufacturing and construction, Port activities and warehousing, Industrial capture fisheries and living resources, Shipping and Transport, Marine R&D and education. The most represented research areas in the emerging marine (ocean-based) industries/sectors in the Black Sea Region (13 BSEC Member States) include: Offshore wind energy, Marine and seabed mining, Ocean renewable energy, Industrial marine aquaculture, Carbon capture and storage.

The total number of publications in the traditional and emerging marine (ocean-based) industries/sectors in the Black Sea Region (in particular, in the BSEC Member States) considered in the analysis significantly exceeds the number of publications in the field of "Blue Economy", "Ocean Economy" and "Blue Growth", even with the publications on the "Ecosystem-Based Management" and "Marine Spatial Planning", as shown on Fig. 2. This is because these concepts or terms are relatively new, while the sectors/industries of the Blue/Ocean Economy have been developing as separate, but interconnected research subject areas for a long time.

Table 1 Representation of scientific research within traditional and emerging marine (ocean-based) industries/sectors in the Black Sea Region (by the number of publications)

	Industry/sector	Number of publications (indexed in the Scopus database over the past 5 years)
Traditional marine (ocean-based) industries/sectors	Marine R&D and education	226
	Shipping and transport	219
	Industrial capture fisheries and living resources	186
	Port activities and warehousing	166
	Marine manufacturing and construction	53
	Offshore oil and gas (shallow water)	47
	Maritime and coastal tourism	34
	Industrial seafood processing	21
	Dredging	21
	Shipbuilding	20
	Marine business services	4
Emerging marine (ocean-based) industries/sectors	Carbon capture and storage	201
	Industrial marine aquaculture	73
	Ocean renewable energy	72
	Marine and seabed mining	63
	Offshore wind energy	51
	Deep and ultra-deepwater oil and gas	41
	Marine biotechnology	25
	Marine monitoring	15
	Maritime safety and surveillance	9
	High-tech marine products and services	8

Source Authors'

The findings of the study show that the majority of countries in the Black Sea Region are involved in the common scientific research agenda related to the Blue/Ocean Economy, including its traditional and emerging marine (ocean-based) industries/sectors, as well as Marine Spatial Planning, while the Ecosystem-Based Management is underrepresented as a research area in the Black Sea Region, as shown in Table 2.

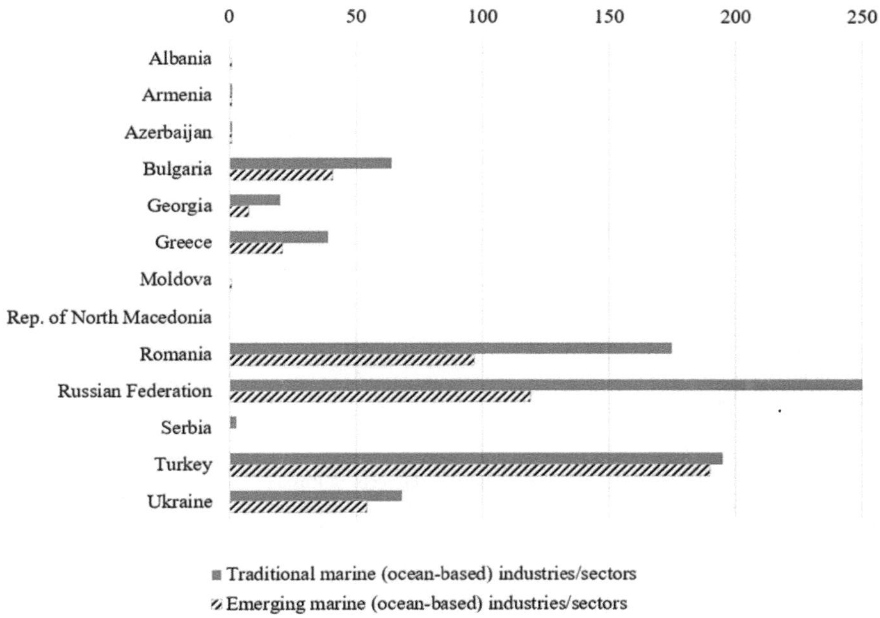

Fig. 2 Number of publications in the traditional and emerging marine (ocean-based) industries/sectors in the Black Sea Region (by country). *Source* Authors'

The number of published articles as a result of academic-corporate collaboration in the research areas, considered in this study, is very low. The areas of Ecosystem-Based Management and Marine Spatial Planning lack academic-corporate collaboration. The subject area of the Blue Economy, Ocean Economy, Blue Growth has the highest share of publications prepared as a result of academic-corporate collaboration (11%). The international cooperation indicator (based on the analysis of coauthored publications) is above 50% for the Blue Economy, Ocean Economy, Blue Growth and Ecosystem-Based Management. Meanwhile, both traditional and emerging marine (ocean-based) industries/sectors show a moderate number of publications prepared as a result of international collaboration (around 25–30%).

4 Conclusion

The findings of the study show that non-regional actors (like the United States, the United Kingdom, Australia, Canada, etc.) have been actively involved in the research agenda in the field of the Blue Economy, inter alia in the Black Sea Region, while the representation of the regional stakeholders (in particular, the BSEC Member States) is relatively low. However, Greece, Turkey, Russia, Romania, Ukraine and Bulgaria could be considered as the main drivers of the development of the Blue Economy

Table 2 Key findings of the bibliometric analysis

	Research area				
	Blue Economy, Ocean Economy or Blue Growth	Ecosystem-Based Management	Marine Spatial Planning	Traditional marine (ocean-based) industries/sectors	Emerging marine (ocean-based) industries/sectors
Number of countries that conduct scientific research in the respective research area in the Black Sea Region (out of 13 BSEC Member States)	9	6	8	10	11
Top-3 countries from the Black Sea Region that conduct scientific research in the respective research area (by the number of publications for the last 5 years)	Greece Russia Turkey	Greece Turkey Russia	Greece Russia Romania	Russia Turkey Romania	Turkey Russia Romania
Number of publications prepared as a result of academic-corporate collaboration in the respective research area (share of publications, in %)	11%	0%	0%	3%	5%
Number of publications prepared as a result of international collaboration in the respective research area (share of publications, in %)	57%	51%	47%	25%	32%

Source Authors'

in the Black Sea Region, as they are actively involved in the development of the scientific agenda on the Blue Economy in the Region.

It has been identified that the Black Sea Region lacks academic-corporate collaboration in the field of the Blue Economy, which is required for the practical implementation of innovative and high-tech solutions, especially in joint projects in the Black Sea Region. To accelerate marine/ocean science and knowledge sharing for sustainable development the involvement of stakeholders across the Black Sea Region in the development of the Blue/Ocean Economy should be increased as well.

The research trends for international cooperation related to the development of Blue/Ocean economy in the Black Sea Region according to the adopted classification of the Blue Economy sectors include marine manufacturing and construction, port activities and warehousing, industrial capture fisheries and living resources, shipping and transport, offshore wind energy, marine and seabed mining, ocean renewable energy, industrial marine aquaculture, marine biotechnology, coastal tourism, carbon capture and storage and marine monitoring.

Each of these trends could be further split into specific subject research areas for a more efficient implementation of joint projects in the Black Sea Region, like ecotourism, alternative and sustainable tourism, marine cultural heritage as an element of Blue Growth, as well as the development of carbon balance calculation systems and carbon polygons to reduce the carbon footprint, or the development of AI-based monitoring systems that predict floods, thermal anomalies and tornadoes. The transformation of basic research into applied innovative projects would require the extensive support of the Blue Economy as an integrated research area from the relevant stakeholders in the Region, in particular on the ministerial level. The above-mentioned research trends could also become the basis for international cooperation in the field of education in the Black Sea Region, in the case of the development of educational programmes in the Blue Economy, for instance, in the shipbuilding sector or the field of state management of maritime activities.

Although, international scientific collaboration in the field of the Blue Economy, Ocean Economy, Blue Growth, as well as the Ecosystem-Based Management and the Marine Spatial Planning could be considered satisfactory (according to the bibliometric analysis), the total number of joint publications related to the Blue/Ocean economy is relatively low in the Black Sea Region (among all BSEC Member States), so further development of international scientific cooperation is required, in particular within research trends and in the perspective subject areas of traditional and emerging marine (ocean-based) industries/sectors that demonstrate relatively high publication activity, reflecting the scale and international character of the research area of the Blue Economy.

Acknowledgements The study was supported by the Ministry of Science and Higher Education of the Russian Federation (project No.730000Ф.99.1.БВ16АА02001) for the Russian implementation of the Black Sea CONNECT CSA project.

References

Brears, R. C. (2021). The Blue Economy. In: *Developing the Blue Economy*. Palgrave Macmillan. https://doi.org/10.1007/978-3-030-84216-1_3

Cristiani, P. (2017). New challenges for materials in the blue economy perspective. *Metallurgia Italiana, 7–8*, 7–10.

European Commission. (2021). The EU Blue Economy Report. Publications Office of the European Union. Luxembourg. https://ec.europa.eu/oceans-and-fisheries/system/files/2021-05/the-eu-blue-economy-report-2021_en.pdf. Accessed 10 September 2021.

Frazão Santos, C., Ehler, C. N., Agardy, T., Andrade, F., Orbach, M. K., & Crowder, L. B. (2019). Marine Spatial Planning. In *World seas: An environmental evaluation*.https://doi.org/10.1016/B978-0-12-805052-1.00033-4

Kabil, M., Priatmoko, S., Magda, R., & Dávid, L. D. (2021). Blue Economy and coastal tourism: A comprehensive visualization bibliometric analysis. *Sustainability, 13*, 3650. https://doi.org/10.3390/su13073650

Konovalov, A., Baturova, G., Tatyana, G., & Grigorenko, O. (2019). Integrated ecosystems management of the coastal zones in the Artic zone of the Russian Federation: Problems and solutions. In *E3S Web of Conferences* (Vol. 120). https://doi.org/10.1051/e3sconf/201912003001

Lappo, A., & Danilova, L. (2015). Pilot projects on maritime spatial planning in the Russian Federation. *Bulletin of Maritime Institute, 2*, 28–33. https://doi.org/10.5604/12307424.1158321

Martínez-Vázquez, R. M., Milán-García, J., & de Pablo Valenciano, J. (2021). Challenges of the Blue Economy: Evidence and research trends. *Environmental Sciences Europe, 33*, 61. https://doi.org/10.1186/s12302-021-00502-1

OECD. (2016). *The Ocean Economy in 2030*. OECD Publishing.https://doi.org/10.1787/9789264251724-en

Singh, V. K., Singh, P., & Karmakar, M. (2021). The journal coverage of web of science, Scopus and dimensions: A comparative analysis. *Scientometrics, 126*, 5113–5142. https://doi.org/10.1007/s11192-021-03948-5

Sousa, C., Fontes, M., & Conceição, O. (2020). Blue Economy as a policy-driven innovation system: Research funding and the direction of ocean-related innovation. In D. Rodionov, T. Kudryavtseva, M. A. Berawi, & A. Skhvediani (Eds.), *Innovations in digital economy. SPBPU IDE 2019. Communications in computer and information science* (Vol. 1273). Springer. https://doi.org/10.1007/978-3-030-60080-8_6

Spalding, M. J., Braestrup, A. E., & Refosco, A. (2021). Greening the Blue Economy: A transdisciplinary analysis. In A. Carpenter, T. M. Johansson, & J. A. Skinner (Eds.), *Sustainability in the maritime domain. Strategies for sustainability*. Springer. https://doi.org/10.1007/978-3-030-69325-1_2

Sumaila, U. R., Walsh, M., & Hoareau, K. (2021). Financing a sustainable ocean economy. *Nature Community, 12*, 3259. https://doi.org/10.1038/s41467-021-23168-y

Features of Chinese Government Policy to Stimulate Demand for Electric Vehicles: The Willingness of Car Owners

Elena I. Lazareva and Yinan Dong

Abstract With the rapid development of China's economy, the total number of cars and per capita ownership in China has also increased rapidly, and the environmental pollution caused by vehicle emissions has worsened. With the development of battery technology, the electric vehicle industry is also receiving more and more attention. The promotion of electric vehicles can effectively solve the environmental pollution caused by vehicle emissions, so the Chinese government has formulated a series of policies to promote the development of electric vehicles, through direct subsidies, tax breaks and other economic policies to stimulate consumer demand for electric vehicles. Consumer demand for electric vehicles is influenced by three main factors: social factors, product factors and personal factors. Government policies as a social factor will have a direct impact on consumers' willingness to purchase electric vehicles, and different policies will have different impacts on consumers' demand. In this paper, 138 valid questionnaires were collected through a questionnaire survey of Chinese car buyers, and the impact of three factors on consumer demand for electric vehicles was analyzed through a Probit model, focusing on the impact of different government policies on willingness to buy an electric vehicle. Through the analysis of the econometric model, we concluded that the subsidies policies have a positive effect on consumers' willingness to purchase an electric vehicle, while the tax breaks policies do not show an effect on the consumers' willingness to buy an electric vehicle. Besides the influence of policies, the results show that gender, education level and awareness of the environment also affect the consumers' willingness. The attributes of the electric vehicle will decline the consumers' willingness. Based on these results we give some suggestions that the Chinese government should formulate a systematic policy system; the Chinese government should implement a wider range of targeted supporting policies; the government should promote a series of campaigns to raise awareness of the importance of the environment.

E. I. Lazareva (✉) · Y. Dong
Southern Federal University, Rostov-on-Don, Russia
e-mail: elazareva@sfedu.ru

Y. Dong
e-mail: yinan.2.dong@uconn.edu

E. I. Lazareva et al. (eds.), *Innovative Trends in International Business and Sustainable Management*, Approaches to Global Sustainability, Markets, and Governance,
https://doi.org/10.1007/978-981-19-4005-7_57

Keywords Demand for electric vehicles · Chinese Government Policy · Willingness of car owners · Econometric analysis · Probit model

JEL Classification J24 · C54 · J64

1 Introduction

The impact of climate change is a serious problem for the global economy and society, and people are becoming aware of the importance of climate issues and are gradually paying more attention to them (Lazareva et al., 2016). One of the most important elements of the climate issue is carbon dioxide emissions, and according to previous studies, automobile emissions are an important cause of global carbon dioxide emissions and air pollution (Lazareva & Dong, 2021; Roorda-Knape et al., 1998). Therefore, the control of vehicle emissions has an important contribution to global CO_2 emissions and air pollution.

Studies have shown that the implementation of the city closure policy during COVID-19 and the reduction of vehicle trips have contributed significantly to CO_2 emissions and air pollution (Singh & Chauhan, 2020). This is a side-by-side verification that controlling vehicle emissions is an effective and important means of solving global climate problems and environmental pollution problems. As the second-largest economy in the world, China's car ownership is growing rapidly with the development of the economy (Wang et al., 2017b), and the exhaust emission of traditional fuel cars has exacerbated the deterioration of environmental problems and climate problems in China to a certain extent. Therefore, effective control of exhaust emissions from fuel vehicles can improve air quality and environmental degradation in China, and further promote sustainable development.

In the past decade, the electric vehicle industry has made tremendous progress in China, and the impact of electric vehicles on environmental pollution and CO_2 emissions is much lower than that of traditional fuel vehicles. The most important reason why fuel cars are harmful to the environment is their exhaust emissions. In terms of tailpipe emissions, electric vehicles can effectively reduce pollutant emissions, reduce greenhouse gas emissions and improve the heat island effect compared to fuel vehicles.

It is an inevitable choice to promote electric vehicles to effectively control environmental pollution, and it is also an inevitable trend to promote the development of the electric vehicle industry and market. Government policies play an important role in promoting the development of the electric vehicle industry and market. In addition to policy support, the most direct factor affecting the purchase of electric vehicles from an economic perspective is consumer demand.

In this article, we will focus on incentive policy and analysis of consumer demand for electric vehicles. Consumer demand analysis is essential for a better policy goals understanding, as well as to justify directions of the industry and the electric vehicle market development. The next following sections of this paper discusses:

Sect. 2, the categories and characteristics of China's electric vehicle policies from the perspective of literature, and the demand factors that influence consumer purchase; Sect. 3, the economic principles of government policies and the economic model of consumer demand factors; collected consumers' willingness data through questionnaires; Sect. 4, the results of econometric analysis of the collected questionnaire data using Probit models; Sect. 5 conclusion and suggestions.

2 Literature Review

The United States, Japan and Europe countries with the early development of electric vehicles have been earlier through a series of policies to promote the development of the electric technology industry and electric consumer market, product technology and market competitiveness have achieved greater development. These include the U.S. Clean Energy and Security Act of 2009, Germany's Electric Vehicle Act, Norway's electric vehicle purchase subsidies, etc. (Steen et al., 2015).

China's electric vehicle industry and market have also made great progress in recent years, also without the support of policies. The development of China's electric vehicle industry started in 2001 when the central government launched the "National "863" Program for Electric Vehicles", which was accompanied by two supporting policies. Then in 2006, China released the "National Medium and Long-term Scientific and Technological Development Plan", the "Plan for the Adjustment and Revitalization of the Automobile Industry" and the "Common Action Plan for the Development of Electric Vehicles". By 2009, the number of policies related to electric vehicles in China had grown very rapidly, and the important policies in 2009 included "The Notice on the Pilot Project of Demonstration and Promotion of Energy-saving and Electric Vehicles", the "Ten Cities and Thousands of Vehicles" Demonstration and Promotion Project of Energy-saving and Electric Vehicles, the "Energy-saving and Electric Vehicles Divisional Promotion Financial Subsidy Management Interim Measures" and many other policies. Starting from the year 2009, the policies showed the characteristics of central to local decentralization, which also laid the foundation for the development of relevant local policies afterwards (Hao et al., 2014).

By 2015, at least 20 policies related to the electric vehicle industry have been released, and the trend of growth is very obvious (Ma et al., 2019). Among the many policies directly related to consumers and consumer demand is the market incentive policy, which can be subdivided into the first type of promotion and demonstration policy, through the implementation of supporting subsidies and incentives, tax breaks and other policies, so that the demand for electric vehicles can be promoted in the demonstration cities. Thus, electric vehicles can not only be promoted in the demonstration cities but also expand the demand for electric vehicles from the demonstration cities to the neighbouring cities through the city cluster effect, so that the demand for electric vehicles can be expanded in a larger area through regional synergistic development.

The second type of market incentive policy is the tax relief policy. In 2006, the first policy related to the consumption tax of electric vehicles was released (Jin & Jianhua, 2017), which gives certain consumption tax benefits to the purchase of electric vehicles.

The third type of market incentive policy is the subsidy incentive policy, which was implemented in 2009 to promote the development of electric vehicles in large and medium-sized cities and to promote the market demand for electric vehicles (Zhang et al., 2011).

Along with these three types of direct market incentives, there are also indirect policies related to subsidies and tax breaks, including incentives and subsidies for charging facilities construction, policies on electricity prices and charging service fees for EVs, and exemptions from road and bridge tolls and parking fees for EVs. Since 2016, direct subsidies and direct tax relief policies have been gradually reduced and withdrawn and replaced by subsidies and incentives for infrastructure construction, electricity consumption exemptions and parking exemptions (Wang et al., 2017b).

In addition to the classification of policies by content, policies can also be divided into three categories according to the way they are implemented: the first category is regulatory policies, in which the government compels the target group to implement orders to achieve policy goals (Greaker, 2021). This is reflected in the electric market, where government regulations are used to guide producers and consumers to the electric market. The second type of policy is incentive policy, in which the government provides incentives to economic agents through economic means, and encourages economic agents to participate in the production and consumption of electric vehicles by tilting policies towards the electric vehicle industry and market (Xue et al., 2021). The last type of policy is information-based policy, in which the government only provides information to economic agents and does not act in any other way, and economic agents can choose their economic behaviour based on the information they obtain (Li et al., 2020).

A variety of policy types and services are important reasons for the tremendous development of China's electric vehicle industry and market in recent years.

Besides the influence of government policies on the purchase of electric vehicles, the most direct influence on the purchase of electric vehicles is the willingness of consumers to purchase. There have been many studies on consumers' willingness to purchase electric vehicles, which can be divided into three main categories: the influence of social factors on consumers' willingness to purchase electric vehicles; the influence of product factors on consumers' willingness to purchase; and the influence of consumers' own information on their willingness to purchase (Liwei, 2015).

The influence of social factors on consumers' willingness to purchase is reflected in values and consumption (Heffner et al., 2005); environmental awareness (McManus et al., 2006); price awareness; group and social norms (Huijts et al., 2012). Product factors are mainly reflected in the attributes of electric vehicles, such as driving range, energy consumption, price, maximum speed, charging time and battery durability, etc. The last category of influencing factors is the consumer's personal factors: gender, age, income level, education level, and other basic information.

3 Materials and Methods

The application of electric vehicles as a new technology in the automotive sector makes them more costly to develop and produce than conventional vehicles. Since the high cost of this technology brings about high environmental benefits that are difficult to compensate for through consumer purchases, the emerging EV market is prone to market failure. In the face of market failure, government policy support is one of the effective means to address market failure. Government policies can help producers and consumers to achieve market equilibrium in a state of market failure. For consumers, government policies mainly promote consumers' willingness to purchase electric vehicles, usually through direct subsidies or tax breaks to achieve the goal of expanding consumer demand, which does not affect the market price, but through subsidies and tax breaks to make consumers purchase electric vehicles at a lower price to achieve the goal of increasing consumer willingness to purchase.

Consumer buying behaviour is determined by demand. In addition to the aforementioned government policies that can have an impact on demand, many other factors influence consumer demand. There are many models in previous studies to analyze consumer demand, and here we choose three models to analyze the factors influencing consumer demand for electric vehicles.

Model 1—Attitude-Behaviour-Situation Model: Study the impact of policy factors and product feature factors as situational factors affecting the purchase intention of electric vehicles (formula (1)) (Lee, 2003).

$$y_i = P_i\beta + \varepsilon_i \tag{1}$$

Model 2—Value-Belief-Normative Theory Model: Consumer behaviour decisions are directly influenced by three types of factors: values, beliefs and norms (formula (2)) (Zhang et al., 2019).

$$y_i = P_i\beta_1 + C_i\beta_2 + \varepsilon_i \tag{2}$$

Model 3—Consumer behaviour decision theory: Analyze the motivations, attitudes and intentions of consumers to reveal the factors that influence consumer behaviour and its development (formula (3)) (Adnan et al., 2017),

$$y_i = P_i\beta_1 + C_i\beta_2 + E_i\beta_3 + \varepsilon_i \tag{3}$$

where y_i represents the respondents' willingness to buy an electric vehicle; P_i represents the respondents' attitudes about the different government policies; C_i represents the basic information about the respondents; E_i represents respondents' answers about the attributes of the EVs; ε_i represents the error terms. We choose subsidies and tax deduction policies as variables for measuring the influence of these two categories of policies on the willingness of the respondents to buy EVs. We choose the driving range; charging time; safety of the EV; charging facilities and the maintenance of EV as variables to measure the attributes of EV.

Consumer purchase intentions can be theoretically divided into antecedent variables, situational variables, household demographic variables, and categorical variables. Among these antecedent variables are in turn composed of cognitive-knowledge factors, psychological factors, normative factors, and perceived behavioural control factors. In our study, we choose cognitive-knowledge factors, which include the respondents' knowledge about the government policy, the cognitive about the environment as our antecedent variables; household demographic variables include the age, gender, education level, the income of the respondents; categorical variables include the attributes of the electric vehicles which are the driving range; charging time; safety; maintenance; charging facilities about the electric vehicles. We use these antecedent variables, household demographic variables and categorical variables as the independent variables.

To analyze the correlation between consumers' willingness to purchase electric vehicles and policies, a Probit model is used in this paper. The first model only considers the influence of different policies on consumers' purchase intention, the second model adds the influence of personal factor of consumers' basic information, and the third model adds the factor of electric vehicle attributes based on the first two models.

The questionnaire survey was conducted among 150 consumers who were interested in purchasing a car, and 138 valid questionnaires were obtained. The questionnaire is divided into two parts, the first part is the respondents' basic personal information, the second part involves the respondents' cognitive level, which includes the respondents' cognitive level of electric vehicles, their understanding of electrically related policies and environmental awareness (Appendix: Survey questionnaires, Table 1).

From Table 1, we can see that the mean value of respondents' willingness to buy electric vehicles is 0.347826, which means that the majority of respondents do not have the willingness to buy electric vehicles. The average education level is 3.405797, which means the average education level of the respondents is high school graduation. The mean gender of the respondents is 0.630435, which means that a higher proportion of the respondents are female. The average age of the respondents is 38.27536 and the average monthly income of the respondents is 5755.072RMB.

From Table 1, we can see also that the mean values of driving range, charging time and charging facilities are 0.55; 0.58; and 0.64 respectively, which are all greater than 0.5, representing that more than half of the respondents believe that these three variables will have an impact on their eventual purchase of an EV, while the mean values of the two variables of safety and maintenance are 0.42 and 0.46 respectively, representing that less than half of the respondents believe that these two the mean values for safety and maintenance were 0.42 and 0.46 respectively, which means that

Table 1 Description data about the demographic variables, the EV, policy, environment

Variable	Obs	Mean	Std. dev	Min	Max
Willingness	138	0.347826	0.478016	0	1
Education	138	3.405797	1.00827	1	5
Gender	138	0.630435	0.484446	0	1
Age	138	38.27536	7.920009	24	51
Income	138	5755.072	1145.672	4100	9600
Range	138	0.550725	0.499233	0	1
Charging	138	0.57971	0.495404	0	1
Safety	138	0.42029	0.495404	0	1
Maintenance	138	0.456522	0.499921	0	1
Facilities	138	0.644928	0.480279	0	1
Subsidies	138	0.456522	0.499921	0	1
Tax	138	0.434783	0.497534	0	1
Environment	138	0.644928	0.480279	0	1

Source Developed by the authors

less than half of the respondents thought that these two variables would not have an impact on their final choice of EV. Regarding the two variables of government policies, the results of the impact of subsidy policies on respondents' willingness to purchase EVs indicate that about 45.7% of respondents believe that subsidy policies affect their final purchase intentions; about 43.4% of respondents believe that tax relief policies affect their final purchase intentions. As for the question on the impact of EVs on the environment, about 64.5% of the respondents thought that EVs would have a positive impact on the environment.

4 Results

The results of the calculations for the three Probit models using the STATA software package are shown in Table 2.

As we can see in Table 2, in the first model, considering only subsidy and tax policies, the results show that subsidy policy produces a significant positive relationship for purchase intentions, while tax policy does not have a significant effect on purchase intentions. This result indicates that government subsidies stimulate consumer demand for electric vehicles, while tax policies do not have a good stimulating effect.

Model 2 adds respondents' personal information to model 1, and the results show that gender, education and environmental awareness have an impact on the purchase intention of electric vehicles, with gender showing a negative correlation at the 99% significant level and education level and environmental awareness showing a positive

Table 2 The results of the calculations for the three Probit models

	(1)	(2)	(3)
Variables	Model 1	Model 2	Model 3
Subsidies	0.849*** (0.230)	0.916*** (0.296)	0.767** (0.336)
Tax	0.334 (0.231)	0.450 (0.294)	0.400 (0.326)
Age		−0.0239 (0.0195)	−0.0177 (0.0212)
Gender		−1.042*** (0.305)	−0.973*** (0.339)
Education		0.841*** (0.207)	0.687*** (0.225)
Income		0.000126 (0.000129)	0.000137 (0.000143)
Environment		1.504*** (0.378)	1.117*** (0.402)
Range			−0.609* (0.362)
Charging			−1.203*** (0.350)
Safety			−0.745** (0.345)
Maintenance			−0.394 (0.349)
Facility			−0.508 (0.361)
Constant	−0.961*** (0.202)	−4.419*** (1.197)	−2.111 (1.374)
Observations	138	138	138

Standard errors in parentheses
***$p < 0.01$, **$p < 0.05$, *$p < 0.1$
Source Developed by the authors

correlation at the 99% significant level, meaning that women have a stronger purchase intention for electric vehicles, and those with higher education level and environmental awareness are more likely to purchase electric vehicles. Respondents with high education levels and strong environmental awareness are more likely to choose electric vehicles, while age and income level do not significantly affect purchase willingness.

Model 3 adds variables related to vehicle attributes to model 2, and the results show that the driving range of electric vehicles has a negative correlation with purchase intention at 90% significance level, charging time at 99% significance level and safety of electric vehicles at 95% significance level. Maintenance and charging facilities of electric vehicles did not have a significant effect on respondents' purchase intentions.

These results indicate that the factors that influence the respondents in terms of vehicle attributes are mainly the driving range, charging time and safety of electric vehicles, and these three attributes are negatively correlated with the purchase intention, indicating that the consumers are not satisfied with the current situation of these three attributes, and these three attributes will reduce the consumers' willingness to purchase electric vehicles.

5 Conclusion

From this study, we analyze the influence of government policies on consumer purchase demand from the perspective of economic principles and analyze the influence of social factors, product factors and personal factors on consumer purchase of electric vehicles from the demand models. The combination of government policies and the consumer willingness model can better stimulate consumers to purchase electric vehicles. This stimulation is done from two aspects, one is the study of government policy itself, and the other is the consumer's willingness to buy, and the effective combination of the two makes the policy better stimulate the consumer's willingness to buy. The results of the econometric analysis show that government policies, social factors, product factors and personal factors all have significant effects on consumers' willingness to purchase electric vehicles. The first point is that the positive impact of policies on consumer willingness is limited to subsidies, while the impact of tax breaks on consumer willingness is not significant in any of the three models. However, three of the attributes have a negative impact on consumers' willingness to purchase, implying that some attributes of electric vehicles are important reasons that prevent consumers from purchasing them; the third point: environmental awareness is gradually changing from social awareness to personal awareness, and consumers with environmental awareness have a higher willingness to purchase electric vehicles.

China's electric vehicle industry and market have seen rapid development in recent years, and this rapid development cannot be achieved without the support of policies. Compared to other countries in the world where electric vehicles are developing faster, China still has significant gaps, for example, in the comprehensiveness and systemic nature of its policies. Based on the three issues mentioned above, we propose three suggestions to better increase Chinese consumers' willingness to buy electric vehicles and to promote the development of China's electric vehicle industry and market. The first recommendation: Although the number of policies related to China's electric vehicle industry and the market has increased significantly, this increase is not comprehensive and therefore leads to a significant reduction in the effectiveness of the policies. The development of a more comprehensive and systematic policy is the basis for ensuring that the policy has the desired effect.

Only by forming a systematic policy system can the Chinese government better promote the development of China's electric vehicle industry and market, stimulate consumer demand and narrow the gap with developed countries. In our findings, government subsidies stimulate consumers' willingness to purchase electric vehicles, but tax breaks do not have an impact on consumers' willingness to purchase electric vehicles, for two possible reasons. The first is that the tax credit policy does not bring actual benefits to consumers, compared to direct subsidies, the policy benefits of the tax credit are limited; the second is that the benefits of the tax credit are comparable to direct subsidies but consumers do not understand the tax credit policy and are not clear about the procedures of the tax credit, resulting in the tax credit policy does not stimulate consumers' willingness to buy.

The second recommendation: In addition to the gap in the comprehensiveness and systemic nature of the policy, China's policy is also inadequate in terms of targeting, and should be more widely implemented with targeted supporting policies. For example, charging time is the most important attribute that reduces consumers' willingness to purchase, so more targeted policies should be developed to address the long charging time, such as subsidies and exemptions for charging electricity; the third suggestion is that environmental awareness plays a significant positive impact on consumers' willingness to purchase electric vehicles. Therefore, the government should promote a series of campaigns to raise awareness of the importance of the environment and the role of electric vehicles in solving environmental pollution.

Appendix

Survey questionnaires

Part 1. Background:

1. **What is your age?**

   ____

2. **Gender:**

   A. Male
   B. Female

3. **What is the highest education level you have attained?**

   A. Primary school
   B. Middle school
   C. High school
   D. Bachelor's degree
   E. Master's degree or PhD

4. **What is your personal income?**

   ____________RMB per month

Part 2. Questions about electric vehicles; policy; environment

5. **Do you think the driving range of electric vehicles is the reason that influences you to buy an electric vehicle?**
   A. No
   B. Yes
6. **Do you think the longer charging time of electric vehicles is the reason that influences you to buy an electric vehicle?**
   A. No
   B. Yes
7. **Do you think the low number of electric vehicles charging facilities is the reason that affects your purchase of electric vehicles?**
   A. No
   B. Yes
8. **Do you think the safety of electric vehicles is the reason that influences you to buy an electric vehicle?**
   A. No
   B. Yes
9. **Do you think the maintenance of electric vehicles is the reason that influences you to buy an electric vehicle?**
   A. No
   B. Yes
10. **Do you think that the electric car can improve the environmental ecology is the main factor influencing whether you buy an electric car or not?**
    A. No
    B. Yes
11. **Do you think direct government subsidies policies will influence you to buy an electric car?**
    A. No
    B. Yes
12. **Do you think the government's tax deduction policies will affect your electric vehicles purchase?**
    A. No
    B. Yes

References

Adnan, N., Noor, S. M. N., Rahman, I., Vasant, P., & Amir, M. (2017). An integrative approach to study on consumer behavior towards plug-in hybrid electric vehicles revolution: Consumer behavior towards plug-in hybrid electric vehicles. In *Applied behavioral economics research and trends. Advances in finance, accounting and economics*. IGI Global. https://research.amanote.com. Accessed 29 November 2021.

Greaker, M. (2021). Optimal regulatory policies for charging of electric vehicles. *Transportation Research Part D: Transport and Environment, 97*, 102922.

Hao, H., Ou, X., Du, J., Wang, H., & Ouyang, M. (2014). China's electric vehicle subsidy scheme: Rationale and impacts. *Energy Policy, 73*, 722–732.

Heffner, T., Kurani, R., & Turrentine, K. (2005). *Effects of vehicle image in gasoline-hybrid electric vehicles*. UC Davis Institute of Transport Studies, University of California. https://escholarship.org. Accessed 29 November 2021.

Huijts, N. M. A., Molin, E. J. E., & Steg, L. (2012). Psychological factors influencing sustainable energy technology acceptance: A review-based comprehensive framework. *Renewewable Sustainable Energy Review, 16*(1), 525–531.

Jin, L., & Jianhua, Z. (2017). Policy changes and policy instruments selection of China's new energy vehicle industry. *China Popular Resource Environment, 27*(10), 198–208.

Lazareva, E., Anopchenko, T., & Lozovitskaya, D. (2016). Identification of the city welfare economics strategic management innovative model in the global challenges conditions. In *SGEM 2016 Conference Proceedings* (pp. 3–10).

Lazareva, E., & Dong Y. (2021). Measuring the value of urban green space using hedonic pricing method. In *ICEST-II 2021: Economic and Social Trends for Sustainability of Modern Society Proceedings: European Proceedings of Social and Behavioural Sciences EpSBS* (Vol. 116, pp. 737–747).

Lee, Y. (2003). *Attitudes of people in Hong Kong to cars and the environment: An application of cognitive dissonance theory*. University of Hong Kong. Centre of Urban Planning and Environmental Management. http://hub.hku.hk. Accessed 29 November 2021.

Li, J., Jiao, J., & Tang, Y. (2020). Analysis of the impact of policies intervention on electric vehicles adoption considering information transmission-based on consumer network model. *Energy Policy, 144*, 111560.

Liwei, J. (2015). Research on the factors influencing the purchase intention of new energy vehicles and guiding policies. *Journal of Climate, 28*(21), 7994–8016.

Ma, S. C., Xu, J. H., & Fan, Y. (2019). Willingness to pay and preferences for alternative incentives to EV purchase subsidies: An empirical study in China. *Energy Economics, 81*(C), 197–215. Elsevier.

McManus, M. A., Berman, S., McInerny, T., & Tang, S. F. (2006). Weighing the risks of consumer-driven health plans for families. *Pediatrics, 117*(4), 1420–1424.

Roorda-Knape, M. C., Janssen, N. A. H., De Hartog, J. J., Van Vliet, P. H. N., Harssema, H., & Brunekreef, B. (1998). Air pollution from traffic in city districts near major motorways. *Atmospheric Environment, 32*(11), 1921–1930.

Singh, R. P., & Chauhan, A. (2020). Impact of lockdown on air quality in India during COVID-19 pandemic. *Air Quality Atmosphere Health, 13*(8), 921–928.

Van Der Steen, M., Van Schelven, R. M., Kotter, R., Van Twist, M., & Van Deventer Mpa, P. (2015). EV policy compared: An international comparison of governments' policy strategy towards E-mobility. *Green Energy Technology, 203*, 27–53.

Wang, N., Pan, H., & Zheng, W. (2017a). Assessment of the incentives on electric vehicle promotion in China. *Transportation Research Part A: Policy and Practice, 101*(4), 177–189.

Wang, S., Li, J., & Zhao, D. (2017b). The impact of policy measures on consumer intention to adopt electric vehicles: Evidence from China. *Transportation Research Part A: Policy and Practice, 105*, 14–26.

Xue, C., Zhou, H., Wu, Q., Wu, X., & Xu, X. (2021). Impact of incentive policies and other socio-economic factors on electric vehicle market share: A panel data analysis from the 20 countries. *Sustainability, 13*(5), 2928.

Zhang, M., Guo, S., Bai, C., & Wang, W. (2019). Study on the impact of haze pollution on residents' green consumption behavior: The case of Shandong Province. *Journal of Cleaner Production, 219*, 11–19.

Zhang, Y., Yu, Y., & Zou, B. (2011). Analyzing public awareness and acceptance of alternative fuel vehicles in China: The case of EV. *Energy Policy, 39*(11), 7015–7024.

Development and Implementation of Digital Technologies in Engineering Surveys to Solve Research and Practical Problems of Rational Nature Management and Environmental Protection When Placing Construction Objects

Nadegda M. Hansivarova, Larisa A. Zolotareva, and Zoya V. Buyko

Abstract The article considers the possibility of using remote digital technologies when conducting engineering surveys on a construction site and the surrounding area to increase the economic and environmental feasibility of an architectural project. The results of the work of the geological portal as a practice-oriented content on a particular site are presented, and the impact of digitalization on the construction sector is described in terms of a possible reduction in time required to perform pre-engineering survey.

Keywords Environmental management · Geotechnical studies · Digitalization in the construction industry · Architectural pre-design analysis · GeoBase geoportal · Multidimensional scientific research

JEL Classification M1 · Q5 · Q13 · Q28 · Q55

1 Introduction

Currently, especially in times of the economic crisis, detailed and accurate engineering surveys of the territories are quite a costly type of research, and sometimes difficult to conduct in conditions of complex terrain and other geological features of the site. The research to which the article is devoted is designed to open the possibility

---

N. M. Hansivarova · L. A. Zolotareva (✉) · Z. V. Buyko
Southern Federal University, Rostov-on-Don, Russia
e-mail: lazolotareva@sfedu.ru

N. M. Hansivarova
e-mail: nmhansivarova@sfedu.ru

Z. V. Buyko
e-mail: zvbuyko@sfedu.ru

E. I. Lazareva et al. (eds.), *Innovative Trends in International Business and Sustainable Management*, Approaches to Global Sustainability, Markets, and Governance,
https://doi.org/10.1007/978-981-19-4005-7_58

of quickly obtaining a sufficiently complete amount of reliable information about the results of previously conducted surveys from the interactive map—geological portal GeoBase, developed by the General Director of LLC Geoelement V. A. Tryukhan together with researchers from the Institute of Earth Sciences of the Southern Federal University. When using Geo-Base, it is also possible to make a geotechnical forecast to determine the values of construction and technological, geomechanical impacts, as well as parameters of geotechnical monitoring and the evaluation criterion "additional subsidence".

The problem and purpose of the article is to study the prospects of the latest augmented and virtual reality technologies in the field of innovative development of engineering and geological surveys in the natural and technical system in the context of digitalization transformation in the construction sector and conservation of the natural environment.

The relevance of the problems of the article is determined by the accelerating development and introduction of information and communication technologies in various sectors of the economy, including in the construction industry and in the educational sphere, as well as a significant reduction in the timing and cost of survey work during the feasibility study for investment, which is especially important in the conditions of the "new reality" and the preservation of the natural-ecological framework of the territory.

The direct goal was to create an ecosystem database entirely in a digital service for geotechnical forecasting and monitoring of geological processes, general assessment of the sustainability of territories and contactless qualitative and quantitative assessment of environmental safety.

The objectives of the study included:

- Formation of a unified information space using the GeoBase information search engine as a means of accumulation, storage, display of the results of engineering surveys for construction.
- Transition to a structural schematic model of the geological environment from the geomechanical model of the soil mass to a new hierarchical level—the soil layer.
- Development of a software product for processing information resources, graphical applications: maps, diagrams, geological, and lithological columns and sections, and further visualization of the processed data with the construction of 3-D models of geological environment sites.
- Creation of a data bank of engineering-geological elements (IGE) typical for the territory of the southern region, soil strata, 3-D models of the geological environment.
- Development of criteria equations for characteristic areas (models) of the geological environment.
- Development of a methodology for calculating, evaluating, and ranking an integral indicator that summarizes the effect of the manifestation of all significant engineering and geological factors that determine the resource potential of the geological environment.

- Mapping of the mineral resource potential of the geological environment of the territory of the south of the European part of Russia.

The object of the study is the geological environment of the territory of the south of the European part of Russia.

The subject of the study is the environment of the proposed construction site.

The problem: The lack of reliable forecasts of the development of negative processes of the geological environment, both in dense urban development and in a relatively free territory.

Research hypothesis: Organization of support for the digital transformation of the construction industry. Creation of a single corporate portal, including a single personal account. The possibility of determining the type of the construction and the functional purpose of buildings based on the analysis of a comprehensive study of the terrain and architectural pre-project analysis to justify investments in the construction of the object.

2 Methodology

In modern conditions of constant shortage of construction sites, developers are forced to develop territories that were previously considered unsuitable for urban construction. One of the parameters that have a direct impact on the degree of complexity of the development of the construction site is the terrain of the site. Many specialists from different countries have devoted their scientific works to solving this problem. From the end of the twentieth century to the present, international experience in the use of the territory located in complex conditions has been studied. Thus, in the book "Urban Planning on the slopes" under the general editorship of the Candidate of Architecture V. R. Krogius, the results of many years of research by Soviet and foreign specialists in this matter are presented (Krogius et al., 1988).

The monograph "Integrated assessment of the territory in urban planning" under the general supervision of S. G. Sheina describes the use of GIS systems in the process of collecting and analyzing initial information for the economic assessment of the studied territory (Sheina et al., 2014). The topic of the above-mentioned monograph is continued by the scientific article by S. G. Sheina and Yu. V. Popova "Evaluation of the suitability of Rostov-on-Don territories for the implementation of integrated development projects" (Sheina & Popova, 2018).

The possibility of constructing an electronic engineering-geological model of the city of Rostov-on-Don based on the analysis of the degree of influence of environmental risk on landslide slopes, as well as geotechnical analysis of the geological environment was proposed by the author A.V. Ishchenko in the article "Complex analysis of built-up areas as a means of effective urban planning in landslide danger zones (on the example of Rostov-on-Don)" (Ishchenko, 2012).

The articles by L. A. Zolotareva, N. M. Hansivarova, V. A. Tryukhan "Expansion of the functions of the geological information portal for joint remote use by various structural units of SFU in teaching students" (Zolotareva et al., 2020) and "Portal of geological information as a tool for remote practical training of bachelors in the field of training 05.03.01—Geology" (Hansivarova et al., 2020) describe the components of the natural-technical system, their interaction, and dynamics. "One of the most important economic and social tasks of our time is the creation of a natural-technical system that is able to meet the needs of society to the maximum extent with minimal disruption of the existing ecological balance. Optimal design and management of the natural-technical system can be provided only by the joint activities of designers and engineering geologists, since the aspects of the decomposition of any natural-technical system are engineering-geological and technical aspects" (Hansivarova et al., 2020).

One of the modern tools for remote study of sites for construction projects is the use of GIS technologies. The use of remote methods of research, survey, and study of territories that do not violate the existing state of the natural environment meets the principles of sustainable development of territories. Among the information resources that allow remote analysis of territories, it is possible to list such platforms as GeoBase, Google Earth, EOS Land Viewer, GIS Panorama.

GeoBase is a geological portal. It is a constantly updated electronic archive of geological information, which was created by a graduate of the Geological and Geographical Faculty (since 2013—the Institute of Earth Sciences) of the Southern Federal University, CEO of LLC Geoelement V. A. Tryukhan. The geological portal contains the following information:

1. A map of the actual material showing the points of engineering-geological and environmental surveys performed on the territories of Russian cities.
2. Brief information about the objects of research.
3. Table of physical and mechanical properties of engineering-geologic elements isolated within the soil layer.
4. Data on the properties of groundwater (Hansivarova et al., 2020).

Google Earth is a geoinformation resource founded by Google, which contains high-quality images of the entire surface of the earth taken by various sources, as well as data of digital elevation model on most of the surface (Google Earth, 2021).

EOS Land Viewer is a platform that provides a set of specific geospatial technologies for extracting valuable information from satellite data, such as quaternary formations, pre-quaternary formations, bathymetry, difference vegetation index (Earth Observing System, 2021).

GIS Panorama is a platform for a spatial data system of digital mapping of cities and other territories, navigation maps (GLONASS), geological survey maps, taking into account digital classifiers. The territorial planning schemes of the Russian Federation—2017 (the classifier is terrplan.v5) are also located with semantic characteristics of objects of topographic plans and attributive characteristics of objects of spatial and urban planning. The emercom.v2.rscz classifier is also presented on the platform for creating electronic maps about the situation with emergencies caused by natural or man-made conditions (GIS "Panorama". KB Panorama—electronic data, 2021).

The applied component of this study is to simplify the procedure for performing engineering-geological and geotechnical surveys, namely a significant reduction in the volume of labor-intensive drilling operations, soil field testing, laboratory soil studies. Assessment of suitability of soils for foundations of buildings and structures will be carried out immediately using quantitative forecasts. The demand for the results of the project is due to the expected economic effect associated with a decrease in the cost of engineering-geological and geotechnical surveys, and, consequently, the cost of construction projects; a reduction in the time of their construction, a decrease in prices for residential, public and industrial facilities.

3 Results

In the first part of the study, the authors' task was to identify methods and techniques suitable for creating an ecosystem of a fully digital service. Within the framework of this part, the following additional tasks were set:

1. Improvement of the algorithms of existing digital platforms, as well as the analysis of the existing state in survey work, using the identified techniques.
2. Schematization, systematization, and classification of the existing state based on LegalTech.
3. Assessment of the current state of the active soil layer and development of a possible assessment of its deformation, as well as scientific and technical forecast of additional deformations.
4. Creation of geotechnical forecasting methodology for remote study of the construction site for the purposes of scientific support of unique, especially dangerous and technically complex objects.
5. Development of methods for assessing deformations and recommendations based on the identified techniques.
6. Preparation of a methodology for providing all survey and construction structures with information on changes in legislative, regulatory, and other systems in order to eliminate delays and conflict situations, as well as improve the quality of services provided to the end user.

In the second part of the study, the authors tested the possibilities of reliable operation of the GeoBase portal as a database containing practice-oriented content. It was proved that both the classification system performed by classes, subclasses, groups, and subgroups, respectively, and the developed scale of the stress–strain state of the layered foundation soil gave an objective assessment and geotechnical forecast for a specific object: "Sewage collector No. 68 of Rostov-on-Don". Within the framework of this part, the following tasks were set:

1. To determine the change in the state of the active zone of the soil layer;
2. Identify changes in the current state of the surrounding development;

3. Determine the boundaries of the deformations of the sewage collector and their impact on the environment.

Based on the results of geotechnical analysis, the boundaries of the impact of deformations of the existing sewage collector on the structures of the surrounding urban development were established (Figs. 1 and 2).

In the same way, the values of additional deformations of the "bases-foundations" system of structures and buildings of adjacent buildings were determined (Table 1).

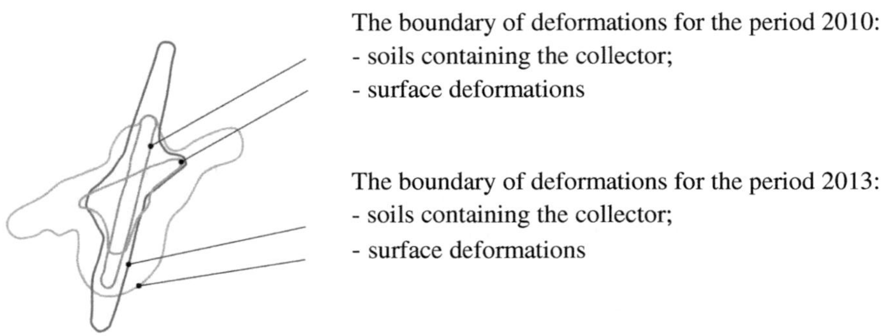

Fig. 1 Boundaries of deformations for the period 2010 and 2013. *Source* Compiled by the authors

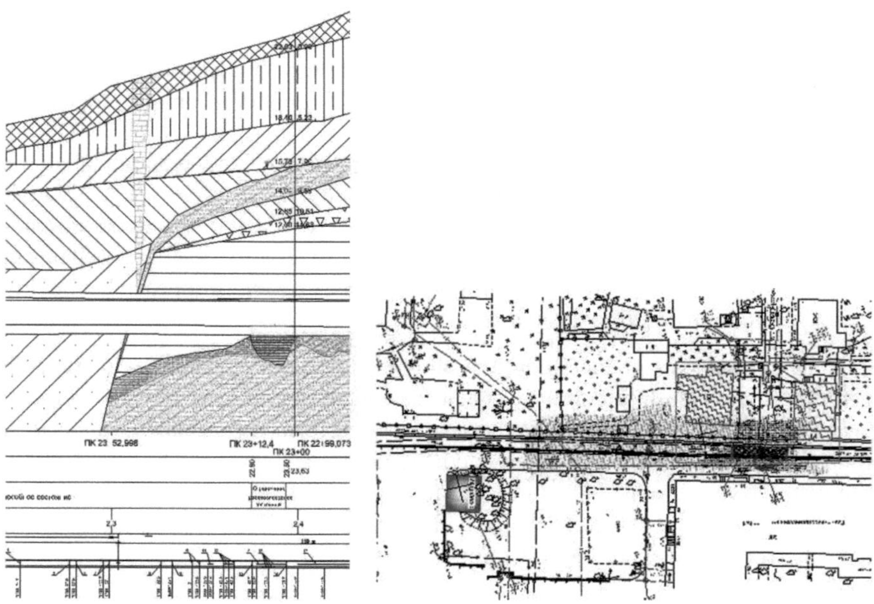

Fig. 2 Geological section and topographic plan of an individual residential building on the street Ofitserskaya, 1 within the vicinity of sewage collector No. 68. *Source* Compiled by the authors

Table 1 Total subsidence under the sole of the foundations according to the materials of 2010, 2017

№	Name of the building/structure	Location	Total subsidence under the sole of the foundations, cm		
			2010г	2017г	доп
1	2	3	4	5	6
1	Private residential house	Ofitserskaya str., 1	19.2	21.45	2.25
2	Multi-apartment building	Zologuicheskaya str., 17	27.28	29.63	2.35

Source Compiled by the authors

Based on the results of testing the work of the geological portal GeoBase, the authors made the following conclusions:

- The GeoBase search and information system, which meets modern requirements, is able to provide complete information about the engineering and geological conditions of the territory of the south of Russia for analytical and informational use in solving scientific and production tasks.
- The creation of software products for processing industrial engineering and geological data with subsequent visualization of some of its elements necessary for mapping and zoning of the city's territory will have a significant impact on the conduct of pre-project engineering studies.
- Generalization of engineering and geological data at the "ground layer" level will allow to supplement the modern classification of soils of Russia with up-to-date information about ground layers typical of the southern regions.
- It is necessary to create and further update digital models of the most characteristic areas of the geological environment according to the main indicators of physical, physico-mechanical, water-physical properties of soils; parameters of dangerous geological processes. The obtained models will be used as the basis for quantitative forecasts of changes in the state, properties, and structure of components of the geological environment during construction development.
- The creation of a database of engineering-geological elements characteristic of the territory of the southern region, as well as soil layers, will make it possible to create a generalized digital model of the geological environment according to the selected criteria, which will give a general idea of the features of the engineering-geological structure of the region, which will highlight the most significant factors in the development of a generalized conceptual model of the geological environment of the region as a whole.
- The results of the study, assessment, and ranking of the resource potential of the geological environment in accordance with the methodology developed by the authors of the project will allow to assess the degree of suitability of a particular section of the lithosphere for the construction of the projected object; to determine the nature of the possible impact of the object on the natural environment, to forecast changes in its components as a result of the expected impact; to

ensure the optimal functioning of the natural and technical system created during construction as a whole of natural and man-made components.

The results obtained from the implementation of the project can be considered breakthrough, corresponding to the level of federal, and with the further development of the project—world leadership.

All of the above is implemented without reducing the quality of the study and evaluation of engineering and geological conditions. In addition, the new knowledge gained about the potential resource of the geological environment is the basis for a broader assessment of the territorial resource of individual sites as a whole, taking into account environmental characteristics, as well as economic calculations of their development, the search for solutions for rational nature management and environmental protection of a certain part of the lithosphere. Such a result can arouse the interest of both the executive authorities of the regional and federal levels, as well as government structures of other countries.

4 Conclusion

The scientific novelty of the conducted research consists in studying the holistic picture of pre-design engineering and architectural studies required to analyze the main factors affecting the process of interaction of a building with the geological environment. Thanks to the joint work of specialists of survey organizations and researchers of the Southern Federal University, the data obtained using the GeoBase search and information system were used for the first time. The results of the conducted comprehensive studies will allow the chief architect and chief engineer of the project to solve the planning structure of the projected object in the most rational and efficient way.

This work is a multidimensional scientific research and the result of practice-oriented developments for the digitalization of the construction industry in the conditions of the "new reality", namely:

- the ecosystem of a fully digital service;
- work in a pair of "surveyor—digital assistant";
- integrated personalized services;
- management and design based on big data research;
- predictive analytics of land plots for construction, including analysis of digital traces;
- industry development management.

The results obtained during various studies on the available maps of the geological portal will allow to make maps of various scales from small construction sites to large territories, such as the Rostov Region and the Southern Federal District, and in the future to cover the entire territory of the Russian Federation.

The declared project initially covers the territory of the European part of the south of Russia, but there is a prospect to expand the boundaries of the project to the level of the region, the federal district, the region of the (BSEC) countries (the Black Sea Economic Cooperation), etc. The methodology for calculating and assessing the resource potential of the geological environment is universal for the territory of any region or country, including the Black Sea Economic Zone. The development of the project requires appropriate funding and involvement in the study of foreign geotechnicians, specialists in other fields of knowledge relevant to the subject of the project, as well as consultations of the President of the Southern Federal University on the creation of a unified interdisciplinary team of interested and competent specialists.

References

Earth Observing System. A platform for the analysis of geospatial data. https://eos.com/ru. Data accessed 01 November 2021.

GIS "Panorama". KB Panorama—electronic data. https://gisinfo.ru/classifiers/classifiers.htm. Data accessed 01 November 2021.

Google Earth. https://www.google.ru/intl/ru/earth/. Data accessed 01 November 2021.

Ishchenko, A. V. (2012). Complex analysis of built-up areas as a means of effective urban planning in landslide danger zones (on the example of Rostov-on-Don). *Network scientific journal "Engineering Bulletin of the Don", 3.* http://www.ivdon.ru/magazine/archive/n3y2012/939. Data accessed 01 November 2021.

Hansivarova, N. M., Zolotareva, L. A., & Tryukhan, V. A. (2020). Portal of geological information as a tool for remote practical training of bachelors in the field of training 05.03.01—Geology. In *Proceedings of the International Scientific and Practical Conference "Current trends in the development of the higher education system: Distance education—problems and advantages"*, Rostov-on-Don, 16–17 June 2020. Southern Federal University Press. https://doi.org/10.18522/801282720

Krogius, V. R., Abbott, D., Pollit, K., Benina, N. B., Ritdorf, V., Arlt, G., Timann, G., Menert, V., Grebennikova, M. A., Penchik, I. F., Gorniak, L., Faytondzhieva, I., Sopilka, V. V., Tevzadze, N. S., Mirzoyan, V. S., & Levitsky, E. Y. (1988). *Urban planning on the slopes.* Stroyizdat.

Sheina, S. G., Babenko, L. L., Matveiko, R. B., & Khamavo, A. A. (2014). *Integrated assessment of the territory in urban planning. Monograph.* Rostov State University of Civil Engineering.

Sheina, S. G., & Popova, Yu. V. (2018). Evaluation of the suitability of Rostov-on-Don territories for the implementation of integrated development projects. *Construction and Technogenic Safety, 13*(65), 29–32.

Zolotareva, L. A., Hansivarova, N. M., & Trukhan, V.A. (2020). Expansion of the functions of the geological information portal for joint remote use by various structural units of SFU in teaching students. In *Proceedings of the International Scientific and Practical Conference "Current trends in the development of the higher education system: Distance education—problems and advantages"*, Rostov-on-Don, 16–17 June 2020. Southern Federal University Press. https://doi.org/10.18522/801282720

China's Sustainable Economic and Environmental Development Strategies: Is There a Correlation?

Libin Ni

Abstract The purpose of this article is to solve the problem of whether there is a correlation between sustainable economic and environmental development strategies in China. Currently, there are few studies on the relationship between sustainable development strategies in the economic and environmental sectors. The main objective of this study is China's sustainable economic and environmental development strategies. The author mainly uses literature research and quantitative analysis to prove if there is a correlation between economic and environmental development strategies. The author divides the development of environmental strategies in China into four phases. The first two phases are characterized by "pollute first, clean up later" development mode, which shows no sign of the correlation between economic and environmental development strategies. The latter two phases are featured by the balance between sustainable economic and environmental development, which clarifies the correlation between sustainable economic and environmental development strategies. It is shown that sustainable economic and environmental development strategies are correlated with each other. There is a mutually reinforcing relationship between sustainable economic and environmental development strategies. They are interdependent and mutually supportive.

Keywords China · Sustainable economic development strategies · Sustainable environmental development strategies · Correlation · Reinforcing relationship

JEL Classification J24 · C54 · J64

L. Ni (✉)
Henan University of Economics and Law, Henan, China
e-mail: 871688596@qq.com

Southern Federal University, Rostov-on-Don, Russia

E. I. Lazareva et al. (eds.), *Innovative Trends in International Business and Sustainable Management*, Approaches to Global Sustainability, Markets, and Governance,
https://doi.org/10.1007/978-981-19-4005-7_59

1 Introduction

Sustainable development is the concept of a relationship between economic growth and the environment. The concept of sustainable development was described by the 1987 Bruntland Commission Report as development that meets the needs of the present without compromising the ability of future generations to meet their own needs (UNESCO, 2021). Over the past 40 years of reform and opening-up, China has maintained a high economic growth rate and become the second-largest economy in the world and its comprehensive strength growing manifold. In the meantime, the environment has also suffered unprecedented damage. The growth rate of Gross Domestic Products in China has been sharply declining since 2010, which is caused by unsustainable economic and environmental development. In this situation, the study of the relationship between sustainable economic and environmental development strategies is of great significance.

In 1983, Environmental protection was set as the national strategy in China. In 1994, sustainable development was set as the national strategy in China. A series of laws and regulations have been established continuously. It evoked the heated discussion of scholars all around the world. On the one hand, scholars have conducted continuous and in-depth research on sustainable development, green low-carbon cycling development and ecological civilization theory in terms of environmental development strategies and policies. On the other hand, the investigation of the environmental policy can be traced back to the 1990s. A new theoretical system on resource economy including resource value theory, resource asset theory, resource industry theory and resource accounting theory has been established. Research and practice on pollution damage measurement have been conducted. In recent years, green finance is also a hot topic of research (Wu, 2019).

However, few people investigate the relationship between sustainable development strategies in the economic and environmental sectors (Anopchenko et al., 2021; Lazareva & Dong, 2020). Based on the research results of the domestic and foreign scholars, this article tries to solve the problem of whether there is a correlation between China's sustainable economic and environmental development strategies.

2 Materials and Methods

The main objective of this study is China's sustainable economic and environmental development strategies. China's environmental development policies can be traced back to 1973. The relevant strategies and policies have moved from environmental protection to the construction of an eco-civilization. China's development history of sustainable economic and environmental strategies make itself representative.

This article analyses the relationship between sustainable economic strategies and sustainable environmental strategies by using the methods of literature research and quantitative analysis.

3 Results

The following China's sustainable economic and environmental development strategies and policies are offered (Table 1).

Up to 2012, China's environmental strategies and policies have formed a relatively complete system structure, and have undergone significant changes in terms of policymaking and policy instruments.

In 1978, at the beginning of the reform and opening up, the central theme in China was economic construction. The coastal areas began to open up to the outside world, accepting the transfer of labour-intensive industries from Japan and Korea in large numbers. Meanwhile, governments at all levels and many social groups focused on attracting investment and running businesses. Economic development and industrial shifts have also brought about increasingly serious environmental problems, which attracted national attention. In 1979, the *Environmental Protection Law (Trial)* was enacted, pioneering the legal regime for environmental protection in China. In 1982, the *Marine Environmental Protection Law* was adopted. In 1983, Environmental protection was set as the national strategy. In 1984 and 1987, the *Water Pollution Prevention and Control Law*, the *Air Pollution Prevention and Control Law* were adopted respectively.

In 1992, former leader Deng Xiaoping, architect of the reforms, delivered a speech during his famous southern tour of China, which promoted reform and opening up. With the construction of Pudong New Area in Shanghai, the Yangtze River Delta region developed rapidly. But at the same time, serious ecological damage and environmental pollution were brought about. Ecological damage, soil erosion and desertification kept deteriorating, with sandstorms intensifying in the northern part of China and disasters such as the flood of the Yangtze River occurring frequently. In this situation, the relevant laws were issued and sustainable development was set as a national strategy.

At the beginning of the reform and opening-up, China's economy was still at the initial stage. The capital was scarce, and almost all products and raw materials were in short supply. The priority of the development was to increase the number of products. It was not possible to impose strict environmental requirements. Though the government issued relevant laws and regulations, the effect was not obvious due to the priority of economic development at that time. The economic and environmental development policies were characterized by "pollute first, clean up later", which conforms to the environmental Kuznets curve. There is no such thing as a correlation between economic and environmental policy in this period.

In 2001, China acceded to the World Trade Organization, which was followed by rapid socio-economic growth, an increasing proportion of heavy industries such as energy, steel and chemicals, with production capacity at the forefront of the world, rapid growth in resource and energy consumption and a significant increase in total emissions of major pollutants. Since 2006, China has listed the reduction of total emissions of major pollutants and energy consumption per unit of GDP as indicators in the *Eleventh Five-Year Plan*.

Table 1 The development of environmental strategies and policies in China since 1973

Phase	Year	The relevant documents
The initial phase (1973–1990)	1973	The First National Conference on Environmental Protection was held in Beijing, which adopted the "Regulations on the Protection and Improvement of the Environment (Trial)"
	1979	The Environmental Protection Law of the People's Republic of China (Trial) was adopted
	1983	Environmental protection was set as the national strategy
The completion phase (1991–2002)	1991	More than 10 laws on resources and environment, including the *Water Pollution Prevention and Control Law*, the *Air Pollution Prevention and Control Law* and more than 20 administrative regulations were issued
	1992	China participated in the United Nations Conference on Environment and Development in Rio de Janeiro and announced that China would adopt a sustainable development strategy
	1994	*China's Agenda 21* was issued and sustainable development was set as the national strategy
	2002	*Law on Desert Prevention and Transformation* was established
The promotion phase (2003–2012)	2003	The scientific outlook on development was proposed
	2005	The establishment of a resource-efficient and environment-friendly society was set as a strategic task in the long-term planning of national economic and social development
	2008	The *Promotion Law of Circular Economy* was introduced
	2005–2012	Based on the *Ninth Five-Year Plan*, the government strengthened the control of the total amount of pollutants, implemented binding target management, promoted the development of environmental economic policies, introduced industrial policies and started piloting environmental economic policies such as ecological compensation, green credit, green insurance and green securities
The reform phase (2013–)	2015	The new *Environmental Protection Law* was revised and came into force, imposing severe penalties on enterprises and institutions for their emissions
	2018	The ecological civilization was written into the *Constitution* and a national conference on ecological protection was held, formally establishing Xi Jinping's ideology of ecological civilization, and technological protection entered a new stage of historical development

(continued)

Table 1 (continued)

Phase	Year	The relevant documents
	2020	"Working Guidance for Carbon Dioxide Peaking and Carbon Neutrality in Full and Faithful Implementation of the New Development Philosophy" "Responding to Climate Change: China's Policies and Actions" "Action Plan for Carbon Dioxide Peak before 2030" were established

Source Compiled by the author based on (Wu et al., 2020)

On the one hand, the environmental economic policy represented by the desulphurization tariff began to drive the construction of desulphurization projects in the power industry, and China has built the world's largest clean coal power system. On the other hand, the strict assessment of targets for energy conservation and emission reduction drove the construction of major local environmental management projects.

In this period, the correlation between sustainable economic development and environmental development began to show up. Sustainable economic development includes environmental protection and ecological civilization. It is about using fewer inputs to produce higher value or to produce products and services of the same value with fewer resources, which is intrinsically linked to environmental protection and ecological civilization. Sustainable economic development cannot be achieved without the alleviation of environmental degradation. Sustainable economic development requires economic efficiency, which implies the reduction of wastage and the prevention of environmental damage (Joshua, 2017). Hence almost all the economic strategies and policies are closely related to environmental strategies and policies. As a part of sustainable development, they are intersected and cannot be separated (Sun, 2019).

Following China's GDP growth rate from 2001 to 2020 is offered (Fig. 1).

According to Fig. 1, the GDP growth rate kept rising before 2007. Influenced by the financial crisis in 2008, the GDP growth rate keeps falling for two years and there is a slight rebound in 2010. Since then, the growth rate has been slightly declining. In 2020, the GDP growth rate plummeted influenced by the COVID-19 pandemic.

There are two fundamental reasons for the decline. Firstly, the transformation drive lags. Secondly, the modern economic system lags. In fact, this is the imbalance of the governance structure caused by the unbalanced and inadequate development as mentioned in the report of the 19th National Congress of the Communist Party of China. The unbalanced and inadequate development at the economic level is reflected in the low quality and unsustainable economic development in recent years (Tian, 2018).

The declining economic growth rate proves that economic development without considering environmental protection can come to a standstill. Sustainable economic and environmental development is undoubtedly correct, but this transformation is a structural and systemic problem that cannot be transformed overnight. Therefore, there are different issues at different stages of sustainable economic development.

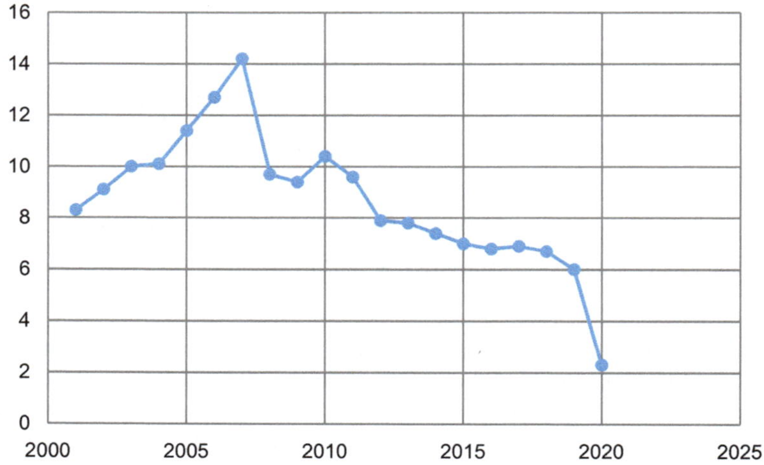

Fig. 1 China's GDP growth rate, 2001–2020. *Source* Compiled by the author based on National Statistics Bureau (2020)

To solve the problem of declining economic growth rate, China attaches great importance to the construction of ecological civilization and ecological environmental protection, incorporating ecological civilization into the overall layout of the "Five-point strategy", making adherence to the harmonious co-existence of man and nature one of the basic strategies for upholding and developing socialism with Chinese characteristics in the new era, making green development a major new development concept, and resolutely declaring war on pollution (Jie, 2019).

Following China's total indicators trend of sustainability index from 2010 to 2017 is offered (Fig. 2).

According to Fig. 2, the total indicators showed a general decline followed by a continuous and steady increase, with the lowest value reached in 2011. Since 2011, the total indicators of sustainable development have shown a steady increase because the government has strengthened the enforcement of sustainable economic and environmental strategies. In the first three quarters of 2021, China's GDP grew by 9.8% year-on-year, with a two-year average growth rate of 5.2% (National Statistics Bureau, 2021).

The relevant strategies and policies have been continuously completed all the time. There are different environmental problems at different stages, and the corresponding stage of economic development and social needs determines the environmental different strategies. Economic development and environmental protection seem to contradict each other. In the short term, they both have an opposite effect, an increase in one leads to a decrease in the other. In the long term, however, environmental protection and economic development are compatible, which means sustainable economic and environmental development strategies can achieve win–win results. It proves that sustainable economic and environmental development strategies benefit both economic development and environmental development.

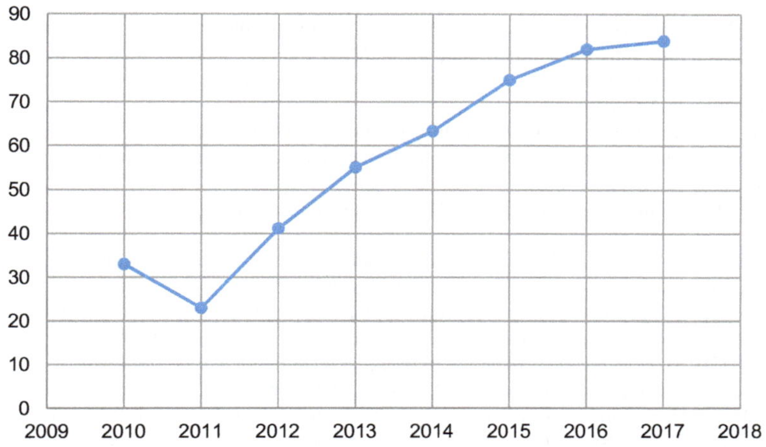

Fig. 2 The total indicators trend of sustainability index in China, 2010–2017. *Source* Compiled by the author based on China Centre for International Economic Exchanges (2019)

4 Conclusion

This article analyses the relationship between sustainable economic and environmental development strategies using the methods of literature research and quantitative analysis.

It is possible to conclude that there is a correlation between sustainable economic and environmental development strategies. There is a healthy interaction between environmental protection policies and sustainable economic development policies. Sustainable economic development strategies and policies serve as the instrument to protect the environment and establish ecological civilization, which can promote the implementation of sustainable environmental strategies and policies.

Because it is difficult to achieve results of sustainable development in the short term, some local governments in China allow some enterprises do damage to the environment. It is recommended that a system of indicators for local environmental protection and ecological construction should be established. The establishment of a timetable is recommended to monitor the implementation of the relevant policies.

References

Anopchenko, T. Y., Lazareva, E. I., Murzin, A. D., Revunov, R. V., & Roshchina, E. V. (2021). Diversification of regulatory powers in social, environmental, and economic relations as a factor for stimulating regional development. In *The challenge of sustainability in agricultural systems. Lecture notes in networks and systems* (Vol. 206, pp. 561–570).

China Centre for International Economic Exchanges. (2019). *Blue book on sustainable development: China sustainable development assessment report*. Social Science Literature Press.

Jie, Z. H. (2019). Historical changes in ecological protection in China in the 40 years of reform and opening up. *China Environmental Management, 11*(04), 4–16.
Joshua, J. (2017). *China's economic growth: Towards sustainable economic development and social justice*. Springer Nature.
Lazareva, E. I., & Dong, Y. (2020). Socio-ecological-economic evaluation of sustainability in managing regional development based on econometric modeling. *Drukerovskiy Bulletin, 5*(37), 76–188.
National Statistics Bureau. (2020). National data. https://data.stats.gov.cn. Accessed 10 November 2021.
National Statistics Bureau. (2021). National economy generally maintains recovery in first three quarters. http://www.stats.gov.cn. Accessed 18 November 2021.
Sun, Q. P. (2019). The role of quality economic development in promoting environmental protection and ecological civilisation. *Contemporary Economic Management, 41*(11), 9–14.
Tian, G. Q. (2018). *How the new voyage of reform and opening up will be stable and far-reaching*. Securities Times. http://physicsweb.org. Accessed 19 November 2021.
UNESCO. (2021). Sustainable development. https://en.unesco.org. Accessed 11 November 2021.
Wu, S. Z. (2019). *Processes, characteristics and prospects of environmental strategy and policy development in China*. China Environment News. https://theory.gmw.cn. Accessed 19 November 2021.
Wu, S. Z., Shen, Y., Guo, L. Q., & Xing, J. J. (2020). Processes, characteristics and prospects of environmental strategy development in China. *Environment and Sustainable Development, 1*, 34–36.

Resource Management of Economic Development of Regional Environmental Management Systems

Jia Hao and Victor N. Ovchinnikov

Abstract The purpose of the article is to develop directions for the development of the resource economy. Large-scale economic development of new areas implies the rational use of natural resources, while it should be understood that the resource potential is not equivalent to economic advantages. In order to receive economic benefits from natural resources, their owners must, first of all, turn them into real factors of production. Currently, the resource-saving model of economic development sets strict imperatives for developers, users of natural resources, and economic development strategists.

Keywords Natural resources · Environmental management · Environmental management system · Economic development · Imperatives

JEL Classification Q57 · F52 · E65

1 Introduction

Relevance. Under conditions of growing scarcity of natural resources and environmental benefits, the change of technological modes, which assumes, along with other imperatives, the dominance of resource-saving industries, intellectualization and innovative social development. This allows us to better understand the laws of ecosystem functioning and scientifically substantiate the practice of their involvement in economic turnover (Lusiunia & Shuantszin, 1987). Green economy, environmentally oriented technologies, and ecosystem clusters of the industry are becoming decisive factors determining the vectors of transformation of the economic space of the country, constituting a new qualitative content of the economy of the Russian

J. Hao · V. N. Ovchinnikov (✉)
Southern Federal University, Rostov-on-Don, Russia
e-mail: vovchinnikov@sfedu.ru

J. Hao
e-mail: hczya@sfedu.ru

E. I. Lazareva et al. (eds.), *Innovative Trends in International Business and Sustainable Management*, Approaches to Global Sustainability, Markets, and Governance,
https://doi.org/10.1007/978-981-19-4005-7_60

regions. *Formulation of the research problem*/ The article attempts to determine the direction of resource-oriented economic development and analyze the production methods of resource-oriented economy, the reasons for the slow development of the resource economy. In Russia, the government is considering development strategies, guided by the principle of "resource advantage", which is associated with its wealth of natural resources. However, experience shows that various scenarios of economic development based on resource advantages do not meet expectations. Therefore, the purpose of this article is to identify the relationship between the dynamics of economic development and the amount of resources provided.

2 Methodology

The methodological basis of this study is the dialectic of cause-and-effect mutual transitions, when at first resource provision acts as a factor of economic development, and then, a new impulse of economic development creates prerequisites for further development and attraction of additional resources to production.

3 Results

1. *Managing the process of transformation of the natural resource potential into real factors of production*

Natural resources are an integral part of material production. For example, raw materials and fuel are factors indispensable for production. Natural resources can become a real production factor and contribute to the growth of wealth and an increase in the standard of living of people only if they are developed and included in the real process of production and economic activity. Such natural resources can be called real; otherwise, they can only be considered as potential resources.

The inclusion of natural resources in the real production process depends on many factors. First of all, it is determined by the products and production technology. Natural resources required for the production of products using a certain technology, as a rule, are transformed into factors of production. Secondly, the change in their status depends on the price level of alternative resources. The quality and relative prices of alternative resources often encourage people to choose other resources as potential factors of production.

With the development of technology, the material elements used in the production of products are in most cases very interchangeable and alternative, which leads to the emergence of many competitors for specific resources (steel, wood, plastics, artificial fibers, etc.), although their physical characteristics differ, but provide excellent interchangeability. As a result, individual resources do not necessarily become real factors of production in specific production processes.

Therefore, in order to determine whether a particular natural resource will become a real factor in the production process from the point of view of the competitiveness of finished products and related production technologies in the market of competing resources, a more accurate assessment of the prospects for the development of the resource market is needed, on the basis of which an appropriate forecast of their development could be made.

2. *Natural resource management for the production of products required by the market*

Along with directly consumed products produced in the field of agriculture and forestry, people use natural raw materials to transform them into final consumer products. The demand for natural resources is stimulated by economic growth as a result of increased demand for the final product.

In order to transform natural resources into a final product, it is necessary to go through many intermediate links of the technological chain, such as extraction, storage, transportation, processing, ultimately through marketing channels in order to enter the market and get into the hands of direct consumers. In the process of transforming a raw material resource into a final product, there should be no "bottlenecks" that limit production volumes or lead to a decrease in its efficiency. That is why when using specific natural resources for the production of a particular product, it is important to take into account not only the state of the resources themselves, but also to implement an integrated approach to assess all conditions of production and economic activity. In a market economy, economic efficiency requires minimizing total production costs. Considerable transportation costs can also significantly affect the difference between the cost of raw materials and finished products, which is an important factor in making management decisions. In addition, the choice of options and sources of investment depend on the quality and cost of labor, as well as on the complexity of the production technology of the final product and various external conditions.

It seems that even if natural resources are not substitutable resources with a high degree of monopoly, they may not necessarily bring significant benefits to the owners. Natural resources are an important, but not the only factor of production, and the production of final products is the result of the interaction of various factors of production. In cases where there are no other conditions, but only natural resources are available, the sale of the latter often becomes an inevitable choice for their owners.

However, today the market situation is such that the resources themselves have limited value, while the cost of finished products depends not so much on natural resources as on the added value during their processing. The added value, in turn, depends on the degree of complexity of the work performed by employees, managers; i.e., basically it is the "crystallization" of human knowledge, the more work requires knowledge, the greater the added value.

Thus, the sale of products in modern markets and the benefits from it depend mainly on the degree of use of production technologies, the level of material conditions, and the availability of highly qualified specialists working in production and management. In addition, as noted above, technological progress has led to a significant reduction in restrictions on the production of natural resources and to a situation where the resource market is in most cases a buyer's market, which makes it difficult to sell resources at high prices. Therefore, owners of natural resources cannot keep the growth of their income only by increasing sales, which, in turn, exacerbates the disadvantageous market environment faced by suppliers of natural resources.

Numerous companies developing deposits often compete with each other, due to the fact that the extraction of many natural resources does not require too complex technologies. Despite the market demand, this leads to a decrease in the supply of natural resources, as a consequence of which suppliers can sell them only at reduced prices, which resulted in the so-called mass production without increasing revenue.

At the same time, since natural resources are commodities, the market demand for them largely depends on the demand for the final product. As soon as the final product market was unfavorable, the demand for the production and sale of natural resources immediately weakened. This causes the vulnerability of the economies of countries providing natural resources to the world market.

3. *Management of the transition to a green economy: saving resources, regulating competition between suppliers of natural resources*

Environmental problems are becoming more and more serious, and many of them are associated with the irrational use of natural resources. According to experts, until the 70s of the twentieth century, the share of final products needed by society accounted for only 20–30% of raw material consumption; that is, 70–80% of resources become waste released into the environment, which led to a significant loss of resources and damage to the environment. In addition, it was recognized that most of the natural resources available to humanity are limited and not renewable, so it is necessary to use these resources very carefully to ensure the sustainable development of mankind. In this regard, calls for the conservation of natural resources became louder, and restrictions on environmental pollution became more severe.

Taking into account such requirements as more efficient use of natural resources, the following main directions of technology development, such as the reuse of resources, the continuous development of new areas of their application, including the identification of new types of their use, and the introduction of resource recovery have become an irreversible trend of sustainable economic development. It has become clear that there is no absolute waste, but there are resources that have not been identified for suitable and economical use. For example, cinder from thermal power plants was originally waste because people did not know how to use it. Huge subsidies were required for its placement, the creation of landfills that occupy significant areas, as well as for the construction of incinerators to neutralize industrial waste that cannot be effectively disposed of, which poses a danger to both the environment and the environment. However, various ways of efficient use of cinder were subsequently identified and implemented, and now, it is considered as a resource for the provision of which a fee is charged. This trend can be observed in developed countries.

More efficient use of resources in developed countries is accompanied by a constant expansion of their scope of application. Back in 1970, Japan received an income of $ 1 billion from secondary resources from waste (garbage). In 1979, the recycling rate was already very high: In the steel industry, it was 75.78%, in the woodworking industry—48.47%, and in publishing—49.12%. The United States achieved 100% use of blast furnace slag and steel slag in the 1950s and 1970s; France has been carrying out complex processing of silver, copper, cobalt, and tin since the late 1970s, which saves 5–20% of raw materials. The Chinese economy is also developing in the direction of saving resources and increasing economic efficiency. For example, energy consumption on average for the production of products worth 10 million yuan (GDP) decreased from 4.79 tons of standard coal in 1991 to 2.06 tons of standard coal in 1996 (Yearbook of Chinese Energy Statistics, 1991–1996, 1998). Currently, environmental imperatives related to environmental protection, the development of a green economy, the achievement of sustainable economic and social development, and technological progress have increased significantly.

This situation has complicated the situation of suppliers of natural resources and led to increased competition between them, since the latter often arises not only because of the availability of the same or similar resources, but also because of the increase in the volume of alternative resources as a result of technological progress. Moreover, technological progress has led to a relative reduction in demand for natural resources for the production of industrial products. Such an expansion of the supply-side capacity of natural resources, on the one hand, and a relative reduction in demand for them, on the other, lead to a double pressure on the supply of natural resources.

4. *An economy that survives only by providing natural resources is an unstable economy*

For all these reasons, areas that have only natural resources and do not have the potential for their extensive processing are often in a less favorable economic situation than those areas where, having no natural resources, there are other advantages, especially in terms of knowledge and technology. Moreover, due to the scarcity of natural resources, the sustainability of a resource-based economy is much lower than that of an economy based on technology and knowledge, and this forces the former to become a vassal of the latter, and the possession of resources is nothing more than a simple supply of raw materials.

Such a perspective allows those areas that possess natural resources to develop their economy only through their development and sale, which will only slow down the relative growth of their economy compared to the areas in which their extensive processing is carried out and will further widen the gap and make them even less developed.

We can summarize this in three equations.

$$\text{A:}\quad \begin{aligned} W_r &= W_{\mathrm{ro}}(1+i_r)^t \\ W_m &= W_{\mathrm{mo}}(1+i_m)^t \end{aligned}$$

$$\text{B:}\quad \begin{aligned} P_r &= P_{ro}(1+k_r)^t \\ P_m &= P_{\mathrm{mo}}(1+k_m)^t \end{aligned}$$

$$\text{C:}\quad \begin{aligned} V_r &= P_r W_r = P_{\mathrm{ro}} W_{\mathrm{ro}}(1+k_r)^t(1+i_r)^t \\ V_m &= P_m W_m = P_{\mathrm{mo}} W_{\mathrm{mo}}(1+k_m)^t(1+i_m)^t \end{aligned}$$

Among them: r—resources, m—products produced by extensive processing of resources, W—production volume, P—unit price, and V—output cost; i—output growth rates, k—price growth rates, O—the base year, and t—the years after the base year. The equations of group A represent the volume of production of resources and products of extensive processing per year t; the equations of group B represent the unit prices of both per year t; the equations of group C represent the output values of both per year t.

This can be seen from the equation of group C: Even if $P_{\mathrm{ro}} \geq P_{\mathrm{mo}}$, $W_{\mathrm{ro}} \geq W_{\mathrm{mo}}$, that is, the place of delivery of natural resources is compared with the place of production of the product of extensive processing, the starting point of the former is not lower than the latter. However, since a resource-saving economy should have $i_r < i_m$, and, as a rule, there are prices for primary products that grow more slowly than prices for manufactured goods, that is, usually $k_r < k_m$, then after t years of development, it should be $V_r(t) \leq V_m(t)$; that is, the latter one will definitely catch up and surpass the former. Not to mention that the starting point of the former is lower than that of the latter.

4 Conclusion

In conclusion, it should be noted that the mere fact of the availability of natural resources for the implementation of long-term development goals is not enough, and therefore, it is necessary that the regions, as part of their strategic development, shift the focus to technological processing of natural resources to increase the added value of the final product and on this basis ensure sustainable socioeconomic development of the country (Akimova et al., 2009).

References

Akimova, T. A., & Mosiekin, Y. N. (2009). *Ecnomics of sustainable development* (pp. 380–432). Economics.

Lusiunia, F., & Shuantszin, L. (1987). *Development and forecast of environmental science and technology* (pp. 147–149). China Science and Technology Press.

Yearbook of Chinese Energy Statistics, 1991–1996. (1998). The *Department of industrial transport statistics of the national bureau of statistics* (Vol. 6, p. 236). China Statistics Press.

Green Transformation and the Concept of Energy Efficiency in the Housing Sector

Aidar B. Assylbayev, Marina V. Safronchuk, Kunduzkul N. Niiazalieva, and Natalia A. Brovko

Abstract *Purpose* The purpose of this paper is to determine the relationship between the growth of the housing stock and limited electricity production within the framework of the concept of energy efficiency in housing. *Design/methodology/approach* The results of a study of the relationship between the dynamics of housing stock development and electricity production in the context of the demographic growth of the region were obtained by the method of correlation analysis of statistical data. Based on the econometric analysis, the necessity of development and implementation of the concept of energy efficiency in the housing sector is proved. As part of the development of energy efficiency in the housing stock, the dynamics of electricity consumption by industry and housing utilities are studied and correlated with the volume of electricity produced and received during the period of independence of the Kyrgyz Republic. *Findings* It is determined, that in 2020 in Kyrgyzstan more than 53% of the total volume of electricity used was accounted for by the industry and the population, 26%—by the agricultural sector, and other sectors accounted for about 21%. This country is on the 83rd level by the total electricity consumption per capita in the world (IEA Statistics). The dynamics of population, the dynamics of housing stock growth and electricity demand are growing and their interdependence is confirmed in the analysis. The negative dynamics in the production of electricity and the positive dynamics in its consumption are obvious. *Originality/value* The concept of energy-profitable housing is suggested. We propose measures to modernize the

A. B. Assylbayev · N. A. Brovko
Kyrgyz-Russian Slavic University, Bishkek, Kyrgyzstan
e-mail: aidaras73@mail.ru

N. A. Brovko
e-mail: nbrovko@list.ru

M. V. Safronchuk (✉)
MGIMO University, Moscow, Russia
e-mail: applied_economics@mgimo.ru

K. N. Niiazalieva
International Kuwait University, Bishkek, Kyrgyzstan
e-mail: kunduz512@mail.ru

E. I. Lazareva et al. (eds.), *Innovative Trends in International Business and Sustainable Management*, Approaches to Global Sustainability, Markets, and Governance,
https://doi.org/10.1007/978-981-19-4005-7_61

energy supply system for housing and transform the consciousness of the population through the formation of environmental responsibility and interest in energy conservation without limiting energy use and reducing the comfort of living. The social and economic effects of the implementation of the concept of construction of energy-efficient and energy-profitable houses are considered, the necessary incentive measures on the part of the state are developed.

Keywords Housing stock · Energy transition · Green transformation · Energy saving · Energy efficiency · Energy system · Population growth · Electricity · Energy profitability · Income effect

JEL Classification D6 · E02 · J11 · J17 · L97 · L94 · O18 · P18 · C82

1 Introduction

The presented investigation is made in the frames of modern directions of scientific and technological progress of national economies adopted in Resolution 'Transforming the World in 2015 and connected with the goals, formulated in The 2030 Agenda for Sustainable Development' at the United Nations (Achieving the Sustainable Development Goals in the Region of the Eurasian Economic Union, 2019). Further developments of the transformations in the economy and society to achieve these goals appeared in the report 'The World in 2050', published by the International Institute for Applied Systems Analysis (TWI2050—The World in 2050, 2018). This study is also associated with the international project 'On the macroeconomic situation in the member states of the Eurasian Economic Union and proposals for ensuring sustainable economic development' (2021). In this context housing and living conditions, the energy intensity of services consumed by residents is important indicators for assessing the quality of life of the population. The quantitative and qualitative consumption of clean energy is a priority and strategic task for developing countries. Achievement of this goal by Kyrgyzstan is impossible without a unified state strategy to improve the energy efficiency of the existing housing stock and those under construction.

The relevance and timeliness of investigation are connected with a catastrophic disproportion between the dynamics of the volume of energy production and its consumption by housing and communal services, new and existing housing stock and other sectors of the industrial economy. This discrepancy is influenced by ineffective construction technologies and the construction of energy-intensive houses, which damages the environment, creates an additional load on the energy system, limiting and complicating access to this service. It must be modernized or replaced with housing that meets the energy-efficient parameters.

The problem of energy transition and saving, energy efficiency improvement in the industrial, transport and residential sectors are linked in the same chain. A comprehensive solution to these problems is necessary. Such an integrated approach (integrated solutions) can create a synergistic effect and positive externalities that extend to other sustainable development goals, including energy transition or green transformation, which will be discussed in the main part of the article.

The purpose of this work is to determine the relationship between the growth of the housing stock and limited electricity production within the framework of the concept of energy efficiency in housing.

This article has the following tasks. The first is to study the dynamics of electricity costs in the region of demographic growth; to study the dynamics of the housing stock, generated and received electricity for the entire period of independence of the Kyrgyz Republic. Then based on the data obtained, simulate and correlate the dynamics of the housing stock, produced and received electricity to determine the degree of their correlation. The third task is to give recommendations on the unified strategy to improve the condition of the housing stock and its energy efficiency.

It should be noted that the improvement in energy efficiency in the housing stock is determined by the reduction in energy consumption per unit of services received. It should take place without deteriorating the quality of life of residents and without harming the ecological environment.

The object of the research is the development of energy efficiency of the housing stock in the framework of the global project for the sustainable and efficient development of environmentally compatible cities and towns. The subject of the research is the dynamics of the energy system, energy efficiency of the growing housing sector in a region with demographic potential.

2 Materials and Methods

Materials for analysis were taken from publicly available data from the National Statistical Committee. When processing statistical material, the method of econometric analysis was used, namely, the method of identifying the correlation relationship between individual factors of the housing stock and energy systems.

Also, the research methodology was based on the review, systematization and synthesis of information in order to deepen the research, better data processing and interpretation of the results.

3 Discussions

Today, energy efficiency in the housing stock is understood as a process of reducing the energy intensity of consumed services without deteriorating living conditions and the quality of life of people. Such a process is possible only with the use of more efficient and modern building materials in the creation of new housing and reconstruction of the old one. However, the concept of an energy-efficient house proposed by us should be transformed into the concept of an energy-profitable house

(Assylbayev, 2014). This concept implies that excessive consumption of various types of energy cannot be considered energy-efficient. Many scientists researched various aspects of energy conservation. But most investigations, connected with the formation of a new policy based on the concept of energy efficiency in the housing sector of the economy, were conducted by (Asaul et al., 2020, 2019; Assylbayev & Kunakunov, 2014; Assylbayev et al., 2016; Kazymova, 2014; Strelyukhina et al., 2018). We consider that with the transition to energy-efficient housing, the problem of energy-intensive housing will be addressed.

The concept of energy efficiency of a housing unit means a decrease in energy costs, quantitative and qualitative comfort maintenance in the process of consuming energy-intensive services and achieving energy profitability not by reducing tariffs, but by optimizing energy consumption using energy-saving technologies and materials. Energy profitability is understood as generating income with profit from the ownership of a residential property as a result of its energy-efficient use. Housing has the properties of economic good and can be a source of income. It can satisfy the material and non-material needs of its residents. As an economic good housing is valued, and the consumption of housing services can be analyzed in terms of income, expenses and profits. Assylbayev (2014), the author of the concept of energy-efficient and energy-profitable housing, offers a basic (or strategic) formula for the energy profitability indicator, which can be calculated both in kW of electricity and in monetary terms at any tariff rate for electricity or gas consumption:

$$E_{\mathrm{hi}} - E_{\mathrm{hc}} = E_{\mathrm{hp}}, \tag{1}$$

where E_{hi}—energy efficiency housing income, E_{hc}—energy consumption housing costs, E_{hp}—energy profitability of housing (Assylbayev, 2014).

Given the principle of ‘acting locally, thinking globally,’ this formula can be extrapolated to the meso- and macro-levels, using it to assess the housing stock at the local, regional and national levels.

It is possible to assess the housing stock for the budget and housing management, as well as to develop a programme for its improvement in order to save energy and transfer energy. Getting to know the proportion of energy-efficient housing, energy-effective and energy-ineffective (or energy-consuming) housing. We can use the same principle, discussed above:

$$E_{\mathrm{eh}} - E_{\mathrm{ch}} = E_{\mathrm{ph}}, \tag{2}$$

where E_{eh}—energy-efficient housing, E_{ch}—energy-consumable housing, E_{ph}—energy-profitable housing (Assylbayev, 2014).

This concept and formula reveal a new understanding of the presence of housing in ownership or in operation, which makes it possible to classify and define it as energy-consuming, energy-efficient and energy-profitable housing.

Soon, as the concept is being implemented, the concern between the energy efficiency of housing and such components of sustainable development of cities and agglomerations as ecological housing, housing demography, housing economics, healthy or safe housing, smart home and smart city, and other indicators of sustainable development would be stronger.

For the implementation of this concept, as well as for the implementation of the SDGs, support is needed at the technological, legislative, and institutional levels. An important role should be played by the institution of responsibility and understanding of the need to introduce energy-saving and 'green' technologies, despite its hard and complex incorporation. That is why state incentives and funding are also needed. The technical parameters developed by scientists and the requirements for energy-efficient housing standards must be incorporated into the regulatory legislation. At the same time, the government at the republican and local levels can act as a customer for such construction, helping to attract investments. It would be effective to use tools to attract investment in housing and infrastructure projects in such a form of cooperation with businesses as PPP in the construction sector, involving national businesses and foreign companies in the construction of housing and its infrastructure (Ivanov & Shamanina, 2021).

For the implementation of the project of energy-efficient and energy-profitable housing, it is necessary to develop appropriate technologies in the field of energy conservation, alternative energy sources, technologies for the production of new energy-saving materials, etc. in the context of green transformation. As incentives for their application, not only legislative initiatives are needed, but also a commitment to these goals on the part of business and other project participants. The development of such behavioural institutions in business as an investment and environmental responsibility, along with external social corporate responsibility, is absolutely necessary for the implementation of projects directly related to the energy transition and 'green' transformation (Ivanov & Shamanina, 2021; Zavyalova et al., 2020).

The implementation of this concept has a social external effect, improving the level of real income of the population. This fits into the goals of increasing welfare and can serve as additional means of poverty eradication methods (Zavyalova & Krotova, 2021).

The concept under consideration is especially relevant not only for the Kyrgyz Republic but also for other countries with low per capita income. The transition to energy-efficient housing will be able to reduce the cost of paying for electricity at unchanged tariffs, creating an income effect. The next step—the transition to energy-profitable housing, will be able to create an additional stream of income from the reverse supply of energy from housing to the network, which is possible with the introduction of special devices into the dwelling itself. At the same time, additional income from the sale of energy by the house can be temporarily tax-free. Later, a regressive energy sales tax for the households could be settled as an additional incentive for energy-efficient housing implementation.

4 Results

Today in Kyrgyzstan the share of per capita electricity costs is growing and has a steady trend towards further growth (Fig. 1).

Figure 1 demonstrates that the dynamics of per capita expenditures have pronounced periods of decline and rise. It makes it quite difficult to describe the trend line functionally. In this regard, the trend line is described by the cubic function:

$$y = 0.0027x^3 - 0.046x^2 + 0.3256x + 1.9904,$$

which has the highest value of the confidence factor equal to $R^2 = 0.6039$. But this corresponds to only 60% of the accuracy of the description. Such a low coefficient of approximation confirms the stochastic behaviour of the dynamics of per capita energy costs. In general, today's electricity costs in the region of 3% are not catastrophic and are relatively low compared to the 10% average for the Eurasian Economic Union.

However, the demographic picture of population growth is positive and has good potential for further growth. The volume of housing construction and, consequently, the housing stock also has all the signs of positive development. But at the same time, the growth of electricity production is steadily slowing down (Fig. 2).

This is undoubtedly a negative factor causing imbalances between the rates of housing stock development, population growth and the volume of electricity production.

The graph (Fig. 2) clearly shows the downward dynamics of energy production and the upward dynamics of the volume of the housing stock. At the same time, an increase in housing facilities inevitably entails an increase in electricity consumption. However, this relationship should not be straightforward. A proportional match with a decreasing proportionality factor between these indicators should be achieved. According to the concept of energy-efficient housing, each newly constructed facility should increase energy efficiency. It means, that energy consumption should decrease, but at the same time, the comfort of living should be maintained or even better.

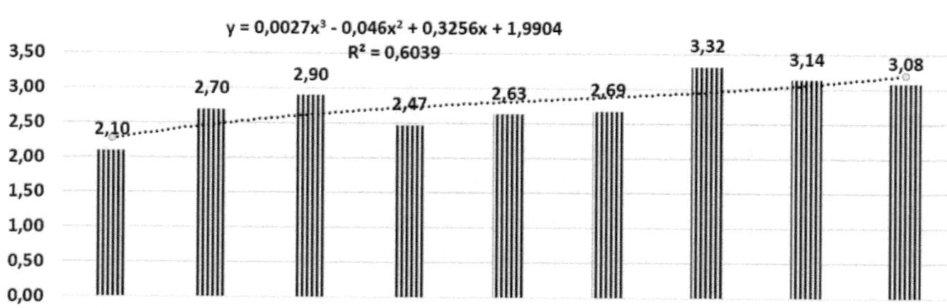

Fig. 1 Share of average per capita electricity costs (percent) in Kyrgyzstan. *Source* Compiled by the author based on Kazymova (2014)

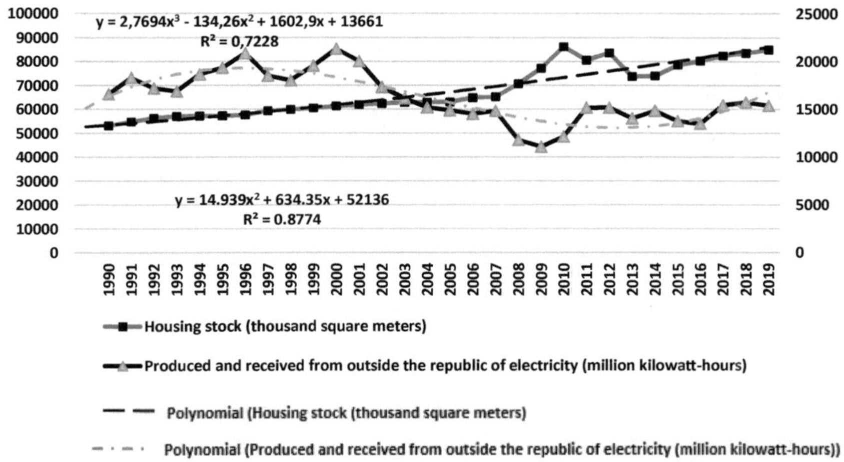

Fig. 2 Dynamics of the housing stock, generated and received electricity for the period from 1990 to 2019. *Source* Compiled by the author based on National Statistical Committee of the Kyrgyz Republic (2021)

The performed correlation analysis showed a negative and weak dependence of the two statistical data: the correlation coefficient is R (correl) = −0.66434902. The result obtained indicates a weak connection between the development of the housing stock and the production of energy. That is, the construction of the housing stock does not have a significant effect on energy production in the republic. At the same time, there is a positive external effect from the energy efficiency of housing, associated not only with the weakening of pressure on the environment but also with the reduction or conservation of electricity.

With an increase in population, the need for energy will also increase. But it should not grow in direct proportion according to the theory of energy efficiency. Below the dynamics of the positive development of the housing stock and the growth dynamics of the population of the Kyrgyz Republic are shown in Fig. 3.

The growth of population can be considered as an electricity demand factor through the development of the housing stock. But in accordance with the concept of energy efficiency and energy profitability of the housing stock, the rate of growth of consumed energy relative to the rate of population growth should decrease or slow down. This is the deep meaning of achieving energy efficiency in the housing stock.

We compared the dynamics of energy production and its consumption in the sector of industry and the sector of housing and communal services (Fig. 4) in order to determine the relationship and the degree of influence of housing on energy production. The negative dynamics in the production of electricity and the positive dynamics in its consumption is visible in Fig. 4.

Correlation analysis of two static data showed a negative and insignificant relationship: the correlation coefficient is R (correl) = −0.569216587. That means that the housing sector of the economy does not affect the volume of energy production

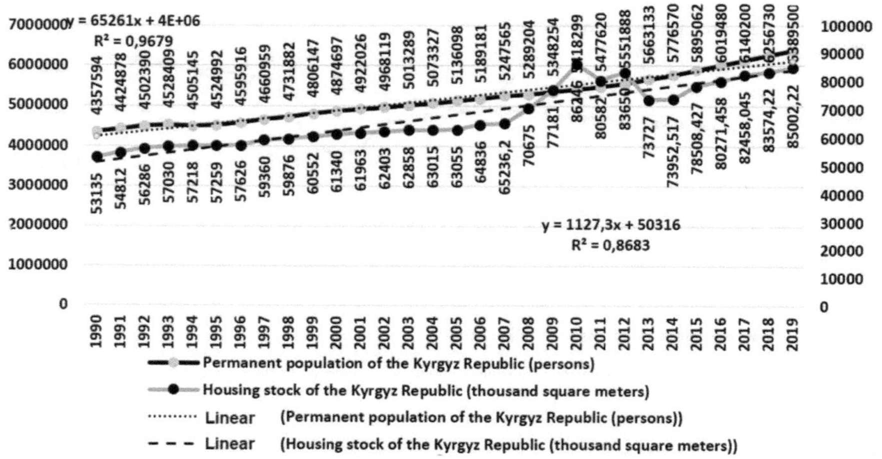

Fig. 3 Diagram of the housing stock and volume of population in Kyrgyz Republic. *Source* Compiled and built by the author based on Kazymova (2014)

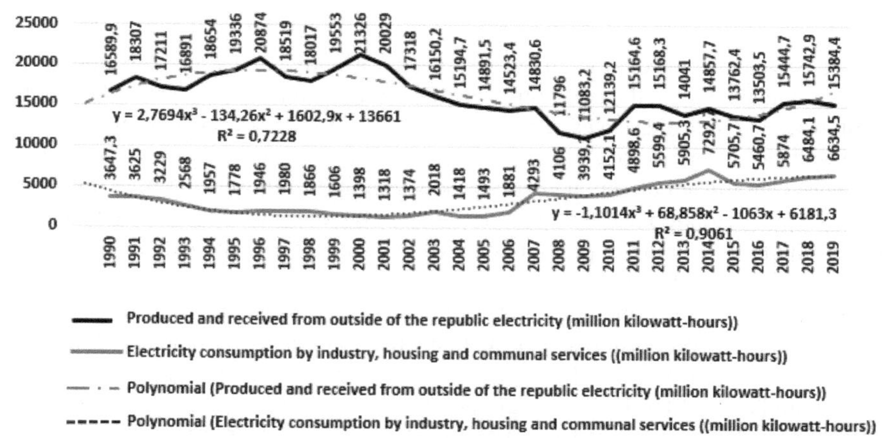

Fig. 4 Dynamics of electricity consumption by industry, by housing and communal services and the dynamics of generated, received electricity for the period from 1990 to 2019. *Source* Compiled and built by the author based on Kazymova (2014)

actively. However, an increase in the volume of construction due to the demographic growth of the population will lead to an increase in electricity consumption (Assylbayev, 2017, 2021; Assylbayev & Niyazalieva, 2018). But there is almost no growth in electricity production in the country (Assylbayev, 2015).

Therefore, it is necessary to pursue a policy aimed at improving the energy efficiency of the housing stock. In 2020 in Kyrgyzstan, more than 53% of the total volume of electricity used was accounted for by the industry and the population,

26%—by the agricultural sector, and about 21%—by others. By the total electricity consumption per person a year, Kyrgyzstan for the analyzed period took the 83rd line in the international rating, Russia—the 28th (IEA Statistics, 2014).

As limited production of electricity in a region with high demographic growth can lead to an energy deficit, the government should stimulate its production and its efficient usage. Raising the energy efficiency of the housing stock will reduce electricity demand and will give the following benefits and socio-economic effects:

- the substitution for cleaner and renewable energy as part of energy efficiency policy will give the climatic benefits for the region;
- the level of energy availability and energy independence will be increased and it will strengthen socio-political stability in general;
- the economic advantages are in saving households' electricity payments. The supplier will reduce losses in the network and the cost of supply. Suppliers and consumers can direct freed-up funds to meet their other needs and preferences.
- renovation and reconstruction of the housing stock will give the comfort of living and the quality of services provided. In general, urban architecture and aesthetics of the settlement will become more interesting and attractive;
- socio-demographic advantages lie in improving the quality of life of the population. The quality of living conditions will increase, which make a positive influence on health and spirit. It will increase the demographic potential;
- finally, the use of incentive tax instruments for the transition to energy efficiency and profitability of housing can have a positive effect on local and regional budgets.

It is necessary to introduce a system of social responsibility and social protection. Social responsibility provides for the obligatory and maximum use of technologies of energy-efficient houses in order to minimize costs, improve the ecology of the area of residence and increase the availability of electricity supply to other households. Social protection involves reducing energy poverty or 'starvation' and energy expenses, including through programmes to promote the development of energy-efficient homes.

The new ways of energy-efficient thinking among the population must be formed by targeted informational work, developing appropriate institutions of economic behaviour and forms of ecological responsibility. Expansion of the social responsibility of business is required. The parameters of compliance with the standards and requirements, necessary for the implementation of sustainable development goals, could be included in a company responsibility report (Starikova & Shamanina, 2021).

Thus, the modernization of housing and industry towards energy efficiency gains strategic importance and requires the introduction of special state investment programmes and legislation criteria for energy efficiency and measures to achieve it in the section on energy-efficient and environmental solutions.

5 Conclusion

The consumption of electricity by the housing stock is growing in the Kyrgyz Republic. The industry and population use more electricity than half of the consumption in all sectors. At the same time, the national energy system isn't profitable due to the lack of new technological equipment and outdated funds. Comprehensive modernization of the energy system and a strategic programme to improve the energy efficiency of the housing stock is important for the economy with a growing population.

It is necessary to legalize special standards, building codes and rules for the use of energy-saving materials and energy-efficient technologies and to conduct an active policy with homeowners' or tenant associations. Collective management forms the collective responsibility for the efficient use of energy. It is necessary to apply the best world technologies and the world's best practices in industrial and investment policies to create better conditions and tools to attract private national and foreign investment.

The concept of energy-efficient housing is the first step in the implementation of a new concept of energy-profitable housing, which will continue development to clean energy and eco-friendly housing in energy-efficient agglomerations.

References

Achieving the Sustainable Development Goals in the Region of the Eurasian Economic Union. Statistical abstract. Eurasian Economic Commission. Moscow, 2019 (p. 95). http://www.eurasiancommission.org/ru/act/integr_i_makroec/dep_stat/econstat/Documents/SDG_abstract2019+cover.pdf. Accessed 2 October 2021.

Asaul, A. N., Asaul, M. A., Levin, Y. A., & Platonov, A. M. (2020). Power supply of isolated territories in the context of attracting investments and development of the regional economy. *Journal of Economy of the Region, 16*(3), 884–895. https://doi.org/10.17059/ekon.reg.2020-3-16

Asaul, A. N., Asaul, M. A., Lyulin, P. B., & Chepachenko, N. V. (2019). Trends in housing construction in Russia and the mid-term forecast. *Journal of Problems of Forecasting, 3*(174), 111–117.

Assylbayev, A. (2021). Study of older households with their living conditions. In *Process Management and Scientific Developments. Part 1 of the international conference in Birmingham*, 21 July 2021, Melbourne (pp. 8–17). https://doi.org/10.34660/INF.2021.40.81.001

Assylbayev, A. B., & Kunakunov, M. K. (2014). Forms of relationship between the state and business in housing and communal services. *Journal of Bulletin of the Kyrgyz-Russian Slavic University, 14*(1), 7–11.

Assylbayev, A. B., & Niyazalieva, K. N. (2018). Interrelation of demographic processes with the housing conditions of citizens in the Kyrgyz Republic. *Journal of Bulletin of the Kyrgyz-Russian Slavic University, 18*(11), 14–22.

Assylbayev, A. B. (2014). Economic proposal for the transition from energy efficient to energy profitable housing. *Journal of Bulletin of the Kyrgyz-Russian Slavic University, 14*(8), 17–19.

Assylbayev, A. B. (2015). Problems and conditions of providing affordable and safe housing to the population of the Kyrgyz Republic. *Journal of Bulletin of the Kyrgyz-Russian Slavic University, 15*(8), 3–7.

Assylbayev, A. B. (2017). Housing demography in the system of demographic sciences: Theoretical and methodological aspect. *Journal of Competitiveness in the Global World: Economics, Science, Technology, 11*(58), 1505–1508.

Assylbayev, K. B., Assylbayev, A. B., & Niyazaliva, K. N. (2016). Diagnostics of unbalanced development of the regions of Kazakhstan and analysis of their convergence using convergence. *Journal of Actual Problems of Economy, 180*(6), 231–245.

IEA Statistics. (2014). Electricity consumption (kWh per capita). https://data.worldbank.org/indicator/EG.USE.ELEC.KH.PC. Accessed 14 October 2021.

Ivanov, O. V., & Shamanina, E. A. (2021). PPP as a tool to achieve sustainable development goals and implement the concept of "Quality Infrastructure Investments". In E. B. Zavyalova, & E. G. Popkova (Eds.), *Industry 4.0*. Palgrave Macmillan. https://doi.org/10.1007/978-3-030-75405-1_28

Kazymova, T. S. (2014). Attraction of investments in the electric power industry of the Kyrgyz Republic. *Journal of Bulletin of the Kyrgyz-Russian Slavic University, 14*(8), 88–91.

National Statistical Committee of the Kyrgyz Republic. (2021). http://www.stat.kg/ru/. Accessed 14 October 2021.

On the draft decision of the Council of the Eurasian Economic Commission "On the draft decree of the Eurasian Intergovernmental Council" On the macroeconomic situation in the member states of the Eurasian Economic Union and proposals for ensuring sustainable economic development". http://www.eurasiancommission.org/en/nae/news/Pages/04-02-2018-1.aspx. Accessed 3 October 2021.

Starikova, E. A., & Shamanina, E. A. (2021). Corporate practice of implementing measures to combat climate change in the Russian oil and gas companies. In E. B. Zavyalova, & E. G. Popkova (Eds.), *Industry 4.0*. Palgrave Macmillan. https://doi.org/10.1007/978-3-030-75405-1_20

Strelyukhina, T. A., Greisukh, G. I., & Nazarov, I. S. (2018). Energy-efficient housing in the eco-quarter "zaprudny" G. Penza. *Journal of Education and Science in the Modern World. Innovation, 2*(15), 256–261.

TWI2050—The World in 2050. (2018). Transformations to Achieve the Sustainable Development Goals. Report prepared by The World in 2050 initiative. International Institute for Applied Systems Analysis (IIASA), Laxenburg, Austria. https://doi.org/10.22022/TNT/07-2018.15347. Last modified 27 August 2021. http://pure.iiasa.ac.at/15347. Accessed 2 October 2021.

Zavyalova, E. B., & Krotova, T. G. (2021). Methods for achieving SDG 1, poverty eradication. In E. G. Popkova, B. S. Sergi (Eds.), *Modern Global Economic System: Evolutional Development vs. Revolutionary Leap. ISC 2019. Lecture Notes in Networks and Systems* (Vol. 198). Springer. https://doi.org/10.1007/978-3-030-69415-9_218

Zavyalova, E., Lee, J. S., & Ostrovskaya, E. (2020). Corporate social responsibility (pp. 173–187). Corporate governance in Russia: Quo vadis? In A. Dementieva, & E. Zavyalova (Eds.), *Volume 3 in the series De Gruyter Studies in Corporate Governance*. https://doi.org/10.1515/9783110695816

Conclusion—A Glimpse into the Future of Sustainable International Business Management in the Age of Neo-globalization

Sustainable management is an indispensable mechanism for ensuring the competitiveness and development of today's international business in the "Decade of Action." As this book showed, sustainable management has no strict boundaries—on the contrary, it is open to change, which is its key advantage. A major challenge and catalyst for new changes in sustainable management have been the transition to neo-globalization, which has now taken clear shape. It replaced the era of global foreign trade cooperation with supranational regulation by international organizations, the key one being the World Trade Organization (WTO).

Neo-globalization represents an era of redefinition of international trade. Entrance barriers to international organizations are increasing, making participation in them elitist. The natural response of world markets is regionalization associated with the formation of regional customs unions. They are widely represented in all world regions and are developing dynamically. Neo-globalization is a good reason to reconsider the sustainable management practices of international business. The questions of determining the future contours of these practices after their reconsideration remain open.

One of the issues is connected with the inclusion of a link to regional institutions as part of the criteria for the sustainability of international business management. The difficulty lies in the fact that binding to a specific region of the world will imply a narrowing of the geographical scope of international business presence and a change in its market strategy, which will also require changes in sustainable management practices as a response.

Another issue is to consider the characteristics of developed and developing countries. The current interpretation of sustainable management from the perspective of the SDGs assumes the promotion of international business to reduce the inequality of countries, which will be difficult with clear regionalization. The issues also include the consideration of the social priorities of digitalization. In societies open to innovation, international business is expected to have a much higher level of automation and greater freedom to adopt advanced technologies than in traditional societies

E. I. Lazareva et al. (eds.), *Innovative Trends in International Business and Sustainable Management*, Approaches to Global Sustainability, Markets, and Governance,
https://doi.org/10.1007/978-981-19-4005-7

with distrust and resistance to change. De-globalization will require international businesses to focus on certain societies, which will mean a shift in the direction of sustainable management.

The presented perspective on the future of sustainable management of the international business in the era of neo-globalization has revealed many specified new and open research questions that merit further research. It is suggested that further research be devoted to these questions, which we hope this book will serve as a basis for.

MIX
Papier aus verantwortungsvollen Quellen
Paper from responsible sources
FSC® C105338

If you have any concerns about our products,
you can contact us on
ProductSafety@springernature.com

In case Publisher is established outside the EU,
the EU authorized representative is:
Springer Nature Customer Service Center GmbH
Europaplatz 3, 69115 Heidelberg, Germany

Printed by Libri Plureos GmbH
in Hamburg, Germany